ethical
space

Journal with a difference:
Celebrating 20 Years

Volume 2.

Published 2024 by Abramis academic publishing

www.abramis.co.uk

ISBN 978 1 84549 833 7

© Ethical Space 2024

All rights reserved

This book is copyright. Subject to statutory exception and to provisions of relevant collective licensing agreements, no part of this publication may be reproduced, stored in a retrieval system, or transmitted in any form or by any means, without the prior written permission of the author.

This book is sold subject to the conditions that it shall not, by way of trade or otherwise, be lent, re-sold, hired out, or otherwise circulated without the publisher's prior consent in any form of binding or cover other than that which it is published and without a similar condition including this condition being imposed on the subsequent purchaser.

Abramis is an imprint of arima publishing.

arima publishing
ASK House, Northgate Avenue
Bury St Edmunds, Suffolk IP32 6BB
t: (+44) 01284 700321

www.arimapublishing.com

Ethical Space – Journal with a difference: Celebrating 20 Years Volume 2.

Foreword

In praise of *Ethical Space* – by Karen Sanders Page 1

Introduction

On the journal's 20th anniversary: Reflecting on the past, looking to the future – by the *ES* editorial team Page 5

Section 1. Directing a critical spotlight on the mainstream

Chapter 1. A sovereign editor: Arthur Mann's *Yorkshire Post* and its crusade against appeasement 1938-1939 – by Tim Luckhurst Page 23

Chapter 2. Richard Hoggart and Pilkington: Populism and public service broadcasting – by Julian Petley Page 41

Chapter 3. Useful idiots or Big Brother's antidote: Analysing the ethical role of the state, the *Guardian* and Edward Snowden in the controversy over surveillance and whistleblowing – by Tim Crook Page 59

Chapter 4. Doublethink in the mass media: Fallujah and the politics of human rights reporting – by Florian Zollmann Page 78

Chapter 5. International fixers: Cultural interpreters or 'people like us' – Colleen Murrell Page 91

Chapter 6. 'A little bit of Salem': Rebekah Brooks, of News International, and the construction of the modern witch – by John Tulloch Page 105

Chapter 7. Dumbs gone to Iceland: (Re)presentations of English national identity during Euro 2016 and the EU referendum – by Roger Domeneghetti Page 112

Chapter 8. Comforting the comfortable: How the corporate media covered Chile's October 2019 social explosion – by Antonio Castillo Page 131

Chapter 9. Trauma in the newsroom: Lessons on the importance of Australia's YZ case – by Alexandra Wake and Matthew Ricketson Page 147

Chapter 10. Ethics and journalism in Brazil: A study of local journalism through Brazilian News Atlas – by Marcelo Fontoura and Sérgio Lüdtke Page 166

Section 2. Alternative voices

Chapter 11. When journalism isn't enough: 'Horror surrealism' in Behrouz Boochani's testimonial prison narrative
– by Willa McDonald — Page 183

Chapter 12. Visibility and cultural voice in Fataluku country Timor-Leste – by Marian Reid — Page 197

Chapter 13. 'Charitable journalism': Oxymoron or opportunity?
– by Judith Townend — Page 216

Chapter 14. Democratic affordances: Politics, media and digital technology after WikiLeaks – by Gerard Goggin — Page 223

Chapter 15. The state of peace journalism in Guatemala – by Lioba Suchenwirth — Page 239

Chapter 16. Enabling environments: Reflections on journalism and climate justice – by Robert A. Hackett, Sara Wylie and Pinar Gurleyen — Page 254

Chapter 17. Navigating journalistic spaces: British Muslim media producers – by Elizabeth Poole — Page 276

Section 3. Public relations: Beyond propaganda

Chapter 18. Integrating the shadow: A Jungian approach to professional ethics in public relations – by Johanna Fawkes — Page 291

Chapter 19. The 'Radical PR' group: Past, present and future
– by Jacquie L'Etang — Page 308

Chapter 20. Taking the BS out of PR: Creating genuine messages by emphasising character and authenticity
– by Kevin Stoker and Brad Rawlins — Page 318

Chapter 21. Communicating mental illness and suicide: Public relations students' perceptions of ethical practice – by Kate Fitch — Page 332

Chapter 22. The object of public relations and its ethical implications for late modern society – a Foucauldian analysis
– by Kristin Demetrious — Page 345

Section 4. And finally: Speaking out on ethics

Chapter 23. Rukhsana Aslam on the Christchurch mosques shooting: Reflections and confessions	Page 363
Chapter 24. Susan Greenberg on the ethics and the poetics of editing	Page 378
Chapter 25. Matthieu Lardeau on the ethical and professional challenges for freelance local sports reporters in France	Page 381
Chapter 26. Richard Lance Keeble pays tribute to Brian Winston	Page 388
Chapter 27. Tony Harcup on why ethics matter	Page 394
Chapter 28. Donald Matheson on the 'long, slow tasks of decolonising communication ethics'	Page 400

Index Page 409

Foreword

In praise of *Ethical Space*

Karen Sanders

Expounding the idea of ethics – let alone communications ethics – has never been a straightforward enterprise. Cynics and nihilists dismiss ethical practice as idealistic or inherently meaningless. Scientific domains such as evolutionary biology, psychology and neurology have provided undoubted insights into some of the empirical bases of human behaviour but have been said by some to have 'biologicized' ethics (Wilson 1975: 562). These reductionist understandings are compounded by a sense of futility about the very possibility of conversations about ethics. This is founded on a widespread assumption that relativism prevails and that shared understandings of ethics based on our common rationality are a discredited project (see Christians 2023). These are important questions: what we think about ethics has substantive implications for our understanding of what it is to be human. If our actions, collectively or individually, are the consequences of biological and/or cultural imperatives, then any judgement of them as freely undertaken acts is misplaced. If agency is illusory, then talk of reasons for actions and attributions of blame and praise become spurious.

The debate about the nature of 'humanness' and any associated ethics has taken on an added urgency with the rapid contemporary developments in Artificial Intelligence (AI) and biotechnology, given prominence in 2023 by the eruption of ChatGPT powered by the new 'large language models' (LLMs). Specialists such as DeepMind's creator, Mustafa Suleyman, alert us to the fact that the radical change which is upon us 'is real, as real as the tsunami that comes out of the open blue sea' (2023: 16). They predict the emergence of 'superintelligence', where machines will outstrip humans' rational capacity (Bostrom 2014), and of what the polymath scientist, John von Neumann, described as the 'singularity', technological acceleration 'beyond which human affairs, as we know them, could not continue' (cited in Ulam 1958). Some point to the existential risk to humans posed by such developments (Tegmark 2017); others are more sanguine and highlight the benefits of AI in areas such as health and education, while also acknowledging the catastrophic risk it can pose (see Wooldridge 2020). Rapid technological change, together with the violent geopolitical context and the pressing imperatives of the climate crisis, make these charged and anxious ethical times. These are times when positing the possibility of discussions about ethics and what it is to be human in relation to technology, to other humans and to the planet is of the utmost importance.

The moral philosopher, Alasdair MacIntyre (1999), memorably described human beings as 'dependent, rational animals' in his book of that name. Particularly marked at our end and our beginning, dependency on others is a condition of human existence. It is in this context that we learn in practice what is necessary to flourish including that most human of 'inventions': language. In language, communication – characteristic of all beings – reaches a new intensity. Among other things, language acts as a vehicle for meaning(s) which, while emerging in community, possesses a quasi-objective status in a similar way as values do for human behaviours (see McCabe 2012 [1968]: 88-89). Words, then, cannot just mean what I want them to mean (unless I am Humpty Dumpty in Lewis Carroll's *Alice in wonderland* who famously said to Alice in rather a scornful tone: 'When I use a word, it means just what I choose it to mean – neither more nor less'). Approving a law that states that a certain country is safe for asylum seekers – as the British government proposed to do in 2023 in the case of Rwanda – does not necessarily make it so. I cannot make rabbits into tigers by just saying they are. In an analogous fashion, values are not just what I state them to be. Describing behaviour by which a small child is starved to death when food is abundant as 'kind' does not make it so.

Humanity is founded on a shared, situated social life that necessarily gives the lie to 'ethical rationalism's subject-object polarity of individuated consciousness' (Christians 2023: 2). It is this situated life – this space – that is made possible and constituted by shared, learned habits and which permits the development of language and of practical reason. In so far as it is configured by human beings, it is potentially an 'ethical space' and, at the very least, a space in which ethics can be studied.

Enabling multidisciplinary debates and conversations about ethics from a diverse multitude of voices and theoretical perspectives was the founding ambition of *Ethical Space: The International Journal of Communication Ethics*. This anniversary edition, bringing together 28 articles, is a fitting tribute to the commitment and achievement of its founders and editors in providing a hospitable venue for debates centred on communication ethics and, ultimately, for the study of ethics itself.

Ethical Space has, indeed, proved to be a journal with a difference. Its mere existence is a testament not only to the tenacity and hard work of its editorial team and contributors but also to the fact that ethics matter and will continue to do so, as Harcup and Matheson eloquently argue in this volume. The journal dares to open its pages to an eclectic range of voices speaking on diverse themes: from news deserts in Brazil where corruption goes uncovered (Fontoura and Lüdtke) or the role of digital visual narratives in creating spaces of dialogue in

Timor-Leste (Reid) to a radical agenda for PR focused on social impact rather than organisational needs (L'Etang) and truth rather than 'bullshit' (Stoker and Rawlins). Alternative theoretical lenses that challenge traditional perspectives and formats (Fawkes; Greenberg; McDonald; Murrell) are welcomed and challenging themes for and about journalists are explored including the reporting of mental health issues and suicide (Fitch), the impact of traumatic events on journalists (Wake and Ricketson) and the contribution of peace and 'charity' journalism (Aslam; Hackett, Wylie and Gurleyen; Suchenwirth; Townend). The journal does not neglect the abiding themes of state, media and individual power and responsibility (Castillo; Crook; Goggin; Lardeau; Petley), media stereotyping, identity and human rights (Domeneghetti; Poole; Tulloch; Zollmann) and the role of outstanding media practitioners and scholars in shaping our ethical narratives (Keeble and Luckhurst). My summary can do scant justice to the richness these pages offer in content, format and viewpoint. The chapters are in and of themselves an articulation of that ethical space the journal has sought always to fashion.

In 1963, Hannah Arendt published in book form her reports for *The New Yorker* on the trial of the Nazi SS apparatchik, Adolf Eichmann (2006 [1963]). She was criticised by some for seeming to underplay the heinous quality of Eichmann's crimes by referring to the banality of evil. In fact, her reference to 'banality', far from trivialising the horror of his actions, sought to capture how the Nazi war criminals strove to efface their existence as humans from the acts they had committed. Their self-effacement amounted to an annulment of their capacity truly to comprehend and, therefore, to be responsible for their actions. They effectively transmuted themselves into killing machines: senior officers would input the orders into their subalterns and they would produce the required outputs. As Arendt wrote:

> The trouble with the Nazi criminals was precisely that they renounced voluntarily all personal qualities, as if nobody were left to be either punished or forgiven. They protested time and time again that they had never done anything out of their own initiative, that they had no intentions whatsoever, good or bad, and that they only obeyed orders (ibid: 114).

In effect, they desisted from key aspects of their humanity and created the dystopia that some have predicted will ensue from the coming technological tsunami. The tragedy of humanity, however, is not only that we are capable of diminishing or renouncing agency, we also frequently misuse it to dominate, control and harm others. These behaviours radically devalue other humans as sources of meaning expressed in communication and have had many damaging historical manifestations such as, for example, colonialism which 'is almost the exact opposite of communication between two cultures' (McCabe 2012 [1968]: 101). The collapse of communication lies at the heart of the collapse of ethics and – to paraphrase – it only takes each of us to fail to create ethical spaces for terrible things to happen. And that is why journals such as *Ethical Space: The International Journal of Communication Ethics* are so vital and the occasion of its twentieth anniversary a cause for celebration.

REFERENCES

Arendt, H. (2003) *Responsibility and judgement*, New York, Schocken Books

Arendt, H. (2006 [1963]) *Eichmann in Jerusalem: A report on the banality of evil*, London, Penguin Classics

Bostrum, N. (2014) *Superintelligence*, Oxford, Oxford University Press

Christians, C. (2023) 'A model of ethical realism', *Ethical Space. Journal with a difference: Celebrating 20 years*, Bury St Edmunds, Abramis pp 1-5

MacIntyre, A. (1999) *Dependent, rational animals: Why human beings need the virtues*, Peru, Illinois, Carus Publishing

McCabe, H. (2012 [1968]) *Law, love and language*, London, Continuum

Suleyman, M. (2023) *The coming wave: AI, power and the 21st century's greatest dilemma*, London, Penguin

Tegmark, M. (2017) *Life 3.0. Being human in the age of artificial intelligence*, London, Allen Lane/ Penguin Books

Ulam, S. (May 1958) Tribute to John von Neumann, *Bulletin of the American Mathematical Society*. Vol. 64, No. 3 part 2: 5

Wilson, E.O. (1975) *Sociobiology: The new synthesis*, Cambridge, MA, Harvard University Press

Wooldridge, M. (2020) *A brief history of artificial intelligence: What it is, where we are, and where we are going*, New York, Flatiron Books

NOTE ON THE CONTRIBUTOR

Karen Sanders is Professor of Politics and Communication and Head of the School of Business and Communication at St Mary's University (UK). She is one of the founding editors of *Ethical Space. The International Journal of Communication Ethics*. She is co-editor of the *Routledge companion to journalism ethics* and has authored key texts including *Ethics & journalism* (Sage) and *Communicating politics in the 21st century* (Palgrave Macmilllan).

Introduction

On the journal's 20th anniversary: Reflecting on the past, looking to the future

The *ES* editorial team

To celebrate the 20 years' anniversary of *Ethical Space: The International Journal of Communication Ethics*, two volumes drawing together papers under various themes are being published by Abramis, of Bury St Edmunds. Appearing in 2023, the first volume covers the topics 'Communication ethics: Philosophical and theoretical reflections', 'New media, new ethical challenges', 'Professionalisation and media ethics: Beyond the rhetoric', 'Communication ethics and pedagogy' and 'Speaking out on ethics'.[1]

In the Foreword, Professor Clifford Christians, one of the world's leading authorities on media ethics, describes *ES* as 'an inspiring model of moral realism'.

Reflecting the broad range of issues and perspectives embraced by the journal, this new volume takes in the topics 'Directing a critical spotlight on the mainstream', 'Alternative voices', 'Public relations: Beyond propaganda' and a collection of essays on the theme 'Speaking out on ethics'.

MAINSTREAM UNDER THE SPOTLIGHT

The journal's 'Aims and scope' outlined at the beginning of every issue highlight its guiding principles, namely internationalism, individual integrity, respect for difference and diversity, interdisciplinarity, theoretical rigour and practitioner focus. Moreover, one of the major strands of *ES* – currently edited by Tom Bradshaw, Sue Joseph, Richard Lance Keeble and Donald Matheson (with David Baines, UK-based reviews editor also attending monthly Zoom meetings) – is to problematise professionalism. It does this, for instance, by focusing on alternative, progressive media and highlighting many of professionalism's underlying myths.

It is thus fitting that this new volume begins with a section looking critically at the mainstream media. Tim Luckhurst examines the anti-appeasement stance taken by Arthur Mann, editor of the *Yorkshire Post* in the lead-up to the Second World War. This was all the more remarkable since the British press was reluctant to criticise government policy – with the most powerful national titles determined to support Neville Chamberlain's efforts to appease Hitler. Mann would not resign his editorship until November 1939 following his newspaper's merger with the *Leeds Mercury*. As Luckhurst concludes:

> He had fought a brave and idealistic battle to preserve his freedom to oppose appeasement. He had denounced the policy and its architect in language so compelling that even his chairman was obliged, in the end, to offer his backing. But Mann could not accept the diminution of his status implied by the merger of his beloved *Yorkshire Post* with its less prestigious stablemate. His hubris meant that he would never test his ideal of editorial independence in the crucible of a democracy at war.

ES was launched in 2003 (essentially as an initiative of Robert Beckett) as the journal of the membership-based Institute of Communication Ethics. This arrangement lasted until Abramis took over distribution and subscriptions after the final, bumper, double issue appeared in 2018 – and following the retirement of the brilliant and hard-working administrator Fiona Thompson. Thus ICE's annual conference, 'Anti-social media' in London in October 2018 was to be its last. Those conferences not only provided the opportunity for members of the *ES* international community to meet and discuss their new projects and teaching challenges. From those conferences a selection of papers would also be drawn to be carried in the following *ES* issue. Julian Petley's chapter, 'Richard Hoggart and Pilkington: Populism and public service broadcasting', is based on the presentation he gave to the ICE annual conference of 2014 that celebrated critically the work of John Tulloch, Stuart Hall as well as Hoggart.

In 1962, the Pilkington Committee, of which Hoggart, author of the celebrated *Uses of literacy* (1957), was an influential member, produced a report extremely critical of ITV and its regulator, the Independent Television Authority. Petley examines in forensic detail the press critique of the Pilkington Report and suggests it prefigures later press interventions into broadcasting controversies – as well as press responses to the Leveson Inquiry report in 2012. The coverage also anticipates the ever-growing hostility of the national press towards the BBC (particularly following the arrival of Rupert Murdoch as a press proprietor in 1969) and the enthusiasm for new broadcasting technologies (a specialism of *The Sunday Times* in the 1980s, when Murdoch was establishing his satellite empire). According to Petley, the national press reporting of Pilkington reflected:

> … the simplistic assumption that new broadcasting technology and an increased number of channels would automatically entail greater diversity of programming. And a raucous populism which regards the state as only ever the enemy of media freedom (understood implicitly as the right of media owners to do with their media whatsoever they will), never as an

enabler of media freedom in the wider sense of helping to make the media more diverse, representative, accessible, accountable, assessable and so on.

Ethical Space has long been concerned over the activities of the secret, surveillance-obsessed states and their impacts on journalism and freedom of expression. But true to its principles, *ES* has carried a range of critical perspectives. In 2013, the *Guardian* published the biggest leak of intelligence in the history of America's National Security Agency and the UK's GCHQ – as provided by the 29-year-old whistleblower Edward Snowden. Tim Crook's fascinating chapter, 'Useful idiots or Big Brother's antidote: Analysing the ethical role of the state, the *Guardian* and Snowden in the controversy over surveillance and whistleblowing', suggests there is a trend for state surveillance bodies, whistleblowers and their receiving journalists and publishers to each claim the moral high ground of public interest. Crook continues: 'The tension remains a struggle between those who claim to be protecting national security and those who claim to be protecting individual privacy and seeking to expose alleged abuse of state power through excessive surveillance and electronic intrusion.'

Crook concludes that, given the absence of clear evidence of impact, it is difficult to prove which side has been responsible for damaging or, indeed, improving the public good:

> Political ideology motivated the journalists Guy Burgess and Kim Philby to infiltrate Great Britain's security establishment to spy for the KGB. They were certainly more than 'useful idiots'. Perhaps history will be the judge of whether Edward Snowden, and the news publisher prepared to publish his leaks will ever qualify as 'useful idiots' for Vladimir Putin and all the other perceived enemies of NSA and GCHQ intelligence gathering operations.

Florian Zollmann's pioneering monograph *Media, propaganda and the politics of intervention* (2017) builds on critical theory, most notably Herman and Chomsky's propaganda model, to dissect US, UK and German media reporting of the military operations in Kosovo, Iraq, Libya, Syria and Egypt. In the process he demonstrates how 'humanitarian intervention' and 'R2P' are only evoked in the news media if so-called 'enemy' countries of Western states are the perpetrators of human rights violations. Here, Zollmann analyses UK press coverage of the US attack on the Iraqi city of Fallujah in 2004. Actions by US/Coalition forces that could be regarded as violations of the Geneva Conventions included the deliberate targeting of a hospital and civilians, the shooting at ambulances, the cutting off of power and water supplies, the use of indiscriminate military force, the prevention of a relief convoy to enter the city, the shooting of wounded soldiers, the use of phosphorous rounds – and assaults on the honour of women.

Violations by the resistance included the occupation of the main hospital, the deliberate targeting of civilians, the improper use of white flags and the use of mosques for hostile purposes.

Zollmann concludes:

> In its coverage of the US assault on Fallujah, the British press instituted the assumption that an otherwise illegal occupation was legitimate. Furthermore, the 'operation' was largely framed as a military endeavour. Most newspapers did not consider it to be a massacre or a crime. … The ability of the press to describe horrific events and place them in a framework of Western benevolence may also amount to what George Orwell defined as doublethink: 'to deny the existence of objective reality and all the while to take account of the reality which one denies'.

Locally hired journalists (often dubbed 'fixers') are increasingly being used by Western media companies abroad to short-circuit newsgathering and gain instant access to local stories and useful contacts. Colleen Murrell analyses data from 20 senior British and Australian television correspondents and from five fixers working in crisis-stricken countries. She finds that the reporters gain a reputation for being able to function well in difficult situations and may go on to reap rewards in terms of promotion, book deals, documentaries featuring their work and access to the lecture circuit. Fixers, on the other hand, will rarely get the kudos of having their name attached to the report, but they may see their experience translated into further paying jobs. And yet, how authentic is the local intervention? Using the social theories of Pierre Bourdieu to examine the 'exchange of cultural capital' that takes place between the Western correspondent and the fixer, Murrell argues:

> Globalisation has made possible this tribe of newsgatherers (be they correspondents or fixers) who have more in common with each other than with the general population of the country being covered. At the end of the day, the correspondent will work with the most effective person who is available and who can deliver the best story for their viewers. In choosing English-speaking professionals, correspondents are broadcasting a tale from abroad, delivered through a filter of Western understanding.

John Tulloch, who sadly died in 2013, was for many years an inspirational speaker at the annual ICE conferences, essayist for *Ethical Space* and the journal's reviews editor. In a tribute, published in *ES* in 2014, Richard Lance Keeble, his colleague at the University of Lincoln and friend, wrote:

> His writings and conference presentations over the years covered a vast range of subjects: peace journalism, Indian newspaper history, press regulation, media coverage of the US 'war on terror', the BBC, investigative reporting, literary journalism, journalism education to name but a few. He wrote beautifully: his prose was bubbling with original ideas and wit. He was able to mix subtle theory, even sections of quantitative analysis, with elegant references to some of the many books he had read. Take for

instance, his *Ethical Space* review of Robert Fisk's *The age of the warrior: Selected writings* (Tulloch 2009) in which the author serenades his cat: John took the opportunity to slip in mention other literary cats – of Keats, Christopher Smart and Dr Johnson for instance, complete with apt quotations, of course. John could even include the word 'bullshit' in an academic essay and make it appear both apt and profound! Indeed, there was a cheeky side to his personality that came out in his writings: while constantly critical of the 'dumbing down' of the media he always wanted to celebrate the tabloids for their mischief-making.

John's contribution to the 2012 ICE annual conference which forms the basis for his chapter here, was so typical of the man. Amidst all the avalanche of media coverage of the Leveson Inquiry into press practices and ethics, John picked on what he called 'the witchifying' of Rebekah Brooks – who might otherwise have been so easily passed over as a Murdoch crony not worth any sympathy or academic attention. So he read carefully from his script:

> Last year, Rebekah Brooks positively willed herself to be my subject. She is, as many have seen fit to tell us, hard to resist. Not the Cotswold-living lady who rides retired police horses, or the tabloid editor and compulsive chum of celebrities. … But the woman in the middle of the bizarre process that seems to happen regularly, when for a short period, they become a subject of press interest, are objectified and, not to be too dainty about it, monstered.

And he continued:

> Apart from the too tempting opportunities for portentous moralising, her case is fascinating for what it can tell us about contemporary media culture, the persistence of class-based attitudes and a sexism so engrained into our public life as to appear 'natural', old boy.

Notice the vitality and wit, the subtle shifts of tone and register of John's prose. How elegantly it mixes subtle theorising, journalese and witty vernacular. All of this crammed into just a few score words.

The ethics of sports reporting has been a constant interest of *Ethical Space* over the years. Next Roger Domeneghetti examines the representation of English national identity in the reporting of the 2016 UEFA European Football Championships. Held in France between 10 June and 10 July of that year against the backdrop of Britain's referendum on membership of the European Union, the tournament took place during a time of heightened debate about national identity. Examining in particular England's three most popular newspapers, the *Sun*, the *Daily Mail* and the *Daily Mirror*, Domeneghetti draws creatively on a range of theoretical approaches including Anderson's (2006) concept of imagined community, Hobsbaum's (1983) notion of invented traditions and Guibernau's (2007) strategies for the construction of national identity. He concludes on a highly critical note:

> Journalists utilised a tried-and-tested formula which employed language that reached back into the shared mythical past of the dominant ethnic group. This language was often overtly militaristic, referencing the Second World War in particular but also the victories of Admiral Nelson and the Armada as well as the 1966 football World Cup success. 'Us' and 'them' narratives were constructed around England's opponents, in particular Wales, which provided the newspapers' readers 'a "fantasy shield" to cement and unify national sentiment for the imagined community'.

Antonio Castillo's chapter draws attention to the remarkable social uprising in Chile in 2019, involving thousands of people in street protests and pitched battles between soldiers and demonstrators, which was largely ignored by the Western corporate media. Castillo argues that the coverage by Chile's corporate media was essentially designed to defend the privileges of the country's elite and criminalise mass public demands for social change and justice. At the same time, alternative media emerged and became spaces of activism, dialogue, political education, direct action and collaboration. They included political podcasts (via YouTube and Spotify), current affairs programmes via university-sponsored media channels, femi-journalism digital platforms (established and managed by feminist organisations) and long-established Indigenous and urban poor media collectives. Castillo concludes:

> In the context of the social explosion, the position of corporate journalism in the Chilean society was not only ethically questioned but it was also rejected. This was the result not only of the demonising coverage, but also the failure to report the massive human rights violations committed against protestors by the police and the military.

The critical spotlight thrown on the mainstream media by Alexandra Wake and Matthew Ricketson focuses on a landmark ruling by an Australian court which put news media companies on notice they faced potential findings of negligence and subsequent compensation claims if they failed to exercise a reasonable duty of care to reporters covering traumatic events. The court ruled that journalist YZ, who worked at one of Australia's oldest metropolitan daily newspapers, *The Age*, be awarded A$180,000 for psychological injury suffered while working between 2003 and 2013. YZ had reported on 32 murders and many more cases as a court reporter. This was in stark contrast to the case from the same newspaper, in 2012, which did not uphold the claim of a news photographer. Wake and Ricketson suggest that the case could have implications for employers not just in Australia but in other countries with similar legal systems. They also consider its relevance for journalism educators who are charged with preparing the next generation of journalists, many of whom will cover traumatic events. And they note approvingly that the World Journalism Education Congress syndicate on journalism and trauma made three broad recommendations on curriculum when it met in Paris in 2019: 'implement classroom training that incorporates theory and practice; provide essential literature, contacts, networks, and resources to students; and promote normalization of reactions to trauma in journalism work'.

The Brazilian News Atlas is a crowdsourcing, non-profit project designed to map local journalism initiatives and news deserts in Brazil. In their chapter, Marcelo Fontoura and Sérgio Lüdtke use the latest data from the Atlas about news deserts, as well as complementary research from the project, to better understand the limitations and challenges to local outlets in Brazil. Their findings highlight a precarious situation in journalism, with the closure of traditional, larger operations, and the emergence of many individual initiatives, mainly in the form of blogs. And they suggest local journalism in Brazil has essentially two major challenges to overcome:

> On one hand, it faces the same financial issues as other parts of industry, and on the other, it still has to tackle the heavy influence of local politics and business. The financial troubles of the industry risk increasing the ethical troubles, since they may encourage newspaper owners to establish even closer ties with potential advertisers. In small towns, where advertising space tends to go to the same companies and to local governments, and where professional culture is weaker, this risk is higher.

ALTERNATIVE VOICES

While directing a critical spotlight on the mainstream media, *Ethical Space* has always aimed to promote the study of alternative voices – and highlight the ethical and political roles of the non-corporate, progressive media within the global alternative public sphere.

Willa McDonald, author of a seminal study of literary journalism in colonial Australia (2023), looks at the prison narrative, *No friend but the mountains* (2018) of journalist, filmmaker and author Behrouz Boochani who had been forcibly detained on Manus Island, Papua New Guinea (PNG), for five years by the Australian government. 'The paradox of Boochani stepping in to fill the place of an Australian journalist writing about Australian government policy and its consequences is that he can only do it because he is an outsider communicating his own outsider status from within the subjective experience of imprisonment.'

Written on a smuggled smart-phone, it was sent out in text messages via WhatsApp to translators in Australia. According to McDonald: 'It is a powerful indictment of Australia's immigration policies, particularly as they affect refugees and asylum seekers arriving at Australia's north by boat from Indonesia.' *No friend but the mountains* follows in the long tradition of 'resistance literature':

> As writing from personal experience, it claims a voice, makes a point, establishes a community and retrieves identity. It seeks redress for injustices and advocates the rights of marginalised communities by speaking out about the actual circumstances of a life or lives.

Marian Reid is an Australian writer and communications adviser whose interests include community-led development, culture, nature and climate change. In her chapter, she focuses on the Fataluku community of Lautem, Timor-Leste, investigating the effect community-driven cultural documentation has on the value, perception and visibility of culture by the community. The case study highlights the fact that digital visual communication is a valuable tool through which to open channels of cultural expression and make visible critically endangered intangible cultural heritage. Reid concludes:

> If the international community feels it has a responsibility to assist in the development of the nation, then it also has a responsibility to support minority, grassroots projects that promote and preserve intangible culture so that it can become part of the footprint for the nation's future. Established in the context of Timor-Leste by local people, the Fataluku Research Project has the culturally appropriate framework to be applied in various communities across the country – and the power to contribute to cultural preservation, revitalisation, dialogue and peace-building.

Judith Townend next examines the question: could the charitable funding of media help reinvigorate topics neglected by the commercial media? Her study takes in the organisations *Full Fact* and *The Conversation UK*, the *Maidenhead Advertiser*, a newspaper run by the private limited company Baylis Media Ltd owned by the Louis Baylis (*Maidenhead Advertiser*) Charitable Trust, and *openDemocracy*, a website published by a private limited company and wholly owned by a private not-for-profit, the openDemocracy Foundation for the Advancement of Global Education, and partially supported by a charity, the OpenTrust. At a local level, the *Ambler*, the *Burngreave Messenger* and the *Lewisham Pensioner's Gazette* are considered.

Townend writes: 'These charitable initiatives share one striking similarity: they all provide content neglected in commercial environments, perhaps because this content does not drive enough traffic to attract online advertising, or is considered unlikely to appeal to paying subscribers and readers.' But there are problems. For instance, it is difficult even for a non-partisan journalism organisation to secure charity status. Indeed, advocates of charitable journalism have suggested that charity law should be capable of recognising the broad public benefit in certain forms of public interest journalism. Townend concludes:

> Charitable status is not a magic bullet for the media industry. Being a charity places particular burdens on organisations as well as granting them reputational and financial benefits. But certain (existing or future) non-profit news organisations, especially those working in local geographic communities, on investigations and specialist topics such as law could greatly benefit from a regime that recognises specified forms of journalistic and news activity as charitable, to a greater extent than it does already.

According to Gerard Goggin, the whistleblowing site, WikiLeaks, launched by the Australian Julian Assange in 2006, was 'perhaps the most singular and spectacular example of innovation in democratic affordances'. A defining story was the *Collateral murder* video (http://www.collateral-murder.com/) and ensuing outcry in 2010. The classified US military video released to the media by WikiLeaks showed a July 2007 incident in which US soldiers in an Apache helicopter attacked and killed Iraqi civilians and two Reuters journalists. 'After the initial shock and dismay at the conduct of the US personnel depicted in the video, there was a backlash against WikiLeaks for the way in which it published the footage with many journalists and commentators questioning the emotional manipulation and de-contextualisation of the video as it was edited for release.'

Goggin also examines WikiLeaks's Afghan war logs, its release of half a million US national text pager intercepts relating to the 9/11 data terrorist attacks – and its Cablegate revelations in November 2010 which involved some 251,287 diplomatic cables from 250 US embassies around the world containing candid assessments by officials about foreign governments. 'To control the reception of the release of the US embassy cables, WikiLeaks again struck agreements with leading press outlets. There were many advantages to this, including the ability to take advantage of the fact-checking, analysis and interpretation skills of leading journalists.' Goggin ends on a critical note:

> For its instigators, the potential capacities of WikiLeaks at its birth appeared revolutionary and straightforward. As it has turned out, however, the interactions among journalism, news, and the digital in this novel platform have not been straightforward at all. The affordances of WikiLeaks as a platform have extraordinary potential to transform journalism and media. Yet the democratic implications of these affordances have been far more ambiguous and at times reactionary than could possibly have been foreseen.

According to Lioba Suchenwirth, much peace journalism theory is too elitist: written from the perspective of international media, meaning Western media outlets based outside the conflict zone, and focusing on foreign correspondents. Drawing on a wide range of theorists including Fraser (1993), Carey (1989), Rodriguez (2000), Harcup (2007), Atton and Hamilton (2008) and Keeble (2009), she directs her attention to alternative, local community media. It is the citizen's media that can give voice to the voiceless and foster empowerment.

Suchenwirth's case study draws on in-depth interviews throughout Guatemala during the summer of 2010 with 26 experts, gathering information on PJ initiatives, alternative and Indigenous media and human rights publications. The experts include journalists, researchers, consultants, community radio broadcasters, activists and government officials as well as a former general and the head of the former guerrilla radio station. She writes: 'Mainstream media appear too far involved with the Guatemalan oligarchy and too absorbed by economic goals to reflect alternative viewpoints, thus failing to give a voice to disenfranchised groups such as Guatemala's Indigenous people. … Alternative media are aiming to fill this gap.'

Robert A. Hackett, Sara Wylie and Pinar Gurleyen also highlight the values of peace journalism and the alternative media in their study of the reporting of the global environmental crisis. In common with climate justice journalism, PJ usefully challenges the epistemological basis for a stance of detachment, urging journalists to reflect more about the institutionalised biases of routine practices, the unavoidably interventionist, political nature of journalism and its potential to become an unwitting accomplice to war propaganda. At the same time, non-corporate media can provide 'a more hopeful picture of environmental communication'. For instance, studies of Vancouver press coverage of the 2009 Copenhagen climate change summit found that two independent news outlets, the online thetyee.ca and urban weekly the *Georgia Straight*, treated climate change as a political issue, without reducing it to official politics – and conveying a sense of agency and hope.

Yet Hackett, Wylie and Gurleyen acknowledge that alternative media and peace journalism are themselves confined to the margins of global communications. In effect, the democratisation of media systems is crucial if climate justice is to be achieved.

Muslim media and the representations of Muslims are the subject of Elizabeth Poole's chapter that is based on 37 interviews with editors and producers in both mainstream and minority outlets. The organisations range from blogs, NGOs, print media such as *Q News*, community magazines, publications aimed at a broader Asian market, publishers and freelances working across the media.

There is complete agreement that the mainstream representation of Muslims was predominantly negative. This is the most discussed topic in the interviews with participants noting the increased volume, simplification, decontextualising, 'formulaic', 'reactionary' and 'xenophobic' coverage that focuses on extremism, radicalism, barbarism, homogenisation and sensationalism. They are 'particularly critical of the Conservative press, Murdoch media, some current affairs programmes such as *Newsnight* and *Dispatches* and some outspoken right-wing commentators'.

Many highlight critically the practice of some news organisations of using extremist sources or self-appointed representatives who failed to represent members of the Muslim community. The precise causes cited, however, vary from a lack of effective media strategies amongst moderate Muslim groups, to tabloidisation and associated stereotyping. Social media are seen as a source of greater diversity – but they had also led to a fragmentation of media sources which could undermine democracy.

Muslim producers believe that Muslim media are increasingly a resource for the mainstream, adding to the diversity of voices available. However, apart from some liberal publications, this view is challenged 'by the results of the interviews with non-Muslim mainstream producers who often had little knowledge of these alternative media'.

Amongst a number of recommendations listed at the end of the chapter, Poole suggests that employers should recognise both the value and importance of employing a wider diversity of people in their workplace while editors should use their journalists as a resource for greater understanding but not always foreground their religious or ethnic identity.

PUBLIC RELATIONS: BEYOND PROPAGANDA

In keeping with its principle of interdisciplinarity, *Ethical Space*, over its 20 years, has covered many aspects of communication: journalism, media pedagogy, computer studies, cultural studies, health communication, hactivism, literary studies, international politics, covert and overt intelligence, sociology of the professions, the ethics of true crime – and Indigenous studies. The journal has also kept in close touch with the developments in public relations research proudly publishing papers by leaders in the field – some of them now collected in this new section of the anniversary text.

Building on her highly original PhD work (later forming the basis for her *Public relations ethics and professionalism: The shadow of excellence*, Routledge, 2014), Johanna Fawkes applies the ideas of Carl Jung (1875-1961) regarding wholeness instead of goodness as the goal of the integrated psyche to a critical study of professional ethics – in particular those of public relations. She suggests Jung's focus on inward dialogue and integration 'offers a new basis for ethical development. It combines a philosophical and psychological approach to the self and highlights the ethical effects of moving away from the ego-defensive split between persona and shadow…'

The Jungian approach to public relations ethics would start by acknowledging its essential propaganda role, 'past and present, without condemnation or judgement'. Moreover, Jung's concept of integration 'offers a way forward for the development of a more coherent professional ethics, not only in public relations but for others grappling with issues of ethics in rapidly changing times'.

'Radical PR' was the name given to an international gathering of like-minded academics from Australia, New Zealand, USA, South America, Scandinavia and Europe at the Stirling Media Research Institute (SMRI) in July 2008. They were scholars who approached the subject of public relations from multi- and inter-disciplinary contexts while they also considered the wider political, ethical and cultural issues and social impacts. In her chapter, Jacquie L'Etang traces the history of the group – and ponders its future.

She begins by providing a brief overview of the history of PR as an academic discipline and stresses how it has long struggled with its identity being located in many different academic 'homes', including marketing, management, communications, media and journalism.

> We sought to liberate the public relations field from its normative, functional, conformist agendas and realise the potential of public relations research to shed new light on contemporary life and inform cultural practice. Our purpose was to establish a network to redress the problems of isolation and generate new bodies of work to replace the current insular body of knowledge centred on narrow positivism that fails to acknowledge the field's power dynamics.

L'Etang ends on a personal note: 'I really hoped that others would be interested in taking the discipline along new and different paths and to be creative, as an antidote to the predictable organisation-management focus of most of the literature.'

Bullshit may at first appear an unusual concept for serious analysis. Yet, in 2005, the American philosopher, Harry G. Frankfurt (1929-2023), published his best-selling *On bullshit* and the topic suddenly achieved academic respectability. In their chapter, 'Taking the BS out of PR: Creating genuine messages by emphasising character and authenticity', Kevin Stoker and Brad Rawlins (drawing from Frankfurt) define bullshit as 'communication that misleads people, short of lying, about the sincerity of the communicator, who is unconcerned and careless about the truthfulness of the message. BS is not false; it is fake'. And public relations, when it is reduced to spin and hype, is BS. So how to remove it?

According to Stoker and Rawlins, a 'more authentic' approach would place responsibility for moral action on practitioners as individuals and organisations as a collective community of individuals. A new stress should also be placed on sincerity: 'If the values communicated differ from the personal values espoused by the communicator, it represents a moral disconnect that deceives the audience as to the communicator's true beliefs.' Finally, striving for more authenticity is crucial.

To reduce disconnects between character and public action, practitioners will need to have moral autonomy. To make authentic moral decisions, they must be able to act independently of all influences that might nullify their humanity and their commitment to character, truth and genuine communication.

Suicide and mental illness are complex issues with significant social and economic implications and their coverage by the media and journalism educators raises a wide range of challenges. Kate Fitch's study examines the perceptions of public relations students in Australia towards the ethics of communicating mental health issues. Her findings suggest students recognise the ambiguities around 'professional' ethics in relation to these issues, the need for personal responsibility in ethical public relations practice, that the growth in ethical awareness is incremental and that they learn most effectively through major assignments.

Amongst her recommendations, Fitch suggests that public relations educators should set a major assessment item on mental illness and suicide. 'In this way, students will research the field and integrate theory with their understanding of professional practice.' In addition, public relations activity needs to be considered in terms of its social impact: 'Some students and, indeed, practitioners, assume that professional responsibility relates to effective business practice, neglecting the social elements implicit in both "social responsibility" and "public relations".'

Another Australian academic, Kristin Demetrious, draws on Foucauldian theory to investigate the object of public relations and its ethical implications for late modern society. As a case study, she looks at the implications for PR of the Timberlands controversy in 1999 when New Zealander Nicky Hager and Australian Bob Burton made a formal complaint to the Public Relations Institute of New Zealand about unethical public relations which, they claimed, had been designed to undermine public debate about the future of West Coast New Zealand's temperate rainforest. Demetrious's paper discusses socially and politically offensive forms of PR and the tension in the field 'which need urgent attention'. 'I believe that reconciling these issues requires innovation and a synthetic approach, drawing on a range of interdisciplinary social, political, communicative and discourse theories...'

AND FINALLY: SPEAKING OUT ON ETHICS

Rukhsana Aslam begins our final section which brings together a diverse range of ethical perspectives with her highly personalised account of the reporting of the Christchurch mosques shooting in New Zealand on 15 March 2019. As a media scholar at the time when the NZ media faced the biggest story of extremism and terrorism in the history of the country, she finds it truly remarkable that the stories in the mainstream media are about people; the talk is about support and compassion; the focus is on peace and diversity and the debate is on how to address the issues. 'The principles of peace journalism were shining bright as they so rarely do.'

Editing is rarely the subject of ethical analysis. In her chapter, Susan L. Greenberg highlights the thinking behind her most recent book (Palgrave Macmillan, 2018), which offers the first ever attempt to define the poetics of editing while also proposing a new academic field of 'editing studies'. She writes:

> Wherever it is found on the political spectrum, anti-MSM 'authenticity' demands the expression of strong, partisan, personal feelings, and opposition to 'experts' or other professional sources of constraint. But I make the case that constraints in a rule-based process can protect the weak and promote agreed public goods. The 'obstacle' of expert editing can help people think critically about what is being put into wider circulation, questioning what is otherwise taken as given.

In 2021, a special double issue of *ES*, edited by Tom Bradshaw and Paul Wiltshire, on 'The ethics of local media across the globe', included an article by Matthew Lardeau, 'Journalist or supporter? The ethical and confessional challenges for freelance local sports reporters in France'. Lardeau, an academic and sports reporter, suggests local press correspondents face special ethical challenges: the closeness to their sources 'often results in the creation of friendly relationships that invite closeness or even familiarity'. But the risk of 'boosterism' can be mitigated by the commitment to fair journalistic treatment by the professional editorial staff who handle the articles. Drawing on his own experience, Lardeau writes: 'I always introduce myself, greet and speak to the managers (president, coach, players) or even the supporters of opposing or visiting teams, giving them even more time than the host team that I already know; likewise, I try to give a fair, if not equal, treatment to the two teams in the article.'

Brian Winston was the first chair of the Institute of Communication Ethics (the original publishers of *ES*) who sadly died aged 80 following a fall on 9 April 2022. A special issue of the journal, dedicated to Brian's memory, included papers by Clifford Christians, Julian Petley and Pratap Rughani – and tributes by John Mair and Ivor Gaber. According to Mair, Winston was 'praxis personified: he did not just talk media, he made it'.

In an editorial, Richard Lance Keeble, his colleague for many years at the University of Lincoln and friend, says there were many Brian Winstons:

> … the polymath, the controversialist and story teller, the expert on media theory, documentaries, journalism ethics, freedom of expression, media technologies and their histories; the distinguished winner of the US Emmy in 1985; the enormously energetic and often provocative speaker at conferences around the world; author, editor and co-author of 20 major books, the last one, on fake news, written with his son, Matthew…

Tony Harcup, Emeritus Fellow at the University of Sheffield, is the author of the seminal text, *Journalism: Principles and practice*, first published in 2004 and now in its fourth edition. In an article specially written for this anniversary text, he says there is sometimes a danger of over-complicating and over-theorising matters. 'Most of ethics can be boiled down to a few simple things such as listening, caring, being respectful, approaching people with a little empathy and humility – and generally trying to put oneself in others' shoes.' Harcup draws from his own experience some fifty years ago with the Basement Writers in Leeds and with the alternative local newspaper, the *Leeds Other Paper* (*LOP*), and suggests they were both inspired by 'an informal set of ethics, starting with listening to people at the bottom of the pile and proceeding to help amplify such voices'.

Finally, Donald Matheson, joint editor of *ES*, in looking ahead to the next twenty years, argues that the journal must tackle the major issue: namely the long legacy of colonialism in ethical thinking. This requires more than an embrace of diversity and more than symbolic actions, such as taking down statues of colonisers like Cecil Rhodes at universities, useful as those moves are. Focusing on Aotearoa New Zealand as a country founded on a bicultural relationship between indigenous and settler cultures, Matheson suggests that one approach is 'to give status and authority to the disempowered indigenous frameworks so as to begin to rework relationships between people'. Indeed, significant changes are being witnessed as Māori perspectives are given centrality in some parts of public life.

> From the national museum to understanding of the country's founding document to the inclusion of the 'more-than-human' in legal definitions of the public, the rules of the game are changing so much that it is no longer possible to think of communication ethics in this place as belonging to Anglo-American traditions.

It is fitting that the Foreword in this anniversary text is composed by Karen Sanders who has been involved with the journal since its launch. Her *Ethics & journalism* (2003), in providing a critical overview of the main ethical approaches in Western journalism, became essential reading. Here she suggests that the debate about the nature of 'humanness' and any associated ethics has taken on an added urgency with the rapid contemporary developments in Artificial Intelligence (AI) and biotechnology, given prominence in 2023 by the eruption of ChatGPT powered by the new 'large language models' (LLMs).

Enabling multidisciplinary debates and conversations about ethics from a diverse multitude of voices and theoretical perspectives was the founding ambition of *Ethical Space: The International Journal of Communication Ethics*. This anniversary edition, Sanders says, 'is a fitting tribute to the commitment and achievement of its founders and editors in providing a hospitable venue for debates centred on communication ethics and, ultimately, for the study of ethics itself'.

NOTE

[1] *Ethical Space: Journal with a difference: Celebrating 20 years, Vol. 1.* See http://www.abramis.co.uk/books/bookdetails.php?id=184549817

**The *ES* editorial team: Tom Bradshaw, Sue Joseph,
Richard Lance Keeble and Donald Matheson**

SECTION 1

Directing a critical spotlight on the mainstream

Chapter 1

A sovereign editor: Arthur Mann's *Yorkshire Post* and its crusade against appeasement, 1938-1939

Tim Luckhurst

During Britain's appeasement of Nazi Germany, the British press was reluctant to criticise government policy and it came under pressure not to do so. The most powerful national titles were determined to support Prime Minister Neville Chamberlain's efforts to appease Hitler. One regional Conservative title, the Yorkshire Post, *stood out against the consensus. This bold stance was the creation of its editor, Arthur Mann. This paper examines the* Yorkshire Post's *editorial opposition to appeasement between the* Anschluss *of March 1938 and the entry of German forces into Prague in March 1939. It explores how Mann resisted pressure from his Conservative proprietors to abandon his stance and examines his understanding of his duty as editor.*

Keywords: Arthur Mann, *Yorkshire Post*, appeasement, proprietorial pressures

INTRODUCTION

Newspapers rarely flatter their rivals. So when, in November 1939, the *Manchester Guardian* praised the *Yorkshire Post*, it was not entirely sincere. The praise marked the merger of the *Yorkshire Post* with the *Leeds Mercury*. This, the *Manchester Guardian* declared, spelled death for a distinctive voice in British public life. Only then did it praise the corpse:

> Soundness in judgement, tenacity of purpose, loyalty to principle, the courage to be unpopular … and even to offend the Party if the Party were not right; these qualities which are the more precious for being rare, have marked the *Yorkshire Post* throughout the long controversy about British foreign policy which began with Mr Chamberlain's Premiership (*Manchester Guardian* 1939).

Responsible for these qualities was Arthur Mann, editor of the *Yorkshire Post* between 1919 and 1939. An austere individual with 'penetrating observation' and 'shrewd judgment' (*The Times* 1972), Mann was the first of thirteen children of Alderman James Mann, twice mayor of Warwick. He attended Warwick School before joining the *Western Mail* as an apprentice reporter. His first editorship was of the *Birmingham Despatch* between 1905 and 1912. In 1915, he moved to London as editor of the *Evening Standard*. His appointment at the *Yorkshire Post* came after the death of John Phillips, editor 1903-1919. The official historians of the *Yorkshire Post*, Gibb and Beckwith (1954: 62), record that Phillips relished leader writing. Mann was content to delegate this task, but he gave precise and detailed instructions to his leader writers. If the words were not his own, the *Yorkshire Post*'s leader columns certainly expressed Mann's opinions.

Mann's bravery over foreign policy was recognised in his lifetime. He was made a Companion of Honour in 1941. And his peers held his work in high regard. James Margach (1978: 53), doyen of the parliamentary lobby for nearly half a century, complimented Mann's *Yorkshire Post* for maintaining 'a robust independence'. Historians, too, have recognised his work (see, e.g., Cockett 1989; Conboy 2011; Hucker 2011; Koss 1990; Meznar 2005). Absent from these assessments have been analyses of the *Yorkshire Post*'s coverage of appeasement and what it can tell us about Arthur Mann's understanding of the role of editor. This paper attempts to fill these gaps, using qualitative content analysis of the newspaper's editorials to examine Mann's policy and style.

APPEASEMENT

My question is not whether appeasement was virtuous. Since the first post-war historians of the era concluded that it certainly was not (see, e.g., Churchill 1948; Namier 1948; Wheeler-Bennett 1948), debate on this topic has been fierce. Revisionists have argued that Chamberlain lacked plausible alternatives and post-revisionists, inspired by Parker's study (1993), have returned to themes first raised in *Guilty men* by Michael Foot, Peter Howard and Frank Owen under the collective pseudonym 'Cato' (1940). Historians in both groups recognise that appeasement as Chamberlain deployed it changed over time, incorporating elements including pacifism, isolationism and deterrence. My purpose is to explore how the editor of one of the few organs of public opinion that challenged it contested its value and purpose.

Gibb and Beckwith (1954) attribute the newspaper's initial opposition to Mann's support for the League of Nation's policy of collective security. Middlemas (1972) shows that this relied upon deterrence, which Chamberlain abandoned in the face of economic weakness and in favour of appeasement. Mann was sceptical about this from the moment Germany reoccupied the Rhineland in March 1936. His antipathy was reinforced by the views of Charles Tower, his chief leader writer, who had been a correspondent in Germany before the First World War. The *Yorkshire Post*'s representative in Vienna, L. R. Murray, who had interviewed the Austrian Chancellor, Kurt Schuschnigg, after the latter had met Hitler, also encouraged him. Murray wrote to Mann that Schuschnigg told him: 'Hitler banged the table and shouted: "I shall get my way because I am ready to run the risk of war and my opponents are not"' (Gibb and Beckwith 1954: 84). This confirmed Mann's view that appeasing Hitler would encourage aggression. And, following the entry of German troops into Austria in March 1938, the *Yorkshire Post*'s criticisms of appeasement intensified. Stedman (2015: 33) notes that Mann also revived his newspaper's advocacy of alliances.

Meznar observes that, in his response to the *Anschluss*, Arthur Mann made his newspaper a critic of the British government. 'It had,' he writes, 'failed to appreciate that Hitler's action followed the plan outlined in *Mein kampf* (Meznar 2005: 161). In its leader column on 16 March 1938, the *Yorkshire Post* accused British ministers of uttering unrealistic words of moderation and reassurance, while 'some of the worst Jew-baiters in Germany were even then arriving in Austria'. It warned that the Cabinet consisted of men, 'some of whom, at least, are temperamentally unfitted to grasp the realities of the national or the international problem, and still less qualified firmly to deal with them' (*Yorkshire Post* 1938a). This was uncompromising stuff at a time when, as Middlemas (1972: 288) explains, a distinct lack of urgency pervaded the mainstream British press. Among the Conservative titles, the *Daily Express, Daily Mail* and *The Times* could be relied upon to champion appeasement, and the left press had grave doubts about any alternative. Mann's position was lonely when, as Hucker (2011: 37) shows, Chamberlain's policy had the support of the majority of British newspapers.

METHODOLOGY

This study examines the *Yorkshire Post*'s opposition to appeasement between 16 March 1938 and 17 March 1939. This period covers the most intense phase of appeasement, beginning with the *Anschluss*, ending with Nazi occupation of Czechoslovakia and including the Munich Crisis. It includes the months during which Adamthwaite (1983: 281) identifies 'a sizable body of opinion critical of Neville Chamberlain's foreign policy' and 'extensive official influence' working to prevent its appearance in newspapers. Hucker (2011: 36) reminds us that, in July 1938, Chamberlain told a National Government rally in Kettering, Northamptonshire, that, when he recalled the Great War, 'I am bound to say again what I have said before … in war, whichever side may call itself the victor, there are no winners, but all are losers.' The British Prime Minister was a zealous appeaser. He believed it was popular and, as Hucker (2011) shows, his belief was reinforced by newspaper support.

Arthur Mann faced stiff opposition and it did not come only from the Cabinet and his rivals. The *Yorkshire Post* was a Conservative newspaper. Its first issue of 2 July 1866 explained: 'The political principles of this journal are Conservative' (*Yorkshire Post* 1866) and these principles had not changed by the late 1930s. Published by the Yorkshire Conservative Newspaper Company Ltd, the appeasement era newspaper was, as Cockett (1989: 100) observes, 'still financially run by and for the Conservative Party in Yorkshire'. Despite this umbilical link to the party of government, Margach (1978: 53) applauds the newspaper's 'robust independence'. Koss (1990) recognises that it went further in its hostility to Chamberlain's foreign policy than any other Conservative title.

A search for all the terms 'appeasement', 'Prime Minister' and 'Hitler' in the *Yorkshire Post*'s online archive between the dates specified above produces 224 hits. From these articles I have analysed leaders and other columns that plainly express the newspaper's opinion.

AFTER THE *ANSCHLUSS*

The leader column of 21 March 1938 reflected on German conduct in Austria, contemplated the emerging Nazi threat to Czechoslovakia and reminded readers of Germany's part in Spain's civil war. It called for a decisive statement as to 'how the power and influence of the whole British Empire shall be used in the preservation of peace and … the preservation of liberty'. It continued:

> Every reasonable man in this country wishes to see appeasement, but no appeasement is worth the name if the whole continent is to continue in a state of uncertainty and terror as to what act of tyranny, heralded by an ultimatum, enforced by invasion, and followed by ruthless inquisition of opinion and expropriation of private property, is to come next (*Yorkshire Post* 1938b).

On 11 April, as the result of the plebiscite endorsing Austria's absorption into the Reich became known, the *Yorkshire Post* turned its fire on Hitler himself:

> He says that Germany has no dictator. But what else is a regime under which the free opinions of an intellectually great people are completely silenced? That intolerance exhibited in Germany, and now also in unhappy Austria, is recognised to threaten also the freedom of other peoples (*Yorkshire Post* 1938c).

Mann was playing with fire. Chamberlain favoured emollient treatment of the Führer and he had the support of Sir Nevile Henderson, Britain's Ambassador to Berlin, who repeatedly warned that Hitler took press criticism extremely seriously. In March 1938, Henderson met Hitler and concluded that any progress towards enduring peace was stymied by British criticism of the Nazi leader. 'Nothing could be done,' Hitler told Henderson, 'until the press campaign against him in England had ceased' (Henderson 1940: 115). Hodgson (2007: 323) notes that the Ambassador later explained: 'It would not have mattered so much had Hitler been a normal individual, but he was unreasonably sensitive to newspaper, and especially British newspaper, criticism.'

Arthur Mann understood the risks. Occasionally he would temper criticism with attempts to understand the new Germany. In May 1938. an example appeared under the headline: 'The lighter side of Nazi Berlin' (*Yorkshire Post* 1938d). It noted that a system of cut-price seats for 'working-class audiences', organised by the Nazi Party's Strength through Joy (*Kraft durch Freude*), had 'benefited the theatres quite considerably'. It was anodyne copy to which even Sir Nevile might have assented. But Mann did not conceal his antipathy towards Nazism for long. In a leader on 20 May, the *Yorkshire Post* warned that Germany's plan was to 'isolate and destroy France as a prelude to colonising Russia' (*Yorkshire Post* 1938e).

Mann's determination to advertise the case against appeasement months before its failure became apparent was made plain in two articles published on the same page in June 1938. The first, a leader, condemned aggression and called for the formation of a 'real league of opposition' to oppose it (*Yorkshire Post* 1938f). The second was a review of a collection of speeches by Winston Churchill. If the rebellious Churchill was a telling choice for a Conservative newspaper, so was Mann's choice of reviewer. John Dundas,[1] a recent graduate in history of Christ Church College, Oxford, was a foreign affairs specialist who had completed his studies in Heidelberg before joining the *Yorkshire Post*. He was already a critic of the Chamberlain government and would go on to report for the newspaper from Czechoslovakia during the Munich crisis. Dundas's review made it plain that he shared his editor's contempt for appeasers:

> Whether one regards Mr Winston Churchill as the heaven-sent leader ... or whether one uses 'Churchillism' as a political swear-word ... all must agree on this – that Mr Churchill makes it perfectly clear where he stands and what he wants. ... In a fog it is so much better to go straight in any direction than to grope in circles (*Yorkshire Post* 1938g).

THE CZECH CRISIS

The *Yorkshire Post*'s hostility was not yet unremitting, but it was persistent. Thus, on 13 July, it warned that neither of the Axis dictators 'interprets "appeasement" in the same sense as it is employed by the British Government'. Indeed, the international outlook could not be improved while Berlin continued 'to point to Czechoslovakia as a thorn in the side of Germany which the Reich, accordingly, has a right in self-defence to rip out and destroy' (*Yorkshire Post* 1938h). Britons wanted their government to assert itself in pursuit of a fair peace. Eight days later, the leader column directed similar criticism against the Prime Minister himself. He was infuriatingly vague and: 'Straightforward utterances are the best way to prepare a stable peace' (*Yorkshire Post* 1938i).

An opportunity for candour arose on 26 July. The Prime Minister had agreed to a debate on 'the international situation' in the House of Commons. The *Yorkshire Post* hoped he would put an end to 'uncontrolled and conflicting versions' of British policy. Appeasement would be tested against two measures: whether Britain would allow Czechoslovakia to be 'so weakened as to involve the dissolution of the state' and whether it would prevent Hitler and Mussolini creating in Spain 'a subservient Fascist-Nazi regime'. To date, requests to Mr Chamberlain for clarity on these issues had elicited 'a perfect and absolute blank'. The *Yorkshire Post* wanted to know 'whether the Dictators are now more minded to pursue a course in all areas which will make the maintenance of peace consistent with the preservation of the fundamental liberties of the Democratic States' (*Yorkshire Post* 1938j).

Arthur Mann reported the debate with a masterpiece of presentation. He foregrounded the speech made by Sir Archibald Sinclair, leader of the Liberal Party. Sinclair warned that allowing the dictators to go on increasing their power 'would undermine the foundations of law, justice and international good faith'. The *Yorkshire Post* contrasted this helpful version of its own opinion with the Prime Minister's Panglossian blandishments. Chamberlain chided Sir Archibald for misrepresenting government polIcy before confirming that the Liberal leader had described it perfectly: 'I cannot imagine anyone in any part of the House who would disagree with what we have so frequently declared to be the main aim of the Government's foreign policy, namely the establishment and maintenance of peace and the removal of all causes of possible conflict, and the amelioration of grievances between one country and another' (*Yorkshire Post* 1938k). The leader lamented the weakness exposed in Chamberlain's approach by its confrontation with the Führer's demands. The Prime Minister had told the House of his plan to send a British mediator to the Sudetenland to make suggestions for a solution to the crisis between the Czech government and the Sudeten Germans. As Cornfield (1964: 101-102) explains, he did not reveal that the Czech government had been placed under irresistible pressure to accept the proposal. Instead, Chamberlain conveyed a misleading impression that the Czechs had requested a mediator. The man chosen for the role was the Liberal Lord Runciman. The *Yorkshire Post* noted that his mission might be achieved 'by virtually forcing Czechoslovakia to accept conditions which would make that country … a mere Nazified vassal of Germany' (*Yorkshire Post* 1938l).

Before the Munich Crisis, the *Yorkshire Post* was not a lone critic of appeasement. Gannon (1971: 154-160) shows that the Liberal *News Chronicle* and Labour-supporting *Daily Herald* advertised the need to oppose German ambitions by force if necessary. He notes that, early in 1938, the *Manchester Guardian* also recognised that the fall of Czechoslovakia would create an intolerable threat to peace. Conservative titles found little to criticise. *The Times* believed Chamberlain could do no wrong and expressed its view in the immediate aftermath of the so-called Weekend Crisis of 21-22 May 1938.[2] 'The British Government's policy is clear to all the world,' it explained. 'It is to urge moderation and peaceful methods, to promote mutual understanding of difficulties, and above all to face the fundamental problem of unrest among the minorities and to press for its solution' (*The Times* 1938a). Chamberlain had equal reason to be happy with the mass-market Conservative dailies, the *Daily Mail* and *Daily Express*. They believed Britain should avoid any entanglement in the affairs of Central and Eastern Europe. The *Daily Telegraph* chose not to question Hitler's good faith (*Daily Telegraph* 1938). Among the Conservative press, the *Yorkshire Post* was lonely and forthright.

But, before the Munich Crisis in September 1938, Arthur Mann avoided irrevocable condemnation of Chamberlain and his policy. No sooner had the *Anschluss* reinforced his scepticism than the Prime Minister and the chairman of the Yorkshire Conservative Newspaper Company encouraged Mann to keep his opinion out of his newspaper. Neville Chamberlain met Mann on 21 March 1938. The editor encouraged the Premier to be robust in his dealings with Hitler and Mussolini. Chamberlain declined, insisted that he was 'much too busy to read the provincial newspapers' and exited announcing: 'I'm afraid I have an appointment at 11.15 and it is now 11.14' (Crowson 1998: 263-264). Chairman of the company Rupert Beckett wrote to his editor on 23 March 1938, warning that he had read 'with growing concern day-by-day the Y.P. leaders devoted to foreign policy', and expressing concern that Mann might believe Chamberlain should be deposed (Mann Papers 1938).

One consequence was that, even as the *Yorkshire Post*'s criticisms became more frequent and direct, the newspaper left open a route to reconciliation. This the editor attempted by deploying a definition of appeasement distinct from the Prime Minister's. Chamberlain's version had come to mean little more than the maintenance of peace at any price short of the surrender of British sovereignty. For Mann it must mean eliminating causes of conflict while adhering to principles of democracy and justice. It would be worthless if it did not permit peoples threatened by Hitler to choose their preferred forms of government. As spring 1938 turned into summer, the tension between these two interpretations became intense. Yet still the *Yorkshire Post* resisted an irrevocable break with government, party and Prime Minister. When Lord Runciman set off for Czechoslovakia it maintained Chamberlain's fiction that his mission was not an instrument of British policy (*Yorkshire Post* 1938m). It showed similar loyalty in coverage of a speech by Sir John Simon, Chancellor of the Exchequer, praising Chamberlain and reaffirming that government policy towards Czechoslovakia was 'to find a solution which is just to all legitimate interests' (*Yorkshire Post* 1938n).

THE ROAD TO MUNICH

Only as the Runciman mission stumbled did Mann move the *Yorkshire Post* towards outright condemnation of government policy. A leader on 29 August warned that the Nazis were 'using the Sudeten Germans as a means of disintegrating Czechoslovakia in the hope that the fatally wounded state could then be used to forward Hitler's plans for domination of Central Europe' (*Yorkshire Post* 1938o). A week later another declared:

> [F]ar from impressing the exponents of power politics with its wisdom, the policy of appeasement was likely to produce on them an impression of weakness rather than strength, and to suggest that we could be blackmailed into paying whatever price was necessary to avoid trouble (*Yorkshire Post* 1938p).

Yet still Mann resisted a final break with Chamberlain. Nothing could be worse, the leader warned, than for dissent at home to undermine the British government's authority at this time of national peril. Now there was palpable tension in Mann's editorial policy. The newspaper had warned that appeasement would bring dangerous consequences. It was delivering them, but Chamberlain did not face the *Yorkshire Post*'s wrath. Conscious of his promise to avoid bullying the government and his proprietors' anxiety, Mann did not declare the Prime Minister unfit for office. Czechoslovakia's plight posed such a threat to peace that the *Yorkshire Post* became temporarily cautious. Reflecting on Hitler's speech at Nuremberg on 12 September, the leader column concluded that, while the Führer shook his 'mailed fist', Britain must simply remain watchful and prepared (*Yorkshire Post* 1938q).

On 15 September, with the crisis approaching boiling point, Chamberlain flew to meet the Führer at Berchtesgaden. Here, without Czech consent, the Prime Minister conceded the transfer of the Sudetenland to Germany. The *Yorkshire Post*'s leader writer did not know this when he penned the paper's analysis for the edition of 16 September. He realised that Sudeten Germans who were demanding incorporation into the Reich were 'a pawn in the Nazi game'. He feared for peace, but he remained cautious. Chamberlain's meeting with Hitler would have 'enabled the British Prime Minister to appreciate the immensity of the problem'. It was 'a clear advantage' that the two men should have exchanged views at a moment of such significance (*Yorkshire Post* 1938r). Scepticism reasserted itself within days. Now the leader column warned that, in the event of any partition of Czechoslovakia, 'there will be recorded another yielding to aggression, and a further tilting of the whole balance of power in Europe on the side of tyranny' (*Yorkshire Post* 1938s).

The *Yorkshire Post* offered comprehensive coverage of the Munich Conference. This included verbatim accounts of the Anglo-French proposals that left the Czechs with no option but to concede to Hitler's demands, and the full text of correspondence between Chamberlain and Hitler (*Yorkshire Post* 1938t). It published on its letters page debate between those who were optimistic about the prospects for appeasement and those who were ashamed. Mann, however, was under intense pressure from his chairman to recognise Munich as a success for Chamberlain. Meznar (2005: 164) records that Beckett wrote to his editor on 30 September insisting that it was the *Yorkshire Post*'s duty 'loyally to support this policy and to cease personal criticisms which alienate Conservative opinion'.

This pressure worked. Mann postponed comment on the Munich Agreement until the House of Commons had heard Chamberlain's explanation of it on 3 October 1938. Now he was scathing. The terms were 'harsh and unconscionable'. Hitler had threatened war to get what he wanted and Britain had bowed to his demands. 'How is it possible that we should feel confident that a man so minded will really prove peace-minded in future?' (*Yorkshire Post* 1938u). But still Mann did not personalise the issue. The *Yorkshire Post* acknowledged that the Prime Minister had been forced to negotiate under constraint. Mere hints of the editor's personal views appeared in two columns. 'Callisthenes' advised readers to pay careful attention to the words of 'the wise, fully informed leader writer' (*Yorkshire Post* 1938v). The 'London Notes and Comment' column recorded that, in the House of Commons, a 'mood of inquiry' had now replaced the euphoria that had greeted Chamberlain's return from Munich. Labour members were sceptical about the course of events and several 'younger members of the Cabinet' shared their misgivings (*Yorkshire Post* 1938w). Leaders published immediately after Munich expose Mann's indecision. Reflecting on four days of parliamentary debate, the *Yorkshire Post* observed 'the nation remains deeply indebted to the Prime Minister for his unsparing and successful efforts to preserve the peace' (*Yorkshire Post* 1938x).

CONDEMNATION AND PROPRIETORIAL PRESSURE

If such praise was the consequence of proprietorial interference, Mann soon recovered his independence of mind and his proprietors intensified their pressure. Meznar (2005: 165) records that, by early November, the *Yorkshire Post* was sure that Hitler did not want peace and concerned that British policy amounted to 'continual retirement'. Mann's anger boiled over in a leader on 8 November 1938. Attacking *The Times* for championing appeasement, the *Yorkshire Post* declared that far from engaging in 'morbid sensationalism' – a criticism levelled by the London title – it was opposing a palpable German menace. It deplored the futility of attempting to do so through 'a policy which has not only yielded to force or the threat of force', but which had 'gravely reduced the total will and strength available in Europe for opposing such menaces'. Government policy risked further weakening of Britain's strategic position (*Yorkshire Post* 1938y). On the twentieth anniversary of the end of the First World War, Arthur Mann published a leader calculated to offend the Prime Minister. It condemned 'a policy of appeasement indistinguishable from a surrender to threats' and accused its architects of a 'tragic lack of conviction'. It concluded: 'We have not cared deeply enough for the things we won in 1918' (*Yorkshire Post* 1938z). The following day's leader promoted Anthony Eden's warnings about the threat to democracy in Europe (*Yorkshire Post* 1938a1).

As news emerged from Germany of the coordinated attacks on Jews known as *Kristallnacht*, the *Yorkshire Post* highlighted reactions from horrified opponents of Nazism. The leader on 16 November demanded a government of national unity. The *Yorkshire Post* acknowledged that it stood accused of 'lack of party loyalty', but insisted it was advancing the best of Conservative values (*Yorkshire Post* 1938b1). A leader on 19 November reflected on the results of five parliamentary by-elections that revealed public opinion to be firmly against the government. The newspaper lamented 'insidious propaganda from London' that continued to promote the government's approach (*Yorkshire Post* 1938c1).

Mann was now under intense pressure from his employer. His leader columns were perceived as accusing Chamberlain of endangering the nation and misleading the public. Cockett (1989: 97) records that the editor told his chairman Chamberlain was a 'commonplace politician' when the country needed 'statesmanship and leadership'. Insisting on editorial freedom, Mann suggested that Beckett should back him or sack him. The chairman declined to demand his editor's resignation. A truce endured until 8 December when the *Yorkshire Post* attacked Chamberlain personally.

Headlined 'Encouragement of aggression', the editorial condemned Chamberlain's foreign policy. By 'repeatedly surrendering to force', he had 'repeatedly encouraged aggression'. The Prime Minister had 'set out with a confident – indeed complacent – belief in his own ability to "talk" the two Dictators into becoming good Europeans'. His approach had invited contempt:

> A Prime Minister who is by nature unfitted to deal with Dictators has habitually disregarded the advice of those most expertly qualified to correct his private judgments. If the fruits of these methods, and the complacency behind them, belonged wholly to the past, we might rightly be urged to refrain from retrospective criticism. It is because we believe that Mr Chamberlain's policy is even now threatening the safety of the realm, and is likely in the near future to threaten it with danger still graver, that we are stating in some detail our case against it (*Yorkshire Post* 1938d1).

On the same page Mann published a second editorial entitled: 'The *Yorkshire Post* and foreign policy – A reply to Conservative critics'. This addressed a motion deploring its criticisms of the Prime Minister that had been passed by the York Conservative Association. It insisted on the newspaper's duty to express its opinion and warned: 'Nothing could finally harm the prestige of the Conservative Party more than that it should, for the sake of a Party advantage, continue to give blind support to a policy which is so gravely endangering national interests as a whole' (*Yorkshire Post* 1938e1).

Mann was at war with his proprietors, and Beckett responded immediately. He wrote to his editor on 8 December, insisting Mann had 'no right … to publish these extreme comments against the P.M. as the considered opinions of the Y. P'. His letter suggested that Mann might tender his resignation:

> I will no longer be a part of the 'bounding down' of the P.M. by day, and this must cease. I have heard you say more than once that you will never 'write to orders', well, if you consider this letter to be an ultimatum to that effect you will of course make your decision as to the course you will adopt (cited in Meznar 2005: 167).

Beckett informed Mann that directors were 'fed up … with this steady spate of personal criticism and recrimination' aimed at the Prime Minister (cited in Cockett 1989: 98). Cockett notes that Mann had revealed in a previous response to Beckett that he was finding it intensely stressful to run the *Yorkshire Post* in the face of criticism from his employers. Now Beckett exploited this information, telling Mann that several directors believed 'this nervous strain to be on the increase'.

Arthur Mann did not buckle. He asked the Yorkshire Conservative Newspaper Company 'whether it is in the true interests of a democratic country that honest expression of opinion by editors and experts trained to study public affairs should be stifled by newspaper proprietors who take their inspiration from interested ministers, from their agents or relatives'. He made a radio programme in which he asserted that responsibility for the editorial content of a newspaper must always reside 'with the man who is responsible for its daily conduct' (cited in Cockett 1989: 99). Here was pure Fourth Estate idealism advanced by an editor who had only occasionally hesitated to operate according to Whig ideals. He explained his principles in a leader column on 3 January 1939. The duty of a journalist 'is to help the public, not to help the statesman'. That other titles were failing to do this was implied by the growing popularity of private newsletters.[3] Concentration of newspaper ownership was reducing the diversity of publications upon which freedom of expression depended. Social contacts between proprietors and Ministers of the Crown were promoting self-censorship. 'Fearlessly to enlighten public opinion on topics of vital national importance is the first responsibility of newspapers' (*Yorkshire Post* 1939a).

EDEN'S FRIEND?

Conservative critics alleged that the *Yorkshire Post*'s hostility to appeasement was informed by Arthur Mann's obedience to the interests of Anthony Eden. His resignation as foreign secretary in February 1938 was taken to imply that Eden opposed Chamberlain's policy. This theory, promoted by the Conservative Whips, asserted that Eden's marriage to Beatrice, third daughter of Sir William Gervase Beckett, a former chairman of the Yorkshire Conservative Newspaper Company, placed Mann under direct pressure to promote Eden's opinions (Gibb and Beckwith 1954: 81). It was superficially plausible. Gervase Beckett was the brother of Rupert Beckett, who served as chairman of the company throughout the period under scrutiny. The Beckett family were the largest shareholders and plainly they were not reluctant to cajole Mann to promote their views. But Sir William had died in 1937 and, by the time of his resignation, Eden was estranged from Beatrice whom he knew to have been serially unfaithful. Nor need we rely on such circumstantial evidence to conclude that Arthur Mann was innocent of promoting Beckett family interests.

Correspondence between Rupert Beckett and Arthur Mann on the editorial treatment of appeasement reveals nothing to suggest that Mann was encouraged to endorse Eden's views. He agreed with aspects of Eden's critique of Chamberlain, but pressure from the Beckett family aimed to force him in the opposite direction. To the extent that Eden opposed appeasement, Mann endorsed Eden's views. His proprietors encouraged him to do the opposite. There is no evidence of favouritism. The *Yorkshire Post* endorsed the views of several opponents of appeasement, including Winston Churchill and Sir Archibald Sinclair.

The assertion that Mann was promoting Eden's career also relies on the belief that Eden was an early and principled critic of appeasement. As Rose (1982) has demonstrated, this is an imperfect description. Though Eden was later identified by Churchill himself as the 'one strong young figure standing up against long, dismal, drawling tides of drift and surrender' (Churchill 1948: 201), his resignation from government was not based on pure principle. In fact, Eden's attitude towards Germany was closely aligned with Chamberlain's. As Rose (1982: 917) notes, one month before his resignation Eden wrote to Chamberlain: 'I entirely agree that we must make every effort to come to terms with Germany.' Eden resigned because he resented Chamberlain's rejection of an offer by US President Franklin Roosevelt to engage in European diplomacy. He felt 'outraged and uneasy' (Avon 1962: 552) because Chamberlain had issued his response to Roosevelt without consulting his foreign secretary. He also disagreed fundamentally with Chamberlain over policy towards Italy. Stedman (2015: 121) recalls that Eden expressed belief in a combination of close Anglo-French co-operation and American support as the best way to keep the peace. Mann agreed with this, but there is no evidence that he did so because Eden asked him to, or that Eden cared about the *Yorkshire Post*'s opinions.

CONSERVATIVE PRESSURE

Mann did not come under pressure from Anthony Eden to oppose appeasement, but he faced persistent imprecations to support it from his proprietors. Less direct was the pressure placed on him by Conservative expectation. The *Yorkshire Post* was accustomed to enjoying excellent contacts with Conservative leaders. Williamson

(1999: 80) shows that Stanley Baldwin had consulted Mann on several occasions during his premiership as had successive chairmen of the Conservative Party. However, Meznar (2005: 159) notes that Mann managed his life so as to avoid compromising his editorial independence. He eschewed personal friendships with politicians and declined political honours lest by accepting them he might appear indebted. Cockett (1989: 62) recalls that Mann wrote to Baldwin following the latter's offer of a knighthood, explaining: 'I feel that a journalist who receives a title, particularly if that title be suggested as a recognition of political services, may … lessen his power to aid the cause he has at heart.'

In 1919, Mann had been tempted away from his editorship of the London *Evening Standard* to edit the *Yorkshire Post*. His time at the London title had been highly successful and he had created such enduring features as 'The Londoner's Diary' (*The Times* 1972). He went to Leeds in the certain knowledge that he was moving to the helm of a powerful bastion of northern Conservatism. Cockett (1989: 62) explains that the Beckett family ran the paper then as later to promote the Conservative cause. Mann was content with this. He was a Conservative, but, above all, he was a journalist inspired by Fourth Estate theory, the key tenets of which he articulated via the leader column of the *Yorkshire Post*. Arthur Mann regarded his newspaper as servant of the public interest, not merely a commercial enterprise.

A SOVEREIGN EDITOR

In opposing appeasement, Arthur Mann performed a role consistent with the model of a sovereign editor (Tunstall 1996: 101) determined to supply the public sphere with watchdog journalism. Conboy (2011: 57) recognises that a few such editors survived into the 1930s, but he attributes their survival to the benevolence of proprietors. Mann had no such protection. He relied on integrity and strength of character to resist pressure from his employers and the Conservative hierarchy. He identified appeasement's flaws and used his office to serve his readers and the body politic. Arthur Mann believed he had a duty to scrutinise politicians and policy. He committed to extended reporting and analysis of appeasement to inform his readers and help them to hold their government to account. These ambitions were aided by his remoteness from London and the pressure to support government policy that was applied there by the Prime Minister's press adviser, George Steward (Cockett 1989: 4-9).

Mann was also able to lean on a team of loyal colleagues, prominent amongst whom was Charles Tower, who possessed 'an unexpurgated copy of *Mein kampf* in the original German' and believed 'Hitler was a reckless megalomaniac bent on war' (*Observer* 1972). Gibb and Beckwith (1954: 86) report that he also took advice on editorial policy and commissioned leaders from: Collin Brooks, later editor of *Truth*; Charles Davy, who subsequently worked as assistant editor of the *Observer*; and Iverach McDonald. No doubt these friends and like-minded employees applauded his independent approach to foreign policy. They had in Mann's *Yorkshire Post* a safety valve through which they could release information and opinion supplied to them by Chamberlain's critics in the Foreign Office.

But Mann alone had to liaise with his proprietors. In his determination to retain undiluted editorial authority he demonstrated his faith in Fourth Estate theory. To him this was no myth invented to glamorise a debased profession. He believed the *Yorkshire Post* had a role to play in political society and that it should 'act as an indispensable link between public opinion and the governing institutions of the country' (Boyce 1978: 21). He considered it his duty to follow where evidence supplied by his correspondents led. His sovereignty as editor compelled him to advance arguments that angered his proprietors and many of his readers. He did not surrender to pressure, though it made him ill, instead he exercised what Stevenson (2002: 26) and Harcup (2004: 6) have defined as agency: the individual journalist's ability to challenge consensus through the exercise of individual conscience. Mann's approach also suggests that a central tenet in the liberal narrative of media history – that agency operating in a free market will ensure diversity of editorial coverage – is of more than theoretical value. Indeed, Arthur Mann believed his *Yorkshire Post* must be 'an educational institution that facilitates the rational public discussion of serious ideas' (Hampton 2009: 27). It was not his fault that, as Hucker (2011: 29) reminds us, Chamberlain chose to ignore press criticism or to dismiss it as misrepresentation. Still less so that he misinterpreted press support that he had won through persuasion as evidence that his policy was popular.

Mann recognised that his work's importance was enhanced by the loyalty offered to Chamberlain by *The Times* and the similarly compliant *Daily Mail*, *Daily Express* and *Observer*. The knowledge that he was standing alone intensified his sense of mission. But his courage and the social value he believed it served were not rewarded by higher sales or profits. Indeed, Arthur Mann's employers believed that his editorial policies damaged sales and contributed to a growing deficit. This financial failure would end his editorship. Beckett told Mann that losses showed, 'it is futile to go on vainly attempting the sale of a newspaper in a form and style that the public have shown consistently they do not want' (Cockett 1989: 128). Meznar (2005: 171) notes that some directors believed 'the paper was losing money because of its long and critical leaders'. Arthur Mann embraced Bentham's theory that the sanction of public opinion should work to protect civil society against misrule. He shared James Mill's certainty that a newspaper could be 'the greatest safeguard of the interests of mankind'.

His courage eventually won his proprietor's respect. Meznar (2005, 169) recalls that in the early months of 1939 Rupert Beckett defended his editor. He told the AGM of the Yorkshire Conservative Newspaper Company the *Yorkshire Post*'s editorial policy was rooted in experience and reason. Answering criticism of Mann, Beckett said: 'In so far as you ask me to say anything which will tie the hands of this newspaper and prevent it giving free and honest expression of its views on policy which may be vital to this country, I shall not sit here and consent to that' (cited in Meznar 2005: 169-170). It had become convenient for Beckett to celebrate in public the principle of editorial independence he had worked to restrict.

THE END OF APPEASEMENT

My content analysis ends on 17 March 1939, immediately after the German seizure of rump Czechoslovakia demonstrated the worthlessness of the Munich Agreement. On this day Neville Chamberlain made a decisive policy speech to the Birmingham Unionist Association. He denounced the German leader's breach of the pledges he had made at Munich and declared Britain's determination to resist Nazism. Chamberlain had lost patience with Hitler (*The Times* 1938b). Much of the remainder of his premiership would be spent seeking to create the very alliances he had long distrusted as more likely to provoke Hitler's wrath than to pacify him. Now deterrence through alliances and rearmament replaced the delusion that Germany might be bought off with territorial concessions. Mann would express approval of this approach, long advocated by the *Yorkshire Post*, but he took every opportunity to snipe at Chamberlain and repeat his calls for a broader government. His criticism of other newspapers remained vivid too. Thus, two weeks after Hitler seized the remnants of sovereign Czechoslovakia, Mann seized on a question raised in the House of Commons. The Prime Minister was asked why, five days before the Prague Coup, the national press had been briefed to understand that he believed the 'international situation gave less cause for concern than for some time'. The *Yorkshire Post* queried why Chamberlain had expressed such confidence only to find 'five days later Czechoslovakia had ceased to exist' (*Yorkshire Post* 1939b). This assault was accompanied by a column which reminded readers of many speeches over the course of the previous year in which the Prime Minister had misinterpreted the mood of the dictators (*Yorkshire Post* 1939c). Beckett's public support appeared to have emboldened Mann.

CONCLUSION: MANN'S BRAVE AND IDEALISTIC BATTLE

Arthur Mann would not resign his editorship until November 1939. He did so then because he could not accept the commercial development the *Manchester Guardian* was so pleased to advertise: the merger of his title with the *Leeds Mercury*. He had fought a brave and idealistic battle to preserve his freedom to oppose appeasement. He had denounced the policy and its architect in language so compelling that even his chairman was obliged, in the end, to offer his backing.

But Mann could not accept the diminution of his status implied by the merger of his beloved *Yorkshire Post* with its less prestigious stablemate. His hubris meant that he would never test his ideal of editorial independence in the crucible of a democracy at war.

- The paper first appeared in *Ethical Space*, Vol 13, No 4 pp 29-39

REFERENCES

Adamthwaite, Anthony (1983) The British government and the media, 1937-1938, *Journal of Contemporary History*, Vol. 18, No.2 pp 281-297

Avon, The Rt Hon. The Earl of Avon (1962) *The Eden memoirs: Facing the dictators*, London, Cassell & Co.

Bingham, Adrian (2004) *Gender, modernity and the popular press*, Oxford, Clarendon Press

Boyce, George (1978) The Fourth Estate: The reappraisal of a concept, Boyce, George, Curran, James and Wingate, Pauline (eds) *Newspaper history from the 17th Century to the present day*, London, Constable & Co. pp 19-40

'Cato' (1940) *Guilty men*, London, Victor Gollancz

Christiansen, Arthur (1961) *Headlines all my life*, London, Heinemann

Churchill, Winston (1948) *The Second World War, Vol. 1*, London, Cassell & Co.

Cockett, Richard (1989) *Twilight of truth: Chamberlain, appeasement and the manipulation of the press*, London, Weidenfeld & Nicolson

Conboy, Martin (2011) *Journalism in Britain: A historical introduction*, London, Sage Publications

Cornfield, Stanley (1964) *Lord Runciman and the Sudeten Germans: A study in appeasement*. Thesis submitted to the Department of History, University of Arizona. Available online at http://arizona.openrepository.com/arizona/handle/10150/318970, accessed on 1 February 2016

Crowson, Nicholas (ed.) (1998) *Fleet Street, press barons and politics: The journals of Collin Brooks, 1932-1940*, Cambridge, Cambridge University Press

Curran, James and Seaton, Jean (2010) *Power without responsibility: Press, broadcasting and the internet in Britain*, London, Routledge, seventh edition

Daily Herald (1938) Leader, 11 April p. 10

Daily Mail (1933) Youth triumphant, by Lord Rothermere, 10 July p. 10

Daily Telegraph (1938) Leader [first item], 2 August p. 8

Gannon, Franklin Reid (1971) *The British press and Germany 1936-1939*, Oxford, Oxford University Press

Gibb, Mildred and Beckwith, Frank (1954) *The Yorkshire Post: Two centuries*, Leeds, Yorkshire Conservative Newspaper Company Ltd.

Goldfarb Marquis, Alice (1978) Words as weapons: Propaganda in Britain and Germany during the First World War, *Journal of Contemporary History*, Vol. 13 pp 467-498

Hampton, Mark (2009) Renewing the Liberal tradition: The press and public discussion in twentieth century Britain, Baily, Michael (ed.) *Narrating media history*, Oxford, Routledge pp 26-35

Harcup, Tony (2004) *Journalism: Principles and practice*, London, Sage Publications

Henderson, Sir Nevile (1940) *Failure of a mission: Berlin 1937-39*, London, Hodder & Stoughton

Hodgson, Guy (2007) Sir Nevile Henderson, appeasement and the press, *Journalism Studies*, Vol. 8, No. 2 pp 320-334

Hucker, Daniel (2011) *Public opinion and the end of appeasement in Britain and France*, Farnham, Surrey, Ashgate Publishing

Koss, Stephen (1990) *The rise and fall of the political press in Britain*, London, Fontana Press

Manchester Guardian (1939) The *Yorkshire Post*, 28 November p. 6

Mann Papers (1938) Ms.Eng. c.3274, Fol. 8: Mann to Pearson, 23 March

Margach, James (1978) *The abuse of power*, London, W. H. Allen

McEwen, J. M. (1983) 'Brass-hats' and the British press during the First World War, *Canadian Journal of History*, Vol. 18 pp 43-67

Meznar, Michael (2005) *The British government, the newspapers and the German problem 1937-39*. Thesis submitted to the University of Durham. Available online at http://etheses.dur.ac.uk/1783/, accessed on 1 February 2016

Middlemas, Keith (1972) *The strategy of appeasement: The British government and Germany 1937-39*, Chicago, Quadrangle Books

Namier, Lewis (1948) *Diplomatic prelude, 1938-1939*, London, Macmillan

Parker, Robert A. C. (1993) *Chamberlain and appeasement: British policy and the coming of the Second World War*, London, Palgrave Macmillan

Rose, Norman (1982) The resignation of Anthony Eden, *The Historical Journal*, Vol. 25, No. 4 pp 911-931

Stedman, Andrew (2015) *Alternatives to appeasement: Neville Chamberlain and Hitler's Germany*, London, I. B. Tauris

Stevenson, Nick (2002) *Understanding media cultures*, London, Sage Publications

The Observer (1972) Obituary of Arthur Henry Mann, 30 July p. 10

The Times (1938a) Anxious moments, 23 May p. 15

The Times (1938b) The Prime Minister's answer, 18 March p. 12

The Times (1972) Obituary: Mr Arthur Mann, an outstanding editor of the *Yorkshire Post*, 28 July p. 18

Tunstall, Jeremy (1996) *Newspaper power: The new national press in Britain*, Oxford, Oxford University Press

Wheeler-Bennett, John (1948) *Munich: Prologue to tragedy*, London, Macmillan

Williamson, Philip (1999) *Stanley Baldwin: Conservative leadership and national values*, Cambridge, Cambridge University Press

Yorkshire Post (1866) 2 July

Yorkshire Post (1938a) There is no other way, 16 March p. 8

Yorkshire Post (1938b) A vital decision, 21 March p. 8

Yorkshire Post (1938c) Hitler's invisible critics, 11 April p. 8

Yorkshire Post (1938d) The lighter side of Nazi Berlin, 3 May p. 8

Yorkshire Post (1938e) The policy of squeeze, 20 May p. 10

Yorkshire Post (1938f) Japan's war burden, 24 June p. 10

Yorkshire Post (1938g) The price of peace: Review by John Dundas of Winston Churchill's *Arms and the covenant*, 24 June p. 10

Yorkshire Post (1938h) Europe and the dictators, 13 July p. 10

Yorkshire Post (1938i) A great French welcome, 21 July p. 10

Yorkshire Post (1938j) The state of Europe, 26 July p. 10

Yorkshire Post (1938k) British government's foreign policy restated, 27 July p. 8

Yorkshire Post (1938l) Foreign affairs debate, 27 July p. 10

Yorkshire Post (1938m) Viscount Runciman's mission, 2 August p. 9

Yorkshire Post (1938n) British aims in Czechoslovakia, 29 August p. 7

Yorkshire Post (1938o) The Czech crisis, 29 August p. 8

Yorkshire Post (1938p) The need for national unity, 6 September p. 8

Yorkshire Post (1938q) Negotiations under threat, 13 September p. 8

Yorkshire Post (1938r) Background to Berchtesgaden, 16 September p. 8

Yorkshire Post (1938s) Face the facts, 19 September p. 8

Yorkshire Post (1938t) Official correspondence on the Czechoslovak crisis, 29 September p. 6

Yorkshire Post (1938u) A momentous debate, 4 October p. 10

Yorkshire Post (1938v) Making up the public's mind, 4 October p. 10

Yorkshire Post (1938w) London notes and comment, 4 October p. 10

Yorkshire Post (1938x) After the debate, 7 October p. 10

Yorkshire Post (1938y) British foreign policy, 8 November p. 10

Yorkshire Post (1938z) Twenty years after, 11 November p. 10

Yorkshire Post (1938a1) Outlook for Britain, 12 November p. 10

Yorkshire Post (1938b1) Call for all-party consultation, 16 November p. 8

Yorkshire Post. (1938c1) Five by-elections, 19 November p. 10

Yorkshire Post (1938d1) Encouragement of aggression, 8 December p. 8

Yorkshire Post (1938e1) The *Yorkshire Post* and foreign policy – A reply to Conservative critics, 8 December p. 8

Yorkshire Post (1939a) A newspaper's first duty, 3 January p. 6

Yorkshire Post (1939b) Government and people, 29 March p. 8

Yorkshire Post (1939c) Essays in over-optimism, 29 March p. 8

Young, G.M. (1952) *Stanley Baldwin*, London, Rupert Hart-Davis

NOTE ON THE CONTRIBUTOR

Tim Luckhurst is Principal of South College and Associate Pro Vice-Chancellor Engagement at Durham University. He is a newspaper historian and an academic member of the university's Centre for Modern Conflicts and Cultures. His most recent book is *Reporting the Second World War: The press and the people 1939-1945* (Bloomsbury Academic, 2023).

Chapter 2

Richard Hoggart and Pilkington: Populism and public service broadcasting

Julian Petley

In 1962 the Pilkington Committee, of which Richard Hoggart was a highly influential member, produced a report which was highly critical of ITV and its regulator the Independent Television Authority. It recommended that the third television channel be allocated to the BBC, and that the authority, once armed with greater seriousness of purpose, should both plan the ITV schedules and sell advertising time, thus greatly reducing the power of the advertisers over the programme makers and schedulers within the companies. The government baulked at the proposals for ITV but, nonetheless, the ensuing 1964 Television Act strengthened the powers of the ITA and allotted the third channel to the BBC. The report was bitterly attacked by most national newspapers, several of which had substantial holdings in ITV companies, and which saw the report's strictures on populism in television programming as an implicit critique of their own journalistic standards and as a threat to press freedom. This paper examines the press critique of the Pilkington Report, and suggests that it prefigures later press interventions in the broadcasting sphere, as well as press reactions to the Leveson Inquiry.

Keywords: Richard Hoggart, Pilkington, populism, ITV, ITA

INTRODUCTION

On 13 July 1960, the Conservative government of Harold Macmillan established a committee under the chairmanship of the industrialist Sir Harry Pilkington 'to consider the future of broadcasting services in the United Kingdom' and, more specifically, 'to advise on the services which should in future be provided in the United Kingdom by the BBC and the ITA' and 'to recommend whether additional services should be provided by any other organisation' (HMSO 1962: 1). It was chaired by the industrialist Sir Harry Pilkington, but the key member of the committee was undoubtedly Richard Hoggart, who had recently written an influential article for *Encounter* entitled 'The uses of television' (Hoggart 1970: 152-162).

The report was commissioned for four reasons. Firstly, ITV had been introduced in 1954 for only a ten year 'experimental' period, mainly because of Labour Party hostility to commercial television, and this would soon be drawing to a close. Second, the channel was attracting mounting criticism from those who believed that the ITV companies were making unacceptably large profits from poor quality programming. Third, there was the looming question of whether there should be a third television channel and, if so, to whom it should be allotted. And fourth, the BBC Charter was due to expire in 1962. However, the resultant report, which was produced in June 1962, went far beyond addressing these specific issues and although, as we shall see, its main recommendations for restructuring ITV were rejected, in 1977 the Annan Committee were able to claim convincingly that 'the Pilkington Report transformed the face of ITV' (p. 146), whilst Jeffrey Milland has argued that 'broadcasting in Britain continued to be based on Pilkingtonian principles for forty years, establishing criteria for judging the performance of broadcasters which few challenged, at least until the 1980s' (2009: 95). For others, the Pilkington Report had an importance that stretched even beyond broadcasting. Thus, as Jean Seaton puts it: 'The committee had been asked to review the development of television. In fact, they did much more, producing a report which judged the nation's culture' (quoted in Freedman 2003: 31), and Michael Bailey, Ben Clarke and John Walton claim that 'insofar as the final report concerned itself with the philosophy of "good broadcasting" and British culture more generally, one could argue that its many appraisals and accompanying proposals belong as much to the "condition of England" tradition as they do to broadcasting history' (2012: 139). Equally, Hoggart himself stated that the report presented an argument not simply about broadcasting but about...

> ... freedom and responsibility within commercialised democracies. It touched on the interrelations between cash, power and the organs for intellectual debate; it had to do with a society which is changing rapidly and doesn't understand its own changes; it had to do with the adequacy of our assumptions and vocabulary to many current social issues (1970: 189).

The main purpose of this paper is to examine the report's attacks on populism in broadcasting, and particularly in ITV programming, and then to analyse the populist counter-attack on the report in significant sections of the national press. But first it is necessary to sketch in something of the context in which the report was commissioned and published.

ITV: PROFIT AND POPULISM

By the late 1950s ITV was becoming increasingly popular – and profitable. By concentrating on the most watched kinds of programmes, ITV companies were making an average annual pre-tax profit of 130 per cent. It was at this point that Roy Thomson, of Scottish Television, coined, extremely unwisely, the phrase about owning an ITV franchise being a 'licence to print money'. ATV's profits increased from less than £450,000 to more than £4m. between 1957 and 1958, and the shares of its deputy chairman, Norman Collins, leapt in value from £2,000 to £500,000. Within three months of ITV's opening night, the controller of programmes for Associated-Rediffusion, which owned one of the two franchises for London, was perfectly blunt about his intention to change the schedules: 'Let's face it once and for all, the public likes girls, wrestling, bright musicals, quiz shows and real-life drama. We gave them the Hallé Orchestra, *Foreign Press Club*, floodlit football and visits to the local fire station. From now on, what the public wants, it's going to get' (quoted in Sendall 1982: 328). For this he was admonished mildly by ITA director-general Sir Ronald Fraser, who responded: 'A television company must have a policy of its own, and that policy must be something more than "giving the public what it wants" unless we are prepared to say that we no more respond to the social significance of television than to the social significance of toffee' (quoted in ibid: 139). However, by 1960 Fraser had changed his tune, averring that: 'If you decide to have a system of people's television, then people's television you must expect it to be, and it will reflect their likes and dislikes, their tastes and aversions, what they can comprehend and what is beyond them' (quoted in Milland 2004: 81).

The Conservatives were divided in their attitude to ITV, as they had been since even before its birth. There were those who supported it because it was a private enterprise, a rival to the BBC (which many Tories, then as now, disliked because it was a public corporation, and one which they perceived to have a liberal bias), and provided freedom of choice in viewing, but others disliked what they saw as its commercial values. On the other side of the political divide, Labour had at one time pledged to abolish ITV, but dropped this idea before the 1959 General Election. Many Labour supporters may have disliked its commercialism, but, equally, others wanted a stake in the burgeoning consumer society and saw nothing amiss in ITV's advertisements and quiz show programmes with their tempting prizes.

When the report was published in June 1962, the Pilkington Committee made it abundantly clear that, in its view, commercial values had exerted a largely negative pressure on television broadcasting. The BBC was given a relatively clean bill of health, but ITV and its regulator the Independent Television Authority (ITA) were very heavily criticised. However, even though the ITA was excoriated for failing to recognise what the committee saw as television's immense power to damage society, the report nonetheless recommended that in future the authority, once armed with greater seriousness of purpose, should both plan the schedules and sell advertising time, thus greatly reducing the power of the advertisers over the programme makers and schedulers within the companies. The report also recommended that the third channel be awarded to the BBC.

'A CANDY-FLOSS WORLD'

Before I go on to examine, and indeed defend, what the report had to say specifically about populism, I do, however, want to acknowledge that aspects of its approach to broadcasting are as likely to evoke as much hostility today within media and cultural studies circles as they did in the case of its many critics at the time of its publication. For example, it pinned its colours firmly to the 'effects' mast[1]: 'Broadcasters must recognise that television affects moral standards by the constant repetition of the values it shows, and by the assumptions underlying its programmes generally. They must remember, too, that their audiences at almost all times include a great many children' (HMSO 1962: 28). It also noted that 'we strongly refute the argument that because an effect has not been conclusively proved the broadcasting authorities need not concern themselves with it' (ibid: 15). One of the report's particular bugbears was 'triviality', which it appeared to think of as an inherent quality of television:

> Programmes which exemplified emotional tawdriness and mental timidity helped to cheapen both emotional and intellectual values. Plays or serials might not deal with real human problems but present a candy-floss world[2] … Our own conclusion is that triviality is a natural vice of television, and that where it prevails it operates to lower general standards of enjoyment and understanding. It is, we were reminded, 'more dangerous to the soul than wickedness'[4] (ibid: 34-35).

This was a judgement with which the committee appeared to concur. It was particularly concerned over ITV quiz shows, of which it opined that:

> In relying upon the appeal to greed and fear, and to the pleasures of watching these emotions roused in others because valuable prizes are at stake, and in relying on an atmosphere of artificial good fellowship, these programmes abandon the objective – light entertainment which amuses because it is good – for light entertainment which is poor in invention and needs the support of extraneous appeals (ibid: 58).

Similarly 'party game' items on ITV variety shows were met with the sniffy response that 'one may, of course, make a fool of oneself among relatives or friends, because one is then participating in an intimate and lively human relationship; to do so for the amusement of millions of others, who are both unseen and unknown, is to risk being merely a foolish spectacle' (ibid: 59).

BROADCASTING AND THE 'MORAL CONDITION OF SOCIETY'

On the other hand, the charge levelled at the time against the report that it took a moralistic line on broadcasting misunderstood what it meant by 'moral' and obscured its valuable contribution to the debate about public service broadcasting, a contribution which is as important now as when it was first published. Much of the relevant material here is contained in Chapter Three of the report, 'The purposes of broadcasting', which was actually written by the committee secretary, Dennis Lawrence, who was a civil servant in the Post Office, then the government department responsible for broadcasting. It is, however, highly Hoggartian in tone, and Hoggart himself referred to it as 'the finest statement in English' on 'the purposes of broadcasting in a democracy' (1992: 65).

The report argues that as it presumes that 'television is and will be a main factor in influencing the values and moral standards of our society', so 'by its nature broadcasting must be in a constant and sensitive relationship with the moral condition of society' (HMSO 1962: 15). This is repeated in slightly different formulations three times (ibid: 28, 31, 39-40). As Hoggart explained in a talk given shortly after the report's publication, aptly entitled 'Difficulties of democratic debate', this did not mean that the report was asserting a 'crudely moralistic relationship' between broadcasting and society, still less that it was suggesting that 'broadcasters had a responsibility for the direct propagation of the Ten Commandments' (1970: 197). Later Hoggart explained that the formulation 'simply stated the inescapable connection with society out there and with the nature of its life, its assumptions, choices and judgements' (1992: 62). 'Moral', then, is used here in a manner which could be seen as synonymous with 'culture' in Raymond Williams's broad sense of the term as denoting a society's 'whole way of life, material, intellectual and spiritual' (1963: 16). As Hoggart himself put it: 'It means that the quality of the life of a society as expressed in its texture – its assumptions and values as bodied out in its habits and ways of life – that these will be reflected and to some extent affected by broadcasting as by other forms of mass communication' (1970: 197). Putting these comments together with the report itself, Bailey, Clarke and Walton argue that what is being suggested here is that …

> Broadcasting is one of many modern technologies of mass communication that are constitutive of 'the life of a society', that shape and are shaped by social relations and processes. Hence the importance that broadcasters respect the medium and assume a responsibility for its output, its listeners, its viewers, indeed, the public at large (2012: 142).

MAJORITIES AND MINORITIES

Central to the report's defence of public service broadcasting is an attack on the populist notion that broadcasting should simply 'give the public what it wants'. In this respect it argues:

The public is not an amorphous, uniform mass; however much it's counted and classified under this or that heading, it is composed of individual people; and 'what the public wants' is what individual people want. They share some of their wants and interests with all or most of their fellows; and it is necessary that a service of broadcasting should cater for those wants and interests. There is, in short, a considerable place for items which all or most enjoy. To say, however, that the only way of giving people what they want is to give them these items is to imply that all individuals are alike. But no two are. ... A service which caters only for majorities can never satisfy all, or even most, of the needs of any individual. It cannot, therefore, satisfy all the needs of the public (ibid: 16).

Furthermore, as Hoggart himself asserted, public service broadcasting ...

... means catering not only for known majorities but also for as many minorities as possible, some small, some almost majorities. An important point here is that these groups are not in watertight compartments separated from each other; they overlap and shift in and out. We are all at some time members of majorities and also of different minorities (2001: 39).

All of which, interestingly, adds up to something of an endorsement of the idea that individuals have multiple identities, which is central to the kind of cultural/media studies that generally take a dim view of Hoggart.

DIVERSITY AND FREEDOM OF CHOICE

Similarly the report emerges as the champion of another quality prized today by these (and other) disciplines, namely diversity. Thus it states:

No one can say he is giving the public what it wants, unless the public knows the whole range of possibilities which television can offer and, from this range, chooses what it wants to see. For a choice is only free if the field of choice is not unnecessarily restricted. The subject matter of television is to be found in the whole scope and variety of human awareness and experience. If viewers – 'the public' – are thought of as 'the mass audience', or 'the majority', they will be offered only the average of common experience and awareness; the ordinary; the commonplace – for what all know and do is, by definition, commonplace. They will be kept unaware of what lies beyond the average of experience; their field of choice will be limited. In time they come to like only what they know. But it will always be true that, had they been offered a wider range from which to choose, they might and often would have chosen otherwise, and with greater enjoyment (HMSO 1962: 17).

This passage also invokes a notion dear to the hearts of latter-day apostles of 'de-regulation', namely freedom of choice, but it does so in a way which is not simply devoid of the 'free market' prescriptions which today habitually attend this idea but is, indeed, diametrically opposed to any such approach. Thus it continues:

> 'To give the public what it wants' is a misleading phrase: misleading because as commonly used it has the appearance of an appeal to democratic principle but the appearance is deceptive. It is, in fact, patronising and arrogant, in that it claims to know what the public is, but defines it as no more than the mass audience; and in that it claims to know what it wants but limits its choice to the average of experience. In this sense, we reject it utterly. If there is a sense in which it should be used, it is this: what the public wants and what it has the right to get is freedom to choose from the widest range of programme matter. Anything less than that is deprivation (ibid: 17-18).

And Hoggart himself was well aware of the economic motives underlying such spurious appeals to democratic principles, noting that 'those who claim to give the public what they already know they want usually mean what it is most profitable to them and the advertisers to offer' (2001: 172).

The report also firmly takes issue with the notion that the only alternative to 'giving the public what it wants' is imposing on the public what someone thinks they ought to like and which will be good for them. In the report's view:

> The role of a broadcasting regulator is not to follow the latter course but to respect the public's right to choose from the widest range of subject matter and so to enlarge worthwhile experience. Because, in principle, the possible range of subject matter is inexhaustible, all of it can never be presented, nor can the public know what the range is. So, the broadcaster must explore it, and choose from it first. This might be called 'giving a lead': but it is not the lead of the autocratic or arrogant. It is the proper exercise of responsibility by public authorities duly constituted as trustees for the public interest (HMSO 1962: 18).

This was a responsibility the committee clearly felt the ITA had shirked, thus helping to deprive the public of the wide range of subject matter which it should have every right to expect from ITV programming. Although, as we shall see, the Pilkington Committee was widely accused of wanting to narrow the range of programmes on television by prescribing a diet of worthy but dull fare, the committee itself saw the pursuit of the largest possible audiences by the ITV companies as limiting viewers' choices and leading to the tyranny of majority tastes, whereas its recommendations 'sought to extend intellectual and imaginative freedom, to give more room for variety and dissent' and encouraged thinking 'not only about what we are but what we might become if we were given more varied chances' (Hoggart 1970: 199-200).

PRESS INTEREST IN ITV

In his 'Difficulties of democratic debate' talk mentioned earlier, Hoggart said of the Pilkington Report: 'Here was a confrontation of an unusually searching kind, and few were ready for it. This has depressing implications, and they go far wider than broadcasting matters alone' (ibid: 200). In particular, the majority of national newspapers were highly critical of the report, and it was not simply in the popular press that the populism which it had attacked in broadcasting answered back, and did so in a particularly raucous and vituperative fashion. However, before we go on to analyse this particular aspect of the press response to the report, it is important to understand what the report itself had to say about the national press, and especially its holdings in ITV companies.

Pages 180-181 of the report contain an extremely valuable, and highly revealing, analysis of such holdings. Thus, for example, Daily Mirror Newspapers owned 13 per cent of Associated Television's (ATV) voting stock, and 8 per cent of its non-voting stock; Thomson Newspapers (which owned *The Times* and *The Scotsman*) and Thomson Television (which was not itself a press group but was wholly controlled by Roy Thomson, who also controlled Thomson Newspapers) between them owned 80 per cent and 100 per cent of the voting and non-voting stock respectively of Scottish Television; News of the World Ltd. owned 21 per cent and 12 per cent of the voting and non-voting stock respectively of TWW (Television Wales and the West); Associated Newspapers, publishers of the *Daily Mail* and *Daily Sketch*, owned 38 per cent of the voting shares in Southern Television; and the Manchester Guardian and Evening News Ltd. owned 21 per cent of both the voting and non-voting shares in Anglia Television.

A THREAT TO DEMOCRACY

The committee was asked by the postmaster general, who had commissioned it in the first place, to consider whether, as some believed, a threat was posed to democracy by the fact that newspapers had shares in ITV companies. The report explains:

> The threat is thought to reside in the fact that, because two of the media of mass communication are owned in some measure by the same people, there is an excessive concentration of power to influence and persuade public opinion; and that if these same people are too few or have broadly the same political affiliations, there will be an increasingly one-sided presentation of affairs of public concern (HMSO 1962: 182).

The report states that the committee had thought it was not for them 'to consider whether or not there has been bias or insufficiency in the presentation by the press of affairs of public concern, because of the association of newspaper interests and television companies', but they did concern themselves with two issues regarding press interests in ITV:

> First, newspapers might unduly publicise and praise, or avoid adverse criticism of, the television service provided by companies in which they had an interest, and might disregard or criticise unfairly the competing service of the BBC; second, newspapers might disregard or criticise unfairly any exercise by the authority of its powers against these companies (ibid: 182).

The committee found no evidence that either of these had taken place. However, they judged that although the risk of the emergence of a threat to democracy was small, 'even so it would be unwise to dismiss it too lightly: in particular, the omission or minimising of news – not necessarily for reasons of bias – might not be easily identified or corrected. But if the likelihood is small, the consequences could be profound' (ibid: 183). They concluded:

> The suspicion of too great a concentration in too few hands of the power to influence and persuade cannot be dismissed by the argument that the power has not been used, and is not very likely to be used. So, some limits must be set. The simplest rule would be to prohibit press participation altogether. But though we believe that the presumption lies against press participation, we do not think it necessary to recommend an absolute ban. That being so, a factual formula is necessary (ibid: 183).

In their view, the press should not be dominant in any company, in the sense of being the largest single interest in it. And in the specific case of Scottish Television, essentially a fiefdom of Roy Thompson, they recommended that the contract should not be renewed on its expiry in 1964 unless the press interest had been sufficiently reduced.

FURY AND DERISION

It is hardly surprising, then, that the report was bitterly rejected by significant sections of the press. It was not that the newspapers avoided 'adverse criticism of the television service provided by companies in which they had an interest': rather, they reacted to it with fury and derision. As Hoggart correctly states, 'the members of the committee were described as authoritarians, socialistic, roundheads, do-gooders, highbrows, puritans, and paternalists; they were, it was said, polemical, smug and naïve' (1970: 189), and elsewhere he notes that certain journalists 'threw every dirty word in their box of cliché abuse at us: "nannying … elitist … patronising … grundyish … do-gooding … superior … schoolmarmish" – all the usual dreary, underdeveloped litany of fear', which he describes as an 'Islamicfundamentalist-like fury' (1992: 61). But it would be simplistic to explain hostile newspapers' ferocious onslaught on the report merely in terms of the threat which they perceived it to pose to their lucrative holdings in ITV companies: what appears to have struck an extremely raw nerve were the report's strictures on populism within broadcasting, strictures which several of the more popular papers perceived as attacking, albeit implicitly, their own populist forms of journalism. Moreover, they also raised the spectre that press regulation might follow in the wake of any successful attempt to require the ITV companies to adhere more closely to the standards of public service broadcasting. That this was beyond unlikely, given successive British governments' allergic reaction to any suggestion that the state should involve itself in some way with press regulation, is beside the point: this was primarily a tactic to scare and scandalise their readers. However, it should be noted that the third Royal Commission on the Press was about to produce its own report.

I will now attempt to show how various national newspapers mobilised populist discourse against the Pilkington Report and, both explicitly and implicitly, in defence of their own forms of journalism and their particular conception of press freedom.

'MULTIPLICATION, ABUNDANCE AND FREEDOM'

On 28 June, the *Daily Telegraph* (which had no shares in ITV companies) published an editorial about the report, headed 'Pride and Prejudice'. Here a critique of the report's anti-populist stance is blended with a defence of competition and private enterprise and an attack on public enterprise, notably the BBC. In the paper's view:

> A form of arrogance ... saturates this amazing document, a haughty conviction that whatever is popular must be bad. Even more deplorable is the committee's assumption that competition has not only done harm but can do nothing else ... The committee's suspicion of any sort of commercial motive becomes at times almost pathological. Throughout the report run the assumptions that commercial disciplines are inimical to, if not actually incompatible with, any sort of objective excellence; that nothing worthwhile can be achieved except by those free of all ignoble desire for gain; above all, that any enterprise deriving revenue from advertisements can only be debased and corrupted in consequence. A serious newspaper, itself deriving revenue from advertisements, could hardly be expected to agree with such nonsense.

Responding to the committee's judgement that local newspapers should not be allowed to own local radio stations for fear of concentrating local media power in too few hands, and that these stations should thus be owned by the BBC, it complains that this would entail 'concentrating more power in even fewer hands. Indeed, it seems to see vices in every private and independent enterprise, virtues in every public enterprise. It sees the least danger where wiser men have seen the most: in the power of the State'.

A similar line, mingling defence of both competition and popular taste was pursued by *The Sunday Times*, 1 July 1961, whose editorial was headed 'An unimaginative report'. This stated that 'only a bigoted few would wish us back in the days of monopoly BBC television' and went on to argue:

> We are at the threshold of an age of enormous expansion and opportunity in this means of information and entertainment. The obvious answer, then, is more competition, with effective control of errors and excesses in the national interest, but without dictation of programmes in the interest of some arbitrary judgement of public needs.

The editorial, which does actually acknowledge the paper's common proprietorship with Scottish Television, also sounds a similarly self-defensive note to that heard in the *Telegraph* in its complaint that 'nowhere do the relevant paragraphs of the report reveal any recognition that the British press is widely varied and demonstrably successful in giving the public what it asks of newspapers for which it freely pays its money' (ibid). But it was the paper's television critic, Maurice Wiggin, in an article entitled 'Going the whole Hoggart', who brought together an attack on the report's anti-populist stance with a warning about its implications for media freedom in general. The report itself is described as 'rich in gobbledegook', the committee as a 'bizarre tribunal', and their conclusions as 'insufferably arrogant'. Wiggin also complains that 'the report reeks of Richard Hoggart. The author of *The uses of literacy* must have signed it with a proud consciousness of having struck a blow for something or other, preferably other'. Wiggin concludes:

> There is a selective switch on every set. Every man has the obligation to use it as he thinks fit. Some will opt for triviality, some for sobriety. Tastes differ. The important thing is that we should be as free as possible to please ourselves. A cultural dictatorship is absolutely unacceptable by free men. If television, then why not the Press, the cinema, the theatre, the publishing of books? Some men love freedom, others fear it. Everything that brings us a step nearer to the standardised state is suspect. Pilkington would bring us a whole stride nearer.

In his view, what is needed is a 'bold and venturesome branching out into every sort of vigorous multiplication, abundance and freedom' and not 'clamping down on free enterprise and erecting yet another smug and impervious State juggernaut'.

'PILKINGTON TELLS THE PUBLIC TO GO TO HELL'

Some of the most forthright attacks on the report were to be found in the *Daily Mirror*, 28 June, which devoted no less than five pages to it (although two of these were largely straightforward accounts of the report's contents). It does also note at the end of one of the articles that the Mirror Group 'is interested' in ATV. Its front page article is headed 'Pilkington tells the public to go to hell', and is more of an editorial than a news story. In its view, the report should have been published on 1 April. The reader is informed that 'Sir Harry, earnest and doleful as he appears to be, has amused his friends by bounding into first place among Britain's Top Ten comedians without a single rehearsal', and that the committee 'are not merely trying to turn the clock back: they want to go back to the hourglass and the sundial', as well as the penny farthing. The article presents what it calls the committee's 'peculiar proposals' thus:

> They tell the public, in 160,000 words, to go to hell. And the public have to pay £45,000 for the privilege of hearing this insult – that was the cost of the report. In effect the committee say: you can't have the TV programmes which a two-thirds majority of you prefer. You must have a different set-up controlled by the government. An 'Uncle' ITA, responsible for planning and selecting programmes – just like 'Auntie' BBC ... By inference they tell the Tory government, which itself set up this deplorable committee, also to go to hell. The Tories had the courage to smash the BBC and set the cathode ray free. Pilkington wants not merely one fettered TV Authority controlling programmes, but two. Both run by the Whitehall Warriors ... The plan is merely to NATIONALISE the lot. They couldn't repeal the Act, so they are trying to repeal the intention of the Act. It is impossible, reading the report, not to conclude that Sir Harry's Eleven were dead against the whole conception of independent television from the start. Public opinion – except that expressed by the vociferous few – has been rudely and crudely ignored. The one and only democratic principle applied is – EQUAL MISERY ALL ROUND.

'BIG BROTHER TV'

Equally vehement in its opposition to the report was the *Daily Sketch*. This was a right-wing publication owned by Associated Newspapers, which folded it into the *Daily Mail* in 1971; interestingly, its highly populist tone prefigures the way in which the *Mail* itself was later to develop. On 28 June, it devoted four pages to the report, all highly negative, and seamlessly blending news and comment in a way which has now become all too familiar in the press. One front and second page article, headlined 'A vicious blow at your choice', consists almost entirely of negative quotations from chairmen of ITV companies, and the other is headlined 'Whose finger on the switch? Beware, it could be Big Brother', thus announcing yet another attack on that favourite populist target: 'Them'. According to the article:

> The people who want to run our lives and tell us what to do came one step nearer to doing it yesterday. By 1964 – they hope – we shall have Big Brother TV telling us what we must see and what we mustn't. They will ration the time for fun and crowd in the time for uplift. If they think you're enjoying yourself too much – well, they'll soon put a stop to that. Make no mistake about it. This is what the Pilkington Report means. They want to wipe out independent television … This is a stupid and biased report. So biased that it would be laughable if it were not so dangerous. The Pilkington Committee want to set up another nationalised television system like the BBC – run by men in black jackets and striped pants.

It then manages to combine an equally distasteful ageism and sexism in one sentence by stating: 'You can almost see the dried up old spinster leaving her tracts at the pub door to go and beat her flimsy breasts at a Pilkington meeting.'

In its coverage, the pre-Murdoch *News of the World*, 1 July, admits that it has a 'fairly large interest in one of the smaller commercial television companies', and its 'Opinion' column, headed 'Not on your telly, sir!', asks:

> What right has any collection of people to decide what is best and proper for others to see and hear when they turn on the television at home? And by what method are these people with total power to be chosen? We do not believe in control of this kind. The ordinary men and women of this country (who will vote for whichever government they want next time) can be trusted to decide for themselves which way to turn the knob on a television set. And it is their right and responsibility to decide for their children, not Pilkington and Co's.

This populist line of attack then turns into a more generalised critique of public enterprise:

> If Pilkington has his way, ITA becomes NTA – the Nationalised Television Authority. A synthetic Siamese twin of the BBC. Surely we have learned by now the lessons of the nationalised industries. Dr Beeching is trying to put some commercial values back into British Railways; Lord Robens is preaching to the miners that they must make profits. Both say the answer is decentralisation, more initiative, more flexibility, more drive.

In the newspaper's view, the NTA bogeyman would, like all public enterprises, 'put up the price, make the product more difficult to get, remove from the public any choice or method of complaint and create an army of inefficient bureaucrats' (ibid).

'PIOUS PURITANS' AND 'PRETENTIOUS PRIGS'

On 1 July in the *Sunday Pictorial* (at that time the Sunday sister paper of the *Daily Mirror*), we find Woodrow Wyatt pre-echoing the hyper-populist tone of the inaptly named 'Voice of Reason' column which he would write for the *News of the World* from 1983 onwards. Thus he refers to the committee members as 'pious puritans' and critics of ITV as 'a tiny handful of pretentious prigs who look down their noses at simple pleasures'. In his view:

> Turning ITV into a parallel BBC and giving the BBC another service would eliminate all serious competition. The BBC would once again become over-complacent, over-governessy. We would all have our heads bored off. Not content with doing this to us on the telly, Pilkington wants to repeat the same prissy pattern for local sound radio. The profound pundits of Portland Place would be allowed to set up stations all over the country, pretending to be local. In practice, they would give us what the director general of the BBC thinks is best for us. Nothing local, nothing jolly, nothing exciting. Why not give them the newspapers to run, too? Then we would make quite sure that there is no variety or freedom of expression whatever. The nation would be told what the genteel residents of South Kensington think we ought to know – *and nothing else.*

Finally, and fittingly for this study of populist attitudes, we turn to the 'Man o' the People' column in *The People*, 1 July. This is entitled 'Hide this page in case Sir Harry sees you!' It warns:

> Now be very careful. If you should be reading this on the beach or on a bus, be ready to slip your copy of *The People* discreetly into your pocket. Sir Harry Pilkington and his pals might be watching you. And at any moment they might decide to get together again to pass judgment on your deplorable taste in newspaper reading. They (the committee) have already agreed that you are a nit-wit and a moron for preferring commercial television to the BBC. Give them another £40,000 of Government money, and they will, I am sure, be delighted also to recommend the suppression of *The People*, the *Daily Mirror* and all the latest popular films.

Complaining about there being five educationalists and a scientist on the committee, the paper argues that 'it is surely frightening to put such eggheads into a position where they can actually recommend the government to rob millions of ordinary people of these simple pleasures. Are we really to be told by a university lecturer and a professor of jurisprudence what we are to enjoy when we nestle into the old arm-chair after the day's work?' However, it reassures it readers:

> The government is not quite so daft as to allow these eggheads to decide the public's viewing. If they were and Sir Harry's cockeyed plan were accepted,

we would be back in the new Dark Ages. For the Culture Boys would then be on the rampage. It would be the *Observer* for you on Sundays by order – and Shakespeare at the cinemas during the week.

A PARANOID FANTASY

In this, inevitably selective, survey of populist attitudes to the Pilkington Report in the press I have deliberately confined myself to the national press. However, I would like to quote a single example from elsewhere – *World's Press News*, July 1962[4] – both because it was written by a Fleet Street journalist, Arthur Christiansen, who edited the *Daily Express* from 1933 to 1957, and because it illustrates particularly clearly the way in which certain journalists attempted to present the committee's proposed reforms of ITV as possible harbingers of some form of 'state control' of the press. Thus Christiansen expresses the fear that after the Pilkington Report anything can happen and asks: 'Is the free press in danger? ... How long will it be before we get a Socialist government which will set up an inquiry into the press that will do a Pilkington on Fleet Street?' Hoggart is identified as 'the *eminence grise* of the Pilkington Report' and as someone who 'loathes the popular press. Way back in 1957 he revealed his prejudices in a book he called *The uses of literacy*'.[5] There then follows a frankly paranoid fantasy about what might happen if Hoggart became the chairman of a government committee to inquire into the press:

> First, editorial content to be subject to a committee composed of representatives of the Home Office, the Foreign Office, the BBC and the Combined Services. Next, newspapers to be non-profit making, surplus revenues from advertising to be turned over to the Treasury ... Inefficient newspapers to be subsidised and printed by the million whether they are purchased by the public or not. 'Popular' papers to be limited to circulations of not more than 50,000. Journalists to be licensed, with sentences of seven years correction detention for indiscretions.

HITTING A RAW NERVE

Hoggart himself argued that the reception of the report by the press was 'an exceptional demonstration of distortion, tendentiousness, personal abuse, half-truth, straight misrepresentation, disingenuousness, pseudo-honesty and irresponsibility' (1970: 191). He also recognised that his critique of populism in broadcasting had hit a particularly raw nerve in a medium much of whose output was largely defined by such an ideology. As he put it:

> Many journalists, even many of those in the 'serious' journals, have been so anxious to avoid aligning themselves with the Establishment, with the idea of superior or patronising powers-that-be, are so anxious to be identified with 'the people', that they have dropped into a sort of wasteland in their

social philosophy, in which they are unable or unwilling to redefine the full nature and responsibility exercised in the public service.[6]

He also noted that journalists, who spend much of their lives criticising others, are peculiarly allergic to criticism of their own practices, and that they …

> … fight back very hard if the system is challenged at the roots. I think they were deeply disturbed by the Pilkington Report because they felt themselves indicted by it. If Pilkington's analysis of the tension between freedom and responsibility demanded by good broadcasting in a democracy was sound, then it had some relevance to the Press also; and the Press would not come out of such an examination lightly (1970: 192).

HARBINGERS OF THE FUTURE

The newspaper response to the Pilkington Report clearly looks back to earlier controversies over the founding of ITV in the first place, and positions taken up in the early 1950s were largely resumed in 1962. But the coverage also prefigures much that was yet to come in the pages of the national press, such as the ever-growing hostility towards the BBC (which would be greatly intensified with the arrival of Murdoch as a press proprietor in 1969); the enthusiasm for new broadcasting technologies (a particular specialism of *The Sunday Times* in the 1980s, when Murdoch was busily laying the foundations of his satellite empire); the simplistic assumption that new broadcasting technology and an increased number of channels would automatically entail greater diversity of programming. And a raucous populism which regards the state as only ever the enemy of media freedom (understood implicitly as the right of media owners to do with their media whatsoever they will), never as an enabler of media freedom in the wider sense of helping to make the media more diverse, representative, accessible, accountable, assessable and so on. Indeed, to read the likes of Wyatt, Christiansen and *The People* is to be flung forward abruptly in time into the all-out hysteria of the press response to the Leveson Inquiry (2012), an examination from which it most certainly did not emerge lightly, and to which it responded with even greater 'distortion, tendentiousness, personal abuse, half-truth, straight misrepresentation, disingenuousness, pseudo-honesty and irresponsibility' than it did to the Pilkington Report, since here it was directly in the firing line.[7]

AFTER PILKINGTON

In the ensuing 1964 Television Act, the ITA was given the responsibility for ensuring that programme output should be 'of a high general standard' and 'properly balanced in subject matter'. It was also granted the power to vet schedules, and even individual programmes, before transmission. The authority insisted that ITV broadcast two current affairs programmes a week, at least one main weekday drama and one documentary, plus regular programmes on art and religion, all in peak time. The number and style of quiz shows were limited, which resulted in admittedly popular programmes such as *Take Your Pick* and *Double Your Money* being cancelled.

It would, of course, be absurd to argue that there was nothing worthwhile in terms of public service broadcasting on ITV before the 1964 Act (both *Armchair Theatre* and *This Week* started in 1956, although *World in Action* did not begin until 1963). It must also be recognised that the coming of ITV forced the BBC to sharpen up its act in numerous significant ways, not least in news and current affairs. And on the downside, the newly empowered ITA not infrequently censored important programmes which dealt with contentious subjects, such as episodes of *World in Action* (Goddard, Corner and Richardson 2007: 185-214). Programmes on the situation in Northern Ireland proved particularly problematic for the ITA (later the IBA) (Potter 1990: 199-213), while *This Week* (Holland 2006: 111-167) and *World in Action* (Goddard, Corner and Richardson 2007: 201-06) not infrequently found themselves in difficulty with the authority when they attempted to tackle this intractable issue. But it should also be recognised that the revamped schedules did strike a better balance between information, education and entertainment, and after Pilkington the channel embarked upon the finest period in its history, which would last until the early 1990s when the ill-judged Broadcasting Act 1990 irrevocably changed the nature of ITV. As Hoggart (1992: 71) put it, the ITV companies had been 'screwed into virtue'.

- This paper was first published in *Ethical Space*, Vol. 12, No. 1 pp 4-14, 2015

NOTES

[1] Although it should be pointed out that at this time Hoggart himself took quite a nuanced view of 'effects'. See in particular 'The argument about effects' in Hoggart (1970: 215-227)

[2] Chapter seven of *The uses of literacy* (1990 [1957]) is called 'Invitation to a candy-floss world'

[3] A remark generally attributed to R. H. Tawney, president of the Workers' Educational Association, which gave evidence to the committee

[4] Item 5/9/42 in the Richard Hoggart archive at the University of Sheffield

[5] In which Hoggart wrote: 'The popular middle-class papers are as trivial and as trivializing as those for the working-classes. For myself I find the dailies aimed particularly at middle-class people more unpleasant than those for working-class people. They tend to have an intellectual smugness, a spiritual chauvinism and snobbery, and a cocktail-party polish which makes their atmosphere quite peculiarly stifling' (1990 [1957]: 244)

[6] 'Pilkington and after', *Christian Broadcaster*, no date. Item 5/9/27 in the Richard Hoggart archive at the University of Sheffield

[7] For a detailed and highly critical account of press coverage of Leveson, see the report by Gordon Ramsay at http://mediastandardstrust.org/wp-content/uploads/2014/09/Final-Draft-v1-040914.pdf

REFERENCES

Bailey, Michael, Clarke, Ben and Walton, John K. (2012) *Understanding Richard Hoggart: A pedagogy of hope*, Oxford/Chichester, Wiley-Blackwell

Freedman, Des (2003) *Television policies of the Labour Party, 1951-2001*, London, Frank Cass

Goddard, Peter, Corner, John and Richardson, Kay (2007) *Public issue television:* World in Action, *1963-98*, Manchester, Manchester University Press

HMSO (Her Majesty's Stationery Office) (1962) *Report of the committee on broadcasting, 1960*, London, Her Majesty's Stationery Office

Hoggart, Richard (1990 [1957]) *The uses of literacy*, London, Penguin

Hoggart, Richard (1970) *Speaking to each other: Volume 1: About society*, London, Chatto & Windus

Hoggart, Richard (1992) *An imagined life*, London, Chatto & Windus

Hoggart, Richard (2001) *Between two worlds: Essays*, London, Aurum Press

Holland, Patricia (2006) *The angry buzz:* This Week *and current affairs television*, London, I. B. Tauris

Milland, Jeffrey (2004) Courting Malvolio: The background to the Pilkington Committee on Broadcasting, 1960-62, *Contemporary British History*, Vol. 18, No. 2 pp 76-103

Milland, Jeffrey (2009) The Pilkington Report: The triumph of paternalism?, Bailey, Michael (ed.) *Narrating media history*, Abingdon, Oxon, Routledge pp 95-107

Potter, Jeremy (1990) *Independent television in Britain: Volume 4: Companies and programmes, 1968-80*, London, Macmillan

Sendall, Bernard (1982) *Independent television in Britain: Volume 1: Origin and foundation, 1946-62*, London, Macmillan

Williams, Raymond (1963) *Culture and society 1780-1950*, Harmondsworth, Penguin

NOTE ON THE CONTRIBUTOR

Julian Petley is Honorary and Emeritus Professor of Journalism in the Department of Social Sciences, Media and Communications at Brunel University London. He has a particular interest in media regulation of all kinds and has published widely in this area. His most recent book is *The Routledge companion to freedom of expression and censorship* (2024), co-edited with John Steel. He is a member of the editorial boards of the *British Journalism Review*, *Ethical Space* and *Porn Studies*, and editor-in-chief of *the Journal of British Cinema and Television*.

Chapter 3

Useful idiots or Big Brother's antidote? Analysing the ethical role of the state, *Guardian* and Edward Snowden in the controversy over surveillance and whistleblowing

Tim Crook

This paper takes a critical approach to the Guardian's *coverage and the British secret state's position on the revelations by Edward Snowden of global surveillance by the NSA and GCHQ. It contextualises the issues and events with reference to intelligence conflicts from the past. How does the position of the* Guardian, *its former journalist Glenn Greenwald and the source Edward Snowden compare to the 'useful idiot' syndrome of the 1930s? This was the failure of some British journalists and public figures to recognise the true nature of Joseph Stalin's regime in the Soviet Union. The analysis focuses on the trend for state surveillance bodies, whistleblowers, and their receiving journalists and publishers to claim the moral high ground of public interest. The tension remains a struggle between those who claim to be protecting national security and those who claim to be protecting individual privacy and seeking to expose alleged abuse of state power through excessive surveillance and electronic intrusion. The opposite sides in this debate appear to delegitimise each other's ethical authority. The paper concludes that in the absence of clear evidence of impact it is difficult to prove which side has been responsible for damaging or indeed improving the public good.*

Keywords: Edward Snowden, useful idiots, surveillance, interception, bugging, *Guardian*

INTRODUCTION

Surveillance and communications interception is a process as old as spying itself – sometimes disparagingly referred to as the second oldest profession. Why should digital cyberspace be any different in the process of intelligence monitoring compared to the age of diplomatic bags, postage, telegraph and radio? Edward Snowden was at the heart of the US National Security Agency system of monitoring and eavesdropping on US domestic and global electronic communications. He decided to betray that system and arguably turned the secret world inside out. The British newspaper and global online news publisher, the *Guardian*, played a key role in publishing his revelations.

A BBC *Panorama* programme has described him as 'the man responsible for the biggest leak of top secret intelligence files the world has ever seen' (Bradburn and Taylor 2015). Intelligence chiefs have had to understand why somebody now judged by them to be so unreliable and dangerous could be recruited and employed by CIA and NSA associated bodies. He has been charged in his absence with criminal offences under the US Espionage Act of 1917. Why did one man so low down in the hierarchy have access to so many intelligence 'crown jewels' capable of causing so much 'irreversible and significant damage' if revealed? (Ackerman and Rushe 2013).

Snowden has broken the magic spell of his profession. The journalist and MI6 intelligence officer Malcolm Muggeridge once said: 'Secrecy is as essential to intelligence as vestments and incense to a mass, or darkness to a spiritualist séance, and must at all costs be maintained, quite irrespective of whether or not it serves any purpose' (Muggeridge 1981: 133). Snowden has exorcised the mystique of clandestine surveillance in the digital information age.

The Snowden affair is not an isolated instance of vigorous challenging of the abracadabra mantra of 'national security' to say and reveal nothing in the face of disturbing evidence of malfeasance, incompetence and controversy. It could be argued that the credibility of UK government intelligence agencies has been seriously questioned in the light of the failure to find weapons of mass destruction following the Iraq invasion of 2003 (Iraq Inquiry 2015), the alleged murder by Russian secret agents of the anti-Putin political exile and MI6 agent Alexander Litvinenko in 2006 (Litvinenko Inquiry 2015), the continuing controversy over British intelligence complicity in torture and 'extraordinary rendition' of alleged Islamist terrorists (Detainee Inquiry 2013), and the unexplained death of MI6/GCHQ cipher expert Gareth Williams in August 2010 (Davies and Meikle 2012).

THE CASE AGAINST EDWARD SNOWDEN AND THE *GUARDIAN*

The digital information age and cyberspace means that the scale and speed of the data field is more retrievable, vast and much more quickly analysable to the extent that trace data of contact can make it easier to focus on what is deemed necessary to fully tap and transcribe in terms of content.

The *Guardian* since 2013 has judged Edward Snowden's revelations to be new insights into the way the United States' NSA and UK's GCHQ harvested massive amounts of macro-data of ordinary people's digital communications for intelligence gathering. Its then-editor-in-chief Alan Rusbridger said publication was 'in the public interest' (Narayan 2015). US journalism culture has legitimised the rectitude of exposure with a Pulitzer prize. A political consensus in America has persuaded Capitol Hill to evaluate greater democratic oversight of information gathering, storage and use of private citizens' data.

Certainly the purpose and imperative of GCHQ and NSA activity is nothing new. It is the medium, technology and exponential vastness of information gathered in a new virtual world of digital finger-printing that has changed. The individual lives, breathes, believes, communicates, trades, acts, performs and intimates in a digital trail and nexus of existence. Individuals have a digital DNA of communicative identity and action that is no longer concealed in the shadows of everyday life. That is why GCHQ spends more of the annual secret budget and employs more people than the UK's other intelligence agencies (GCHQ 2015). Its capabilities and role in the global eavesdropping infrastructure is so important it receives an extra £100 million every year in funding from the US NSA – a fact that was secret up until 2013 (Hopkins and Borger 2013).

- The UK intelligence world's indictment against the *Guardian* is that they have been a conduit for Snowden's breach of the national security of the USA and UK in multiple dimensions. The home secretary, Theresa May, said in a hearing before the House of Commons home affairs select committee the secret techniques revealed by the subsequent leaks to the *Guardian* newspaper have made it easier for terrorists, jihadis and organised criminals to avoid detection;

- the leaks have 'damaged' intelligence agencies across the world and drained vital resources from MI5, MI6 and GCHQ;

- security officials have had to abandon buildings used to house top-secret sources for fear they have been compromised – at huge cost to the British taxpayer;

- the self-styled Islamic State has seized on the Snowden leaks and has passed on information to its operatives – making it harder to track them down;

- al Qaeda were able to produce a training video on how its followers can avoid being tapped by 'FBI Secret Spying technology' when communicating, can identify technology companies who are co-operating with the UK and other countries so they can be avoided, and can access software packages which can be used to thwart digital surveillance (Slack 2015).

It can be argued a distinction needs to be made between the *Guardian* as a news publisher that exists to challenge power and hold governments and authority to account, and Edward Snowden who says he betrayed his obligations as a computer specialist at an intelligence centre in Hawaii for the wider good of letting the public know of the extent and scale of information gathering by the secret world which, in his opinion, is a threat to democracy.

Snowden made the decision to take 1.7 million NSA and GCHQ files first to Hong Kong, then Russia, (Cole 2014) where he has been granted asylum and now lives in a secret location. From these locations it would appear he originally chose to leak some of these files to the *Guardian* via Glenn Greenwald living in Brazil, the filmmaker Laura Poitras, living in Berlin, and the US *Washington Post*.

The *Guardian*'s position is interesting because it has through its online presence the third-largest English-language readership in the world (Rusbridger 2013). It has editorial spheres of original publication in Britain and the USA. In the UK legal jurisdiction there is a doctrine of prior restraint for national security revelations and a government-funded Defence and Security Media Advisory Committee (previously known as the Defence Press and Broadcasting Committee) which seeks to advise on the security risks with journalists and editors before publication of intelligence sensitive material. In the Snowden affair the *Guardian* did not engage the system for the first day of its revelations. Subsequently it did and there were many consultations. The view of the secretary of the committee, Rtd Air Marshall Andrew Vallance, was that much of the *Guardian* material was politically embarrassing rather than national security sensitive (Petley 2014: 12). The paper also agreed to have computer discs containing Snowden leaked documents smashed and destroyed by government technicians in its basement (Rusbridger 2013). It is legally contesting the seizure of electronic devices containing Snowden material taken from its courier David Miranda, the partner of Glenn Greenwald, who was passing through Heathrow airport (Cole 2014).

By contrast, in the US jurisdiction there is no hinterland and practice of media prior restraint over national security revelations. The very principle was discouraged by the Supreme Court in the Pentagon Papers case of 1971 (Crook 2009: 331-333). There is no Defence and Security Media Advisory Committee nor even any system of press and online media regulation. Both countries do pursue criminal prosecution and punishment of state intelligence sources with vehemence and punitive ruthlessness (ibid: 316-333). The *Guardian* has, therefore, been performing its role in two entirely different theatres of public culture and law but where reception and access is clear between one and the other.

It could be said that there appear to be three conflicting but also overlapping interests: the *Guardian*'s 'public interest' in exercising freedom of expression, the US and UK state national security interest, and the democratic interest – what is necessary in a democratic society and constituting a pressing social need either for concealment or disclosure.

The US and UK intelligence world can argue that there is a democratic interest in national security. The *Guardian* can argue that the public interest of its global readership in print and online is an important exercise of the democratic interest through freedom of expression. The *Guardian* has been criticised by its rival UK newspapers such as the *Sun*, *Mail*, *Telegraph* and *Times* for not being able to cite specific examples where spooks have wrongly and unjustly used NSA/GCHQ metadata collecting operations to violate the human rights and privacy of identifiable private individuals (Glover 2013). Specific content snooping examples have related to the political leaders of NATO countries (Cole 2014). In turn, Snowden has criticised the intelligence agencies for not being able to explicitly prove one case where a life has been lost that can be directly attributable to his revelations (Bradburn and Taylor 2015). When they talk of serious damage they are being challenged to provide quantitative and qualitative evidence of this (Crook 2013b).

HISTORICAL AND CONTEMPORARY PARALLELS

The *Guardian*'s Edward Snowden scoops do have their equivalence in intelligence history. The fate of insiders leaking from the intelligence profession because of what they regarded as the public interest is varied. In the US, Daniel Ellsberg, who sought to reveal the secrets of US military and government assessment of the Vietnam War in what was known as the Pentagon Papers case, was prosecuted but acquitted under the 1917 Espionage Act in 1973 (Ellsberg 2002 and Goodale 2013). CIA officer Philip Agee's exposure of plots to overthrow central and Latin American governments led to his permanent exile in Cuba (Agee 1975). In 1980, a CIA officer in Vietnam, Frank Snepp, was defeated at the US Supreme Court over his revelations of service at the US Embassy in Saigon and had to surrender all of the royalties from the publication of his 1977 book *Decent interval* (Snepp 1999).

In more recent times, Edward Snowden could understandably appreciate the trend of prosecution of intelligence sources. US soldier Chelsea (formerly Bradley) Manning provided WikiLeaks with about 720,000 secret documents from the State and Defense Departments. In 2013, she was tried and convicted for violating the Espionage Act and sentenced to thirty-five years in prison (Cole 2014). Manning's online publisher, Julian Assange, fears US retribution to the extent that he has resisted extradition to Sweden on sexual offence allegations and lived in the one room sanctuary of London's Ecuadorian Embassy for more than three years (ibid). NSA whistleblower Thomas Drake was criminally prosecuted in 2012 resulting in a conviction for misusing the agency's computer system (Aftergood 2011). CIA analyst and case officer, John Kiriakou, became the first CIA officer to be convicted for passing classified information to a reporter and received 30 months imprisonment in 2013 (Schmidt 2013). In 2005, Russell Tice was dismissed by the NSA after publicly lobbying for stronger protections for federal intelligence agency whistleblowers (Ross 2006). Lawyer and former CIA employee

Jeffrey Sterling, arrested, charged and convicted of violating the Espionage Act for revealing classified information to a journalist, received three and a half years' imprisonment in 2015 (Apuzzo 2015; Associated Press 2015).

In Britain, state intelligence officials and civil servants who leak are also pursued vigorously with criminal sanctions. MI5's David Shayler lost any public interest argument in law for revealing the failures and incompetence of anti-terrorist operations, spying on politicians, and a plot to assassinate Libya's Colonel Gaddafi. He was jailed at the Central Criminal Court for six months in 2002 (Crook 2009: 325). Former MI6 officer Richard Tomlinson was jailed for a year in 1997 for trying to write a book about operations he had taken part in and his employment dispute with MI6 (ibid: 329). The Hutton Inquiry of 2003 posthumously condemned the late Dr David Kelly for briefing BBC reporter Andrew Gilligan about his views on the accuracy and reliability of a government published dossier assessing the risk of Saddam Hussein's regime deploying weapons of mass destruction prior to the invasion of Iraq (ibid: 330).

In 2004, the UK Attorney General announced that he would not pursue an Official Secrets Act prosecution of GCHQ translator Katharine Gun who had leaked information about the NSA's eavesdropping operation on countries tasked with passing a second United Nations resolution on the invasion of Iraq (Burkeman and Norton-Taylor 2004). In 2007, Downing Street civil servant David Keogh was jailed for six months for leaking a memo of a conversation between the then-UK Prime Minister Tony Blair and US President George W. Bush and a reporting ban prevents the media speculating about its contents (Crook 2009: 355-356). As in the Gun case, in 2008 the prosecution dropped the case against Foreign Office civil servant Derek Pasquill for leaking documents on the US practice of secretly transporting terror suspects to places where they risked being tortured (Pasquill 2008).

Snowden is not alone in being an insider who has decided to sound the alarm about the extent of mass National Security Agency intrusion into individual privacy. William Binney resigned his senior role in the agency in 2001 and argued subsequently that the NSA is in deliberate violation of the US Constitution (Shorrock 2013). In 2005, former AT&T technician Mark Klein exposed the company's cooperation with the NSA in installing network hardware that retrieved and processed American telecommunications (Klein 2009).

It could be argued that the implications of mass state surveillance of bulk electronic communications data had been exposed and criticised many years before Snowden's actions. The Cryptome website, created in 1996 by John Young and Deborah Natsios, has been a consistent conduit for revealing state abuse of privacy, misuse of cryptography, dual-use technologies and oppressive policies of national security, intelligence gathering and government secrecy (Young and Natsios 2015). In 2009, investigative journalist James Bamford focused on the heightening of domestic surveillance by the National Security Agency after the failures to detect and disrupt the 9/11 attack. His book *The shadow factory* argued that the extent of data mining of US citizens had become disproportionate (Bamford 2008).

Edward Snowden has exposed the ability of the NSA/GCHQ to access on fibre-optic cable 50,000 DVDs' worth of data transiting the UK in any hour (Bradburn and Taylor 2015). GCHQ's TEMPORA program, shared with the NSA, harvested this data from its base near Bude, in Cornwall (ibid). Bulk or meta-data is more valuable in intelligence analysis than content (ibid).

WHO ARE THE 'USEFUL IDIOTS'?

The term 'useful idiots', was apparently coined by Lenin to identify Westerners who had been deceived into acting as apologists for oppressive political regimes (Coombs and Sweeney 2010a and 2010b). The term is often applied to Soviet sympathisers who would in turn be nurtured and given generous hospitality by the Soviet government in Moscow (ibid). It can be argued that the concept of the 'useful idiots' can be drawn much wider to include anyone or, indeed governments and states, that give their support to tyrannies and tyrants for cynical, ideological and near evangelistic reasons. Instead of seeing Gulag Archipelagos, Belsens and Dachaus, they see utopias and holiday camps. Professor Donald Rayfield, the author of *Stalin and his hangmen: The tyrant and those who killed for him* (2005), has offered a more up-to-date definition: 'The phrase seems to have been around for about 70 years. It's someone who doesn't think they are an idiot, who thinks they are highly intelligent, but is so easily persuaded by flattery from people in power that they're prepared to serve their purposes and allow themselves to be duped or even just to lie for the sake of advantage' (Coombs and Sweeney 2010a).

To what extent is Edward Snowden a 'useful idiot' to terrorist groups and countries opposed to the USA, the UK and the West? Has not his blatant exposure of the inner-most secrets of NSA/GCHQ information warfare given comfort, advantage and succour to Beijing, Moscow, Tehran, al Qaeda and the Islamic State? To what extent has the *Guardian* been the oxygen giving heat and destructive force to Snowden's collaboration with those forces inimical to the West's best interests? On the other hand, have not the US and UK governments also been 'useful idiots' in failing to supervise, negotiate and determine the correct boundaries between protecting national security and individual privacy and liberty? By adopting a clandestine totalitarian method of controlling and monitoring their citizens with inadequate judicial, legislative and executive oversight have they not surrendered the democratic imperative of consent? As a result how can the USA and UK offer themselves up as models of liberty and democracy to differentiate and indeed condemn outside regimes for abuse of human rights? Does that not make them 'useful idiots' too?

In the early 1930s, Joseph Stalin engineered the Ukrainian famine to crush millions of peasants who resisted his policies. The British correspondent for *The*

New York Times, Walter Duranty, did all he could to discredit other correspondents' reports of mass starvation even though he was secretly aware of the full scale of the tragedy. He actively supported the cover-up of this politically constructed human disaster. His dispatches from Moscow were awarded with the Pulitzer Prize, and when the extent of his deception later became apparent, were never withdrawn (Taylor 1990).

John Sweeney argued that Hitler's apologists in the 1930s did not know about the Holocaust to come, but Stalin's 'useful idiots' did know about the millions starving through the Soviet dictator's enforced famine (Coombs and Sweeney 2010a). The Liverpool-born journalist Walter Duranty briefed the British Embassy in 1933 that he believed 10 million people had perished through starvation in the previous year, but he lied about this in his reports for *New York Times* readers (Taylor 1990: 220-221).

The socialist playwright George Bernard Shaw met Stalin in the Kremlin in 1931 and praised him with enthusiasm afterwards. Shaw is certainly seen as a 'useful idiot'. Professor Rayfield observed: 'Shaw had a really dictatorial instinct. He was in favour of very summary solutions to the world's problems and he rather liked the idea of a revolution that swept unnecessary people away. It's something like very many of the characters in his plays' (Coombs and Sweeney 2010a). Shaw's penchant for murderous dictators even extended to being filmed expressing support for Adolph Hitler in 1935 (Holroyd 1998: 568).

It was described as appeasement. But the large body of public figures from the 1930s who sought to brush away the ghastly realities of Hitler's regime in the cause of avoiding another world war and promoting Anglo-German relations certainly qualifies them for the sobriquet 'useful idiot' (Kershaw 2004). There is an argument for applying the term to Prime Ministers Stanley Baldwin and Neville Chamberlain and their national coalition governments until the decision to engage fully with rearmament. The former Great War Prime Minister, David Lloyd George, visited and legitimised relations with Hitler in 1936 (Kershaw 2004: 64, 174-175). The former King Edward VIII, as the Duke of Windsor, made a sensational visit to Nazi Germany in 1937 and his sympathy and apparent public endorsement of the regime could be considered the actions of another of Hitler's 'useful idiots' (ibid: 170).

The application of the 'useful idiot' analogy of the 1930s to the present day narrative involving the *Guardian* is not based on any evidence of lying or deliberate duplicity concerning the journalists and sources involved. But it could be relevant in terms of potential conflicts of interest and the evaluation of journalistic impartiality and intrinsic British interests.

Snowden's revelations specifically relating to GCHQ have been judged to be a potential attack on British national interests (Petley 2014). The *Guardian*'s journalism was a complicated team project involving staff specialists such as Ewen MacAskill and the non-British based freelance contributor Glenn Greenwald. The information gathering and contacts operated in a global sphere. It would seem Snowden originally leaked files to Greenwald, American film-maker Laura Poitras and Barton Gellman, of the *Washington Post*.

Greenwald is an American attorney, columnist and author based in Rio de Janeiro, Brazil, where he lives with his partner David Miranda. He allegedly used Miranda as a courier for British classified intelligence files provided by Edward Snowden. Miranda had not met Snowden in Moscow but he had been in contact with Laura Poitras in Berlin (Martinson 2015). Miranda was detained under UK terrorism legislation at Heathrow Airport and all the digital files in his possession were seized for forensic examination (Miranda v. Home Office 2013 and 2014). The British courts have so far ruled that the actions of the British authorities were legal. After Miranda was reunited with his partner in Brazil the day after his detention, Greenwald was perceived to threaten the UK with comments in Portuguese that he would 'be much more aggressive than before in my reporting. I will publish many more documents than before. I will publish many things on Britain as well. I have many documents on Britain's spying system. Now my focus will be that, they will regret what they have done' (*Telegraph* 2013).

Snowden is an American fugitive from justice given sanctuary by Russia, which is by no means a friendly nation to NATO, the USA or the UK. Greenwald left the *Guardian* in October 2013 to join with eBay founder and PayPal owner Pierre Omidyar on the independent news venture First Look Media. This launched the online publication the *Intercept* in February 2014 that is also edited by Laura Poitras.

The ethical dynamics of the *Guardian*'s coverage are, therefore, complicated by the nexus of international agency and ideological imperatives of main source and freelance journalists involved. It should also be noted that the paper shared the 2014 Pulitzer Prize for public service journalism with the *Washington Post* (Pulitzer 2014).

FREEDOM OF EXPRESSION AND NATIONAL SECURITY: THE CONTRAST IN CRIMINAL RESPONSIBILITIES

The interception of communications is undoubtedly a manifestation of Machiavellian 'ends justifies the means' ethics. In itself it is an immoral practice. Justification demands that the invasion of privacy is serving a greater good. The efficacy of such a device is dependent on concealment. If used by the journalist or spy neither can reveal the involvement of their 'unclean hands'. Perhaps this is one of the reasons why telephone and data interception evidence remains inadmissible in the courts. Equally news publishers engaging in phone hacking were anxious to hide what they were doing behind the shield of 'protection of sources' (Davies 2014). The legal and ethical connection between media corporation phone hacking and state intelligence body snooping is fully represented by the Regulation of Investigatory Powers Act 2000. The statute gives licence to state bodies to intrude covertly and criminalises journalistic publications for doing so in pursuit of information for stories.

In the tabloid field, it would appear journalists convinced themselves that the covert pursuit of private information about public celebrocrats and people involved in news events was justifiable in the public interest. RIPA 2000 rendered such state investigatory interception as legally permissible and additionally enabled police forces to identify the sources of journalists when investigating unauthorised government and public body leaking without any of the safeguards of judicial scrutiny established in the 1984 Police and Criminal Evidence Act (Ponsford 2015b). The dark art of journalistic phone hacking appears to have been rendered acceptable for a while by the idea that mobile phone messages could be legally monitored if they had been previously read and heard by their recipients. This cynical legal interpretation was struck down by a Court of Appeal ruling in 2013 that excluded any possibility of a public interest defence for journalists (Coulson and Kuttner 2013).

However, the use of such surveillance powers by state investigation agencies to identify the journalistic sources of public interest stories is currently subject to legal challenges. The violation of the confidential journalistic source by public bodies is regarded in most British and European legal jurisprudence as an example of national security unjustifiably negating democratic interest (Newman 2015).

The UK state police and secret world spend millions of pounds of its annual budget buying and receiving information from participating criminals and agents who are inevitably breaching confidentiality. If the agents are public officials then they would also be likely committing misconduct in public office (Robinson 2013). Yet the practice by journalists and their sources is judged to be criminal albeit now requiring proof of damaging the public interest on the part of journalists (Chapman and others 2015). Offering rewards for any breach of confidentiality is now a potential offence under the 2010 Bribery Act. The offence of misconduct in public office is a common law construction by the courts and the Director of Public Prosecutions. It has never been a statutory decision by parliament. It began as a method of criminalising unlawful communication of official information after the statutory offence under Section 2 of the Official Secrets Act was abolished in 1989. This was in the wake of the failure to prosecute and convict MoD senior civil servant Clive Ponting who had leaked documents to an MP that challenged the veracity of government ministers about the sinking of the Argentine battleship, the Belgrano, during the Falklands War of 1982 (Ponting 1985).

It may well be the case of Thomas Lund-Lack in 2007 that became the tipping point for prosecuting authorities to use misconduct in public office rather than the Official Secrets Act in the pursuit of public officials leaking documents to journalists. The common law offence had a more elastic application. It was not hidebound by clumsy statutory construction and ambiguous judicial interpretation in subsequent case law. And the punishment was not capped and could in theory extend to life imprisonment. Mr Lund-Lack was a former Special Branch Inspector and civilian defence specialist at Scotland Yard. His lawyer told the court his client had been suffering from severe post-traumatic stress disorder and personal difficulties. He had 'blundered' by leaking information about a planned al-Qaeda attack on the West to a *Sunday Times* journalist. He was jailed for eight months. The journalist was neither arrested nor prosecuted (Levy 2007).

The arrest and prosecution of Milton Keynes local newspaper journalist Sally Murrer by Thames Valley Police in 2008 could be described as the first full dress-rehearsal for using the misconduct in public office offence against journalists. Police had bugged her everyday crime reporting contact with a police officer, but the Surveillance Commissioner giving permission had not been told she was a journalist and the police were seeking to identify a confidential source (*PA Media Lawyer* 2014). The trial was halted on the grounds of breaching Article 10 of the Human Rights Act 2000 relating to freedom of expression.

The extension of the common law offence to include systematic prosecution of journalists arose after Director of Public Prosecutions, Keir Starmer QC, established guidelines on when it was not against the public interest to apply the offence against journalists. In 2011, arrests began of a total of 34 *Sun* and former *News of the World* journalists in Operation Elveden for receiving and paying for stories sourced by public officials working in government departments, the armed services, prisons and the police. Trials began in 2013. Most have been acquitted, one pleaded guilty, and another's conviction faces challenge at the Court of Appeal (Ponsford 2015a).

The pendulum of criminal disincentive for leaking has clearly swung the way of state interests and beyond the realm of what would be regarded as national security matters. Public misconduct arrests and prosecutions are now being applied to issues and information that journalists regarded as everyday and popular public interest journalism. Many of the juries that acquitted the *Sun* and *News of the World* journalists on trial heard arguments and defences that they had been researching and talking to their public official sources for stories that they believed were of importance and significance to their readers (Greenslade 2014). This would suggest the lay opinion of randomly selected jurors from the electoral registers agreed with the journalistic construction of 'public interest' (ibid). However, the successful prosecution and conviction of the sources have included the jailing of a detective chief inspector in February 2013 who only anonymously contacted a journalist once by mobile phone to complain that the multi-million phone hacking was draining her counter-terrorism unit of much-needed detective resources (Crook 2013a).

JOURNALISTS AND SPIES: ISSUES OF PARALLEL ETHICS

Any suggestion that the ethical reputations of journalists and spies are somewhat problematical is clearly something of an understatement. The *Guardian* has a reputation in British journalism for being 'the bishops of Fleet Street'. The newspaper's campaign to expose mobile phone hacking at the News International tabloid titles *News of the World* and the *Sun* led to the Leveson Inquiry and a 'perfect storm' of moral panic over journalism ethics that is unprecedented in modern history. Metropolitan Police inquiries have led to prosecutions of journalists and their sources for the criminal offences of unlawful interception of communications and misconduct in public office in relation to paying and using public official information (Ponsford 2015c). No other Western democratic society has experienced this level of public expenditure and criminal investigation of journalistic conduct and publication. The *Guardian* has also published powerful interventionist investigative journalism on the role of UK undercover policing of political activists. It has politically and morally questioned the use of participating agents having intimate and child-bearing relationships with intelligence targets (Lewis and Evans 2013).

The *Guardian*'s phone-hacking reporting has placed UK journalism and its ethics under a media, political, legal and social microscope since 2011. Yet the same could not be said for national security and intelligence bodies. No Leveson Inquiry for spooks has been able to address the fact that very little in the way of ethical self-examination of the spying trade has been published. The *Oxford handbook of national security intelligence* has 28 out of 888 pages devoted to 'Ethics and professional intelligence'. Its author, Michael Andregg, described as 'an intelligence professional who also teaches at the University of St Thomas in St Paul, Minnesota', says in his opening paragraph:

> The terms 'ethics' and 'spies' do not combine easily since spies routinely break the laws of target countries and sometimes engage in many practices that polite society deems immoral from theft to extortion, blackmail, murder and other crimes. Yet every government employs spies when it feels that vital interests are at stake (Andregg 2010: 235).

Andregg begins his concluding section by admitting:

> Let us be realistic for a moment. No government is likely to hire you to be an intelligence professional (or spy) based on your resume as an ethical leader. In fact, while they are not moral morons and always claim to hire only people of the highest integrity, intelligence administrators are actually a bit afraid of real 'ethics' and discussion thereof (ibid: 750).

This honest appraisal of his profession is rounded up with the reflection: 'But enough talk and philosophy; the innocents of the earth need practical protection and even civilization itself is under siege today by the barbarians of our time. Be professionals and protect them' (ibid).

The intriguing history of journalists and spies interchanging between their respective roles as poachers and gamekeepers is fully charted by Phillip Knightley in his seminal text *The first casualty: The war correspondent as hero and myth-maker from the Crimea to Iraq*. Kim Philby is perhaps one of the most notorious (Knightley 2004: 243-244). He was already a Soviet agent when the longest serving foreign correspondent during the Spanish Civil War, and he was the *Observer*'s Middle East correspondent when he finally defected to Moscow from Beirut in 1963.

What Edward Snowden has in common with Philby is that they were both granted political asylum in Russia. Snowden says he is motivated by a libertarian imperative to help preserve democracy: 'My sole motive is to inform the public as to that which is done in their name and that which is done against them' (Greenwald 2013a). Yet he is sheltered by a regime waging war in the Ukraine, that has revived the Cold War, that is suspected of suffocating freedom of the media and speech through intimidation and violence within its own borders, and is accused of carrying out assassinations in London of its political dissidents (Lucas 2014). The death by polonium poisoning of Alexander Litvinenko is the subject of a UK judicial public inquiry where Putin and his intelligence services are accused by Litvinenko's widow of murdering on the streets of London. 'Body in the bag' GCHQ and MI6 officer Gareth Williams died from unlawful killing according to the inquest into this death, from an accident according to the Metropolitan Police, and from a Russian secret service assassination according to a former KGB agent (Penrose 2013).

Snowden is not in Moscow because he admires Vladimir Putin and Russian authoritarianism. He is there because he wishes to avoid US criminal sanctions for what he regards as whistleblowing for democracy (Bradburn and Taylor 2015).

Political ideology motivated the journalists Guy Burgess and Kim Philby to infiltrate Great Britain's security establishment to spy for the KGB. They were certainly more than 'useful idiots'. Perhaps history will be the judge of whether Edward Snowden, and the news publisher prepared to publish his leaks, will ever qualify as 'useful idiots' for Vladimir Putin and all the other perceived enemies of NSA and GCHQ intelligence gathering operations.

But the Snowden affair, like past surveillance scandals in British history, has been an issue that transcends any context of appeasement of a former Cold War adversary, asymmetric terrorist groups, and a self-styled state in Iraq and Syria. The *Guardian* is not the source. It is the traditional messenger. The intense political debates and legislative changes arising from the story demonstrate that as a global news publisher it has challenged potential abuse of state surveillance power. This is true of media corporations ruining lives by grotesquely and unlawfully breaching personal privacy (Davies 2014), secret police units infiltrating *agent provocateur* undercover officers into law-abiding groups of political activists (Lewis and Evans 2013) or state intelligence agencies harvesting and exploiting data without judicial or credible executive oversight (Harding 2014).

CONCLUSION

Rather than publish with the foolishness of an idiot, it can be argued that the *Guardian* has exercised the courage of tenacious journalism – something that is wholly necessary in a democratic society and for which there will always be a pressing social need. In the United States it received a joint Pulitzer Prize because the political debate arising from publication questioned the effectiveness of the country's infrastructure of judicial oversight of mass surveillance. In the United Kingdom, despite the *Guardian* being condemned as traitors to the country's national interest (Petley 2014), the political debate arising resulted in a new Investigatory Powers Bill that proposes an infrastructure of judicial oversight that did not exist before and the further extraordinary revelation that MI5, the UK Security Service, began bulk collection of all telephone data from 2005 without any legislative or judicial approval or scrutiny (Wintour 2015).

It can be argued that both Snowden and the *Guardian* have advanced a public interest of knowledge and understanding of what had been going on covertly and there has now been a political debate about where the boundaries of state surveillance should be drawn. The UK's Independent Reviewer of Terrorism Legislation, David Anderson QC, said:

> Edward Snowden has done harm to the ability of this country to protect itself, particularly in the short term. But I think you could also say that he's done us a service by ensuring that these intrusive powers will be publicly debated and properly provided for in law (Bradburn and Taylor 2015).

This observation may be touching on a more paradoxical truth about the affair. State intelligence bodies, whistleblowers and news publishers have succeeded in advancing and reducing each other's public interest credibility. It is certainly arguable that greater transparency and understanding of how everyday digital communicative life can be recorded, observed and scrutinised by the state advances democratic identity through consent, while at the same time informing those who wish to undermine stability and democratic values how they can avoid detection and prosecution.

- This paper was first published in *Ethical Space*, Vol. 12, Nos 3 and 4 pp 14-24, 2015

REFERENCES

Agee, Philip (1975) *Inside the Company: CIA diary*, London, Penguin

Andregg, Michael (2010) Ethics and professional intelligence, Johnson, Loch K. (ed.) *The Oxford handbook of national security intelligence*, Oxford, Oxford University Press pp 735-753

Bamford, James (2008) *The shadow factory: The ultra-secret NSA from 9/11 to the eavesdropping on America*, New York, Doubleday

Bunyan, Tony (1977) *The political police in Britain*, London, Quartet Books

Crook, Tim (2009) *Comparative media law and ethics*, London, New York, Routledge

Davies, Nick (2014) *Hack attack: How the truth caught up with Rupert Murdoch*, London, Chatto & Windus

Ellsberg, Daniel (2002) *Secrets: A memoir of Vietnam and the Pentagon Papers*, New York, Viking Press

Goodale, James C. (2013) *Fighting for the press: The inside story of the Pentagon Papers and other battles*, New York, Cuny Journalism Press

Greenwald, Glenn (2015) *No place to hide: Edward Snowden, the NSA and the surveillance state*, London, Penguin

Harding, Luke (2014) *The Snowden files: The inside story of the world's most wanted man*, London, Guardian Faber Publishing

Holroyd, Michael (1998) *Bernard Shaw: A biography*, London, Vintage

Kershaw, Ian (2004) *Making friends with Hitler: Lord Londonderry and the roots of appeasement*, London, Allen Lane

Klein, Mark (2009) *Wiring up the Big Brother machine ... and fighting it*, Charleston, South Carolina, BookSurge

Knightley, Phillip (2004) *The first casualty: The war correspondent as hero and myth-maker from the Crimea to Iraq*, Baltimore, Maryland, Johns Hopkins University Press, third edition

Lewis, Paul and Evans, Rob (2013) *Undercover: The true story of Britain's secret police*, London, Guardian/Faber Publishing

Lucas, Edward (2014) *The new Cold War: Putin's threat to Russia and the West*, London, Bloomsbury

Muggeridge, Malcolm (1981) *The infernal grove: Chronicles of wasted time Vol. II*, London, Fontana

Petley, Julian (2014) The state journalism is in: Edward Snowden and the British press, *Ethical Space: The International Journal of Communication Ethics*, Vol. 11, Nos 1 and 2 pp 9-18

Ponting, Clive (1985) *The right to know: The inside story of the Belgrano affair*, London and Sydney, Sphere Books Limited

Rayfield, Donald (2005) *Stalin and his hangmen: The tyrant and those who killed for him*, London, Random House

Snepp, Frank (1999) *Irreparable harm: A firsthand account of how one agent took on the CIA in an epic battle over free speech*, Lawrence, Kansas, University Press of Kansas

Taylor, Sally J. (1990) *Stalin's apologist, Walter Duranty: The New York Times' man in Moscow*, Oxford, Oxford University Press

COURT RULINGS AND INQUIRIES

Coulson & Kuttner v. Regina (2013) EWCA Crim 1026, 28 June. Available online at http://www.bailii.org/ew/cases/EWCA/Crim/2013/1026.html, accessed on 10 November 2014

Chapman & Others, v. Regina (2015) EWCA Crim 539, 26 March. Available online at http://www.bailii.org/ew/cases/EWCA/Crim/2015/539.html, accessed on 1 May 2015

Miranda, R. (on the application of) v. Secretary of State for the Home Department and Commissioner of Police for the Metropolis (2013) EWHC 2609 (Admin) 23 August. Available online at http://www.bailii.org/cgi-bin/markup.cgi?doc=/ew/cases/EWHC/Admin/2013/2609.html

Miranda v Secretary of State for the Home Department & Others (2014) EWHC 255 (Admin) 19 February. Available online at http://www.bailii.org/cgi-bin/markup.cgi?doc=/ew/cases/EWHC/Admin/2014/255.html

The Litvinenko Inquiry (2015) Available online at https://www.litvinenkoinquiry.org/, accessed on 15 October 2015

The Detainee Inquiry (2010-2013) Available online at http://www.detaineeinquiry.org.uk/, accessed on 15 October 2015

WEBSITE REFERENCES

Ackerman, Spencer and Rushe, Dominic (2013) NSA director: Edward Snowden has caused irreversible damage to US, *Guardian*, 23 June. Available online at http://www.theguardian.com/world/2013/jun/23/nsa-director-snowden-hong-kong, accessed on 20 April 2015

Aftergood, Steven (2011) In Drake leak case, govt seeks to block unclassified info, FAS, Federation of American Scientists, 12 May. Available online at https://fas.org/blogs/secrecy/2011/05/drake_unclassified/, accessed on 1 November 2015

Apuzzo, Matt (2015) CIA officer is found guilty in leak tied to *Times* reporter, *New York Times*, 26 January. Available online at http://www.nytimes.com/2015/01/27/us/politics/cia-officer-in-leak-case-jeffrey-sterling-is-convicted-of-espionage.html, accessed on 1 November 2015

Associated Press (2015) Former CIA man Jeffrey Sterling gets 42 months in prison over Iran leaks, *Guardian*, 11 May. Available online at http://www.theguardian.com/us-news/2015/may/11/former-cia-man-jeffrey-sterling-42-months-prison-iran-leaks, accessed on 1 November 2015

Bradburn, Howard and Taylor, Peter (2015) Edward Snowden: Spies and the law, *Panorama*, 5 October. Available online at http://www.bbc.co.uk/iplayer/episode/b06h7j3b/panorama-edward-snowden-spies-and-the-law, accessed on 20 October 2015

Burkeman, Oliver and Norton-Taylor, Richard (2004) The spy who wouldn't keep a secret, *Guardian*, 26 February. Available online at http://www.theguardian.com/politics/2004/feb/26/interviews.iraq, accessed on 1 November 2015

Cole, David (2014) The three leakers and what to do about them, *New York Review of Books*, 6 February. Available online at http://www.nybooks.com/articles/archives/2014/feb/06/three-leakers-and-what-do-about-them/, accessed on 10 September 2015

Coombs, David and Sweeney, John (2010a) *The documentary: Useful idiots*, Episode 1, CTVC Production for BBC World Service, 8 August 2010. Available online at http://www.bbc.co.uk/programmes/p008vd41, accessed on 30 March 2015

Coombs, David and Sweeney, John (2010b) *The documentary: Useful idiots*, Episode 2, CTVC Production for BBC World Service, 15 August 2010. Available online at http://www.bbc.co.uk/programmes/p008z6sg, accessed on 30 March 2015

Crook, Tim (2013a) The legal case for protecting April Casburn, *Press Gazette*, 11 February. Available online at http://www.press-gazette.co.uk/content/legal-case-protecting-april-casburn, accessed 20 August 2015

Crook, Tim (2013b) Alan Rusbridger evokes First Amendment to backward UK, *The Conversation*, 4 December. Available online at https://theconversation.com/alan-rusbridger-evokes-first-amendment-to-backward-uk-21129, accessed on 20 September 2015

Davies, Caroline and Meikle, James (2012) Gareth Williams's death was 'criminally mediated', says coroner, *Guardian*, 2 May 2012. Available online at http://www.theguardian.com/uk/2012/may/02/gareth-williams-coroner-never-solved, accessed on 10 October 2015

GCHQ (2015) GCHQ funding and controls. Available online at http://www.gchq.gov.uk/how_we_work/running_the_business/Pages/Funding-financial-controls.aspx, accessed on 1 November 2015

Glover, Stephen (2013) Stupendous arrogance: By risking lives, I say again, the *Guardian* is floundering far out of its depth in realms where no newspaper should venture, *Daily Mail*, 9 October. Available online at http://www.dailymail.co.uk/debate/article-2451532/STEPHEN-GLOVER-By-risking-lives-The-Guardian-floundering-far-depth.html, accessed on 10 January 2015

Greenslade, Roy (2014) Juries in *Sun* reporters' trials unworried by payments for information, *Guardian*, 10 December. Available online at http://www.theguardian.com/media/greenslade/2014/dec/10/juries-in-sun-reporters-trials-unworried-by-payments-for-information, accessed on 4 September 2015

Greenwald, Glenn, MacAskill, Ewen and Poitras, Laura (2013a) Edward Snowden: The whistleblower behind the NSA surveillance revelations, *Guardian*, 11 June. Available online at http://www.theguardian.com/world/2013/jun/09/edward-snowden-nsa-whistle-blower-surveillance, accessed on 20 August 2014

Hopkins, Nick (2013) UK gathering secret intelligence via covert NSA operation, *Guardian*, 7 June. Available online at http://www.theguardian.com/technology/2013/jun/07/uk-gathering-secret-intelligence-nsa-prism, accessed on 7 May 2014

Hopkins, Nick and Taylor, Matthew (2013) Alan Rusbridger and the home affairs select committee: The key exchanges, *Guardian*, 3 December. Available online at http://www.theguardian.com/world/2013/dec/03/rusbridger-home-affairs-nsa-key-exchanges, accessed on 13 December 2014

Hopkins, Nick and Borger, Julian (2013) Exclusive: NSA pays £100m in secret funding for GCHQ, *Guardian*, 1 August. Available online at http://www.theguardian.com/uk-news/2013/aug/01/nsa-paid-gchq-spying-edward-snowden, accessed on 10 September 2015

Levy, Megan (2007) Scotland Yard man jailed for terror leak, *Telegraph*, 27 July. Available online at http://www.telegraph.co.uk/news/uknews/1558648/Scotland-Yard-man-jailed-for-terror-leak.html, accessed on 5 September 2015

MacAskill, Ewen, Davies, Nick, Hopkins, Nick, Borger, Julian and Ball, James (2013a) GCHQ intercepted foreign politicians' communications at G20 summits, *Guardian*, 17 June. Available online at http://www.theguardian.com/uk/2013/jun/16/gchq-intercepted-communications-g20-summits, accessed on 20 May 2014

MacAskill, Ewen, Davies, Nick, Hopkins, Nick, Borger, Julian and Ball, James (2013b) GCHQ taps fibre-optic cables for secret access to world's communications, *Guardian*, 21 June. Available online at http://www.theguardian.com/uk/2013/jun/21/gchq-cables-secret-world-communications-nsa, accessed on 20 May 2014

Martinson, Jane (2015) *Sunday Times* drops claim that Miranda met Snowden before UK detention, *Guardian*, 15 June. Available online at http://www.theguardian.com/media/2015/jun/15/sunday-times-drops-claim-david-miranda-edward-snowden, accessed on 1 November 2015

Narayan, Hari (2015) 'Not only can the state intercept your communication, it does', *Hindu*, 17 July Available online at http://www.thehindu.com/opinion/interview/an-interview-with-alan-rusbridger-about-edward-snowden/article7430262.ece, accessed on 4 November 2015

Newman, Melanie (2015) Boost for press freedom campaign as European court prioritises Bureau's legal challenge to UK snooping laws, Bureau of Investigative Journalism, 20 January. Available online at https://www.thebureauinvestigates.com/2015/01/20/boost-press-freedom-european-court-bureau-case-snooping-laws/, accessed on 10 March 2015

PA Media Lawyer (2014) QC: Alarm bells should have rung with bugging of Sally Murrer, UK journalists need 'shield law' to stop RIPA abuse, *Press Gazette*, 12 November. Available online at http://www.pressgazette.co.uk/alarm-bells-should-have-rung-bugging-sally-murrer-uk-journalists-need-shield-law-stop-ripa-abuse, accessed on 20 January 2015

Pasquill, Derek (2008) I had no choice but to leak, *New Statesman*, 17 January. Available at http://www.newstatesman.com/politics/2008/01/british-muslim-story-case, accessed on 1 November 2015

Penrose, Justin (2013) Spy in the bag Gareth Williams was killed to protect Russian 'mole' in MI6, ex-KGB agent claims, *Daily Mirror*, 17 November. Available online at http://www.mirror.co.uk/news/uk-news/former-kgb-agent-boris-karpichkov-2800352, accessed on 3 March 2015

Ponsford, Dominic (2015a) Elveden unravels: After four years and 34 arrested/charged journalists, one conviction stands, *Press Gazette*, 20 April. Available online at http://www.pressgazette.co.uk/elveden-unravels-after-four-years-and-34-arrestedcharged-journalists-one-conviction-stands, accessed on 25 October 2015

Ponsford, Dominic (2015b) The careless way Plebgate police helped themselves to journalists' call records was a Stasi-style nightmare, *Press Gazette*, 22 July. Available online at http://www.pressgazette.co.uk/content/careless-way-plebgate-police-helped-themselves-journalists-call-records-was-stasi-style, accessed on 10 August 2015

Ponsford, Dominic (2015c) The betrayal of newspaper sources jailed under Operation Elveden casts a shadow over our industry, *Press Gazette*, 28 July. Available online at http://www.pressgazette.co.uk/content/betrayal-newspaper-sources-jailed-under-operation-elveden-casts-shadow-over-our-industry, accessed on 1 August 2015

Pulitzer (2014) The 2014 Pulitzer Prize Winners: Public Service. Available online at http://www.pulitzer.org/citation/2014-Public-Service, accessed on 1 November 2015

Robinson, Martin (2013) Police forces pay £25million to informants and nearly half is spent by London's Met, 18 June. Available online at http://www.dailymail.co.uk/news/article-2343764/Police-forces-pay-25million-informants-nearly-half-spent-London-s-Met.html#ixzz3qjINdvrV, accessed on 15 September 2015

Ross, Brian (2006) NSA whistleblower alleges illegal spying, *ABC News*, 10 January. Available online at http://abcnews.go.com/WNT/Investigation/story?id=1491889, accessed on 1 November 2015 Rusbridger, Alan (2013) The Snowden leaks and the public, *New York Review of Books*, 21 November. Available online at http://www.nybooks.com/articles/archives/2013/nov/21/snowden-leaks-and-public/, accessed on 1 November 2015

Schmidt, Michael (2013) Ex-CIA officer sentenced to 30 months in leak, *New York Times*, 25 January. Available online at http://www.nytimes.com/2013/01/26/us/ex-officer-for-cia-is-sentenced-in-leak-case.html, accessed on 1 November 2015

Shorrock, Tim (2013) Obama's crackdown on whistleblowers, *Nation*, 26 March. Available online at http://www.thenation.com/article/obamas-crackdown-whistleblowers/, accessed on 1 November 2015

Slack, James (2015) Snowden leaks 'put spies at risk': May says traitor has damaged intelligence agencies across the world including MI5 and MI6, *Daily Mail*, 18 March. Available online at http://www.dailymail.co.uk/news/article-2999878/Snowden-leaks-spies-risk-says-traitor-damaged-intelligence-agencies-world-including-MI5-MI6.html, accessed on 20 August 2015

Telegraph (2013) Glenn Greenwald threatens UK after partner's Heathrow detention, *Telegraph*, 19 August. Available online at http://www.telegraph.co.uk/news/worldnews/northamerica/usa/10253544/Glenn-Greenwald-threatens-UK-after-partners-Heathrow-detention.html, accessed on 1 November 2015

Wintour, Patrick (2015) Only 'tiny handful' of ministers knew of mass surveillance, Clegg reveals, *Guardian*, 5 November. Available online at http://www.theguardian.com/world/2015/nov/05/nick-clegg-cabinet-mass-surveillance-british-spying, accessed on 6 November 2016

Young, John and Natsios, Debora (1996-2015) Cryptome. Available online at https://cryptome.org/cryptome-archive.htm, accessed on 1 November 2015

NOTE ON THE CONTRIBUTOR

Tim Crook is Emeritus Professor of Media, Communication and Cultural Studies at Goldsmiths, University of London. He has authored a number of books on media law, journalism and radio.

Chapter 4

Doublethink in the mass media: Fallujah and the politics of human rights reporting

Florian Zollmann

Florian Zollmann examines the UK press coverage of the US attack on Fallujah in 2004 and concludes that they conformed to the predictions of the 'propaganda model' by playing down serious violations of international law.

Since World War II the importance of human rights has significantly increased and a diverse range of human rights standards has been institutionalised in international accords (Donnelly 2007). The formalised agreements can be placed within two categories: international human rights law (i.e. a set of laws aimed at protecting human rights) and international humanitarian law (i.e. a set of laws aimed at protecting human rights during armed conflicts). International human rights law and international humanitarian law are subsets of international law which incorporates a further range of treaties, conventions, principles and customs (Rehman 2010: 19-26, 765).

The basic tenet of international law is the United Nations Charter (UN Charter) which came into force on 24 October 1945 and has since become binding law for all signatory states including the US and United Kingdom. The UN Charter's preamble proclaims a determination 'to save succeeding generations from the scourge of war'. Any use of force in violation of the UN Charter can be termed unlawful aggression. Christian Tomuschat (2008: 154) sees a connection between the UN Charter's focus on the prevention of war and the preservation of human rights ... war and armed conflict have been placed under the regime of the [UN] Charter because they are susceptible of bringing 'untold sorrow to mankind'. This is tantamount to saying that prevention of war constitutes indirect protection of human rights.

Tomuschat seems to echo the judges of the Nuremberg Tribunal, at which the Nazis were convicted, who saw Germany's illegal war as the major crime of World War II. In their seminal verdict, the judges concluded:

To initiate a war of aggression, therefore, is not only an international crime; it is the supreme international crime differing only from other war crimes in that it contains within itself the accumulated evil of the whole (Judgment, Trial of the Major War Criminals before the International Military Tribunal, Nurnberg [sic], Germany, 1947 (Official Text), cited in Gerhart 1998: 1109).

The Nuremberg verdict includes an important argument: wars are prerequisites for human rights abuses and should thus be avoided. Today, the body which has the law enforcement power to stop wars and maintain 'international peace and security' is the United Nations Security Council (Bailey and Daws 1998: 19). By using their veto power, however, the permanent members of the Security Council are able to avert the council's capability to act (for a discussion of the veto system see Bailey and Daws 1998: 226-230).

International enforcement to prevent human rights violations has rarely been applied because human rights are regarded as state affairs (Forsythe 2006: 58). This gap was filled by non-governmental organisations and advocacy groups who monitor human rights and shame their abusers. Accordingly, Thomas Risse and Stephen C. Ropp (1999: 275) argue that:

> … transnational human rights pressures and policies, including the activities of advocacy networks, have made a very significant difference in bringing about improvements in human rights practices in diverse countries around the world.

In conjunction with these developments, various courts, mandated to prosecute violations of international law and human rights, were established during the last decade of the 20th century thus signalling an end of the era of immunity: they include two UN ad hoc criminal courts, the International Criminal Tribunal for the Former Yugoslavia (ICTY) and the International Criminal Tribunal for Rwanda (ICTR), a range of hybrid criminal courts for Kosovo, East Timor, Sierra Leone and Cambodia, and, as a permanent institution, the world's highest legal authority, the International Criminal Court (ICC) (Forsythe 2006: 96-112).

It could be argued, then, that at the beginning of the 21st century human rights have become a defining aspect of Western culture valued among governments, NGOs, academia and the media (Chandler 2002: 1). Nonetheless, David Chandler (ibid: 2) points out that 'rather than challenging political and economic inequalities in the international system, the human rights framework is facilitating new hierarchies of control and regulation'.

THE POLITICS OF LAW ENFORCEMENT

The current practice of law enforcement suggests that the human rights model has been geared towards the interests of Western imperialism. Edward S. Herman and

David Peterson (2010: 20) describe how a process of selective prosecution has been set in motion:

> ... it turns out that all fourteen of the ICC's indictments through mid-2009 had been issued against black Africans from three countries (the Democratic Republic of Congo, Uganda, and the Sudan), while carefully excluding Uganda's Yoweri Museveni and Rwanda's Paul Kagame, perhaps the most prolific tandem of killers to rule on the African continent during the current era, but highly valued clients of the West.

Additionally, while several courts were created under UN auspices to prosecute violations of international law (see discussion above), no courts have been established to prosecute violations of international law conducted by Western states in the former Yugoslavia (1999), Afghanistan (2001-2010) and Iraq (1991-2010) (see Herman and Peterson 2007, 2010; Mandel 2005), as well as by Western allies such as Israel, Colombia, Turkey or Indonesia. This has been accompanied by a legal culture that neglects to focus on the crime against peace: the ICC, the ICTY and the ICTR exclude the crime of aggression from their jurisdiction. Similarly, leading human rights organisations such as Amnesty International (AI) and Human Rights Watch (HRW) reject aggression as a framework for their inquiries. The same applies to great parts of Western intellectual and media culture for which 'the supreme international crime' is of no concern (see Herman and Peterson 2010: 17-27).

THE POLITICS OF HUMAN RIGHTS REPORTING

Critical literature on media coverage has also identified double standards in media treatment of human rights abuses. Edward S. Herman and Noam Chomsky's (e.g. 1979a, b; 2008) studies reveal how the mass media selectively focuses on human rights depending on Western economic and military relations to a country. As a result, coverage on Western states and their 'clients', who have this status because they provide a favourable investment climate to Western corporations, is remarkably different from coverage of so called 'enemy' states of the West.

Herman and Chomsky (2008) compared coverage of victims of state-violence by 'enemy' countries (such as the former Soviet Union, Poland, North Vietnam, Cambodia and the former Republic of Yugoslavia) with victims of state violence by the US or 'friendly' countries (such as Guatemala, El Salvador, Turkey and Indonesia). They concluded (ibid: 34) that 'differential treatment occurs on a large scale' and 'that the US mass media's practical definitions of worth are political in the extreme and fit well the expectations of a propaganda model' which assumes the media to 'consistently portray people abused in enemy states as *worthy* victims, whereas those treated with equal or greater severity by its own government or clients will be *unworthy*'. A growing body of literature has identified similar media patterns in the US, Canada and United Kingdom (e.g. DiMaggio 2010; Edwards and Cromwell 2006; Herman and Peterson 2010; Klaehn 2005). Such comparisons involve an ethical dimension: As Gilbert Achcar (2006: 30) writes: 'Putting a vile act in the context of acts of the same kind does not trivialize it. ... Rather, to put the act in context is to reject selective indignation.'

Dichotomised media choices can be illustrated when comparing coverage of the Iraq and Bosnian Wars. According to former UN Human Rights Coordinator Denis Halliday, the US/UK-imposed sanctions on Iraq following the 1991 conflict, had 'almost certainly' killed 'well over a million' Iraqis (cited in Pilger 2004). Additionally, Les Roberts (2007), co-author of the most authoritative surveys on mortality in Iraq, points out that the Iraq War has 'triggered an episode more deadly than the Rwandan genocide'. These atrocities have virtually been excluded from media coverage (see Edwards and Cromwell 2006, 2009).

In stark contrast to Iraq, during the Bosnian War journalism operated in a modus of attachment highlighting atrocities – but mainly those conducted by the Serbs (see Hammond 2007). The Research and Documentation Center in Sarajevo and the UN prosecutor's office at the war crimes tribunal in the Hague estimate that during the Bosnian War up to 110,000 people were killed on all sides (BBC News 2007). This is about 1/15th of the deaths for which the West is responsible in Iraq. Isn't that evidence for media bias?

FALLUJAH AND THE POLITICS OF HUMAN RIGHTS REPORTING

On 8 November 2004, US/Coalition forces launched a full-scale military attack against the Iraqi city Fallujah to crush the resistance which had rooted in the town. Official discourse depicted the 'operation' as a quick military success. Accordingly, Eric Schmitt (2004) wrote in *The New York Times* on 15 November: 'Military commanders point to several accomplishments in Fallujah. A bastion of resistance has been eliminated, with lower than expected American military and Iraqi civilian casualties.' In contrast, *Democracy Now's* Amy Goodman situated the assault 'among the most violent and devastating attacks on a civilian population in recent decades' (cited in Jamail 2007: xi). The documentary record supports the latter perspective. Up to 6,000 people were slaughtered and 36,000 houses demolished. Numerous violations of the Geneva Conventions have since been documented (see Holmes 2007; Jamail 2004a, 2004b, 2007; Marqusee 2005; Zollmann 2010). Today, the use of poisonous weapons has caused, according to one study, 'increases in infant mortality, cancer and leukaemia in the Iraqi city of Fallujah [that] exceed those reported by survivors of the atomic bombs' (Cockburn 2010).

This research explores how the British 'quality' press reported the November assault in consideration of international law. The newspaper sample comprises the *Independent*, the *Guardian*, and *The Times* as well as their respective Sunday titles including the *Observer*. The set of newspapers was selected in accord with a 'best-case approach' which looks at those media having 'large foreign news staffs, high prestige and sophistication, and a record of willingness to take on the government' (Entman 2004: 77). The study incorporates all published material during the first two weeks after the November 2004 attacks unfolded. The period was chosen because it includes the indicative peak coverage of the assault and is long enough to capture critical angles that might have developed later (see Esser, Schwabe and Wilke 2005: 320; Mermin 1999: 42). A 'qualitative' content analysis of 143 articles was conducted using David Altheide's (1996: 7) method to analyse 'multiple documents' with a research protocol. This approach allows for contextual and frequency analyses and enables systematic structuring of the data and the disclosure of the research procedure.

OFF THE AGENDA 1: AGGRESSION

At first we should consider how the media referred to the US/Coalition occupation of Iraq because the assault on Fallujah was a direct outcome of this event. The number of legal experts who saw the Iraq War as a violation of international law far exceeded the few who depicted the invasion as legal (see Mandel 2005: 33). And if the invasion of Iraq was illegal, then so is the occupation. Accordingly, Article 3 (a) of UN Resolution 3314 (XXIX) defines aggression as: 'The invasion or attack by the armed forces of a State of the territory of another State [in contravention of the UN Charter], or any military occupation, however temporary, resulting from such invasion.' The media sample did not contain any reference suggesting that the US/Coalition occupation could have constituted a case of aggression.

During the invasion/occupation of Iraq, Britain was the junior partner of the US. When covering British foreign policy, it is usually the case that the media applies the concept of 'basic benevolence' or 'the idea that Britain promotes high principles – democracy, peace, human rights and development' (Curtis 2003: 380). Furthermore, coverage was influenced by the codification of UN Resolution 1483 which was implemented on 22 May 2003 to formally legitimise the occupying powers (see Boyle 2005). As a result, the basic assumption underlying coverage under review was that the US/Coalition was the legitimate occupant of Iraq.

OFF THE AGENDA 2: THE INITIAL VIOLATION OF THE GENEVA CONVENTIONS

When General George Casey, Commander of the Multinational Forces in Iraq, announced the beginning of the attack at the official US Department of Defense meeting on 8 November, he said:

> Our estimates are that, again, 50 [per cent] to 70 per cent of the population has departed. That is borne out by heat signatures and generator signatures that we observe there during darkness. That's about as good an estimate as I can give you on what's there inside of Fallujah (US DoD 2004).

Hence, US military planners must have expected that between 60,000-100,000 civilians were inside Fallujah, a densely populated city with a size of roughly 3 x 3,5 square kilometres. It seems beyond comprehension how a full-scale military attack on such a city involving the use of heavy weaponry such as artillery, tanks, helicopters, jets, heavy bombs and other explosives (such as explosive coils to clear minefields, which were detonated in residential areas, and the use of thermobaric weapons and white phosphorus) (see Zollmann 2010) can be conducted in accord with the Geneva Conventions which demand that civilians 'shall in all circumstances be treated humanely' (Article 3, Convention IV, 1949) and that 'indiscriminate attacks are prohibited' (Article 51, Protocol I, 1977).

The press did not discuss this issue. This is not to say that coverage was monolithic. All newspapers under review published some deviant commentaries. Haifa Zangana, for instance, described the assault as 'collective punishment' in the *Guardian* on 17 November. 'Western governments, led by the US and UK, supported Saddam's regime against the will of the Iraqi people for decades. They are committing a similar crime now,' Zangana concluded.

THE LAWS OF WAR: NOT TO SEE THE WOOD FOR THE TREES

Some articles carried very critical statements suggesting that the assault was a crime. An editorial in the *Guardian*, on 9 November, stressed: 'Critics of the US have already written [the assault] off as a war crime.' However, the editorial's conclusion still acknowledged the basic legitimacy of the 'operation': 'The most we can probably hope for is that this Iraqi battle will be fought with care, restraint and speed.' The newspapers also featured highly critical statements by Iraqi opposition groups suggesting that military actions were not justified. In *The Times*, on 9 November, Richard Beeston cited 'Muhammad Bashar al-Faidhi, of the Association of Muslim Scholars, a Sunni group close to the insurgency' saying: 'The attack on Fallujah is illegal and illegitimate.' Such statements were often buried somewhere down the inverted pyramid of the news report between pronouncements by US officials.

When covering the assault, the press also discussed or mentioned actions in relation to possible violations of the laws of war. Many of these articles referred to a US Marine's shooting of an unarmed, wounded resistance fighter in a mosque which was filmed by NBC reporter Kevin Sites. Gary Younge and Brian Whitaker discussed the execution on 17 November in the *Guardian*: 'The protection of wounded combatants is a basic tenet of the Geneva Conventions which govern the rules of war.' *The Times*'s Philippe Naughton wrote on 20 November: 'The Marine was suspended and is under investigation for possible war crimes...' Andrew Buncombe's description in the *Independent*, on 16 November, suggested that the shooting might not have been an isolated event:

> Other footage has shown troops shooting wounded fighters lying in open ground as well as attacks on Iraqis – some said to be civilians – by US

aircraft and helicopters. This latest footage is among the most shocking given that it apparently shows without obstruction the Marine shooting the prisoner in the head at close range.

Furthermore, two articles described the US raid of a hospital, which was one of the first actions of the assault, pointing out that the institution was under protection of the Geneva Conventions. And finally, various articles included critical statements by the UN or human rights groups. The article by Younge and Whitaker, for example, cited 'Louise Arbour, the UN high commissioner for human rights' saying 'all those responsible for violations should be brought to justice'. Similarly, Tim Reid and James Hider paraphrased Amnesty International in *The Times* on 17 November announcing that 'both sides in the Fallujah fighting had broken the rules of war governing the protection of civilians and wounded combatants'.

While the resistance certainly had conducted crimes, such statements indicated equal responsibility. No newspaper, however, made the effort to inquire about the extent of human rights violations and the perpetrators of these atrocities. Only the mosque shooting was investigated in detail. Other possible violations of the Geneva Conventions were mentioned *en passant*, many more were ignored. Strikingly, the press described numerous incidences that could literally be regarded as violations of the Geneva Conventions without actually labelling them as such. They were depicted in at least 39 articles (27 per cent of all coverage). With regard to US/Coalition actions, they included:

- the seizure of a hospital (Article 19, Convention I; Article 18 Convention IV): 'The main hospital was captured by US and Iraqi government forces on Monday, when, according to government figures more than 40 "terrorists" were killed.' *Independent*, 10 November;

- the bombing of a hospital and killing of patients and staff (Articles 19, 24 Convention I; Article 18 Convention IV): 'Twenty Iraqi doctors and dozens of civilians were killed in a US air strike that hit a clinic in Fallujah, according to an Iraqi doctor who said he survived the strike.' *Independent*, 11 November;

- the deliberate targeting of a hospital (Article 19, Convention I; Article 18 Convention IV): 'US forces launched several raids overnight… In one operation they attacked the Zaharawi hospital, from which they believed militants were operating.' *Guardian*, 20 November;

- the deliberate targeting of civilians (Article 3, Convention I; Article 51, Protocol I, 1977): 'We see active and well-trained young men using deadly force, perhaps against a population we cannot see, and certainly against enemy fighters…' *The Times*, 15 November;

- the deliberate targeting of driving vehicles (Article 3, Convention I): 'During the fight, rules of engagement allow US troops to shoot and kill anyone ... driving in Fallujah...' *Independent*, 8 November;

- the shooting of ambulances (Article 21, Convention IV; Article 12, Protocol I, 1977): 'We had one ambulance hit by US fire and a doctor wounded. There are scores of injured civilians in their homes whom we can't move. A 13-year-old child just died in my hands.' *Independent*, 14 November;

- the prevention of citizens from leaving the city (Article 35, Convention IV): 'Tens of thousands of civilians are thought to have stayed behind. Under the terms of a curfew imposed on Monday they cannot leave their homes.' *Guardian*, 10 November;

- the cutting off of power and water supplies (Article 54, Protocol 1, 1977): 'Once the attack began, power was cut off to the city and some residents said the water supply had also been cut.' *Guardian*, 10 November;

- the use of indiscriminate military force (Article 51, Protocol I, 1977): 'The reaction of US troops to attacks, say residents, have been out of all proportion; shots by snipers have been answered by rounds from Abrams tanks, devastating buildings, and, it is claimed, injuring and killing civilians.' *Independent*, 15 November;

- the prevention of a relief convoy to enter the city (Article 3, Convention I; Article 63 Convention IV): 'Fardous al-Ubaidi, head of the Iraqi Red Crescent Society, said her organisation had asked permission from the Iraqi government to deliver aid supplies to people in the city but the request was turned down.' *Independent*, 13 November;

- the prevention of doctors and ambulances treating wounded people (Article 20, Convention IV; Article 15 Protocol I 1977): 'Dr Salih al-Issawi, the director of Fallujah Hospital, said he asked US officers to allow doctors and ambulances go inside the main part of the city to help the wounded, but they refused.' *Independent*, 9 November;

- the establishment of free-fire zones during night time (Article 51, Protocol I, 1977): 'Fallujah, blacked-out since the onslaught began, was under a strict night-time shoot-to-kill curfew. Anyone spotted in the soldiers' night-vision sights would be shot.' *The Times*, 12 November;

- the shooting of wounded fighters (Articles 3, 12 Convention I): 'He shot the man in the stomach: he fell, but kept crawling, so Sergeant Veen shot him again in the shoulder. Still the man tried to move away, so the sergeant blasted him with his 50-calibre machinegun.' *The Times*, 15 November;

- the symbolic use of force (i.e. terrorism) (Article 33, Convention IV): 'Lieutenant Fares Ahmed Hassan said that the destroyed city would send a strong message. ... "When the people of Fallujah come back and see their houses, they will kick out any terrorists. This will be an example to all Iraqi cities," the Kurdish officer said.' *The Times*, 15 November;

- the use of phosphorous rounds (Article 2, Protocol III, 1980): 'As the battle degenerated into wild exchanges of thousands of rounds of small arms fire, one tank fired a phosphorus shell that inadvertently rained flaming debris on American troops.' *The Times*, 14 November;

- Assaults on the honour of women (Article 27, Convention IV): '... survivors of the fighting in Falluja ... accused the Iraqi national guard [a US proxy force] of seizing young female refugees "like hungry dogs".' *The Times*, 21 November.

There were also instances depicting actions by the resistance, they included:

- the occupation of the main hospital (Article 12, Protocol I, 1977): 'The Iraqi interim Prime Minister Iyad Allawi claimed that troops had detained 38 insurgents entrenched at Fallujah Hospital.' *Guardian*, 10 November;

- the deliberate targeting of civilians (Article 3, Convention I; Article 51, Protocol I, 1977): 'He said that some civilians had said that insurgent snipers had shot anyone trying to leave their homes.' *The Times*, 15 November;

- the improper use of white flags (perfidy) (Article 37, Protocol I, 1977): '... insurgents waved a white flag of surrender before opening fire on US troops and causing a number of casualties, Marine spokesman Lt. Lyle Gilbert said.' *Observer*, 21 November;

- the illegal use of booby-traps (Article 6, Protocol II 1980): 'Mujahidin regularly boobytrap themselves when dying.' *The Times*, 17 November;

- the use of mosques for hostile purposes (Article 53, Protocol I, 1977): 'Officially, soldiers cannot attack mosques unless they are being used by insurgents for hostile purposes. Which of course they have been.' *Independent*, 15 November.

Clearly, the assault on Fallujah could not be justified under international law and many of the incidents described above may amount to war crimes and crimes against humanity (for legal definitions see Rehman 2010: 736-745). The press's investigations into the conduct of the 'operation' were poor. The Geneva Conventions demand from 'Each High Contracting Party ... to search for persons alleged to have committed, or to have ordered to be committed, such grave breaches, and shall bring such persons ... before its own courts' (Article 49, Convention I). A party to the conflict may also request the establishment of an inquiry (Article 52, Convention I). Evidence suggests that the US prevented legal inquiries in Fallujah (see Zollmann 2009). The press could have campaigned on this issue. It didn't.

CONCLUSION

The newspapers under review certainly covered a diverse range of views, thus highlighting civilian suffering and violations of the laws of war. Nevertheless, even such critical coverage can be explained within a propaganda paradigm: an instrumental approach does not necessarily expect facts to be excluded from coverage because 'successful propaganda is that based directly on obvious facts' (Ellul 1973: 84). More important is the framework in which these facts are placed and how certain contexts are emphasised over others. Furthermore, dynamics of media campaigns amount to 'the playing down and rationalization of "own" crimes and repression in friendly client states [thus allowing for the] maintenance of the image of national beneficence...' (Herman 1986: 177).

Hence, a propaganda approach assumes the media will apply a politicised human rights model. It would anticipate the media to be highly critical of 'enemy' states and uncritical in the 'acceptance of certain premises in dealing with self and friends' (Herman and Chomsky op cit: 32). In its coverage of the US assault on Fallujah, the British press instituted the assumption that an otherwise illegal occupation was legitimate. Furthermore, the 'operation' was largely framed as a military endeavour. Most newspapers did not consider it to be a massacre or a crime.

A propaganda model would further expect 'the [search for] responsibility of high officials for abuses in enemy states, but diminished enterprise in examining such matters in connection with one's own and friendly states' (Herman and Chomsky op cit: 32). Accordingly, this study suggests the press only acknowledged that low level military personnel might have been responsible for violations. Legal documents suggest, however, that official planners were mainly accountable (see article 28 of the ICC Statute).

And finally, a propaganda framework would assume 'different criteria of evaluation to be employed, so that what is villainy in enemy states will be presented as an incidental background fact in the case of oneself and friends' (Herman and Chomsky op cit: 32). As documented above, descriptions of acts which literally amounted to war crimes largely remained decontextualised and scattered.

The ability of the press to describe horrific events and place them in a framework of Western benevolence may also amount to what George Orwell (2004 [1949]:

265) defined as doublethink: 'to deny the existence of objective reality and all the while to take account of the reality which one denies'.

- This paper was first published in *Ethical Space*, Vol. 8, Nos 1 and 2 pp 25-31, 2011

REFERENCES

Achcar, Gilbert (2006) *The clash of barbarisms: The making of the New World Disorder*, Boulder, Paradigm Publishers

Altheide, David L. (1996) *Qualitative media analysis*, London, Sage

Bailey, Sydney D. And Daws, Sam (1998) *The procedure of the Security Council*, Oxford, Clarendon Press

BBC News (2007) Bosnia war dead figure announced, 21 June. Available online at http://news.bbc.co.uk/1/hi/world/europe/6228152.stm, accessed on 22 November 2010

Boyle, Francis A. (2005) US as belligerent occupant, *Counterpunch*, 22 December. Available online at http://www.counterpunch.org/boyle12222005.html, accessed on 25 November 2010

Chandler, David (2002) Rethinking human rights, Chandler, David (ed.) *Rethinking human rights: Critical approaches to international politics*, New York, Palgrave Macmillan, pp 1-15

Chomsky, Noam and Herman, Edward S. (1979a) *The Washington connection and Third World fascism: The political economy of human rights: Volume I*, Nottingham, Spokesman

Chomsky, Noam and Herman, Edward S. (1979b) *After the cataclysm: Postwar Indochina and the reconstruction of imperial ideology: The political economy of human rights: Volume II*, Nottingham, Spokesman

Cockburn, Patrick (2010) Toxic legacy of US assault on Fallujah 'worse than Hiroshima', *Independent*, 24 July p. 28

Curtis, Mark (2003) *Web of deceit: Britain's real role in the world*, London, Vintage

DiMaggio, Anthony (2010) *When media goes to war: Hegemonic discourse, public opinion and the limits of dissent*, New York, Monthly Review Press

Donnelly, Jack (2007) *International human rights*, Boulder, Westview Press, third edition

Edwards, David and Cromwell, David (2006) *Guardians of power: The myth of the liberal media*, London, Pluto Press

Edwards, David and Cromwell, David (2009) *Newspeak in the 21st century*, London, Pluto Press

Ellul, Jacques (1973) *Propaganda: The formation of men's attitudes*, New York, Vintage Books

Entman, Robert M. (2004) *Projections of power: Framing news, public opinion, and US foreign policy*, Chicago, University of Chicago Press

Esser, Frank, Schwabe, Christine and Wilke, Jürgen (2005) Metaber ichterstattung im Krieg. Wie Tageszeitungen die Rolle der Nachrichtenmedien und der Militär-PR in den Irakkonflikten 1991 und 2003 framen, *Medien & Kommunikationswissenschaft*, Vol. 53, Nos 2-3 pp 314-332

Forsythe, David P. (2006) *Human rights in international relations*, Cambridge, Cambridge University Press, second edition

Gerhart, Eugene C. (1998) *World reference guide to more than 5,500 memorable quotations from law and literature*, New York, William S. Hein and Co

Hammond, Philip (2007) *Framing post-Cold War conflicts: The media and international intervention*, Manchester, Manchester University Press

Herman, Edward S. (1986) Gatekeeper versus propaganda models: A critical American perspective, Golding, Peter, Murdock, Graham and Schlesinger, Philip (eds) *Communicating politics: Mass communications and the political process*, New York, Holmes and Meier pp 171-196

Herman, Edward S. and Chomsky, Noam (2008) *Manufacturing consent: The political economy of the mass media*, New York, Pantheon Books, third edition

Herman, Edward S. and Peterson, David (2007) The dismantling of Yugoslavia: A study in humanitarian intervention (and a Western liberal-left intellectual and moral collapse), *Monthly Review*, Vol. 59, No. 5. Available online at http://www.monthlyreview.org/1007herman-peterson1.php, accessed on 10 November 2010

Herman, Edward S. and Peterson, David (2010) *The politics of genocide*, New York, Monthly Review Press

Holmes, Jonathan (2007) *Fallujah: Eyewitness testimony from Iraq's besieged city*, London, Constable

Jamail, Dahr (2004a) 800 civilians feared dead in Fallujah, Inter Press Service, 16 November. Available online at http://dahrjamailiraq.com/800-civilians-feared-dead-in-Fallujah, accessed on 1 June 2009

Jamail, Dahr (2004b) Fallujah refugees tell of life and death in the kill zone, *New Standard*, 3 December. Available online at http://dahrjamailiraq.com/fallujah-refugees-tell-of-life-and-death-in-the-kill-zone, accessed on 1 June 2009

Jamail, Dahr (2007) *Beyond the Green Zone: Dispatches from an unembedded journalist in occupied Iraq*, Chicago, Haymarket Books

Klaehn, Jeffery (2005) *Filtering the news: Essays on Herman and Chomsky's propaganda model*, Montreal, Black Rose Books

Mandel, Michael (2005) *Pax Pentagon: Wie die USA der Welt den Krieg als Frieden verkauft*, Frankfurt am Main, Zweitausendeins

Marqusee, Mike (2005) A name that lives in infamy: The destruction of Fallujah was an act of barbarism that ranks alongside My Lai, Guernica and Halabja, *Guardian*, 10 November. Available online at http://www.guardian.co.uk/world/2005/nov/10/usa.iraq, accessed on 12 December 2008

Mermin, Jonathan (1999) *Debating war and peace: Media coverage of US intervention in the post-Vietnam era*, Princeton, Princeton University Press

Orwell, George (2004 [1949]) *Nineteen eighty-four*, Fairfield, IA, 1st World Library – Literary Society

Pilger, John (2004) John Pilger on why we ignored Iraq in the 1990s, *New Statesman*, 4 October. Available online at http://www.newstatesman.com/200410040012, accessed on 23 November 2010

Rehman, Javaid (2010) *International human rights law*, Harlow, Pearson, second edition

Risse, Thomas and Ropp, Stephen C. (1999) International human rights norms and domestic change: Conclusions, Risse, Thomas, Ropp, Stephen C. and Sikkink, Kathryn (eds) *The power of human rights: International norms and domestic change*, Cambridge, Cambridge University Press pp 234-278

Risse, Thomas and Sikkink, Kathryn (1999) The socialization of international human rights norms into domestic practices: Introduction, Risse, Thomas. Ropp, Stephen C. and Sikkink, Kathryn (eds) *The power of human rights: International norms and domestic change*, Cambridge, Cambridge University Press pp 1-38

Roberts, Les (2007) Iraq's death toll is far worse than our leaders admit, *Independent*, 14 February. Available online at http://www.independent.co.uk/opinion/commentators/les-roberts-iraqs-death-toll-is-far-worse-than-our-leaders-admit-436291.html, accessed on 23 November 2010

Schmitt, Eric (2004) A goal is met. What's next?, *New York Times*, 15 November p. 1

Tomuschat, Christian (2006) *Human rights: Between idealism and realism*, Oxford, Oxford University Press

US Department of Defense (2004) DoD briefing: Iraq security forces and multinational forces offensive actions in Fallujah, Iraq, 8 November. Available online at http://www.defenselink.mil/transcripts/transcript.aspx?transcriptid=2087, accessed on 11 October 2010

Zollmann, Florian (2009) Falludscha. Das verschwiegene Massaker, *Publik-Forum*, No. 24 pp 54-59

Zollmann, Florian (2010) Paper of record or paper of power? How *The New York Times* covered the second US assault on Fallujah, *Z Magazine*, September. Available online at http://www.zcommunications.org/paper-of-record-or-paper-of-power-by-florian-zollmann, accessed on 20 November 2010

NOTE ON THE CONTRIBUTOR

Florian Zollmann is a Senior Lecturer in Journalism at Newcastle University, UK. His research areas include war reporting, news media and journalism, communication power, persuasion and propaganda, critical political economy of the media, and the sociology of news production. Zollmann's research has been widely published in international academic journals and edited collections. With Richard Lance Keeble and John Tulloch, he jointly published the volume *Peace journalism, war and conflict resolution* (New York: Peter Lang, 2010). His latest monograph is *Media, propaganda and the politics of intervention* (New York: Peter Lang, 2017).

Chapter 5

International fixers: Cultural interpreters or 'people like us'?

Colleen Murrell

Western television correspondents working abroad usually employ 'fixers' to short-circuit newsgathering and gain instant access to local stories and useful contacts. These people are often employed in an ad-hoc fashion with apparent serendipity or they are chosen on the recommendations of friends, colleagues, Facebook contacts or via databases in newsrooms. But are these people representative of local views in the particular country in question or are they instead representative of a particular socio-economic class, whose globalised cultural viewpoints are replicated through each chosen fixer from country to country? In class or cultural terms are they, in fact, 'people like us' (PLU)? This paper analyses data from twenty senior British and Australian television correspondents and from five fixers working in crisis-stricken countries. The social theories of Pierre Bourdieu are employed to examine the field of journalism and the exchange of cultural capital that takes place between the Western correspondent and the locally employed fixer.

Keywords: foreign correspondent, fixer, news gathering, Pierre Bourdieu, television news, globalisation

HYPOTHESIS

This paper is concerned with how Western television correspondents go about the day-to-day tasks of finding and reporting stories when abroad. It asks if the employment of a 'fixer' opens a window on to local perspectives and stories or if fixers are, by their very nature and selection, 'people like us' (PLU), who will tend to reinforce Western news values? A fixer is the common name for people who are hired mostly on an *ad-hoc* basis by visiting foreign correspondents, although in recent years some companies such as the BBC have begun to call these people 'local producers'. The 24/7 news cycle means that television correspondents have little time to prepare their reports when they parachute into each new destination, and this is why they need to employ fixers. According to Hamilton and Jenner (2004: 41): 'These fixers, generally paid on an as-needed basis, brief reporters when they arrive, arrange interviews and transportation and translate when language is a problem.'

LITERATURE REVIEW

The literature review was aimed at understanding the 'journalistic field' – a concept of Pierre Bourdieu's, which describes how the contest for power happens within different fields of influence. According to Bourdieu the field is 'a metaphor for the (metaphorical) space in which we can identify institutions, agents, discourses, practices, values and so on' (Webb et al. 2002: 86). This project, therefore, sought out the literature that explored the macro, meso and micro influences on the journalist within the field of foreign correspondence. At the macro level, research on international newsgathering is split between those scholars who see globalisation as a positive force, through the opening up of the 'global public sphere' to a wider selection of voices (Volkmer 1999; McNair 2006; Flew 2007), and another group, who are gathered under the umbrella of the 'global dominance paradigm' (Cottle 2009: 28). These latter scholars believe that globalisation has led to an intensification of 'media imperialism' (Boyd Barrett 1998). They include Fred Fejes (1981), Peter Dahlgren and Sumitra Chakrapani (1982), Robert McChesney (1999) and Daya Kishan Thussu (2007). Dahlgren and Chakrapani argue that news programmes offer 'ways of seeing' that are always in line with 'the needs and interests of the social classes and groups who command economic and political power' (1982: 62).

For this argument to hold sway it would negate any local influence that is brought to bear on correspondents and their stories by fixers. Extending this belief would imply that all Western foreign correspondence is nothing more than a means of continuing imperial domination, to the extent that it serves as a means for a limited, non-indigenous worldview to be placed upon local conflicts as the basis of its narration of them. The findings of the data in this project suggest a more nuanced understanding of the effect of local intervention in the news agenda is warranted.

At the meso and micro levels of influence on international reporting, the correspondent is affected in his or her news production by having to work in tandem with news agencies (Boyd-Barrett 1980; Patterson 1998); 24-hour news cycles (Cottle 1999; Ursell 2003; Garcia Aviles et al. 2004); cheaper technology (Duffield et al. 1998) and an exponential growth in multi-skilling and citizen journalism (Sambrook 2010). Add to this the efforts of broadcast companies to lower the fixed costs associated with international bureaux – by either employing cheaper, local reporters or by targeted 'parachute journalism' (ibid: 98). All of these forces, which come together within the field of journalism, mean that the correspondent has to work ever quicker and be an instant expert on arrival at every new foreign destination.

The mythology of the lone, single-handed correspondent, cut-free from the demands of head office to pursue at leisure the higher calling of journalism has been around since the nineteenth century (Knightley 2002: 2). Countless journalists' autobiographies speak of a striving for both adventure and autonomy (Weisberger 1961; Caputo 1991; Simpson 2002; Keane 2006). Aldridge argues this mythologising of the brave explorer in unfriendly lands is the product of a 'professionalising strategy' (1998: 113), as it is linked to an assertion of high social worth. According to scholars such as Schlesinger (1978), and Erickson and Hamilton (2006), foreign correspondents are some of the most important and influential people in journalism: 'From the inception foreign correspondents have been elites in their profession' (ibid: 34). According to Pierre Bourdieu, being able to exercise autonomy is a sign of power (1998: 69). In this respect foreign correspondents are powerful insofar as they remain fairly autonomous from newsroom control, even if they have less autonomy now in the connected, digital age.

But as this research project has demonstrated (Murrell 2009), correspondents are not agents acting alone: they are part of a team and this team includes fixers. A few scholars have ascribed some importance to fixers (Hannerz 2000; Hamilton et al. 2004; Tumber 2006; Palmer and Fontan 2007), describing them as important helpers or aides but arguing that they mostly fulfil a logistical or translating function. However, this researcher has demonstrated that correspondents believe the fixers' role is both editorial and logistical (Murrell 2009: 10) and that fixers play a central role in helping to initiate and craft the local stories told from their countries (Murrell 2010: 133). Fixers can turn up as bit-players in some journalists' autobiographies. However, they are again mostly portrayed as logistical helpers, rather than central editorial players initiating local stories. Occasionally journalists do place more importance on the centrality of the fixer (Keane 2006; Willacy 2006; McGeough 2003) in their newsgathering.

Mostly, in order to stress their own power and autonomy, journalist-authors have tended to downplay their fixers' achievements. Television reporters need fixers more than print journalists because the logistical and filming demands are so great. According to Joris Luyendijk (2009: 136):

> When I first found out about fixers, I found it scandalous. But after I'd tried making television a few times myself, my shock waned. With television you had to adapt as best you could to the circumstances as they were, if only because the warring parties were doing that too.

This paper will consider whether the fixers' news perspective is likely to be compromised by the effects of globalisation. Since the dawn of Marshall McLuhan's 'global village' decreased the distances between people, giving them an enhanced 'understanding and a sense of belonging to a shared place or community' (Cottle 2009: 174), some have seen a tendency towards homogenisation of culture that stems from the 'dominant flows of Americana' (Thussu 2007: 14). And these global, cultural movements can affect the local, professional job market of many of the countries that correspondents visit. As Dick Hebdidge states (in Flew 2007:

145) we are 'living in a world where "mundane cosmopolitanism" is part of the ordinary experience [as] all culture, however remote temporally and geographically, [is] becoming accessible to us today as signs and/or commodities'.

THEORY

The theories that underpin the examination of this close, working relationship between the correspondent and the fixer are first based on the work of Pierre Bourdieu, concerning the journalistic field (Neveu 2005) and the acquisition of cultural capital (Bourdieu 1986). Bourdieu stressed that everything in cultural production is relational, as 'part of what is produced in the world of journalism cannot be understood unless one conceptualizes this microcosm as such and endeavours to understand the effects that the people engaged in this microcosm exert on one another' (Neveu 2005: 33). Successful and creative people in the media or arts scenes are the ones who manage to borrow or acquire 'cultural capital' (Bourdieu 1986) that is unique to the particular field and then trade it until they can succeed in their domain. Bourdieu's theory of capital can be applied to foreign correspondents as they continually borrow their fixers' 'embodied', 'objectified' and 'institutionalised' cultural capital (ibid: 243, 244, 248) in order to function effectively as journalists at different datelines, gaining access to language skills, contacts, stories and expert opinion that they would have difficulty accessing if working by themselves.

The other theory underpinning this research project is the emphasis, borrowed from scholars in the sociology of journalism tradition, on the importance of examining news production – the making of news – as the key set of practices that inform the reporter's working day. Scholars in this tradition include Phillip Schlesinger (1978), Jeremy Tunstall (1970, 1971 and 1993), Gaye Tuchman (1978), Herbert Gans (1979), Mark Fishman (1980), Michael Schudson (1996), Brian McNair (1998), Stephen Reese (2001), Simon Cottle (2003) and Jose Garcia Aviles (2004). While most of these studies are based on work carried out in newsrooms, this project examines the complexities and challenges of working 'on the road' and reflects how these are navigated by a working partnership of staff correspondents and fixers. This paper examines the 'intake' side of news production, rather than the 'output' side favoured by scholars such as Lilie Chouliaraki (2006) who examine narratives, messages and the abilities of stories to encourage public mediation on crisis issues.

METHODOLOGY

This project used semi-structured interviews to reveal the detailed, working norms of the two key players. According to Kathryn Bowd (2004: 118), semi-structured qualitative interviewing is the closest kind of interviewing in the academy to the kind used by journalists, and as such it is an ideal method to use when journalists are the sources of the data being collected. Television foreign correspondents with plenty of international experience were sought and in the end a purposive sample of ten Australian and ten British television correspondents was chosen from a variety of commercial channels plus the public service media. Five fixers were also tracked down and selected – from Iraq, Kosovo, Gaza and Indonesia. The project used a mirroring technique by questioning both sides of the newsgathering relationship in order to unearth similarities and differences in the field, as interpreted by the correspondents and as interpreted by the fixers.

The central hypothesis of the whole study (Murrell 2011) asked to what extent, and how, is the relationship between a correspondent and a fixer important to international television newsgathering. However, in this paper, we are more narrowly concerned with what the data reveal about the ways in which fixers deliver new story insights or simply reflect back on journalists their own worldview. The questions sought answers about what constituted the particularities of the job of newsgathering abroad that necessitated the hiring of fixers in order to successfully carry out the understood rules (or 'doxa') of the game. The questions were loosely grouped around five central areas, which probed:

- general background of both players (including their education, travel and journalistic experience, thus reflecting their position in their professional 'habitus');

- production – locating fixers (how and where journalists make contact with fixers and where fixers go looking for work – these questions were designed to reveal information about the specific type of people being sought out);

- identifying the kinds of help that fixers provide (editorial, logistical or both);

- crisis coverage (issues of danger and security in newsgathering and whether this meant that fixers were needed more, due to limitations on journalists' capacity to travel) and

- stories/editorial (the minutiae of day-to-day work which reveals the role played by fixers in how stories are sourced and influenced).

FINDINGS

The questions put to the fixers' group (a) showed that they had all pursued tertiary studies in one form or another. Four of them had had their studies cut short due to fighting breaking out in their countries. All of them spoke excellent English. According to the correspondents, within each of the countries where fixers are hired, the over-riding purpose is to access translation of the local language into English. English is, therefore, the specific embodied capital being sought in people who also speak the local language. If you live in a developing country and have attended a university, then you are part of the professional classes within that country and you have many things in common with Westerners. Ibrahim Adwan had become a fixer in Gaza through family connections as his uncles used to work as camera operators for Western media and since childhood he found himself:

> … chatting with friends or foreigners who speak English. They used to come to my home, or go out for a coffee or something. So I used to chat with them, so I started to like the field itself. And this is how I started working as a fixer with different guys.

The data from area (b) show that fixers are often found in newspaper offices and in universities. Even when correspondents choose fixers from outside the professional classes, they still select people who have experience of working with Westerners – for example, taxi drivers, people in the tourism industry or people who have been influenced by the transnational media. One of the correspondents said he had employed a teenage boy in Northern Albania who had 'somehow learned really quite competent English, basically from watching CNN as far as I can work out'.

The data from areas (c), (d) and (e) suggest that fixers have taken on the message of Western journalistic concepts of 'objective' reporting. As the fixers from Iraq and Gaza pointed out, this is interpreted as laying out the views of many people, rather than just giving their own views. This can also involve putting forward beliefs from people whose religious or political viewpoints are seen as showing the country in an unfavourable light. According to Ahmed Hussein*:

> But our main job is not reflecting our personal in the job, our personal views. We have to reflect the truth on the ground. We have to tell [the correspondents], this is since we work with them, and we learn this from them. That our own views are respected but in work you have to be impartial, you know. You have to be independent. You have to tell us, you should tell us what is on the ground.

However, even when these factors are taken into consideration, fixers (like journalists) will fall back on interviewees whom they know, like or respect and for whom they have contacts. These interviewees also tend to hail from the professional classes and are usually the most important people whom the fixers can locate. The fixers interviewed (and many of the fixers mentioned by correspondents) have travelled abroad and are, therefore, able to understand culturally the view of 'outsiders'. ITN's Alex Thomson commented:

> Chances are they've spent a portion of their time out of the country, so they've seen things from a different perspective. Are those the sort of people who are necessarily blindly going to go along with the allegiances of a civil war or international war? Not necessarily. … They quite often sit

around taking the piss about their own brethren.

In other words, they have absorbed Western cultural values and Western news values. Other data from area (b) 'locating fixers' show that patterns could be found in the hiring of fixers, depending on the country involved, the particular skills needed for a certain kind of story, the types of media companies employing the journalists (commercial or state) and the size of their wallets. The five correspondents from the BBC all had access to country-by-country databases which hold contact information on fixers and are kept up-to-date either centrally at BBC HQ in London or in the hub bureaus of their respective regions of operation. These resources immediately give these correspondents an advantage over colleagues who do not have such resources, while it also means that some fixers were seen as 'tried and tested', as previous 'gatekeepers' had welcomed them into the 'employable enclosure'. Sometimes these databases also contained information on the fixer's ethnic and religious background and political views. All of these correspondents talked of employing fixers whom the BBC had used for many years. Even when BBC correspondents were not working with people from the databases, they still favoured people who came with a recommendation from other colleagues or competitors. According to the BBC's Jeremy Bowen:

> I prefer a fixer whom someone has recommended, probably a local journalist. Not necessarily a local journalist, maybe just a very bright young student or something. These things are generally by word of mouth.

The BBC's Clive Myrie said he would use the BBC database, followed by the BBC World Service network of local bureaus around the world. If this still did not provide a name, then he would turn to journalist colleagues from other organisations, as 'two or three phone calls should get you someone'. For Caroline Hawley, Andrew North and Mark Glover (all of whom had worked for the BBC in Baghdad), the employment of fixers in this difficult security situation still echoed the *leitmotif* of colleague recommendation. According to Glover:

> You can't do any kind of positive vetting worth the name – you're hoping that the candidates that you are looking for are usually very well known to somebody else you trust and that's the way we've tried to do it.

For ABC Australia's journalists, the employment of fixers was not done via databases but by recommendations (when not on an *ad-hoc* basis). Peter Cave explained the process thus:

> Fixers tend to be swapped between news organisations. For example, if it's a place where people aren't going all the time, you know, you'll use the same fixer as the BBC or CNN or NBC or someone like that. You know you'll call around, you'll find out who's got a good fixer, or you will ask a reliable fixer to recommend a friend. So say the BBC has a good fixer, we'll

ask the BBC to ask their fixer if he or she has a friend who can fix for us.

This demonstrates that the fixers the reporters were keen to employ were those who had already been tried and tested by other, similar reporters. In other words, the friend of a fixer would probably be in the same PLU class as the original fixer and would have the same characteristics. In answers to questions from areas (b) and (c), correspondents overwhelmingly showed the preferred type of fixer was the local journalist. These people were seen to have localised but similar cultural capital to the correspondent, although, fortunately for the correspondents, they had a lesser economic status, which had put them on the job market in the first place. These local reporters reveal they understand the particular nature of the journalistic field, including its objectives, competitiveness and obstacles. The 24-hour news cycle is also familiar to them as is an understanding of what makes a good news story for journalists from the West.

Correspondents revealed that when employing a local journalist they mostly chose someone with similar views, who would not try to push a political preference too hard and who would demonstrate they were striving for objectivity. In favouring local journalists as fixers, correspondents show a marked preference for PLU fixers. These people have the knowledge and skills to find the particular interviewees needed, and they also understand the media prism through which this data information is passed. These media professionals can get access to the highest people in the land (the Indian prime minister for Adrian Brown, the Argentine president for Bill Neely or the everyday activists in the South African communities for Zoe Daniel).

A related theme running through correspondents' responses regarding fixers with whom they enjoy working is that they like to employ people with an understanding of their needs. For example, ITN's Juliet Bremner talked in pleased tones about the fixers in Kabul who 'knew exactly the kind of stories we want'. These stories included ones about women who went out to work and did not wear a burqa or a female MP who had been harassed because of her job. In a similar vein, her colleague at ITN, Alex Thomson, said that his fixer Abdullah* suggested one day that they do a story on suicide bombers in Kabul, so that they could 'understand what goes on in the heads of these mother****ers'. Hiring these kinds of 'globalised fixers' in Afghanistan does deliver stories that will be in tune with UK sensibilities, but these fixers do not necessarily represent how many of the people think (or vote) in Afghanistan.

For Bremner, safety was an important issue as a woman in Afghanistan, and so hiring people who could see the world in a similar way to her made for more comfortable working conditions. Hugh Riminton said he would make decisions instantly about whether he was going to be able to work with someone 'straightaway, on face' and added that he had to believe that he could trust someone. He estimated it usually took him about 36 hours to decide whether or not the team dynamics were working well and then he would make 'pretty hard assessments' and get rid of fixers if necessary. The journalists from the BBC and CNN in Baghdad all mentioned working with a team of locals who came from each one of the ethnic or religious groups – to show that they did not favour one group over another.

However, Caroline Hawley and Mark Glover said that having 'a sense of humour' was also very important, as was being a 'team player'. These concepts, hiring 'on face', team playing and having a sense of humour, would appear to go to the core of what makes foreign correspondents feel happy to work in close proximity with others during difficult circumstances. If the streets of Baghdad are tense and dangerous then correspondents want to be holed up in the office with people who make them feel comfortable. Having people around you who are similar to yourself in outlook appears to be an important factor in composing a team.

A number of correspondents argued strongly in favour of employing academics for assistance, when faced with complicated political stories that required the context of a situation to be understood and properly explored. On the plus side, academics are seen by journalists to represent knowledgeable and 'objective' sources, due to their long-term study of particular topics. According to Pierre Bourdieu, tenured professors have high levels of cultural capital, as opposed to true economic power. Due to their institutionalised capital and regular income, he placed them above writers and artists but below captains of industry (1988: 36). The ABC's Chris Clark recounted hiring a Chechen academic 'because of his understanding of both the layers of political history in recent times down there and his analysis of the personalities involved'. He also valued him for not being part of the 'descent into tribalism' but said, instead, that he was a 'very urbane, highly intelligent, somewhat detached person'. This was an academic with the traits of a detached observer – i.e. someone who has the qualities of a journalist (according to a journalist).

His colleague, Tim Palmer, described his academic-fixer in Bali as, 'this sort of highly educated Brahman, who has written three or four academic texts in Indonesia'. CNN's Hugh Riminton recounted how, if you were a reporter from Channel 9 in the Balkans, you did not stand a chance of getting 'the professor of political science from the university to become your fixer, with perfect English and a deep understanding of local realities', but rather you were stuck with the lesser mortals. Academics are, therefore, highly prized when context is needed but are not as sought after in an everyday sense as local reporters, especially if they have knowledge of television.

MANAGING THE ERRANT VIEWS

Even when the fixers are not 'PLU' and are known to hold different views to the correspondents (for example, the fixers used from Hezbollah or IRA sympathisers) correspondents still believe they can be employed if care is exercised. The argument put forward by the journalists was that these fixers had specific strengths and that they could be partially 'managed' for the purposes of newsgathering. When correspondents choose people for particular political, ethnic or religious contacts, it is because they feel that they can master any possible dangers that may come from association with people with differing points of view. Correspondents in this project exhibit great self-belief in their abilities to see through skewed editorial influence. They consider that the access they can get, via these people, to Hezbollah training camps or IRA leaders, is worth the risk. Sometimes, as Tim Palmer points out, there is no alternative. If you want to get through to the Free Aceh Movement (GAM) in Indonesia, then you must inevitably deal with people with dangerous connections.

Therefore, even 'people who are not like us' can serve their newsgathering purpose and become honorary and temporary PLU. What is notable here is that, where it could be argued that such fixers might bring alternative or radical perspectives into the news, correspondents, on the grounds of their professional disposition (what Bourdieu called 'habitus'), seek to minimise this possibility. In this way Sky's Stuart Ramsay admitted employing someone who turned out to be an 'occasional sniper' in Afghanistan and on another occasion he hired someone he suspected of being a 'Hezbollah terrorist' in Lebanon. Alex Thomson hired 'khat dealers' to help him get into Mogadishu, Somalia, while Bill Neely happily used a fixer in Moscow whom he knew was ex-KGB.

CONCLUSION

All the correspondents talked of the lack of time for original newsgathering, the difficulties of parachuting into news crisis areas at the last minute, and the pressures caused by the 24-hour news clock and the attendant need to furnish stories for multimedia outlets in TV, radio and online. The interesting link in this project's data is that correspondents drew a clear connection to solutions to these problems centring on the employment of a fixer. Most thought that even a bad fixer was better than no fixer at all. These people help initiate stories and are influential in terms of how stories are covered.

From an ethical point of view, the data show that these correspondents are willing to admit that they get significant help from fixers, which greatly increases their stores of cultural capital. The reporters gain a reputation for being able to function well at difficult datelines and they go on to reap rewards in terms of promotion, book deals, documentaries featuring their work and access to the lecture circuit. Fixers trade their skills for a successful work record and reputation in the field of foreign correspondence. They will rarely get the kudos of having their name attached to the report, but they may get to parlay their experience into further paying jobs. The role of the fixer in injecting his or her local views and stories into the international news flow shows that not all decisions are made at HQ and then followed slavishly by bumbling hacks, as has been suggested by van

Ginneken (1998: 135). Fixers can get to propose a news agenda even if it is the correspondents who make the final decisions.

Nonetheless, this local intervention is not entirely authentic as it is mediated by 'globalised fixers' who have been affected by Hebdige's 'mundane cosmopolitanism' (in Flew 2007: 145) and are essentially PLU. These fixers, whose habitus gradually comes to resemble that of the Western foreign correspondent, know what kinds of stories work for the various journalists from different broadcast companies. Globalisation has made possible this tribe of newsgatherers (be they correspondents or fixers) who have more in common with each other than with the general population of the country being covered. At the end of the day, the correspondent will work with the most effective person who is available and who can deliver the best story for their viewers. In choosing English-speaking professionals, correspondents are broadcasting a tale from abroad, delivered through a filter of Western understanding.

The help of PLU fixers effectively gives reporters the same access to stories that they would have in their own countries. A reporter may not be able to completely understand or translate the lives of people in impoverished areas of Bradford in the UK or of Redfern in Sydney, but they are able to access these places and talk to the inhabitants. A working relationship with a PLU fixer in Aceh or Cairo gains you access to these local people, even if their stories may not always be perfectly handled. The view enabled through working with fixers is still closer to a genuine local view than correspondents would be able to get if they were working on their own in the countries concerned, and without a working knowledge of the language or norms.

INTERVIEWS (CONDUCTED IN 2007-2008)

Ibrahim Adwan (fixer who worked in Gaza)
Jeremy Bowen (Middle East Editor, BBC)
Juliet Bremner (former Europe Correspondent, ITN)
Adrian Brown (foreign correspondent, Channel 7)
Matt Brown (Middle East correspondent, ABC)
Mark Burrows (former US correspondent, Channel 9)
Peter Cave (foreign affairs editor, ABC)
Chris Clark (foreign correspondent in London, Moscow and Jerusalem, ABC)
Zoe Daniel (former Africa correspondent, ABC)
Dian Estey (fixer who worked in Indonesia)
Mark Glover (Baghdad bureau chief, BBC)
Leith Hashim* (fixer who worked in Iraq)
Caroline Hawley (former Baghdad correspondent, BBC)

Ahmed Hussein* (fixer who worked in Iraq)
Allan Little (World Affairs correspondent, BBC)
Brett McLeod (former London correspondent, Channel 9)
Clive Myrie (Europe correspondent, BBC)
Bill Neely (international editor, ITN)
Andrew North (Baghdad correspondent, BBC)
Tim Palmer (former correspondent in Jerusalem and Jakarta, ABC)
Stuart Ramsay (chief correspondent, Sky News)
Hugh Riminton (correspondent in Hong Kong, CNN)
Pranvera Smith (fixer who worked in Albania and Kosovo)
Alex Thomson (chief correspondent, Channel 4 News, ITN)
Dominic Waghorn (Middle East correspondent, Sky News)
Michael Ware (Baghdad correspondent, CNN)
Adrian Wells (head of foreign news, Sky)

*The fixers and the BBC Baghdad bureau chief who worked in Iraq asked to have their names changed to protect their anonymity.

Mark Glover and Adrian Wells were interviewed for specific details related to BBC Baghdad and to Sky News – their answers did not form part of any of the correspondents' quantitative data responses, published previously.

- This paper was first published in *Ethical Space*, Vol. 10, Nos 2 and 3 pp 72-81, 2013

REFERENCES

Adams, W. (ed.) (1982) *Television coverage of international affairs*, New Jersey, Ablex

Aldridge, M. (1998) The tentative hell-raisers: identity and mythology in contemporary UK press journalism, *Media, Culture and Society*, Vol. 20 pp 109-127

Bowd, K. (2004) Interviewing the interviewers: Methodological considerations in gathering data from journalists, *Australian Journalism Review*, Vol. 26, No. 2 pp 115-123

Boyd-Barrett, O. (1980) *The international news agencies*. London, Constable

Boyd-Barrett, O. (1998) Media imperialism reformulated, Thussu, D. K. (ed.) *Electronic empires: Global media and local resistance*, London and New York, Arnold pp 157-176

Bourdieu, P. (1986) The forms of capital, Richardson, J. (ed.) *Handbook of theory and research for the sociology of education*, New York and London, Greenwood Press pp 241-58

Bourdieu, P. (1988) *Homo academicus*, Stanford, Stanford University Press

Bourdieu, P. (1998) *On television*, New York, Free Press

Bourdieu, P. (2005) The political field, the social science field, and the journalistic field, Benson, R. and Neveu, E. (eds) *Bourdieu and the journalistic field*, Cambridge, Polity Press pp 29-47

Caputo, P. (1991) *Means of escape: Memoirs of the disasters of war*, UK, Simon & Schuster

Chouliaraki, L. (2006) *The spectatorship of suffering*, London, Sage Publications

Cottle, S. (1999) From BBC newsroom to BBC newscentre: On changing technology and journalist practices, *Convergence: The International Journal of Research into New Media Technologies*, Vol. 5, No. 3 pp 22-43

Cottle, S. (2003) *Media organisation and production*, London, Sage Publications

Cottle, S. (2009) *Global crisis reporting: Journalism in the global age*, New York, McGraw-Hill

Dahlgren, P. and Chakrapani, S. (1978) The third world on TV news: Western ways of seeing the 'other', Adams. W. (ed.) (1982) *Television coverage of international affairs*, New Jersey, Ablex pp 45-66

Duffield, L. and Cokley, J. (2006) *I, journalist: Coping with and crafting media information in the 21st century*, Frenchs Forest, Pearson Education Australia

Erickson, E. and Hamilton, J. (2006) Foreign reporting enhanced by parachute journalism, *Newspaper Research Journal*, Vol. 27, No. 1 pp 33-47

Fejes, F. (1981) Media imperialism: An assessment, *Media, Culture and Society*, Vol. 3, No. 3 pp 281-289

Fishman, M (1980) *Manufacturing the news*, Austin, University of Texas Press

Flew, T. (2007) *Understanding global media*, New York, Macmillan

Gans, H. (1979) *Deciding what's news: A study of CBS Evening News, NBC Nightly News, Newsweek and Time*, New York, Pantheon Books

Garcia-Aviles, J. et al. (2004) Journalists at digital television newsrooms in Britain and Spain: Workflow and multi-skilling in a competitive environment, *Journalism Studies*, Vol. 5, No. 1 pp 87-100

Hannerz, U. (2000) *Foreign news: Exploring the world of foreign correspondents*, Chicago, University of Chicago Press

Hamilton, J. M. and Jenner, E. (2004) Redefining foreign correspondence, *Journalism*, Vol. 5, No. 3 pp 301-321

Keane, F. (2006) *All of these people*, London, HarperCollins

Knightley, P. (2002) *The first casualty: The war correspondent as hero and myth-maker from the Crimea to Kosovo*, Baltimore, Johns Hopkins Paperback Edition

Luyendijk, J. (2009) *People Like Us: Misrepresenting the Middle East*, New York, Soft Skull Press

McChesney, R. (1999) *Rich media, poor democracy: Communication politics in dubious times*, Chicago, University of Illinois Press

McNair, B. (1998) *The sociology of journalism*, London, Arnold

McNair, B. (2006) *Cultural chaos: Journalism, news and power in a globalised world*, London, Routledge

Murrell, C. (2009) Fixers and foreign correspondents: News production and autonomy, *Australian Journalism Review*, Vol. 31, No. 1 pp 5-17

Murrell, C. (2010) Baghdad bureaus: An exploration of the inter-connected world of fixers and correspondents at the BBC and CNN, *Media, War and Conflict*, Vol. 3, No. 2 pp 125-137

Murrell, C. (2011) Foreign correspondents and fixers: An investigation of teamwork in international television newsgathering. Doctoral thesis, University of Melbourne

Neveu, E. (2005) Bourdieu, the Frankfurt School, and cultural studies: On some misunderstandings, Benson, R. and Neveu, E. (eds) *Bourdieu and the journalistic field*, Cambridge, UK, Polity Press pp 195-213

Palmer, J. and Fontan, B. (2007) 'Our ears and our eyes': Journalists and fixers in Iraq, *Journalism*, Vol. 8, No. 1 pp 5-24

Paterson, C. (1998) Global battlefields, Boyd-Barrett, O. and Rantanen, T. (eds) *The globalisation of news*, London, Sage pp 79-103

Reese, S. (2001) Understanding the global journalist: A hierarchy-of-influences approach, *Journalism Studies*, Vol. 2, No. 2 pp 173-187

Sambrook, R. (2010) *Are foreign correspondents redundant? The changing face of international news*. Oxford, RISJ Challenges, University of Oxford

Schlesinger, P. (1978) *Putting 'reality' together: BBC news*, London, Constable

Schudson, M. (1996) The sociology of news production revisited, Curran, J. and Gurevitch, M. (eds) *Mass media and society*, London and New York, second edition pp 151-159

Simpson, J. (2002) *A short walk to Kabul*, London, Macmillan

Thussu, D. K. (2007) Mapping global media flow and contra-flow, Thussu, D. K. (ed.) *Media on the move: Global flow and contra-flow*, New York, Routledge pp 11-32

Tuchman, G. (1978) *Making news: A study in the construction of reality*, New York, the Free Press

Tumber, H. and Webster, F. (2006) *Journalists under fire: Information war and journalistic practices*, London, Sage

Tunstall, J. (1970) *The Westminster lobby correspondents: A sociological study of national political journalism*. London, Routledge and Kegan Paul

Tunstall, J. (1971) *Journalists at work: Specialist correspondents; their news organizations, news sources, and competitor-colleagues*, London, Constable

Tunstall, J. (1993) *Television producers*, London, Routledge

Ursell, G. (2003) Creating value and valuing creation in contemporary UK television: Or 'dumbing down' the workforce, *Journalism Studies*, Vol. 4, No. 1 pp 31-46

van Ginneken, J. (1998) *Understanding global news: A critical introduction*. London: Sage

Volkmer, I. (1999) *News in the global sphere: A study of CNN and its impact on global communication*, Luton, University of Luton Press

Weisberger, B. (1961). *The American newspaperman*, Chicago, University of Chicago Press

NOTE ON THE CONTRIBUTOR

Professor Colleen Murrell moved to Dublin City University in 2020 after 20 years as an academic in Australia. She is the lead researcher of the annual Reuters Digital News Report Ireland (2021-2026). Following this paper for *Ethical Space*, Colleen went on to publish more articles and a book on the subject, *Foreign correspondents and international newsgathering: The role of fixers* (Routledge: 2015). Colleen continues to research international news and is currently finishing a book on BBC newsgathering. Before her career as an academic, she worked as a senior journalist for several international news organisations including the BBC, ITN, AP and ABC Australia. She can be reached on the following email: colleen.murrell@dcu.ie.

Chapter 6

'A little bit Salem': Rebekah Brooks, of News International, and the construction of a modern witch

John Tulloch

INTRODUCTION

Nothing in this article should be understood as having any bearing on current or future legal proceedings. My subject is emphatically *not* hacking of 'phones or computers, the alleged bribery of officials by journalists nor other wrong-doing. Rather, it is about one small aspect of how we make sense of the world – or rather, how we use the press to make sense of the world for us. And how that press reflects one of the most persisting sources of inequality that we negotiate day by day: the differential construction of images of men and women.

Last year, Rebekah Brooks positively willed herself to be my subject. She is, as many have seen fit to tell us, hard to resist. Not the Cotswold-living lady who rides retired police horses, or the tabloid editor and compulsive chum of celebrities, or the CEO of News International, the erstwhile 'most powerful woman in British media'. But the woman in the middle of the bizarre process that seems to happen regularly, when, for a short period, they become a subject of press interest, are objectified and, not to be too dainty about it, monstered.

Schadenfreude – taking pleasure in others' disasters – is too weak a word to describe the savouring of the extraordinary and delicious irony of Rebekah Brooks's fall by large sections of the media class and academia. That a person who had been responsible for editing the *News of the World* (2000-2003) and the *Sun* (2003-2009), those great engines for reproducing sexist stereotypes of women and promulgating the idea of human evil, should be herself turned into a witch or a Medusa, was a dream so wet, an irony of such purest poetry, that description was not just beggared, but hung, drawn and quartered. But rejoicing in the tokens of her fall, though delicious, diminishes all women – and Brooks has the same rights to imaginative fair-dealing as the most virtuous feminist. And apart from the too tempting opportunities for portentous moralising, her case is fascinating for what it can tell us about contemporary media culture, the persistence of class-based attitudes and a sexism so engrained into our public life as to appear 'natural', old boy.

THE MAKING OF A WITCH

The process of 'witchifying' Brooks was given an elegant start signal on BBC2's *Newsnight* by Charlotte Harris, a prominent lawyer representing alleged victims of phone hacking. The occasion was the appearance by Rebekah Brooks in front of the Leveson Inquiry on 12 May 2012. Ms Harris, of course, might be construed to have ample grounds for anger:

> **Rebekah Brooks compared to witch by hacking lawyer: Critic says former News International chief looked 'a little bit Salem', Mail Online, 13 May 2012**
>
> Rebekah Brooks' outfit at the Leveson Inquiry has been compared to the clothes worn by 17th-century witches by a top phone-hacking lawyer. In an interview on BBC2's *Newsnight*, Charlotte Harris seized on the plain black dress with a white Peter Pan collar worn by the former News International chief executive as she gave evidence last week.
>
> Ms Harris, who has represented a series of phone-hacking victims, said: 'Her appearance was interesting because she appeared to be dressed quite innocently. But with the contrasting collar, it did look a little bit Salem.'
>
> The show's presenter, Gavin Esler, interrupted to check she was referring to the infamous Salem witch trials in Massachusetts in the 1690s.
>
> Ms Harris then replied: 'A little bit. She is a very dramatic and iconic figure and there was that drama with the inquiry. She turned up with her mass of red hair, wearing a black outfit with a white collar and white cuffs.'
>
> The unflattering description was followed up by another guest, who described Mrs Brooks's appearance as 'Puritan chic'.
>
> He said the look was 'straight out of Arthur Miller's *The Crucible*', referring to the well-known dramatisation of the witch trials written by the celebrated American playwright.

The cue was speedily taken up by Guido Fawkes (aka Paul Staines, the conservative political blogger): 'Guido can't help but notice Rebekah Brooks has gone for the classic Salem Show Trial chic for her turn on the stand…' (Fawkes 2012).

And numerous others soon followed, as the witch image, along with 'Medusa', speedily went viral. The cover of *Private Eye* – that reliable barometer of the British media climate – of 31 May featured Brooks in the notorious dress, with the caption:

> THE STORY SO FAR: It is new England in the Year of Our Lord 2012, and diabolical goings-on have led to the Witchfinder-General being called in to determine who is guilty of bewitching whom. A simple girl, Rebekah, confesses to being a disciple of the Devil, known to all as Murdoch…

Brooks was also involved in spinning the story herself and with her husband Charlie claimed angrily that a 'witch hunt' was being perpetrated (*Mail on Sunday* 2012).

Apart from the joys of pure mischief, what was the attraction of the witch image? And what was involved in constructing it? Following Brooks's appearance in court on 12 May, key elements were mortared into position. Rebekah Brooks's background was described as somewhat mysterious, with an evasive *Who's who* entry masking 'umble origins, a tugboat-man father and an identity speedily nailed by *Daily Mail* journalists, courtesy of innumerable Victorian novels, as a sharp-elbowed social climber, a 21st century Becky Sharp. 'She never introduced us to people from her past,' an informant told *Vanity Fair*. 'That was a little creepy, as if there was no past' (*Vanity Fair* 2012). Not for her the traditional English (male) networks – school, university, clubs – but an adroit use of the dark (feminine) arts. According to one of her more assiduous pursuers, Geoffrey Levy in the *Daily Mail*, her:

> … remarkably swift rise in the company was due not so much to her talents as a journalist but to her single-minded ruthlessness and her dazzling, feline ability to charm (Levy 2011).

Her alleged mysterious hold on powerful men, we are nudgingly told, involves an attempt to substitute for their natural daughters. 'I wouldn't think Rupert stood a chance,' one of her 'oldest acquaintances' told Levy (Levy 2012). The formation of the witching identity draws on some ancient myths and theories. For instance:

- the witch's background is mysterious – sired perhaps by the devil;
- witches breach natural relations;
- witches emanate malevolence – notably in the form of Medusa whose stare paralyses;
- she gets access to the powerful in a mysterious way, using wiles, charms and the power of prophecy;
- she threatens patriarchal systems with her special abilities;
- she is in touch at a mysterious level with the community – gossip, remedies, old skills;

- other women look to her skills e.g. for abortions, female maladies, child illnesses, contraception, impotence cures;
- men can't compete with her intuitive qualities: she is in touch with the pre-Christian pagan self, and knows how to captivate and capture male attention.

The longest, most sustained analysis of her mysterious powers appeared in *Vanity Fair*:

> 'She'd get you to do things,' says another former *News of the World* reporter. 'She had this charisma, this magnetic attraction,' he says. 'She would praise to high heaven, make you feel like you were on top of the world. It was only afterwards that you realised you were manipulated.' In a largely male tabloid world – a business in which Brooks was once asked at a corporate golf gathering to sew a senior executive's button back on his shirt, which she did – perceptions counted for a lot (Andrews 2012).

UTILISING HER FEMINITY

For the BBC's Edward Stourton, Brooks utilises her feminity in an extraordinary, upfront way, combining self-confidence with a magical quality:

> Colleagues at her first serious job in journalism remember her appearing as suddenly and mysteriously as a genie from a lamp. Graham Ball was the features editor on Eddie Shah's famously short-lived *Post* newspaper when the 20-year-old Rebekah approached him in its Warrington offices. 'She came up to me and said: "I am going to come and work with you on the features desk as the features secretary or administrator." I said: "I'm afraid that's not going to be possible because next week I'm going to London," and I thought nothing more of it. The following Monday I got to our new office in London, and there she was,' he said. 'She did everything with great finesse, she was very clever' (Stourton 2012).

Edward Stourton's tale celebrates her mystery and seemingly superhuman cleverness. Not, of course, conventional cleverness – her 'childhood friend' Louise Weir describes Rebekah Brooks as more emotionally intelligent than academic.

> She's been very charming and she's always been able to get what she wants out of people, even if they don't really like her. 'She is a typical Gemini; she's got her lovely fluffy side and then her angry side,' Louise recalls (ibid).

How appropriate the horoscope should be deployed for a tabloid editor. A chap like Stourton can't compete with that, with a clear above-board CV which shows he's gone to the right educational establishments, touched all the right journalistic bases … he is one of us:

- born 1957, Lagos Nigeria;
- educated Ampleforth and Trinity College, Cambridge;
- BA English Literature;
- graduate trainee ITN;
- founder member Channel 4 News;
- 1983 reported from Beirut;
- 1986 Channel 4's Washington correspondent;
- 1988 BBC Paris correspondent;
- 1990 ITN diplomatic editor;
- 1993 BBC *One O'Clock News*;
- 1999-2009 *Today* programme.

Of course, what is played with some nuance and sensitivity by Edward Stourton turns into an exercise in the bleedin' obvious in the coarser tones of the *Daily Mail*:

> **Rebekah Brooks, the schmoozer hated by Murdoch's wife and daughter**
>
> Who would have imagined when Lewis Carroll wrote *Alice's adventures in wonderland* in 1865 that the Cheshire village of Daresbury where he lived would one day produce its own real-life Alice? Her name was Rebekah Wade (now Brooks) and her tugboat-man father could have had no idea when his only child was born in 1968 that she would step – or rather schmooze – into a world of princes, prime ministers and proprietors, every bit as hazardous as Alice's. This was the media wonderland run by Rupert Murdoch, and until yesterday he made sure that no harm would come to the girl he has virtually treated as another daughter (he has four real daughters, from three marriages) (Levy 2011).

And then there's wee Peter McKay, also of the *Daily Mail*, the journalist as frustrated screen-writer:

> As a story, it has everything – larger-than-life characters, seedy villains, bewitching women, protesting celebrities who feel ill done-by, and a thrice-married, 80-year-old billionaire media mogul who said his chief aim was to stand by his Medusa-haired chief executive, who rose from the typing pool to the boardroom (McKay 2011).

Imagine 'Medusa-haired George Entwistle…' Medusa, of course, is usually described as 'having the face of a hideous human female with living venomous snakes in place of hair. Gazing directly upon her would turn onlookers to stone…' The *Guardian*'s Simon Hoggart was captured playing the same game, in a radio interview about the *News of the World*, angering at least one female listener:

> Nothing struck me until Hoggart brought up News International chief executive Rebekah Brooks, describing her as having 'curly red hair, rather like Medusa'. That's almost all he said about her. Maybe I'm over-reacting, but that description rubbed me the wrong way. Powerful women are too often stereotyped in unflattering ways. Even though [she] may allegedly have overseen a hacking scandal [which she denies] couldn't Hoggart have stuck to the allegations rather than critiquing Brooks's appearance by comparing her to a monster of Greek myth? (Milne-Tyte 2012).

CONCLUSION

Harmless tabloid mischief? Maybe. A defining feature of British tabloid culture is its tendency to create objects of hatred by a process of dehumanisation and the routine invocation of 'evil' as an explanatory tool. As I have argued elsewhere (Tulloch 2009), this essentially Manichean view of the world deploys monsters and saints, angels and devils, and witches. In these moral fables of villainy, the demonisation and public execution of women has a special place.

No less a figure than Paul Dacre, editor of the *Daily Mail*, publicly embraced this role, when he told the Society of Editors in November 2008: 'Since time immemorial public shaming has been a vital element in defending what are considered acceptable standards of social behaviour ... For hundreds of years, the press has played a vital role in that process' (Dacre 2008).

Dacre's analysis shows this process is no mere populist reflex but a deliberate strategy. Circulations are built, and maintained, by creating the most powerful of Northcliffean 'talking points' – human evil (Tulloch 2000).

- This paper was first published in *Ethical Space*, Vol. 10, No. 1 pp 4-7, 2013

REFERENCES

Andrews, Suzanna (2012) Untangling Rebekah Brooks, *Vanity Fair*, February. Available online at http://www.vanityfair.com/business/2012/02/rebekah-brooks-201202, accessed on 8 December 2012

Dacre, Paul (2008) Speech at Society of Editors Annual Conference, 9 November 2008. Available online at http://image.guardian.co.uk/sysfiles/Media/documents/2008/11/07/DacreSpeech.pdf, accessed on 18 December 2008

Fawkes, Guido (aka Paul Staines) (2012) Guido Fawkes: Brooks at Leveson edition. Available online at http://order-order.com/2012/05/11/guidos-fashion-tips-brooks-at-leveson-edition/, accessed on 8 December 2012

Levy, Geoffrey (2011) Rebekah Brooks, the schmoozer hated by Murdoch's wife and daughter, *Daily Mail*, 17 July. Available online at http://www.dailymail.co.uk/femail/article-2015257/Rebekah-Brooks-hated-Rupert-Murdochs-wife-Wendi-daughter-Elisabeth.html, accessed on 8 December 2012

Mail Online (2012) Rebekah Brooks compared to witch by hacking lawyer.... Available online at http://www.dailymail.co.uk/news/article-2143599/Rebekah-Brooks-compared-witch-phone-hacking-lawyer-Charlotte-Harris.html, accessed on 8 December 2012

Mail on Sunday (2012) It's a witch hunt: Rebekah Brooks and husband Charlie lash out after they are charged with perverting the course of justice in phone-hacking scandal, 12 May. Available online at http://www.dailymail.co.uk/news/article-2144615/Phone-hacking-Rebekah-Brooks-husband-Charlie-charged-perverting-course-justice.html, accessed on 8 December 2012

McKay, Peter (2011) Sucking up to the Sun King is a sign of *The Times*, Mail Online, 18 July. Available online at http://www.daily-mail.co.uk/debate/article-2015816/Phone-hacking-scandal-Sucking-Rupert-Murdoch-Sun-King.html, accessed on 8 December 2012

Milne-Tyte, Ashley (2011) Rebekah Brooks – Medusa-like?, 12 July. Available online at http://www.ashleymilnetyte.com/ashleymilne-tyte/2011/07/rebekah-brooks-medusa-like.html, accessed on 8 December 2012

Private Eye (2012) Salem witch trial Day 94. Available online at http://www.private-eye.co.uk/covers.php?showme=1314, accessed on 8 December 2012

Stourton, Edward (2012) Profile: Rebekah Brooks, ex-News International chief, BBC News. Available online at http://www.bbc.co.uk/news/uk-politics-13117456, accessed on 8 December 2012

Tulloch, John (2000) The eternal recurrence of the New Journalism, Sparks, Colin and Tulloch, John (eds) *Tabloid tales*, Boston and London, Rowman and Littlefield pp 131-146

Tulloch, John (2009) Printing devils: Reflections on the British press, the problem of 'evil' and fables of social disease, *Ethical Space: The International Journal of Communication Ethics*. Vol. 6, No. 1 pp 17-250

NOTE ON THE CONTRIBUTOR

John Tulloch sadly died of cancer, aged 67, in October 2013. He was Professor of Journalism at the University of Lincoln from 2004-2013. Previously (1995-2003) he was Head of the Department of Journalism and Mass Communication, University of Westminster. His edited books included *Tabloid tales* (2000) (with Colin Sparks), *Peace journalism, war and conflict resolution* (2010) (with Richard Lance Keeble and Florian Zollmann), and *Global literary journalism, Vols 1 and 2* (with Richard Lance Keeble, 2012 and 2014). As Prof. Keeble wrote: 'John was critical of the standards of the corporate media, but loved the tabloids for their cheeky irreverence. He had a healthy suspicion of authority and an enormous curiosity about life. The breadth and depth of his knowledge never ceased to amaze me: music (of all genres), films, history, literature, art, politics, war and peace journalism, travel, robots – these were just a few of his interests. He claimed to own 20,000 books. His home in Finchley, north London, the small house he rented in Lincoln and his office at the university were certainly bursting with them' (see https://www.theguardian.com/media/2013/oct/22/john-tulloch-obituary).

Chapter 7

Dumbs gone to Iceland: (Re)presentations of English national identity during Euro 2016 and the EU referendum

Roger Domeneghetti

This paper analyses (re)presentations of English national identity during the 2016 UEFA European Football Championships which were held in France between 10 June and 10 July of that year. Set against the backdrop of Britain's referendum regarding membership of the European Union, the tournament took place during a time of heightened debate about English national identity. Employing inductive textual analysis and drawing on Anderson's (2006) concept of imagined community, Hobsbaum's (1983) notion of invented traditions and Guibernau's (2007) strategies for the construction of national identity, England's three most popular newspapers, the Sun, *the* Daily Mail *and the* Daily Mirror, *were examined. While the papers' narratives employed familiar tropes which referenced England's past history and employed militaristic metaphors and the 'us' and 'them' cliché, there was also demonstrable uncertainty regarding the articulation of 'English' (and 'British') national identity.*

Keywords: England, Euro 2016, football, media discourse, media sport, national identity

INTRODUCTION

Due to the referendum on the UK's continued membership of the European Union (EU), the 2016 UEFA Football Championship (Euro 2016) was played during a period of heightened debate about English national identity. On Thursday 23 June, three days after England's final group match against Slovakia, the referendum took place with 51.9 per cent voting in favour of 'Brexit' – for Britain to leave (or exit) the EU. Hobolt's (2016) analysis of the vote showed a deeply divided nation split along demographic lines with young graduates living in large multi-cultural cities voting to 'Remain' whereas those living in the English countryside and northern post-industrial towns voted in large numbers to 'Leave'. There was also a geographical split with England and Wales voting to 'Leave' while Scotland and Northern Ireland voted to 'Remain'.

Although some commentators, such as Gapper (2014), have argued that 'The era of the Fleet Street tabloids, the populist and fearsome emblems of British culture and politics, is over', research conducted by Loughborough University (2016) showed that the press played a prominent – and partisan – role during the referendum campaign. Less than an hour after the result was announced, Tony Gallagher, editor of the *Sun*, told the *Guardian*: 'So much for the waning power of the print media' (Martinson 2016) which was indicative of the feeling that, despite declining sales and falling revenues, newspapers still had a significant impact on the result (Seaton 2016). This study seeks to examine the narratives employed by the three best-selling English newspapers: the *Daily Mail*, the *Sun* and the *Daily Mirror* (Ponsford 2016) and their Sunday counterparts in covering the England men's football team during Euro 2016. While it must be acknowledged that these newspapers articulate a particular form of Englishness, they had a combined readership in excess of four million at the time of the referendum[1] and, therefore, provide fertile ground for exploring the manner in which the articulation of English national identity reflects both the real and imagined versions of Englishness during Euro 2016 in the context of the build-up to and aftermath of the EU Referendum.

(ENGLISH) NATIONAL IDENTITY, FOOTBALL AND THE MEDIA

A nation is, as described by Anderson, an 'imagined political community' (2006: 6). In Anderson's conceptualisation, nations are inherently *limited* because no nation identifies with the entire human race, and even the most populous have geographical boundaries beyond which lie other nations from which they are separated. They are also *sovereign* because the conceptual roots of the nation can be traced back to the age of Enlightenment and the French Revolution when the sovereign state and the concept of liberty began to usurp and replace supposedly divinely-ordained dynasties and feudalism (ibid: 6-7). Nations are imagined, Anderson argues, because even people living in the smallest will never meet or know the majority of the rest of the population in that nation 'yet in the minds of each lives the image of their communion' (ibid: 6).

This perception of a unique national community is created through cultural phenomena such as a shared language, a mass education system and mass media which both create and relay narratives concerning the nation's culture (Gellner 1983). According to Womack et al., 'national identity is thus the product of discourse' (2009: 22) or, as Stuart Hall put it: 'National cultures construct identities by producing meanings about "the nation" with which we can *identify*' (1996: 613, italics in the original). This discursive national culture is compromised of what Hobsbawm refers to as 'invented traditions' which he defined as:

A set of practices, normally governed by overtly or tacitly accepted rules and of a ritual or symbolic nature, which seek to inculcate certain values and or norms of behaviour by repetition, which automatically implies continuity with the past (2012: 1).

Wherever possible these invented traditions, which can range from national anthems, flags and emblems to the British monarch's Christmas broadcast, are associated with an idealised past. For example, in Britain, 'the war is taken to evoke the British at their best, the qualities of Churchill's "island race". This … helps construct a sense of nation and nationality …' (Cesarini 1996: 69). They are, in turn, bolstered through discourses articulated by both politicians and journalists. Guibernau (2007) outlined five strategies which, she argues, the state employs to construct and disseminate a definitive national identity in an attempt to unite its citizens.

- Firstly, the image of nation is defined and represented in stories about the dominant ethnic group within the nation's borders and reinforced by stories of that group's common history and culture.

- Secondly, this shared history, culture and sense of belonging is reinforced through the use of national symbols and rituals.

- Thirdly, a clearly defined set of civic rights and duties are created at the same time establishing who is entitled to those rights and is thus accepted as a citizen and who is not.

- Fourthly, a nation's identity is made distinct and reaffirmed through the creation of common enemies, thereby separating out and distinguishing the national identity (us) from the identity of other nations (them).

- Finally, the media and education systems are utilised to disseminate the above, namely: the image of the nation; its shared history and culture; its civil rights and duties, and its distinction from the common enemy thereby defining what it is to be a 'good citizen'.

As Guibernau argues, by 'strengthening a sentiment of belonging to an artificial type of extended family, the nation' (ibid: 169), this shared notion of national culture and history supersedes other social identities such as class, race and gender. Because of this, 'individuals identify with and … regard as their own the accomplishments of their fellow nationals' (ibid). Hobsbawm expresses a similar sentiment and directly applies the idea to sport which, he argues, is 'uniquely effective' in instilling feelings of national belonging (2012). Few, if any, cultural events provide a more fertile environment for the communal expression of national identity than mediated sports events such as a football World Cup or European

Championships. Thus, any national football team (which, lest we forget, begins each match by singing its national anthem) becomes a powerful symbol of the relevant nation because, to repeat Hobsbawm's oft-quoted phrase: 'the imagined community of millions seems more real as a team of eleven named people. The individual, even the one who only cheers, becomes a symbol of his nation himself' (ibid: 143).

BRITISH BULLDOG OR ENGLISH LION?

When James VI of Scotland became King of England in 1603 he declared that he was not King of England and Scotland but King of Great Britain. However, it was not until the Act of Union in 1707 that the term 'Great Britain' was formally adopted (Kumar 2003a). Cesarini draws out the development of this process of 'forging a nation', arguing that the confused history of British citizenship means that British national identity has never been clearly defined and in many respects 'was formed in opposition to foreign countries that were considered repressive and "backward"' (1996: 61). Crucially, this notion of 'Britishness' became synonymous with a mythologised 'Englishness' that dominated the Celtic nations of Scotland, Wales and Northern Ireland (Fulbrook and Cesarini 1996: 212) which, in turn, 'clung to their national identities as a kind of compensation …' (Kumar 2003a: 187).

Consequently, following the loss of the *British* Empire, *English* national identity which, unlike Scottish, Welsh or Northern Irish identity, was intrinsically associated with that Empire was hit by crisis (Kumar 2003a; Nairn 2003). In the years before the 2016 EU referendum, scholars of English national identity argued that this crisis was reinforced by political devolution of the Celtic nations (Bryant 2003), scepticism about politics in general (Kenny 2014) and also increased integration with Europe (Wellings 2012). So it is little surprise that since the early 1990s, perceived internal and external threats such as Celtic devolution and greater European integration have, in turn, led to a heightened awareness and articulation of English national identity of which football and, in particular, the men's national team has become a fulcrum. One example of this revival of populist English nationalism is the manner in which since the Euro 96 football tournament England fans have increasingly displayed the (English) flag of St George instead of the (British) Union flag, an action 'seen by many as a positive re-affirmation of an English nationalism in response to the collapse of a coherent British identity' (Carrington 1999: 76). The notion of Englishness has been further reinforced in opposition to the perceived threat of 'radical Islam' in the aftermath of both the 9/11 attacks in America in 2001 and the 7/7 bombings in London in 2005 (Garland and Treadwell 2010).

HOLD THE BACK PAGE!

The cultural representation of a nation state's identity through mediated sport is described by Rowe et al. (2000) as the 'sport-nationalism-media' troika. The potent emotive and dramatic mix provided by sport (and in the context of this study football) means that English newspapers do not just report on matches and their results. Instead, 'the football Press plays a part in the production of a shared set of experiences or in the establishment of an "imagined community"' (Crolley and Hand 2001). Coverage of the sport has become an extension of the country's norms and values providing a representation of the perceived characteristics of English national identity (Crolley and Hand 2002: 19). This mediation of football plays a crucial role in reproducing and amplifying key characteristics associated with fans and their clubs, cities or countries, in turn helping to develop a wider collective identity among the group (Boyle and Haynes 2000: 13). Blain et al. refer to this as a 'form of discursive paralysis' (1993: 64) in which sports journalists construct images of their own country's national identity (autotypification) and that of other nations (heterotypification). Therefore, and crucially in the light of the 2016 EU Referendum, football match reports and related articles 'may be read, partly at least, as weaving a story about how Europeans interact with each other and how they reflect upon their own national, regional and group identities' (Crolley and Hand 2002: 2). This content is aimed at what Blain and O'Donnell (2000), citing Umberto Eco, call 'the model reader': a constructed, idealised figure partially extrapolated from actual readers – in essence an individual representation of Anderson's (2006) 'imagined community'. However, the football press does not simply passively reproduce existing societal attitudes, nor do its readers passively receive the content. Instead, they are both 'part of a tripartite structure consisting of readers/viewers who are interpreting the world(s) represented or implied, and those who are doing the representing' (Rowe et al. 2000: 121).

This interaction is complicated by the fact that those producing the texts (the journalists) and those consuming them (the readers) may not necessarily have the same political agenda, share the same socio-economic backgrounds nor be of the same race and/or gender. The producers' interpretation of the meanings embedded in the texts may be different from the consumers' interpretation of the same meanings. Therefore, sports-media texts are polysemic and do not possess a fixed, single meaning (Kennedy and Hills 2009: 21) but are, instead, a site for negotiation of socio-cultural identity. For the purpose of this paper, the focus is on the (re)presentation of that identity by the English tabloid print media *not* the readers' interpretation of that (re)presentation.

50 YEARS OF HURT

The 1966 World Cup, which was both hosted and won by England, has become '… a powerful, self-sustaining myth that has been wired into the nation's collective consciousness' (Silk and Francombe 2011: 265). One of the key elements of the 'myth of 1966' (Critcher 1994: 86) was nostalgic nationalism which 'conjures up the supremacy of Britain on the international stage and an acceptance and enactment of mythical English "values"' (Silk and Francombe 2011: 264). Weight argues that victory for England in the final over Germany cemented the Germans as 'an opponent' (2002: 457) while at the same time compensating for England's decline since the Second World War, making the England men's football team a touchstone for the health of the nation. Colley and Hand (2002) have drawn out the manner in which the 'denigration of the Other' has become more prevalent in English football reports during the second half of the 20th century at the same time arguing that representations of English national identity and, in particular, the England men's football team, draw on a range of perceptions which 'derive from and feed into wider assumptions in the national imagined community dating from the imperial era that serve to define "Englishness"' (Crolley and Hand 2002: 31).

In many respects this reached a peak in coverage of the 1996 UEFA Football Championship (Euro 96). Maguire et al. (1999) and Garland and Rowe (1999) found that English national identity was defined by both the Second World War and England's 1966 World Cup triumph. The tabloid (and to a lesser extent broadsheet) press coverage invoked English national symbolism and employed 'us' and 'them' rhetoric which drew heavily on the aforementioned conflict in both its narratives and imagery, particularly in the build-up to England's semi-final defeat to Germany. By far the clearest example of this was the *Daily Mirror's* declaration of 'football war' on Germany in a front page which used pictures of England players Stuart Pearce and Paul Gascoigne in World War Two army helmets along with the headline 'ACHTUNG SURRENDER: For you Fritz, ze Euro 96 Championship is over' (*Daily Mirror*, 24 June 1996 as quoted in Maguire and Poulton 1999: 25).

Analysis of the 1995 Rugby World Cup found similar coverage of the England team. Reportage employed national stereotypes in adversarial 'us' v. 'them' narratives in which players were 'highly visible embodiments [of England] – they are "patriots at play"' (Tuck 2003: 180-181).

Various studies have found that many of these narrative techniques were in evidence in the coverage of the England men's football team at subsequent tournaments. These included the invocation of the memories of British military successes (Alabarces et al. 2001) and the use of military metaphors and the negative characterisation of 'traditional enemies' (Garland 2004). Vincent et al. (2010) found that 40 years after the 1966 World Cup, the discursive construction of English national identity at the 2006 World Cup drew heavily on invented traditions and previous military successes and had '… barely moved beyond the shadow of the Second World War' (2010: 219). Similar narratives, particularly surrounding the Second World War and the 1966 World Cup victory, were also in evidence during the coverage of the last European Championships in 2012

(Euro 2012) (Vincent and Harris 2014). However, Kennedy found that in marked contrast to what had come before the newspaper discourses generated since the 2010 World Cup and, in particular, in the run-up to and during the Euro 2012 tournament, were 'uncharacteristically muted' (2014: 276). They were, he argued, dominated by a narrative of 'low expectations' mirroring the wider societal preoccupation with austerity which was part of a long-term 'complex and largely non-linear dialectic of decline and renewal' (2014: 281).

METHODOLOGY

To solicit data for the research, a qualitative discourse analysis was undertaken of three English so-called 'tabloid' newspapers: the *Sun*, and the *Daily Mail*, the country's two best-selling daily papers which both sit on the right of the political spectrum, and the *Daily Mirror*, the third best-selling paper which sits to the left of the political spectrum, plus their Sunday counterparts. The newspapers were chosen because of their popularity, their extensive coverage of football, and because tabloid newspapers produce more race-focused sports stories than their broadsheet counterparts (Law 2002). They are also characterised by the national stereotypes that they employ which articulate and reinforce myths and perceptions of national identity (Garland 2004). Furthermore, the *Sun*, in particular, but also to a lesser extent the *Daily Mirror* and the *Daily Mail*, have been the subject of a range of earlier research on the narratives employed in media texts focused on the England men's team at major international football tournaments (Garland 2004; Vincent et al. 2010; Vincent and Harris 2014). Mirroring such previous research in this paper will make comparisons easier, which is important as the concept of (English) national identity is fluid and changes over time and in relation to the contemporary socio-cultural environment (Crolley and Hand 2002: 25).

Hard copies of the newspapers were analysed for a period of 40 days from 2 June, the day of England's final warm-up 'friendly' match and eight days before the tournament's start, until 11 July, the day after the tournament final. The newspapers were read twice and articles and comment pieces which included text and/or photographic imagery concerning:

(1) the England men's team both on and off the pitch;

(2) England supporters both at the tournament and in England or elsewhere; and

(3) English national identity in the context of Euro 2016.

All these were subject to coded content analysis. The articles were organised by newspaper and date. The transcripts were re-read twice with the aim of identifying dominant and/or contradictory narratives. To facilitate this a constant comparison methodology using two levels of coding – open and axial – was used to inductively interpret the emerging themes and relationships (Corbin and Strauss 2015; Cresswell 1998). The codes which emerged from this process were subsequently interpreted using Guibernau's strategies of national identity, Anderson's concept of an imagined political community (2006) and Hobsbawm's notion of invented tradition (2012). Barthes (2006) argues that the myth does not need to be deciphered or interpreted to be understood or to be effective. On the contrary, if the ideological content of the text is obvious the myth ceases to have power – it stops being a myth. Therefore, myth only works when the denotative meaning of a text and its underlying socio-cultural connotations blur into one. This methodology allowed these dual interpretations to be unpackaged by first identifying the denotative meaning of the articles examined and secondly by identifying their social meaning. The aim of the paper, therefore, is not to define 'Englishness' or English national identity but to examine how this national identity is articulated in the tabloid press at a particular moment in time against a backdrop of major socio-cultural flux (the EU membership referendum), through the coverage of the country's men's football team at a major international tournament.

RESULTS

'FUCK OFF EUROPE – WE'RE ALL VOTING OUT'

Guibernau (2007) argued that the construction of national identity united citizens around stories regarding the dominant ethnic group which drew upon a sense of shared history and were reinforced through the use of nationally recognised symbols. In the context of Euro 2016, the papers focused on white, Anglo-Saxon fans and their performance of Englishness, which was anchored in the nation's idealised common heritage. Typical of this theme was a *Daily Mirror* article headlined 'To-knight is the night Hodgson starts Crusade' which featured fans enacting a playful parody of an idealised version of Englishness in which they greeted England boss Roy Hodgson while 'dressed up as Crusaders … decked out in chainmail and St George's cross tabards' (11 June: 7). Several scholars (e.g. Vincent and Harris 2014; Vincent et al. 2010) have noted that the increased articulation of English nationalism in the 1990s was mirrored by the 'resurrection' (Heffer 1999: 33) of the flag of St George into English football during the 1996 European Championships, held in England, and subsequent tournaments during which the flag became 'a powerful statement of national pride and solidarity' (King 2006: 250). The flag was also in evidence during coverage of Euro 2016. On the day of England's first match, team captain Wayne Rooney was pictured on the back pages of all three analysed papers in front of the flag of St George (the *Sun*, *Daily Mirror*, *Daily Mail*, 11 June 2016). The following day Rebecca Vardy, the wife of England striker Jamie Vardy, was pictured in a Cross-of-St-George vest top in the *Sun* (12 June) to advertise her tournament diary.

However, the cultural significance of the flag of St George was complicated by its association with England fans who engaged in violence in the two days leading up to the team's first match, against Russia, as well as on the day of the game itself. Many of these fans were pictured draped in the flag or in front of St George cross flags which they had attached to the walls of local bars. Poulton has argued that in the English media's coverage of football hooliganism 'As soon as trouble breaks out, almost all distinctions between the violent, minority and non-violent majority is lost in the media coverage that emphasises the behaviour of the former. Consequently, the majority loses all sense of identity, voice and presence' (2001: 124). At Euro 2016, this meant that those fans whose behaviour fit the 'hooligan' narrative were soon foregrounded at the expense of those fans whose behaviour was, by contrast, relatively benign. However, this (re)presentation of the England hooligans as typical of all England fans meant that their aggressively xenophobic performance of Englishness complicated the signifiers they were associated with, such as the flag of St George.

Furthermore, as well as singing songs about the IRA and German bombers being shot down – familiar refrains from previous tournaments (Vincent and Hill 2011) – the fans regularly sang 'Fuck off, Europe – we're all voting out' (Gysin 2016), a crude articulation of the campaign to 'Leave' the EU. This meant the flag of St George and associated symbols, such as the Crusader costume, became antagonising symbols of English national identity. Their ambiguous and contested meanings were evident in several stories in which anxiety about the extremes of English nationalism were both articulated and rebutted. Two days before Euro 2016 began, the *Daily Mail* featured a story about a blog post on the BBC's *iWonder* website which questioned whether the 'Crusader' costumes worn by some fans might offended Muslims. The newspaper quoted Conservative MP Philip Davies saying: 'I don't think an England supporter dressing up as a crusader is offensive to anyone other than these do-gooders. It's ludicrous.' The article also quoted several fans who claimed the BBC piece would only spur them on to wear the costume – 'anything to annoy the BBC PC Brigade' (8 June: 14).

Garland and Treadwell have outlined how the English Defence League (EDL), a high-profile group formed in 2009 and opposed to radical Islam, with loose links to the English football hooligan milieu, has adopted the flag of St George, incorporating it into their own insignia as well as clothing that they sell. Garland and Treadwell argue that the EDL's adoption of the flag is 'loaded with symbolism' (2010: 29) due to its historical links to the Crusades – a conflict between Christian Europe and Islam – and 'in many ways … this flag as a symbol encompasses much of the message of these groups' (2010: 29). Gimson et al. argue that this link with the EDL has meant the flag has become 'toxified' (2012: 6) with 24 per cent of people associating the flag of St George with 'racism' (2012: 2). This association was evident in a separate story later in the tournament, on the day before the

EU referendum, in which the *Sun* told how a father-of-two had been branded a 'pathetic racist' for adorning his car with England flags (22 June: 17).

LAUNCHING THE VARMARDA

Guibernau (2007) argued that a national consciousness is created through narratives which disparage foreigners thus creating common 'enemies'. These narratives draw upon 'invented traditions' (Hobsbawm 2012) and due to the legacy of the British Empire they are often 'imbued with military metaphors and references' (Crolley, Hand and Jeutter 2000: 110). In the 'tabloid' press this is done by 'bludgeoning the readership with exaggerated insular, parochial, "little Englander" "us vs. them" ideologies' (Vincent and Harris 2014: 233). Before England's first game at Euro 2016, the *Sun* (9 June: 5) sent Lee Chapman, a lookalike of the England player Jamie Vardy, to 'see off [a] Russian sub' that had sailed towards the English Channel. Under the headline 'VLAD'S BOYS THINK IT'S ALL DOVER…', the article echoed narratives identified by Vincent and Harris in their analysis of the coverage of Euro 2012 which were employed to 'capture the interest of the English "imagined community"' (2014: 229), which is 'English and, with few exceptions, white' (Crabbe 2004: 700), as opposed to the country's wider multi-ethnic population. The words 'think it's all Dover' drew upon the famous BBC commentary of Kenneth Wolstenholme during England's 1966 World Cup final victory in which he said: 'Some people are on the pitch … they think it's all over… It is now!' as Geoff Hurst scored the final goal of the game. At the same time, the headline evoked the popular World War Two song 'There'll be bluebirds over / the white cliffs of Dover' sung by Dame Vera Lynn. Furthermore, Chapman was 'dressed as Lord Nelson' and was said to be leading a 'VARMARDA' – a play on the name of the England forward, Jamie Vardy, which evoked memories of the English navy's victory over France and Spain at the Battle of Trafalgar in 1805, and the English navy's defeat of the Spanish Armada in 1588.

The wider coverage of the England team drew on nostalgic myths rooted in the Second Word War. England's match against Wales was referred to as 'The battle of Britain' by both the *Daily Mail* (16 June 16: 96) and the *Sun* (June 15: 61). On the day of the game, Martin Samuel, of the *Daily Mail*, referred to the conflict again, claiming that 'the Phoney War is over' – a reference to the period after Britain declared war on Germany in 1939 but before the two countries engaged in combat. However, the militaristic narratives never reached the xenophobic heights of the Euro 96's 'Achtung Surrender' rhetoric. This may have been, as Vincent et al. (2010) noted in their analysis of the coverage of the 2006 World Cup, due to England's poor early performances and a draw which meant that, apart from Wales, they did not meet any of their historic on-(or off-)field rivals.

ST GEORGE SLAYS THE DRAGONS

In 1998, fulfilling a manifesto pledge, New Labour established the devolved Welsh Assembly (as well as the Scottish Parliament and Northern Ireland Assembly). At the same time as giving the Celtic nations a louder political voice, some argued that the move led to the 'death of Britain' (Kumar 2003b: 7) with which English national identity had been synonymous. This, in turn, according to some commentators, led to a heightened desire among the English to formulate a cultural identity distinct from that of their Celtic neighbours (Gibbons and Malcolm 2017). Thus, the nationalistic 'us' vs 'them' tone of the papers' coverage reached a crescendo during the build up to, and immediate aftermath of, England's second group game against Wales.[2]

This antagonism was articulated explicitly in a *Daily Mirror* article concerning the comments of England midfielder Jack Wilshere which was headlined 'THEY DON'T LIKE US AND WE DON'T LIKE THEM' (14 June: 60). The coverage of the game drew heavily on both countries' 'invented traditions', with the *Daily Mirror* (16 June: 69) billing it as 'Lions vs Dragons'. Crolley and Hand (2006) have argued that the lion became a key signifier of English patriotism and national identity following the exploits of King Richard I, otherwise known as Richard the Lionheart, during the Crusades in the 12th Century. The Football Association (FA) adopted the three lions (drawn from Richard I's heraldic emblem) as their logo and regularly refer to the England men's team as 'Lions' (and the women's team as 'Lionesses'). This symbolism gained wider resonance during Euro 96 thanks to the song *Three Lions (Football's coming home)*, released by comedians David Baddiel and Frank Skinner along with Ian Broudie of the *Lightning Seeds*, which became a popular fan anthem. During Euro 2016, the team and individual players were referred to as 'Lions' (the *Sun*, 14 June: 48 and 49) with the most overt example being published on the day of the England-Wales match when the *Sun* used a picture of England captain Wayne Rooney's face superimposed on to the head of a lion. In the accompanying article, headlined 'FREE LIONS: Come on Roy, get 'em roaring', the paper implored the England manager, Roy Hodgson, to 'make us proud' (16 June: 68).

In a similar manner the papers referred to the Welsh team as 'Dragons' or 'The Dragon' (e.g. the *Sun*, 16 June: 60; *Daily Mirror*, 15 June: 63) drawing on that country's national symbol, the red dragon, which was first referenced in the ninth century text *Historia Brittonum* and was incorporated into the Welsh flag in 1959, eight years after it first featured on the crest of the Football Association of Wales. After England's victory, the *Sun* declared 'ST GEORGE SLAYS THE DRAGONS' (17 June: 9), a reference to England's patron saint who supposedly fought and killed a dragon. Crolley and Hand suggest that, for sports journalists, the Lionheart attitude of the English encoded within the symbolic representation of the lion seems to embody 'both the identity of the English people and the desired spirit of the England team' representing an 'overt communication of courage and pride' (2006: 20).

The overarching narrative constructed around the game focused on which of the two (British) teams demonstrated these characteristics most passionately. For example, in the *Daily Mirror* on the day before the game, James Nursey wrote about how Welsh player Gareth Bale insisted 'Wales had more pride and passion than their English counterparts' (15 June: 62 and 64). In the event England came from behind to win the match 2-1 courtesy of an injury-time goal from Daniel Sturridge. The *Sun* greeted the victory with the headline 'ROAR PASSION', pointedly asking: 'How was that for pride then, Gareth?' (17 June: 88) while the *Daily Mirror* declared the England team a 'PRIDE OF LIONS' (17 June 17: 70-71) and the *Daily Mail* captioned a picture of Sturridge celebrating as a 'Lion's roar' (17 June: 96).

PATRIOTS AT FAIR PLAY

Guibernau (2007) noted that national identity is reinforced by a clearly defined set of civic rights afforded to a nation's citizens as well as duties and responsibilities expected of them. This means that in their roles of 'patriots at play' and 'embodiments of the nation' (Tuck 2003) the England players and their coaches are held to a certain standard of behaviour and level of achievement. Vincent et al. argue that one of the ways in which this is articulated is through the ethos of fair play, which they argue is 'one of the defining features of English sporting identity' (2010: 212) and which is frequently constructed in opposition to the supposed 'cheating' of foreign players.

This theme was identified in several articles before the tournament. For example, in a *Daily Mail* article headlined 'I'd never tell my players to dive, insists Hodgson' (6 June: 73), Matt Lawton detailed how the England manager 'has insisted he will not encourage his players to employ the dark arts to succeed' as he did not 'think it was part of our culture'. Hodgson's stance was contrasted with that of England player Eric Dier – who, it was pointed out, had been brought up in Portugal – who suggested 'England needed to be more "streetwise".' Writing in the *Sun* about Hodgson's comments, Neil Ashton wrote that 'English football is renowned for honour and integrity' and that 'the dark arts can be left to the dirty rotten scoundrels' (6 June: 58). It is notable that, by contrast, the *Daily Mirror*, which unlike the *Sun* and *Daily Mail* took a pro-EU stance during the referendum, did not devote as much space to the story, nor offer any editorialised comment about it.

After England lost to Iceland in the competition's second round, a defeat the *Sun* labelled 'the most humiliating in the nation's history' (28 June: 1), this scrutiny intensified. None of the papers' post mortems offered detailed analysis of the long-term structural problems within the English game such as, for example, the impact of the competing demands of the Premier League, England's top football competition. Instead, the narratives were anchored within the long-term 'discourse of renewal and decline' (Kennedy 2014: 281). The result came just three days after the United Kingdom voted to leave the EU and, although the long-term political and economic ramifications of the vote were unknown, the tone taken reflected the papers' stances on the referendum and whether or not they felt leaving the EU would increase the country's fortunes.

Following the resignation of England manager Roy Hodgson, Dave Kidd, the chief sports writer of the *Daily Mirror*, wrote: 'In keeping with recent events, an England without a functioning government, opposition, nor any future plan, no longer has a manager for its national football team either' (28 June: 54-55). Thus for the *Daily Mirror*, which had campaigned to remain within the EU, the anxiety about the uncertain future of the England team mirrored anxiety about the future of the United Kingdom in the aftermath of victory for the 'Leave' campaign. By contrast, the pro-Leave *Daily Mail* published a brief, light-hearted editorial which implied that Iceland's unexpected victory was comparable to the unexpected victory of the 'Leave' campaign:

> In the week after the referendum, this paper salutes the people of a proud seafaring island in the North Atlantic, who refused to be cowed by 'expert' predictions and emerged victorious against opponents who threw millions at their campaign. Well played, Iceland. And oh dear, England! (29 June: 16).

The sports journalists 'spoke as if a still great nation was being betrayed by the bunglers and shirkers who ran, or were, its football team' (Wagg 1991: 222). The *Daily Mirror* reported on a press conference the day after England's defeat in which Hodgson said he was not sure why he was in attendance while Martin Glenn, the FA's chief executive, said he was 'not a football expert' under the headline 'WE DON'T KNOW WHAT WE'RE DOING' (29 June: 64) which evokes the terrace chant of disgruntled football fans 'You don't know what you're doing!' This mirrored invective aimed at politicians on both sides of the Brexit argument. For example, the *Sun* took aim at chancellor George Osborne for his economic warnings during the campaign in an article headlined 'YOU IDIOT, GEORGE' (28 June: 8-9*)*, while the *Daily Mirror* criticised Boris Johnson, a prominent 'Leave' campaigner, for failing to attend a debate on the referendum result under the headline 'No-show BoJo [a] political pygmy' (28 June: 6-7). Although the focus was on Hodgson, the manager, and members of the Football Association, the players were also subject to criticism which renewed the narrative developed in the build-up to the game against Wales about whether they demonstrated the right 'spirit' or demonstrated enough 'pride'. For example, ex-England player-turned-pundit Jamie Carragher claimed that the players were 'too soft', arguing that 'We think we are making them men but actually we are creating babies' (*Daily Mail*, 29 June: 74).

HISTORY BOYOS

While the England players were castigated for their perceived failure as 'patriots at play', Wales, who unexpectedly reached the semi-finals before losing to the eventual champions Portugal, were (re)presented as heroes. Euro 2016 was the first international men's football tournament finals in which another Home Nation team[3] had progressed further than England since the 1978 World Cup (when Scotland qualified but England failed to). With the absence of England, which had become synonymous with the formation and maintenance of British identity (Gibbons and Malcom 2017; Kumar 2003a, 2003b), the Welsh team became the embodiment of Britain, albeit framed within the context of England's failure. The Welsh were compared favourably to England in a *Sun on Sunday* article headlined 'Wales v Wallies' which looked at 'How Dragons got it right 'n Lions lost the plot' (3 July: 68).

The following day, the *Sun* claimed that whatever happened in Wales' semi-final they would 'be crowned the best of British … to further humiliate England' by overtaking them in the FIFA rankings (4 July: 56). And, despite their defeat, the 'Welsh heroes' were declared to be the 'Pride of Britain' (the *Sun Goals*, 7 July: 1; *Daily Mirror*, 7 July: 62 and 63). Furthermore, the Welsh team were encoded with the quintessential characteristics usually reserved for the English players. After their quarter-final victory over Belgium, the *Sun's* chief football reporter, Neil Ashton, wrote of the Welsh team's 'pride and passion and enthusiasm' (7 July: 58). Similarly, the *Daily Mirror's* chief sports writer, Dave Kidd, wrote that Wales had 'been everything Roy Hodgson's flops were not in France. Confident. Courageous. Cunning. Thrilling. And winning' (2 July: 69).

CONCLUSION

The aim of this research was to examine how the English popular press (re) presented English national identity through its coverage of the country's men's national football team and the team's fans immediately before and during Euro 2016 in light of the fact that the tournament coincided with the run-up to and aftermath of the EU membership referendum in the UK. The study found that where English national identity was (re)presented the newspapers' coverage adhered to Guibernau's (2007) framework for creating a national identity by employing 'invented traditions' (Hobsbawm 2012) that drew on the country's heritage and culture to speak to and reinforce an 'imagined community' (Anderson 2006).

In various ways the findings in this study support those of previous research dating back to the early 1990s which have analysed the articulation of 'Englishness' through coverage of the England men's team (e.g. Wagg 1991; Garland and Rowe

1999; Maguire, Poulton and Possamai 1999; Garland 2004; Vincent et al. 2010; Vincent and Harris 2014) thus showing that 'the sport-nationalism-media troika is no passing fad' (Rowe et al. 1998: 133). Journalists utilised a tried-and-tested formula which employed language that reached back into the shared mythical past of the dominant ethnic group. This language was often overtly militaristic, referencing the Second World War in particular but also the victories of Admiral Nelson and the Armada as well as the 1966 football World Cup success. 'Us' and 'them' narratives were constructed around England's opponents, in particular Wales, which provided the newspapers' readers 'a "fantasy shield" to cement and unify national sentiment for the imagined community' (Vincent et al. 2010: 219).

Furthermore, these narratives clung to out-dated monocultural notions of English national identity with no acknowledgement of the country's ethnic diversity. As Blain et al. argue, there was reliance on the language of nationhood in which 'the will to construct a historically continuous account of ... national character prevails against the contrary indications of everyday experience' (1993: 192). Given that Blain et al. drew this conclusion more than 20 years ago, it might seem as if there is 'nothing new' to report. But these finding are useful in emphasising which narratives endure in the formation of national cultures in general and English national identity in particular.

However, Euro 2016 took place at a time of social and political flux in England (and Britain) when the meaning of 'Englishness' was hotly contested between those at ease with the country's multi-cultural population and its place within a united Europe and those who sought to limit immigration and leave the EU. Sports writers may have been re-employing formulaic narratives used in the past but they did so with less confidence. It was no longer clear whether symbols which had been used as positive expressions of 'Englishness' in the past, such as the flag of St George, continued to be benign representations of patriotism or had instead become racialised articulations of an insular English national identity.

Underpinning this crisis of identity was a 'new realism of low expectations within the wider political and cultural economy' (Kennedy 2014: 285) which dealt a further blow to the confidence with which 'Englishness' was expressed. Following England's defeat to Iceland the sense of national humiliation mirrored the wider socio-economic and political uncertainty created by the referendum result. And, as the Welsh team progressed to the tournament semi-finals the 'us' and 'them' invective employed about Chris Coleman's Welsh team gave way to a feeling that England, once uniquely synonymous with Britain, was no longer the best of British.

- This paper was first published in *Ethical Space*, Vol. 15, Nos 3 and 4 pp 75-85, 2018

NOTES

[1] According to the circulation figures for March 2016, the *Sun* sold 1.7m. copies, the *Daily Mail* sold 1.5m. copies and the *Daily Mirror* sold 784,000 copies

[2] It is important to note that this match took place on the same day as the murder of Jo Cox, the Labour MP for the constituency of Batley and Spen. Thus the coverage of the game, particularly at the front of the newspapers, was almost certainly less extensive than it might otherwise have been

[3] The so-called home nations are England, Wales, Scotland and Northern Ireland

REFERENCES

Alabarces, P., Tomlinson, A. and Young, C. (2001) Argentina versus England at the France '98 World Cup: Narratives of nation and the mythologizing of the popular, *Media, Culture & Society*, Vol. 23, No. 5 pp 547-566

Anderson, B. (2006) *Imagined communities: Reflections on the origins and spread of nationalism*, London, Verso

Barthes, R. (2006) Myth today, Storey, J. (ed.) *Cultural theory and popular culture: A reader*, Harlow, Essex, Pearson Education pp 293-302

Blain, N, Boyle, R. and O'Donnell, H. (1993) *Sport and national identity in the European media*, Leicester, Leicester University Press

Blain, N. and O'Donnell, H. (2000) European sports journalism and its readers during Euro 96, Roche, M. (ed.) *Sport, popular culture and identity*, Oxford, Meyer & Meyer Sport pp 37-56

Boyle, R. and Haynes, R. (2009) *Power play: Sport, the media and popular culture*, Edinburgh, Edinburgh University Press

Bryant, C. G. (2003) These Englands, or where does devolution leave the English?, *Nations and Nationalism*, Vol. 9, No. 3 pp 393-412

Carrington, B. (1999) 'Football's coming home' but whose home? And do we want it? Nation, football and the politics of exclusion, Brown, A. (ed.) *Fanatics, power, identity and fandom in football*, London, Routledge pp 101-123

Cesarini, D. (1996) The changing character of citizenship and nationality in Britain, Cesarini, D. and Fulbrook, M. (eds) *Citizenship, nationality and migration in Europe*, London, Routledge pp 57-73

Corbin, J. and Strauss, A. (2015) *Basics of qualitative research: Techniques and procedures for developing grounded theory*, London, Sage

Cresswell, J. W. (1998) *Qualitative inquiry and research design: Choosing among five traditions*, London, Sage

Crabbe, T. (2004) *englandfans* – A new club for a new England? Social inclusion, authenticity and the performance of Englishness at 'home' and 'away', *Leisure Studies*, Vol. 23, No. 1 pp 63-78

Crolley, E. and Hand, D. (2001) France and the English other: The mediation of national identities in post-war football journalism, *Web Journal of French Media Studies*, Vol. 4, No. 1

Crolley, E. and Hand, D. (2002) *Football, Europe and the press*, London, Frank Cass

Crolley, E. and Hand, D. (2006) *Football and European identity: Historical narratives through the press*, London, Routledge

Crolley, E., Hand, D. and Jeutter, R. (2000) Playing the identity card: Stereotypes in European football, *Soccer & Society*, Vol. 1, No. 2 pp 107-128

Critcher, C. (1994) England and the World Cup: World Cup willies, English football and the myth of 1966, Sudden, J. and Tomlinson, A. (eds) *Hosts and champions: Soccer cultures, national identities and the USA World Cup*, Aldershot, Arena pp 77-92

Fulbrook, M. and Cesarini, D. (1996) Conclusion, Cesarini, D. and Fulbrook, M. (eds) *Citizenship, nationality and migration in Europe*, London, Routledge pp 209-217

Gapper, J. (2014) The market has written a requiem for the tabloids, *Financial Times*, 25 June. Available online at https://www.ft.com/content/b6e43e54-f8a3-11e3-befc-00144feabdc0, accessed on 23 October 2017

Garland, J. (2004) 'The same old story?' Englishness, the tabloid press and the 2000 football World Cup, *Leisure Studies*, Vol. 23, No. 1 pp 79-92

Garland, J. and Treadwell, J. (2010) 'No surrender to the Taliban!' Football hooliganism, Islamophobia and the rise of the English Defence League, *Papers from the British Criminology Conference 2010*, Vol. 10 pp 19-35

Garland, J. and Rowe, M. (1999) War minus the shooting? Jingoism, the English press, and Euro 96, *Journal of Sport and Social Issues*, Vol. 23, No. 1 pp 80-95

Gellner, E. (1983) *Nations and nationalism*, Oxford, Blackwell

Gibbons, T. and Malcolm, D. (2017) Nationalism, the English question and sport, Gibbons, T. and Malcolm, D. (eds) *Sport and English national identity in a 'Disunited Kingdom'*, London, Routledge pp 1-16

Gimson, A., Jolley, R., Katwala, S., Kellner, P., Massie, A. and Miranda, R. (2012) *This Sceptred Isle: Pride not prejudice across the nations of Britain*, British Future. Available online at http://www.britishfuture.org/wp-content/uploads/2012/04/BritishFutureSceptredIsle.pdf, accessed on 20 February 2018

Guibernau, M. (2007) *The identity of nations*, Cambridge, Polity

Gysin, C. (2016) New battle of Marseille, *Daily Mail*, 11 June p. 8

Hall, S. (1996) The question of cultural identity, Hall, S., Held, D., Hubert, D. and Thompson, K. (eds) *Modernity: An introduction to modern societies*, Oxford, Wiley pp 595-634

Heffer, E. (1999) *Nor shall my word. The reinvention of England*, London, Weidenfeld & Nicolson

Hobolt, S. (2016) The Brexit vote: A divided nation, a divided continent, *Journal of European Public Policy*, Vol. 23, No. 9 pp 1259-1277

Hobsbawm, E. J. (2012) *Nations and nationalism since 1780: Programme, myth, reality*, Cambridge, Cambridge University Press

Kennedy, E. and Hills, L. (2009) *Sports, media and society*, Oxford, Berg

Kennedy, P. (2014) 'Sometimes you go into competitions with little or no expectations': England, Euro 2012 in the context of austerity, *Soccer & Society*, Vol. 15, No. 2 pp 272-289

Kenny, M. (2014) *The politics of English nationhood*, Oxford, Oxford University Press

King, A. (2006) Nationalism and sport, Delanty, G. and Kumar, K. (eds) *The Sage handbook of nations and nationalism*, London, Sage pp 249-259

Kumar, K. (2003a) *The making of English national identity*, Cambridge, Cambridge University Press

Kumar, K. (2003b) Britain, England and Europe: Cultures in contra-flow, *European Journal of Social Theory*, Vol. 6, No. 1 pp 5-23

Law, I. (2002) *Race in the news*, Basingstoke, Palgrave

Loughborough University (2016) *EU referendum 2016. Media analysis from Loughborough University Centre for Research in Communication and Culture*. Available online at https://blog.lboro.ac.uk/crcc/eu-referendum/uk-news-coverage-2016-eu-referendum-report-5-6-may-22-june-2016/, accessed on 13 October 2017

Maguire, J. and Poulton, E. K. (1999) European identity politics in Euro 96: Invented traditions and national habitus codes, *International Review for the Sociology of Sport*, Vol. 34, No. 1 pp 17-29

Maguire, J., Poulton, E. and Possamai, C. (1999) The war of the words? Identity politics in Anglo-German press coverage of Euro 96, *European Journal of Communication*, Vol. 14, No. 1 pp 61-89

Martinson, J. (2016) Did the *Mail* and *Sun* help swing the UK towards Brexit?, *Guardian*, 24 June. Available online at https://www.theguardian.com/media/2016/jun/24/mail-sun-uk-brexit-newspapers, accessed on 13 October 2017

Nairn, T. (2003) *The break-up of Britain: Crisis and neo-nationalism*, Melbourne, Common Ground

Ponsford, D. (2016) Bulks helped *Times* and *Telegraph* grow their print circulations year on year in March, *Press Gazette*, 21 April. Available online at http://www.pressgazette.co.uk/bulks-help-times-and-telegraph-grow-their-print-circulations-year-year-march/, accessed on 1 June 2016

Poulton, E. (2001) Tears, tantrums and tattoos: Framing the football hooligan, Perryman, M. (ed.) *Hooligan wars: Causes and effects of football violence*, London, Mainstream pp 122-140

Rowe, D., McKay, J. and Miller, T. (1998) Come together: Sport, nationalism, and the media image, Wenner, L. (ed.) *MediaSport*, London, Routledge pp 119-133

Seaton, J. (2016) Brexit and the media, *The Political Quarterly*, Vol. 87, No. 3 pp 333-337

Silk, M. L. and Francombe, J. (2011) All these years of hurt: Culture, pedagogy and '1966' as a site of national myths, Wagg, S. (ed.) *Myths and milestones in the history of sport*, London, Palgrave Macmillan pp 262-286

Tuck, J. (2003) The men in white: Reflections on rugby union, the media and Englishness, *International Review for the Sociology of Sport*, Vol. 38, No. 2 pp 177-99

Vincent, J. and Harris, J. (2014) 'They think it's all Dover!' Popular newspaper narratives and images about the English football team and (re)presentations of national identity during Euro 2012, *Soccer and Society*, Vol. 15, No. 2 pp 222-240

Vincent, J. and Hill, J. (2011) Flying the flag for the En-ger-land: The *Sun*'s (re)construction of English identity during the 2010 World Cup, *Journal of Sport & Tourism*, Vol. 16, No. 3 pp 187-209

Vincent, J., Kian, E. M., Pedersen, P. M., Kuntz, A. and Hill, J. S. (2010) England expects: English newspapers' narratives about the English football team in the 2006 World Cup, *International Review for the Sociology of Sport*, Vol. 45, No. 2 pp 199-223

Wagg, S. (1991) Playing the past: The media and the England football team, Williams, J. and Wagg, S. (eds) *British football and social change: Getting into Europe*, Leicester, Leicester University Press pp 221-239

Weight, R. (2002) *Patriots: National identity in Britain 1940-2000*, London, MacMillan

Wellings, B. (2012) *English nationalism and Euroscepticism: Losing the peace*, Bern, Peter Lang

Wodack, R., de Cillia, R., Resign, M. and Liebhart, K. (2009) *The discursive construction of national identity*, Edinburgh, Edinburgh University Press, second edition

NOTE ON THE CONTRIBUTOR

Dr Roger Domeneghetti is an assistant professor and programme leader in Journalism at Northumbria University. His first book, *From the back page the front room: Football's journey through the English media*, was shortlisted for the British Society of Sport History's Lord Aberdare Prize for the best sports history book in 2015. His second book, *Everybody wants to rule the world: Britain, sport and the 1980s*, was published in May 2023 by Yellow Jersey Press. He is the editor of *Reporting sports in the digital age: Theoretical and ethical considerations in a changing media landscape*, the first entry in Routledge's *Journalism Insights* series, published in 2022. Before his career as an academic, he worked as a journalist at local and national levels in print and online media. A Fellow of the Royal Historical Society, he continues to write for the *New European, BBC History Magazine* and the *Blizzard* among other publications.

Chapter 8

Comforting the comfortable: How the corporate media covered Chile's October 2019 social explosion

Antonio Castillo

In a land of devastating earthquakes, Chile experienced a tremor of historical proportions on 18 October 2019 when thousands of protestors flooded the streets and squares of this long and narrow South American country. It became known as the 'estallido social' – the social explosion. The protests reflected mass discontent with the political and financial elite – and its strong grip on the commercial mainstream media. This paper examines the media's coverage of the social explosion and argues that it was essentially designed to defend the privileges of the country's elite and criminalise the Chileans' demands for social change and justice. It also highlights the distinctive role played by the alternative media in challenging the consensus of the corporate media.

Keywords: protest, media coverage, Latin America, Chile, October 2019 social explosion, journalism, social movements

INTRODUCTION

The celebrated Uruguayan journalist, writer and novelist, Eduardo Galeano (1940-2015), yearned that one day the television set would no longer be the primary member of the Latin America family circle. Galeano was a constant critic of the Latin American commercial media's portrayal of the progressive social movement. And he damned the media for its role in propelling and defending the neoliberal economic system that has been destroying the livelihoods of so many Latin Americans over the last 40 years.

Indeed, in this region, the media – with its ability to set the news agenda – is the most powerful tool used by conservative forces to maintain the status quo and criminalise people demanding social change and justice. And the medium Galeano loathed, the television set, is still the chosen vehicle of information and entertainment for Latin American families. It is through the television screen that most Latin Americans get to know, understand, construct and participate in the political, economic and social reality.

From Mexico's streets to Chile's plazas, the demonstration is one of the most visually symbolic and potentially powerful acts undertaken to demand social change and justice. They are public acts of protest that cry out for mainstream media attention. Yet when that attention is given by the ideologically reactionary media the social, economic and political demands are frequently demonised with protestors commonly portrayed as deviants.

This paper examines the commercial news media coverage of Chile's October 2019 mass mobilisation. It goes on to argue that professional journalists not only in Chile but throughout Latin America have failed ethically in their reporting on the street protests which have recently engulfed the continent.

THE PROTEST PARADIGM

Spirited mass mobilisations, thunderous protests and clashes with the police are never too far away in the buzzing Latin American streets and plazas. Historically, streets and plazas have been the site of collective dissent, resistance and democratic ferment. The street protest is, as Sidney Tarrow suggests (2012 [1998]), potentially disruptive while collective actions such as rallies, marches and sit-ins capture in unique, visual ways people's demands and aspirations.

In 2019, Latin America experienced the highest number of protests globally. In fact, many spoke of a 'Latin American spring'. While the Covid-19 pandemic slowed down the intensity of the region's mass mobilisations, they have not gone away. Writing in *Foreign Policy*, Joe Daniel Parkin forecast that Latin America would see 'new or further unrest in the next few years' (2020). This prediction certainly applies to Chile.

Paraphrasing Todd Gitlin (2003), demonstrators need the 'whole world to watch' in order to get their message across to the public. In this context, news coverage becomes a vital component of the act of protesting. As Danielle Kilgo points out, 'the role journalists play can be indispensable if movements are to gain legitimacy and make progress' (Kilgo 2020).

In the streets and plazas of Latin America, the news media's presence – especially given its agenda-setting role – is both sought and needed. However, this demand tends to collide with the 'symbiotic but imbalanced relationship between activists and the press' (Kilgo and Harlow 2019: 509). Ideally, gaining favourable news media coverage from the mainstream media is one of the six goals a social movement must achieve (McAdam and Snow 1997). However, achieving such coverage is extremely difficult. Research has shown that mainstream news organisations struggle to portray accurately and fairly actions that challenge the status quo (Gitlin 1980; Gamson and Wolfsfeld 1993).

From Chile to Hong Kong, media coverage of recent protests, it could be argued, has seriously damaged the aspirations of the progressive social movement. A study by Grassau et al. (2019) showed that news coverage of the social explosion was largely unreliable. Participants in this study also expressed their disappointment at the media's failure to scrutinise the major political powers (ibid).

As far back as 1984, Joseph M. Chan and Lee Chin-Chuan highlighted the concerted stigmatisation of protesters as deviants and the exaggerated focus on any violent element of any demonstration (Chan and Chin-Chuan 1984). This is reflected today in the media emphasis on the drama and the social and economic disruptions the protests may cause.

Rather than covering the activists' grievances, the mainstream media's narrative effectively serves to trivialise their actions. As seen during the Chilean protests that began on 18 October 2019, according to the president of Chile's College of Journalists Margarita Pastene, the coverage gave a seriously distorted picture of the events – highlighting the rare scenes of violence, the destruction of public amenities and clashes with the police (Pastene, personal communication, 11 December 2019).

This kind of news coverage is reproduced across Latin America. In Guatemala, for instance, a country with deep scars from the brutal 1960-1996 civil war, human rights activists have been systematically demonised by the commercial media, which portrayed them as 'terrorists' engaged in an armed struggle against the government. As Abbott points out, this media labelling serves to criminalise human rights activists and aims, ultimately, to silence dissent (2016).

Furthermore, Douglas McLeod and James Hertog's 'protest paradigm' (1999) demonstrates that protests and social movements, mostly progressive and left-wing, will not be favourably reported by the commercial media. In Chile, during the 2019 mass protests, the media coverage aimed above all to defend and maintain the country's neoliberal and right-wing government. As one Chilean television journalist told me anonymously: 'The executives instructed us that the "defence of democracy" was the main aim of our news coverage' (personal communication, 3 December 2019).

In the 1970s, the Glasgow University Media Group showed the mainstream media in capitalist countries was aligned to the economic, social and political interests of the most powerful sectors of society. In addition, their research showed that the mainstream media was behind the marginalisation and delegitimisation of mass mobilisation – strikes, rallies, sit-ins (Glasgow University Media Group 1976).

Chile has one of the most concentrated media ownerships in Latin America. In this long, narrow country of approximately 19 million, the commercial mainstream media is tightly aligned to the country's political and financial elite. The latter own television channels, radio stations, newspapers and magazines. As Chilean journalist and author María Olivia Mönckeberg points out, it is a media system characterised by high levels of homogenisation and concentration – with close ties to dominant political and economic interests (2009). A journalistic investigation by the Chilean digital platform *Interferencia* showed that the right-wing *Channel 13*, *Megavision* and the state-funded *National Television Channel* were the primary sources of journalists employed as media advisers by the then government of Sebastián Piñera, a right-wing financial speculator and tycoon (*Interferencia* 2021).

The other main source of journalists turned media advisers and spin doctors is *El Mercurio* (ibid). *El Mercurio* is Chile's most influential newspaper. In Chile, two newspaper companies, COPESA and El Mercurio S.A.P (Public Limited Company) control approximately 95 per cent of the newspapers (Gumucio and Parrini 2009). COPESA publishes *La Tercera*, the second-largest newspaper, and El Mercurio S.A.P. publishes *El Mercurio*. These are newspapers where the interests of the financial and political elite converge and can be heard. More about *El Mercurio* later in this essay.

A study by Ximena Orchard (2019) showed that 85 per cent of newsmakers cited or interviewed by *El Mercurio*, *La Tercera*, and *La Segunda* (a tabloid owned by El Mercurio S.A.P.) were part of the country's institutional elite – right-wing politicians, state bureaucrats and members of the state legislature. By comparison, the same study showed that only 7 per cent of newsmakers cited and interviewed in these newspapers were from the country's progressive left-wing social movement.

From the start of the social explosion, on 18 October 2019, protestors focused their anger – and demands for change – on the Chilean mainstream media. 'The rich own everything – the banks, the water and the media,' according to Javier, a street artist who, during the second day of the protest, was painting colourful political messages on the walls around the epicentre of the social explosion – Plaza Baquedano – in downtown Santiago, Chile's capital (Javier, personal communication, 19 October 2019).

Significantly, demonstrators re-baptised Plaza Baquedano as Plaza Dignidad – or Dignity Plaza. However, journalists working for the commercial media were instructed not to use the new name in their stories – thus demonstrating how the Chilean corporate media is the custodian of the neoliberal economic system left in place by the 1973-1989 military dictatorship of Pinochet. Any narrative that challenges this orthodoxy is either regarded as a 'conspiracy theory' or snubbed.

Among the many grievances that came to light against the Chilean media during the social explosion was the news treatment of the financial scandals involving high-ranking businesspeople and politicians. Chileans used to boast proudly – even with a sense of arrogance – that the country was 'not like the rest of Latin America', that it was a society 'free from corruption and impunity'. Whether this was once true or just a national myth, Chileans are tightening their jaws angrily in the face of grotesque cases of corruption and impunity.

Largely, these are cases that implicate Chile's political and economic elite, and even the police and military. These scandals, including the commercial collusion of significant companies and the illegal funding of political parties, have been either ignored or played down by the media (Castillo 2019).

COMFORTING THE COMFORTABLE

Mr Dooley was a fictional 19th-century Irish bartender. He coined one of the most memorable phrases about the alleged role of journalism in society. 'The job of the newspaper is to comfort the afflicted and afflict the comfortable,' Mr Dooley said (Shedden 2014). In Chile, the commercial newspapers are doing just the opposite, especially *El Mercurio* – the newspaper mentioned earlier in this piece.

Any examination of the news treatment of the Chilean progressive left-wing social movements would be incomplete without referring to the role played by *El Mercurio*. It is the most influential voice of the Chilean elite. Serving the interests of the most powerful and demonising the progressive left-wing movement is what *El Mercurio* has been doing since it was set up in 1827. Considered the oldest Spanish language newspaper still in circulation, *El Mercurio* exercises, paraphrasing Slavoj Žižek, a devastating 'media violence' (2012) against those who challenge the neoliberal capitalist system.

The newsroom practice in *El Mercurio* echoes the organisational ideologies and professional routines as highlighted in Herman and Chomsky's notions of the 'propaganda model' and 'manufacturing consent' (1988). The role of *El Mercurio* in the US-sponsored 11 September 1973 coup d'état against the democratically elected socialist government of President Salvador Allende has been widely documented (Constable and Valenzuela 1991; Spooner 1999).

Years before the 1973 coup, in 1967, a group of journalism students had already denounced the journalistic ethics of *El Mercurio*. On a gigantic banner displayed in the Catholic Pontifical University's main building, in the heart of the Chilean capital Santiago, the students wrote: '*El Mercurio* Miente' (*The Mercurio* Lies). It became a majestic ethical judgement against the newspaper (Araya 2008).

Then, in September 2019, a month before the social explosion, a group of journalism students from the prestigious Catholic Pontifical University again displayed in front of the university building a banner that proclaimed: '46 years on, *El Mercurio* continues to lie.'

El Mercurio is part of a media system that, as the Glasgow University Media Group suggests, has not only demonised the country's progressive social movement, but has also made it invisible. Kristin Sorensen describes this invisibility as a media 'structuring absence' (2010). This means that television coverage also of controversial issues, such as human rights and social justice demands, is either sporadic or ignored.

In the last few years, this 'structured absence' has been observed in the coverage of several strikes and protests demanding social justice. One of them goes back to 2009, to the strike of Farmacias Ahumada, or Ahumada Pharmacies – one of the three largest pharmacy chains in Chile and owning a network of around 1,000 chemist shops overall in Chile, Peru, Brazil and Mexico. For several months, workers demonstrated in daily peaceful picket lines in front of the pharmacy's shops across the country. The protestors were demanding better working conditions and salary rises. Yet these protests were totally ignored by the media. Reflecting Martín Barbero's notion of media 'citizen exclusion' (2001: 51), the Chilean media denied the fundamental right of this social movement – to be seen and heard.

While a few journalists from the commercial media expressed their disappointment at the lack of coverage of the strike, they had to accept – as one of them told me back in 2009 – that 'they were facing mighty economic enemies' (personal communication, 2 October 2009). Ahumada Pharmacy owners had threatened to withdraw television advertising contracts worth millions if the workers' strike was covered.

The decision not to cover the strike was widely condemned by civil society, unions and activists. Hundreds of workers of Ahumada Pharmacies protested in front of the studios of *Channel 13* and Chilevisión. On the other hand, the College of Journalism, the leading organisation of Chilean journalists, and the National Television Council condemned the lack of coverage of the pharmacy workers' strike (Journalism Students 2019).

CRIMINALISING THE OCTOBER 2019 SOCIAL EXPLOSION

'Chile is finally awake,' read one of the thousands of placards protestors displayed at the epicentre of the social explosion – in Plaza Baquedano or Dignity Plaza, on 18 October 2019. At first, discontent was directed at the price rises for travel on the Santiago metro. However, when the price rise was cancelled by Sebastián Piñera, the Chilean President, mobilisations demanding increased investment in health, housing, wages and pensions continued (Castillo 2019). Moreover, throughout the country, demonstrations demanded changes to the country's constitution so that it guarantees free education and consumers' rights, a health system that benefits the poor and an end to the privatisation of water and the pension system. And the demonstrations went on for months.

As the social explosion spread across the country, the government began a media offensive. According to a leaked statement from the Federation of Television Workers, the leading television channels' top executives were invited to La Moneda, the government house. Here they met the former interior minister, Andrés Chadwick, who advised them on coverage. The Federation of Television Workers described the meeting as a totally unacceptable intervention in the reporting of the social explosion (Tabilo Castillo 2020).

As witnessed in previous acts of mass mobilisations, such as the ground-breaking high school students' movement of 2006, protestors singled out the commercial mass media as an instrument used by the elite to criminalise the demands for justice and social change. In contrast to *Time* magazine that, in 2011, described the 'protestor' as the personality of the year, the Chilean media dubbed protestors as deviants and lawbreakers. In addition, the media opted to ignore the brutal police repression against activists. News framing, as Robert Entman (2007 [1993]) points out, is an instrument of power. This means that the distribution and interpretation of events favours certain groups in society – in the case of Chile, it favoured the ruling financial and political elite. The news frame constructed by the commercial media, as Márquez suggests (2019), presented a stereotypical picture of the protestors as television footage and newspaper photographs constantly highlighted scenes of looting, the destruction of shops, the erection of street barricades and violent clashes with the police. In the process, the social explosion's causes and aims were ignored (see Bourdieu 2005) encouraging the audience to perceive the protests as futile, pointless and even irrational.

Santander points out that the Chilean mainstream media's handling of the social explosion used two noticeable and related frameworks (2019). First, the protests were represented as a problem of law and order. Second, the damage to buildings, private property and even traffic lights was given top news priority. Indeed, a year after the October 2019 protests, traffic light stories still featured prominently in the mainstream media. On 4 September 2020, under the by-line of José Ignacio Gutiérrez, *La Tercera* newspaper published a story with the following headline: 'It has been reported that 85 per cent of vandalised traffic lights in Santiago have been repaired' (Gutiérrez 2020).

While *La Tercera* was concerned about the fate of Santiago's traffic lights, this newspaper – owned by the powerful Said Group – has given no coverage at all to the fate of around 200 protesters who were blinded, some of them partially and others entirely, by pellets fired by state security agents (*dw.com* 2019). It is not surprising, then, that Chilean journalists, as reported in a Reuters Institute study, are regarded as part of an unrepresentative political class (2020). In addition, 'there is a profound resentment on the streets about the news coverage of the social explosion on both television and in the press' (ibid: 91).

By and large, the mainstream coverage of the social explosion was, from a media manipulation standpoint, relatively unsophisticated. However, there were some instances of sophistication, as pointed out by Claudia Lagos and Antoine Faure (2019) with commercial television channels using split-screen images of shops being looted next to shots of protesters marching and shouting. This double-screen strategy constructed a story where looting and peaceful demonstrations were the two sides of the same coin (ibid).

The social explosion did not have visible leaders. Parties and movements associated with progressive social demands, the Communist Party, or unions, for example, were not seen. Party flags were replaced by the Mapuche indigenous nation's flags or even by the flags of the country's two most popular football clubs, Colo-Colo and the University of Chile. This absence of identifiable leaders was a matter of concern for Iván Martinic, the *El Mercurio* newspaper's national editor. 'The lack of leaders on the streets worried us,' he said during an online media symposium at the Universidad del Desarrollo, or Development University (2019). 'We failed to find the leaders of what was happening, and this led us to a sense of disconnection with the events,' he said.

As a result, the commercial television channels and photojournalists turned their cameras on to the 'Primera Linea' or the front line – a group of women, men, gender activists, young and old who erected barricades to shield protestors from the actions of the police. Accompanied by her daughter, a protestor told me she was one of the many pensioners who flooded the country's streets demanding better social security. 'They are heroes,' she told me (personal communication, 21 October 2019).

While the 'Primera Linea' activists rapidly became folk heroes among the protestors, the main television channels depicted them as arsonists, looters and anarchists. A young, long-haired male, usually wearing a mask, clashing with special police forces was the most recurrent image on television and in the newspapers.

Television never showed any 'noble actions', such as members of the 'Primera Linea' using shields to protect protestors from the police's rubber bullets and teargas. One photojournalist who requested anonymity was filing for a mainstream commercial newspaper. He told me he could take any shot he wanted. 'However, I needed to file photos showing violent acts committed by the Primera Linea,' he said (personal communication, 22 October 2019).

The Chilean financial elite severely punished those news organisations that dared to have an ethical and fairer approach to the social movement of October 2019. This was the case of CNN Chile. The agricultural holding company of the Sutil Family, one of the wealthiest in Chile, ceased its advertorial and financial support of CNN's programme 'Agricultural agenda' (Cárdenas 2019). Juan Sutil is the patriarch of the Sutil family. He represents the oligarchic National Agricultural Society and is president of the Confederation of Production and Commerce. In a letter to CNN Chile and Chilevisión, Sutil condemned the coverage of the protests by both televisions channels as 'deplorable' (ibid).

For media scholar Enrique Núñez, of the Faculty of Communications at the Pontifical Catholic University of Chile, the way the media covered the protests directly impacted on the way in which the population reacted (quoted by Saleh 2019). Professor Núñez told Saleh that the protests were manufactured as an inner enemy's actions in a country in a state of war (ibid). The statement of President Sebastián Piñera that Chile was at war and that foreign secret agents were behind the social explosion was published and re-published.

La Tercera newspaper, for example, published a verbatim police statement, dated 27 October 2019, alleging the protestors were Venezuelan and Cuban secret service agents. *La Tercera*, initially, insisted the story was a matter of public interest – 'it contained information relevant to 2019'. However, the newspaper was quickly forced to do a volte-face. In a statement, *La Tercera* (2019) said:

> It was not the intention of *La Tercera*, nor has it ever been, to criminalise foreign citizens who are living in Chile. Regardless of the progress of police investigations, we recognise that we failed – as a journalistic team – to corroborate that information with third sources who would support the story. We should not have published the story without first corroborating whether it was accurate. We apologise for that.

THE PEOPLE AGAINST THE MEDIA: AN ETHICAL BACKLASH

Eduardo Galeano, who was cited at the beginning of this paper, once said: 'The walls are the publishing press of the poor.' During the social explosion of October 2019, the walls next to the mass mobilisation's epicentre, in downtown Santiago, became the canvas of protest against the commercial media. 'Television lies', 'Turn the television off', 'Traitor journalists', 'The street screams what the TV shuts up' were some of the most expressive graffiti protestors scribbled on the walls.

Journalists covering the protest became the target of the protestors' anger. Protestors verbally questioned them for their role in criminalising the social explosion. Writing in the Spanish edition of *The New York Times*, Argentinean journalist and academic Roberto Herrscher pointed out that 'as the popular protest grew, a new culprit emerged: the media' (2019).

As the rage against the media grew, protestors headed to the studios of the leading television channels. In fact, and perhaps symbolically, protests in front of the television studios became more numerous than the demonstrations in front of La Moneda, the Chilean government house. On streetlights, the photographs of some of the most well-known television presenters were hung along with banners labelling them liars.

One of the television stations targeted was *Megavision*. On 21 October, more than 500 protestors demonstrated in front of the television studio. Moreover, the mass mobilisation's negative coverage attracted thousands of complaints to the National Television Council, the broadcast watchdog. The channels that attracted the highest volume of complaints, together with *Megavision*, were the state-funded *National Television Channel* and *Channel 13*. This latter is owned by the Luksic Group, the most powerful business conglomerate in Chile. On the web site of Chile's College of Journalism, a group of journalism students commented:

> We condemn *Channel 13*, the *National Television Channel*, *Megavision* and *Chilevision* for their role of criminalising protest, resorting to censorship, prioritising government sources and misrepresenting information by showing only violence on the streets, but not human rights violations committed by the police and military special forces.

The coverage of the social explosion did not please some journalists employed by the corporate media. Kevin Felgueras, a journalist from the state-funded *National Television Channel*, said: 'The television channels had to accept errors were committed, errors on how the story was told,' during an online discussion organised by the School of Journalism at the Pontifical Catholic University of Valparaiso (2020).

Reporters on the ground were often highly critical of their employers – senior executives and business management (Aguilar 2019). They were considered disconnected from the reality (ibid). However, this critical view is rarely publicly expressed. Chilean journalists live in a profound state of job precarity. In the last four years, at least 2,460 media professionals have lost their jobs (Herrera et al. 2020). The largest number of job losses has happened in *Channel 13*, *Megavision* and the *National Television Channel*.

The only publicly dissenting voices in the media come largely from independent journalists and journalism students. On 29 October, a group of journalists and journalism students rallied in front of the Theatre of the University of Chile, in the vicinity of Plaza Baquedano or Dignity Square – the epicentre of the social explosion. 'It is not possible for the media to disseminate the statement of official sources without questioning them,' said a statement of Chile's Journalists and Communicators Organised, an independent media collective (2020). 'We must never forget that we have first and foremost a social responsibility' (ibid). The statement continues: 'Ethics does matter' (ibid).

ALTERNATIVES FILL ETHICAL VACUUM

The social explosion of October 2019 showed that the Chilean corporate media failed to meet even the minimum journalistic ethical guidelines (Enrique Ortega 2020). In this ethical journalistic vacuum, an alternative, non-commercial media began thriving and gaining new audiences. This is an alternative media characterised by its abundance and diversity (Ortega 2020). As Paola Nalvarte points out, this 'alternative media emerged to keep citizens informed about the reality on the ground' (2020).

While alternative journalism is not new in Chile – it goes back four decades – this new media scenario propelled by digital platforms has managed to challenge the corporate media. As Enrique Ortega points out: 'The programming of the alternative scene is larger and more diverse, which gives voice to the audiences that are not represented in the corporate media – not their voices, images nor their experiences' (2020).

The social explosion did not only expose the alignment between the elite and the corporate media, but it also brought about an emerging hybrid media space (Chadwick 2013). This media hybrid scenario is reflected by the increasing popularity of political podcasts (via YouTube and Spotify), media spaces of conversation (current affairs programmes via university-sponsored media channels), femi-journalism digital platforms (established and managed by feminist organisations) and long-established indigenous and urban poor media collectives.

In this hybrid media ecology, as suggested by Chadwick, these media platforms are not simply spaces of news. They are spaces of activism, dialogue, political education, direct action and collaboration. One example of this media hybridity is a podcast called *La Cosa Nostra*. During the social explosion of 19 October, it became the media space where a large section of the community sought to know, understand and make sense of the social explosion.

This podcast is an example of a hybrid media initiative. It is not just a podcast where news and current affairs are discussed. It goes beyond that. It is a digital workshop for civic and political education, a space of activism and resistance. It is also a micro-media business led by three well-known Chilean personalities: sociologist and academic Alberto Mayol, sociologist and union adviser Dario Quiroga and journalist Mirko Macari. The podcast has reached an unprecedented level of influence in mediating, and more fundamentally, keeping in the Chilean public discussion, the social explosion of October 2019 (Palma 2021).

CONCLUSION

The Chilean corporate media coverage of the social explosion of October 2019 was an ethical failure with profound ramifications for the country's journalism. The coverage obscured and concealed the legitimacy of the protestors' demands while, at the same time, giving high levels of prominence to violence and deviance. Philosopher Judith Butler (1998) warns against systematic exclusion and stigmatisation. This is exactly what the corporate media attempted while covering the social explosion – exclusion and stigmatisation.

As argued in this paper, the Chilean commercial media, closely aligned to the political and financial elite, played a central role in either demonising or ignoring the demands of the country's progressive movement during the social explosion of October 2019. The legitimacy of the country's corporate media and individual journalists has been seriously eroded (Reuters 2020). The Reuters Institute's study shows that the percentage of Chileans who claim to trust the corporate media fell from 53 in 2018 to 30 per cent in 2020. According to the study, people associate the media with the elite, powerful groups and even to the spread of fake news (ibid).

From the beginning of the social explosion, the Chilean corporate media – especially the commercial television channels – broadcast almost uninterrupted the protests that started on October 18. During the days and months that followed, the news coverage focused on the spectacular – the emphasis of the narrative was placed on acts of vandalism, looting and disorder.

In the context of the social explosion, the position of corporate journalism in the Chilean society was not only ethically questioned but it was also rejected. This was the result not only of the demonising coverage, but also the failure to report the massive human rights violations committed against protestors by the police and the military. As the distinguished Chilean journalist and academic Faride Zeran pointed out: 'Journalism didn't live up to the magnitude and seriousness of the events' (2020).

The social explosion has now turned into a national social movement seeking a new and more democratic constitution (Chile is still under the 1980 Constitution imposed by Pinochet, the former dictator). But it is also seeking a more democratic and ethically vigorous media system. And while the corporate media is lagging in this respect, the alternative media are rapidly and inexorably expanding – being an essential part of a crucial 'movement from below'. It is a movement embedded within a hybrid media ecology and deeply connected to the social demands that sparked the historical social explosion of October 2019.

- This paper was first published in *Ethical Space*, Vol. 18, Nos 1 and 2 pp 24-32, 2021

REFERENCES

Abbott, Jeff (2016) Across Latin America, governments criminalise social movements to silence dissent, *Waging nonviolence*, March. Available online at https://wagingnonviolence.org/2016/03/across-latin-american-governments-criminalize-social-movements-to-silence-dissent, accessed on 21 November 2019

Aguilar, Marcela (2019) Periodismo, hoy más que nunca [Journalism, today more than ever], CIPER, October. Available online at https://www.ciperchile.cl/2019/10/26/periodismo-hoy-masque-nunca, accessed on 5 March 2021

Araya, Pedro (2008) El Mercurio miente 1967: Siete notas sobre escrituras expuestas [El Mercurio lies 1967: Seven notes on exposed scriptures], *Revista Austral de Ciencias Sociales*, Vol. 14 pp 157-172

Bourdieu, Pierre (2005) *On television and journalism*, London, Pluto Press

Butler, Judith (1998) Merely cultural, *New Left Review*, Vol. 1/227 pp 33-44

Cárdenas, Leonardo (2019) Sutil companies cut sponsorships to CNN Chile's Agricultural Agenda programme in disagreement over coverage of protests, *La Tercera*. Available online at https://www.latercera.com/la-tercera-pm/noticia/empresas-sutil-corta-auspicios-a-programa-agenda-agricola-de-cnn-chile-en-discrepancia-porcobertura-a-ola-de-protestas/89340, accessed on 1 December 2019

Castillo, Antonio (2019) The collapse of Chile's model: The people have had enough, *Globe Post*, 18 November. Available online at https://theglobepost.com/2019/11/18/chile-economic-model, accessed on 8 December 2020

Chadwick, Andrew (2017) *The hybrid media system: Politics and power*, Oxford, Oxford University Press

Chan, Joseph M. and Chin-Chuan, Lee (1984) The journalistic paradigm on civil protests: A case study of Hong Kong, Arno, Andrew and Dissanayake, Wimal (eds) *News media in national and international conflict*, Boulder, Westview Press pp 193-202 dw.com (2019) Hundreds of Chileans blinded by police since protests began, *dw.com*, 15 November. Available online at https://www.dw.com/en/hundreds-of-chileans-blinded-by-police-since-protests-began/a-1260524#:~:text=The%20principle%20medical%20organization%20 in,in%20the%20South%20American%20country, accessed on 12 February 2021

Constable, Pamela and Valenzuela, Arturo (1991) *A nation of enemies: Chile under Pinochet*, New York, Norton

Entman, Robert (2007 [1993]) Framing: Toward clarification of a fractured paradigm, *Journal of Communication*, Vol. 43, No. 4 pp 51-58

Herrera, Polet, Aguilera, Patricio and Echegoyen, Maximilano (2020) Despidos y precariedad laboral: Los datos tras la profunda crisis de los medios de comunicación en Chile [Dismissals and job precariousness: Data after Chile's deep media crisis], *Puro Periodismo*, August. Available online at http://www.puroperiodismo.cl/despidos-y-precariedad-laboral-los-datos-tras-la-profunda-crisis-de-los-medios-de-comunicacion-en-chile, accessed on 3 March 2021

Gamson, William A. and Wolfsfeld, Gadi (1993) Movements and media as interacting systems, *The Annals of the American Academy of Political and Social Science*, Vol. 1, No. 528 pp 114-125

Gans, Herbert J. (1979) *Deciding what's news: A study of* CBS Evening News, NBC Nightly News, Newsweek, *and* Time, New York, Pantheon Books

Gitlin, Todd (2003) *The whole world is watching: Mass media in the making and unmaking of the new left*, California, University of California Press

Glasgow University Media Group (1976) *Bad news*, London, Routledge and Kegan Paul

Grassau, D., Valenzuela, S., Bachmann, I., Labarca, C., Mujica, C., Halpern, D. and Puente, S. (2019) Estudio de opinión pública: Uso y evaluación de los medios de comunicación y las redes sociales durante el estallido social en Chile [Public opinion study: Use and evaluation of media and social media during the social explosion in Chile], Faculty of Communications of the Pontifical Catholic University of Chile. Available online at http://bit.ly/EncuestaMediosFComUC, accessed on 2 January 2021

Gumucio, M. and Parrini, V. (2009) Political communication during the concertation, Quiroga, Y. and Ensignia, J. (eds) *Chile during the concertation 1990-2010: A critical view, balance and perspectives*, Santiago, Friedrich-Ebert-Schtiftung pp 301-331

Gutiérrez, José Ignacio (2020) It has been reported that 85 per cent of vandalised traffic lights in Santiago have been repaired, *La Tercera*. Available online at https://www.latercera.com/mtonline/noticia/ministerios-de-transportes-y-de-vivienda-informan-que-el- 85-de-semaforos-vandalizados-en-el-gran-santiago-fue-reparado/ SRAMBKUHZVFP3ITHTANR5ZNXIE, accessed on 2 November 2020

Herman, Edward S. and Chomsky, Noam (1988) *Manufacturing consent: The political economy of the mass media*, New York, Pantheon

Herrscher, Roberto (2019) Chile woke up, it's time for journalism to wake up, *New York Times*, 12 December. Available online at https://www.nytimes.com/es/2019/12/12/espanol/opinion/medios-protestas-chile.html, accessed on 3 January 2021

Interferencia (2021) *El Mercurio, Canal 13, La Tercera, TVN y Mega*: Los medios favoritos del gobierno para reclutar periodistas [*El Mercurio, Channel 13, La Tercera, TVN and Mega*: The government's favourite media to recruit journalists]. Available online at https://interferencia.cl/articulos/el-mercurio-canal-13-la-tercera-tvn-y-mega-los-medios-favoritos-del-gobierno-parareclutar, accessed on 17 January 2021

Journalists and Communicators Organized of Chile (2019) Periodistas, estudiantes y comunicadores convocan a marcha hoy martes [Journalists, students and communicators call for a march on Tuesday], National College of Journalists of Chile, October. Available online at https://www.colegiodeperiodistas.cl/2019/10/ periodistas-estudiantes-y-comunicadores.html, accessed on 2 March 2021.

Journalism Students (2019) We demand an end to the communication barrier, College of Journalism. Available online at https://www.colegiodeperiodistas.cl/2019/10/estudiantes-deperiodismo-exigimos-el.html, accessed on 5 September 2020

Kilgo, Danielle K. and Harlow, Summer (2019) Protests, media coverage, and a hierarchy of social struggle, *The International Journal of Press/Politics*, Vol. 24, No. 4 pp 508-530

Kilgo, Danielle K. (2020) Riot or resistance? How media frames unrest in Minneapolis will shape public's view of protest, *The Conversation*, 29 May. Available online at https://theconversation.com/riot-or-resistance-how-media-frames-unrest-in-minneapolis-will-shape-publics-view-of-protest-139713, accessed on 2 October 2019

Lagos, Claudia and Faure, Antoine (2019) Precarious journalism: Can/does the press want to protect citizens? CIPER. Available online at https://www.ciperchile.cl/2019/10/31/periodismo-precarizado-puede-quiere-la-prensa-proteger-a-los-ciudadanos/, accessed on 7 December 2019

La Tercera (2019) Aclaración sobre artículo publicado por *La Tercera*: Un error del que nos hacemos cargo [Clarification on article published by *La Tercera*: An error we take care of]. Available online at https://www.latercera.com/nacional/noticia/aclaracion-articulo-publicado-la-tercera-error-del-nos-hacemos-cargo/881975/, accessed on 4 December 2020

Márquez, Francisca (2019) What the neighbour sees, and the TV doesn't, CIPER. Available online at https://www.ciperchile.cl/2019/10/27/lo-que-el-vecino-ve-y-la-television-no, accessed on 3 November 2019

Martín Barbero, Jésus (2001) *South of modernity: Communication, globalisation, and multiculturalism*, International Institute of Ibero-American Literature, University of Pittsburgh

McAdam, Doug and Snow, David, A. (1997) *Social movements: Readings on their emergence, mobilisation, and dynamics*, Los Angeles, Roxbury

McLeod, Douglas M. and Hertog, James (1999) Social control, social change, and the mass media's role in the regulation of protest groups, Demers, David and Viswanath, Kasisomayajula (eds) *Mass media, social control, and social change: A macrosocial perspective,* Ames, Iowa State University Press pp 305-330

Mönckeberg, María Olivia (2009) *The press magnates: Media concentration in Chile*, Santiago, Random House Mondadori

Nalvarte, Paola (2020) Social protest and crisis of traditional media in Chile leads to creation of alternative media and fact-checking outlets, *LatAm Journalism Review*, November. Available online at https://latamjournalismreview.org/articles/social-protest-chile-fact-checking-alternative-media, accessed on 23 February 2021

Orchard, Ximena (2019) Political press: The echo chamber of elites, CIPER. Available online at https://www.ciperchile.cl/2019/10/29/prensa-politica-la-camara-de-eco-de-las-elites, accessed on 3 January 2021

Ortega, Juan Enrique (2020) Comunicación alternativa y popular: La importancia de multiplicar los relatos [Alternative and popular communication: The importance of multiplying stories], *Revista Palabra Pública*, April. Available online athttps://palabrapublica.uchile.cl/2020/04/27/comunicacion-alternativa-y-popular, accessed 27 February 2021

Palma, Sebastian (2021) El poder de la Cosa Nostra: el boyante negocio de Macari, Mayol y Quiroga [The power of Cosa Nostra: The buoyant business of Macari, Mayol and Quiroga], *The Clinic*, January. Available online at https://www.theclinic.cl/2021/01/16/el-poder-de-la-cosa-nostra-el-boyante-negocio-de-macari-mayol-y-quiroga, accessed on 24 February 2021

Parkin, Joe Daniel (2020) Latin America's wave of protests was historic – then the pandemic arrived, *Foreign Policy*, June. Available online at https://foreignpolicy.com/2020/06/25/latin-america-protest-pandemic-informal-economy, accessed on 10 October 2020

Ramonet, Ignacio (2001) *Tyrannie de la communication*, Paris, Gallimard Education

Reuters Institute (2020) *Reuters Institute digital news report*. Available online at https://reutersinstitute.politics.ox.ac.uk/sites/default/files/2020-06/DNR_2020_FINAL.pdf

Saleh, Felipe (2019) The day the public got bored of TV: The critical coverage of channels opens to social explosion in Chile, *El Mostrador*. Available online at https://www.elmostrador.cl/destacado/2019/10/23/el-dia-en-que-el-publico-se-aburrio-de-la-tele-la-criticada-cobertura-de-los-canales-abiertos-al-estallido-social-en-chile/?fbclid=IwAR0RcWNGs-dnH3YPywQBARG4kx1wZgcRA9MBY2OhkSPVBbXn1UpA-nDL3Fk, accessed on 24 November 2019

Santander, Pedro (2019) TV sucks, radio reporting, networks fighting, *El Desconcierto*. Available online at https://www.eldesconcierto.cl/opinion/2019/10/24/la-tv-una-mierda-la-radio-informando-las-redes-luchando.html, accessed on 4 December 2019

School of Journalism at the Pontifical Catholic University of Valparaiso (2020) Conversation: Media, journalists and one-year communication of the social explosion, School of Journalism at the Pontifical Catholic University of Valparaiso. Available online at https://www.youtube.com/watch?v=ZrdouZbFMz4&t=168s&ab_channel=EscueladePeriodismoPUCV, accessed on 10 January 2021

Shedden, David (2014) Mr Dooley: 'The job of the newspaper is to comfort the afflicted and afflict the comfortable', *Poynter.org*, 7 October. Available online at https://www.poynter.org/reporting-editing/2014/today-in-media-history-mr-dooley-the-job-of-the-newspaper-is-to-comfort-the-afflicted-and-afflict-the-comfortable/, accessed on 12 February 2021

Sorensen, Kristin (2010) The case of Chilevisión: Negotiating difficult speeches in the Chilean television, Information Notebooks. Available online at http://cuadernos.uc.cl/uc/index.php/CDI/article/view/14/10, accessed on 3 January 2021

Spooner, Mary Helen (1999) *Soldiers in a narrow land, the Pinochet regime in Chile*, Los Angeles, University of California Press

Tabilo Castillo, Luis (2020) One year after the explosion: The secret meetings of Piñera and his ministers with senior television executives and presenters, *La Voz de los que Sobran*. Available online at https://lavozdelosquesobran.cl/a-un-ano-del-estallido-la-reuniones-secretas-de-pinera-y-sus-ministros-con-altos-ejecutivos-y-rostros-de-television, accessed on October 29, 2020

Tarrow, Sidney (2012 [1998]) *Power in movement: Social movements and contentious politics*, Cambridge, Cambridge University Press

University for Development [Universidad del Desarrollo] (2019) Journalism Department holds forum on the social explosion and the role of the media. Available online at https://www.udd.cl/noticias/2019/11/14/periodismo-realizo-foro-sobre-el-estallido-social-y-el-rol-de-los-medios, accessed on 15 December 2019

Zeran, Faride (2020) El periodismo no ha estado a la altura de la magnitud y gravedad de los acontecimientos [Journalism didn't live up to the magnitude and severity of events], University of Chile, January. Available online at https://portaluchile.uchile.cl/noticias/161360/el-periodismo-no-han-estado-a-la-altura-de-los-acontecimientos, accessed on 1 March 2021

Žižek, Slavoj (2012) *Violence*, London, Profile Books

NOTE ON THE CONTRIBUTOR

Dr Antonio Castillo is a journalist and academic. Antonio has occupied, at different universities, high-ranking teaching, leadership and management positions and has taught in Latin America, Asia, Australia and Europe. He currently teaches journalism at RMIT University in Melbourne. He also supervises PhD, Honours, and MA students. At RMIT, Antonio has been the Director of the Journalism Program and Communications, Politics and Culture Research Centre (CPC). He founded and convened the Latin American Research Community (LARC) at RMIT. As a journalist, Antonio has written about major internal events, people and places. He covered the 'Arab Spring' in Cairo and witnessed the peace process in Sri Lanka. He has written about Mexico's war on drugs and the collapse of the Chilean economic model. Antonio is the author of *Journalism in the Chilean transition to democracy*, co-author of *Cosmopolitan Sydney* and co-managing founding editor of *Global Media Journal*. His next book, *Up to the neck in contradictions*, is a work of journalistic reportage where he examines the last two decades of Latin American history, economics, politics and culture.

Chapter 9

Trauma in the newsroom: Lessons on the importance of Australia's YZ case

Alexandra Wake and Matthew Ricketson

A landmark ruling by an Australian court has put news media companies on notice they face potential findings of negligence and subsequent compensation claims if they fail to exercise a reasonable duty of care to journalists who cover traumatic events. Drawing on legal doctrinal methodology, we look at the successful case and compare it to an earlier unsuccessful case at the same newspaper where a journalist sought damages from their employer for injury caused by their work. The case before the Victorian County Court in 2019 was the first to recognise the risk of psychological damage on those who report on traumatic events. The court ruled that YZ, a journalist at one of Australia's oldest metropolitan daily newspapers, The Age, *be awarded A$180,000 for psychological injury suffered while working between 2003 and 2013. YZ had reported on 32 murders and many more cases as a court reporter. She covered what were colloquially called Melbourne's gangland wars, was threatened by one of its notorious figures and found it increasingly difficult to report on events involving the death of children, such as the case of a four-year-old who was murdered by her father by being thrown from a bridge in 2009. The court's ruling – and ratification of the decision at appeal – was in stark contrast to the case from the same newspaper, in 2012, which did not uphold the claim of a news photographer. Apart from the intrinsic importance of the cases, it is relevant for journalism educators who are charged with preparing the next generation of journalists, many of whom will cover traumatic events. Educators and others have been urging cultural change in newsrooms for years but this ruling shows that it may well be now required by law. This paper asks: Can educators find sufficient space in a crowded curriculum to prepare students?*

Keywords: trauma, journalists, occupational post-traumatic stress disorder, PTSD, newspapers, journalism practice, journalism education

INTRODUCTION

In 2020, Facebook agreed to a US$52 million settlement for thousands of content moderators because their job exposed them to hour upon hour of viewing disturbing material (Marantz 2020: 22; Newton 2020). As Steven Levy writes in *Facebook: The inside story*: 'The presence of all that stomach-churning content was an uncomfortable fact for Facebook, which preferred to keep its armies of scrubbers out of sight' (Levy 2020: 445). The experience (and financial recognition) of the issue for content moderators at Facebook stands in stark contrast to the experience of journalists and news media workers who have long been exposed to unedited footage of terrorist attacks, crime and accidents to ensure the public is not affronted by the reality of what can be a traumatising world.

It is only in the past three decades or so that the potential impact on journalists and photographers of witnessing traumatic events, and moderating online content for news outlets, has become a topic of research. It is even more recently that journalists have begun bringing claims against their employers for occupational PTSD, and it was only in 2020 that a successful claim was brought. To the best of the authors' knowledge, the case central to this paper is the first successful one of its kind in Australia, the United Kingdom or the United States. This is also the considered view of Bree Knoester, the lawyer who acted for YZ and before that, for AZ in her unsuccessful claim for occupational PTSD.

This paper uses legal doctrinal methodology to describe and analyse the YZ and AZ legal cases to focus on the implications on the long overdue recognition by a court of occupational PTSD in newsrooms. In the expert opinion of Bruce Shapiro, the executive director, US Dart Center for Journalism and Trauma based at Columbia University's Graduate School of Journalism, YZ is unquestionably a historic case, not just for Australia but for journalists and news organisations worldwide:

> It is the first judgment on record anywhere in which a major news organisation has been found liable for a journalist's avoidable, work-related psychological injury. The judgment's rigorous analysis has found its way on to the desks of news executives and attorneys across the globe, and has sped a growing industry consensus that news organisations have significant responsibility for the psychological safety of trauma-exposed staff, just as they do for those facing physical risk (Shapiro, personal communication, 28 January 2021).

Whether the decision at the County Court in Victoria, Australia, in 2019 will spur media companies to take more seriously occupational PTSD is an open question and a vexed one but, in the first instance, it is necessary to document the case of a journalist working for *The Age* newspaper (known in court as YZ to protect her identity) who successfully sued her employer for occupational PTSD and won damages of A$180,000. The case confirms that media companies have a duty of care to their journalists to protect them against the foreseeable risk of mental injury. The questions we ask about the case are as follows:

1. How did the plaintiff, YZ, succeed where the plaintiff in an earlier case in Australia, known as AZ, did not?

2. What are the implications of the court decision for the news media industry?

We seek to answer these questions primarily by analysing the two court cases and to a lesser extent by drawing on news media articles about the cases, as well as the academic literature.

TRAUMA AND JOURNALISM

The impact that experiencing or witnessing traumatic events may have on people has been long understood even if PTSD was only included in the American Psychiatric Association's official manual of mental disorders in 1980 (Herman 1992: 27-28). The disorder features recurrent, distressing memories of or dreams about the traumatic event, hyper-arousal, emotional numbness, sharp alterations in mood and avoidance of places or events that trigger memories of the traumatic event (American Psychiatric Association 2013: 271-272). The manual recognises that a person's occupation may increase the risk of traumatic exposure and singles out police officers, firefighters and emergency medical personnel (ibid: 276). There has been growing awareness of the impact on journalists and photographers reporting on traumatic events, after many years of ignorance or avoidance of discussing journalists' experience of witnessing trauma (Castles 2002). Journalists have been 'hidden first responders': commonly, they arrive at car crashes, crimes or bushfires at the same time as paramedics, police and firefighters, or soon after, or, occasionally, before. Where it is well understood that journalists write 'the first rough draft of history', in the words of the former publisher of the *Washington Post*, Phil Graham, the implications of that memorable phrase are less well understood (Shafer 2010). That is, to write the first draft of history journalists need to be on the scene to observe and report, and what they see and hear and, for that matter, smell, is the raw reality of horrible events. What effect witnessing such events has on journalists themselves rarely forms the first rough draft of history. For every emotive cry of 'Oh, the humanity' as the German passenger airship, the *Hindenburg*, crashed in front of a radio announcer's eyes in 1937 (*National Geographic* 2015), there are hundreds of reports written in the formal language and institutional voice of standard daily journalism. It is illuminating that the *Wikipedia* (2020) entry for the Hindenburg disaster radio announcer, Herbert Morrison, lists ten instances of his phrase 'Oh, the humanity' in popular culture, most of which are intended as humorous. Morrison is actually witnessing the deaths of 35 people as the Zeppelin explodes into flames. His voice cracks, he falters as he hears the people on the ground screaming for their friends aboard and he is then unable to go on, saying: 'This is the worst thing I've ever witnessed.' Morrison's broadcast is celebrated in media history and analysed in the academic literature but far less has been written about the effect this experience had on Morrison (Miller 2003: 60-61).

As part of their duties, though, journalists are commonly required to seek out traumatic events (Derienzo 2016; Ricketson 2017). Even when journalists are in news roles that do not on the surface appear to be specifically related to trauma (such as sports reporters or fashion writers) the nature of breaking news means that such journalists can be thrust into bearing witness to a traumatic event, as Herbert Morrison was; his usual work was as an announcer on live musical programmes. However, there is a human cost of bringing crimes, disasters and other traumatic events and issues to the attention of the world at large. Studies have found that the prevalence of PTSD is higher among journalists than the general population, with up to 33 per cent of journalists reportedly suffering from probable PTSD (Aoki et al. 2013: 380; Backholm and Björkqvist 2012; Dworznik 2011; Hatanaka et al. 2010; Newman, Simpson and Handschuh 2003; Pyevich, Newman and Daleiden 2003; Weidmann, Fehm and Fydrich 2008).

Research has found that journalists and other media workers, such as video editors, are also vulnerable to PTSD through vicarious exposure to trauma. Their vulnerability may arise in interviewing victims of crime or, in the case of court reporters, listening to the testimony of distressed survivors of violence (Barnes 2016) or by viewing unedited videos or photo files through the news desk (Feinstein, Audet and Waknine 2014; Weidmann and Papsdorf 2010). Attending at the scene of a traumatic event can be predictive of negative outcomes for the journalist (Hatanaka et al. 2010). The frequency with which traumatic events are experienced has been found a major risk factor for journalists (Newman, Simpson and Handschuh 2003). Despite this and a range of other research work over the past three decades, the preparation of journalists for reporting traumatic events is patchy and underdeveloped. Worse, young graduates fresh out of journalism programmes may well find themselves exposed to covering crimes or flying off into conflict zones (Wake 2016). Programmes to prepare, support and de-brief other first responders, such as paramedics, police and firefighters, or those whose work brings them into contact with human suffering, such as social work, nursing, psychology, psychiatry, mental health, disability or aged care, are common (Quitangon and Evces 2016; Dorfman, 2007; Barnes 2016).

Journalists will immerse themselves in investigations for extended periods about, say, child sexual abuse, or attend months-long murder trials without the kind of thorough-going professional practice or regulation around self-care such as that which has been incorporated within other professions. Where the work of first responders such as police, paramedics or firefighters requires them to take direct action to solve a problem, journalists can feel powerless to alleviate human suffering at a traumatic event. Offsetting this sense is the beneficial effect for journalists of having the ability and training to express themselves about what they are witnessing on behalf of the general public (McMahon 2016; Lyall 2012: 217). Complicating this picture further is that exemplary coverage of traumatic events may well be rewarded, as even a cursory viewing of the list of winners for Australia's most prestigious prize, the Walkley awards, shows (see https://www.walkleys.com/ awards/walkley-winners-archive/). Historically, the prevailing culture in newsrooms has been that journalists are reluctant to express vulnerability when witnessing trauma, partly because the bigger the traumatic event the bigger the news event, and partly because journalists worry they will not be given these sought-after assignments if they complain (Lyall 2012).

THE CASE OF AZ VS *THE AGE*

The YZ case was preceded by the case of a Walkley award-winning photographer who had been working for 28 years at *The Age*, one of the leading metropolitan newspapers in Australia. It is necessary to outline the case in detail as it was the first of its kind in Australia (Ricketson 2017), and because the experiences of the plaintiff are similar in many ways to those of the plaintiff in the later case. But the judges in the two cases reached diametrically opposed conclusions. The photographer, known in the Supreme Court case only as AZ to protect her identity, sued for negligence, arguing that the newspaper had done little to prevent her suffering PTSD from her duties and claiming between $700,000 and $1 million in loss of earnings (Deery 2012; Caldwell 2012). Information about the case is drawn primarily from the judgement handed down by Justice Kate McMillan in September 2013 (AZ (a person under a disability who sues by her litigation guardian BZ) v. *The Age* (2013) VSC 335) which was reported and discussed in an article in the *Australian Journalism Review* (Ricketson 2017). AZ's experience was a common one in that she photographed numerous traumatic events during her career alongside many other assignments that were not at all traumatic. In her personal life, AZ had experienced trauma; one brother died in an industrial accident while another died of an AIDS-related illness. Her long-term partner suffered from bi-polar disorder. She was the primary income earner (AZ (a person under a disability who sues by her litigation guardian BZ) v. *The Age* (2013) VSC 335 at 16-18).

Her problems at work began in 2003 when she was asked to contribute to a series of reports commemorating the first anniversary of the Bali bombings. This meant photographing between 10 and 16 families who had lost loved ones in the bombings. AZ found it a difficult, distressing assignment; often the still-grieving interviewees would be looking at her for extended periods while the journalists, heads down, took notes. At the end of the day she and the journalist would share a meal together and talk about the interviews, but she worked with several journalists on the assignment and one of them would go and sit in his car straight after the interview, leaving AZ with the family to finish taking photographs. He would retreat to his hotel room, leaving her alone. By the time she completed her photographs for the anniversary series she was beginning to experience flashbacks and nightmares about the bombings. She experienced panic attacks and began drinking to excess. In early 2004, the journalist who had retreated to his hotel room after the anniversary interviews committed suicide. In December 2004, AZ refused an assignment to travel to Aceh to cover the Boxing Day tsunami. Early the following year she took sick leave and began seeing a psychiatrist who diagnosed her as suffering from depression.

In April 2005, AZ met her direct line supervisor at *The Age* to tell her about the problems she was experiencing at work. The supervisor, Louise Graham, offered to move her to *The Sunday Age*, where unfortunately one of her first assignments was to attend an interview with a family whose son had shot a policeman and then killed himself. AZ found the job distressing and later that year, during another period of leave, she was offered a voluntary redundancy from the newspaper. She accepted the need for it as by this time she felt unable to do her job, but it was not until 2008 that her employment with *The Age* was terminated. Between 2005 and 2012 her physical and mental health deteriorated; she began to self-harm. She saw several doctors who all diagnosed her as suffering from PTSD (AZ (a person under a disability who sues by her litigation guardian BZ) v. *The Age* (2013) VSC 335 at 18-47).

AZ claimed the newsroom culture at *The Age* discouraged anyone from discussing their emotional response to stories they covered. To refuse an assignment was regarded as unprofessional. Her claim stated that she had received no trauma-awareness training, that there was no peer-support programme in place, that no advice was given before photographers and journalists embarked on difficult stories, that there was no monitoring of their state of mind during these jobs and no follow-up afterwards. Evidence was provided in court that by 2003 there was sufficient knowledge of trauma, from academic studies and from programmes implemented in at least some other news organisations, such as the BBC, that *The Age* should have been doing more to safeguard its employees' health and safety when covering traumatic events (AZ (a person under a disability who sues by her litigation guardian BZ) v. *The Age* (2013) VSC 335 at 47-55).

In addition, 15 months before the anniversary series, *The Age* had commissioned an international expert to report on the workplace's safety, including the psychological impact of the work required of journalists and photographers. In October 2002, associate professor David Caple recommended the introduction of a peer-support programme and that the newspaper's health centre include psychological issues in its incident reporting system. *The Age* did not implement Caple's recommendations (AZ (a person under a disability who sues by her litigation guardian BZ) v. *The Age* (2013) VSC 335 at 55-57).

The Age rejected the plaintiff's claim, on several grounds: that AZ had not been exposed to covering traumatic events 'such as would sensitise her to psychiatric injury' (AZ (a person under a disability who sues by her litigation guardian BZ) v. *The Age* (2013) VSC 335 at 91); that she did not raise concerns about the Bali assignment until after the second Bali bombings occurred in October 2005; that there was no evidence any measure taken by the defendant would have been likely to protect the plaintiff from injury; that there was little agreement among experts about the preferred model of support for employees, but that in any case the newspaper (it argued) had in place adequate measures to support the plaintiff. The plaintiff's claim of negligence had been brought under common law. Employers have a duty to take reasonable care for the safety of their employees, including prevention of psychiatric harm. For an action to succeed, two arguments need to be made: first, that the injury or in this case psychiatric harm was foreseeable and, second, that the employer breached its duty. The judge agreed with *The Age*'s arguments and dismissed the photographer's claim (AZ (a person under a disability who sues by her litigation guardian BZ) v. *The Age* (2013) VSC 335 at 114).

THE CASE OF YZ VS *THE AGE*

In 2019, a journalist who had worked for *The Age* from 2003 to 2013 sued the newspaper for negligence, on the same grounds as AZ. Their careers at the newspaper overlapped but only for a couple of years, as AZ had begun taking extended periods of leave in 2005. Material in this section draws on the judgement in the Victorian County Court by Justice Chris O'Neill. From 2003 to 2009 YZ reported on crime, covering at least 32 murders and other serious crimes. She reported on some of the key figures in Melbourne's notorious 'gangland wars', such as Carl Williams and Mick Gatto, which she found 'pretty frightening' (YZ (a pseudonym) v The Age Company Limited (2019) VCC 148 at 13). She found even more difficult attending crime scenes where she saw dead bodies, some of them badly mutilated, and was required to find relatives and friends of the deceased to interview. Particularly difficult was reporting on the deaths of children, such as the 16-month-old girl who was murdered by her father with a spear gun (YZ (a pseudonym) v. The Age Company Limited (2019) VCC 148 at 9).

The cumulative effect of witnessing so much trauma eventually became too much for YZ to bear in 2009. On 29 January YZ attended a crime scene where four-year-old Darcey Freeman was thrown by her father from the 58-metre-high West Gate bridge into the Yarra River below. YZ witnessed the ambulance officers, visibly distressed after they administered CPR to the girl. After spending several hours reporting from the scene, in a state of shock, YZ returned to the office and said to the news desk: 'I'm done. I can't do this anymore. I have had enough of death and destruction' (YZ (a pseudonym) v. The Age Company Limited (2019) VCC 148 at 12).

As a result of the concerns she expressed, YZ was transferred to the sports desk where she reported on sport until April the following year when the newspaper's deputy editor, Mark Baker, asked her to take up a role covering the Supreme Court. YZ declined, saying she had had her 'fair share of death and destruction' (YZ (a pseudonym) v. The Age Company Limited (2019) VCC 148 at 14) but Baker persisted. YZ declined again but was told 'it was going to happen' (YZ (a pseudonym) v. The Age Company Limited (2019) VCC 148 at 15) and was offered a pay rise and a date to begin at the court. She eventually accepted.

She found reporting on crime in the Supreme Court equally harrowing. Not only was she required to report on numerous murders but the methodical laying out of evidence could be highly distressing. In one trial, CCTV cameras had recorded close-up footage of Carl Williams's head after he had been bashed to death with a metal pole by a fellow inmate in prison. YZ was also required to cover the trial of Darcey Freeman's father, Arthur, which included the police video of Darcey's six-year-old brother recounting how he pleaded with his father not to throw her off the bridge as Darcey could not swim. Jurors and journalists were in tears watching this, YZ testified. The judge offered the jurors counselling (YZ (a pseudonym) v. The Age Company Limited (2019) VCC 148 at 16). YZ had previously sought support through the Employee Assistance Program (EAP) provided by *The Age* but found she had to wait too long for appointments and that the counsellor, while helpful, did not understand the nature of journalism nor the demands of the newsroom. She began seeing a psychologist and then a psychiatrist but was also drinking heavily at times and unable to concentrate on her work. As Justice O'Neill commented, the plaintiff's testimony in court about her exposure to trauma was chilling:

> She was regularly distressed and unable to go on. That reaction was no doubt as a result of the PTSD. Neither this brief summary of the evidence, nor a reading of the transcript, properly reflects YZ's description of the trauma she observed and wrote about, nor its impact upon her (YZ (a pseudonym) v. The Age Company Limited (2019) VCC 148 at 19).

In her statement of claim, YZ argued that *The Age*:

- had no system in place to enable her to deal with the trauma of her work;

- failed to provide support and training in covering traumatic events, including from qualified peers;

- did not intervene when she and others complained;

- transferred her to court reporting after she had complained of being unable to cope with trauma experienced from previous crime reporting.

For its part, *The Age* contested whether the journalist was actually suffering from PTSD. It argued that, even if a peer-support programme had been in place, it would not have made a material difference to the journalist's experience. *The Age* denied it knew or should have known there was a foreseeable risk of psychological injury to its journalists while at the same time arguing that the plaintiff knew 'by reason of her work she was at high risk of foreseeable injury' (YZ (a pseudonym) v. The Age Company Limited (2019) VCC 148 at 6).

Justice O'Neill found in favour of YZ; he accepted her evidence that she had been exposed to a 'wide range of disturbing and graphic traumatic events' (YZ (a pseudonym) v. The Age Company Limited (2019) VCC 148 at 87). He found her symptoms of PTSD had emerged over time, but accepted that 'she suffered over the years, a range of very significant and disabling symptoms' (YZ (a pseudonym) v. The Age Company Limited (2019) VCC 148 at 87) including depression, anxiety, panic attacks, broken sleep, nightmares and flashbacks. 'I accept that while it is possible she may return to journalism, she would not be able to work in the field of crime or court reporting' (YZ (a pseudonym) v. The Age Company Limited (2019) VCC 148 at 87). The judge found YZ received no training in how to deal with the trauma of the incidents she was required to report on. The PTSD, anxiety and depression she experienced stemmed directly from her work for *The Age*.

The employer could have foreseen the risk of psychological injury and could have prevented it but did not, Judge O'Neill found. Therefore, *The Age* had breached its duty of care to its employee. He found that to fulfil its duty of care, *The Age* should have:

- trained the journalist, both at the outset and on a continuing basis;

- trained editors and senior managers to identify symptoms that may indicate psychological injury;

- implemented a formal peer support programme involving journalists and others trained in such work, on the ground that journalists are best placed to understand the stresses of the newsrooms and their support is more likely to be accepted by other journalists who historically have been wary of counselling;

- provided instructions about how to conduct 'intrusions' (that is, interviews with grieving relatives) and debriefing afterwards for those who wanted it;

- expanded the Employee Assistance Programme, to avoid delays for journalists seeking appointments;

- changed the culture at *The Age* so editors could encourage journalists to talk openly about the difficulties of being exposed to traumatic events, and feel able to report symptoms of stress, anxiety and depression to their managers;

- ensured journalists knew they had the option to move to another area in the newsroom, where reasonably practicable, if they felt the trauma associated with the work became too much (YZ (a pseudonym) v. The Age Company Limited (2019) VCC 148 2019 at 70-71).

One of the newspaper's own witnesses, the editorial training manager, Colin McKinnon, gave evidence of his frustration at being unable to persuade management to implement a suitable training and support programme. Judge O'Neill found him a convincing witness. Further, Justice O'Neill found there was sufficient evidence the reporter had complained to several editors and human resources managers about the level of trauma she was being exposed to and the impact it was having, yet adequate training and support were not provided. The judge was also satisfied that the reporter's injury was worsened by being 'persuaded' to transfer to the court reporter role from sport in 2010 after she repeatedly refused the transfer:

> It must have been obvious to management at *The Age* that something was wrong, more than an isolated emotional reaction to a traumatic story, but a clear indication of the emergence of an underlying psychological disorder. She should never have been requested, let alone persuaded, to undertake work as a court reporter given her complaints to *The Age* after the Darcey Freeman incident (YZ (a pseudonym) v. The Age Company Limited (2019) VCC 148 at 50).

The plaintiff asked for $250,000 in 'pain and suffering damages' while the defence argued damages should be no more than $50,000. In the judgement handed down on 22 February 2019, YZ was awarded $180,000 in damages.

APPEAL OF THE DECISION IN THE YZ CASE

The ruling in the YZ case was a landmark as it was the first time a journalist had won a case for occupational PTSD in Australia. The case received little coverage in the mainstream Australian news media except a report on the national broadcaster, the ABC's legal affairs programme (Edraki and Carrick 2019), a media-focused online publisher *Crikey* (Watkins 2019) and *news.com.au* (Smith 2019). This reinforced the comment of Ricketson in his article about the AZ case that this may have stemmed from the judge granting the journalist anonymity, and also 'perhaps because the media was squeamish about covering a case that called into question the industry's heroically stoic self-image' (Ricketson 2017: 186). The case was, however, discussed in *The Conversation*, the global online website whose articles are written by academics and edited by journalists (Ricketson and Wake 2019).

The Age lodged an appeal that was heard by the Victorian Supreme Court of Appeal on 30 October 2019. The newspaper argued that it had not breached its duty of care to its employee and it challenged the judge's formulation of an employer's duty of care, arguing that it was too vague and did not take into account 'the need to respect the autonomy and privacy of employees' (The Age Company Limited v. YZ (a pseudonym) (2019) VSCA 313 at 27). The three appeal court justices upheld part of the appeal but also upheld Justice O'Neill's core finding that YZ suffered from PTSD and that *The Age* had failed in its duty of care to her. The appeal court justices distinguished between YZ's experiences before and after she told the news desk in 2009 that she had 'had enough of death and destruction'. They were not persuaded that *The Age* had breached its duty of care in the period YZ was reporting on crime but were persuaded that once she had made her views clearly known and a year later had been assigned to court reporting against her wishes that the risk of psychological injury was foreseeable and the newspaper had breached its duty of care. Because the damages awarded in the original judgement did not distinguish between these two periods, the appeal court justices referred the matter back to the county court for further consideration of the appropriate amount of damages.

In March 2020, the parties settled the matter out of court. In September 2020, the online news website *Crikey.com.au* published an article written by Dean Yates, a former journalist with the international news agency Reuters, who had been diagnosed with occupational PTSD and who had then headed Reuters' mental health and wellbeing strategy until earlier that year. For it, he interviewed both YZ and a spokesperson for *The Age*. The former said the five days of cross-examination in the trial 'nearly broke me. During the county court trial I was forced to relive a lot of the trauma I'd been exposed to' (Yates 2020). She said she had pursued her case because she wanted to change the way media organisations treated journalists who are repeatedly exposed to trauma so that other journalists did not have to suffer as she had. *The Age* spokesperson said the newspaper and its parent company, the Nine Entertainment Company, took 'the mental welfare of its employees seriously and has a range of support and training measures in place to ensure the wellbeing of our people', including its Employee Assistance Programme and training provided by the Asia-Pacific arm of the Dart Center for Journalism and Trauma (ibid).

Table 1: Summary of the judge's main findings in the YZ decision

YZ suffered from post-traumatic stress disorder (PTSD) as a result of the reporting work she did.
The nature of journalistic work meant the risk of psychological injury was foreseeable.
YZ made it clear to her employer that she could no longer report on traumatic events and needed to move to another role.

The Age persuaded YZ against her will to return to reporting on traumatic events.
The judge rejected the contradictions in the defendant's arguments. *The Age* did not accept it could foresee the risk of psychological injury but argued YZ should have been able to.
The judge found convincing the evidence of the newspaper's former training editor who testified about his frustration at being unable to introduce a properly resourced trauma-awareness programme.

DISCUSSION OF THE YZ CASE

The decisions in the YZ case are of international significance, even if that seems to be belied by the muted response to it in the Australian news media and the broader public. In effect, the decision puts media companies on notice that a core part of their business – reporting on crime, disasters and other traumatic events – exposes them to legal risk from the journalists who do that work. As the Dart Center's Bruce Shapiro wrote:

> The last several years have seen significant growth in trauma-support efforts in major newsrooms. While the reasons for this far-reaching culture change are complex, one motivation is clearly companies' fear of liability, as a growing and well-publicized consensus of research illuminates the cost of occupational PTSD, burnout and other psychological injury among news professionals. YZ made those fears real and sent ripples far beyond the Victoria courts (Shapiro, personal communication, 28 January 2021).

The Age spokesperson quoted above said the newspaper took seriously its employees' mental health and wellbeing, but that claim flies in the face of the judgements in the County Court and the Supreme Court of Appeal. Equally important, there was no public acknowledgement by *The Age* that it had failed in its duty of care to YZ, nor any public commitment to improve its processes in future. The newspaper's refusal to acknowledge that it lost the appeal suggests it did not accept the court's decision but the spokesperson did not say that, nor did the newspaper appeal the decision further. No representative of the newspaper contacted YZ after the case to apologise to her, although 'plenty of colleagues I worked with got in touch after reading the county court decision to express their disgust at the way I'd been treated' (see Yates 2020). Further, the newspaper's lawyers had subpoenaed YZ's Employee Assistance Programme counselling records to use in their cross-examination of her even though '*Age* management had constantly assured staff [they] were completely confidential sessions' (ibid). If the case had involved another company, other than *The Age*, it may well have found itself featured in the newspaper itself. However, the company acted to protect its commercial interests rather than uphold its masthead values of being 'Independent. Always'. It is possible that inside *The Age* the implications of the court judgements have been digested and programmes to support journalists improved. It is also possible other media organisations are improving their employee wellbeing programmes but at the time of writing this paper there has been no public evidence of this. Even assuming there was the will to do so, it is highly unlikely substantial resources would be devoted to employee wellbeing and training because of the threat posed to the viability of the media's business model by the global digital behemoths Google and Facebook (Australian Competition and Consumer Commission 2019). Therefore, news organisations leave themselves open to further action from traumatised staff.

If putting the media companies on notice is the most important implication of the judgements in the YZ case, there are other less obvious implications that merit discussion. First, the two judgements delineate more clearly what kind of reporting work is most likely to damage a journalist's mental health. In the AZ case, Justice McMillan was not satisfied the photographer had been exposed to sufficient traumatic events to significantly increase the likelihood of psychological injury. It is possible to agree in general with that finding while noting the judge did not appreciate the extent to which general photographers (such as AZ), as distinct from war photographers, are exposed to traumatic events. Even more than journalists, photographers are first responders who must be on the scene of an event to do their job. Journalists may well be on the scene but can gather news in a range of ways, including by phone, email and, sometimes in a war zone, from a hotel room (Anderson and Young 2016). In the YZ case, Justice O'Neill, in contrast to Justice McMillan, was more willing to accept the potential for psychological injury created by reporting traumatic events. As mentioned earlier, he found YZ's testimony about her experience 'chilling'. It is certainly clear cut that YZ was exposed regularly to traumatic events as she reported on crime between 2003 and 2009 and that was her primary role; AZ, on the other hand, was exposed to traumatic events amid a wide range of photographic duties. Does that mean she was not exposed to enough traumatic events to damage her psychologically? That is a fine judgement and depends on other elements which we will come to.

Before that, it needs to be noted the Supreme Court of Appeal judges acknowledged YZ had been exposed to a substantial amount and level of traumatic events but they were not persuaded *The Age* had breached its duty of care in the 2003 to 2009 period. After she complained about being done with 'death and destruction' and was assigned against her wishes to court reporting, the risk of psychological injury was foreseeable and the newspaper had breached its duty of care. As the appeal court judges put it: 'The issue became whether to transfer an employee to a traumatic environment, rather than a failure to transfer an employee *away* from a traumatic environment' (The Age Company Limited v. YZ (a pseudonym) (2019) VSCA 313 at 48, emphasis added). A clear implication of this for journalists is that their legal standing is bolstered once they express their concerns clearly to their editors and direct line managers. The problem is the culture in newsrooms which mitigates against journalists speaking freely about their experience of work, especially their emotional experience, as was acknowledged in both the trial judgement and the appeal (YZ (a pseudonym) v. The Age Company Limited (2019) VCC 148 at 62-63; The Age Company Limited v. YZ (a pseudonym) (2019) VSCA 313 at 49) from the testimony of two journalists as well as YZ. Liz Minchin needed to take a period of leave because her mental health was suffering at work but found few in the newsroom willing or able to discuss 'depression and anxiety' (YZ (a pseudonym) v. The Age Company Limited (2019) VCC 148 at 52), while it took six months for the news desk to act on concerns raised by Adrian Lowe about difficulties he experienced covering courts (YZ (a pseudonym) v. The Age Company Limited (2019) VCC 148 at 46).

What is alarming about the court's finding about the newsroom's culture is that it concerns a newspaper long regarded as committed to high-quality journalism (Nolan 2014: 12-14). Moreover, the events occurred in the last decade rather than in the distant past when young journalists were routinely sent out to do intrusive interviews with grieving relatives as a way of 'blooding' them (Oakham 2004). Equally alarming is evidence of the extent to which these attitudes still held sway in contemporary newsrooms. YZ testified that as a crime reporter she worked in a 'blokey environment' where the implicit message was to 'toughen up, princess' rather than to express any qualms or seek help (YZ (a pseudonym) v. The Age Company Limited (2019) VCC 148 at 42).

In this context, it is worth noting that when YZ returned to the newsroom after attending the scene of Darcey Freeman's murder – a day that she later described as the worst of her life – she still managed to finish and file her story for the paper (YZ (a pseudonym) v. The Age Company Limited (2019) VCC 148 at 12). When a colleague of YZ, Lara O'Toole, confronted the deputy editor, Mark Baker, about YZ's difficulties she testified that he was unsympathetic, saying journalists are 'meant to be tough and hardy' (YZ (a pseudonym) v. The Age Company Limited (2019) VCC 148 at 52). An inability to reflect on the impact of covering traumatic events was also exhibited in the newsroom. YZ testified that after she wrote a feature article for the newspaper's weekend edition about Arthur Freeman's murder trial, the editor of *The Saturday Age*, Steve Foley, told her he was not going to publish it because he could no longer read anything about this 'awful' trial, to which she replied: 'Well, try sitting through every single day of the trial having covered it [Darcey's murder] when it happened' (YZ (a pseudonym) v. The Age Company Limited (2019) VCC 148 at 47).

Coming back to the point raised earlier about other elements that come into play when assessing the impact of covering traumatic events, not all journalists are the same, either by temperament or background. Some journalists are untroubled by reporting traumatic events while others may be distressed by what they witness but are resilient and able to continue such work. Dr Cait McMahon, then managing director of the Dart Center Asia Pacific, provided expert evidence at both the AZ and YZ trials. The likelihood that journalists could do the important work of reporting traumatic events was increased significantly, she testified, when news organisations had in place well-resourced programmes to prepare journalists beforehand, to support them while on assignment and to help them debrief afterwards (The Age Company Limited v. YZ (a pseudonym) (2019) VSCA 313 at 25-26). That said, some journalists may struggle when exposed to traumatic events, because of mental health issues experienced earlier in life or in the present day. Historically, the law in this area has struggled to account for the difference between physical and mental injuries in the workplace and to find a balance between safeguarding an employee's privacy and protecting them from psychological injury, as was evident in Justice McMillan's judgement in the AZ case (Ricketson 2017: 185). In the Supreme Court appeal judgement for the YZ case, the judges revisited the 2016 case of State of New South Wales v. Briggs that concerned a police officer who sued his employer for negligence over occupational PTSD caused by his witnessing of traumatic events. The police officer was successful in his claim but lost the case on appeal. One of the appeal court judges, Justice Ruth McColl, accepted that issues of an employee's privacy and autonomy were important but 'so too is the proper discharge of an employer's duty to avoid foreseeable harm' (The Age Company Limited v. YZ (a pseudonym) (2019) VSCA 313 at 34). She continued:

> The solicitude the 'employer' must exhibit concerns an actual, or potential workplace injury. The fact that it entails a worker's mental health does not immunise it from the employer's responsibility to discharge the relevant duty of care. Nor, with respect, should it be characterised as an intrusion into an employee's private life (The Age Company Limited v. YZ (a pseudonym) (2019) VSCA 313 at 34).

Having made these points, Justice McColl agreed with the decision of the other two appeal court judges to uphold the state of New South Wales' appeal.

CONCLUSION

The decision in the case of YZ v. *The Age* to award damages to journalist YZ for suffering occupational PTSD is important for a number of reasons: it is the first of its kind in Australia and could have implications for employers not just in Australia but in other countries with similar legal systems. Whether the YZ case opens the door for similar cases brought by journalists at other news media outlets remains to be seen just as it is not clear yet whether media companies have been jolted into improving their training and support programmes or whether most companies' financial difficulties, aggravated by the impact of Covid-19 in 2020 and beyond, will constrain their ability to improve such programmes.

What is most important from this case is that media companies and their journalists are now in no doubt that they must adopt a multi-faceted approach to psychological well-being of all who work in the news space including, but not only, the journalists, photographers, editors and online comment moderators.

News outlets must firstly acknowledge the need and value of reporting on trauma-including events such as disasters, crime, grief and the like; second, that witnessing traumatic events does have psychological consequences on journalists; third that any impact will intensify if journalists and managers try to ignore it; fourth that journalism educators have a key role to play in preparing a new generation of trauma-informed journalists who are open to peer support; and, fifth, that most journalists are resilient.

The importance of educators in this space is increasingly being recognised with scholars noting the need to ensure journalism graduates not only have the news skills when entering the profession but also the skills to manage trauma (Hill 2020). The World Journalism Education Congress syndicate on journalism and trauma made three broad recommendations on curriculum when it met in Paris in 2019: 'implement classroom training that incorporates theory and practice; provide essential literature, contacts, networks, and resources to students; and promote normalization of reactions to trauma in journalism work' (Hill 2020: 66-67). Further, a group of 60 international educators have formed a Journalism Education and Trauma Research Group (JETREG) to address what they say is a 'lack of knowledge, lack of resources and lack of reading materials as barriers to inclusion of trauma literacy in journalism curricula' (Ogunyemi 2021).

The literature shows that, with good support systems in place, journalists will successfully absorb the impact of traumatic events and be able, willing even, to continue their work. That's important because we need journalists to do the work that sadly must also expose them to deeply traumatic events such as the aftermath of the 2004 Boxing Day tsunami or clerical child sexual abuse. Sadly, serious, perhaps irrevocable damage has been done to many journalists, including YZ and AZ, but that underscores the importance for media companies to have in place strong systems to support and advise their journalists to do their job – a job that benefits not just the companies but society as well.

ACKNOWLEDGEMENT

The authors would like to acknowledge the advice of Bree Knoester, lawyer for YZ and AZ.

- This paper was first published in *Ethical Space*, Vol. 19, No. 1 pp 39-49, 2022

REFERENCES

American Psychiatric Association (2013) *Diagnostic and statistical manual of mental disorders*, American Psychiatric Publications, fifth edition

Anderson, Fay and Young, Sally with Henningham, Nikki (2016) *Shooting the picture: Press photography in Australia*, Miegunyah Press, Carlton

Aoki, Yuta, Malcolm, Estelle, Yamaguchi, Sosie, Thornicroft, Graham and Henderson, Claire (2013) Mental illness among journalists: A systematic review, *International Journal of Social Psychiatry*, Vol. 59, No. 4 pp 377-390. DOI:10.1177/0020764012437676

Australian Competition and Consumer Commission (ACCC) (2019) *Digital platforms inquiry, final report*, 20 June. Available online at https://www.accc.gov.au/system/files/Digital%20platforms%20inquiry%20-%20final%20report.pdf

AZ (a person under a disability who sues by her litigation guardian BZ) v. *The Age* (2013) VSC 335

Backholm, K. and Björkqvist, K. (2012) The mediating effect of depression between exposure to potentially traumatic events and PTSD in news journalists, *European Journal of Psychotraumatology*, Vol. 3 pp 183-188

Barnes, Lyn (2016) *Journalism and everyday trauma: A grounded theory of the impact from death-knocks and court reporting*, PhD thesis, Auckland University of Technology, Auckland, NZ. Available online at http://aut.researchgateway.ac.nz/handle/10292/10228, accessed on 27 January 2021

Caldwell, Alison (2012) *The Age* sued by traumatised photographer, *PM*, radio programme, Australian Broadcasting Corporation (ABC), 19 November. Available online at http://www.abc.net.au/pm/content/2012/s3636143.htm, accessed on 27 January 2021

Castles, P. (2002) *Who cares for the wounded journalist? A study of the treatment of journalists suffering from exposure to trauma*. Unpublished Master's thesis, Queensland University of Technology, Brisbane

Deery, Shannon (2012) Former *Age* photographer sues over trauma from covering anniversary of Bali bombings, *news.com.au*, 19 November. Available online at https://www.perthnow.com.au/news/nsw/former-age-photographer-sues-over-trauma-from-covering-anniversary-of-bali-bombings-ng-d981cc2e60c00503c64a0 0109090b7e3, accessed on 27 January 2021

Derienzo, M. (2016) Trauma journalism, *Editor & Publisher*, Vol. 149, No. 10 pp 22-23

Dorfman, William. I. (2007) *First responder's guide to abnormal psychology applications for police, firefighters and rescue personnel*, New York, Springer US

Dworznik, G. (2011) Factors contributing to PTSD and compassion fatigue in television news workers, *International Journal of Business, Humanities and Technology*, Vol. 1, No. 1 pp 22-32

Edraki, Farz and Carrick, Damien (2019) Trauma of news journalism in focus after *The Age* found responsible for reporter's PTSD, *The Law Report*, radio programme, Australian Broadcasting Corporation (ABC), 22 March. Available online at https://www.abc.net.au/news/2019-03-22/ex-age-journalist-awarded-damages-for-ptsd-world-first/10896382, accessed on 27 January 2021

Feinstein, Anthony, Audet, Blair and Waknine, Elizabeth (2014) Witnessing images of extreme violence: A psychological study of journalists in the newsroom, *Journal of the Royal Society of Medicine*, Vol. 5, No. 8 pp 1-7

Hatanaka, Miho, Matsui, Yutaka, Ando, Kiyoshi, Inoue, Kako, Fukuoka, Yoshiharu, Koshiro, Eiko and Itamura, Hidenori (2010) Traumatic stress in Japanese broadcast journalists, *Journal of Traumatic Stress*, Vol. 23, No. 1 pp 173-177

Herman, Judith (1992) *Trauma and recovery: The aftermath of violence – from domestic abuse to political terror*, New York, Basic Books

Hill, Desiree, Luther, Catherine A. and Slocum, Phyllis (2020) Preparing future journalists for trauma on the job, *Journalism & Mass Communication Educator*, Vol. 75, No 1 pp 64-68. Available online at https://doi.org/10.1177/1077695819900735

Levy, Steven (2020) *Facebook: The inside story*, London, Penguin

Lyall, Kimina (2012) Covering traumatic events without traumatising yourself or others, Ricketson, Matthew (ed.) *Australian Journalism Today*, South Yarra, Palgrave Macmillan pp 28-44

McMahon, Cait (2016) *An investigation into post-traumatic stress and post-traumatic growth among trauma reporting Australian journalists*, PhD thesis, Swinburne University, Melbourne, Australia

Marantz, Andrew (2020) Explicit content: Facebook's failure to control toxic speech, *New Yorker*, 19 October pp 20-27

Miller, Edward (2003) *Emergency broadcasting and 1930s American radio*, Philadelphia, Temple University Press

National Geographic (2015) Hindenburg disaster: Emotional reporter reacts in real time, *nationalgeographic.com*, 27 September. Available online at https://video.nationalgeographic.com/video/news/00000150-0641-dd38-ab58-ff45504a0000#:~:text=Modern%20History-,Sept.,with%2097%20people%20on%20board, accessed on 27 January 2021

Newman, Elana, Simpson, R. and Handschuh, D. (2003) Trauma exposure and post-traumatic stress disorder among photojournalists, *Visual Communication Quarterly*, Vol. 58, No. 1 pp 4-13

Newton, Casey (2020) Facebook will pay $52 million in settlement with moderators who developed PTSD on the job, *Verge*, 12 May. Available online at https://www.theverge.com/2020/5/12/21255870/facebook-content-moderator-settlement-scola-ptsd-mental-health, accessed on 27 January 2021

Nolan, Sybil (2014) *The Age*, Griffen-Foley, Bridget (ed.) *A Companion to the Australian media*, Australian Scholarly Publishing, North Melbourne pp 12-14

Oakham, Katrina Mandy (2004) *Was there too much blood kid? Cadet journalists in Australian media*, PhD thesis, Deakin University, Melbourne, Australia

Ogunyemi, Ola (2021) Safe space for journalists and journalism educators to talk about trauma. Available online at https://staffnews.lincoln.ac.uk/2021/11/30/safe-space-for-journalists-and-journalism-educators-to-talk-about-trauma/

Pyevich, C., Newman, E. and Daleiden, E. (2003) The relationship among cognitive schemas, job-related traumatic exposure, and post-traumatic stress disorder in journalists, *Journal of Traumatic Stress*, Vol. 16, No. 4 pp 325-328

Quitangon, Gertie and Evces, Mark R. (2016) *Vicarious trauma and disaster mental health: Understanding risks and promoting resilience*, New York, New York, Routledge

Ricketson, Matthew (2017) Taking journalism and trauma seriously: The importance of the AZ case, *Australian Journalism Review*, Vol. 39, No. 2 pp 177-189

Ricketson, Matthew and Wake, Alexandra (2019) Media companies on notice over traumatised journalists after landmark court decision', *Conversation*, 6 March. Available online at https://theconversation.com/media-companies-on-notice-over-traumatised-journalists-after-landmark-court-decision-112766, accessed on 27 January 2021

Shafer, Jack (2010) Who said it first? Journalism is the 'first rough draft of history', *Slate*, 30 August. Available online at https://slate.com/news-and-politics/2010/08/on-the-trail-of-the-question-who-first-said-or-wrote-that-journalism-is-the-first-rough-draft-of-history.html, accessed on 27 January 2021

Smith, Rohan (2019) *The Age* journalist paid $180,000 compensation after 10-year service on Melbourne crime desk, *news.com.au*, 6 March. Available online at https://www.news.com.au/national/victoria/crime/the-age-journalist-paid-180000-compensation-after-10year-service-on-melbourne-crime-desk/news-story/0feaec242a01b104f5c1a0751ef0d3fa, accessed on 27 January 2021

The Age Company Limited v. YZ (a pseudonym) (2019) VSCA 313

Wake, Alexandra (2016) Distant, disconnected and in danger: Are educators doing enough to prepare students for frontline freelance risks?, *Pacific Journalism Review*, Vol. 22 pp 52-73

Watkins, Emily (2019) 'Psychologically scarred': *Age* crime reporter wins $180,000 for workplace trauma, *Crikey*, 10 April. Available online at https://www.crikey.com.au/2019/02/27/psychologically-scarred-the-age-crime-reporter-wins-180000-for-reporting-trauma/, accessed on 27 January 2021

Weidmann, Anke, Fehm, Lydia and Fydrich, Thomas (2008) Covering the tsunami disaster: Subsequent post-traumatic and depressive symptoms and associated social factors, *Stress and Health*, Vol. 24 pp 129-35

Weidmann, Anke and Papsdorf, Jenny (2010) Witnessing trauma in the newsroom: Post-traumatic symptoms in television journalists exposed to violent news clips, *The Journal of Nervous & Mental Disease*, Vol. 198 pp 264-271. Available online at https://doi.or/0.109/MD.0b013e3181d612bf

Wikipedia (2020) Herbert Morrison. Available online at https://en.wikipedia.org/wiki/Herbert_Morrison_(journalist)#:~:text=Herbert%20Oglevee%20%22Herb%22%20Morrison%20(,%2C%201937%2C%20killing%2036%20people, accessed on 26 November 2020

Yates, Dean (2020) Inside story: How *The Age* dragged a traumatised reporter through the courts, *Crikey*, 4 September. Available online at https://www.crikey.com.au/2020/09/04/the-age-workers-compensation-trauma/, accessed on 27 January 2021

YZ (a pseudonym) v. The Age Company Limited (2019) VCC 148. Available online at http://www.austlii.edu.au/cgi-bin/sign.cgi/au/cases/vic/VCC/2019/148, accessed on 22 January 2021s

NOTE ON THE CONTRIBUTORS

Alexandra Wake is an Associate Professor in Journalism at RMIT University in Melbourne, Australia. She is an active leader, educator and researcher in journalism. Her work sits at the nexus of journalism practice, journalism education, equality, diversity and mental health. Dr Wake has taught journalism at RMIT, Deakin University, Dubai Women's College, and was a trainer on international aid projects including at the South African Broadcasting Corporation. Dr Wake has been an education advisor for Mindframe for Journalists since 2012 and was a Dart Center for Journalism and Trauma Academic Fellow in 2011. She is also part of the Journalism Education and Trauma Research Group (JETREG) based at the University of Lincoln, UK, and the team of researchers in the International UNESCO UniTWIN Network on Gender, Media and ICTs promoting and developing international co-participative projects together with the National Autonomous University of Mexico.

Matthew Ricketson is an academic and journalist. He is a Professor of Communication at Deakin University in Melbourne, Australia. Before that he was inaugural Professor of Journalism at the University of Canberra between 2009 and 2017. He ran the Journalism programme at RMIT for 11 years. He has worked on staff at *The Age*, *The Australian* and *Time Australia* magazine, among other publications. He is the author or co-author of four books and editor or co-editor of three more. He has been a chief investigator on three Australian Research Council-funded projects about the media and journalism. Between 2012 and 2019 he was chair of the board of directors for the Dart Centre Asia-Pacific.

Chapter 10

Ethics and journalism in Brazil: A study of local journalism through the Brazilian News Atlas

Marcelo Fontoura and Sérgio Lüdtke

This paper addresses the relation between news deserts and ethics in the ecosystem of Brazilian news. For that, we first analyse specific historical factors of Brazilian journalism in terms of ethics, employing ideas from Bucci (2000), Seligman (2009) and Christofoletti (2018). The research is done empirically by a description and analysis of the Brazilian News Atlas, a crowdsourcing, non-profit initiative designed to map local journalism initiatives and news deserts in Brazil. The paper describes the latest data from the Atlas about news deserts, as well as complementary research from the project, to better understand the limitations and challenges to local outlets. We conclude that news deserts are endemic in Brazil and while a recent increase in digital outlets may change this scenario, the over-reliance on advertising as a source of revenue poses challenges to a journalism ecosystem already historically damaged by ethical issues.

Keywords: local journalism, News Atlas (Atlas da Notícia), Brazilian journalism, ethics

INTRODUCTION: THE BRAZILIAN NEWS ATLAS AND ITS CONTEXT

An annual census carried out in Brazil by Instituto para o Desenvolvimento do Jornalismo – Projor (Institute for the Development of Journalism) has shown over the past four years the precariousness of journalistic activity in the country. Atlas da Notícia, or the Brazilian News Atlas (https://www.atlas.jor.br/english/), has demonstrated in its first four editions a picture of the difficulty in financing organisations that produce local journalism, which culminated in the closing of activities of hundreds of traditional newsrooms in the country. For the purposes of this paper, the project will henceforth be referred to simply as Atlas.

The Atlas showed that six out of every 10 Brazilian municipalities were news deserts, that is, places where people do not have journalistic information about where they live. The weak presence of journalism – or its absence – could do little to prevent the sudden deterioration of the informational environment taken over by misinformation during the 2018 presidential elections and beyond. That was the environment when the Covid-19 pandemic arrived in the country. But the most recent census, published nearly a year after the first Covid-19 cases appeared in Brazil, unveiled a surprising picture. Although traditional newsrooms continued to close their doors, many others emerged in the digital environment, taking advantage of the lack of entry barriers to the online business and the growing demand for reliable information about the health crisis. The interest in quality information, at a time when the pandemic was captured by politics and the informational environment was contaminated by misinformation, gave a new breath to journalism.

Although the pandemic has worsened the situation for local media companies, the health crisis has shown that connecting with audiences is a path to find economic sustainability. This commitment to audiences, which is now being strengthened, can guarantee journalistic performance based on ethical and transparent editorial guidelines designed to oversee the government and bring quality information for citizens everywhere in the country.

This paper analyses the scenario of local journalism in Brazil through the lenses of the Brazilian News Atlas. For that, it encompasses a discussion on recurring ethical issues in Brazilian journalism, with ideas from Bucci (2000), Seligman (2009) and Christofoletti (2018), among others. Then, it describes the history and methodology of the Atlas, as well as its latest results, in order to understand the current ecosystem of local journalism in Brazil and its challenges. Mainly, we have identified that news deserts are endemic in the country, and that an over-reliance on classical revenue models poses ethical challenges.

ETHICS IN BRAZILIAN JOURNALISM: A BRIEF OVERVIEW

As a country with a large area of countryside but developed cities closer to the coast, Brazil has a difficult geography for local journalism. Beyond the usual challenges for news production in the 21st century, such as monetisation, new platforms and active audience behaviours, local Brazilian news production suffers with the control of local authorities and has not been able to make other financial avenues, beyond advertising, viable. Connected to this, ethical issues have become a major point of concern. Christofoletti (2019: 92) argues that a new ethics of journalism may not save the profession from its crisis, but could 'remove the edges of the commitments it intends to maintain with society'. That is, working towards a more ethical exercise of journalism would make clearer its purpose for society, which is especially important amid a convergence of crises for the profession. However, one should not understand ethics monolithically nor on a specifically local basis. Rather, it combines global references with local adaptations. Wasserman (2011: 801) refers to the African context:

Furthermore, the negotiation of ethical frameworks takes place not only internally in African countries but is also linked to cultural flows and contraflows between Africa and the rest of the world in a globalized media landscape. Influences from Northern media ethics are adopted, adapted and resisted in local contexts, and take on new social and political meanings.

Similarly, Wasserman and Rao (2008) discuss a trend of 'glocalization' of the journalistic ethos, or the adaptation of global trends with local emphasis.

At the turn of the century, journalism in Brazil had to navigate a context of freedom and new challenges. After a violent and repressive military dictatorship that lasted 20 years and finished in 1985, journalists and outlets had to deal with the long-sought freedom to report. This freedom was accompanied by developments in professionalisation and improvements in technical infrastructure. In the next 10 years, the rise of the web would pose another challenge to this fast-developing journalism. Overall, Brazilian society had to adapt quickly to a context of democracy and representation (Christofoletti 2008). However, this period was also marked by major ethical faults by Globo, the country's leading broadcaster (Bucci 2000). These included ignoring pro-democracy demonstrations, as well as openly supporting candidate Fernando Collor for presidency, since he would promote policies favoured by Globo, thereby going against the principle of broadcaster impartiality. Thus, the industry was facing a period that combined both freedom and ethical challenges. In fact, the very discourse of freedom of the press may serve to conceal ethical faults (Seligman 2009), when it shields journalists from critiques, by casting its critics as pro-censorship.

Another specific issue regarding professionalisation of newspeople in Brazil is the fact that, for several decades, being a journalist required a specific licence, through an undergraduate degree in journalism. Such restriction was removed by a decision from the Supreme Court in 2009, but has provided an enduring self-image of professionalism among journalists in the country, although this requirement has not always been enforced, especially in distant cities (Nascimento 2011).

It was 1988, when the country was in the midst of approving a new constitution, after the totalitarian period, when the journalist and academic Perseu Abramo (2016) wrote a typology of manipulations of the Brazilian press. It was developed specifically with the Brazilian context in mind, and can still be observed today, representing a valuable summary of the ethical issues that affect Brazilian journalism to this day (Christofoletti 2018). They are:

1) concealment pattern – when outlets choose not to cover a given topic, effectively silencing it from the public sphere;

2) fragmentation pattern – when outlets disconnect a fact from its consequence;

3) inversion pattern – when aspects of a news report are inverted, thus changing their interpretation. May also mean to invert opinion and fact;

4) induction pattern – when the media, reporting on an issue, creates and insists on a certain social context, where it is difficult for the audience to escape this interpretation. The media, thus, induces an interpretative framework on the audience;

5) global pattern – specific to broadcasters. Refers to the structure of news reports and their tendency of searching for answers to social problems by listening to an authority.

For the scope of this paper, the first four are the most important ones, since they evoke steps of both planning and producing journalism, and are more widely observable. Christofoletti (2018), noting their enduring usefulness, adds three other types of manipulation: softening – strategies to soften the impact of facts and declaration, with flexible, moderate language; blanketing – when outlets conceal specific details on a report; and shuffling – narrative or aesthetic strategies that confound the understanding of the issues at play.

This typology demonstrates that ethical issues are frequent and diverse in Brazilian journalism, notwithstanding the professionalisation process the industry experienced in the last decades. At the same time, those issues are diverse and can happen at different stages of the journalistic process, both from economic and political biases. 'Structural aspects, such as market concentration, cross-ownership and electronic coronelismo,[1] are decisive not only in the production of informative content, but also in distribution, balance, plurality and diversity' (ibid: 78). Indeed, a strong market concentration and a lack of professional regulatory boards are major historical factors in the ethical issues affecting Brazilian journalism (Lelo 2020), which limit the ability of individual journalists to resist unethical demands by bosses and companies. In the countryside, where overall conditions are worse and economic interference in journalism is greater, this context is intensified.

Another frequent mark of the ethical faults of local journalism is the constant use of sensationalism as a strategy for gathering readership (Seligman 2009). This happens with the use of suggestive pictures, *double entendres* and the exploration of tragedy – usually city crime and traffic accidents. One major example was the popular newspaper *Notícias Populares*, from São Paulo, which in the 1970s and 1980s reached a circulation of 180,000 copies daily, and became infamous for inventing stories (ibid). However, Seligman (ibid) points to a trend of local papers to divert from crime and violence to provide service to the audience regarding local issues.

Although journalistic companies emphasise ethics as being a challenge that can be met by hiring ethical, upright professionals, Bucci (2000) captures the importance of scaling this discussion to the company level as well. Journalistic ethics should be tied not only to the individuals and their mistakes, but to the actions of the news organisations involved. At least, the audience seems to have followed this interpretation. As Mick (2019) demonstrated, there are two parallel trends occurring in terms of trust and media in the country: on the one hand, a decrease in overall trust in media outlets and, on the other hand, an increase in trust in individual journalists. The author suggests that an explanation can be found in a distrust of the owners of media outlets, as well as of the advertisers and the relation between the two groups. Journalists, however, are seen as 'experts' who are 'fundamental for the social, contemporary experience' (ibid: 257), acting under the constraints of power structures and everyday work. This reading will be further complicated in a media ecosystem where journalists launch their own initiatives, being both owner and news professionals, a trend identified by the Atlas.

Thus, media ethics, especially in small towns in Brazil, tends to be touted by companies as a strong value, being bound to the traditional notions of journalism. However, practice tends to be influenced by resources and professional and audience restrictions. In order to better understand the distribution and characteristics of local media in Brazil, we must now turn to the aspects of the Brazilian News Atlas.

THE BRAZILIAN NEWS ATLAS AND ITS METHODOLOGY

This section highlights the inception of the Brazilian News Atlas, as well as the methodology employed to execute the mapping. The main inspiration for the Atlas was the project on America's growing news deserts, in the *Columbia Journalism Review*.[2] The American project, done in 2017, proved a useful way to highlight a widespread problem that was easily forgotten in big metropolitan areas: most cities do not have local, journalistic coverage of what happens there. This trend seemed even bigger in a developing country such as Brazil, with higher poverty and a potentially tougher scenario for local newsrooms. Then, Projor decided to create a similar project, adapting it to the local context of Brazil. Since its inception, the Atlas has been supported by a fellowship from Facebook, also receiving institutional support from Abraji, the Brazilian Association for Investigative Journalism. So far, the Atlas[3] has had four editions, being updated annually since the initial edition in 2017. Usually this involves adding more data for outlets that are in the mapping, marking the ones that have closed, and adding more outlets. During the writing of this paper, the fifth edition was in the making. The technical development of the platform is done by the consultancy Volt Data Lab, and is licensed under a Creative Commons licence. The Atlas has been used as source by several academic studies, including Serpa et al. (2019), which uses the Atlas to describe and analyse new business models, Da Silva Deolindo (2018), which studies news deserts and how people in them access information, and Reis (2018), which maps and analyses news production in medium-sized towns in Northern Brazil.

Given that Brazil is the fifth largest country in the world, a mapping that intends to cover all its territory involves difficulties and choices. As such, the methodology was adapted to fit a context of a large country, with a rural, developing countryside, and where ethical perspectives in journalism are blurred.

Brazil is divided administratively into five regions – North, Northeast, Central-West, Southeast and South – made up of 26 states, plus the Federal District. The number of states per region varies from three to nine. Every region has a research coordinator on Atlas, who has experience as a journalist, and frequently a graduate degree in the area. Those professionals are responsible for gathering volunteers, guiding them and overseeing the submission process.

The first edition of the project was based on lists of outlets from industry organisations, government press offices and similar departments. This allowed for the construction of a beta mapping that could be updated later on. Currently, the Atlas works mainly via crowdsourcing. Local teams of volunteers are organised to do the basic aspects of identifying outlets and submitting them to the platform. Usually, teams of volunteers are created through contact with local schools of journalism, where undergraduate students have an incentive to learn more about the ecosystem of local news that surrounds them, in their cities and nearby regions. If students are in low numbers other volunteers may be sought, for instance among journalists. Overall, the local teams are responsible for a given region or set of towns and are tasked with three main activities:

- identifying new outlets that are still not on Atlas, whether because they were created recently or because they were not mapped before;
- identifying outlets that have closed (especially common with print papers);
- adding more details to outlets already on Atlas;
- reviewing regions of news deserts, to check if they are indeed still deserts.

This division of tasks ensures that the mapping remains relevant and is the reason why the project is updated annually.

The very nature of the Atlas brings about the question of what counts as a news outlet. Indeed, during the course of the project, this issue proved to be a point of debate, although a stable idea was agreed upon. The working definition of a news outlet, for the Atlas, is a publication of socially relevant, recent, original and journalistic content. Thus, the outlet needs to have been updated in the last month, and needs to publish original content (even if just partially), so outlets that just republish information are not counted. In addition, the Atlas does not count initiatives that are part of an institution, such as a paper from a church, a union, or an organisation, since those are not considered as independent. Those initiatives may be added via the submission form, but are checked as 'non-journalistic'. All

Atlas's calculations regarding news deserts and the distribution of outlets are done based on the number of journalistic initiatives. Radio and TV stations are added via a general list, from a freedom of information request, since every broadcaster in the country needs to have an authorisation from the government.

One important point regarding the methodology is the division of outlets by media. An outlet may be marked as print, online, TV or radio (exclusive choice). However, in the case of a print newspaper with a webpage, it is counted as two separate outlets: a print one and an online one. In this fashion, if a print newspaper closes, but continues its online counterpart – a common scenario – the print entry in Atlas is checked as closed, but the online entry stays the same. The same goes for radio and TV stations. Podcasts, online radio stations and YouTube channels are interpreted as online. All the definitions were discussed and agreed upon among the team at the beginning of the project.

All submissions to the Atlas database are made through an online form,[4] which has fields involving general aspects of the outlet, their business model, journalistic aspects used (such as opinion pieces, blogs, newsletter, data journalism etc), frequency of publication, ownership, staff size and social network links. Most of the fields, however, are non-mandatory, since this information can be hard to come by, especially in deep corners of the country. All submissions from each region are reviewed and approved/complemented by the researcher responsible, in order to ensure standardisation and quality. The next section reviews the distribution of news deserts in the country according to the Atlas's data.

NEWS DESERTS ACROSS BRAZIL

Brazil is the fifth largest country in the world, with a territorial extent of more than 8.5 million square kilometers, an area equivalent to 86 per cent of the territory of the United States. This vast territory is divided into 5,570 municipalities distributed in the five major regions mentioned above. Brazil is also the sixth most populous country in the world, with an estimated population of 213 million inhabitants (IBGE 2021). Almost 70 per cent of this population is concentrated in the south-east and north-east regions.

Brazilian geography is fundamental to understanding the presence of local journalism in the country. The news deserts, mapped annually by the Atlas da Notícia, are six in every ten Brazilian municipalities, but affect around 16 per cent of the total population. According to the survey, around 34 million Brazilians do not have journalistic information about where they live. Currently, 3,280 Brazilian municipalities have no record of any journalistic means of communication to produce and disseminate local information. These municipalities have an average of 10,200 inhabitants and are distributed throughout the territory, especially in areas farther away from large centres, such as the Amazon region and the semi-arid region of the north east. Deserts are also found in the interior of the richest states and in municipalities located on the outskirts of large cities, as shown in the map below.

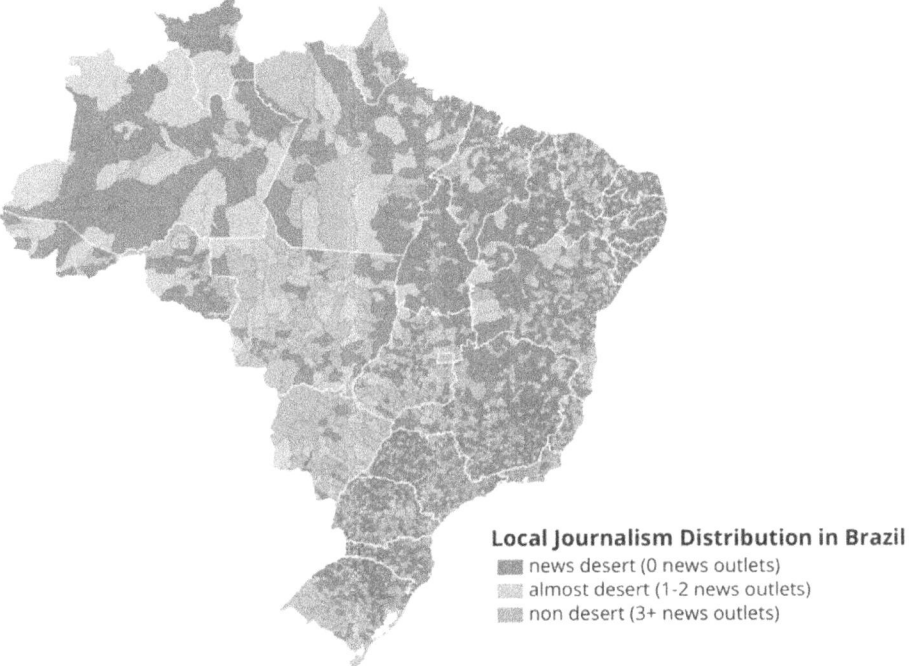

In addition to news deserts and areas irrigated by local information, the Atlas also distinguishes what it has come to call 'almost deserts', places that have only one or two media organisations with local coverage and risk becoming deserts. These semi-deserts are inhabited by another 28.9 million Brazilians. According to the survey, 1,187 municipalities are currently in this condition, which represents two in every ten municipalities in the country.

Geography also partly explains the means used to distribute journalistic content. The Atlas mapped 13,092 active journalistic outlets in 2020. Of these, 4,403, or one-third of the total, are radio stations. Another 4,221 are online newsrooms. Radio stands out in more remote regions, but the preponderance of online initiatives is understandable in the contemporary media ecosystem. The emergence of digital native journalistic initiatives has given new impetus to local journalism. The 2020 census identified a growth in online journalism and incorporated 1,170 new digital native vehicles to the base, most of them in the north-east region of the country. In terms of context, according to the TIC Domicílios[5] survey, 134 million people regularly access the internet in Brazil, which is equivalent to three in every four inhabitants over 10 years old. Brazilians are also heavy users of social networks. According to the Global Web Index 2020 Q2-Q3 study,[6] each person in Brazil spends an average of 3 hours and 42 minutes a day connected to social networks.

The flourishing of digital journalism caused a reduction in 2020 of 5.9 per cent in the number of municipalities considered local news deserts in Brazil, largely offsetting the closure of 272 media outlets, mainly print, also registered by the census. The results of the fourth edition of the Atlas contradicted expectations. Although 2020 was an atypical year, with a series of restrictions imposed by the Covid-19 pandemic, drastic routine changes, the adoption of remote work and a deepening of the economic crisis with an immediate impact on the revenue of the media dependent on advertising, the desire of the population for information prevailed. The 2020 census showed a 10.6 per cent growth in the number of journalistic organisations in the country compared to the previous survey.

The growing participation of digital media in the local information ecosystem and the occupation of old news deserts should, however, be viewed with some caution. If, on the one hand, it is possible to perceive a vitality and renewal of the information environment, with media more diverse and connected to the populations, the Atlas also points to a precarious situation in journalism, with the closure of traditional, larger operations, and the emergence of many individual initiatives, mainly in the form of blogs.

With few barriers for entry, digital entrepreneurship presents itself as a natural path for journalists who leave traditional newsrooms behind. These professionals, who usually bring with them journalistic experience, specialisation in one or more topics, and knowledge of sources and audiences, among other things, are not always qualified for running a business. When they take the path of pursuing the initiative individually without associating with experts or organisations of wider business competencies, this becomes an even greater risk for the initiative's survival. Individual ventures are also in danger when these entrepreneurs' ability to influence is co-opted by politics or even used to serve as a springboard to their owners' own political careers, recalling the ethical constraints mentioned by Christofoletti (2018) and Abramo (2016).

Two lines of action need to be explored by the digital native outlets willing to irrigate news deserts with information. One of them is to espouse and follow the editorial principles and ethical commitments that serve to light the path for the evolution and maturity of the news outlet. The other is to train its actors or seek external competences to strengthen the business aspect of the enterprise and give it the economic independence that will guarantee editorial independence. These two lines must go together. Business model and editorial model must be seen as inseparably linked to each other. The consistency of these two interdependent models lies on the capacity that the new digital vehicles will have to flourish in deserts or to revitalise the ecosystem of already 'forested' areas. The next subsection deals with this debate, addressing the challenges that local media, especially digital native outlets, faced in Brazil during the pandemic.

CHALLENGES FOR THE ECOSYSTEM: REVENUE SOURCES AND AUDIENCE

The Atlas involves a quantitative, broad look at local Brazilian journalistic production. In order to complement this perspective, the team carried out a survey of 179 native digital communication media or those with an online presence. Held in March and April 2021, the objective was to take a closer look at the daily reality of these media outlets and their relationship with the reality of the pandemic.

The Covid-19 pandemic caused significant changes in the ecosystem of local Brazilian journalism. The study's conclusion is that, while the health crisis took journalists off the streets, imposed new routines, reduced advertising revenues and weakened businesses, on the other hand it expanded the reach of the work produced by journalists and their audience, and as such strengthened journalism. During the pandemic, audience and revenue took opposite paths. As local media saw their audience and interest in their content grow, revenue plummeted. With no means to address both fronts, these organisations run the risk of losing the audience and the relevance they have achieved. Instead of investing in maintaining this new audience, they feel the need to pay full attention to the recovery of revenues and find new sources of financing, a fundamental condition for them to continue operating. The chart shows, in the media organisations' view, their priorities for the next 12 months.

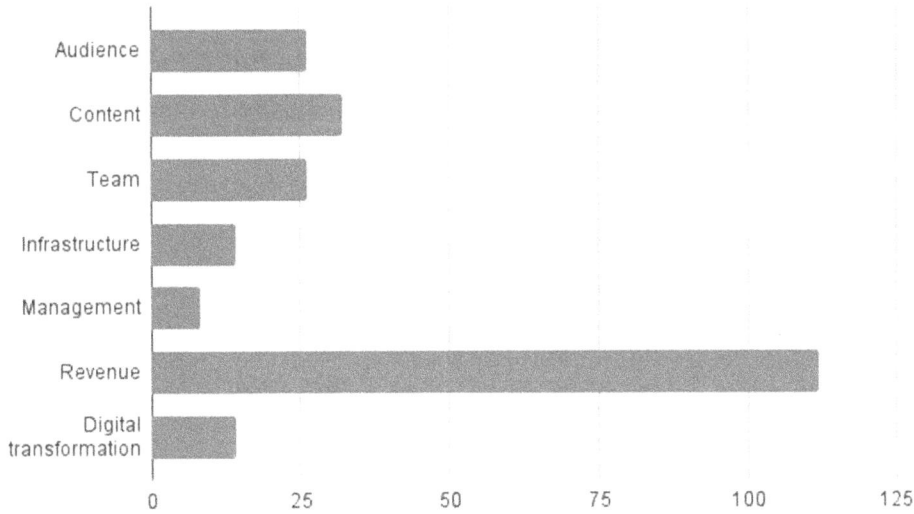

**Priorities for media organisations in the next 12 months.
Source: survey by Atlas (2021). N = 179**

CHANGES AND ACHIEVEMENTS DURING THE PANDEMIC PERIOD

The pandemic encouraged both journalistic activity, with expansion of coverage, and the launch of new outlets. Of the 1,170 new ventures identified by Atlas da Notícia in Brazil in 2020, four responded to the complementary survey. A fifth reopened as print, four years after the print edition stopped. Of the 179 organisations that participated in the survey, 26 per cent expanded editorial coverage during the pandemic. These outlets rushed digital transformation processes that were already underway, reorganised newsrooms, and their teams had to learn to cover science and work remotely. More than half of the initiatives (55.1 per cent) adopted remote work throughout the pandemic period and another 27 per cent only in some periods.

The change in routine forced the learning of new techniques and tools that can continue to be used in the post-pandemic period to improve journalistic work and gain productivity. Remote working is likely to be more common in these organisations in the future. Almost half of the newsrooms that adopted the remote working model admit the possibility of keeping the entire team or part of it remote in the post-pandemic age. A quarter of the outlets intend to return completely to face-to-face activities in the newsroom and another 27 per cent had not yet defined how they would work again after the health crisis. One in five of the newsrooms surveyed reduced the size of teams in 2020, while 8.9 per cent expanded the team of employees and 6.1 per cent of the respondents kept the staff at the same size, but, in order to do so, reduced the coverage of other topics. The remaining 64.8 per cent of the companies kept their editorial and coverage teams unchanged.

What really grew in the pandemic were audience numbers and followers on social media. This finding reinforces the idea that, during this period, the audiences recognised the importance and usefulness of journalistic work, which strengthened the relationship of trust between readers and media.

But, despite this apparently very favourable environment to consolidate these relationships and appeal for the support of this audience, there were few organisations that saw the numbers of paying subscribers and supporters increase.

FINANCING SOURCES

The survey identified 13 revenue sources that give sustainability to local journalism. Of these, three are based on advertising. Ad revenue ranks in the top two positions of the most explored sources. This dependence on advertising explains the financial crisis experienced by many. The temporary closures of trade, the economic crisis and the migration of advertising budgets from advertisers to technology platforms are pointed out by them as the causes of the reduction in revenue.

Source of income	Explored by (companies)
Advertising (other types)	110
Graphic advertising (banners, pop-ups etc.)	83
Partnerships	75
Sponsored content	71
Services provision	61
Native advertising (paid journalistic content)	42
Institutional financing (e.g., Foundations, companies etc.)	27
Direct donations	26
Financing by project	19
Sale of copies	16
Subscription/paywall	15
Crowdfunding	12
Selling reports/content licensing	2

Table 1 - Sources of income of the respondents. Source: survey by Atlas (2021)

All organisations that lost advertising revenue during the health crisis have made it a priority to recover their revenues and return to at least to pre-pandemic levels, but many are sceptical about this possibility. A fact revealed by the research explains this scepticism. Despite advertising being the main source of revenue for the interviewed newsrooms, 61.5 per cent of them no longer have their own structure dedicated to the commercial sector, and 39.5 per cent of those who still have a sales department reduced the number of personnel during the pandemic. Note that the ethical difficulties of Brazilian local journalism, as seen before, are often related to an intense search for revenue. With the Brazilian local press mainly structured around the pillar of advertising, and with that pillar especially susceptible to the pandemic and progressively abandoned as a journalistic subsidy method globally, a remarkable space is opened for a closer relationship between journalism and potential advertisers than between journalism and the public.

The solution may lie in exploring new financing models, taking advantage of the increase in audience that many had during the health crisis. The relationship that has been strengthened between the media and reader communities, and the level of trust that has been established, create favourable conditions for exploring new financing models, with greater support from readers and reducing dependence on funds from advertising.

The urgency for revenue, which emerges in this survey as the main challenge for local journalism in the country, should not hide nor minimise other equally important challenges that are in the path of local journalism, such as improving management, implementing the digital transformation, training qualified professionals, increasing transparency and giving more visibility to the ethical commitments of organisations.

If the search for financing overlaps with the organisation's other challenges, there is a risk of breaking the association between the business model and editorial principles and commitments. Putting all the effort into revenue can create new dependencies that lead newsrooms to destroy a considerable part of the appreciation gained during the pandemic, an especially sensitive period for Brazil and which showed Brazilians that quality information is a valuable service.

FINAL CONSIDERATIONS

As in other places, local journalism in Brazil has experienced two different trends: an increase in audience and relevance of journalism, but a decrease in revenue, associated with a lack of resources to pursue funding. Although they were focusing on digital native outlets, Salaverría et al. (2019) identified that news managers do not usually have experience in business, a very useful skill in such a scenario.

In this paper, we have seen how journalism in Brazil has a history of ethical troubles. We have also detailed the Brazilian News Atlas and how it has identified news deserts across the country.

Although Brazilian journalism has passed through professionalisation, specialisation and improvements in technological aspects, historical factors such as market concentration and political influence facilitate the crossing of ethical limits. Thus, local journalism in Brazil has two challenges to overcome. On one hand, it faces the same financial issues as other parts of industry and, on the other, it still has to tackle the heavy influence of local politics and business. The financial troubles of the industry risk increasing the ethical troubles, since they may encourage newspaper owners to establish even closer ties with potential advertisers. In small towns, where advertising space tends to go to the same companies and to local governments, and where professional culture is weaker, this risk is higher.

This danger may result in a lack of critical coverage, concealment of corruption and self-censorship. News deserts enter as another element of repression, since they represent a decline in places where journalists can exercise their profession. Of course, they also represent opportunities for journalists eager to create their own experiments and serve audiences that are neglected, but there are financial, political and even safety issues. This paper has contributed to the discussion on how the ecosystem of local news in a developing country is faring in a time of change, but more research is needed, especially in the convergence between ethical faults and the reliance on advertising as a main source of revenue.

- This paper was first published in *Ethical Space*, Vol. 18. Nos 3 and 4 pp 71-85, 2021

NOTES

[1] A Brazilian expression, common in politics, denoting a power structure where local figures, especially in the countryside, control local politics, public work and money, usually spanning across generations

[2] https://www.cjr.org/local_news/american-news-deserts-donuts-local.php

[3] https://www.atlas.jor.br/english/

[4] https://www.atlas.jor.br/plataforma/formulario/ (in Portuguese)

[5] https://cetic.br/pesquisa/domicilios/

[6] https://www.gwi.com/hubfs/Downloads/Market%20Snapshot%20Brazil%20 2021%20-%20 GWI.pdf

REFERENCES

Abramo, Perseu (2016) *Padrões de manipulação na grande imprensa* [*Patterns of manipulation in the mainstream press*], São Paulo, Fundação Perseu Abramo

Bucci, Eugênio (2000) *Sobre ética e imprensa* [*On ethics and the press*], São Paulo, Companhia das Letras

Christofoletti, Rogério (2019) *A crise do jornalismo tem solução* [*The crisis in journalism has a solution*], São Paulo, Estação das Letras e Cores

Christofoletti, Rogério (2008) *Ética no jornalismo* [*Ethics in journalism*], São Paulo, Contexto

Christofoletti, Rogério (2018) Padrões de manipulação no jornalismo brasileiro: Fake news e a crítica de Perseu Abramo 30 anos depois [Patterns of manipulation in Brazilian journalism: Fake news and Perseu Abramo's criticism 30 years later], *RuMoRes*, Vol. 12, No. 23 pp 56-82

Da Silva Deolindo, Jacqueline (2018) O deserto da notícia no interior Brasil– apontamentos para uma pesquisa [The news desert in Brazil's interior – research notes], *41º Congresso Brasileiro de Ciências da Comunicação* pp 1-15

IBGE (2021) Populacão [Population], *Instituto Brasileiro de Geografia e Estatística*. Available online at https://www.ibge.gov.br/estatisticas/sociais/populacao.html, accessed on 22 September 2021

Lelo, Thales (2020) O sofrimento ético no mundo do trabalho dos jornalistas [Ethical suffering in the workplace for journalists], *E-Compós*, Vol. 23 pp 1-17

Mick, Jacques (2019) Profissionalismo e confiança: o curioso caso do país que acredita mais nos jornalistas do que na mídia [Professionalism and trust: The curious case of a country that believes more in journalists than in the media], *Política & Sociedade*, Vol. 18, No. 43 pp 242-260

Nascimento, Lerisson (2011) Um diploma em disputa: a obrigatoriedade do diploma em jornalismo no Brasil [A diploma in dispute: The obligation of a diploma in journalism in Brazil]. *Sociedade e Cultura*, Vol. 14, No. 1 pp 141-150

Projor – Instituto para o Desenvolvimento do Jornalismo [Projor – Institute for the Development of Journalism] (2021) *Atlas 4.0*. Available online at: https://www.atlas.jor.br, accessed on 2 December 2021

Reis, Thays (2018) Mapeamento dos serviços de mídia das cidades médias da região norte [Mapping of media services in médium-sized cities in the north region], *41º Congresso Brasileiro de Ciências da Comunicação* pp 1-15

Salaverría, Ramón, Sádaba, Charo, Breiner, James and Warner, Janine (2019) A brave new digital journalism in Latin America, Túñez-López, Miguel, Martínez-Fernández, Valentin-Alejandro, López-García, Xosé, Rúas-Araújo, Xosé, Campos-Freire, Francisco (eds) *Communication: Innovation & Quality*, London, Springer pp 229-247

Seligman, Laura (2009) Jornais populares de qualidade-ética e sensacionalismo em um novo fenômeno no mercado de jornalismo impresso [Popular newspapers of ethical quality and sensationalism in a new phenomenon of the print journalism market], *Brazilian Journalism Research*, Vol. 5, No. 1 pp 1-15

Serpa, Leoni, Weber, Patrícia and Sousa, Jorge Pedro (2019) Cenários e alternativas na viabilidade econômica da atividade jornalística no Brasil [Scenarios and alternatives for the economic viability of journalistic activity in Brazil], *REVISTA ESTUDOS DE JORNALISMO SOPCOM*, No. 10 pp 35-49

Wasserman, Herman (2011) Towards a global journalism ethics via local narratives: Southern African perspectives, *Journalism Studies*, Vol. 12, No. 6 pp 791-803

Wasserman, Herman and Rao, Shakuntala (2008) The glocalization of journalism ethics, *Journalism*, Vol. 9, No. 2 pp 163-181

NOTE ON THE CONTRIBUTORS

Marcelo Fontoura is an adjunct professor of data journalism and disinformation studies at PUCRS. He is a PhD on Social Communication from PUCRS with a dissertation on the impact of the digital transformation on the boundaries of journalism. He also acts as consultant, as researcher for the Brazilian News Atlas, and as assessor for the International Fact Checking Network. He has also worked at the non-profits Meedan and News Product Alliance.

Sérgio Lüdtke is the editor-in-chief of Projeto Comprova, a coalition formed by 41 media outlets that investigates collaboratively misinformation in Brazil. He also coordinates the training area of Abraji (Brazilian Association of Investigative Journalism) and the team of researchers at Atlas da Notícia. He is also president of Projor Institute for Development of Journalism.

SECTION 2

Alternative voices

Chapter 11

When journalism isn't enough: 'Horror surrealism' in Behrouz Boochani's testimonial prison narrative

Willa McDonald

The journalist, filmmaker and author, Behrouz Boochani, has been forcibly detained on Manus Island, Papua New Guinea (PNG), for the past five years at the direction of the Australian government. His prison narrative, No friend but the mountains *(2018), uses prose, poetry, allegory and political theory to depict the conditions the refugees and asylum seekers endure in detention. Described by his translator as 'horrific surrealism' (2018a: xxx, 2018b: 367), it was written on a smuggled smart-phone hidden in Boochani's mattress and sent out bit by bit in text messages via WhatsApp to translators in Australia. Written in Farsi, the language of the oppressors of the Kurds, and translated into English, the language of his jailers, it is a powerful indictment of Australia's immigration policies, particularly as they affect refugees and asylum seekers arriving at Australia's north by boat from Indonesia. This paper examines* No friend but the mountains *as an example of a politically motivated text that functions not only as prison narrative but also as literary memoir and testimonial literature. It is the latest in Boochani's ongoing efforts to witness the experience of imprisonment on Manus Island, while resisting Australian government policy, and calling for the humane treatment of refugees and asylum seekers.*

Keywords: Behrouz Boochani, testimonial prison narrative, *No friend but the mountains*, refugees

INTRODUCTION

The reporting of asylum seeker and refugee issues traditionally has been negative in Australia and is growing increasingly negative over time (Cooper et al. 2017: 78). While migrants have enriched much of contemporary Australian society, racism has played a significant role in Australian immigration history (Jayasuriya, Walker and Gothard 2003; Jupp 2007; Markus 1994; Yarwood and Knowling 1982).

It continues to underpin immigration policy, regardless of the persuasion of the government (Bolger 2016). With the federal government in control of the media narrative, the political rhetoric, particularly since 2001, casts asylum seekers, most pointedly the 'irregular' arrivals coming by boat, as 'illegals' who threaten the social cohesion, affluence and security of the Australian way of life (Cooper et al. 2017: 78). This is despite Australia signing the *Convention Relating to the Status of Refugees 1951.*

Because of Australia's location close to Asia and the Pacific Islands, and the largely unacknowledged ownership of the land by the First Peoples, Australians historically have harboured a deep fear of the alien and foreign 'Other' (Jayasuriya, Walker and Gothard 2003; Jupp 2007; Markus 1994; Yarwood and Knowling 1982). In colonial times, fears of a 'yellow peril' and invasion by 'hordes' from the north dominated Australian thinking, manifesting in the exclusionist White Australia policy that was an important ideological component for the push towards federation and nationhood in 1901 (Griffiths 2006). It was not until after the Second World War and the need for population-driven economic growth that immigration restrictions were relaxed. However, the racially selective White Australia policy continued with successive governments assessing prospective immigrants on their suitability for integrating into Australian society (Bolger 2016).

Despite the move to multiculturalism in 1973, immigration policies continued to conform to a racialised agenda where potential immigrants who were sufficiently 'westernised' and 'white' were welcome and others remained excluded (ibid). This has been underpinned post-9/11 by anti-Muslim fears. While the majority of people who seek protection in Australia arrive through authorised channels and with valid visas, a smaller number arrive by boat from countries such as Iraq, Afghanistan and Sri Lanka without proper travel documents after fleeing persecution, most often at the hands of their own governments (Refugee Council of Australia 2016; Bolger 2016). This latter group is the most affected by the policy of mandatory detention of asylum seekers and refugees. The policy has been a highly contentious issue in Australia for almost twenty years, yet it remains in place despite successive governments of different persuasions. While its purpose is ostensibly administrative – to allow for health and security checks to mitigate risks to the community – it is kept in place as a deterrent to other would-be asylum seekers contemplating similar journeys to Australia.

Information about the conditions in the detention centres is difficult for Australians to come by. Visas are charged at $8000, the cost is non-refundable and they are rarely granted to journalists, preventing reporters from describing conditions first-hand (Jabour and Hurst 2014). While visas to Manus Island are granted or denied by the PNG government, journalists say the responsibility lies with the Australian government (Al Jazeera 2017), which has admitted the denial of visas is one of a number of 'operational disciplines' needed to secure Australia's borders and prevent intelligence being shared with 'people smugglers' (Karp 2016).

The Australian government has also clamped down on whistleblowers. In May 2015, the government passed a law preventing disclosure to the public of 'protected information' by Australian Border Force employees, including medical personnel (Killedar and Harris 2017). A two-year prison sentence was threatened for anyone working in an Australian immigration detention facility, whether on the mainland or offshore, if they disclosed what they saw while working. The secrecy laws were ameliorated in September 2016 when an amendment excluded 'health professionals' from the ban. A year later, the legislation was again changed allowing service workers to speak out as long as the information could not threaten Australia's security (Coady 2017). It remains difficult, however, for service workers and media outlets to assess what the government will regard as threatening to the nation.

To challenge the government's control of the narrative and imposition of secrecy, Behrouz Boochani has been reporting directly from detention, becoming a principal source of information for the media as well as acting as a journalist in his own right. At considerable risk, he witnesses conditions in detention, using social media prolifically and writing for media including the *Huffington Post*, the *Guardian*, the *Sydney Morning Herald*, the *Financial Times* and the *Saturday Paper*. His is also a key source for journalists around the world who are prevented from visiting the offshore detention centres to obtain information. His work has earned him three human rights awards: the Amnesty International Australia 2017 Media Award, the Diaspora Symposium Social Justice Award, and the Liberty Victoria 2018 Empty Chair Award as well as the Anna Politkovskaya Award for journalism. He is non-resident Visiting Scholar at the Sydney Asia Pacific Migration Centre (SAPMiC) at the University of Sydney.

For the first two years he was in detention, Boochani wrote his journalism under a false name for fear of retaliation, using a smuggled smartphone. With the help of Reporters Without Borders and Pen International, he eventually started to use his real name (Hazel 2016). At the same time, he began to realise that the language of journalism was not powerful enough to convey the suffering of the detainees 'and to tell the history of this prison, and what Australian government is doing in this island' (Germian 2017). His translator, Omid Tofighian, quotes him as saying:

> With journalism I have no choice but to use simple language and basic concepts. I need to consider diverse audiences when writing news articles … they're for the general public so it isn't possible to delve as deeply as I would like. And this is the problem right here. I can't analyse and express the extent of the torture in this place… (Tofighian 2018a: xv).

Continuing the tradition of Kurdish resistance, Boochani eschews journalistic and political jargon, refusing to endorse the rhetoric of the Australian government and disdaining such terms as 'border protection', 'Pacific Solution' and 'mandatory detention'. Instead, with the help of Tofighian, he has experimented with language and form, interweaving poetry, memoir, monologues, dreams, political theory and commentary, in the process stretching the boundaries of accepted genres while breaking free from the book's own textual genesis, the restrictions of torture and imprisonment, and the language of Australia's immigration policy. The turn to literature has been liberating. He says that, through literature:

> … I can do whatever I like. I create my own discourse and do not succumb to the language of oppressive power. I create my own language for critically analysing the phenomenon of Manus Prison (Boochani 2018: 367).

His aim in turning to literary memoir is primarily to move 'readers to resist the colonial mindset that is driving Australia's detention regime and to inspire self-reflection, deep investigation and direct action' (Tofighian 2018a: xxxiv). By calling the Manus Island Regional Processing Centre the Manus Prison, he makes clear its purpose as a place of punishment, rather than 'processing'.

> Can it be I sought asylum in Australia only to be exiled to a place I know nothing about? And are they forcing me to live here without any other options? I am prepared to be put on a boat back to Indonesia: I mean the same place I embarked from. But I can't find any answers to these questions. Clearly, they are taking us hostage. We are hostages – we are being made examples to strike fear into others, to scare people so they won't come to Australia. What do other people's plans to come to Australia have to do with me? Why do I have to be punished for what others might do? (Boochani 2018: 107).

As hostages of the government, the men on Manus Island are being mistreated for political purposes.

BEHROUZ BOOCHANI

Born in Ilam, western Iran, in 1983, Behrouz Boochani first wrote journalism for the student newspaper while attending Tarbiat Madares University, from which he graduated with a Master's degree in Political Science, Political Geography and Geopolitics. Later he wrote freelance on Middle East politics and Kurdish culture for the Iranian newspapers *Kasbokar Weekly*, *Qanoon* and *Etemaad* and the Iranian Sports Agency (Zable 2015; Hazel 2016; Pen International 2017). His writing and his membership of the National Union of Kurdish Students and the outlawed Kurdish Democratic Party brought him to the attention of the Islamic Revolutionary Guard Corps, the paramilitary intelligence agency known as Sepah. In 2011, he was arrested, interrogated and forced by Sepah to give an undertaking he would stop writing and teaching Kurdish culture and language.

In 2013, when Boochani was writing for the Kurdish language magazine, *Werya,* Sepah raided the magazine's offices, arresting 11 people and imprisoning six. Boochani was in Tehran at the time of the raid. Having escaped arrest and interrogation, he drew attention to Sepah's actions and the plight of his colleagues by writing about the incident for the website *Iranian Reporters*. Consequently, he was forced into hiding. He fled Iran on 23 May and made his way to Indonesia. From there, he paid people smugglers to join a group of asylum seekers crossing the Arafura Sea to Australia. The boat sank. Rescued by fishermen, he returned to Indonesia where he was jailed. Escaping, he attempted the dangerous sea crossing again and in July, was one of a group of 75 asylum seekers picked up by the Australian Navy. On board, he asked, legally, for asylum under Article 1 of the Refugee Convention (Zable 2015; Hazel 2016; Pen International 2017).

Boochani and his fellow asylum seekers were taken to Christmas Island, one of Australia's external territories, in the Indian Ocean, south of Java, Indonesia. They arrived only days after the Labor government under Julia Gillard decided to transfer all 'boat people' to Manus Island or Nauru, where they would be indefinitely detained (Zable 2017; Davidson 2016). After a month, Boochani was transferred to the men-only detention centre on Manus Island, in Papua New Guinea. The decision by Gillard's government to reintroduce 'offshore processing' after a hiatus of several years was in response to increasing arrivals by boat of asylum seekers with 5,175 arriving in 2011 (Australian Human Rights Commission 2012).

Although the majority of asylum seekers on Manus Island have been found to be refugees (Kenny 2017), they have been told by the Australian government that there is no possibility of their being granted entry visas to Australia. The choices for the 700 men are stark – return to the countries they fled from or remain on the island permanently. The release of the men into the Manusian community is not acceptable to many locals as the small island does not have the economy nor social supports to sustain them (Zable 2015; Hazel 2016; Pen International 2017). Boochani has indicated he cannot return to Iran, which is one of the world's most repressive countries in terms of censorship of the media, as the state controls information and news through the persecution of journalists with intimidation, arrest and jail (Reporters Without Borders n. d.). Boochani, in a 2016 interview with Inter Press Service, says:

> The political situation in Iran does not change especially for Kurdish people. There are about 20 journalists still in prison there. In November, the United Nations General Assembly adopted a resolution against the Iranian regime for violating human rights. Last year they hanged more than 1,000 people. How can I go back? (Hazel 2016).

Australia is repeatedly condemned for its treatment of refugees and asylum seekers by the United Nations Human Rights Council (Doherty 2018; Human Rights Watch 2018). The principle of non-refoulement under the Refugee Convention provides that asylum seekers and refugees cannot be sent to a place where they may be persecuted (Refugee Council of Australia 2016), yet, it is now well-documented that conditions on Manus Island and Nauru (where families with children who have arrived 'irregularly' are detained) have resulted in acts of self-harm including self-immolation, abuse, riots and deaths (Davidson 2016; Doherty 2016; Farrel, Evershed and Davidson 2016). Fifteen people are known to have died in offshore detention on Manus Island, Nauru and Christmas Island. This number includes Reza Barati, the 23-year-old asylum seeker and friend of Boochani who was killed during a riot in February 2014 (Tofhigian 2018a: xii). Although others, including Australians, were also thought to be involved, two Papua New Guineans – a guard and a former worker at the detention centre – were found guilty of his murder (Tlozek 2016).

An enquiry by the Australian Senate into the riot, in which 70 detainees were injured, found the violence was foreseeable and its cause was the failure of the Australian government in its duty to protect the detainees and to process asylum seeker claims (Griffiths 2014). Eighteen months later, the detention centre on Manus Island was closed following an earlier ruling by the PNG Supreme Court that it was unconstitutional. With no option of leaving the island except to return to the countries from which they originally fled, most of the men refused to leave in a stand-off that lasted several weeks. During that time, the power, water and food were shut off. The reasons for the stand-off were the men's fear of increasing violence from the islanders, as well as frustration at the lack of any real solution to their detention (Human Rights Watch 2018). Eventually, the PNG government used force to clear the men out. With Australian reporters mostly excluded from reporting on the incident, Boochani was one of the main sources of information, despite being arrested by PNG security during the forced closure. Since the shutting down of the Manus Island Regional Processing Centre, the men have been resettled in lower-security facilities but are still prevented from leaving the island.

NO FRIEND BUT THE MOUNTAINS

Boochani's book begins with the perilous sea voyage taken by the asylum seekers by leaking fishing boat from Indonesia to Australia. Once picked up by the Australian Navy, they are taken to Christmas Island, where they are subjected to the initiation ritual of being stripped, body-searched and re-clothed.

> A grim-looking officer gives a set of clothes to anyone who passes through the strip-and-search stage, even though the clothes do not match the size of the person in any way whatsoever. There is no choice. We have to wear whatever they issue …. they transform our bodies, they utterly degrade us (Boochani 2018: 85).

Jeff Sparrow (2018), comparing Boochani's text with Alexander Berkman's *Prison memoirs of an anarchist* (1970 [1912]) and Victor Serge's *Men in prison* (1981 [1930]), has noted 'the vignette is immediately recognisable as a key generic element of the prison narrative' in the way the humiliation is designed to strip prisoners not only of their citizenship but also of their dignity and selfhood. Says Boochani: 'No matter who I am, no matter how I think, in these clothes I have been transformed into someone else' (op cit: 97).

It is on Christmas Island that Boochani first befriends Reza Barati, whom he calls 'The Gentle Giant'. They shared sleeping quarters for a month until they were transferred to Manus Island. On Manus, the men – who have fled mountainous landlocked countries with no experience of the sea prior to this journey – are housed 'in a boiling hot and filthy cage, still traumatised by the terrifying sound of waves' (ibid: 126-127). Hoping for fair treatment under the Refugee Convention, they are instead imprisoned indefinitely with repeated statements by successive Australian governments that they will never be settled in Australia. The destruction of hope acts as a form of torture, which is exacerbated by the way power is used by the prison authorities to unsettle and destabilise the detainees through hunger, surveillance and the micro-control of their daily lives.

There is no privacy in the detention centres. The men are constantly watched via CCTV as well as by Australian and Papua New Guinean guards known as Papus. Prison routines are frequently changed, without pattern or reason beyond disorienting the detainees. Food is inadequate and insufficient, as is medical care. Contact with the outside world is restricted; phone calls are limited to three minutes once a week. Toilets overflow and the smell of excrement is overpowering. Games are forbidden, reinforcing the use of boredom as punishment. The generator regularly breaks down increasing tensions. Despite the lack of food, cigarettes are distributed, even to those who don't smoke, and are used as prison currency. The detainees are required to queue for even the most basic requirements including meals, ablutions, washing powder and razors. The queues take on their own agency, encouraging violence by ensuring that the most brutish prisoners are those who dominate the scarce resources to end up with the most comfort. 'The spectacle of the prison queue is a raw and palpable reinforcement of torture' (ibid: 193).

Violence is rife. The guards, trained in prisons on the mainland, treat the detainees as if they are hardened criminals rather than people in need of sanctuary and protection. 'Without question, crime, criminal courts, jail, prison violence, physical violence and knife attacks have become part of their everyday routine and mindset' (ibid: 142). While conflict between the inmates is usually ignored (ibid: 195), the guards frequently intervene to insist that the rules of detention are followed. Describing a scene where the guards enforced the prohibition on games, Boochani says: 'It seemed that was their only duty for the entire day; to shit all over the sanity of the prisoners, who were left just staring at each other in distress' (ibid: 126).

The capricious and callous nature of the detention centre bureaucracy is demonstrated in another scene involving the use of the phones. Referring to a man he calls 'The Father of the Months-Old Child', Boochani describes an instance where the guards refuse him a phone call to speak to his father who is dying on the other side of the world. Repeated requests by the man, with the support of the other prisoners, are rejected. When he is finally allowed to make the call during his officially scheduled turn three days later, he discovers his father has died. Enraged and grief-stricken, he smashes the phones. The guards force him to the ground and then punish him by imprisoning him in Chauka, the secret high-security seclusion cells within the detention centre used to punish troublemakers (ibid: 223-232). The existence of the cells was revealed in Boochani's feature-length documentary film *Chauka, please tell us the time,* shot clandestinely on a contraband smartphone and made with Iranian filmmaker Arash Kamali Sarvestani in the Netherlands. In an act of colonial insensitivity, the cells are named after a bird, native to the island and sacred to the Manusians.

Tofighian points out that Boochani's book intends to 'expose the prison as a neo-colonial experiment' while performing as a 'decolonial intervention' (Tofighian 2018a: xxvi). That colonialism underpins the policy of mandatory detention is a key theme of the text. Says Tofighian:

> I don't think readers can truly appreciate the depth of Behrouz's thought and writing unless they recognise and understand the impact and consequences of colonialism on Kurdistan, Iran, Australia and Manus Island … and also the relationship between coloniality and forced migration (ibid: xxv).

Reflecting the colonialism underpinning the prison structure, the detention system is hierarchical and made up of three tiers: the Australian prison officers at the top, the Papus (locals brought in as guards and service workers) and at the bottom the prisoners. 'The Australians' perspective is a mixture of abhorrence, envy and barbarism…' (Behrouz 2018: 136). The Papus are expected to obey orders and are paid less than the Australians. It creates a fragile alliance between the Papus and the detainees, but the alliance crumbles during the violent prison riot that ends the book where the Papus joined forces with the Australians, resulting in severe injuries for many and the death of Reza Barati.

Boochani applies the feminist theorist Elisabeth Schüssler Fiorenza's principle of the Kyriarchal System to the way the prison is governed. She coined the term in 1992 to describe a 'theory of interconnected social systems established for the purposes of domination, oppression and submission' (ibid: 124). The principle is to turn the prisoners:

… against each other and to ingrain even deeper hatred between people. Prison maintains its power over time; the power to keep people in line. Fenced enclosures dominate and can pacify even the most violent person – those imprisoned on Manus are themselves sacrificial subjects of violence. We are a bunch of ordinary humans locked up simply for seeking refuge. In this context, the prison's greatest achievement might be the manipulation of feelings of hatred between one another (ibid: 124-125).

In another scene that illustrates the way the Kyriarchal System operates, a detainee known as 'The Prime Minister' because of his virtues and the strength of his character, is forced by the toilet queue to defecate in public. It destroys his dignity, his reputation and his ability to continue to withstand the ritual humiliations. He decides to return to the country from which he fled and where he faces persecution. The Kyriarchal System demands the men 'accept, to some degree, that they are wretched and contemptible – this is an aspect of the system designed particularly for them' (ibid: 184). Sparrow (2018) argues that for Boochani, the detention centre is merely the extreme manifestation of the Kyriarchical System that already applies in Australia and pits its citizens against each other in its anti-refugee sentiment. Pointing to the universality of the book's themes, he says its 'logic extends beyond the camp, with Manus merely one aspect of a "border-industrial complex" that functions to atomise and control subaltern classes across the globe'.

THE PROCESS OF WRITING AND TRANSLATING

No friend but the mountains incorporates influences from Western literature, including, according to Tofighian, Kafka's *The trial* (1925), Camus's *The stranger* (1942), and Beckett's trilogy *Molloy* (1951), *Malone dies* (1951) and *The unnameable* (1953), texts which Boochani was reading at the time he was writing his book (Tofighian 2018a: xxiii). It also references 'Kurdish folklore and resistance, Persian literature, sacred narrative traditions, local histories and nature symbols, ritual and ceremony' with reference as well to Manusian 'thought and culture' (ibid). Each chapter bears a double title, underlining that it is both factual and parabolic. Poems are used throughout the manuscript with Arnold Zable (2018) recognising them as having 'the power of a Greek chorus', revealing 'the terror of imprisonment from another perspective'. To protect the men on Manus Island, Boochani has created composite characters, giving them allegorical names.

Boochani found support from a number of writers and public intellectuals who helped him to complete and publish including the poet Janet Galbraith, who facilitates the writing group Writing Through Fences; the author Arnold Zable who, with Galbraith, introduced Boochani's work to Pen International, and the academic and artist Kirrily Jordan who provided feedback on draft chapters. The refugee advocate Moones Mansoubi began working with Boochani in 2015. It was she who mostly compiled the original material sent to her by Boochani via WhatsApp messages. Once it was in a format of which Boochani approved, she sent PDFs of the full chapters to Omid Tofighian for translation (Tofighian 2018a: xvi).

There was no real-time communication to facilitate the translation process (ibid). Text and voice messages were the most reliable way to communicate because the internet connection on the island was so poor. Occasionally, Boochani would directly communicate with Tofighian via WhatsApp. Later, he would text Tofighian new passages to add to the translated work. Says Tofighian: 'The full draft of each of Behrouz's chapters would appear as a long text message with no paragraph breaks. It was this feature that created a unique and intellectually stimulating space for literary experimentation and shared philosophical activity' (ibid).

At the time Mansoubi began working with Boochani, security in the detention centre was tight and the men were kept under continuous surveillance. 'Brutal' raids to confiscate smartphones and other contraband, were staged regularly in the pre-dawn (ibid: xxxiii). Boochani's first phone was confiscated. 'For two to three months he would write his book by hand and use [his friend] Aref Heidari's phone to send voice messages to Moones for transcribing' (ibid). He managed to acquire another phone which he hid in his mattress but it was stolen in 2017, suspending his ability to continue to work on the book until he could secure a third smartphone. There were other delays sometimes dragging on for weeks and months, including when the authorities suspended his communications. 'During phases of extreme securitization and surveillance he was forced to leave his phone hidden for long periods' (ibid). The forcible closure of the detention centre in October 2017 also caused a delay while Boochani turned his attention to reporting on the three-week siege.

BOOCHANI AND THE LITERATURE OF RESISTANCE

The title Boochani chose for his memoir – *No friend but the mountains* – comes from a Kurdish proverb that speaks to the long history of persecution and isolation of the Kurds. The application of the proverb to the situation of the refugees and asylum seekers on Manus Island internationalises and universalises the writing. Boochani, using the tropes of testimonial literature to speak to the circumstances endured by all the men on Manus Island, is not writing as the citizen of any nation. While they share different ethnicities, he and his fellow detainees are stateless, stripped of belonging to anything except humanity at its rawest and most elemental.

The notion of testimony is an important aspect of a literature of resistance. It is literature as a response to cultural violence. As writing from personal experience, it claims a voice, makes a point, establishes a community and retrieves identity. It seeks redress for injustices and advocates the rights of marginalised communities by speaking out about the actual circumstances of a life or lives. As the black lesbian writer Audre Lorde (1982) said: '[I]f I didn't define myself for myself, I would be crunched into other people's fantasies for me and eaten alive.' Refusing to be objectified, Boochani uses his writing to challenge the identities imposed on him and the other refugees and asylum seekers in detention who are stereotyped in the disempowering dominant narrative as binary opposites, either criminal or victim.

In *No friend but the mountains*, Boochani is a human being speaking through the universality of literature to policy and practices that are condemned under international agreements. According to the barrister and human rights activist Julian Burnside (2018), they are also condemned under Australian law, specifically the *Criminal Code Act, 1995* which categorises the taking of hostages as a war crime. Says Burnside:

> There is no doubt that our use of indefinite detention is a breach of section 268.12. And it is strongly arguable that offshore processing as it is presently done is a breach of section 268.12 and section 268.13. ... The only difficulty is that prosecutions for these offences can only be instituted with the Attorney-General's written consent (ibid).

CONCLUSION

The paradox of Boochani stepping in to fill the place of an Australian journalist writing about Australian government policy and its consequences is that he can only do it because he is an outsider communicating his own outsider status from within the subjective experience of imprisonment. He uses *No friend but the mountains* to explore that ground of subjectivity and rebel against the Kyriarchal System, not through violence but through creativity. Like the character 'Maysam the Whore' who regularly entertains the other inmates with humour and satire, singing and dancing, he uses art to disrupt the system and its violence, claiming:

> [T]he only people who can overcome and survive all the suffering inflicted by the prison are those who exercise creativity. That is, those who can trace the outlines of hope using the melodic humming and visions from beyond the prison fences and the beehives we live in (Boochani 2018: 128).

Detainment strips prisoners of their autonomy and sense of self, as well as their connection to broader society, yet the act of self-narration is crucial to a person's selfhood, identity and well being (Eakin 1999). In writing *No friend but the mountains*, Boochani has used creativity to reassert his agency and resist the Kyriarchal System. In creative resistance lies liberation. As he tells Arnold Zable in 2018: 'In those moments, when I was writing, I was completely free ... those moments were the most exciting ... because I found myself out of the prison as a free man.'

- The paper first appeared in *Ethical Space*, Vol. 15, Nos 3 and 4 pp 17-24, 2018

REFERENCES

Al Jazeera (2017) Manus Island: Australia pulling the media strings, *The Listening Post*, 19 November. Available online at www.aljazeera.com/programmes/listeningpost/2017/11/manus-island-australia-pulling-media-strings-171118083724605.html?xif=et, accessed September 2018

Australian Human Rights Commission (2012) Face the facts (2012), chapter 3. Available online at www.humanrights.gov.au/publications/face-facts-2012/2012-face-facts-chapter-3, accessed September 2018

Berkman, A. (1970 [1912]) *Prison memoirs of an anarchist*, New York, Schocken

Bolger, D. D. (2016) *Race politics: Australian government responses to asylum seekers and refugees from White Australia to Tampa*, PhD Thesis, School of Humanities and Communication Arts, Australia, Western Sydney University

Boochani, B. (2018) *No friend but the mountains* (trans. by Tofighian, O.), Sydney, Australia, Picador/Pan Macmillan

Burnside, J. (2018) Fear is the great threat to multiculturalism in Australia, Walter Lippmann Oration, *Daily Review*, 14 September. Available online at www.dailyreview.com.au/julian-burnside-oration/78065/, accessed September 2018

Cooper, S., Olejniczak, E., Lenette, C. and Smedley, C. (2017) Media coverage of refugees and asylum seekers in regional Australia: A critical discourse analysis, *Media International Australia*, Vol.162, No. 1 pp 78-89

Coady, D. (2017) Government to relax secrecy rules for detention centre workers in 'humiliating backdown', *ABC News* online, updated 14 August. Available online at www.abc.net.au/news/2017-08-14/government-to-scrap-whistleblower-protections-immigration-centre/8802902, accessed September 2018

Davidson, H. (2016) Offshore detention: Australia's recent immigration history a 'human rights catastrophe', *Guardian Australia*, 13 November. Available online at www.theguardian.com/australia-news/2016/nov/13/offshore-detention-nauru-immigration-history-human-rights, accessed September 2018

Doherty, B. (2016) United Nations reiterates demand for Australia to close 'dire' detention centres, *Guardian Australia*, 13 August. Available online at www.theguardian.com/australia-news/2016/aug/13/united-nations-reiterates-demand-for-australia-to-close-dire-detention-centres, accessed September 2018

Doherty, B. (2018) UN body condemns Australia for illegal detention of asylum seekers and refugees, *Guardian Australia*, 8 June. Available online at www.theguardian.com/world/2018/jul/08/un-body-condemns-australia-for-illegal-detention-of-asylum-seekers-and-refugees, accessed September 2018

Eakin, J. (1999) *How our lives become stories*, New York, Cornell University Press

Farrel, P., Evershed, N. and Davidson, H. (2016) The Nauru files: Cache of 2,000 leaked reports reveal scale of abuse of children in Australian offshore detention, *Guardian Australia*, 10 August. Available online at www.theguardian.com/australia-news/2016/aug/10/the-nauru-files-2000-leaked-reports-reveal-scale-of-abuse-of-children-in-australian-offshore-detention, accessed on 28 September 2018

Germian, R. (2017) Film shot entirely on Manus detainee's mobile gets public screening, *In Focus*, SBS Kurdish, 12 April. Available online at www.sbs.com.au/yourlanguage/kurdish/en/article/2017/04/12/film-shot-entirely-manus-detainees-mobile-gets- public-screening, accessed September 2018

Griffiths, E. (2014) Reza Barati death: Senate committee report says violence at Manus Island was 'eminently foreseeable', *ABC News* online, 11 December. Available online at www.abc.net.au/news/2014-12-11/violence-at-manus-eminently-foreseeable-senate-report/5960752, accessed September 2018

Griffiths, P. (2016) *The making of White Australia: Ruling class agendas, 1876-1888*, PhD thesis, Canberra, Australian National University

Hazel, A. (2016) Reporting from inside a refugee detention centre, Inter Press Service, December 29. Available online at www.abc.net.au/news/2014-12-11/violence-at-manus-eminently-foreseeable-senate-report/5960752, accessed September 2018

Human Rights Watch (2018) Australia: Events of 2017, *World Report*. Available online at www.hrw.org/world-report/2018/country-chapters/australia, accessed September 2018

Jabour, B. and Hurst, D. (2014) Nauru to increase visa cost for journalists from $200 to $8,000, *Guardian Australia*, 9 January. Available online at www.theguardian.com/world/2014/jan/09/nauru-visa-to-cost-8000, accessed September 2018

Jayasuriya, L., Walker, D. and Gothard, J. (2003) *Legacies of White Australia: Race, culture and nation*, Crawley, University of Western Australia Press

Jupp, J. (2007) *From White Australia to Woomera: The story of Australian immigration*, Cambridge, Cambridge University Press, second edition

Karp, P. (2016) Keeping journalists out of detention centres helps stop boats, says Cormann, *Guardian Australia*, 14 June. Available online at www.theguardian.com/australia-news/2016/jun/14/keeping-journalists-out-of-detention-centres-helps-stop-asylum-boats-mathias-cormann-bill-shorten-election, accessed September 2018

Kenny, M. A. (2017) Three charts on: What's going on at Manus Island, *Conversation*, 17 November. Available online at www. theconversation.com/three-charts-on-whats-going-on-at-manus-island-87354, accessed September 2018

Killedar, A. and Harris, P. (2017) Australia's refugee policies and their health impact: A review of the evidence and recommendations for the Australian Government, *Australia and New Zealand Journal of Public Health*, Vol. 41, No. 4. Available online at www.onlinelibrary.wiley.com/doi/full/10.1111/1753-6405.12663, accessed September 2018

Lorde, A. (1982) *Learning from the '60s*. Address delivered at Harvard University as part of the celebration of the Malcolm X weekend, February. Available online at www.blackpast.org/1982-audre-lorde-learning-60s, accessed September 2018

Markus A. (1994) *Australian race relations, 1788-1993*, St Leonards, NSW, Allen & Unwin

Pen International (2017) On Human Rights Day: Take action for journalist Behrouz Boochani, stranded on Manus Island, 7 December. Available online at www.pen-international.org/news/on-human-rights-day-take-action-for-journalist-behrouz-boochani-stranded-on-manus-island, accessed September, 2018

Refugee Council of Australia (2016) The Refugee Convention, 14 May. Available online at www.refugeecouncil.org.au/getfacts/international/internationalsystem/the-refugee-convention/, accessed September 2018

Reporters Without Borders (n. d.) Iran. Available online at www.rsf.org/en/iran, accessed September 2018

Serge, V. (1981 [1930]) *Men in prison* (trans. by Greeman, R.), New York, Writers and Readers Publishing

Sparrow, J. (2018) A place of punishment: *No friend but the mountains*, by Behrouz Boochani, *Sydney Review of Books*, 21 September. Available online at www.sydneyreviewofbooks.com/a-place-of-punishment-no-friend-but-the-mountains-by-behrouz-boochani/, accessed September 2018

Tlozek, E. (2016) Reza Barati death: Two men jailed over 2014 murder of asylum seeker at Manus Island detention centre, *ABC News*, 19 April. Available online at www.abc.net.au/news/2016-04-19/reza-barati-death-two-men-sentenced-to-10-years-over-murder/7338928, accessed September 2018

Tofighian, O. (2018a) Translator's tale: A window to the mountain, Boochani, Behrouz, *No friend but the mountains* (trans by Tofighian, O.), Sydney, Australia, Picador/Pan Macmillan

Tofighian, O. (2018b) *No friend but the mountains*: Translator's reflections, Boochani, Behrouz, *No friend but the mountains* (trans by Tofighian, O.), Sydney, Australia, Picador/Pan Macmillan

Yarwood A. T. and Knowling, M. J. (1982) *Race relations in Australia: A history*, North Ryde, NSW, Methuen Australia

Zable, A. (2015) Iranian journalist Behrouz Boochani tells of the horrors of Manus Island: Out of sight, out of mind, *Sydney Morning Herald*, 21 September. Available online at www.smh.com.au/opinion/iranian-journalist-behrouz-boochani-tells-of-the-horrors-of-manus-island-out-of-sight-out-of-mind-20150921-gjrdi8.html, accessed September 2018

Zable, A. (2017) 'This republic breaks all borders': A dialogue with Behrouz Boochani on Manus, *Sydney Morning Herald,* 22 December. Available at www.smh.com.au/national/this-republic-breaks-all-borders-a-dialogue-with-behrouz-boochani-on-manus-20171221-h08bx1.html, accessed September 2018

Zable, A. (2018) Australia's barbaric policy confronted by Boochani's prison memoir, *Sydney Morning Herald* online, 25 August. Available online at www.smh.com.au/national/australia-s-barbaric-policy-confronted-by-boochani-s-prison-memoir-20180821-p4zyt7. html, accessed September 2018

NOTE ON THE CONTRIBUTOR

Dr Willa McDonald is Senior Lecturer in Media at Macquarie University where she teaches and researches creative non-fiction writing and literary journalism. A former journalist, she has worked in print, television and radio, including for the *Sydney Morning Herald, The Bulletin*, the *Times on Sunday,* ABC TV and ABC Radio National. She completed her doctorate at UNSW in Australian Studies. Willa's books are: *Literary journalism in colonial Australia* (2023, Palgrave Macmillan), *Literary journalism and social justice* (2022, Palgrave Macmillan, with Robert Alexander), *Warrior for peace: Dorothy Auchterlonie Green* (2009, Australian Scholarly Publishing) and *The writer's reader: Understanding journalism and non-fiction* (2007, Cambridge University Press, with Susie Eisenhuth). Willa is co-editor of Palgrave Macmillan's literary journalism book series.

Chapter 12

Visibility and cultural voice in Fataluku country Timor-Leste

Marian Reid

This study explores the intersection of digital visual communication and traditional culture in the Fataluku community of Lautem, Timor-Leste. Focusing on the Fataluku Research Project as a case study, this paper investigates the effect that community-driven cultural documentation has on the value, perception and visibility of culture by the community, and makes a conceptual link between increased cultural visibility and its potential to contribute to social cohesion in the context of Timor-Leste. This paper highlights how being on camera through a collaborative process can create spaces of dialogue, open channels of cultural expression and reinforce identity for Fataluku people. This paper also explores digital visual communication as a framework that can be applied to other ethnic communities in Timor-Leste and more broadly.

Keywords: digital visual communication, Fataluku, identity, intangible culture, participatory research, Timor-Leste, visibility

INTRODUCTION

For the Fataluku community in Lautem District, Timor-Leste, a lost culture amounts to a lost identity. With increasing evidence of the evaporation of ancestral knowledge and disconnection from culture in a post-conflict and developing context (De Carvalho 2011; Arnott 2012; ETWA 2015), people in Lautem are concerned about the preservation of their culture – and their identity. In response, a small group of local Fataluku community members were supported in 2012-2013 by Australian-Timor organisation Many Hands International to seek out, document and digitally re-tell some of the hidden stories and knowledge that make up Fataluku culture. The Fataluku Research Project trained local people in media and research skills, enabling them to work with knowledge custodians in the documentation of critically endangered intangible cultural heritage over 12 months. The process aimed to contribute to the revitalisation, safeguarding and sustaining of intangible culture by increasing its visibility and raising cultural voice. It was also a process of reclaiming identity and building community capacity to include culture in the nation's growth.

Long before it became the heart of the Timorese Resistance Movement, Lautem was a distinctly unique region inhabited by Fataluku, Lero, Makasa'e and Lovaia people with strong cultures of the same names (Valentim and Pereira 2013). Deeply embedded across these cultural groups and languages were a set of systems, beliefs and values that made up the rich identities of each culture – complex kinships, spiritual ceremonies, animatism, agriculture, medicine, architecture, song, music, instruments and weavings (Brandao 2011; McWilliam 2011; Brown 2013; O'Conner Pannell and Brockwell 2013).

Today in Lautem's lush, green capital, Lospalos, the single main street shows signs of past conflict and neglect, and a victory statue symbolising the district's role in independence marks an intersection. The Catholic church, which still holds three services each Sunday, has merged the shape of an *umu-lulig* (traditional spirit house) where a steeple or cross would normally be. Walls near the church showcase street art as an emotional expression of development, harmony, past, present and hope (Parkinson 2010). Most people walk – motorbikes are few and cars even more so. Some children sell boiled eggs and vegetables in the streets so they can afford school, and unemployment rates are high. Since Timor-Leste's independence, Lospalos has been peaceful, but there have been few opportunities for the local people, and the underlying pressures of development have placed strain on community and cultural survival.

In Timor-Leste, the shift towards development can translate as a disconnection from ancient stories, traditional social norms and community capacity for the younger generation who are interested in pursuing a more progressive life in the city or overseas (De Carvalho 2011; Arnott 2012; ETWA 2015). When Timor-Leste gained independence from Indonesia in 2002, the country was inundated by international agencies working on 'nation building' (UNDP 2015). Yet many of the international development strategies have been poorly administered and are not suitable to the culture and context of the nation, with the disconnect between Western and traditional approaches threatening to destroy customary institutions and practices (Moxham 2005; Batterbury 2006; Niner 2007).

Cultural loss in Timor-Leste is not just the discarding of dress or artefacts – it's the loss of a deep-rooted and complex system that is intangible in nature and yet essential for the social fabric of the people who live it. It's a loss of kinships, sacred stories, symbols, ancestry, ritual and ceremony, relationships with land and, importantly, relationships between people (Brandao 2011). It's these intangible cultures that disappear first when the younger generation is met with new social and economic pressures (Arnott 2012). This is not to say people should not engage in development. Rather, it's a concern with what happens when a lack of employment opportunities is coupled with expectations of economic gains resulting in a disillusioned youth population who are also losing their culture (Horta 2013).

Intangible culture is closely aligned with the formation of identity over time. It relates to 'the practices, representations, expressions, knowledge, skills – as well as the instruments, objects, artefacts and cultural spaces associated therewith – that communities, groups and, in some cases, individuals recognise as part of their cultural heritage' and it provides communities with a sense of continuity (UNESCO 2015). For example, specific to the people of Iliomar on Timor-Leste's south-east coast is the practice of *Fulidaidai*, a living socio-cultural system that fosters collective community action and the generational passing of wisdom and traditional knowledge (ETWA 2015). For Fataluku people, there is also *Ratu*, the kinship to which someone belongs and a key social institution that can help form cooperation and social unity through shared spiritual obligations and values (McWilliam 2011). Intangible culture can even be a resource for peace-building. For example, the practice of *Fetosaa-umane* establishes relationships between intermarried families and, while not always ideal, can promote a strong social identity when values and traditions from *umalisan* (clan traditional houses) are passed between generations (Brandao 2011).

In a globalising society, these practices are inherently fragile, and the tragedy of contemporary cultural loss in Timor-Leste is even greater when we acknowledge local people were able to retain an incredibly strong sense of cultural identity throughout more than 400 years of colonisation and more than 20 years of occupation. This enabled them to nurture a collective identity where narratives were passed down through generations, and recognise key aspects of their culture that were essential for the long-term sustaining of communities (Grenfell et al. 2009). Specific to Timor-Leste's cultural struggle has been the freedom struggle built on the desire for independence and cultural identity. The sense of legitimacy that arrived with independence is embedded in the history of place and ancestors, and 'Timorese culture was powerfully entwined with the drive for resistance and independence' (Brown 2013: 12).

THE DIGITAL DOCUMENTATION OF INTANGIBLE CULTURE

Increasingly there are examples of societies facing cultural loss turning to digital visual communication and storytelling to help preserve their traditions. Mulka Arts has been using film and photography since 2007, for example, to record and protect Yolngu cultural knowledge in Australia's North-East Arnhem Land (Mulka 2015). Similarly, photographer Jeff Young answered a call by Maasai tribes for 'technologists' to help them preserve their culture – they saw digital storytelling as one way to balance technology with their traditional storytelling practices (Young 2010).

Often stories hold power for the storyteller as a form of survival, causing people to consider how stories inform their present and future lives (Lambert 2013), and technology – particularly in the form of digital storytelling – can be engaged as a creative tool through which to explore life narratives (Lambert 2015). Not only applicable to personal survival, the ability to tell a visual story creates a way for people to share what they value within culture and community, and can act as a powerful visual tool for sharing ancient and contemporary knowledge systems with others as a counter to modern culture (Photovoices 2015; Snyder 1996).

The enthusiasm for merging digital storytelling and culture is evident, but there is more to the process than just the sharing of knowledge. Ricouer suggests identity can actually be produced when elements of culture and life are re-narrated (in Reitmaier et al. 2011), while the telling of stories in whatever form they take can actually reaffirm them as 'embodied history' (Clandinin and Connelly 1998; Couldry 2010). Laurel Smith refers to an Indigenous video project in Mexico with *Grupo Solidaro d Quiatoni* to emphasise the relevance of culture now, and the role of visual communication in keeping culture moving and creating space for local identities in the global sphere (Paulson and Calla 2000; Smith 2008). On placing culture and identity in the context of development, the *Grupo Solidaro d Quiatoni* said: 'We need to know who we are today in order to study our own knowledge and wisdom. This is how we want to progress' (Smith 2008: 183).

But despite the good intentions and possibilities, transferring culture through digital visual communication comes with tensions, especially in regard to less visible intangible culture, which often forms the social fabric, relationships and customs that contribute to a holistic identity. Reitmaier et al. (2011) discuss the importance of oral storytelling for Lwandilean communities, where culture can be obscured in every day interactions and cultural-linguistic contexts. Although the Lwandilean people were enthusiastic to document their culture, they noted 'that recording must be compatible with the features of orality that construct their identity … [they] felt outsiders did not articulate the meanings that entwine their identity with a setting in which their kin have resided for generations' (Reitmaier et al. 2011: 660).

There is also the question of whether digitising culture can bring about cultural preservation or a change in the community perception of culture, and we cannot expect that technology and community-driven media will automatically save culture, transform communities or create social change (Ramella and Olmos 2005; Zoetti 2013). Robbins (2010: 115) sees an 'uneasy balance between the globalisation this technology brings and the preservation of Indigenous cultures'. He acknowledges there are many Indigenous cultural preservation projects that utilise film and photography but suggests it is naive to imagine documentation alone can revitalise culture – this is just one component of a bigger, integrated project (ibid). Instead, supporting structures in various forms can contribute to a more dynamic cultural preservation rather than documenting tradition as a static end (ibid).

THE FATALUKU RESEARCH PROJECT

The Fataluku Research Project in Timor-Leste was initiated to help re-invigorate critically endangered Fataluku culture by recording forms of traditional expression, such as music, rituals, ceremonies, traditional knowledge and crafts. The project also set out to build local capacity to preserve cultural heritage and provide Fataluku people with an opportunity to learn more about their cultural heritage (Valentim and Pereira 2013).

While historically, outsiders have recorded Timorese culture for 'safe-keeping', this project was dedicated to putting the power in the hands of local community members and allowing the owners of culture to be the sole documenters of their heritage. Four local Fataluku people – three men and one woman – with no prior media experience, were hired and trained as cultural researchers and 'filmmakers'. They attended workshops in interviewing, research, film, photography and video editing.

For the next 12 months, the filmmakers worked with *Chefe de Sukus* (village chiefs) to meet local knowledge custodians in three Lautem sub-districts: Lospalos, Lautem/Moru and Tutuala. Custodians worked with the filmmakers to decide what was appropriate to record and how they would do it. The process included photography, video and written records, and films were shown back to participating communities. The filmmakers interviewed 64 men and 84 women over the 12 months (Valentim and Pereira 2013). Currently the content is shared through an online resource, on social media, and is in the slow process of being archived in the Lospalos Cultural Centre.

SITUATING THE PROJECT IN PARTICIPATORY MEDIA

The Fataluku Research Project utilised elements from participatory video, participatory research and visual anthropology to form community-driven digital documentation of intangible cultural narratives. Participatory video is a tool often used to explore self-transformative narrative and representation (Rodriguez 2001; Bradden 1999), and can work to capture the unique expressive nature of community stories as a contribution to cultural diversity. According to Browne (2005) and Pietikainen (2008), it is close collaboration within a community, for a community – as demonstrated in the Fataluku project – that will truly contribute to communal and linguistic revitalisation where culture is endangered.

The process of participatory video can also be aligned with participatory research and visual anthropology (High et al. 2012), which requires participants to create and project their own images (Yang 2012; Pink 2001). Pink makes correlations between what she terms visual anthropology and collaborative film process similar to the Fataluku project. In particular, she refers to a project with Carlos Flores and Maya Q'eqchi filmmakers in Guatemala where the collaborative process brought about important ethnographic and cultural insights, new levels of engagement and self-awareness and social healing in the post-war context (Flores 2004; Pink 2007).

For Evans and Foster (2009: 105), 'participatory research is fundamentally about transforming communities from passive subjects, objects or victims of the research gaze into agents', which is very much about supporting community members as researchers themselves, as found in the Fataluku Research Project. Community-led research allows those at the centre of the research to navigate cultural norms and establish spaces of safety and understanding that can support the participation and reflection of local community participants (Wheeler 2009; Low et al. 2012; Miller and Smith 2012; Mistry and Berardi 2012).

Zoetti (2013: 216) writes that 'being on camera is not only important for the recognition of a group's culture and identity, it can also be of great relevance to the non-dominant sectors of society, simply because of the gain in visibility, which may bring people back from oblivion and into public existence'. This idea is extremely relevant in the context of intangible culture, where 'being on camera' can, for knowledge custodians and community, project images and culture from the forests and villages into another sphere. Being on camera renders culture semi-permanent and present, so long as recordings are viewed and used in supporting structures.

According to Rodriguez (2001), the digital expression of social and cultural content by marginalised people can lead to the survival of cultural identities. For Zoetti (2013: 217), this visibility is a form of 'symbolic power'. He believes the survival of minority cultures is linked to their 'recognition as a distinct group', often best served through broadcasting and reaffirming a group's culture (ibid: 216). Yet Zoetti is also careful to point out that video does not magically empower those without voice, and acknowledges grassroots communities are often already powerfully vocal (Zoetti 2013; see also Gadihoke 2003). Regardless, he highlights the use of video – and other visual communication – as a tool for marginalised cultural communities to reaffirm their identity and their traditions. His writings come with a warning too: 'While filming culture can be seen a first step towards giving marginalised communities a say in their public image, it can also easily connive in their further objectivation-folklorization, once again serving the dominant sectors of society' (Zoetti, 2013: 221).

Testament to the power of digital visual communication, Timor-Leste released its first locally made feature film, *Beatriz's war*, in 2014, which told the story of resistance using local people as actors, many of whom had experienced the conflict first-hand. One of the Timorese producers, Lurdes Pires, said:

> 450 years of Portuguese colony, then 24 years of Indonesian ruling – we haven't been able to tell our story. When you put the screen up in the districts and the people can see their faces, their people, their story, their language … it's quite exciting (Radio National 2014).

Yet, like *Beatriz's war*, much of Timor's visual imagery – such as the Tekee Media content produced by Max Stahl and his team that documents the freedom struggle (Tekee 2015) – remains saturated with images of the occupation and resistance, with less space for culture, self-expression or creative arts. The engagement of local content producers in the construction of their own identities – where visual media is used to explore the relationship between culture and their communities (Ginsburg 2002) – is a relatively new concept in Timor-Leste. In the space of the new nation, where the freedom of cultural expression and storytelling has come with freedom from occupation, the power of stories about local people by local people has particular poignancy.

CASE STUDY: INVESTIGATING THE FATALUKU RESEARCH PROJECT

Considering these approaches to participatory-based digital documentation, this case study set out to capture the experiences of the Fataluku Research Project filmmakers and community members and investigate the power of cultural voice and visibility. This case study asked: does the use of digital visual communication to document critically endangered intangible culture by local community members contribute to a shift in how that culture is valued? And what is the potential of this practice to contribute to social cohesion?

Four filmmakers from the Fataluku Research Project participated in a focus group discussion that explored their experiences documenting intangible cultural heritage. Three Lospalos-based knowledge custodians and five members from a cross-section of the Lospalos community participated in semi-structured interviews exploring the relationship between culture, development, community and social cohesion. Participants included artists, elders, business people, youth workers and non-government workers. This case study also employed itinerant ethnography as a research tool, where community members became informal interviewees who shared anecdotal data and shed light on certain ways of life by their daily actions, comments and movements (Schein 2000). The following section explores themes relating to the findings of this research.

FINDINGS

THE EXPERIENCE OF CULTURAL LOSS

The gradual loss of culture in Lautem began to accelerate during the Indonesian occupation, a period of more than 20 years during which cultural practices were discouraged and destroyed. Displacement and the mobilisation of *Fretilin* (freedom) fighters caused both women and men to leave their villages and established cultural systems. But even for those left in the villages, rituals and ceremonies were stifled and homes and *umu-luligs* destroyed (Brown 2013). As one Fataluku Research Project film-maker explained:

> During Indonesian occupation, we didn't feel free to practice our culture. We couldn't do our culture anymore, because the Timorese people were oppressed by the Indonesian people (focus group discussion, 26 November 2013).

Yet, participants also acknowledged the significant role culture played in driving the Resistance Movement, and that it was the deep desire for identity that gave fighters a cause. For one film-maker, the feeling that they secured freedom '*because of our culture*' remains central to his quest to preserve culture. For him, life after independence is equated with a sense of 'loss' without his (Resistance) leader, potentially indicating a loss of clarity around social systems. This loss could also be exacerbated by the context of development. The cultural drivers that led to national freedom can be easily forgotten with the promise of economic opportunity. What some members of the Lospalos community are now experiencing is a wave of outside influences – being free from colonisation and occupation does not necessarily mean a strengthening of identity. One community member explained:

> [Now] in the freedom times, there are many people from outside, like the UN, they come to Timor-Leste. Coming are many people with many cultures ... the culture is in danger because of modern development because the young people are focused on the modern. It is in danger because most people don't transfer their knowledge to others (focus group, 26 November 2013).

This can translate specifically to the loss of practices that have been passed down from ancestral times, and that have the potential to contribute to community diversity and be built on for future community strength and enterprise. For example, Assaleino, just outside Lospalos, was once known for its pottery. But these days, those who have the skills to produce pottery are limited. 'The making of pottery comes from our ancestors until now but now it is endangered,' said a local potter. 'Not many people here make pottery, just about 10 people' (personal communication, 20 November 2013). Yet the village is home to hundreds. Many of the girls and boys are going to school, which is wonderful, but which means they are not learning the art of pottery from their mothers and grandmothers. 'If children want to learn we will teach them. But because they go to school they don't have time to learn,' explained the potter. Education, although important, removes young people from the traditional models of learning arts and cultural practices, leaving a gap in the transmission of cultural knowledge between generations. It is hard for people to grapple with because, while they want their children to learn their tradition, the old modes of transmission have been broken with no replacement. One local weaver said:

> The first thing my mother taught me is weaving. ... I am happy because my mother taught me about the weaving. For now, because my children

are at school they just watch me. It is important for my children to learn, if I don't teach it to my children they will forget. It's … not good for us, because it's our culture and we will forget it (personal communication, 20 November 2013).

What some are noticing is that losing culture is not just about the evaporation of a unique identity, but that it is a threat to social unity as well, because aspects of culture contribute so integrally to respect and understanding. All community members and film-makers alike repeatedly articulated the notion of culture and respect during the research. As one Many Hands International local staff member said:

If we lose culture there will be many problems, like people don't respect each other and there is no unity. From my observation, when we have strong culture, old people, young people, women and men have a strong relationship because of the culture (personal communication, 21 November 2013).

Everyone who was interviewed believed culture was essential to life in Lospalos, and Timor-Leste more generally. The passion for their traditions and identity was overwhelming, and yet all stated their culture is in danger. This sentiment translated strongly during the Fataluku Research Project filmmaking process because the film-makers come from a place where culture is paramount to their identity.

THE PROCESS OF FILMING: SAFEKEEPING AND SURVIVAL

What was also emphasised during this case study was the mutual learning and social connection that occurred between the film-makers and the custodians/community during the Fataluku project. For example, after working with knowledge custodians, the filmmakers spent time showing the films and images back to the community. What became evident through this experience was the potential for this process to arouse community pride, and a re-evaluation of what they had shared. According to one film-maker, the viewing of the intangible culture by custodians and community on screen evoked the idea of beauty and significance:

When we showed the films to the community again, they felt happy because they said 'ooohhh all our culture is very beautiful'. Some people don't think about the process of culture, they just know that [we are] documenting them, but they don't really understand about the process of their culture. But when they see the films again, they appreciate that our culture is important. The process is like that (focus group, 26 November 2013).

Equally important for custodians and community was the representation of themselves on screen, particularly because they have not previously been asked to talk on camera about their culture. This was a positive experience for the film-makers, as expressed by one when he said:

> When the research team played the films again, we felt proud because everyone has the opportunity to show their face on film and it's the first time. The people are very proud of this (ibid).

What was also common was a sense of permanence that the films were creating. By recording culture, it is perceived as captured and 'safe' – both by the film-makers and custodians. One film-maker explained: '…they saw that the culture we are filming is not in danger because we have films, photos and writing so it doesn't disappear' (ibid).

Significantly, cultural learning occurred for the film-makers themselves. One film-maker knew very little about the culture of Lautem and the process raised her own awareness and understanding about ancestral knowledge:

> I can now know many cultures because even though I am from Lospalos, I didn't know much about the local culture. So this project really helped me learn more about my own culture (ibid).

VOICE, VISIBILITY AND SOCIAL COHESION

One of the biggest outcomes from the Fataluku Research Project was a sense of increased visibility of culture for the filmmakers themselves, and their communities, although how far this goes is discussed further on. There was a feeling among the film-makers that the project facilitated a greater understanding of local culture, and created connection within community. One film-maker said:

> We are happy because we are talking about our culture or we are recording the information about our culture by ourselves. I can show to everyone what makes our culture (ibid).

Beyond this was a process of connection between local people who may never otherwise have met. For example, there is distance between the film-makers who live in Lospalos and members of more remote communities. Meeting these people, sharing ideas, ancestral stories and commonalities, as well as inviting collaboration, created a space for dialogue not otherwise available. Expressed simply, one film-maker said: 'I was able to meet people who live in the rural areas,' while another mentioned he 'discussed about how people can share and talk about their *Ratu*' (focus group discussion and personal communication, November 2013).

This idea of talking about *Ratu* (kinship) relates strongly to the theme of respect, which emerged throughout the interviews conducted for this case study. When asked why culture even matters these days, there was an overwhelming correlation between culture and unity from community members. It's not just about upholding traditions, but it's a glue for the fabric of society. Culture and respect were inherently interconnected for one local weaver who said: 'In Timor-Leste, especially in Lospalos, culture is important because if there is culture we can respect each other. If there is no culture we cannot respect each other' (personal communication, 20 November 2013). The idea of respect, culture and *Ratu*, and the role of all these elements in the promotion of social cohesion was beautifully articulated by a local dance teacher:

> Culture can bring *Ratus* together, and from that we can know each other, and we can have good relationships between different *Ratus*. From culture we can create peace, unity. Culture is not just ritual and dancing. But culture is how we can respect each other (ibid).

There was also a sense of expectation by community about the impact filming their endangered cultures could have. Both film-makers and custodians saw the process of recording stories and knowledge as pivotal to increasing their voice and visibility, and pivotal to cultural preservation where – as the dance teacher said: 'When the young people look for recordings, maybe they can be motivated to share their knowledge about culture' (personal communication, 20 November 2013). The expectations of some custodians reached further afield than just Lautem. A local potter said:

> From the film I hope the children and young people can continue to make the pottery. Culture and life go together, so the children and young people have to know the culture. When they [filmmakers] came to interview, maybe they think it's good for us. I hope this will continue. Many people in outside countries can know about our culture (personal communication, 20 November 2013).

Despite perceptions of safekeeping, preservation and impact, the members of the Fataluku Research Project remained grounded in what they believed the project could achieve on its own. They recognised the project alone would not achieve the outcomes of cultural preservation, but that it was a contributor to a more supported and holistic approach through the structures of Many Hands International, networks and the Lospalos Cultural Centre. Preserving culture was an integrated process. 'We have to archive files, recordings and photos and we can keep it in a safe place … because if we don't have an archive about culture the next generation won't know what is our culture,' said one of the film-makers. But he added:

> Just films don't encourage young people to learn. But if we can also do the training according to the files that we collect, like learning the *keko* (wooden music instrument), we can prepare many people to learn to play

the *keko*. When they know how to play, they can conserve the culture (personal communication, 20 November 2013).

DISCUSSION

The findings from the Fataluku Research Project support the notion put forward by Zoetti (2013) surrounding the relationship between being on camera and visibility for culture and identity. One theme that commonly arose during this case study was a fear of culture and identity 'disappearing'. There was also a belief that by recording this disappearing culture, they were counteracting cultural oblivion. If only it was as simple as being 'visible'. Even so, increasing the visibility of intangible cultural heritage through a project like the Fataluku Research Project can contribute to cultural survival, where being on camera through a collaborative and community-driven process creates spaces of dialogue and the reinforcing of cultural identity. Although incredibly grassroots and limited in its impact, the Fataluku Research Project has contributed to a community creation of 'self and environment', as well as a certain level of conscientisation as defined by Rodriguez (2001) and Freire (1970). The presence of a shift in perception by participants indicates there could be far greater levels of change if, for example, the project was ongoing and bigger in scale, more collaborative and employed even greater participatory practices.

When it comes to situating the project within the theory of participatory video, participatory research and visual anthropology, where to place the Fataluku Research Project is arguable. It must be remembered that the project did not set out to be a participatory video project and, in many ways, the outcomes are equally valuable where the indirect results are just as interesting and relevant (High et al. 2012). We certainly see a process of self-representation (Bradden 2009) by knowledge custodians, which can illuminate the value of their intangible cultural heritage and the importance of transmission. The project also retains strong threads of visual anthropology, which can contribute to transformative change (Pink 2007). It is not only the final product that has meaning but the collaborative processes to get to that point gives rise to 'new levels of engagement in thematic issues and of self-awareness' (ibid: 112). Where the Fataluku Research Project has the strongest fit is as participatory research, which is more closely aligned to the project's purpose and which incorporates key elements of participatory video and visual anthropology. The film-makers as researchers – or researchers as film-makers – are researching intangible cultural heritage first and foremost, are driven by community interests, and collaborate with various participants along the way.

The researcher-film-makers also become involved in the process of transformation, as illustrated by one film-maker when he said: 'When the research team played the films again, we felt proud because everyone has the opportunity to show their face on film and it's the first time. The people are very proud of this' (focus group, 26

November 2013). This links strongly with the emerging theory of participatory research as having a 'real and positive impact for communities' (Low et al. 2012: 53) because we can see the process has created 'pride' and, therefore, a strong sense of cultural value. It is also an example of inclusiveness, where community has the rare opportunity to be on camera and be seen by others – which can be a potential contributor to better cross-community understanding and social cohesion. Additionally, the film-makers are novice researcher-film-makers who, by being given the training and tools to undertake this project, are themselves participants.

Coming back to the question of whether digital cultural documentation changes how culture is valued, the recorded experiences of the Fataluku Research Project participants highlight the simple but transformative effect filming culture can have through a two-fold process. Firstly, for example, when culture is played back to community members and they said 'ooohhh our culture is very beautiful', this indicates that spotlighting 'culture' in a community that has lived it for generations can ignite an appreciation of something previously internalised in normal life, therefore increasing value. Secondly, the project has been pivotal in drawing out some of the hidden elements of intangible culture that have previously been protected by custodian knowledge holders. This is instrumental in making these hidden cultural narratives more visible.

The potential flow-on effect from the project ties in with Zoetti (2013), Couldry (2010) and Reitmaier's (2011) ideas that the retelling of narratives can bring about a reaffirmation of identity, and aligns with Smith's (2008) experiences of cultural narratives as key for shaping local identities and for re-framing community purpose and place. The Fataluku Research Project is actually quite powerful as a process because it allows local community members the freedom to explore their cultural assets their way, and with their own voice. It's poignant when one of the film-makers exclaimed that he was 'happy because we are talking about our culture … and we can show to everyone what makes our culture' (focus group, 26 November 2013). Even if the reach is not great, and immediate change cannot be clearly seen or measured, there was a sense among participants that this is an important step in reclaiming their identity.

Not only about the process, but the creation of a product as a result of the Fataluku Research Project also holds significance. The project was invited to present its work at UNESCO's Workshop for the Implementation of Intangible Cultural Heritage in Jakarta in 2013, for which they created a short film of some of the important cultural narratives they had captured. On returning, one of the film-makers and community cultural researchers told, with pride, of the applause and praise for their work. They were the only team to present work visually. This is significant in placing both the Fataluku people and Timor-Leste on an international platform where they are able to promote their intangible cultural heritage in the public sphere. Not lost is the presence of a Timor-Leste cultural preservation group presenting in Indonesia, a country that for so long had been instrumental in the destruction of Timorese culture.

Culture and social cohesion (respect and peace) in Timor-Leste have a symbiotic relationship – which highlights the importance of allowing space for the representation of culture. This case study makes a conceptual link between increased cultural visibility and the *potential* it has to strengthen society and, therefore, contribute to social cohesion. What is clear in this case study is that among the film-makers there is a sense that their unity was destroyed during occupation along with their culture, and that this is ongoing in the face of modernisation. Through the promotion of culture, a project like the Fataluku Research Project promotes mutual respect and trust through existing cultural systems. As Brandao (2011: 6-7) suggests, 'culture and traditional practices continue to represent the primary means of conflict resolution and peace building in most Timorese communities' and should 'aim to preserve the spirit and values represented by customs unique to each cultural group as a way to enhance local and national identity'.

At the same time the Fataluku project can act as a mechanism for 'instilling a sense of identity for community members and fostering linkages between generations' (Brandao, 2011: 15). Brandao gives an example of the 2006 crisis in Timor-Leste where tensions arose between those living in the East (Lorosa'e) and those in the West (Loromonu). According to interviews conducted by Brandao these divisions were political and not cultural, and many community members expressed the desire to 'reunite the people of Timor-Leste by reminding them of their interwoven cultural relationships in order to restore a broken peace' (Brandao 2011: 23).

In this space, it is important to acknowledge the role projects like the Fataluku Research Project could have in contributing to this reminder.

Of course, there is danger in the perceived magic of the camera (Zoetti 2013). One film-maker said: 'When they see the films again, they appreciate our culture is important. The process is like that' (focus group discussion, November 2013). However, the Fataluku Research Project is too small-scale to realise such change on its own and there is little evidence to suggest that any one film project can bring about cultural survival. As the film-makers themselves acknowledge, just creating a self-narrative about endangered culture is not enough to preserve it. It is, therefore, important to look at the project in its supporting structure of Many Hands International, and include the organisational mission when understanding the project. As Couldry suggests, voice is most valued when there are diverse, interlinked and sustainable processes of being heard (2010).

Culture is never a final and static entity and the Fataluku Research Project is just one part of an integrated approach to the preservation and revitalisation of intangible culture in Lautem, similar to Robbins' (2010) integrated approach. The Fataluku project is an important process in the capturing of cultural narrative, yet relies on the existence of the Lospalos Cultural Centre, which opened in 2014 as a joint project between Many Hands International and the Timor-Leste Ministry of Culture. Here the cultural narratives will be archived for the community to access and hopefully make more visible in various forms. There are also other cultural-based development projects led by Many Hands International, dedicated to exploring and valuing culture in the community such as cultural festivals, youth arts programmes and music exchange programmes.

Robbins (2010) also highlights a series of risks with the digitisation of intangible cultural heritage that relate to the Fataluku Research Project. Within communities there are fears of 'killing tradition through its flattening into a disconnected media' (Robbins 2010: 118) and the danger of relegating culture to museum status to be viewed from a distance. Archiving material in the Lospalos Cultural Centre and online does pose a risk of ossification if the project stops there. It is important the project is ongoing, allows culture to be revisited and retold, and enables people of all ages to use the recordings and stories to develop knowledge and new forms of cultural expression. Perhaps some of this will bring about inauthentic practice for asset-based development, but that is more desirable than the disappearance of an ancient and unique culture, and it creates space for culture to be rightly included in the development process. Within the Timorese community, a subtle determination prevails to explore and express culture in the spaces left in the post-conflict context. There are many young people engaging with culture and trying to define their identity in different ways. This force is part of the supporting structure needed to celebrate culture and keep it living and breathing. To influence cultural change, projects like the Fataluku Research Project need to better engage young people in the filming process and as the tellers of stories, creating inter-generational sharing.

CONCLUSION

This case study has highlighted that digital visual communication is a valuable tool through which to open channels of cultural expression and make visible critically endangered intangible cultural heritage. There is power in its form that can realise a certain level of conscientisation for participants, and there is great potential for it to contribute to social cohesion where the recognition of culture is key to bridging divides created in a neoliberal context. If, as Robbins (2010: 118) suggests, the goal of digitising intangible cultural heritage is 'to preserve, develop and learn from endangered traditions, so that not only the form but the goals and experiences live on, finding a growing place in a changing world', then the Fataluku Research Project is an important example of this at play in the unique context of Timor-Leste. While it is a microcosm of what could be achieved, it provides a unique framework from which to build, grow and be reapplied in the nation's context.

In shining a light on the relationship between intangible cultural heritage and social cohesion, this study highlights the significant role that digital visual communication can play in strengthening this relationship in a post-conflict and modernising context. It is widely hoped by community members that 'cultural practices in Timor-Leste can preserve their legitimacy and importance as a positive force for social cohesion, respect and harmony within with a modern democratic state, while also encouraging families to invest in the health, education and development opportunities of their members' (Brandao 2011: 7). As communities consider how to meet development while retaining a connection to and respect for cultural values (ibid), the potential of participatory-based digital visual communication to help facilitate this discussion has been demonstrated in this case study and by the Fataluku Research Project.

The Fataluku project presents an element of diversity that – like so many aspects of life – is important because it invites collaboration and creates channels of voice for people who may otherwise remain oblivious in the context of development. Essentially, those people involved in the project are people who care for and create their community, and who are legitimate custodians of their living culture. Their work deserves to be given space. They should not have to struggle to secure the means to have cultural voice simply because it's not within a dominant economic and technological framework. Intangible cultural heritage deserves a place in the future development dialogue and public sphere in Timor-Leste by increasing its visibility.

If the international community feels it has a responsibility to assist in the development of the nation, then it also has a responsibility to support minority, grassroots projects that promote and preserve intangible culture so that it can become part of the footprint for the nation's future. Established in the context of Timor-Leste by local people, the Fataluku Research Project has the culturally appropriate framework to be applied in various communities across the country – and the power to contribute to cultural preservation, revitalisation, dialogue and peace-building.

- This paper was first published in *Ethical Space*, Vol 14, No 4 pp 25-33, 2017

REFERENCES

Arnott, K. (2012) East Timor's secret stories unlocked on stage, *ABC News*, October. Available online from www.abc.net.au/news/2012-10-05/an-east-timor27s-secret-stories-unlocked-on-stage/4297120, accessed on 15 April 2015

Batterbury, S. (2006) Final reflection, Palmer, L., Niner, S. and Kent, L. (eds) *Exploring the tensions of nation building in Timor-Leste – Proceedings of a forum*, Melbourne, School of Social and Environmental Enquiry, University of Melbourne p. 15

Bradden, S. (1999) Using video for research and representation: Basic human needs and critical pedagogy, *Journal of Educational Media*, Vol. 24, No. 2 pp 117-129

Brandao, C. E. (2011) Culture and its impact on social and community life: A case study of Timor-Leste, *EWER Policy Brief No. 5*, Belun and Centre for International Conflict Resolution

Brown, A. M. (2013) *Addressing legitimacy issues in fragile post-conflict situations to advance conflict transformation and peacebuilding: Timor-Leste report supported by the Berghof Foundation*, Germany, Berghof Foundation

Browne, D. R. (2005) *Ethnic minorities, electronic media and the public sphere: A comparative study*, Cresskill, NJ, Hampton Press

Clandinin, J. and Connelly, M. (1998) Personal experience methods, Denzin, N. and Lincoln, Y. (eds) *Collecting and interpreting qualitative materials*, Thousand Oaks, Sage pp 150-178

Couldry, N. (2010) *Why voice matters: Culture and politics after neoliberalism*, London, Sage

De Carvalho, D. (2011) Local knowledge of Timor-Leste, *UNESCO Jakarta*. Available online at http://unesdoc.unesco.org/images/0021/002145/214540E.pdf, accessed on 15 April 2015

ETWA (2015) East Timor Women's Association. Available online at www.etwa.org.au, accessed on 20 April 2015

Evans, M. and Foster, S. (2009) Representation in participatory video: Some considerations from research with Metis in British Colombia, *Journal of Canadian Studies/Revue d'études Canadiennes*, Vol. 43, No. 1, Winter pp 87-108

Flores C. Y. (2004) Indigenous video, development, and shared anthropology: A collaborative experience with Maya Q'eqchi' filmmakers in post-war Guatemala, *Visual Anthropology Review*, Vol. 20, No. 1 pp 31-44

Freire, P. (1970) *Pedagogy of the oppressed*, New York, Herder and Herder

Gadihoke, S. (2003) The struggle to 'empower': A women behind the camera, White, S. (ed.) *Participatory video: Images that transform and empower*, New Delhi, Sage pp 271-285

Ginsburg, F. (2002) Mediating culture: Indigenous media, ethnographic film and the production of identity, Askew, K. and Wilk, R. R. (eds) *The anthropology of media: A reader*, Malden: Blackwell pp 187-209

Grenfell, D., Walsh, M., Trembath, A., Norohona, C. and Holthouse, K. (2009) *Understanding community: Security and sustainability in four Aldeia in Timor-Leste*, the Globalism Research Institute, Melbourne, RMIT

High, C., Singh, N., Petheram, L. and Nemes, G. (2012) Defining participatory video from practice, Milne, E. J., Mitchell, C. and de Lange, N. (eds) *Handbook of participatory video*, Lanham, Altamira Press pp 35-48

Horta, L. (2013) Timor-Leste: A fragile peace, International Relations and Security Network, *ISN Zurich*, 7 August. Available online at www.isn.ethz.ch/Digital-Library/Articles/Detail/?id=167662, accessed on 15 April 2015

Lambert, J. (2013) *Digital storytelling: Capturing lives, creating community*, New York, Routledge, fourth edition

Lambert, J. (2015) Centre for Digital Storytelling. Available online at www.storycenter.org, accessed on 19 October 2015

Low, B., Brushwood, C., Salvio, P. and Palacios, L. (2012) Reframing the scholarship on participatory video: From celebration to critical engagement, Milne, E. J., Mitchell, C. and de Lange, N. (eds) *Handbook of participatory video*, Lanham, Altamira Press pp 49-65

McWilliam, A. (2011) Fataluku Forest tenures and the Conis Santana National Park in East Timor, *Land and life in Timor-Leste: Ethnographic essays*, McWilliam, A. and Traube, E. G., *press.anu.edu*. Available online at http://press.anu.edu.au/austronesians/sharing/pdf/ch11.pdf, accessed on 20 April 2015

Miller, E. and Smith, M. (2012) Dissemination and ownership of knowledge, Milne, E. J., Mitchell, C. and de Lange, N. (eds) *Handbook of participatory video*, Lanham, Altamira Press pp 331-348

Mistry, J. and Berardi, A. (2012) The challenges and opportunities of participatory video in geographical research: Exploring collaboration with Indigenous communities in the North Rupununi, Guyana, *AREA*, Vol. 44, No. 1 pp 110-116

Moxham, B. (2005) The World Bank's land of kiosks: Community driven development in Timor-Leste, *Development in Practice*, Vol. 15. Nos 3/4 pp 522-528

Mulka (2015) The Mulka Project. Available online at http://yirrkala.com/the-mulka-project, accessed on 30 July 2015

Niner, S. (2007) A reassertion of customary practices in Timor-Leste, Palmer, L., Niner, S. and Kent, L. (eds) *Exploring the tensions of nation building in Timor-Leste*, Melbourne, University of Melbourne pp 10 and 41-46

O'Conner, S., Pannell, S. and Brockwell, S. (2013) The dynamics of culture and nature in a 'protected' Fataluku landscape, Brockwell, S., O'Conner, S. and Byrne, D. (eds) *Transcending the culture – Nature divide in cultural heritage: Views from the Asia-Pacific region, Terra Australis*, Canberra, ANU Press pp 203-234

Parkinson, C. (2010) *Peace of wall: Street art from East Timor*, South Melbourne, Affirm Press

Paulson, S. and Calla, P. (2000) Gender and ethnicity in Bolivian politics: Transformation or paternalism?, *Journal of Latin American Anthropology*, Vol. 5, No. 2 pp 112-149

Photovoices (2015) Photovoices International: Empowering people through photography. Available online at www.photovoicesinternational.org/index.html, accessed on 17 April 2015

Pietikainen, S. (2008) To breathe two airs: Empowering indigenous Sami media, Wilson, P. and Stewart, M. (eds) *Global indigenous media: Cultures, poetics and politics*, Durham, NC, Duke University Press pp 197-213

Pink, S. (2001) More visualising, more methodologies: On video, reflexivity and qualitative research, *Sociological Review*, Vol. 48, No. 4 pp 586-599

Pink, S. (2007) Video in ethnographic research, Pink, S. (ed.) *Doing visual ethnography*, London, Sage, second edition pp 96-117

Radio National (2014) East Timor's first feature film, *Drive*, 14 July

Ramella, M. and Olmos, G. (2005) *Participant authored audiovisual stories (PAAS): Giving the camera away or giving the camera a way?*, 10 Qualitative Series, London, LSE

Reitmaier, T., Bidwell, N. J. and Marsden, G. (2011) Situating digital storytelling within African communities, *International Journal of Human-Computer Studies*, Vol. 69, No. 10 pp 658-668

Robbins, C. (2010) Beyond preservation: New directions for technological innovation through intangible cultural heritage, *USA International Journal of Education and Development using Information and Communication Technology* (IJEDICT), Vol. 6, No. 2 pp 115-118

Rodriguez, C. (2001) *Fissures in the mediascape: An international study of citizen's media*. Cresskill, NJ, Hampton Press

Schein, L. (2000) *Minority rules: Miao and the feminine in China's cultural politics*, Durham, North Carolina, Duke University Press

Smith, L. (2008) The search for well-being: Placing development with indigenous identity, Wilson, P. and Stewart, M. (eds) *Global indigenous media: Cultures, poetics and politics*, Durham, North Carolina, Duke University Press pp 183-196

Snyder, G. (1996) *A place in space: Ethics, aesthetics and watersheds*, Washington DC, Counterpoint Press

Tekee (2015) The Audio Visual Archive and Cultural Centre, Tekee Media. Available online at http://tekeemedia.com/camstl/, accessed on 30 July 2015

UNDP (2015) United Nations Development Programme in Timor-Leste. Available online at www.tl.undp.org/content/timor_leste/en/home/ourwork/overview.html, accessed on 25 October 2015

UNESCO (2015) Text of the Convention for the Safeguarding of Intangible Cultural Heritage. Available online at www.unesco.org/culture/ich/?lg=en&pg=0006, accessed on 11 April 2015

Valentim, J. and Pereira, N. (2013) *Cultural assets-based community development in Timor-Leste*, Lospalos, Many Hands International

Wheeler, J. (2009) The life that we don't want: Using participatory video in researching violence, *IDS Bulletin*, Vol. 40, No. 1 pp 10-18

Yang, K. (2012) Reflexivity, participation and video, Milne, E. J., Mitchell, C. and de Lange, N. (eds) *Handbook of participatory video*, Lanham, Altamira Press pp 100-114

Young, J. (2010) Digital storytelling: Preserving a cultural tradition, *Education Canada*, Vol. 50, No. 1 pp 22-25

Zoetti, P. A. (2013) Images of culture: Participatory video, identity and empowerment, *International Journal of Cultural Studies*, Vol. 16, No. 2 pp 209-224

NOTE ON THE CONTRIBUTOR

Marian Reid is an Australian writer and communications adviser. Led by participatory media principles and local solutions, she elevates local stories that support communities and non-government organisations. Her thematic focus includes community-led development, culture, nature and climate change.

Chapter 13

'Charitable journalism': Oxymoron or opportunity?

Judith Townend

Resource intensive journalism considered likely to attract small audiences has been particularly vulnerable to industry cuts. Could charitable funding help reinvigorate topics neglected by commercial media? And what are the benefits and drawbacks?

Keywords: charitable journalism, media plurality, public interest journalism, media policy and regulation

My recent research investigating the possibility of charitably funded journalism has prompted a few bemused responses. Surely journalism and charity are mutually exclusive? This view is part of a general suspicion of public or state intervention in the news business; politicians such as Lord Stoneham of Droxford have been unconvinced 'that the state should get involved in subsidising the industry' (*Parliament.uk* 2012). Despite this perception, there is a range of existing journalistic projects that are funded charitably and opportunities to add more to this list.

As author of the UK section of a new five-country report co-produced by the Reuters Institute for the Study of Journalism and the Yale Information Society Project,[1] I was tasked with finding out whether any 'news' is sustained by charities in the UK, and if so, how. This exercise required flexible thinking. Certainly there are no national news organisations operating in this way. It is unlikely that any national operation could achieve such status without radical change to its structure and output. As a Charity Law Association working party identified in 2011, 'a commercial undertaking such as a conventional newspaper company is likely to be disqualified from charitable status because its underlying purpose is to generate a financial return for its owners, regardless of any beneficial effect on the public that might result from some of its work' (CLA 2011). This would make it difficult to meet the 'public benefit' requirement, by which a charity must not give rise to more than an incidental personal benefit.

CHARITABLE JOURNALISM IN PRACTICE

This restriction would not, however, preclude a not-for-profit organisation seeking charitable status. And if one thinks beyond national news outlets to other types of organisations producing news-like or journalistic-style content, then there is convincing evidence of charitable funding being used to support journalism. In 2011 Robert Picard (co-editor of the new report) identified three possible models: 'Charitable ownership and control', 'Charitably supported media' and 'Trust ownership and control'. For the new research, I adapted and updated these as follows:

1. charitable ownership and control, in which a charity directly produces journalism as a core activity;

2. charitable ownership and control, in which a charity owns or controls a non-charitable journalism-producing organisation;

3. charitably-supported journalism in which non-charitable journalism-producing organisations and individuals receive some support from charities and charitable individuals (recipient may be taxed on grants received).

There were examples for each of these models, although some organisations might be better described as 'hybrid' with overlap between the categories depending on the nature of its set-up and operations. The national organisations *Full Fact* and *The Conversation UK* fall in category one, in which the charity produces journalism as a core activity. Both organisations are registered charities, employ journalists and writers, and have charitable purposes strongly connected to the mission of journalism. *Full Fact*, a non-partisan fact-checking website, provides tools, advice and information to allow people to assess claims made about public issues. It was originally rejected twice by the Charity Commission before successfully securing charitable status in 2014 after a third application (Sharman 2014). It aims to advance public education 'in the fields of crime, health, immigration, economy, education, environment and social welfare, through education, research and training' to 'promote and advance public understanding and inform public debate … by making available to the public, through a process of objective, impartial research and rigorous factual analysis, full, accurate and relevant information' (Charity Commission 2015).

Meanwhile, *The Conversation UK*, part of an initiative that started in Australia, is publisher of an online news analysis and commentary website where all articles are written by academics for a general non-academic audience. Authors and editors sign up to an Editorial Charter and contributors must abide by its community standards policy. All its articles are available for republishing free of charge under a Creative Commons licence. Its charitable object is, like *Full Fact*, the advancement of education. As non-profits, rather than commercial enterprises, they were able to show that they would not give rise to more than an incidental personal benefit

In the second category, where the relationship is less direct, and the charity owns or controls a non-charitable organisation, examples include *Which?* magazine, published by the charity the Consumers' Association through its trading company Which? Ltd, which is registered as a private limited company; and the *Maidenhead Advertiser*, a newspaper run by the private limited company Baylis Media Ltd owned by the Louis Baylis (*Maidenhead Advertiser*) Charitable Trust. The charitable trust receives at least 80 per cent of the newspaper's profits. The benefits of being a charity are less obvious in this category: for example, the private entity would not necessarily enjoy the tax relief available for charities.

The last category allows for arrangements whereby an organisation receives charitable funding, but without necessarily being tied to one charitable owner. The boundaries are not clearly defined: categories two and three may overlap to some extent. Examples within this group include *openDemocracy*, a website published by a private limited company and wholly owned by a private not-for-profit, the openDemocracy Foundation for the Advancement of Global Education, and partially supported by a charity, the OpenTrust. This arrangement allows a publishing entity to engage in different types of activity, some charitably funded – with specific charitable purposes and for the public benefit – and some non-charitably funded, and therefore unconstrained by restrictions on political activity.

Finally, outside the three categories of what might be called charitable journalism, there are examples of *media*-supporting charities; charities such as BBC Action or the Media Trust which support media training and education. There are also charities that produce media content as part of their wider work: human rights charities, universities and churches, for example.

Not only is charitable journalism already being done, it is successful. At a local level, the *Ambler*, the *Burngreave Messenger* and the *Lewisham Pensioner's Gazette* are charitable initiatives producing local media content, part of a useful response to the 'democratic deficit' caused by local news closures and cuts. Academics have been able to share their work with public audiences through *The Conversation UK* without relying on commercial news organisations constrained by news agendas and a lack of time (or inclination) to commission and edit academic work for non-specialist audiences. *China Dialogue* is publishing a dual language website highlighting under-covered environmental issues. *Full Fact* is injecting reliable information into the media and political system by systematically checking the claims that are made by politicians, newspapers and other powerful people and institutions.

These charitable initiatives share one striking similarity: they all provide content neglected in commercial environments, perhaps because this content does not drive enough traffic to attract online advertising, or is considered unlikely to appeal to paying subscribers and readers. One such neglected area is law for general public audiences: it is notable that specialist legal and courts coverage has declined in recent years, with fewer expert correspondents and full-time court reporters employed by commercial national and local news organisations (see, for example, Magrath 2012). *Full Fact* has, however, bucked the trend and increased its output on legal topics after the Legal Education Foundation funded its first legal researcher post (McKinney 2015). Charitable status helps attract funding for public interest content that is being cut in other quarters.

A SUITABLE MODEL?

These forms of charitable journalism are not appropriate for all kinds of public interest content, however. According to Charity Commission guidance based on the common and statutory law, a charity's purposes cannot be political; political campaigning, or political activity, must be undertaken by a charity only in the context of supporting the delivery of its charitable purposes (Charity Commission 2008). A partisan newspaper offering strong political commentary would not be suitable for charitable status. It is only a particular type of tightly structured non-partisan organisation that would be able to fit within the constraints of the existing charity regime.

One concern raised by critics is that charitable trustees and funders would be able to put pressure on editors and journalists working for their publications, risking editorial autonomy. In counterpoint, it can be argued that the robust structure required for a charity, with guidelines and a system of regulatory enforcement, could, in fact, help protect journalism from editorial interference – offering greater safeguards than in commercial environments, where editorial interference from powerful owners is well-documented. Tom Murdoch, partner at the charity-specialist law firm Stone King LLP, believes that greater recognition of charitable forms of journalism could equip community news providers and investigative journalists to more easily survive in the new environment, strengthen local communities and meet an important democratic need to disseminate information which enables citizens to participate more fully in society.[2]

OBSTACLES TO REGISTERING AS A CHARITY

It is not easy for a non-partisan journalism organisation – even if designed to meet a charitable purpose and provide public benefit – to secure charitable status. It took *Full Fact* three attempts. The Bureau of Investigative Journalism has also been rejected twice, and has delayed a third application until it can be more confident of success.

Among the issues is the Charity Commission's requirement to see evidence that the organisation's input to investigative journalism translates into democratic participation and engagement; the Bureau felt it needed clearer guidance on this before proceeding with a further application. The Bureau was also concerned that changing trustee roles and operating procedures, as it has been advised to do, could affect the editorial independence of the editor and constrain the range of its journalism. A revised structure could potentially introduce delays in committing to stories. According to its chairman James Lee, 'these constraints would not necessarily have been prohibitive, but they were certainly far from ideal'.[3]

POLICY AND LAW

Proponents of charitable journalism, such as an *ad hoc* group of lawyers and practitioners that submitted written evidence to the Leveson Inquiry in 2012, have suggested that charity law 'should be capable of recognising the broad public benefit in certain forms of public interest journalism, subject to conditions that would not open the floodgates to the registration of news organisations that are pursuing commercial benefit or political objects' (Heawood et al. 2012). This followed recommendations by the House of Lords select committee on communication that the Charity Commission should 'provide greater clarity and guidelines on which activities related to the media, and in particular investigative journalism, are charitable in the current state of the law'. The committee also asked that the body 'take into consideration both the current pressures on investigative journalism as well as its democratic importance when interpreting the relevant legislation' (House of Lords 2012: para. 201).

The previous Coalition government was reluctant to engage on this issue. At the time of the House of Lords committee hearings Jeremy Hunt, then culture secretary, indicated that the government was not 'inclined to legislate' (ibid: para. 198). And, it would seem, disinclined to take any action at all, as neither the government nor the Charity Commission appears to have officially responded to the House of Lords report. There has been no indication of further consultation on this issue, at least not publicly.

AN OPPORTUNITY FOR JOURNALISM

To return to the question posed in the title: is charitable journalism an oxymoron or an opportunity? The research discussed here, and in my wider work (Townend 2016; Barnett and Townend 2015), indicates that models of charitable journalism provide an opportunity for producing public interest content under-served by commercial organisations. It would only be oxymoronic if the journalism were partisan, existed for a political purpose and provided more than incidental personal benefit to owners: these characteristics – which define many commercial news operations – would conflict with a common social and legal understanding of charitable work. As the *ad hoc* group wrote in its evidence to Lord Justice Leveson, there need to be conditions preventing news organisations which further commercial and party political interests from becoming charities.

Charitable status is not a magic bullet for the media industry. Being a charity places particular burdens on organisations as well as granting them reputational and financial benefits. But certain (existing or future) non-profit news organisations, especially those working in local geographic communities, on investigations and specialist topics such as law could greatly benefit from a regime that recognises specified forms of journalistic and news activity as charitable, to a greater extent than it does already. The structures and approach required for charitable status would strengthen rather than undermine the quality and independence of journalism, and especially so in areas neglected by commercial media organisations.

- This paper was first published in *Ethical Space*, Vol 13, Nos 2 and 3 pp 81-87, 2016

NOTES

[1] *The impact of charity and tax law/regulation on not-for-profit news organizations*, edited by Robert Picard, Valerie Belair Gagnon and Sofia Ranchordás and published by the Reuters Institute for the Study of Journalism, University of Oxford, and the Yale Law School Information Society Project, was published in March 2016. The research for my chapter in that report is partly based on work completed for an AHRC-funded project on media power and plurality at the University of Westminster, 2013-2014

[2] Tom Murdoch advised on the full RISJ/ISP report, in which his views are set out more fully

[3] Information taken from discussion seminar notes at the University of Westminster in 2014 and personal correspondence with James Lee

REFERENCES

Barnett, S. and Townend, J. (eds) (2015) *Media power and plurality: From hyperlocal to high-level policy*, Palgrave Global Media Policy and Business, London, Palgrave Macmillan

Charity Commission (2008) *Speaking out: Guidance on campaigning and political activity by charities*. Available online at https://www.gov.uk/government/publications/speaking-out-guidance-on-campaigning-and-political-activity-by- charities-cc9/speaking-out-guidance-on-campaigning-and-political-activity-by-charities, accessed on 15 September 2015

Charity Commission (2015) *1158683: FULL FACT, Charitycommission.gov. uk*. Available online at http://apps.charitycommission.gov.uk/Showcharity/RegisterOfCharities/CharityFramework.aspx?RegisteredCharityNumber=1158683& SubsidiaryNumber=0, accessed on 15 September 2015

Charity Law Association (CLA) (2011) *Written evidence to House of Lords select committee on communications' inquiry into the future of investigative journalism*. Available online at http://charitylawassociation.org.uk/api/attachment/576?_output=binary, accessed on 15 September 2015

Heawood, J., McCarthy, R., Simanowitz, L. and Overton, I. (2012) *Good news? A report by the Advisory Group on Journalism and Charitable Status: Representation to the Leveson Inquiry*. Available online at http://www.mediaplurality.com/wp-content/uploads/2013/10/Leveson-submission-Good-News.pdf, accessed on 15 September 2015

House of Lords (2012) *House of Lords Communications Committee Third Report: The future of investigative journalism*, House of Lords. Available online at http://www.publications.parliament.uk/pa/ld201012/ldselect/ldcomuni/256/25602.htm, accessed on 15 September 2015

Parliament.uk (2012) *Daily Hansard*, 25 July 2012: Column GC305, *Parliament.uk*. Available online at http://www.publications.parliament.uk/pa/ld201213/ldhansrd/text/120725-gc0001.htm#12072541000330, accessed on 15 September 2015

Picard, R. G. (2011) Charitable ownership and trusts in news organisations, Levy, D. A. L. and Picard, R. G. (eds) *Is there a better structure for the news providers? The potential in charitable and trust ownership*, Oxford, Reuters Institute for the Study of Journalism

Magrath, P. (2012) Law reporting in a new media age, ICLR. Available online at http://www.iclr.co.uk/law-reporting-in-a-new-media-age/, accessed on 14 January 2016

McKinney, C. J. (2015) *Full Fact on family law*, The Transparency Project. Available online at http://www.transparencyproject.org.uk/full-fact-on-family-law/, accessed on 14 January 2016

Sharman, A. (2014) Full Fact gets charity status after being rejected twice, *Civilsociety.co.uk*. Available online at http://www.civilsociety.co.uk/governance/news/content/18563/full_fact_gets_charity_status_after_being_rejected_twice, accessed on 15 September 2015

Townend, J. (2016) The United Kingdom: The impact of charity and tax law/regulation on not-for-profit news organizations, Picard, R.G., Belair-Gagnon, V. and Ranchordás, S. (eds) *The impact of charity and tax law/regulation on not-for-profit news organizations*, Reuters Institute for the Study of Journalism, University of Oxford; Information Society Project, Yale Law School

NOTE ON THE CONTRIBUTOR

Judith Townend is Reader in Digital Society and Justice at the University of Sussex. At the time of writing this article, she was lecturer in information law and policy and director of the Information Law and Policy Centre at the Institute of Advanced Legal Studies, University of London. She was co-editor (with Steven Barnett) of *Media power and plurality* (Palgrave Macmillan, 2015) and she is co-author (with Lucy Welsh) of *Observing justice* (BUP, 2023). She continues to research and write on topics related to civic access to information and the protection and resourcing of public interest journalism.

Chapter 14

Democratic affordances: Politics, media and digital technology after WikiLeaks

Gerard Goggin

This paper considers the role of digital technologies and cultures in re-envisioning democratic media and ethics. Much hope is being invested in the potential of digital technologies to provide the way forward to addressing the impasse in democratic communication, especially through innovative online news and journalism tools and projects. In the context of such discourses and initiatives, this paper argues that we need to develop a serviceable notion of 'democratic affordances', the qualities of digital technologies, and the media ecologies in which they take shape, that allow individuals and collectivities to pursue democracy, ethics and justice. I explore this idea via an analysis of the celebrated case of Julian Assange's WikiLeaks, perhaps the most singular and spectacular example of innovation in democratic affordances. For its instigators, the potential of WikiLeaks at its birth appeared revolutionary and straightforward. As it has turned out, however, the interactions between journalism, news and the digital in this novel platform have not been straightforward at all. The case of WikiLeaks thus reveals the need to take a much broader view of the pluralistic system in which such digital technologies now unfold. In particular, the paper argues for a comprehensive, pluralistic approach to designing the communicative architecture for ethical and truth-telling practices that go hand-in-hand with the struggle for democracy, justice and the good life.

Keywords: democracy, digital technology, democratic communication, affordances, WikiLeaks

The power of people speaking up and resisting together terrifies corrupt and undemocratic power. So much so that ordinary people here in the West are now the enemy of governments, an enemy to be watched, an enemy to be controlled and to be impoverished. True democracy is not the White House. True democracy is not Canberra. True democracy is the resistance of people, armed with the truth, against lies, from Tahrir to right here in London. Every day, ordinary people teach us that democracy is free speech and dissent.

Julian Assange (2012a)

The whole trend [of the 'truth paradox'] is fed by a growing abundance of platforms where power is interrogated and chastened, so that monitory democracies tend to nurture uncertainty, doubt, scepticism, modesty, irony, the conviction that truth has many faces, the recognition that the meaning of the world and its dynamics are so complicated that, ultimately, its true meaning and significance cannot be fully grasped.

John Keane (2013a)

INTRODUCTION: DIGITAL HOPES FOR DEMOCRACIES

Around the world in the 2010s, discourses, plans and experiments for re-imagining democratic media and ethics centre on the prospects of digital technologies and digital cultures. In recent uprisings and social upheavals, new kinds of media devices and practices have being hailed as the signature of a new form of social action and political mode.

When Philippines President Joseph Estrada was forced from office by a popular uprising in 2001, he felt it was due to protests organised by text messaging which he dubbed a *coup de texte* (Goggin 2006). Mobile phones and the internet were widely used in the 2007 Burmese 'Saffron revolution'. Iran's 2009 'Green revolution' was nicknamed the 'Twitter revolution' (Ash 2009; Sreberny and Khiabany 2010). Egypt's 'Arab spring' of 2011 was styled the 'Facebook revolution' (Beaumont and Sherwood 2011; Shenker 2011; Ghonim 2012). A central theme in how such movements for democracy are understood revolves around a novel digital technology as incubator in revolutions and societal uprisings (Castells 2012).

More broadly, the subject of digital technology's use for democracy is the subject of a large and still inconclusive body of experimental practice and research across many countries, political systems and cultures, and social settings. It is beyond the scope of this paper to provide an adequate assessment of these adventures in democracy via digital technology and their associated research and debates (Chadwick and Howard 2008; Kies 2010; Dahlberg and Siapera 2007). Instead, the focus is on the increasing effort being invested in the prospects of digital technologies for a more democratic media. As Robert Hackett and collaborator Yuezhi Zhao point out, there exists a complex set of intersections between global media and processes of democratisation. This involves both 'democratisation through the media – the use of communications by civil society or states to promote democratic processes elsewhere in society' and 'democratisation of the media themselves' (Zhao and Hackett 2005: 2). Clearly digital technology is the media of our time most widely credited with enabling great strides in democratisation.

We can say with conviction and evidence that digital technology is a key factor in the transformation of contemporary media – with far from obvious implications. Contemporary media are in extraordinary flux in many societies, especially in the West. Traditional roles in journalism and media, and their assumed entailments for ethics, are being fundamentally reworked. As the business models for journalism and news dramatically shift in the face of internet-based search, with many traditional journalism positions lost, all media organisations, but especially newspapers, are grappling with the rise of online, mobile, and social media devices, applications, forms and platforms.

Increasingly, professional journalists and media workers, existing and new media organisations, citizens, activists, politicians, leaders, civil society, government, business and others interested in democracy wish to take the opportunity of the 'creative destruction', as economist Joseph Schumpeter (1975) termed it, of existing media, to find better ways to remodel these institutions in the service of existing or imagined democracies. There are diverse positions on these new nexus of democracy and media – from the fit between digital platforms and John Keane's notion of 'monitory democracy' (Keane 2009) to projects of 'open democracy', 'open government' (using computer culture notions of open source) or 'gov 2.0'. Much attention has concentrated on the potential of the widely available digital network technologies to support democratic communication – starting with the early internet, moving through the web, and blogging, and then focusing on mobile media and social media such as Twitter and Facebook.

If we examine digital platforms for journalism in particular, a project with a long genealogy is the use of websites and blogs, suitably modified, to publish quality journalism. Forerunners of such sites, which have enjoyed financial viability and longevity, include the *Huffington Post* and Slate.com. There are now many such blogs around the world that have taken over from independent newspapers, small magazines and journals in providing journalism and news, commentary, reviews, essays and critique. Sometimes these seek to run on a subscription basis, as the Australian website Crikey.com sought to do. Others start as free blogs, underpinned by funds from foundations and universities (such as another Australian title *inside story*) and then solicit donations, or even provide printed copies and compendium via newsagents and bookshops. A new initiative is the Dutch digital news site called De Correspondent (https://decorrespondent.nl/). It attracted a great deal of attention in March 2013 for its mission to value quality over quantity, and publish long-form journalism on a bespoke digital platform – but also for raising a substantial amount of capital via crowdsourcing.

A new kind of project that uses digital technology to rethink one particularly salient mission of democratic media and ethics is PolitiFact.com, a project of the *Tampa Bay Times*. PolitiFact.com aims to 'to help you find the truth in American politics' (Politifact 2013). To do so, *Times* reporters and editors 'fact-check statements by members of Congress, the White House, lobbyists and interest groups and rate them on our Truth-O-Meter' (ibid). The Truth-O-Meter is central to Politifact, and involves analysing statements in their context, dividing them into individual claims, which are independently verified. Then the statement is given one of six ratings: true; mostly true; half true; mostly false; false; pants on fire (ibid). With PolitiFact Mobile the Truth-O-Meter comes as an app to provide fact-checking on a smartphone or table device. PolitiFact is a North American incarnation, but former *Sydney Morning Herald* publisher and editor-in-chief Peter Fray has the rights to introduce it into Australia in mid-2013.

These are but two tendencies among a raft of digital experiments. The general problem besetting most of these, as I have already suggested, is that it is typically unclear whether digital technology is bringing about improvements in democracy, let alone playing a much more creative, transformative role in constituting new modes of democracy (Sykes 2012; Curran 2011; Fenton 2010; Hindman 2009; Papacharissi 2010). Despite the many reasons for scepticism, digital technology is still widely believed to be critical in achieving a breakthrough in the impasse of democratic communication. And experiments in digital technology and democracy are imbued with much hope and excitement.

In the context of such discourses and initiatives, this paper argues that we urgently need to develop a serviceable notion of 'democratic affordances'. The concept of affordance was developed by psychologist James J. Gibson (1977) and is widely used in design and analysis of digital technology to indicate the elusive zone of the quality of an object, environment, technological system, application or artefact that allows an individual to perform a particular action. An affordance in effect, is what kind of use is suggested by a technology. By democratic affordance, I wish to raise the question of how we identify, evaluate, debate, select and modify the qualities of digital technologies, and the media ecologies in which they take shape, that allow individuals and collectivities to pursue democracy, ethics and justice.

My framework for understanding and proposing democratic affordance as a useful concept in this project of re-envisioning democratic media and ethics draws on media and cultural studies research on digital technology and cultures, but also from the extensive science and technology studies (STS) literature on the shaping and politics of technology. In particular, there was a famous debate kicked off by US scholar Langdon Winner, in his article 'Do artifacts have politics?' (Winner 1980). This paper received at least two dedicated rebuttals (Woolgar and Cooper 1999; Joerges 1999), and his argument has now receded in the face of a wide range of approaches that emphasised the open-ended nature of technology, the deeply enmeshed mutual constitution of society and technology, and the complex, recursive non-linear politics that is conducted through the design, implementation and appropriation of technology (Latour and Weibel 2005; Latour 2005). Despite the emerging consensus in these research fields that it is rarely possible to read the politics of technology, there is also a strong view that such a project is important.

These ideas are behind my proposal of the concept of democratic affordance as something that would bring a much-needed focus on how we can evaluate, critique, abandon or adapt, modify and refine the many digital platforms now being born under the sign of democracy.

In what follows, I explore the idea of democratic affordances via an analysis of the celebrated case of Julian Assange's WikiLeaks, perhaps the most singular and spectacular example of innovation in democratic affordances. For its instigators, the potential capacities of WikiLeaks at its birth appeared revolutionary and straightforward. As it has turned out, however, the interactions among journalism, news and the digital in this novel platform have not been straightforward at all. What the case of WikiLeaks reveals is the need to take a much broader view of the pluralistic system in which such digital technologies now unfold.

WIKILEAKS: STRATEGY AND TACTICS

Launched in late 2006, WikiLeaks became a *cause célèbre*: an independent, non-profit organisation that publishes news documents from anonymous news sources and leaks. Loosely modelled on the participatory platform Wikipedia, WikiLeaks is primarily a platform for a time-honoured tradition: leaking documents. It makes public the new kinds of data government and corporate agencies were able to record and store, that previously would neither have been regarded as worthy of release for scrutiny of citizens, nor as sources for journalists. WikiLeaks established its reputation relatively quickly, receiving an *Index on Censorship* Freedom of Expression award in 2008, cited as 'an invaluable resource for anonymous whistleblowers and investigative journalists' (*Index on Censorship* 2008). Considering what WikiLeaks represents, it is clear its affordances, as well as its strategics and tactics, go well beyond previous platforms. Let us consider WikiLeaks's tactics and strategies first.

To be sure, WikiLeaks has been able to solicit, obtain and release documents of the type that are sometimes available to journalists. Following in the wake of internet news ventures before it (notably the Drudge Report: www.drudgereport.com), it showed a bold unconventionality in being prepared to release unfiltered documents. The Drudge Report was one of the first, best-known experiments of its kind in the Anglophone world, because its founder, Matt Drudge, was prepared to release stories on the basis of sources that would usually not be deemed credible according to the norms of journalism. Such norms still influence online news. As I finished this paper (in April 2013), the story about allegations of sexual abuse by another famous expatriate Australian, the entertainer Rolf Harris, broke. Rumours concerning this had been circulated on blogs for some days, before the mainstream media were prepared to name Harris – and only then because the police had arrested him for questioning on suspicion of committing sexual offences.

WikiLeaks stakes out a different position on releasing documents online because of its insistence that it deals with 'leaks', rather than unsubstantiated stories *per se*:

WikiLeaks accepts *classified, censored* or otherwise *restricted* material of *political, diplomatic or ethical significance*. WikiLeaks *does not accept* rumour, opinion or other kinds of first hand reporting or material that is already publicly available … Over 100,000 articles catalyzed world-wide. Every source protected. No documents censored. All legal attacks defeated (WikiLeaks 2013b).

As such, WikiLeaks makes a strong claim to be an organisation underpinned and oriented by ethical principles:

> … multi-jurisdictional organization to protect internal dissidents, whistleblowers, journalists and bloggers who face legal or other threats related to publishing. Our primary interest is in exposing oppressive regimes in Asia, the former Soviet bloc, Sub-Saharan Africa and the Middle East, but we are of assistance to people of all nations who wish to reveal unethical behavior in their governments and corporations … WikiLeaks opens leaked documents up to stronger scrutiny than any media organization or intelligence agency can provide. WikiLeaks provides a forum for the entire global community to relentlessly examine any document for its credibility, plausibility, veracity and validity (Visser 2009).

A defining story for WikiLeaks was the *Collateral murder* video (http://www.collateral-murder.com/) and ensuing outcry. On 5 April 2010, WikiLeaks released a classified US military video showing a July 2007 incident in which US soldiers in an Apache helicopter attacked and killed Iraqi civilians. After the initial shock and dismay at the conduct of the US personnel depicted in the video, there was a backlash against WikiLeaks for the way in which it published the footage. Severe criticism emanated from the US government, but serious concerns were also raised by wide range of commentators, including comedian Stephen Colbert in a much-noted interview with Assange. Colbert echoed the concerns of many journalists and commentators in questioning the emotional manipulation and de-contextualisation of the video as it was edited for release (Kennedy 2010).

In response to the criticism it received over its *Collateral murder* video, WikiLeaks modified its tactics. This is most evident in its July 2010 release of US military internal logs of the Afghanistan conflict dating 2004-2010 (http://wikileaks.org/afg/). These were reports written by soldiers, military and intelligence personnel, covering US Army and US Special Forces actions. WikiLeaks's editorial board summary of the Afghan logs states:

Unless otherwise specified, the document described here:

- was first publicly revealed by WikiLeaks working with our source;

- was classified, confidential, censored or otherwise withheld from the public before release;

- is of political, diplomatic, ethical or historical significance.

Any questions about this document's veracity are noted (WikiLeaks 2010a).

Until mid-2010, WikiLeaks represented itself as fiercely independent – capable of, and willing to, publish exactly what it wished to, for the interest and examination of the readers and internet users of the world. With the Afghanistan war logs, it formed partnerships with some of the best-known and respected press organs, including the *Guardian*, *New York Times*, and *Der Spiegel*. These media partners made an agreement with WikiLeaks to publish simultaneously their reports regarding the Afghanistan war logs, at the same time as WikiLeaks released the full database on the internet (*Guardian* 2010). WikiLeaks was widely believed to have turned to these lions of the established press to garner credibility (Kennedy 2010). Yet, as it turned out, this was not wholly successful.

The release of the secret material that comprised the Afghan logs not only drew the expected condemnation from the US government, its military, security agencies and allies. WikiLeaks also attracted strong criticism from journalists and organisations defending press freedom for carelessly releasing the names of many Afghan informants assisting coalition forces. Reporters without Borders and Amnesty International were two respected organisations that criticised WikiLeaks for failing to redact names of individuals at risk from the release of the documents (Siddique 2010). WikiLeaks rejected the criticisms at the time, but later took these on board – as was evident in its next sensational and long-running release: Cablegate.

From November 2010 onwards, WikiLeaks steadily released tranches of cables with revelations pertinent to various countries unfolding daily. In total, there were 251,287 diplomatic cables from 250 US embassies around the world containing candid assessments by officials about foreign governments (WikiLeaks 2010b). The material released caused severe discomfiture to many governments around the world, too numerous to mention.

To control the reception of the release of the US embassy cables, WikiLeaks again struck agreements with leading press outlets. There were many advantages to this, including the ability to take advantage of the fact-checking, analysis and interpretation skills of leading journalists. Also, the newspapers were able to pick out the aspects of the cables most germane to their national publics and zero in on the points of maximum embarrassment and outrage to their own governments. Last but not least, when Assange was being threatened with assassination and imprisonment, he was able to point to the fact that others – highly regarded newspapers no less – had also published the cables.

With Cablegate, WikiLeaks found a rapprochement with the press. Indeed, WikiLeaks went so far as to cloak itself in the honourable, truth-telling traditions of the Fourth Estate:

> WikiLeaks has combined high-end security technologies with journalism and ethical principles. Like other media outlets conducting investigative journalism, we accept (but do not solicit) anonymous sources of information. Unlike other outlets, we provide a high security anonymous drop box fortified by cutting-edge cryptographic information technologies … We are fearless in our efforts to get the unvarnished truth out to the public. When information comes in, our journalists analyse the material, verify it and write a news piece about it describing its significance to society. We then publish both the news story and the original material in order to enable readers to analyze the story in the context of the original source material themselves (WikiLeaks 2013a).

Elsewhere Assange, with a characteristic flourish, termed this approach 'scientific journalism':

> In 1958 a young Rupert Murdoch, then owner and editor of Adelaide's *The News*, wrote:

> 'In the race between secrecy and truth, it seems inevitable that truth will always win.' … I grew up in a Queensland country town where people spoke their minds bluntly. They distrusted big government as something that could be corrupted if not watched carefully … These things have stayed with me. WikiLeaks was created around these core values. The idea, conceived in Australia, was to use internet technologies in new ways to report the truth. WikiLeaks coined a new type of journalism: scientific journalism. We work with other media outlets to bring people the news, but also to prove it is true. Scientific journalism allows you to read a news story, then to click online to see the original document it is based on. That way you can judge for yourself: Is the story true? Did the journalist report it accurately? Democratic societies need a strong media and WikiLeaks is part of that media (see Kennedy 2010).

Here we see how Assange wishes to present WikiLeaks as disruptive to the existing regime of news and journalism. However, he also insists on the continuity of WikiLeaks within the traditional role of media. Thus, WikiLeaks positions itself clearly as an integral yet critical part of democracy's mainstream media institutions.

WHAT WIKILEAKS AFFORDS DEMOCRACY (SO FAR)

Thus far, I have focused on the tactics and strategies that WikiLeaks used between 2008 and 2010 when it achieved international fame. Let me now turn an analysis of the affordances of WikiLeaks and what lessons we might draw from these for the broader account of democratic affordances I am seeking to outline. An obvious affordance of WikiLeaks as a platform is the way it deploys the internet and related information and communication technologies to offer a new kind of online, anonymous conduit for leaking. Different kinds of technologies are deployed to ensure those wishing to leak documents can securely submit a file online (WikiLeaks 2013b). As John Keane notes:

> This 'intelligence agency of the people' (as Assange calls his organisation) did more than harness to the full the defining features of the unfinished communications revolution of our time: the easy-access multi-media integration and low-cost copying of information that is then instantly whizzed around the world through digital networks ... For the first time, on a global scale, WikiLeaks created a custom-made mailbox that enabled disgruntled muckrakers within any organisation to deposit and store classified data in a camouflaged cloud of servers (Keane 2013b).

Despite this achievement, ironically, the tried-and-tested postal service still receives WikiLeaks's highest recommendation: 'Submissions to our postal network offer the strongest form of anonymity and are good for bulk truth-telling' (WikiLeaks 2013b). What is most interesting about how this particular affordance of WikiLeaks has developed is that it is now precisely coupled with a long-standing legal understanding of the status of leaks in journalism:

> All staff who deal with sources are accredited journalists. All submissions establish a journalist-source relationship. Online submissions are routed via Sweden and Belgium which have first rate journalist-source shield laws (ibid).

A submission is no longer simply posted or uploaded to WikiLeaks. Rather, all submissions are deemed to 'establish a journalist-source relationship'. In addition, WikiLeaks is a global media platform, but it becomes a 'glocal' form when it chooses the most desirable potential defence of sources. While WikiLeaks has chosen to limit its conceptualisation of its role, the affordances of the platform potentially go much wider. To appreciate the scope of WikiLeaks, it is helpful to return to a less well-known episode in the WikiLeaks story so far.

In 2009, Wikileaks released a set of data containing a distinctive record of the events of the terrorist attacks of 9/11:

> From 3am on Wednesday November 25, 2009, until 3am the following day (US east coast time), WikiLeaks released half a million US national text pager intercepts. The intercepts cover a 24-hour period surrounding the 11 September 2001 attacks in New York and Washington. The messages were broadcast 'live' to the global community – sychronized to the time of day they were sent ... Text pagers are usually carried by persons operating in an official capacity. Messages in the archive range from Pentagon, FBI, FEMA and New York Police Department exchanges, to computers reporting faults at investment banks inside the World Trade Center. The

archive is a completely objective record of the defining moment of our time. We hope that its entrance into the historical record will lead to a nuanced understanding of how this event led to death, opportunism and war (WikiLeaks 2009).

As released by WikiLeaks, the intercepted messages represent a mosaic of communications responding to the breaking event, flows of everyday media from individuals and organisations:

7:05:57 am

Please don't leave the building. One of the towers just collapsed! Please, please be careful. Repeat,

11:00:30 am

BOMB SQUAD PLS REPORT TO EDIC...PER T913..OPS/JL ...

5:20:30 pm

Honey wanted to tell you how much i love you. I was a little worried. I Don't want to lose you now that I got you back. You mean everything to me. You have my whole heart and life. I love you so much,

6:05:05 pm

We are bombing Afganistan. Pene 6:58:58 pm

1) my nephew's ok, 2) there's a dead body at the main gate, 3) US denies responsibility for bombing in Afghanistan. Over and out (quoted in *Huffington Post* 2009).

The messages show the banality as much as the vivid, poignant nature of reaction to 9/11, in this slice of US society.

If we consider how the 9/11 text pager data of WikiLeaks fits into accounts of journalism and news, the obvious starting point is the long-established role of the press in uncovering and reporting news, based on new caches or archives of documents. Such documents themselves serve as the basic, factual evidence to ground the veracity of such stories and clinch their legitimacy. With the rise of notions of open government and, specifically, the concept of freedom of information *vis-à-vis* government and public sector information, journalists and newspapers have often reproduced and discussed sets of documents. The advent of the world wide web has provided greater capacity for the press to provide the underlying or accompanying documents themselves for readers to consult and interpret. This direction in openness is greatly extended by WikiLeaks's release of the 9/11 text pager data.

News stories often rely on intercepts of many telephone calls, emails or text messsages. Usually, however, a few key telephone calls or messages are described and reproduced – as a 'smoking gun', to provide the establishing evidence. It is typically then left to archiving, collecting or cultural institutions – libraries, national archives, museums – to serve as repositories for such information, so it can be preserved for historical, research and cultural heritage purposes. WikiLeaks's release 'disintermediates' the gamut of institutions, from the press through to libraries and archives and universities. It makes available to anyone who has access and can use the internet to peruse, download and make sense of these records. The 9/11 text pager data release is an early sign of the extraordinary affordances of WikiLeaks's platform. We might extend this argument further, however.

As WikiLeaks made plain at the time, the 9/11 message data release is only possible because of the routine surveillance of citizens in everyday life. The source of the messages was a US organisation that intercepts all manner of data communications traffic, from the commanding heights of state security organisations such as the Pentagon and FBI, through police and emergency organisations, to interpersonal communications and computer generated communications. This kind of networked, informational society operates on data networks and data communications, that, in turn, may be surveilled, aggregated, archived and analysed. In this sense, WikiLeaks has drawn attention to the lineaments of the data-intensive architecture of everyday life in polities such as the US; then, through its release of a sample of the data, is able to make a signal intervention, to pierce the veil of this 'dataveillance' (Amore and de Goede 2005; Clark 1994). Thus it adds a further twist to the 'social life' of such data (Brown and Duguid 2000), creating a democratic temper from its affordances.

To sum up, in a relatively short space of time, WikiLeaks has moved from being a radical outlier, experimenting with the potential of the internet to create a new media force – to something that works much more hand-in-glove with the organs of the press it hoped to trump with 'higher scrutiny' (cf. Allan 2013). There are, then, two principal lessons to be drawn from this case study in digital technology, media and democracy.

Firstly, there is extraordinary potential for socio-technical innovation in creating digital platforms. WikiLeaks's affordances in their 'raw' form – witness the *Collateral murder*, war logs and 9/11 data releases – clearly disrupted the existing circuits that connect democracy with media. In a powerful, stark, profound and troubling sense, WikiLeaks has sketched the possibility for a new communicative architecture for democracy.

Secondly, the social and cultural shaping of WikiLeaks's platform and the power relations in which they unfolded, revealed the complexity of designing and implementing such platforms for democratic means and ends. For its instigators, the potential capacities of WikiLeaks at its birth appeared revolutionary and straightforward. As it has turned out, however, the interactions among journalism, news and the digital in this novel platform have not been straightforward at all. The affordances of WikiLeaks as a platform have extraordinary potential to transform journalism and media. Yet the democratic implications of these affordances have been far more ambiguous and at times reactionary than could possibly have been foreseen (cf. Lovink 2011; Brevini et al. 2013).

An obvious test of the democratic potential and effects of media relates to a judgement concerning the closely linked issues of accountability, transparency and governance. Especially once WikiLeaks became a household name, the transparency of WikiLeaks was not only being assailed by governments (most spectacularly in US elected representatives' threats to the liberty and life of Assange) – it was also questioned by a range of independent commentators and civil society actors. The secretive nature of WikiLeaks, the complexity of its organisational, financial and legal status, and the closeted, cell-like nature of its governance model, raised legitimate queries (Domscheit-Berg 2011). These critiques of WikiLeaks occurred before Julian Assange was required by authorities to return to Sweden for questioning in relation to allegations of sexual assault.

Assange's attempt to evade the Swedish authorities led him in June 2012 to seek asylum in Ecuadorian embassy in London. Ecuador's President Rafael Correa has been widely regarded as a lion of the left, but since at least 2010 has sought to muzzle his country's press. As a *Guardian* journalist noted, serious concerns about Ecuadorian press freedom emerged from the very US diplomatic cables published by WikiLeaks in Cablegate (Assange 2012b). Yet Assange has pointedly declined to discuss Ecuador's woeful recent record on press freedom (Carter 2012). Assange and WikiLeaks are certainly not alone in exhibiting such contradictions on freedom of expression and press freedom. The fact that Assange is not prepared to address satisfactorily such central issues raises further doubts about the potential of WikiLeaks to realise its own vision to integrate the traditional conceptions of journalism and media's relationship to democracy, on the one hand, with new ideas and affordances.

CONCLUSION: DIGITAL ARCHITECTURES FOR DEMOCRATIC COMMUNICATIONS

The case of WikiLeaks is an important reminder of how much imaginative work needs to be done in order to make such digital platforms genuinely democratic in their affordances. It is with good reason that WikiLeaks has exerted such fascination and controversy alike among those interested in how to design digital technology to make contemporary media a much more powerful, ethical force for democracy and justice.

The problem with WikiLeaks, as I see it, is not just its questionable approach to media ethics and accountability which is, it could be argued, an inevitable consequence of an organisation beseiged by the might of the US and other Western countries, and their intelligence, security and finance agencies (Leigh and Harding 2011). Nor is the issue with WikiLeaks simply the problems that come from having such a charismatic and compelling defining figure as Assange. Rather, I suggest the main problem with WikiLeaks is that not enough attention has been given by its creators – or, indeed, its supporters, analysts or detractors – to considering what its affordances are, and how they might be skewed, or inflected, towards democratic media and ethics.

This may seem an unfair criticism to make of a project such as WikiLeaks which has made such inroads into lifting the lid on some of the most explosive and important issues of the day. I certainly am keen to acknowledge the remarkable success of WikiLeaks in shining such a bright light on the fissures of contemporary mainstream politics. However, as I hope my analysis has shown, in the passage of WikiLeaks towards a rapprochement with traditional journalism and news, something has been lost in capturing, extending and refining the democratic affordances of its platform.

WikiLeaks is but one of many platforms currently emerging or evolving – along with Politifact, crowdsourcing in elections, text messaging, Facebook and the new blog and web-based independent quality journalism. Indeed, we need a mix of digital platforms which, taken together, could make an important contribution to a reliable, enduring, open media ecology in which democracy flourishes. It is widely agreed that our traditional media can no longer provide what citizens require, even with the balance of public service media, community, alternative and personal media thrown into the bargain. We are certainly in the heyday of innovation of digital platforms for democracy, so I would be the last to put a dampener on this ferment. However, we do need a much more rigorous and vigorous debate about the democratic affordances they provide. And where such platforms fit into the ensemble of media we need in order to create, recreate and sustain democratic private and public life.

- This paper was first published in *Ethical Space*, Vol. 10, Nos 2 and 3 pp 6-14, 2013

ACKNOWLEDGEMENT

The context and inspiration for many of the ideas in this paper have come from various conversations with Professor John Keane and Peter Fray, Visiting Professor of Politics and Media, both in the Institute of Democracy and Human Rights, the University of Sydney. In addition, I am grateful to Associate Professor Jake Lynch and Professor Robert A. Hackett for the generative seminar in late 2012 that also shaped and gave rise to this paper.

REFERENCES

Allan, Stuart (2013) Journalism as interpretive performance: The case of WikiLeaks, Peters, Chris and Broersma (eds) *Rethinking journalism: Trust and participation in a transformed news landscape*, London and New York, Routledge pp 144-159

Amoore, Louise and de Goede, Marike (2005) Governance, risk and dataveillance in the war on terror, *Crime, Law & Social Change*, Vol. 43 pp 149-173

Assange, Julian (2012a) Statement after six months in Ecuadorian Embassy. Available online at http://wikileaks.org/Statement-by-Julian-Assange-after.html, accessed on 21 April 2013

Assange, Julian (2012b) WikiLeaks cables paint chequered picture of Ecuador, *Guardian*, 19 June. Available online at http://www.guardian.co.uk/world/2012/jun/19/wikileaks-cables-ecuador-julian-assange, accessed on 21 April 2013

Beaumont, Peter and Sherwood, Harriet (2011) Egypt protesters defy tanks and teargas to make the streets their own, *Guardian*, 28 November. Available online at http://www.guardian.co.uk/world/2011/jan/28/egypt-protests-latest-cairo-curfew, accessed 21 April 2013

Brown, John Seely and Duguid, Paul (2000) *The social life of information*, Boston, Harvard Business School Press

Brevini, Benedetta, Hintz, Arne and McCurdy, Patrick (eds) (2013) *Beyond WikiLeaks: Implications for the future of communications, journalism and society*, London, Palgrave

Carter, Chelsea J. (2012) Assange disregards questions on free press, his reported ill health, CNN, 29 November. Available online at http://edition.cnn.com/2012/11/29/world/europe/uk-assange-interview, accessed on 25 April 2013

Castells, Manuel (2012) *Networks of outrage and hope: Social movements in the internet age*, Cambridge, Polity

Chadwick, Andrew and Howard, Philip N. (eds) (2008) *Routledge handbook of internet politics*, New York, Routledge

Clarke, Roger (1994) Dataveillance by governments: The technique of computer matching, *Information Technology & People*, Vol. 7 pp 46-85

Curran, James (2011) *Media and democracy*, Oxford and New York, Routledge

Dahlberg, Lincoln and Siapera, Eugenia (eds) (2007) *Radical democracy and the internet: Interrogating theory and practice*, Basingstoke, UK, Palgrave Macmillan

Domscheit-Berg, Daniel (2011) *Inside WikiLeaks: My time with Julian Assange at the world's most dangerous website*, New York, Crown

Fenton, Natalie (ed.) 2010) *New media, old news: Journalism and democracy in the digital age*, Los Angeles, Sage

Garton Ash, Timothy (2009) Twitter counts more than armouries in this new politics of people power, *Guardian*, 17 June. Available online at http://www.guardian.co.uk/commentisfree/2009/jun/17/iran-election-protests-twitter-students, accessed on 25 April 2013

Ghonim, Wael (2012) *Revolution 2.0: The power of the power is greater than the people in power*, New York, Houghton Mifflin Harcourt

Gibson, James J. (1977) The theory of affordances, Shaw, Robert and Bransford, John (eds) *Acting and knowing: Toward an ecological psychology*, Hillsdale, NJ, Lawrence Erlbaum pp 67-82

Goggin, Gerard (2006) *Cell phone culture: Mobile technology in everyday life*, London and New York, Routledge

Guardian (2010) Afghanistan war logs: How the *Guardian* got the story, *Guardian*, 25 July. Available online at http://www.guardian.co.uk/world/2010/jul/25/afghanistan-war-logs-explained-video, accessed on 25 April 2013

Hindman, Matthew (2009) *The myth of digital democracy*, Princeton, NJ, Princeton University Press

Huffington Post (2009) 9/11 text messages released: WikiLeaks publishes intercepted government pager texts as they were sent, 25 November. Available online at http://www.huffing-tonpost.com/2009/11/25/911-text-messages-release_n_370085.html, accessed on 2 May 2013

Index on Censorship (2008) Winners of *Index on Censorship* Freedom of Expression Awards announced. Available online at http://www.indexoncensorship.org/2008/04/winners-of-index-on-censorship-freedom-of-expression-award-announced/, accessed on 25 April 2013

Joerges, Bernward (1999) Do politics have artefacts?, *Social Studies of Science*, Vol. 29 pp 411-431

Keane, John (2009) *The life and death of democracy*, London and New York, Simon and Schuster

Keane, John (2013a) Does truth really matter in politics?, The Conversation, 10 April. Available online at http://theconversation.com/does-truth-really-matter-in-politics-7866, accessed on 26 April 2013

Keane, John (2013b) Lunch and dinner with Julian Assange in prison, The Conversation, 18 February. Available online at http://theconversation.com/lunch-and-dinner-with-julian-assange-in-prison-12234, accessed on 26 April 2013

Kennedy, Dan (2010) Why WikiLeaks turned to the press, *Guardian*, 27 July 2010. Available online at http://www.guardian.co.uk/commentisfree/cifamerica/2010/jul/27/why-wikileaks-turned-to-press, accessed on 25 April 2013

Kies, Raphaël (2010) *Promises and limits of web-deliberation*, London, Palgrave Macmillan

Latour, Bruno (2005) *Reassembling the social: An introduction to actor-network-theory*, Oxford, Clarendon

Latour, Bruno and Weibel, Peter (eds) (2005) *Making things public: Atmospheres of democracy*, Cambridge, MA, MIT Press

Leigh, David and Harding, Luke (2011) *WikiLeaks: Inside Julian Assange's war on secrecy*, London, Guardian Books

Lovink, Geert (2011) *Networks without a cause: A critique of social media*, Cambridge, Polity

Papacharissi, Zizi (2010) *A private sphere: Democracy in a digital age*, Cambridge, Polity

Politifact (2013) About Politifact. Available: http://www.politifact.com/about/, accessed on 25 April 2013

Schumpeter, Joseph A. (1975) *Capitalism, socialism, democracy*, New York, Harper

Shenker, Jack (2011) Egyptian protesters are not just Facebook revolutionaries, *Guardian*, 28 January. Available online at http://www.guardian.co.uk/world/2011/jan/28/egyptian-protesters-facebook-revolutionaries, accessed on 25 April 2013

Siddique, Haroon (2010) Press freedom group joins condemnation of WikiLeaks' war logs, *Guardian*, 13 August. Available online at http://www.guardian.co.uk/media/2010/aug/13/wikileaks-reporters-without-borders, accessed on 25 April 2013

Sreberny, Annabelle and Khiabany, Gholam (2010) *Blogistan: The internet and politics in Iran*, London, I. B. Tauris

Sykes, Helen (ed.) (2012) *More or less: Democracy and new media*, Sydney, Future Leaders

Visser, Gerrit (2009) *WikiLeaks opens leaked documents*. Available online at htAtp://www.smartmobs.com/2009/11/26/wikileaks-opens-leaked-documents/, accessed on 25 April 2013

WikiLeaks (2009) *9/11 tragedy pager intercepts*. Available online at http://911.wikileaks.org/, accessed on 21 April 2013

WikiLeaks (2010a) *Afghan war diary*. Available online at http://www.wikileaks.org/wiki/Afghan_War_Diary,_2004-2010, accessed on 21 April 2013

WikiLeaks (2010b) *Secret US embassy cables*. Available online at http://wikileaks.org/cablegate.html, accessed on 21 April 2014

WikiLeaks (2013a) About us. Available at http://wikileaks.org/About.html, accessed on 21 April 2013

WikiLeaks (2013b) Submissions. Available at http://www.wikileaks.org/wiki/WikiLeaks:Submissions, accessed on 21 April 2013

Winner, Langdon (1980) Do artifacts have politics?, *Daedalus*, Vol. 109 pp 121-136

Woolgar, Steve and Cooper, Geoff (1999) Do artefacts have ambivalence? Moses' bridges, winner's bridges and other urban legends in S and TS, *Social Studies of Science*, Vol. 29 pp 433-449

Zhao, Yuezhi and Hackett, Robert A. (2005) Media globalization, media democratization: Challenges, issues and paradoxes, Hackett, Robert A. and Zhao, Yuezhi (eds) *Democratizing global media: One world, many struggles*, Lanham, MD, Rowman and Littlefield pp 1-33

NOTE ON THE CONTRIBUTOR

Gerard Goggin is Professor of Media and Communications at the University of Sydney. His recent books are *Apps: From mobile phones to digital lives* (2021) and (co-authored) *Mobile media methods* (2024).

Chapter 15

Oligarchy reloaded and pirate media: The state of peace journalism in Guatemala

Lioba Suchenwirth

This paper presents a case study of the state of peace journalism (PJ) in Guatemala, based on the critical assumption that analysts need to broaden the definition of PJ to encompass current local level and alternative media initiatives. It investigates current PJ in Guatemala through interviews with those who analyse the media (media experts), produce the media (journalists and volunteers) and those whose representation in the media is essential for the peace process (indigenous groups). While profound racism and a violent environment hamper peace journalistic work for both mainstream and alternative outlets, the paper argues that the opening for media for the people and by the people in Guatemala is to be found within alternative channels rather than commercial outlets.

Keywords: peace journalism theory and practice, Guatemala, alternative media

METHODOLOGICAL CONSIDERATIONS

In this paper, I will conduct a case study of the state of peace journalism (PJ) in present day Guatemala, based on the critical assumption that analysts need to broaden the definition of PJ to encompass current local level media initiatives. My criticism of current PJ theory and practice is that it is:

a) too heavily based on international (i.e. Western) media and does not take local media into sufficient account;

b) too elitist in its tendency to concentrate on the work of professional, mainstream journalists, at the cost of alternative media outlets (both based on Keeble 2010).

I investigate PJ in Guatemala through interviews with those who analyse the media (media experts), produce the media (journalists and volunteers) and those whose representation in the media is essential for the peace process (indigenous groups). I will test how my critique of PJ applies to the Guatemalan case by looking at the dominant themes appearing in my interviews, thus contrasting PJ theory with Guatemalan reality. I will look at the political economy of the mainstream media in Guatemala, different alternative media outlets and then explore two features distinctive to the country: racism and security. To limit the scope of this paper, I will not examine internet journalism projects.

The material collected is the result of in-depth interviews throughout Guatemala during the summer of 2010 with 26 experts in their respective fields, focusing on the Guatemalan media, and gathering information on PJ initiatives, alternative and indigenous media and human rights publications. The experts included journalists, researchers, consultants, community radio broadcasters, activists and government officials as well as a former general and the head of the former guerrilla radio station. This is complemented by a literature review which allowed me to crosscheck some claims made by the interviewees. However, there are some obvious limitations, as there is little up-to-date literature available on the media in Guatemala, and even less on the alternative media in the country.

My approach to the expert interviews is based on 'sociological naturalism' which holds that the goal is to uncover reality as it appears for interviewees (see Kidd Olsen 2009: 26). According to this approach, 'a relatively stable perception of reality exists with each interviewee, and the challenge becomes to extract it as data' (ibid). For Rubin and Rubin the purpose of qualitative interviewing is theory building, and contrary to a positivist approach to research, qualitative researchers build theory step by step from the examples and experiences collected during the interviews (1995: 56).

WHAT IS PJ?

Peace journalism is a normative journalistic school critiquing mainstreaming 'war journalism' as introduced by Johan Galtung in 1965 (see McGoldrick and Lynch 2000: 6). By using conflict analysis techniques in reporting, its main purpose lies in both mapping out and actively supporting peaceful solutions to conflict. Rather than modelling its reports on sports journalism with its zero sum games and focus on who is winning or losing, Galtung suggests that the PJ approach should be modelled on health journalism, which does not focus on disease, but on possible ways to overcome it (2002: 259). The core of the theory is formed by an awareness of conflict dynamics and an understanding that no information can be neutral. According to PJ theory, every time a report goes public, it has an impact on the particular conflict. When reporting in a manner that gives undue attention to violence, journalists' reports may actually spawn a new chain of violent behaviour, a mechanism called the *negative feedback loop* (Lynch and McGoldrick 2005).

While the definition of PJ provided by Lynch and McGoldrick remains vague, they provide a clear list of practical/professional activities for peace journalists (ibid: 5). They are supposed to have the perspective of the vulnerable groups, report the background of the conflict rather than single sensational events, seek 'stories which maximise the chance for peace building' and get out 'messages crafted to foster peaceful resolutions of conflict'. Journalism will be 'intended outcome programming' used as a tool for transforming attitudes, promoting reconciliation, putting the conflict sides together for resolution, maintaining 'a duty for journalists to use their potential for mediation between conflict parties' (see also Spurk 2002: 16), thus emphasising the responsibilities of the journalistic actors to respond in ways that are supposed to maximise the chances for peace (Lynch 1997).

INTERNATIONAL AND WESTERN VS LOCAL MEDIA

Richard Lance Keeble points out that current PJ theory is 'too elitist in its definition of journalism' (2010: 52). Indeed, much peace journalism theory is written from the perspective of international media, meaning Western media outlets based outside the conflict zone and focusing on foreign correspondents (e.g. Blaesi 2004; Lynch and McGoldrick 2005). Yet Keeble, while pointing to the limitations of Western corporate media, names a number of local media outlets campaigning for social and political reforms, among them the British unstamped press of the early 19th century, underground communication networks in South Africa during the 1970s and 1980s, Bolivian miners' radio stations from 1963 to 1983 and current web-based movements in Burma (2010: 54-55).

When talking about peace-building within a society, it is the local media which are of special importance, because they are concerned most directly on the communication between the different military antagonists and civil groups (see for example Blondel 2004). A sustainable peace can only be built when these crucial groups are willing to do so. It is in the local settings that the soft power[1] of the media can fully fulfil its potential as peace building efforts must have as overarching goal 'to enhance the indigenous capacity of a society to manage conflict without violence' (ibid) in which 'external support for peace building is an adjunct to local peace building efforts and not a substitute for them' (Howard et al. 2003: 24). Wolfsfeld proposes four major types of political impact by local media on peace processes:

- defining the political atmosphere;

- influencing the nature of debates;

- influencing the strategies and behaviour of the antagonists;

- and raising and lowering the public standing of antagonists (2004: 11-14).

Carey (1989) adds a cultural element by defining communication as having two primary functions: control – leading, for example, to political representation in the public sphere – and also community building underlining consensus. The latter, so-called ritual view of communication, includes the sharing and formation of personal values, sentiments and worldviews, thus providing the basis on which to construct and maintain collective identities. Cultural knowledge, the knowledge of cultural codes, is seen as paramount to reach this consensus, and its focus on Western output may limit the validity of PJ theory. Thus, I will focus on local instead of foreign media outlets.

MEDIA FOR THE PEOPLE AND BY THE PEOPLE – A CITIZENS' MEDIA

Analysts should also look at the people who are producing peace journalism. While proposing that PJ can be an *alternative* coverage method (an alternative to a supposed mainstream war journalism technique) (see for example Galtung 2002; Lynch and McGoldrick op cit; Mandelzis 2007: 2), PJ theorists tend to focus on mainstream media, and neglect alternative media outlets. Keeble writes:

> Thus a dominant strand in PJ theory focuses closely on the notion of journalism as a privileged, professional activity and fails to take into account the critical intellectual tradition which locates professions historically and politically, seeing them as essentially occupational groupings with a legal monopoly of social and economic opportunities in the marketplace, underwritten by the state (2010: 51).

He continues: 'We need to move away from the concept of the audience as a passive consumer of a professional product to seeing the audience as producers of their own (written or visual) media' (ibid: 56). Keeble calls for 'a radical broadening of the definition of journalism to include intellectuals, campaigners and citizens – all of them articulating their ideas within the dominant and alternative, global public spheres' (ibid: 53).

While alternative media can consist of very diverse groups and organisations, they can be explicitly partisan, characterised by efforts to disclose issues of exclusion, elite-bias and gaps in information left by the mainstream by providing room for alternative views and a voice to those who are not otherwise heard (Atton and Hamilton 2008: 79, 86; Harcup 2007: 85). They are seen to 'challenge accepted news values and ethical frameworks of mainstream media' (Harcup ibid: 127), thus creating counter-public spheres (Fraser 1993 cited in Keeble 2009: 197). Alternative media are often linked to identity and community building:

> … the strength of alternative media lies not only in their counter-information role but also in the provision of opportunities for ordinary people to tell their own stories, and to reconstruct their culture and identity using their own symbols, signs and language. In this way, they challenge social codes, validate identities and empower themselves and their communities (Atton and Hamilton 2008: 122).

Thus PJ can learn from development journalism, which has long argued for a transformation from *imposition* to *collaboration*. In her theory of citizens' media,

Clemencia Rodriguez writes: 'Only when citizens take their destiny in their own hands and shape it using their own cultures and strengths will peace and social change be viable. In both cases power has diffused from being concentrated in a few experts into the everyday lives and cultures of civil society' (2000: 150). It is the citizens' media, not the news media which in her opinion can 'give voice to the voiceless', foster empowerment, connect isolated communities, foster conscientisation and serve as alternative sources of information (ibid: 151). She is adamant that peace media can learn from citizens' media – and address a gap which peace journalism has so far not addressed appropriately. These producers of peace journalism could be radical alternative journalists, radical intellectuals, some research centres and political activists, moving away from the narrow idea of the 'professional journalist' as the only producer of media output (Keeble 2010).

PJ INITIATIVES IN GUATEMALA: HISTORICAL CONTEXT

Fifteen years after the end of Guatemala's infamously brutal civil war, armed groups and clandestine security networks have merged with criminal organisations deeply entrenched in state institutions. Murders and death threats to civil society activists undermine democracy, and homicide rates have almost doubled since 2000. The UN development report comments: 'To put it bluntly: Central America is the most violent region of the World, with the exception of those regions where some countries are at war or are experiencing severe political violence' (UNDP 2010:14).

Meanwhile, international actors such as the World Bank, OAS, IMF, UNDP, religious organisations as well as numerous NGOs and state development agencies have been heavily involved in the country's affairs, though the effects of their efforts remain doubtful. Poverty rates remain at 51 per cent with 34 per cent living in extreme poverty. 23 per cent of children are malnourished. At least 26 per cent of the population is illiterate (World Bank 2010). Indigenous people, mainly Mayan groups, are affected the most, because although they make up the demographic majority, they are excluded politically, socially, economically and culturally.[2] In short, the civil war is over, but violence and the underlying causes for the conflict continue to exist.

The signing of the Guatemalan Peace Accords in December 1996 marked the official end of a 36-year conflict between army and guerrilla groups. A CIA-sponsored coup had overthrown the democratically elected government in 1954, justifying the intervention in the light of a US Cold War interventionist strategy to contain 'communist menace'. Land reforms seeking to redistribute unused land from large holdings to landless peasants were immediately reversed. Reformist dissidents were gradually eliminated as civil society was destroyed through targeted repression by the subsequent military dictatorship. Receiving extensive military and economic assistance from the USA, Guatemala became a security state par excellence.

The consequent civil war took a tremendously heavy toll: a minimum of 200,000 deaths, in addition to 40,000 people who 'disappeared' after being arrested. More than 400 villages were destroyed, 200,000 people were forced to flee to neighbouring Mexico and, of Guatemala's 10 million inhabitants, about one million were displaced internally (Handy 2002; Carey 2004: 70). Around 93 per cent of the killings were inflicted by the army, according to the Guatemalan truth commission. As over 83 per cent of the dead were Mayans, the army had committed 'acts of genocide' since they 'contemplated the total or partial extermination of the group' (Handy 2003: 279). Although the conflict had its origins in Cold War ideological differences, it soon took on distinct ethnic dimensions.

Clearly, the rift between population of European descent (and those who would have adopted a European identity), so-called Ladinos and the majority indigenous populations did not appear overnight. Shortly after the arrival of the Spanish conquistadores in 1524, Spanish distinctiveness was sharply separated from 'Indian' identity through the provision of different rights. During centuries to come, racism was rife, while political indigenous identification was discouraged at best and brutally suppressed at worst (Colop 1996; Watanabe 2000). 'To be indigenous was to be treated as the dangerous "Other" who had to be kept under control – if necessary by all means' (Warren 2003: 108).

GUATEMALA MAINSTREAM MEDIA SCENE: IT'S A FAMILY THING

Media ownership in Guatemala is marked (and marred) by monopoly, which both perpetuates the oligarchic system and prevents democratic change (Monzon 2010; Rockwell and Janus: 2001). Monzon speaks of an 'ideological embrace' of media and company interests (2010: 60) and concludes: 'They are companies, not communication media' (ibid: 59).

All of Guatemala's national newspapers[3] are owned by two competing news groups, both of which are affiliated with *the famous twenty*: elite Guatemalan families who control the country's major sources of income and have considerable political influence (Casaus Arzu 2002). In addition, there is a 'monopoly of gate-keeping' (Silvio Gramajo, personal interview 2010). One example is the family Marroquin, who own the smaller publishing group, as well as providing the editor of *Prensa Libre*, the biggest broadsheet in the country, and the editor of another broadsheet, *elPeriodico*. 'They are not a very powerful family as such, but it looks as if they might soon have the entire print output under control' (ibid). While the Guatemalan readership is low due to the country's high illiteracy rates, newspaper influence among the elites is deemed to be considerable (ibid).

Infamously, the Mexican Angel Gonzalez (nicked-named 'the Angel of Democracy'), brother in law of the former minister of communication, owns all four commercial TV licences, as well as the main radio news channel, Radio Sonora, and a large part of the commercial radio stations. When journalist and social scientist Gustavo Berganza wrote of favours exchanged between the Mexican and certain politicians, he was made 'the target of a relentless attack of the news programs of the "national TV" channels owned by this Mexican' (*Guatemala Times* 2008). In a personal interview, Berganza said: '[Angel Gonzalez] doesn't distort reality as such, making up news that is pure government propaganda, but he omits information that could harm them' (2010).

Radio ownership is similarly concentrated in a few major groups which mainly repeat the news broadcast in Radio Sonora, or printed in newspapers including the Catholic and evangelical church and the state. Due to the high illiteracy rate, radio is of particular importance, and more than 90 per cent of the population of Central America is exposed to radio on a daily basis (Rockwell and Janus cited in Salzman and Salzman 2010: 8).

Regional journalists often work part-time as the PR people for local authorities, and part-time as correspondents for media in the capital, since the media organisations do not pay them sufficiently (Gramajo, personal interview 2010). Hence journalists do not appear to stay in the profession for very long, as they receive low wages and have few career opportunities (Berganza, personal interview, 2010).

A recent government drive saw the recruitment of large numbers of former mainstream journalists to government media outlets to increase its quality (ibid). Consequently, the newspaper *Diario de Centroamerica* and various radio stations have risen in popularity. Silvio Gramajo elaborates:

> In this country government media were basically pro-government propaganda. But now they also report from a different view: to put it simply, there is journalistic work being done now, when before it was propaganda work. ... That is a step forward (personal interview, 2010).

A positive side-effect of their increased popularity and wider reach is that the government is less dependent on placing advertisements with commercial media to distribute official information, thus making them less vulnerable to corruption and favouritism (ibid).

PIRATES, PRIESTS AND COMMUNISTS: ALTERNATIVE MEDIA OUTLETS

Although the right to indigenous and participatory media is actually part of the Peace Accords signed in 1996, community radio stations are illegal if they have not competed for their frequency in regular commercial auctions, which they can hardly ever afford. Yet there are more than 800 self-declared community radio stations in the country. Some promote mainly missionary content rather than news, such as the evangelical stations in association with Radio Cultural (Sywulka, personal interview 2010). Others are essentially commercial pirate radio stations with local reach. Yet according to Martina Richards, country director of the German national development agency DED, community radio is at present the best media outlet for Guatemala, because 'it's where its audience is' (personal interview, 2010).

During the conflict, community radio was used both by guerrilla groups to keep in touch with their fighters and supporters as well as a non-violent means of opposition (Viscidi 2004). Former broadcaster with legendary guerrilla radio station La Voz Popular, Tino Recinos is now coordinating Mujb'ab'l yol, a network of 205 community radio stations. Programmes focus on human, indigenous and children's rights, freedom of speech, and other social and political themes (personal interview 2010). Mujb'ab'l yol sees its role clearly as community building. Its website states:

> From our point of view a means of communication shouldn't just be about distributing and sharing information but rather it should be orientated around getting close to the community it serves. In this way it can supply the conditions needed to benefit society as a whole in terms of increased community awareness and cohesion. Establishing members of radio stations and other people as pillars of the community who can promote progressive change, means leaving behind the image of just being distributors of information to being progressive activists who promote development within the community (2010).

One of the biggest problems community radio is facing in Guatemala is that there exists no clear definition of what a community radio station is. They are too divided among themselves, which will make it hard for them to get legislation passed. This is why most community stations remain illegal to this day, believes Gramajo (personal interview, 2010).

In terms of alternative television, the former military channel was given to the Academy of Mayan Languages as part of the Peace Accords, and is now known as TV Maya. Expectations and demand were high, yet TV Maya is currently being kept in an economic limbo, as – being a public channel – it is not allowed to sell advertising space, yet it receives little public funding and cannot broadcast beyond its neighbourhood.

A rather more successful venture is independent *EntreMundos*, a free magazine aiming to publish 'news and commentary on human rights and development in Guatemala'. Originating as a society magazine in Quetzaltenango, its current focus vastly increased its popularity and readers can now be found all over Guatemala. Theme-specific issue subjects include mining (May and June 2010), education (July and August 2010), gender (March and April 2010) and its 2,000 copies are distributed in cafés, universities, libraries as well as the internet. Valeria Ayerdi, editor of *EntreMundos*, elaborates:

> [I want] to give a voice to news you normally wouldn't see or wouldn't notice. ... You see, I read the newspapers every day, and I take important news that

I know the normal media won't cover and we publish it ... and sometimes small news items become big articles for us. ... In the mainstream, you see indigenous people just being used, or see them as patronising postcards but they don't really tell about their story. In contrast, we are focused: whenever we talk about a project or something from indigenous people or rural areas we try to show the human side of them (personal interview 2010).

According to Ayerdi, *EntreMundos* is actively encouraging its readership to contribute with articles. Yet talking about terms such as freedom or civil liberties is difficult, as they are often associated with communism. 'I want to be critical about both sides, both left and right so that they can see that, if you are talking about human rights, it doesn't mean that you are a communist' (ibid).

Unsurprisingly, funding is a major point of worry to alternative media outlets. The axiom that 'community media lack power, because they lack economic power' (Evelyn Blanck, personal interview 2010) was expressed commonly in the interviews, especially by those who work in and with alternative media. Lucia Escobar, for example, laments that while their project, Radio Ati, is trying to change Guatemalan society as a whole, she often does not even have the fare to send a journalist to report from the next village (personal interview, 2010).

A lack of funding for alternative media means that their employees need to have second and third jobs. These might influence their journalistic output, or vice versa. Valeria Ayerdi tells of the repercussions of her journalistic work for her second job, teaching English. After publishing an *EntreMundos* edition on mining, a particularly sensitive subject in Guatemala, she was called into the principal's office. Parents were apparently concerned about what she was teaching their children. She was given an official warning and told to stick 'only to teaching English' (personal interview, 2010).

However, besides these findings, interviewees also recounted positive side-effects of economic pressure. Indeed, the tight financial situation appears to increase collaboration between activists. Julia Cajas, coordinator for AMOIXQUIC, an NGO for indigenous women's rights, explained how she turned to community radio stations to broadcast their women's rights programme, since AMOIXQUIC had no money to pay for space in a commercial station. Community radio makers taught the women how to produce a programme and distributed the results using their wide network of community stations. Since the organisation had no funds to produce professional material, the women had to produce the shows themselves. '[I]t was problematic because I too didn't know how to do many of these things, but still we managed and that has more value than anything else because we learned it by doing it and between the women there were a lot of skills and originality.' Women did not only acquire more skills, but also gained self-esteem, said Cajas (personal interview, 2010).

The precarious economic situation could also foster an increased sense of ownership and community for those involved, says volunteer co-ordinator Ruben Dominguez. When the community radio station, Doble Via, had to raise 4,000 Quetzales for equipment, the bill was footed by its 37 volunteers. This increased the sense of belonging to the community (personal interview, 2010).

RACISM AND INDIGENOUS INCLUSION

Racism in the media was rampant during and before the civil war. While certain expressions are no longer in use since the Peace Accords in 1996, there was little inclusion of indigenous identity in the written mainstream press ten years later (Suchenwirth 2006). This is even more evident in the case of indigenous women (Tubin Sotz 2007). Even for political advertisements aimed at Mayans, indigenous people play subordinate roles (Connolly-Ahern and Castells i Talens 2010). The director of a comprehensive study of the Guatemalan media over the last three years, Amilcar Davila, concluded:

> The racism has transformed a lot. But it does not disappear, it adapts, it camouflages. Very few people would now say strong insults in public ... but is this progress? ... You can see it very well when there is a crisis of sort, let's say a demonstration. Nobody is a racist until there is a crisis ... and everything comes out: [They say that the indigenous people] are behind the times, they don't want progress, they don't think about the future etc. ... For me the biggest topic, more than the insults and stereotypes, which do still happen, is the exclusion of indigenous people. They are not covered. Not important topics, not their points of view, they don't even think about them: the discourse goes in a different way. ... The news is not aimed at them (personal interview, 2010).

It was difficult for the professional journalists to accept the outcome of the study. 'One reason mainstream journalists give is that the country is racist, so therefore the media will be racist, and that if sources are racist, that translates to the article, but this, they claim, is not the journalists' fault' (ibid).

However, interviewees agreed that there had been improvements in employment policy, with more journalistic openings for indigenous people, though they may often not campaign on indigenous causes. Mayan professor of anthropology Lina Barrios commented: 'We have had some success in the promotion of indigenous identity [in the last five years], for example now there are TV programmes which talk about the meaning of the Mayan calendar. This is some progress, but there is no significant progress' (personal interview, 2010).

SECURITY

Legally, freedom of speech is part of the Guatemalan constitution, though Salzman and Salzman conclude: 'Media freedom is protected only in law. Even the application of that legal protection is not guaranteed' (2010: 10). Guatemala is regularly featured among the most dangerous countries to work as a journalist. In particular, threats related to drug trafficking and organised crime are having a serious impact on freedom of speech, as self-censorship is pervasive. Three journalists were killed in 2009 (CERIGUA 2010). Media outlets in the interior are particularly targeted. One common explanation is the increased visibility of the journalist. Cesar Perez Mendez, chief editor of *El Quetzalteco* (the largest regional newspaper in Guatemala) recounts:

> Here in the region, they have killed journalists. There is one well known case of Jorge Merida whom they killed when he was at home writing a news article [in 2008]. We have had complicated issues regarding the topic of safety here at the *Quetzalteco*. We have received death threats. Last month one of our editors quit her job because she felt threatened, and it was true, they were threatening her, and also the director of the newspaper, with death threats. So she said: 'I'd rather go home and be alive and don't expose myself' (personal interview, 2010).

There is a consensus among those interviewed that solely politically motivated threats seem to have given way to those stemming from a general sense of insecurity in the country (such as organised crime). Valeria Ayerdi states that for publishing *EntreMundos*, 'ten years ago, I would have been killed'. She described relations with the police now as passive aggressive (personal interview, 2010). Yet that same violent climate and the widespread impunity make threats based on political differences easier.

Feminist journalist Lucia Escobar feels she has received a public death threat from a member of the Catholic Church after writing a column about women's productive rights (personal interview, 2010). Evelyn Blanck, director of Centro Civitas, tells of a burglary, despite the office being in a compound guarded constantly by security guards, as well as having its own security guard. The only thing that was stolen was the NGO's computer hard drives and a USB stick, leaving everything else behind (personal interview, 2010).

Conversely, Gramajo warns that many of the journalists working in the media now were around during or directly after the war, when politically motivated violence against journalists was common. He speaks of a myth of a 'hero journalist' and is not sure how many threats are *bona fide*. In addition, he thinks journalists may actively seek danger. 'Some might even say: "I want to die in service" and they go for whatever there is. ... There can be a lack of consciousness' (personal interview, 2010).

Violence can not only be directed towards journalists, but can also stem from the media. Tino Recinos recounts how a visitor from a commercial radio station threatened to shut down the community station Doble Via, since they were a pirate station. Doble Via broadcast this threat – and asked for support from the population. When the man returned, there were about three hundred people waiting for him, armed with machetes and stones, ready to kill him. Recinos called the police, and warned that the situation could get out of hand, while trying to calm the irate listeners. 'He realised what was going on and tried to escape, but they caught him. He was scared. In the end, he signed a paper that the commercial station would be left in peace, and we have not heard from them since' (personal interview, 2010).

PJ IN GUATEMALA: IT AIN'T WHAT IS SAYS ON THE BOX

I examined peace journalism in Guatemala, as seen through the eyes of those who analyse the media (media experts), produce the media (journalists and volunteers), and those whose representation in the media is essential for the peace process (indigenous groups). Testing my assumption that analysts need to broaden the definition of PJ to encompass current local level media initiatives I voiced two main points of critique.

Conducting the case study of the state of PJ in present day Guatemala, I looked at the political economy of the mainstream media in Guatemala, different alternative media outlets and then explored two features distinctive to the country: racism and security. Mainstream media appear too far involved with the Guatemalan oligarchy and too absorbed by economic goals to reflect alternative viewpoints, thus failing to give a voice to disenfranchised groups such as Guatemala's indigenous people. While there are examples of good journalism and voices of dissent, mainstream media output can hardly count as PJ and is, in fact, mostly counter-productive to peace building in post-conflict Guatemala.

Alternative media are aiming to fill this gap. Community radios such as the Mujb'ab'l yol network are actively promoting human rights and social change while giving voice to those least heard. Situated within small communities, the stations have ideal access to local knowledge and cultural codes. However, community radio efforts are threatened by their legal situation and lack of definition. Since every station can be a self-declared 'community radio', news value for peace has to be scrutinised carefully in each individual case. Indeed, on occasion community stations may even incite violence. TV Maya has so far failed to reach out to its audience. *EntreMundos* appears the most successful project so far, as it is constantly growing, focusing more and more on peace journalistic issues. The country's high illiteracy rates, however, mean that the magazine is not for all. Profound racism and a violent environment hamper peace journalistic work even further for both mainstream and alternative outlets.

Yet despite these difficulties, the opening for media for the people and by the people in Guatemala is to be found within alternative channels rather than commercial outlets. The success of *EntreMundos* and the ever increasing number of community radio stations tells of the population's interest. Peace journalism emphasises the moral responsibility of media involved in conflict, and it is the people who should be able to express their own voice to determine their fate.

- This paper was first published in *Ethical Space*, Vol 8, Nos 1 and 2 pp 44-52, 2011

NOTES

[1] Soft power is a phrase coined by Joseph Nye to describe a power that is not physical, but works on the basis on persuasion (2004)

[2] Statistics of Guatemala are considered to be extremely unreliable for a variety of reasons, yet Mayans are believed to be in the region of six million people meaning that, by all accounts, they comprise one half or more of the total population (Handy 2002). In addition, there are around 2,000 Xinca (a different indigenous group) and 4,000 Garifuna, whose ancestors were African slaves settling on the Caribbean coast at the end of the 19th century

[3] Cooperacion de Noticias owns the broadsheet *Siglo Veintiuno* as well as the tabloid *Al Dia*. They are in fierce competition with the larger of the two groups, a news conglomerate controlling the biggest-selling broadsheet *Prensa Libre,* also holding the most successful tabloid *Nuestro Diario*, as well as *elPeriodico*, another broadsheet. In addition, the Prensa Libre group also owns *El Quetzalteco*, Quetzaltenango's bi-weekly regional paper, the biggest regional in the country

REFERENCES

Atton, Chris and Hamilton, James F. (2008) *Alternative journalism*, London, Sage

Blaesi, Burkhard (2004) Peace journalism and the news production process, *Conflict and Communication Online*, Vol. 3, No.1/2. Available online at http://www.cco.regener-online.de

Blondel, Yvla Isabelle (2004) International media get the most attention, but don't ignore local media in defusing conflict, *Media conflict prevention and reconstruction*, Paris, UNESCO

Carey, David (2004) Maya perspectives on the 1999 referendum in Guatemala: Ethnic equality rejected?, *Latin American Perspectives*, Issue 139, Vol. 31, No. 6 pp 69-95

Carey, James W. (1989) *Communication as culture: Essays on media and society*, London, Routledge

Casaus Arzu, Marta (2002) *La metamorfosis del racismo en Guatemala* [*The metamorphosis of racism in Guatemala*], Guatemala, Cholsamaj, third edition

CERIGUA (2010) *Estado de Situacion de la Libertated de Expresion* [*The state of freedom of expression*] *2009*, CERIGUA, Guatemala. Available online at http://cerigua.info/nuke/especiales/informe_primer_semestre_2009_estado_situacion_de_la_libertad_de_expresion_en_guatemala.pdf, accessed on 15 November 2010

Colop, Sam Enrique (1996) The discourse of concealment and 1992, Fisher, Edward and McKenna Brown, R. (eds) *Maya cultural activism in Guatemala*, Austin, University of Texas pp 146-156

Connolly-Ahern, Colleen and Castells i Talens, Antoni (2010) The role of indigenous peoples in Guatemalan political advertisements: An ethnographic content analysis, *Communication, Culture & Critique*, Vol. 3 pp 310-333

Fraser, Nancy (1993) Rethinking the public sphere: A contribution to the critique of actually existing democracy, Robins, Bruce (ed.) *The phantom public sphere*, Minneapolis, University of Minnesota Press pp 1-32

Galtung, Johan (1996) *Peace by peaceful means*, London, Sage for PRIO

Galtung, Johan (2002) Peace journalism: A challenge, Kempf, Wilhelm and Luostarinen, Heikki (eds) *Journalism and the New World Order: Studying war and the media*, Göthenburg, Nordicom

Guatemala Times (2008) In solidarity to Guatemalan journalist Gustavo Berganza, 16 December. Available online at http://www.guatemala-times.com/news/guatemala/644-in-solidarity-to-guatemalan-journalist-gustavo-berganza.html, accessed on 15 November 2010

Handy, Jim (2002) Democratizing what? Some reflections on nation, state, ethnicity, modernity, community and democracy in Guatemala. Paper presented at the Conference on threats to democracy in Latin America. Available online at http://www.iir.ubc.ca, accessed on 10 November 2010

Handy, Jim (2003) Reimagining Guatemala: Reconciliation and the indigenous accords, Prager, Carol A.L. and Govier, Trudy (eds) *Dilemmas of reconciliation: Cases and concepts*, Waterloo, Ontario, Wilfried Laurier University Press pp 279-306

Hackett, Robert A. and Carroll, William K. (2006) *Re-making media: The struggle to democratize public opinion*, London, Routledge

Harcup, Tony (2007) *The ethical journalist*, London, Sage

Howard, Ross, Rolt, Francis, van den Veen, Hans and Verhoeven, Juliette (2003) *The power of the media: A handbook for peace-builders*, Utrecht, European Centre for Conflict Prevention

Keeble, Richard Lance (2009) *Ethics for journalists*, Oxon, Routledge, second edition

Keeble, Richard Lance (2010) Peace journalism as a political practice: A new, radical look at the theory, Keeble, Richard Lance, Tulloch, John and Zollmann, Florian (eds) P*eace journalism, war and conflict resolution*, New York, Peter Lang pp 49-67

Kidd Olsen, Tarjei (2009) *Running Radio Selam: Constraints facing an Ethiopian peace radio project*. Master's thesis in Peace in Conflict Studies, University of Oslo. Available online at http://www.duo.uio.no/publ/statsvitenskap/2009/98154/NEWTHESIS.pdf, accessed on 29 November 2010

Lynch, Jake (1997) *The peace journalism option*. Available online at http://www.transcend.org, accessed on 23 May 2006

Lynch, Jake and McGoldrick, Annabel (2005) *Peace journalism*, Stroud, Hawthorn Press

Mandelzis, Lea (2007) Representations of peace in news discourse: Viewpoint and opportunity for peace journalism, *Conflict and Communication Online*, Vol. 6, No.1. Available online at www.cco.regener-online.de, accessed on 18 October 2010

McGoldrick, Annabel and Lynch, Jake (2000) *Peace journalism. How to do it?* Available online at http://www.reportingtheworld.org, accessed on 23 May 2006

Monzon, Marielos (2010) Guatemala: Con los Mismos Anteojos, Rincon, Omar (ed.) *Porque nos odian tanto. Estado y medios de comunicación en América Latina*. Bogota, Centro de Competencia en Comunicación para América Latina, Friedrich Ebert Stiftung pp 55-70

Nye, Joseph S. Junior (2004) *Soft power*, New York, Public Affairs

Retolaza Eguren, Inigo (2008) Moving up and down the ladder: Community-based participation in public dialogue and deliberation in Bolivia and Guatemala, *Community Development Journal*, Vol. 43, No. 3 pp 312-328

Rockwell, Rick and Janus, Noreene (2001) Stifling dissent: The fallout from a Mexican media invasion of Central America, *Journalism Studies*, Vol. 2, No. 4 pp 497-512

Rodriguez, Clemencia (2000) Civil society and citizens' media: Peace architects for the new millennium, Wilkins, Karin (ed.) *Redeveloping communication for social change: Theory, practice, power*, Boulder, Rowman and Littlefield pp 147-160

Rubin, Irene and Rubin, Herbert (1995) *Qualitative interviewing: The art of hearing data*, Thousand Oaks, CA, Sage

Salzman, Ryan and Salzman, Catherine (2010) Central American media: Testing the effects of social context, *Journal of Spanish Language Media*, Vol. 3 pp 5-23

Spurk, Christoph (2002) KOFF – *Media and peacebuilding: Concepts, actors and challenges*, Schweizerische Friedensstiftung. Available online at http://www.swisspeace.ch/typo3/fileadmin/user_upload/pdf/KOFF/Reports/medienstudie.pdf, accessed on 1 December 2010

Suchenwirth, Lioba (2006) Mayans in the news. A study of the formation of post-conflict identities in Guatemala. Master's thesis in Peace in Conflict Studies, University of Oslo. Available online at http://www.duo.uio.no/publ/statsvitenskap/2006/42403/42403.pdf, accessed on 22 November 2010

Tubin, Sotz and Aurora, Victoria (2007) *Mujeres mayas, racsimo y medios de comunicacion [Mayan women, racism and the media]*, Guatemala, Fundacion para Estudios y Profesionalizalion Maya FEPMAYA. Available online at http://www.racismoenlosmedios.com/img/articulo_2.pdf , accessed on 10 October 2010

UNDP (2010) *Opening spaces to citizen security and human development: Human development report for Central America*, HDRCA, *2009-2010*. Available online at http://www.idhacabrirespaciosalaseguridad.org.co, accessed on 20 November 2010

Viscidi, Lisa (2004) *The people's voice: Community radio in Guatemala*, Americas Program of the Interhemispheric Resource Center. Available online at http://www.americaspolicy.org/articles/2004/0410radio.html, accessed 18 May 2005

Watanabe, John (2000) Culturing identities, the state, and national consciousness in late nineteenth century western Guatemala, *Bulletin of Latin American Research*, No. 19 pp 321-340

Warren, Kay (2003) Culture, violence and ethnic nationalism, Ferguson, R. Brian (ed.) *The state, identity and violence*, London, Routledge pp 102-114

Wolfsfeld, Gadi (2004) *Media and the path to peace*, Cambridge, Cambridge University Press

World Bank (2010) *Guatemala data*. Available online at http://data.worldbank.org/country/guatemala, accessed on 29 November 2010

NOTE ON THE CONTRIBUTOR

Lioba Suchenwirth is a press spokesperson for the German Aerospace Center near Munich and a lecturer for Science Communication at the Hochschule München. She previously worked as a lecturer at the Lincoln University's School of Journalism, focusing on peace journalism projects in post-conflict societies. Lioba holds an MPhil in Peace and Conflict Studies from the University of Oslo and a degree in journalism. She has been working as a freelance journalist from Central America and Mexico since 2005.

Chapter 16

Enabling environments: Reflections on journalism and climate justice

Robert A Hackett, Sara Wylie and Pinar Gurleyen

What kind of journalism is relevant for a world beset by potentially catastrophic climate change? While democratic engagement remains a relevant touchstone for journalism in conditions of planetary emergency, we argue that journalism should adopt a crisis-orientation organised around effective frames for climate justice, such as urgency plus agency, climate change as a political issue, environmental citizenship, fossil fuel industry as rogue, and localisation. While such frames may find some openings within hegemonic (Western) media, they face a range of structural and professional constraints. We therefore argue for greater attention to such potentially transformative models and venues as peace journalism and alternative media.

Keywords: climate justice, media frames, democratic communication, crisis journalism, peace journalism, alternative media

If the dystopic projections of climate change scientists are not mitigated by collective remedial action, future generations will be enquiring why catastrophe overwhelmed 21st century global civilisation. The answers are complex and contested, ranging from the incremental nature of global warming and the futility of consumption reduction by isolated individuals, to the failures of governments and the destructive/expansionist dynamics of capitalism. But part of the answer is the enormous disjuncture between the growing crisis and modern culture's most important form of storytelling – journalism as 'the textual system of modernity' (Hartley 1996 cited in Hartley 2008: 312). Journalism plays a two-fold role in regards to crisis communication. It contributes to the discursive construction of crisis by selecting, defining and publicising certain issues over others to be characterised as crisis (Cottle 2009:165). It can also potentially help to prevent or mitigate the actual destructive impacts of crisis by providing the public with adequate information, and facilitating government and civil society initiatives.

That kind of cultural and political power makes journalism an inescapable player in addressing the causes and impacts of human-made climate change. Discounting fantasies of magical technological solutions, any feasible approaches require collective action and state policy, backed by an 'environment' of public communication that enables and encourages people to act, and to overcome the hostility of powerful interests and inertia of daily habits entrenched in the carbon economy.

Climate change is not just a scientific, technical, economic and political matter. It poses profoundly *ethical* challenges to human institutions, including journalism. The concept of 'climate justice' combines the need for urgent action with the promotion of the rights and voices of ordinary people affected by climate change. For its advocates, climate justice entails such principles as placing the main burden of adjustment on the wealthy countries of the global North that have contributed most to the crisis; leaving fossil fuels in the ground; planning a transition to a low-carbon society that protects people's rights, jobs and well-being; and conserving natural resources for the common good, not private and unsustainable exploitation (*New Internationalist* 2009, cited in Lee 2009).

This paper reflects upon what media frames best fit with an ethos of climate justice, and speculates about the conditions under which they might be realised.

THE 'DEMOCRATIC PUBLIC SPHERE' AS A TOUCHSTONE

In Western debates about journalism ethics, journalism is evaluated above all about how well it makes democracy work. In that regard, its putative functions include monitoring power, facilitating public deliberation, opposing concentrations of social power in the interests of equality, and (more contentiously) collaborating with the state and other social institutions to achieve shared objectives (Christians et al. 2009). But in a global 'risk society' (Beck 2009[2007]), is democracy still a relevant and productive benchmark? A world of multiple and intersecting crises (Cottle 2009: 1-25) – climate change and resource depletion; actual and potential political violence, exemplified by a decade of 'terror war' (Kellner 2003); stateless refugees and economic migration; financial instability and periodic meltdowns; globalised inequality and poverty – may be in a state of planetary emergency. Some commentators see a state of emergency as an appropriate political response. James Lovelock, the formulator of the Gaia hypothesis, the planet as a self-regulating single complex system, argued in 2010 that 'even the best democracies agree that when a major war approaches, democracy must be put on hold for the time being ... Climate change may be an issue as severe as a war. It may be necessary to put democracy on hold for a while'.

The multiple difficulties with this view include the assumption that the world is already democratic, that 'everyone can have their say' (Lovelock's phrase). On the contrary. Under existing relations of power, and the global hegemony of neoliberal capitalism, planetary emergency law would yield regimes of plunder more naked and brutal than we already have, generating even faster ecological decline unchecked by the cries of its victims. Climate justice requires more, not less, democratic communication.

That recognition does not necessarily mean accepting conventional notions of democracy and of journalism's role, however. For instance, the Habermasian model of the 'public sphere' contained within individual states may need rethinking. Historically, in Habermas's narrative, public spheres developed in the context of shared (bourgeois) class interests (Calcutt and Hammond 2011: 152-153) and relatively culturally homogeneous European nation-states. Given the exclusion of workers (not to mention women), participants did not need to dispute and attempt to resolve fundamental conflicts of interest, and could thus potentially operate in a consensual, rule-bound way. How can this model of equal, rational deliberation be transposed to any transnational public sphere, where cultural, ethnic, national and class contradictions co-exist with the homogenising logic of capital accumulation; where there is no single centralised authority yet where the necessity of co-ordinated action is urgent?

To overwork the Titanic metaphor, humanity has a shared interest in keeping the ship afloat, but conflicting interests over claims to the few lifeboats, to which first-class passengers already have privileged access. In a climate justice perspective, perhaps the concept of 'public sphere' needs to be conceptualised as operating within transnational social movements (rather than nation-states), and *against* the political and economic sponsors of ecocide. This implies a rather expanded role for subaltern counter-public spheres (Fraser 1997), capable of developing and articulating the interests of subaltern groups on a transnational basis, before re-engaging and challenging the keepers of the global order.

Similarly, global crisis calls for a rethinking of conventional liberal rationales for democracy itself. The classic theories of democracy stemming from the European Enlightenment differ in important respects – for example, whether they privilege the protection of rights against tyranny, or the more positive goal of promoting the development of human creative capacities (Held 2006). But they have in common the value of expanding individual autonomy and freedom, arguably premised upon not only the political defeat of tyranny but the spread of material prosperity.

The condition of planetary ecological emergency, however, forces a re-think. What if we have reached the 'end of growth'? Instead of the Enlightenment's exaltation of human development, suppose our starting point is instead the inherent embeddedness of human civilisation in the broader ecosphere – and the realisation that our abuse of that relationship is jeopardising the continuation of the human project? New criteria are then raised: how does political decision-making incorporate accountability to future generations, and to non-human species? What kinds of restrictions do majorities need to place upon their own freedom now, in order to facilitate future freedoms for others? (One harbinger is Ecuador which, in

2008, became the first country to enshrine constitutionally the rights of nature 'to exist, persist, maintain and regenerate its vital cycles, structure, functions and its processes in evolution', defining nature as 'a rights-bearing entity that should be treated with parity under the law' (Phillips and Huff with Project Censored 2009: 83-84)). None of this entails the replacement of democracy with eco-dictatorship. But it does imply a new task, and perhaps an alternative rationale, for democracy – obtaining consent and legitimacy for the shared sacrifices that societies, particularly in the global North, need to make in the interests of a sustainable common future.

Such weighty considerations are beyond further elaboration here. But they afford a glimpse into an ethical framework for journalism consistent with climate justice. We propose that such an ethical re-orientation for journalism could draw from recent work in environmental communication.

CRISIS ORIENTATION FOR CLIMATE JOURNALISM

One starting point is the notion of environmental communication as a 'crisis discipline', one that accepts both an explicit obligation to the public, and the ideological standpoint inherent in the practice. If climate change is articulated as an urgent social problem that must be addressed through proactive government policy, then an environmental crisis-discipline is inherently political; it will favour ideological positions favourable to collective action while scanting others, particularly the free market agenda (Klein 2012). It is thus important that environmental communication present itself as a complex theoretical discipline, whose effectiveness is ultimately evaluated by its ecological impact (Schwarze 2007: 91).

What are the ethical obligations of environmental communication to the public? Robert Cox, a leading scholar in the field, offers the beginnings of a model, based on four ethical principles:

- 'enhance the ability of society to respond appropriately to environmental signals' for the benefit of human and environmental health;

- make relevant information and decision-making processes 'transparent and accessible to members of the public' while those affected by environmental threats 'should also have the resources and ability to participate in decisions affecting their individual or communities' health....';

- engage various groups 'to study, interact with, and share experiences of the natural world';

- critically evaluate and expose communication practices that are 'constrained or suborned for harmful or unsustainable policies toward human communities and the natural world' (Cox 2007: 15-16).

Could Cox's proposed criteria be transposed to journalism? Many journalists find themselves striking an uneasy balance between the 'objectivity' standards of a reporter and the 'advocacy' work of an alarmed citizen. Cox's principles can potentially span that divide. They are reasonably consistent with the recognised democratic functions of journalism in monitoring power, surveying the (social and physical) environment for threats to well-being and facilitating public conversation on issues of public importance.

At the same time, Cox's second principle, in particular, parallels climate justice. The link between action that is both *effective* and *just* entails special efforts to ensure that the victims of climate change are heard. This concept also resonates with equality as a cornerstone of democratic communication. Journalism should help to offset the inequalities that are prevalent elsewhere in the social, economic and political system, argues Robert McChesney, a prominent American communication scholar. Indeed, 'unless communication and information are biased toward equality, they tend to enhance social inequality' (McChesney 1999: 288).

Whether journalism could follow environmental communication down the academic path of becoming a *discipline* is a debatable matter, beyond the scope of this paper. The argument here is that an ongoing crisis-orientation in journalism is possible, which means rejecting certain once-standard explanations of public communication, such as Anthony Downs's model of the information-attention cycle. It portrays a simplified process of communication by which the media and public react to news temporarily at the centre of public attention through several predictable phases, while never addressing or resolving the core issue (Boykoff and Boykoff 2007: 6). Rejecting such a deterministic model, Hansen (2011: 14) argues that journalists must capture climate change within diversified discourses and not rely only on external events to make climate change a relevant public issue.

The information-deficit model makes similar one-dimensional assumptions, assuming a linear progression from individuals' exposure to a problem, to their comprehension of the issue, to some form of collective action to bring about change. These assumptions over-emphasise the connection between individual knowledge, and the desire and ability to effect change. Furthermore, the model over-emphasises individual responsibility at the expense of the 'multiple structural and institutional constraints on the response of individuals to climate change imperatives' (Potter and Oster 2008:120).

CLIMATE JUSTICE FRAMES

A more appropriate guideline for thinking about climate justice journalism is the concept of 'framing', much used in contemporary media theory. Todd Gitlin (1980: 7) defined 'media frames' as 'persistent patterns of cognition, interpretation and presentation, of selection, emphasis and exclusion, by which symbol-handlers routinely organise discourse, whether verbal or visual'. Framing processes occur not only at the level of media texts, but also in the culture, and in the minds of elites, professional political communicators and individual citizens (Entman, Matthes and Pellicano 2009: 176). More complex and sustained than a mere persuasive message, a frame:

> … repeatedly involves the same objects and traits, using identical or synonymous words and symbols in a series of similar communications that are concentrated in time. These frames function to promote an interpretation of a problematic situation or actor and (implicit or explicit) support for a desirable response, often along with a moral judgment that provides an emotional charge (ibid: 177).

Framing is a contentious topic within the discipline of environmental communication. Proponents argue that framing is essential for any campaign aiming to effect social change (Lakoff 2010). A coherent framing strategy could communicate climate change and the destruction of nature as an ethical crisis. By contrast, critics of framing-as-strategy consider it an elitist approach that prevents a wider public dialogue around climate change (Brulle 2010: 90) and reinforces 'industrialised communication' in the same pattern of industrial production which produced climate change in the first place (López 2010: 103).

Such debates are a tempest in a teacup, however. Frames are inherent in the socially-constructed processes of media, *and* are essential for mobilising any social movement. Scholarly and grassroots constructions are not mutually exclusive. Framing emphasises the active agency of various stakeholders in forging responses to global warming, avoids the determinism of the information-deficit and issue-attention models, and ethically challenges the 'frame-blindness' (Maras 2012) associated with journalism's regime of objectivity. It calls attention to contestation over frames as a key aspect of political and ideological power, and to the strategies and unequal distribution of resources that influence the outcomes of such contests. Framing nevertheless holds open the possibility of sustained attention to climate change through successful strategic communication, thus overcoming the media's fragmentation bias. Robert Entman (2010) suggests some specific tactics, such as 'continuity editors' in news organisations – but the key need is for an overarching long-term narrative, much like 'fiscal restraint' or 'the war on terror' that have worked so well for the political right.

One strategic starting point is to recognise the 'psychological, social and structural barriers' to effective *societal* action on climate change (Ockwell, Whitmarsh and O'Neill 2009: 311), including lack of legislative action or business interest; the 'high carbon infrastructure and institutions' (ibid: 308) and other structural barriers; as well as common social norms and practices that are harmful to the environment. Obstacles to *individual* action include not a lack of information about climate change, but to the contrary, information overload, the intimidating scientific nature of the evidence, and the reception of information that may conflict with values or behaviour – all contributing to a 'value-action' gap in which people are aware of climate change but have not changed behaviour sufficiently. If there is a relevant information deficit, it concerns the *local* impact of climate change.

So, what frames are likely to be both effective and compatible with the ethics of climate justice? Extrapolating from the environmental communication literature, we suggest several.

CRISIS ORIENTATION: URGENCY PLUS AGENCY

People need information about the scientific consensus on the process of global warming and the urgency of combating it, without being paralysed by stories of melting ice caps, rising sea levels, expanding deserts, extreme weather, shrinking food supplies, dying oceans and uprooted environmental refugees. We need to know about such consequences of inaction, but we also need stories about successes and feasible solutions. We need publics with a strong sense of both urgency and empowerment.

Understanding climate change journalism as a crisis-based discipline raises the question of fear and sensationalism. For many activists, apocalyptic frames are an attractive tactic to communicate a sense of urgency. But over-reliance on 'climate porn' (Russill 2008: 147), a fear narrative based on 'tragic' ultimatums (Foust and Murphy 2009: 163) can leave the audience feeling overwhelmed and disengaged from meaningful solutions (O'Neill and Nicholson-Cole 2009: 376). Furthermore, such tactics would allow opponents to discredit climate change journalism's inconvenient truths. On the contrary, human agency must be 'at the heart of the narrative' to prevent disengagement and highlight opportunities for change (Foust and Murphy op cit: 163). Fear-appeals or dramatic narratives have their place, but they should be connected to people's everyday experiences and to 'feasible coping responses' for individuals (O'Neill and Nicholson-Cole op cit: 376).

CLIMATE CHANGE AS A POLITICAL ISSUE

While reduced consumption (especially in the global North) and technological innovation are key to greenhouse gas reductions, these processes are not likely to occur through market mechanisms alone. The incentives and subsidies that only governments can provide, and more broadly 'a hospitable legislative, regulatory, and policy environment', are necessary catalysts (Gunster 2012: 248).

That means avoiding representing policy-making as merely a self-interested game played by insiders, in which failures, stalemates and shortfalls are nearly inevitable. If climate change is a *political* issue, a *democratic* perspective highlights opportunities for popular agency, engagement within various local and global sites, and the development of popular political efficacy (ibid), while fulfilling Cox's criterion (noted above) of monitoring decision-making processes.

Climate justice journalism could challenge the dominant political narrative that climate change mitigation is in opposition to the economy, employment and industry. A political frame can integrate these problems into the larger systemic issue of environmental destruction and emphasise the potential for green energy policy developed through democratic involvement. This narrative could be extended to question the logic of infinite economic growth and its political implications (ibid). Newsworkers should, indeed, highlight policy-making failures, but juxtaposed with empowering stories within a political solutions frame. While such a frame endorses conservation and individual consumption reduction, it prioritises democratic participation in developing more systemic solutions.

ENVIRONMENTAL CITIZENSHIP: CLIMATE CHANGE AS A MORAL ISSUE

Environmental communication could promote the notion of 'environmental citizenship', reinforcing the ethical notion that our environmental rights are contingent on our environmental responsibilities (Ockwell et al. 2009: 316).

The discourse ought to move past the appeal to financial or materialist values as reasons for citizens to 'go green' and, instead, encourage a greater sense of social responsibility in their communities, even of beneficial sacrifice – an opportunity for renewal and to contribute with others in meeting a shared challenge. If barriers to individual engagement on environmental issues can be challenged and overcome, then citizens are more likely to mobilise for stronger top-down legislation on climate change mitigation (ibid: 320).

Put differently, this frame entails 'normalising' activism – representing civic engagement as common, pleasurable and politically effective; seeking stories about and from people who have become politically active, and highlighting how it affects their feelings, identity, understanding and engagement with the world (Gunster 2012: 262-263).

IDENTIFYING AN 'ENEMY'

A leading American environmentalist, Bill McKibben (2012), recently suggested that the main strategies of the environmental movement against global warming have failed. Big oil corporations have not been persuaded to switch to sustainable energy. Persuading individuals to change lifestyles takes far too long, and notwithstanding the moral appeal to shared sacrifice noted above, given our shared dependence on cheap fossil fuel, it is 'like trying to build a movement against yourself'. Likewise, the political process (at least in the US, still the world's largest greenhouse gas emitter) has yielded at best very limited results. The missing key, he suggests, is to frame the fossil fuel sector as a reckless rogue industry, because rapid transformative change 'would require building a movement, and movements require enemies'. That approach worked for the successful non-smokers' rights movement, which targeted not individual smokers but the tobacco industry as industrial purveyors of a lethal and addictive product – albeit one much less hard-wired into the global economy than fossil fuels.

Some versions of social movement theory, such as the Resource Mobilisation tradition, support McKibben's strategy. Movements need 'collective action frames' that identify certain conditions as grievous, identify sources responsible for those conditions and propose remedies (Klandermans 2001). Climate change is surely a shared grievance, albeit one with decidedly differential regional, racial and class impacts; the fossil fuel industry could credibly be framed as an enemy not only of the movement(s), but of the planet itself.

'LOCALISING' THE GLOBAL CHALLENGES OF CLIMATE CHANGE

Local frames could situate people within a greater social environment, implicating the community in its role in environmental degradation, the subsequent effects on its locality, and opportunities for change. Shared experience over rising food or gas prices in a community, for example, can be opportunities to contribute to local climate change awareness. Journalists could leverage the public awareness of local consequences towards the systematic and seemingly abstract processes of climate change.

While climate justice journalism should not be excessively scientific, overly focused on arcane scientific debates to the exclusion of analysing the contending values at stake (Moser and Dilling 2007), it is also important not to relate too glibly local events like unusual weather directly to climate change. (Not that corporate media in northern America have needed much encouragement to avoid the topic altogether.) Instead, environmental journalism could identify locals' shared experiences, beliefs and attitudes and frame climate change coverage to appeal to these cultural values (Schweizer et al. 2009), and to situate people within the multifarious and interconnected spaces being affected by environmental change. Highlighting people's relation to their community helps to 'implicate all of us within the im/material networks' of climate change (Potter and Oster 2008: 124).

Cultural resonance gives environmental issues vital anchorage, and can 'activate existing chains of cultural meaning' to improve coverage, gain legitimacy and nurture political efficacy (Hansen 2010: 101). Climate change solutions can be associated with cultural values of health and quality of life, instead of being framed as a force of deprivation in conflict with cultural practices.

Framing can help to encourage interpersonal dialogue and relationship-based sharing of information among a specified audience. Nisbet (2009) argues that peer-sharing of selectively-framed information, facilitated by a media source, can advance a discourse on climate change in a trusting and safe space, and can also create agreement on how certain solutions could address that group's particular needs.

Being situated within a network of humans similarly affected by climate change allows 'our cultural stories [to] give shape to the real' (Potter and Oster 2008: 121). Furthermore, strategic framing allows the media to identify localised points of leverage as opportunities to anchor climate change within a larger cultural context (Cox 2010: 130). This encourages the public to view environmental challenges as part of a greater system influenced by dynamic and interconnected forces operating on different levels (natural, social, economic, political) where change can take place, thus providing multiple points of intervention (instead of multiplying the gravity of the problem). Such a re-conceptualisation could generate better understanding of the crisis, more potential for innovating solutions, and more awareness of other actors (and potential allies) within the system, like organisations, politicians and communities.

FROM ENVIRONMENTAL COMMUNICATION TO JOURNALISM?

Some caveats are now necessary. First, effective frames cannot necessarily be universalised. Our list above is neither exhaustive nor definitive; it is drawn from environmental communication scholarship and arguably under-represents the 'justice' aspect of responding to the climate crisis – viz. the need for specific frames from and for mobilising groups most vulnerable to the impact of climate change. Frames work differently for particular groups. The conventional literature is arguably too glib about 'public', 'democracy' and 'community' as singular entities.

Second, frames are not everything. The ethical responsibility of journalism cannot be reduced to the question of appropriate textual representations. It also involves structure – ownership, control, financing, access to the means of communication, including the internet – the self-formation of social movements and counter-public spheres, and the distribution of different forms of cultural, social and economic capital which different parties bring to bear in producing 'credible' accounts.

Third, the environmental communication frames we have identified do not clearly distinguish between those appropriate for journalism, as distinct from advocacy campaigns and social movements. Journalism has a societal function, a capacity for an independent gaze that separates it from propaganda (Calcutt and Hammond 2011).

Yet these frames do provide an initial benchmark of the performance of leading news media. Could a crisis orientation, combined with empowering narratives and dialogic forms of news production, take root within corporate news organisations? To the extent that 'coherent narratives sell', Entman (2010: 110) suggests that a crisis orientation could help alleviate northern American journalism's own crisis of legitimacy, relevance and underinvestment. Media sociology, such as Shoemaker and Reese's (1996) model of a hierarchy of influences on news content, identifies possible space for climate justice frames. Many journalists personally have 'liberal' or environmentalist views. Everyday routines like the professional concepts of 'balance' provide opportunities for environmental groups to become media sources. Such news values as novelty, human interest and spectacle can facilitate coverage of some kinds of climate change news, such as dramatic or disruptive protests (although often at the cost of conveying a 'serious' message).

News organisations have their own legitimation imperatives; to retain credibility with audiences, while middle or mass-market media cannot be seen as propagandists, particularly on issues (such as the proposed northern Gateway pipeline in British Columbia, intended to export Alberta tar sands oil) where public opinion is polarised and mobilised. The funding, expertise, communication strategies and/or perceived public support of organisations such as the Suzuki Foundation can also sometimes be effective 'extra-media' influences on the news, backed by the new possibilities for agenda-shaping afforded by social media and online citizen's journalism.

And yet, powerful organisational and professional forces militate against climate justice frames in the still-dominant corporate media. The well-known 'propaganda model' of Edward Herman and Noam Chomsky (1988) highlights five causal factors or 'filters' on hegemonic American news media – large- scale corporate ownership of media, corporate advertising, high dependence on elite political and institutional spokespeople as sources, ongoing 'flak' from well-financed conservative media critics, and unreflective ideological frameworks, such as anti-communism – all render the US media into conduits for the issue agendas and worldviews of political and economic elites. There is diversity and debate within the press, but generally within the limits of disagreements within the elites themselves.

The propaganda model has been understandably criticised as reductionist (Hackett 2006), but in some respects, it actually understates the degree of current integration between media conglomerates and financialised global capitalism (Almiron 2010). One implication of the global dominance of commercial media is an ideological bias in favour of affluent urban consumers, muting the voices of the rural poor, environmental refugees, Aboriginal people in the Arctic and others who disproportionately bear the brunt of climate change. Commercial media's pursuit of profitable audiences may not be compatible with crisis journalism's challenges to aspects of hegemonic culture, such as acquisitive individualism. The reluctance of consumers to contemplate doomsday scenarios or their own role in creating them makes climate change a topic potentially difficult to market. Moreover, in calling for diversification of news sources, climate justice journalism challenges the legitimacy of a 'news net' (Tuchman 1978) anchored on government and corporate elites, such as the military and carbon industry establishments.

Corporate lobbying, and the manipulation of media and of scientific reports by conservative think tanks (CTTs), are related influences on media and political agendas. One survey of fifty international CTTs found that 90 per cent of them advocated environmental scepticism in their publications and online, in order to 'undermine the environmental movement's efforts to legitimize its claims via science' (Jacques et al. 2008: 364; with respect to Canada, see Gutstein 2009, Chapter 7).

Given such structural pressures, as well as the professional practices of 'objectivity' noted below, how receptive are hegemonic media to climate justice frames? A television meteorologist told us that news media overall are doing an 'abysmal' job on climate change because they do not devote sufficient resources to the issue, and have 'the attention span of a gnat'. Academic research tends to support that dismal observation. Dominant media typically treat climate change haphazardly, in an 'episodic' way that focuses on particular events (such as an iceberg breaking, or a summit conference), rather than as an ongoing process. Hansen (2011: 16) found that, rather than emphasise the responsibility or consequences of climate change as did Dutch and French newspapers, American newspapers used a 'conflict' frame; they highlighted divergent views on the certainty of climate science, thus minimising both the sense of urgency and the vested interests of carbon-emitting industries. The phase of climate denial is largely behind us, but we are left with journalism that implicitly assumes that economic growth and consumerist culture are good, that 'the economy' and 'the environment' are mutually exclusive, and that the politics of climate change is a spectator sport that ordinary people observe from the outside as elite actors at international summit meetings decide our futures (Gunster 2011).

Adapting the propaganda model, Jennifer Good (2008) found that Canadian, American and international newspapers tiptoed around the climate change issue. Notwithstanding national differences, the press in all three venues was more likely to finger 'greenhouse gases' rather than 'fossil fuels' as causes; to avoid linking weather extremes with climate change; to minimise the themes of decreasing or differential energy use; to privilege a science frame over political/economic frames in such a way as to convey 'a sense that the science of climate change is uncertain' (ibid: 248); and to offer a solutions-oriented frame in less than 2 per cent of articles, implying that 'there is no alternative to the *status quo*' (ibid: 247). Hegemonic media's ties with the fossil fuel industry, not only through advertising, but also ownership and mutual integration into financialised global capitalism (Almiron 2010), may lead to self-censorship in journalism (Anderson 2009: 170).

To be sure, the hegemonic media sometimes offer respectful coverage of environmental protests and in-depth reporting on environmental issues. The *Vancouver Sun*'s nine-part series on the Northern Gateway pipeline project in January 2012 is an example. But the overall pattern is one of disjointed coverage of climate change at best, with the carbon industries' preferred frames (fossil fuel development is essential to economic prosperity and jobs; oil companies are developing alternative energy; climate change activists are hypocrites for using fossil fuels) usually well-represented, and often dominant.

ALTERNATIVES FOR CLIMATE CHANGE JUSTICE JOURNALISM

If the existing media field is barren ground for climate justice frames, what alternatives are available? Hackett (2006) suggests three logical possibilities: change the media field from within; construct a new 'parallel' field of alternative media, independent from but potentially influencing dominant media; and build reform movements that can influence the field from outside. Here, we sketch examples of the first two approaches.

CHANGE FROM WITHIN: PEACE JOURNALISM

Peace journalism (PJ) is an instructive example of the first approach. Since the late 1990s, advocates of PJ have accumulated a wealth of experience in journalism training and media production. Remarkably similar to environmental communication, PJ is an analytical method for evaluating reportage of conflicts, a set of practices and ethical norms that journalism could employ in order to improve itself, and a rallying call for change. In sum, PJ's public philosophy 'is when journalists make choices – of what stories to report and about how to report them – that create opportunities for society at large to consider and value non-violent responses to conflict' (Lynch and McGoldrick 2005: 5).

PJ draws upon the insights of conflict analysis to look beyond the overt violence that is the stuff of conventional journalism, which is often tantamount to war journalism. PJ calls attention to the context, of Attitudes, Behaviour and Contradictions, and the need to identify a range of stakeholders broader than the 'two sides' engaged in violent confrontation. If war journalism presents conflict as a tug-of-war between two parties in which one side's gain is the other's loss, PJ invites journalists to re-frame conflict as a cat's cradle of relationships between various stakeholders, and to distinguish between stated demands, and underlying needs and objectives. Journalists should identify and attend to voices working for creative and non-violent solutions; to ways of transforming and transcending the hardened lines of conflict; and to aggression and casualties on all sides, avoiding the conflict-escalating trap of emphasising 'our' victims and 'their' atrocities. PJ looks beyond the direct physical violence that is the focus of war journalism, to include the structural and cultural violence (e.g. racism, militarism) that may underlie conflict situations (Hackett 2006).

In common with climate justice journalism, PJ challenges key aspects of journalism's 'regime of objectivity' (Hackett and Zhao 1998). It challenges the epistemological basis for a stance of detachment, calling instead for journalists to be more reflective about the institutionalised biases of routine practices, the risks posed by certain framing and sourcing choices, the stratagems of sources, the unavoidably interventionist nature of journalism, and its potential to become an unwitting accomplice to war propaganda (Lynch 2008: 10-14; Hackett 2011: 42). It challenges the conventional news emphasis on violence, negativity, unambiguity and timeliness, calling for more attention to long-term processes and contexts of conflict formation and resolution. PJ calls for the broadening of sources beyond officials and politicians, to include the voices and options for peaceful resolution. PJ even arguably challenges the entire global war system and its 'deadly forms of propaganda' (Falk, in Lynch 2008: viii).

PJ's advocates can lay claim to some of Western journalism's vaunted proclaimed ideals – such as comprehensiveness, accuracy, fairness and truth-seeking. Yet given its semi-oppositional and transformative nature, it is not surprising that PJ has not found much fertile soil in established Western corporate media. It has had more uptake in societies like Indonesia and the Philippines, where the media are perceived to have exacerbated internal conflict and where the political roles and professional norms of journalism are in greater flux (Hackett 2011: 45).

The parallels with climate justice journalism are evident. Both paradigms call attention to victims, to change-makers and long-term contexts, and challenge powerful institutions and norms. Arguably, they even have a common 'enemy' – militarism and imperialism – that both profligately uses, and seeks to control, fossil fuel resources. It has been suggested that PJ may find more fruitful ground in alternative than commercial media (Suchenwirth and Keeble 2011; Hackett 2011). The same may apply to climate justice communication.

ALTERNATIVE MEDIA

Throughout modern history, subaltern social groups have produced their own media, giving expression to the voices and interests of those ignored or attacked in the hegemonic media (Downing et al. 2001). Debates abound concerning how to define or even label such 'alternative' media, but an ideal type might include these characteristics: participatory models of production; aesthetic experimentation; challenges to established media power (including the professionalisation and highly capitalised economy of commercial journalism, and the division between media producers and audiences); bottom-up rather than top-down ways of scanning and reporting the world, challenging elite definitions of reality; an intention to represent subaltern communities and develop counter-public spheres; openness to advocacy or campaigning journalism; and/or a positive orientation to social change, social movements and/or marginalised communities (Hackett 2011; Atton and Hamilton 2008: 1; Atton 2009). Often launched through discontent with dominant media or with the social order itself, alternative media constitute 'a critique in action' (Atton 2009: 284).

Not surprisingly then, the burgeoning research on alternative media provides a more hopeful picture of climate change communication. For instance, studies of Vancouver press coverage of the 2009 Copenhagen climate change summit found that two independent news outlets, the online *thetyee.ca* and urban weekly the *Georgia Straight*, substantially differed from the corporate dailies (Gunster

2011, 2012). Both publications treated climate change as a political issue, without reducing it to official politics. They conveyed a sense of agency and hope, offering news articles that 'invited readers to actively participate in imagining how (easily) a better world might be built' (Gunster 2012: 250).

What characteristics of alternative media render them relatively conducive to climate justice communication? Very briefly, we suggest four.

1. *counter-hegemonic content* is often accepted as the quintessence of alternative media, and some scholars consider them to be 'critical media' that show:

   …. the suppressed possibilities of existence, antagonisms of reality, and potentials for change. It questions domination, expresses the standpoints of the oppressed and dominated groups and individuals and argues for the advancement of a co-operative society (Fuchs 2010: 173).

   Alternative media *sourcing routines* broaden or even invert the hierarchy of access prevalent in conventional media, one dominated by politicians, government and business, rather than NGOs, charities or pressure groups (Lewis and Franklin 2008: 14). By contrast, through giving access as legitimate news sources to environmental groups and to those adversely affected by the fossil fuel industry and by climate change, alternative media can challenge existing frames (Brulle 2010: 82).

   Moreover, to varying degrees, alternative media *qualify or reject the practices of objectivity*, such as balance and impartiality. For several years, the American corporate news media contributed to scientifically unwarranted climate scepticism through the practice of balancing climate scientists with 'experts' from fuel industry-funded think tanks (Antilla 2005; Boykoff and Boykoff 2004). Many alternative journalists reject not only such false balance, but more broadly objectivity as a journalistic ideal that 'is not only unrealistic but also masks relations and structures of domination' (Atton and Hamilton 2008: 84). The tradition in some alternative media of 'advocacy' or 'campaigning' journalism makes it easier to frame climate change as a political issue and to analyse the interests of contending stakeholders. At the same time, like peace journalism, alternative media often pursue certain aspects of objectivity – accuracy, comprehensiveness, truthfulness – that mesh well with climate justice journalism.

2. Alternative media often have a *positive (though independent) relationship with social movements*, and a *mobilisation-orientation*:

   In contrast to mainstream media's liberal democratic ideal of the 'informed' citizenry, alternative media promote the participatory democratic ideal of the 'mobilized' citizenry (Haas 2004: 116; citing Atton 2002).

Beyond the critical role of providing counter-information and oppositional frames, this entails the 'creative, positive action of proposing, debating and putting into practice new kinds of social relationships, and ultimately, a new social order' (Hamilton 2000: 363).

3. Some commentators regard *participatory and dialogical forms of communication* as more important than the content. While we should not dismiss framing strategies as inherently elitist, we agree with Brulle (2010: 91) that political mobilisation campaigns 'are more effective and legitimate if they engage citizens in a sustained dialogue rather than treating them as mass opinion to be manipulated'. Historically, alternative media are more likely to 'break down the producer/consumer binary' (Platon and Deuze 2003: 218), to involve audiences in decision-making and ownership as well as content production, and arguably to constitute 'citizens' media' where people are 'reshaping their identities, reformulating established social definitions, and legitimising local cultures and lifestyles on the personal as well as the local level' (Rodriguez 2001: 158).

4. Overlapping with horizontal and dialogical communication, many alternative media are *local in orientation*. We suggested above that localised frames are relatively effective in engaging publics on the climate change issue. 'Organic', 'small' and 'slow' media environments can be ideal spaces for communities to engage; examples include a 'community radio station, media literacy workshop, or a discussion group around an independently made documentary' as well as 'poetry slams, or community film festivals that draw in local businesses and community members' (López 2010: 101,106). Cultural and physical proximity to audiences helps local media to generate frames that resonate with communities (Segnit and Eraut 2007: 32).

These considerations are especially relevant for climate justice. Agyeman et al. (2007: 130) stress the importance of adopting 'socio-cultural perspectives' that account for 'injustice' in climate change communication, particularly when interacting with low-income and minority communities. They find that the rural poor and people in disinvested inner urban cores are likely to be sceptical of programmes and 'experts' that originate outside of their community (ibid: 133). Their recommendations concern partnerships between climate change communicators and community organisations, but could be extrapolated to media organisations.

To be sure, some 'mainstream' commercial media (such as 'community' weekly papers) also have a local orientation, and sometimes excellent environmental news. But given their dependence on commercial revenue, increasing reliance on agency copy and civic boosterism, they are less likely than movement-oriented alternative media to promote mobilising frames that challenge the fossil fuel industry (Gurleyen and Hackett, forthcoming).

Yet while offering promising models and venues for climate justice communication, alternative media and peace journalism are themselves confined to the margins of global media. Neither is likely to find much scope for growth through market mechanisms, corporate media that are integrated with global capital or political elites committed to neoliberalism. We have suggested that pro-environmental communication, effective climate change policy and democratic engagement are mutually supportive. All three goals would benefit through the success of a fourth – the democratisation of media systems so that they enhance participation and equality (Hackett and Carroll 2006: 88). In turn, the fate of these intertwined objectives depends upon the revitalisation of broader popular movements for radical social change, including climate justice.

- This paper derives from the Climate Justice Project, a SSHRC-CURA research study led by the Canadian Centre for Policy Alternatives – British Columbia, and the University of British Columbia. For projects entitled 'The climate of discussion: News media and the politics of climate change in British Columbia' and 'Paradigms for contention: Journalism for a world in crisis', funding was provided by the Social Sciences and Humanities Research Council of Canada, the office of the Vice-President, Research at Simon Fraser University, and the office of the Dean, Faculty of Communication, Art and Technology. The authors wish to thank Shane Gunster (SFU) and Shannon Daub (CCPA) for comments and advice; Joey Chopra, Nicole Keith, Wendee Lang, Vojtech Sedlak, Josh Tabish and Maegan Thomas for invaluable research assistance; and Angelika Hackett for editorial assistance. With thanks to Jake Lynch, an earlier version was presented by invitation at the 'New media, new journalism: Challenges and opportunities' conference, University of Sydney (13 September 2012).

- This paper was first published in *Ethical Space*, Vol 10, Nos 2 and 3 pp 34-46, 2013

NOTE

[1] Chris Nash (2011) suggests that a discipline entails a relational rather than essentialist approach, the use of theoretical abstractions that generate operational definitions for practitioners and robust criteria for assessing the efficacy of the theorisation. Whether the conditions of journalism, including timeliness, are conducive to disciplinary status is debatable, but that does not preclude journalism that is anchored in other academic disciplines

REFERENCES

Agyeman, J., Doppelt, B., Lynn, K. and Hatic, H. (2007) The climate-justice link: Communicating risk with low income and minority audiences, Moser, S and Dilling, L (eds) *Creating a climate for change: Communicating climate change and facilitating social change*, Cambridge, Cambridge University Press

Almiron, N. (2010) *Journalism in crisis: Corporate media and financialization*, trans McGrath, W., Cresskill, NJ, Hampton Press

Anderson, A. (2009) Media, politics and climate change: Towards a new research agenda, *Sociology Compass*, Vol. 3 pp 166-182. Available online at http://onlinelibrary.wiley.com/doi/10.1111/j.1751-9020.2008.00188.x/abstract, accessed on 1 March 2013

Antilla, L. (2005) Climate of scepticism: US newspaper coverage of the science of climate change, *Global Environmental Change*, Vol. 5, No. 4 pp 338-352

Atton, C. (2009) Why alternative journalism matters, *Journalism*, Vol. 10, No. 3 pp 283-285. Available online at http://jou.sagepub.com/cgi/content/refs/10/3/283, accessed on 1 March 2013

Atton, C. (2002) *Alternative media*, London, Sage

Atton, C. and Hamilton, J. (2008) *Alternative journalism*, London, Sage

Beck, U. (2009 [2007]) *World at risk*, trans Cronin, C., Cambridge, Polity Press

Boykoff, M. and Boykoff, J. (2007) Climate change and journalistic norms: A case-study of US mass-media coverage, *Geoforum*, Vol. 38, No. 6 pp 1190-1204. Available online at http://www.eci.ox.ac.uk/publications/downloads/boykoff07-geoforum.pdf, accessed on 1 March 2013

Boykoff, M. and Boykoff, J. (2004) Balance as bias: Global warming and the US prestige press, *Global Environmental Change*, Vol. 14 pp 125-136

Brulle, R. (2010) From environmental campaigns to advancing the public dialogue: Environmental communication for civic engagement, *Environmental Communication*, Vol. 4, No. 1 pp 82-98. Available online at http://www.informaworld.com.proxy.lib.sfu.ca/smpp/section?content=a919927306&fulltext=713240928, accessed on 1 March 2013

Calcutt, A. and Hammond, P. (2011) *Journalism studies: A critical introduction*, London and New York, Routledge

Christians, C. G., Glasser, T. L., McQuail, D., Nordenstreng, K. and White, R. A. (2009) *Normative theories of media: Journalism in democratic societies*, Urbana and Chicago, University of Illinois Press

Cottle, S. (2009) *Global crisis reporting: Journalism in the global age*, Maidenhead, UK, Open University Press

Couldry, N. and Curran, J. (2003) *Contesting media power: Alternative media in a networked world*, Lanham, MD, Rowman and Littlefield

Cox, R. J. (2010) Beyond frames: Recovering the strategic in climate communication, *Environmental Communication: A Journal of Nature and Culture*, Vol. 4, No. 1 pp 122-133. Available online at http://www.informaworld.com.proxy.lib.sfu.ca/smpp/ftinterface-content=a919926348-fulltext=713240928-frm=content, accessed on 1 March 2013

Cox, R. J. (2007) Nature's 'crisis disciplines': Does environmental communication have an ethical duty?, *Environmental Communication: A Journal of Nature and Culture*, Vol. 1, No. 1 pp 5-20. Available online at http://www.informaworld.com.proxy.lib.sfu.ca/smpp/section?content=a778982174&fulltext=713240928, accessed on 1 March 2013

Downing, J. D. H., Ford, T. V., Gil, G. and Stein, L. (2001) *Radical media: Rebellious communication and social movements*, Thousand Oaks, CA, Sage

Entman, R. M. (2010) Improving newspapers' economic prospects by augmenting their contributions to democracy, *International Journal of Press/Politics*, Vol. 5, No. 1 pp 104-125. Available online at http://hij.sagepub.com/cgi/reprint/15/1/104, accessed on 2 March 2013

Entman, R. M., Matthes, J. and Pellicano, J. (2009) Nature, sources, and effects of news framing, Wahl-Jorgensen, K. and Hanitzsch, T. (eds) *The handbook of journalism studies*, New York, Routledge pp 175-190

Foust, C. R. and Murphy, W. O. (2009) Revealing and reframing apocalyptic tragedy in global warming discourse, *Environmental Communication: A Journal of Nature and Culture*, Vol. 3, No. 2 pp 151-167. Available online at http://www.informaworld.com.proxy.lib.sfu.ca/smpp/content-db=all-content=a912388367, accessed on 2 March 2013

Fraser, N. (1997) *Justice interruptus*, New York, Routledge

Fuchs, C. (2010) Alternative media as critical media, *European Journal of Social Theory*, Vol. 13, No. 2 pp 173-192. Available online at http://fuchs.uti.at/wp-content/uploads/altmedia.pdf, accessed on 3 March 2013

Gitlin, T. (1980) *The whole world is watching: Mass media in the making and unmaking of the new left*, Berkeley, University of California Press

Good, J. (2008) The framing of climate change in Canadian, American, and international newspapers: A media propaganda model analysis, *Canadian Journal of Communication*, Vol. 33, No. 2 pp 233-255. Available online at http://web.ebscohost.com.proxy.lib.sfu.ca/ehost/pdfviewer/pdfviewer?vid=2&hid=13&sid=a4656176-3b35-446d-98f0-1d23d967fb22%40sessionmgr10, accessed on 4 March 2013

Gunster, S. (2012) Radical optimism: Expanding visions of climate politics in alternative media, Carvalho, A. and Peterson, T. R. (eds) *Climate change politics: Communication and public engagement*, Amherst, N.Y., Cambria Press pp 239-267

Gunster, S. (2011) Covering Copenhagen: Climate change in B. C. media, *Canadian Journal of Communication*, Vol. 36, No. 3 pp 477-502

Gurleyen, P. and Hackett, R. A. (forthcoming) Who needs objectivity? Journalism in crisis, journalism for crisis, Gasher, M. and Brin, C (eds) *Deliberation, diversity and dollars: Public strategies for journalism in the Canadian media ecology*, Toronto, University of Toronto Press

Gutstein, D. (2009) *Not a conspiracy theory: How business propaganda hijacks democracy*, Toronto, Key Porter

Haas, T. (2004) Alternative media, public journalism and the pursuit of democratization, *Journalism Studies*, Vol. 5, No. 1 pp 115-121. Available online at http://dx.doi.org/10.1080/146167003200017478 3, accessed on 5 March 2013

Hackett, R. A. (2011) New vistas for peace journalism: Alternative media and communication rights, Shaw, I. S., Lynch, J. and Hackett, R. A. (eds) *Expanding peace journalism: Comparative and critical approaches*, Sydney, Sydney University Press pp 35-69

Hackett, R. A. (2006) Is peace journalism possible?, *Conflict and Communication Online*, Fall, Vol. 5, No. 2

Hackett, R. A. and Carroll, W. K. (2006) *Remaking media: The struggle to democratize public communication*, New York, N. Y., Routledge

Hackett, R. A. and Zhao, Y. (1998) *Sustaining democracy? Journalism and the politics of objectivity*, Toronto, Garamond

Hamilton, J. (2000) Alternative media: Conceptual difficulties, critical possibilities, *Journal of Communication Inquiry*, Vol. 24, No. 4 pp 357-378. Available online at http://jci.sagepub.com/cgi/content/abstract/24/4/357, accessed on 22 February 2013

Hansen, A. (2011) Communication, media and environment: Towards reconnecting research on the production, content and social implications of environmental communication, *International Communication Gazette*, Vol. 73, No. 1 pp 7-25

Hansen, A. (2010) *Environment, media and communication*, New York, Routledge

Hartley, J. (2008) Journalism and popular culture, Wahl-Jorgensen, K and Hanitzsch, T. (eds) *The handbook of journalism studies*, New York, Routledge pp 310-325

Hartley, J. (1996) *Popular reality: Journalism, modernity, popular culture*, London, Arnold

Held, D. (2006) *Models of democracy*, Stanford, CA, Stanford University Press, third edition

Herman, E. and Chomsky, N. (1988) *Manufacturing consent*, New York, Pantheon

Jacques, J., Dunlap, R. E. and Freeman, M. (2008) The organisation of denial: Conservative think-tanks and environmental scepticism, *Environmental Politics*, Vol. 17, No. 3 pp 349-385. Available online at http://pdfserve.informaworld.com/605724_770885140_793291693.pdf, accessed on 21 February 2013

Kellner, D. (2003) *From 9/11 to terror war: The dangers of the Bush legacy*, Lanham, MD, Rowman and Littlefield

Klandermans, B. (2001) Why social movements come into being and why people join them, Blau, J. (ed.) *Blackwell companion to sociology*, Malden, MA, Blackwell pp 268-81

Klein, N. (2012) Serious climate agenda means scrapping free market agenda, *CCPA Monitor*, March, Vol. 18, No. 9 pp 8-10

Lakoff, G. (2010) Why it matters how we frame the environment, *Environmental Communication*, Vol. 4, No. 1 pp 70-81. Available online at http://www.informaworld.com.proxy.lib.sfu.ca/smpp/section?content=a919923726&fulltext=713240928

Lee, P. (2009) *The no-nonsense guide to communication, climate justice and climate change*, Toronto, World Association for Christian Communication

Lewis, J, Williams, A. and Franklin, B. (2008) A compromised fourth estate? UK news journalism, public relations and news sources, *Journalism Studies*, Vol. 9, No. 1 pp 1-20

López, A. (2010) Defusing the cannon/canon: An organic media approach to environmental communication, *Environmental Communication*, Vol. 4, No. 1 pp 99-108. Available online at http://www.informaworld.com.proxy.lib.sfu.ca/smpp/section?content=a919925653&fulltext=713240928, accessed on 22 February 2013

Lovelock, J. (2010) Interview. Available online at http://www.guardian.co.uk/environmenet/blog/2010/mar/29/james-lovelock, accessed on 22 February 2013

Lynch, J. (2008) *Debates in peace journalism*, Sydney, Sydney University Press

Lynch, J. and McGoldrick, A. (2005) *Peace journalism*, Stroud, UK, Hawthorn Press

Maras, S. (2012) *Objectivity in journalism*, Cambridge, UK, Polity Press

McChesney, R. W. (1999) *Rich media, poor democracy: Communication politics in dubious times*, Urbana and Chicago, University of Illinois Press

McKibben, B. (2012) Global warming's terrifying new math, *Rolling Stone*, 2 August. Available online at http://www.rolling-stone.com/politics/news/global-warmings-terrifying-new-math-20120719?link=mostpopular1, accessed on 22 February 2013

Moser, S. and Dilling, L. (eds) (2007) Introduction, *Creating a climate for change: Communicating climate change and facilitating social change*, Cambridge, Cambridge University Press pp 1-30

Nash, C. (2011) Izzy Stone, James Carey and beyond: Universities in the new journalistic order. Paper presented to Crossing Boundaries Conference, University of California, Berkeley, 17-18 March

New Internationalist (2009) January/February, No. 419

Nisbet, M (2009) Communicating climate change: Why frames matter for public engagement, *Environment: Science and policy for sustainable development*. Available online at www.environment-magazine.org/March-April%202009/Nisbet-full.html, accessed on 25 February 2013

Ockwell, D., Whitmarsh, L. and O'Neill, S. (2009) Reorienting climate change communication for effective mitigation, *Science Communication*, Vol. 30, No. 3 pp 305-327. Available online at http://scx.sagepub.com/cgi/content/abstract/30/3/305, accessed on 26 February 2013

O'Neill, S. and Nicholson-Cole, S. (2009) Fear won't do it: Promoting positive engagement with climate change through visual and iconic representations, *Science Communication*, Vol. 30, No. 3 pp 355-379. Available online at http://scx.sagepub.com.proxy.lib.sfu.ca/cgi/content/abstract/30/3/355

Phillips, P. and Huff, M. with Project Censored (2009) *Censored 2010*, New York, Seven Stories Press

Platon, S. and Deuze, M. (2003) Indymedia journalism: A radical way of making, selecting, sharing news?, *Journalism*, Vol. 4, No. 3 pp 336-355. Available online at http://jou.sagepub.com/cgi/content/abstract/4/3/336, accessed on 27 February 2013

Potter, E. and Oster, C. (2008) Communicating climate change: Public responsiveness and matters of concern, *Media International Australia*, Vol. 127 pp 116-126. Available online at http://www.emsah.uq.edu.au/mia/secure/resources/127/13-potter_oster.pdfm accessed on 26 February 2013

Rodriguez, C. (2001) *Fissures in the mediascape: An international study of citizens' media*, Cresskill, NJ, Hampton Press

Russill, C. (2008) Tipping point forewarnings in climate change communication: Some implications of an emerging trend, *Environmental Communication*, Vol. 2, No. 2 pp 133-153. Available online at http://www.informaworld.com/smpp/content-db=all?content=10.1080/17524030802141711, accessed on 27 February 2013

Schwarze, S. (2007) Environmental communication as a discipline of crisis, *Environmental Communication: A Journal of Nature and Culture*, Vol. 1, No. 1 pp 87-98. Available online at http://www.informaworld.com/smpp/content-db=all?content=10.1080/17524030701334326, accessed on 2 March 2013

Schweizer, S., Thompson, J. L., Teel, T. and Bruyere, B. (2009) Strategies for communicating about climate change impacts on public lands, *Science Communication*, Vol. 31, No. 2 pp 266-274. Available online at http://scx.sagepub.com.proxy.lib.sfu.ca/cgi/content/abstract/31/2/266, accessed on 3 March 2013

Segnit, N. and Eraut, G. (2007) *Warm words ii: How the climate story is evolving and the lessons we can learn for encouraging public action*, London, Institute for Public Policy Research

Shoemaker, P. and Reese, S. (1996) *Mediating the message: Theories of influences on mass media content*, White Plains, NY, Longman, second edition

Suchenwirth, L. and Keeble, R. L. (2011) Oligarchy reloaded and pirate media: The state of peace journalism in Guatemala, Shaw, I. S., Lynch, J. and Hackett, R. A. (eds) *Expanding peace journalism: Comparative and critical approaches*, Sydney, Sydney University Press pp 168-190

Tuchman, G. (1978) *Making news: A study in the construction of reality*, New York, Free Press

NOTE ON THE CONTRIBUTORS

Robert A. Hackett is Professor Emeritus of Communication, Simon Fraser University. He has written extensively on media democratisation and journalism as political communication. Bob's most recent collaborative books include *Journalism for climate crisis: Public engagement, media alternatives* (2017), *Expanding peace journalism: Comparative and critical approaches* (2011) and *Remaking media: The struggle to democratize public communication* (2006). He is on the editorial advisory board of *Journalism Studies* and the *Journal of Alternative and Community Media*. He has co-founded several community-oriented media education and advocacy initiatives, including Newswatch Canada and Media Democracy Days. Bob is a research associate with the Canadian Centre for Policy Alternatives and has been involved in pro-climate and anti-pipeline activism since 2014. He now lives in Powell River and writes periodically for *National Observer, Canadian Dimension, the Tyee, rabble.ca* and other online outlets.

Sara Wylie graduated from Simon Fraser University with a BA Honours in Political Science in 2012. She has experience working with a range of climate and social justice non-profit organisations.

Pinar Turan (née Gurleyen) is a communications instructor at Columbia College in Vancouver, BC. She received a Master's degree in communications from Galatasaray University in Istanbul, Turkey, and a Master's degree in communications from Simon Fraser University in Vancouver, BC. Her research interests include alternative media and alternative journalism.

Chapter 17

Navigating journalistic spaces: British Muslim media producers

Elizabeth Poole

Much has been written about changes to media production brought about by a wide range of phenomena including technological developments and processes of globalisation. These have had an impact on both professional practices and media content. These trends have taken place against a background of transnational migration increasing cultural diversity across Europe. This chapter is based on the findings of a research project that aimed to explore the role of Muslims in media production in the UK in a range of media contexts. The research shows how Muslims negotiate their identities in various media environments in order to create a space in which to construct their own narratives and the challenges they face in doing so.

Keywords: Muslim media, minority media, production, journalism practice, diasporic media

INTRODUCTION

In the last decade or so there has been a growth of media produced by and targeted towards Muslim audiences in the UK. This is partly driven by the growth of cultural politics in the post 9/11 era but also the explosion of media forms due to technological developments. A healthy literature on minority media in Britain already exists focusing initially on Black media from the 1970s and later British Asian communities (see Cottle 2000). Criticisms of fixing audience positions by race resulted in a shift to ethnographic research on transnational diasporic communities and their media consumption from the 1990s onwards (see Gillespie 1995, 2002) which included audiences of the expanding Arab satellite media (Miladi 2006). Perhaps for this reason there has been little attempt to study what we have termed 'Muslim media' in the UK (see following section for discussion).

This label does not seek to reify this aspect of identity but is helpful in differentiating media that aims specifically to address Muslim issues. Two previous studies of Muslim media have focused on consumption (Ahmed 2006) and representation (Gilewicz 2012).

More recently Muir and Smith (2011) have studied the experience of journalists with a Muslim heritage working in mainstream media whilst Rigoni's (2006) earlier work on producers in Britain and France's minority media provides an important precursor to our research. These studies have shown how minority media offers British Muslims a platform to voice their diverse concerns over social and political issues, to counter negative mainstream discourse about Muslims and Islam, and provides a positive and diasporic space for identity and community building (Ahmed 2006). This chapter details the main findings of 'Muslims in the European Mediascape' a project which examined the production and consumption of news about Muslims. In this paper I will focus only on the producers findings from the UK.

MUSLIMS IN THE EUROPEAN MEDIASCAPE[1]

The project had two primary aims, to:

- analyse comparatively patterns in the media use and production of people of Muslim and non-Muslim background in Europe (Germany and the UK);
- identify possible relationships between perceptions, views about and attitudes to various groups in society and patterns in the use and production of media in view of further key variables which may include socio-economic background, education, gender, ethnicity, religion, generation, personal and private inter-cultural relationships and age.

In meeting these aims, the project sought to:

- explore how Muslim and non-Muslim (including minority) populations in Germany and the United Kingdom relate to media content involving diversity issues;
- document radio, print, television and internet media outlets targeted at, produced by and significantly consumed by audiences of Muslim background in Europe;
- investigate diversity and equality practices within mainstream and minority/community media institutions;
- explore the dynamics of journalistic work, particularly in relation to the coverage of issues related to diversity and inclusion;
- explore the professional practices and experiences of Muslim journalists and their relationship to the production of various types of content in different media outlets.

METHODOLOGY

Editor and producer interviews took place with producers working in mainstream and minority media. The majority of these were individual semi-structured interviews with some focus groups. It was necessary to shift from face-to-face to telephone interviews when time constraints became a limitation to professionals' ability to take part. Specific outlets were targeted including large, well-known media organisations but also regional, local and wider, especially for Muslim media, blogs etc, supplemented with a snowballing technique. This resulted in 37 interviews overall with the sample of mainstream producers being slightly larger (23 compared to 14 working in Muslim media), reflecting the greater number of these organisations in the UK.

CONCEPT OF 'MUSLIM MEDIA'

The term 'Muslim' is obviously problematic but here is used as shorthand for media which are largely produced for and by Muslims and address 'Muslim' issues. That this may be a problem was picked up by the German team (with a large Turkish demographic). Whilst some outlets, such as some Asian publications, are obviously aimed at a wider audience (and many others had that intention), most of the UK participants, were comfortable with the term. Most had a positive perception:

> It was the first Muslim media product I should say that I found was confidently Muslim. And I'm unashamed to see the world through Muslim eyes. And that was very, very exciting. I'd never seen that before. So there'd be movie reviews of *Terminator 2*, but written, you know, with a kind of a sensibility of how we would see it (producer).

The aim was not to essentialise identity and suggest that Muslim identity is at the forefront of and central to all decision-making taking place in these producers' professional lives. However, the aim of this project was to explore when and how this does impact on reporting. It is clear that in the current political climate these producers (who were self-selecting) do consider the politics of Muslim identity when reporting on specific issues.

MUSLIM MEDIA PRODUCERS: WHO ARE THEY?

The producers we interviewed were predominantly male (only three were female), about 10 years into their career, and were working as generalists. Participants were mainly of an Asian background, British and Muslim. Two identified themselves as converts. Of the people who talked about their career routes all had gone to university and then taken a varied path, working across a range of media gaining experience before entering their current job. This included mainstream and specialist organisations. Whilst they all worked as generalists now, it was their experience writing on ethnic issues that had often led to openings, in particular for writing in more mainstream organisations such as the *Guardian* and *Channel 4*.

WHOM DO THEY WORK FOR?

Many of the media outlets these producers worked for were not specifically newsgathering organisations but social/cultural creative organisations producing media for education religious/ purposes etc. for example, resources (film and photography exhibitions) for public/educational/community events. Because they tend to be smaller outlets with a mainly freelance staff the lines between editor and producer were more blurred than in larger mainstream organisations. However, six were editors (as well as having a role in production) and nine solely producers. Five of these producers were freelances.

The type of organisations they were working for ranged from blogs, NGOs, print media such as *Q News*, community magazines, publications aimed at a broader Asian market, publishers and freelances working across the media. Al-Jazeera (English) was not represented in this sample because it does not define itself as an Islamic media organisation, but rather a global mainstream news and broadcaster based in the Middle-East.[2]

The organisations could be described as 'progressive' in their politics (only one used the term left-wing) dealing with humanitarian issues, social and cultural policy, identity, race relations:

> So we try and keep a broad issue range of what stories we cover. We do have a core interest in human rights, the Muslim world and minority communities in Europe (editor, internet).

Audience profile

Ranging from small (5,000 a month readers) to medium-sized organisations (publications with monthly circulations of 60,000 with some supporting websites reaching 1.5 million hits a month). Most, however, were on the smaller end of the scale. All the organisations described Muslims as being their core audience but were keen to emphasise their outward facing content. Most talked of their 'broad', 'wide' and varied content that would have a wider interest. One editor emphasised the desire not to 'ghettoise'.

Most of these have a national focus and so were also largely aimed at the South Asian diaspora. Only one organisation described itself as being international (a publisher). Most did not have an accurate way of measuring their audience (due to costs) but talked about mixed age ranges (as the content was already specialist) with two organisations targeting a younger market.

Staff profiles/diversity policy

Being small organisations, they did not appear to have formal policies on this but talked about having a 'mixed race' profile. This is partly due to the size of the organisations that rely on voluntary contributions and freelances. Whilst there was a tendency towards a greater number of staff from ethnic minority groups this was due to the content of the output.

Amongst those who had worked for mainstream organisations there was a difference between those who had worked in the print media and those who had worked in broadcasting. Those who had worked in newspapers did not appear to know what their organisations' policies on diversity and equality were (and felt it was not their remit) other than that they took it seriously. There was a sense that the organisations they worked for felt that they had the integrity to work independently (issue of trust) and editors would only intervene if necessary. This may reflect the outlook of the organisations that employ them that actively promote diversity. Those who had worked in broadcasting felt it was much more about meeting regulations and quotas:

> Yeah, yeah, that's why you'll find a lot of presenters not on the main show for example *London Tonight*, but the late bulletin or the early bulletin, a Black or Asian, and why do you think that is? Because they have this kind of quota where they've got to tick boxes – how many Asians or Black people do you vox pop, how many women, and they're very strict (producer).

It was also claimed that the local media were more sensitive to local demographics:

> Whereas what I found with *London Tonight* there was much more of an awareness that we have a mixed audience in London in particular and I found their stories quite balanced and the coverage quite balanced and there are a lot of stories about ethnic minorities, not really pushed by the editor (producer).

MAIN FINDINGS: MUSLIM MEDIA PRODUCERS

Representational issues: Mainstream media

There was complete agreement that the mainstream representation of Muslims was predominantly negative. This was the most discussed topic in the interviews despite the emphasis on production in the research. Participants noted the increased volume, simplification, decontextualising, 'formulaic', 'reactionary' and 'xenophobic' coverage that focused on extremism, radicalism, barbarism, homogenisation and sensationalism. They were particularly critical of the Conservative press, Murdoch media, some current affairs programmes such as *Newsnight* and *Dispatches* and some outspoken right-wing commentators.

As the research was carried out around the time of the death of Osama Bin Laden in May 2011 there was much criticism of coverage of this:

> And as a journalist I know that's poor journalism. It's shoddy ... But why does it pass muster these days? No one asked, you know, the basic questions. Where's the evidence for ... did you actually see this happen? Have these reports been corroborated? Are there any independent observers of this thing? ... Journalism should be – cleverly, in a pithy way, with expertise – giving us the context (producer).

Sources
Many were against the practice by some news organisations of using extreme sources or a number of self-appointed representatives who do not represent members of the Muslim community. They argued that the consistent use of these minority sources caused a lot of frustration. The precise causes cited, however, varied from a perceived lack of effective media strategies amongst moderate Muslim groups, to tabloidisation and associated stereotyping:

> There are quite a few so-called Muslim community leaders, so-called representatives that are just rabble-rousing attention seekers, they're ... (unclear) allowed to dominate headlines. The obvious example are people who have got zero following in the Muslim community, they have got a handful of individuals if that, that are presented as if they are mainstream voices and essentially they are no more representative of Muslim communities than the grand wizard of the Klu Klux Klan represents Christian communities (producer).

What is missing in the coverage?
Spiritual aspects of Islam, its diversity, achievements and contributions to civilisation, attacks on Muslims, depth, detail and Muslim voices:

> I often feel that the very interesting realities and contours of Muslim communities in Europe or in Britain on the ground are often missed (producer).

Generally, it was the critical awareness that these journalists had of changes in recent decades – global geopolitics, migration that had led to social fracture and religious diversity – which were felt not to frame the debates about diversity issues in the press.

However, there was some praise in places, for the *Guardian*, for example, although it was also criticised for having a 'liberal' agenda (exclusive liberalism) and the *New Statesman*. Britain, in general, was felt to be a positive and diverse cultural and social environment particularly in comparison to the rest of Europe.

> Apart from a couple of awful institutions that tend to be the Murdoch press, the *Daily Star*, there is quite a grown-up attitude toward race in Britain and diversity in Britain. Primarily because such a large part of Britain's population is Black or Asian, primarily because most people in Britain are fair minded and recognise the history of the relationships between Britain and India and Pakistan and the West Indies (producer).

Overall, the participants felt negative media coverage had led to Muslims being suspicious/sceptical of the media: hence a loss of credibility, even for the BBC.

Internal representation (how do Muslims represent themselves?)

Almost all of the producers working in these outlets felt it was somewhat their responsibility to counter mainstream representation not so much with positive images (rejected as promotion) but with a more nuanced approach.

However, there was a general keenness to make the content more widely accessible with as many references made to providing an 'open view', 'different sides of the picture' a 'broad range of content' and 'complexity'. Participants also felt a responsibility to criticise minorities but again to do so in a more nuanced way than the mainstream media. The aim appears to be to provide a critical journalism which may appeal to a wider public rather than be engaged in the 'promulgation of Islam' whilst focusing on diversity issues given the core audience:

> ... so a lot of the ideas that I write about are things which don't explicitly try and offer a positive viewpoint but which try and offer a more complicated portrayal of Islam, whether that's to do with, you know, speaking with Muslim comedians or whether that's to do with talking about my own wedding or whether it's to do with Muslim girls who are learning about British fashion. I try and tell stories which haven't been heard, which kind of add something to the more perennial and familiar tropes that are present in Muslim portrayal in the media (producer).

Few if any of the Muslim media outlets engage in regular newsgathering. They tend to offer more features-based stories of a human interest or religious nature. This was partly due to the publication cycle which may not follow established news routines, for example bi-monthly publications. Some felt it was their duty not to focus specifically on ethnic issues but to include features on universal issues such as relationships and marriage, financial matters, medical concerns, environmental issues and how these relate to their religion. Those with a greater religious focus explored facets of the religion and teaching and how these related to everyday life whilst some of the diasporic media had a strong focus on countries of origin such as Pakistan. Each outlet emphasised a contextualised approach (exploring meaning and significance of experience within a specific context).

The process of choosing stories is quite spontaneous. None of the outlets was big enough to have specialist correspondents who were sent out to cover specific stories. Rather, they are specialists in a different way following their own interests. In other words, many of these outlets relied on the interests of others to send stories in or followed their own interests when coming up with ideas. It may not be possible, therefore, to follow a media agenda such as the Middle East as they did not have the resources to do this. Those with a team of writers also pursued their own interests. Some of the coverage was a reaction to mainstream media coverage. One of the producers who also worked in the mainstream media was also able to pursue his own ideas as he had the profile and networks to be able to do this. He maintained that what he was offered by the mainstream media was always 'ethnic issues' and the only way he could balance this out was by being proactive.

Role of new media
Whilst some highlighted the increase in coverage post 9/11 with a continuing negative narrative, some also highlighted improvements in the diversity of voices partly due to social media which had extended the coverage of and become a source for mainstream outlets. There were frequent references to social media as a source of greater diversity. However, this was not only perceived as a positive development but had also led to a quantity of media sources over quality and increasing fragmentation which could undermine democracy:

> And I do think that new media – new media as shorthand for all the other stuff that's out there – is really challenging the way in which things are being covered. But also we're creating – you know the analysis is old now but it doesn't mean it's not true – we're creating a whole bunch of echo chambers that exist, echo chambers-silos, that exist next to each other. You know that … we're speaking to ourselves because now given the media choice we have we can just go to the places that reflect our opinions and ideas and perspectives to begin with (producer).

In this regard it is becoming increasingly difficult to categorise audiences (Muslim media) in the contemporary fragmented media environment because people are getting their media content from a variety of sources and are able to mix and match across a range of local, national, international, print, broadcast and digital media.

Journalist backgrounds
Journalists of a Muslim background working in the mainstream press affirmed that this was of benefit for engaging with and relating to sources. But it was also suggested that it enabled a more critical take on Muslim issues (being insulated from accusations of Islamophobia):

> But I think that sometimes as journalists and society in general we recognise institutions or someone that sets up an organisation, but we don't recognise individuals, we don't recognise people, so I try to just go out of my way and try to speak to individual people, and the contacts that I had in the community (producer).

The majority of journalists interviewed also said that their background meant that they would be more equipped to cover stories relating to Muslims and Islam because they would have a greater understanding (and interest) of the complexities involved in the issues. In the main this was viewed positively although most were reflexive about this:

> It's important and I think journalists, whatever they are and whatever things they bring to the job, need to abide by, I mean hopefully the highest levels of professionalism and practice and investigation. But I'd be a liar if I said that my faith or my values or my principles, my ethics, my morals don't impact on what I choose to report, how I choose to report it. In fact quite the opposite, I try not to gloss over nasty things when I find it, and because that's the journalist in me. You know those are things I wanna expose. At the same time I'm always careful about context, so for me personally it's always about … you can't simply understand X without the context around it (producer).

The journalist's social class was also an issue with many stating that a non-white who was very middle class would fit in and not be able to relate to ordinary Muslims. Only one of these journalists felt background was not an issue a view more in keeping with the mainstream reporters interviewed (based on an idea of professional objectivity).

Impact of coverage
There was complete agreement that media coverage has an impact on attitudes on the ground and on inter-group and community relations. This included an increase in antagonism, tension and even racial violence. This was felt to be inappropriate in sensitive times:

Negative coverage leads to frustrations amongst Muslims and a feeling of exclusion (some went as far as saying that it breeds extremism). Most journalists did say they have adapted or carefully considered the way they covered a story because of community tensions they were aware of on the ground:

> Q: Are there times when you have not reported or been careful about the way that you have edited a particular story because of concerns about potential impacts on community tensions?
>
> A: Yes absolutely. The major, very very sensitive thing is desecration of the Koran. As someone who spends a lot of time in Pakistan and is involved minority rights and human rights work in Pakistan I am very aware that the actions of a mob and the actions of lunatics wanting to create a response in Europe lead to the reactions and a consequential impact of activity of mobs in Karachi and Lahore, so we tread very carefully because some of these things are incendiary and have an impact on the streets (producer).

It was felt that by giving Muslims a voice, these media can have a positive impact on integration. Muslim media provides a channel for the articulation of frustrations but these participants thought that they should also be represented in mainstream media.

MAINSTREAM MEDIA PRODUCERS

In this section I will briefly discuss some of the findings from the producers working in mainstream media. Almost half of these were from a minority background and so illustrate the kind of dilemmas these journalists face on a daily basis. Out of 23 people interviewed 12 were from a minority background. Only four self-identified as Muslim. They gave their ethnicity as British Asian (two), Pakistani and Iranian. The organisations these producers worked for tended to be larger but also more liberal based on the method of self sampling. Only one had at some point worked on a tabloid newspaper. Most came from the print media although the majority of media forms were at least represented. Interestingly, the results from the non-Muslim minority producers concurred more with that of the Muslim producers than with that of other colleagues in the mainstream media on this issue.

Staff profiles

As this sample included more employees from large national organisations respondents were more aware of diversity policies especially at the BBC. Despite this, other than at al-Jazeera English, most observed that newsrooms were predominantly white, male and middle-class, and felt this to be problematic. There was a suggestion of tokenism being evident in some broadcast organisations, particularly on the presenting side of the camera. As was the practice in larger newsrooms, local newsrooms would occasionally use freelance reporters to cover stories that required a particular angle or access to a particular community, but local media did not always have this resource available.

Background

Here mainstream producers from minority groups contradicted the notion that any good journalist could cover any story presented by white British producers (within the norms of journalist professionalism and values of objectivity). Instead, they suggested that they were often pushed (however nicely) into covering stories about minorities or indeed pushed into minority or specialist media itself. Only one minority producer disagreed, a reporter at al-Jazeera thought background was not an issue and that the organisation did not send 'a Muslim looking reporter' to do a Muslim story. This policy was supported by having 'fixers' who enabled access to various communities across the world. This reveals a fascinating, though not necessarily surprising, dynamic at play in the newsrooms of mainstream media. Unlike those working in minority media, minority producers working in mainstream media were keen to escape the foregrounding of this identity. This is partly a result of the differing objectives of these organisations. Mainstream producers suggested it was not their job to cater for specific audiences and some questioned the notion that minority groups should be regarded differently to other audience members.

The project illustrates the tensions felt by producers of a Muslim background both in making production decisions and covering Muslim stories. For those working in the mainstream they have to struggle with the 'burden of responsibility' – the tension between not wanting to be pigeon-holed and taking the opportunity to provide positive images to counter the negative. These are the kind of struggles they have to deal with on a daily basis.

Representation
Most respondents felt that their organisations' coverage of stories related to Islam and Muslims was well-done and even-handed, with those working in the liberal broadsheet press and national broadcast media praising its coverage highly. However, all acknowledged that negative representation existed in certain sections of the media. The tabloid press was held up for particular scrutiny.

Social impact
Here we can see the difference between those producers of a migratory/non-migratory background illustrated further in relation to questions about the potential impact of their news stories:

> I don't think it's the journalist's responsibility to spend too much time worrying about the impact of their story on community relations. For instance after the Bradford riots you go up there and you have to tell the story what happened in the Bradford riots, why did it blow up this way. Now by doing that you may inflame tensions further, but it's definitely in the public interest to tell the public how on earth the situation got as bad as it did (non-migratory background mainstream producer).

There was considerable criticism of what is perceived to be Muslim media by mainstream media producers based on quality, its effect on fragmentation – 'people talking amongst themselves' – and failing to have an impact or political significance. Many producers from non-minority backgrounds had little knowledge of the existence of these media revealing the dissonance between Muslim media producers' perception of their impact and actual impact.

CONCLUSIONS

This project demonstrates the growth of media organisations and content aimed at minority audiences. The range of organisations that exist have different functions and are aimed at religious, ethnic and/or diasporic communities. However, they all seek to address what is lacking in mainstream media.

Muslim media producers demonstrate a professional, critical and intelligent journalistic approach. Their aim is to have a positive impact countering negative media coverage and providing a more nuanced understanding of diversity issues which reflects their own acute understanding of these. These outlets are not sectarian and are keen to differentiate themselves from 'religious' media that might seek to propagate Islam. They should be seen as part of a wider process of diversification and personalisation of the media offering more consumer choice.

They believe that Muslim media are increasingly a resource for mainstream media adding to the diversity of voices available. However, apart from some liberal publications, this view was challenged by the results of the interviews with non-Muslim mainstream producers who often had little knowledge of these alternative media. We could call this a 'difference of perception' narrative or a dissonance between the views of those working in minority and mainstream media.

On this basis we could offer some possibilities for change:

- There should be greater interaction between minority/mainstream media. This should be used as a source for mainstream media to share a more nuanced history of relations between Islam and the West.

- Research such as this should feed into journalist education.

- There should be clear and formal policies on diversity and editorial policy. Evidence from broadcasting shows that these can have a positive benefit. Whilst informal arrangements may work at small or progressive organisations, a more rigorous approach demonstrated by the regulation of broadcasting could have a positive impact on other organisations. Clear communication of these policies to staff is also needed.

- Employers should recognise both the value and importance of employing a wider diversity of people in their workplace.

- Editors should use their journalists as a resource for greater understanding but should not always foreground their religious or ethnic identity.

- There could be further regulation of the industry to instil ethical responsibility.

Acknowledgements to my co-investigator Siobhan Holohan, Keele University and researchers Joanna Redden, Ryerson Infoscape Research Lab and Justin Schlosberg, Goldsmiths.

- This paper was first published in *Ethical Space*, Vol. 9, Nos 2 and 3 pp 32-44, 2012

NOTES

[1] Muslims in the European Mediascape was a year-long project funded by the Institute of Strategic Dialogue. Some of this material is taken from Holohan and Poole (2012) *Muslims in the European mediascape*, UK Country Report, ISD

[2] See http://english.aljazeera.net/aboutus

REFERENCES

Ahmed, Sameera (2006) The media consumption of young British Muslims, Poole, Elizabeth and Richardson, John (eds) *Muslims and the news media*, London, I. B. Tauris pp 167-176

Cottle, Simon (2000) *Ethnic minorities and the media*, Buckingham, Open University Press

Gilewicz, Magdalena (2012) *The construction of Muslim community and British Muslim identity in two British newspapers*, PhD submission, University of Aberdeen

Gillespie, Marie (1995) *Television, ethnicity and cultural change*, London, Routledge

Gillespie, Marie (2002) Dynamics of diasporas: South Asian media and transnational cultural politics, Stald, Gitte and Tufte, Thomas (eds) *Global encounters: Media and cultural transformations*, University of Luton Press pp 151-173

Holohan, Siobhan and Poole, Elizabeth (2012) *Muslims in the European mediascape: UK country report*, Institute of Strategic Dialogue

Miladi, Noureddine (2006) Satellite TV news and the Arab Diaspora in Britain: Comparing al-Jazeera, the BBC and CNN, *Journal of Ethnic and Migration Studies*, Vol. 32, No. 6 pp 947-960

Muir, Hugh and Smith, Laura (2011) Keeping your integrity and your job: Voices from the newsroom, Petley, Julian and Richardson, Robin (eds) *Pointing the finger: Islam and Muslims in the British media*, London, Oneworld pp 152-168

Rigoni, Isabelle (2006) Islamic features in British and French Muslim media, Poole, Elizabeth and Richardson, John (eds) *Muslims and the news media*, London, I.B.Tauris pp 74-86

NOTE ON THE CONTRIBUTOR

Elizabeth Poole is a Professor of Media and Communications at Keele University. Her research interests include media representations of Muslims, news contexts, online hate speech and social media activism. She is author of *Reporting Islam* (2002), co-editor of *Muslims and the news* (2006) and co-author of *Media portrayals of religion* (2013) and is currently working on an AHRC project #Contesting Islamophobia: Representation and appropriation in mediated activism.

SECTION 3

Public relations:
Beyond propaganda

Chapter 18

Integrating the shadow: A Jungian approach to professional ethics in public relations

Johanna Fawkes

The paper suggests that professional ethics might benefit from consideration of the ideas of Carl Jung (1875-1961) regarding wholeness instead of goodness as the goal of the integrated psyche. The whole self then becomes the basis for ethics in contrast to the ideal-typical self at the heart of many approaches to professional ethics. It looks briefly at current debates into the legitimacy of professions and suggests that professional ethics have acquired increased importance in a time of diminishing deference to professionals. Contemporary approaches to professional ethics suggest a search for deeper common values, looking to intrinsic rather than external guidance for ethical behaviour. This is the context for suggesting Jung's focus on inward dialogue and integration offers a new basis for ethical development. It combines a philosophical and psychological approach to the self and highlights the ethical effects of moving away from the ego-defensive split between persona and shadow, ideas which are explored in the paper. Finally, questions raised by taking a Jungian approach to professional ethics in the field of public relations – in which the author has practised and taught for 30 years – are briefly explored.

Keywords: Carl Jung, professional ethics, integration, shadow work, public relations

INTRODUCTION

This paper is the first of three summarising the main planks of my PhD thesis that Jung's concept of integration, through working with the shadow, suggests a new approach to professional ethics that could be applied to public relations as an example and by extension to other professional groups. This paper concentrates on the area of professional ethics and the narrowness of the 'ideal-typical' approach which underpins many ethical approaches and is strongly evident in public relations writing. The second (Fawkes 2009a) considers Jungian approaches to ethics at a philosophical level; the third (Fawkes 2009b) delves more deeply into the potential impact of these ideas on public relations' ethics.

The research approach is fundamentally hermeneutic, or interpretive, drawing on the ideas developed in the past few decades primarily by Ricoeur and Gadamer. Schweiker (2004) outlines the main hermeneutical approaches from the pre-critical (literal interpretations of the Bible, for example), through historical-critical hermeneutics (which contextualise interpretation) to post-critical hermeneutics which examine the assumptions underpinning texts, as in critical approaches, but then move on to construct new meanings or interpretations: 'The point of interpretation for any post-critical theory is to show the contemporary meaning and truth of the work. It is to open the text or symbol of event for renewed engagement within the dynamics of current life' (p. xx). Hermeneutics seems suited as a means of discussing Jung's complex and shifting ideas and insights: firstly because so much of Jung's writing is deeply interpretive, seeking meaning in patient experience and finding resonances in vast reading across centuries and cultures; secondly, hermeneutics has been used as an approach to ethical thinking by scholars (Schweiker 1990, 2004; N.H. Smith, 1997; P.C. Smith, 1991) exploring similar issues to those in this paper, but without considering Jung's work.

This paper sets out the current crisis in professional confidence, the centrality of ethics to the professional 'project' and the dependence on idealised self-images as the benchmarks for ethical standards. It then explores Jung's core concepts, particularly of individuation and working with the shadow, as an alternative approach to the dualistic good/bad basis of most Western ethics. Finally, these ideas are briefly related to the field of public relations to illustrate the impact such an approach might have on the field.

BACKGROUND

The status and legitimacy of professions is challenged at the start of the twenty-first century by technological changes to the acquisition and dissemination of knowledge and by structural changes in society (Broadbent, Deitrich and Roberts 1997; Dent and Whitehead 2002; Watson 2002; Cooper 2004). Moral philosophy, meanwhile, is grappling with unease at the post-Enlightenment – and post-modern – compartmentalising of the totality of human experience to focus on rationality and textual analysis, respectively (MacIntyre 1984; Oakley and Cocking 2001; Cooper 2004; Jones 2007). Issues of character, self and identity in a fragmented culture are the subject of urgent discussion leading to, inter alia, the re-emergence of Aristotelian virtue ethics in the late twentieth century (MacIntyre op cit; Oakley and Cocking op cit) and a renewed interest in hermeneutics and moral identity (Smith 1997; Seidler 1994; Schweiker 2004). These authors express common concerns regarding lost moral anchors, over-reliance on inadequate rules and codes and the predominance of emotivist and relativist individualism in ethical decision-making.

The two fields meet in professional ethics. A central element of the professional narrative is the responsibility of the professional to society at large, as well as to the particular client or patient. Professionals are perceived as 'possessing some of the characteristics of community' (Larson 1977: x). In order to justify the social credit enjoyed by professions, they appeal to general ideological rationales, according to Larson (ibid), as promoters of social values, rather than simple monetary reward, for example. But Cooper (op cit: viii) argues that professional ethics are failing to respond adequately to societal changes, and that professions tend to claim either that there are no moral frameworks any more or create situation-specific codes lacking an underlying philosophy, leading to 'moral drift and banal choices'.

PROFESSIONALISM

One reason for the confusion is the changing nature of the professional and the idea of professionalism in the early twenty-first century. The claim to be a professional traditionally rests on certain precepts: esoteric knowledge – theoretical or technical – not available to the general population; commitment to social values, such as health or justice; national organisation to set standards, control membership, liaise with wider society; extra-strong moral commitment to support professional values (Cooper op cit). The sociology of the professions encourages analysis of the role of professions in society, their historical development and their view of themselves (Larson op cit; Abbott and Meerabeau 1998). There is agreement that professions embody ideological attitudes and contain preferred readings or constructed meanings which are intended to promote the profession and its institutions. It would seem reasonable to suppose that all professions embody some persuasive or promotional role (Wernick 1991).

However, as Sommerlad (2007: 191) points out the 'aura of mystery' enjoyed by the perceived or claimed superiority of technical and theoretical knowledge referred to earlier has been eroded by the decline in deference traditionally offered to professions by the general public. What Larson (1977) calls the 'professional project' is under threat, as is the idea of a professional identity which many see as experiencing a crisis in the twenty-first century (Broadbent, Deitrich and Roberts 1997; Dent and Whitehead 2002; Watson 2002). Given the range and source of these threats it is not surprising that many professional bodies are looking to ethics for validation.

PROFESSIONAL ETHICS

The traditional approach to professional ethics was – and in many cases, still is – based on what Larson (1977) calls the ideal-typical practitioner, usually involving codes and other embodiments of best practice. She is concerned that these display elements of the ideal-typical constructions 'do not tell us what a profession is, only what it pretends to be…' (1977: xii). Fligstein (2001) and Suddaby and

Greenwood (2005) show how professional institutions act as entrepreneurs using discourse and rhetoric to influence the social construction of legitimacy (cited in Bartlett et al. 2007). Codes are the primary choice for establishing this legitimacy in most professions, particularly where the professional body does not control the licence to practise. The rhetorical role of codes of conduct is outside the scope of this paper but one analysis of public relations codes (Parkinson 2001) suggests that the main function of codes of practice is (still) to improve the reputation of the professional organisation rather than change the behaviour of members.

Traditionally, codes – like much other discussion of ethics – have relied on a combination of utilitarian and deontological approaches, as developed by Bentham and Kant respectively. However, their main thrust is normative rather than philosophical or reflective. In recent years virtue ethics, as described by MacIntyre (1984) and others, has had an impact on the field of professional ethics, shifting the discussion from behaviour to character.

The virtue approach is particularly useful in its lack of reliance on external codes' rules to prescribe acceptable ethical behaviour, relying instead on character and reflection. The central precepts of virtue ethics are summarised as:

(a) an action is right if and only if it is what an agent with a virtuous character would do in the circumstances;

(b) goodness is prior to rightness;

(c) the virtues are irreducibly plural intrinsic goods;

(d) the virtues are objectively good;

(e) some intrinsic goods are agent-relative;

(f) acting rightly does not require that we maximise the good (Oakley and Cocking 2001: 9).

Harrison and Galloway (2005) have sought to apply virtue ethics to public relations practice but highlight problems in finding agreement about the nature of the internal and external goods of the profession. Others have looked to questions of personal and social identity as a source of ethical guidance (Mount 1990). This approach allows deeper discussion of the character of the professional and raises the possibility of investigating the less-than-ideal aspects of the individual professional and, by extension, their organisations. The focus on professional character offered by virtue ethics and social identity theory may be contrasted with discourse ethics with their emphasis on texts rather than persons. Post-modern approaches have usefully revealed the power structures operating within and beneath professions (e.g. Sommerlad 2007) building on Weberian analyses of the professional role in supporting the dominant ideology.

However, some writers on ethics (such as MacIntyre 1984; Baumann 1993; Cooper 2004) have expressed concern that post-modern approaches have led to anomie and moral drift, as suggested earlier. This concern is also articulated by the business ethicist Goodpaster (2007) who has coined the term 'teleopathy' to describe business's fixed, amoral drive for profit-related goals, and argues for the reintegration of moral purpose into the corporate agenda. The question of where to look for that purpose is deeply explored by Schweiker (2004) who argues that the contemporary culture or *Weltanschaung* is 'over-humanised', that is over-reliant on human powers, having lost contact with any sense of the sacred.

To summarise: professions are widely viewed as playing a key part in the maintenance of the general social order; they have common factors which distinguish them from non-professionals, though these boundaries are blurred and under stress; the role of ethics is one of the platforms that makes a profession but there is wide disagreement about the underlying moral philosophy of professional ethics and confused responses to post-modern approaches to ethics. There is urgency in these debates. This paper argues that the ideal-typical concept provides an inadequate basis for professional ethics and is designed more to promote the profession and its leading organisations than actually engage with ethical dilemmas.

The continual emphasis on best practice, like that offered by the Excellence project in public relations, discussed below, leads to a dualistic separation from the 'darker' aspects of professional behaviour. While the virtue ethics approach offers a subtler, more inwards focus for debate, there is room for a deeper exploration of the role of the self – both individually and collectively in professions – in locating the inner source of ethics. For this, the paper turns to Jung and his ideas on the self, the shadow and integration as the foundation of ethics.

A JUNGIAN APPROACH: WHY JUNG?

Jung's potential contribution to the field of professional ethics stems from his commitment to integration as a moral journey, requiring courage and commitment to face and own the 'shadow' or denied aspects of the personality or group (Singer 1999). Storr (1998) calls this his greatest original contribution to analytic psychology. What is striking about Jung's approach is that it does not stress goodness but *wholeness* as the key to moral development and integrity and it is this insight I wish to pursue as the possible basis for a new approach to professional ethics.

It is worth stating here that Jung's extensive works (over 20 volumes) do not constitute an explicit theoretical foundation; there is repetition, contradiction, interpretation and reinterpretation throughout the writing. Jones (2007) suggests that Jung is hard to read and best explored by following a thread through his writing. The thread I propose to follow is that of individuation – the process by which an individual builds a relationship with the unconscious and comes to terms with the different, often conflicting elements of the psyche. Jung sees this as essentially a moral journey (CW 9ii/13-19). Arguments will be provided to support the extrapolation from the individual unit of study to the group level of the profession (Singer and Kimbles 2004).

Jungian concepts permeate the culture: we talk of introverts and extraverts, archetypes, collective unconscious, shadow dynamics, animus/anima, Self and other terms taken from his extensive writings. Yet many consider his contribution to thought has been undervalued by academics in recent decades, leaving the 'cause' to proselytisers (Bishop 1999) or philosophers and literary scholars (especially in film and genre-studies) rather than psychologists (Storr 1999), though, of course, his work forms the basis of analytical psychology as practised throughout the world (Samuels 1985). The central idea to be investigated here is that of individuation, the process of integrating the shadow and developing a more transcendent, less ego-dominated view of the self and others. As Solomon (2000: 198) puts it, 'a Jungian approach to understanding how the self may achieve an ethical attitude can be located within the context of the unfolding of the self over the stages of an entire life'. To clarify the connections between the evolution of the self and professional ethics I need to explore Jung's architecture of the psyche a little further here.

INTEGRATING THE SHADOW

While there is some contradiction between different parts of Jung's writing (he revised some lectures and articles but left others to stand as testimony to his evolving ideas, and never wrote a definitive summary) he perceives the psyche as consisting of personal consciousness (with the ego at the centre), the personal unconscious and the collective unconscious (CW 8/317-21).

Personal consciousness includes everything of which the individual is aware, with the ego acting as the main organiser for managing external and internal stimuli; the personal unconscious includes forgotten and repressed material and peripheral, low interest contents; and the collective unconscious includes the possibilities of representations common to all people (archetypes) which may constellate differently according to the particular cultures and epoch and which form the basic structure underpinning the individual psyche. These elements are seen as compensatory; that is, the more the personal conscious refuses to deal with unwelcome thoughts or insights, the more powerful the unconscious becomes. The relationship between these elements can be antagonistic but resolving the opposing forces in the psyche can also be a source of joy and fulfilment. Jung saw the unconscious, both personal and collective, as a more benign presence than did his one-time mentor, Freud: 'The unconscious is immensely old and capable of continuing to grow indefinitely' (CW 9i/489-524).

Jung described the public face of the individual as the 'persona', drawing on the Greek masks of ancient drama. Persona is a complicated system of relations between individual consciousness and society, a kind of mask designed to 'impress and conceal', and to meet societal demands (CW 7/305-309). As the ego gravitates to the public 'approved' view, unconscious activity starts to compensate. The personal unconscious is 'organised' around a series of archetypal images, the templates of which are located in the collective unconscious. The most powerful archetypes are those of Shadow and Animus/anima. Solomon describes the concept of the shadow as 'central to Jung's understanding of the self as an ethical entity' (2000: 199), and I will concentrate on the shadow dynamics rather than other archetypal struggles. The shadow comprises those elements of the personal unconscious which are not considered acceptable to the conscious self (CW 11/130-134). They are not necessarily 'bad', simply rejected, as a workaholic might reject relaxation, for example. However, part of this rejection can be *projected* on to others, making them 'carry' the unlived elements (Storr 1999: xv). To continue the example, the compulsive worker may perceive his/her colleagues as skivers and lightweights whom he/she both despises and envies.

This characterisation is particularly germane to public relations both in its professional identity (the emphasis on excellence as Persona) and in the content of practice, which often engages with issues of blaming others and polishing one's own image.

JUNG AND ETHICS

The result of this journey is the development of the Self, an undertaking in which the shadow is confronted, acknowledged as one's own material (so no longer projected onto others) and the ego shifts from the centre of the personality to make room for the presence of the mysterious, the unknown and still unconscious. In recognising and accepting the limits of consciousness, the individual can conduct internal dialogue with his or her own shadows and archetypes before taking action. As Samuels (1985: 65) says: 'There is a compelling moral aspect to integration of the shadow: to unblock personal and communal relationship and also to admit the inadmissible, yet human.' I suggest that this dialogue is a precondition to ethical behaviour: in its absence the individual or group is likely to respond defensively to any threat to the dominance of the ego or persona; others are likely to be blamed for the unexamined assumptions or consequences and the individual or group will remain stuck in immature responses to the world.

Solomon (2000) is also surprised at how little is written about Jung and ethics, given his emphasis on the moral importance of the development of the self, as outlined above. There is of course material on the ethics of the analytical relationship but less which extends these ideas out of the consulting room. The following observations are based on a variety of commentaries on Jung as a psychologist and philosopher and seek to construct the core elements of a Jungian approach to ethics.

Jung thought that ethics and morality are innate but that the individual has to free himself from the collective norms to experience this (Samuels 1985: 61). Like Nietzsche, Jung rejects the 'performance' of morals and refers back to classical ethics and Gnosticism in which morality was intrinsic rather than extrinsic (CW 11/130-134). Solomon (2000) cites Jung's distinction between morality and ethics, suggesting that the former relies on rules and codes, while the latter is 'reflective ... subject to conscious scrutiny...' and is engaged when 'a fundamental conflict arises between two possible modes of moral behaviour' (CW 10/855). While Jung's definitions are not always consistent, it is clear that he locates ethics as an inward, esoteric journey, rather than the application of externally generated rules: the ethical is linked to the integral, in that the whole person is less conflicted or ego driven and has greater access to their own 'moral channels in the psyche' (CW 10/825-857).

Indeed, Jung contrasts the Eastern philosophy of going inwards for ethical guidance with the Christian tradition of reliance on externals, such as rules, law and texts (1957: 75), though he doubts the ability of the post-Enlightenment European ego to embrace an Eastern approach and instead urges acceptance of both the order of the rational mind and the chaos of the unconscious (CW 9i/489-524).

The process of developing an integrated self involves bringing opposing elements together in consciousness so that they become creative sources of energy, rather than generators of distress, denial and neurosis. The uniting of opposites is a central theme of Jung's work – though he was a devout Christian, Jung rejected the either/or, good/bad morality of the Church. 'The criterion of ethical action can no longer consist in the simple view that good has the force of a categorical imperative, while so-called evil can resolutely be shunned. Recognition of the reality of evil necessarily relativises the good, and the evil likewise, converting both into halves of the paradoxical whole' (1983 [1963]: 361). Indeed, he is clear that neglecting one's capacity for evil, creates the conditions for it (1957: 95). However, this does not lead to moral relativism as Jung is clear that the purpose or teleology of understanding one's own shadow is not to treat all actions as morally equal but to step outside the narrow considerations of ego and persona to envision the greater potential for behaving according to higher principles.

Here, Solomon (2000: 204) is describing the gestation of ethics in the consulting room but it has wider implications: 'The ethical attitude develops, personally and professionally, through the self progressing from a narcissistic mode of relating.' Schweiker (2004: 37) does not refer to Jung but does endorse the importance of integrity of life as central to 'the moral meaning of creation'. This integrity is described as 'characterised by richness and yet also coherence or wholeness' and Schweiker's exploration of the core and uniting values which might underpin twenty-first-century pluralist approaches to ethics seems, to me, to belong to the same debate that Jung was engaged with a century ago. The next question is: can the psychology of the individual be applied to groups and, by extension, professions?

JUNGIAN APPROACHES TO THE PROFESSIONS

The leap from the individual to the group is well established in organisational psychology, which looks at both the psychology of the individual and groups in workplaces and at organisational characteristics or personality as a whole (Haslam 2004; de Vries 1991, for example). Some scholars have looked specifically at the application of Jungian psychology to groups and organisations, (e.g. Henderson 1990; Feldman 2004; Abramson 2007; Matthews 2002), Singer and Kimbles (2004: 2) developed the idea of the cultural complex, and comment that: 'Although Jung included the cultural level in his schema of the psyche, his theory of complexes has never been systematically applied to the life of groups and to ... the "collective".'

Jungian analyst Guggenbuhl-Craig (1972 [1968]) comes the closest to my intentions in his analysis of the shadow side of healing professions, particularly physicians, priests and, of course, analysts. He describes how infatuation with images of healing or saving others can fuel darker figures of quack and false prophet, before discussing the shadow dynamics of the consulting room. There is scope for a wider discussion about how this dynamic might have played out in the cases of serial killer GP Harold Shipman or the many child abuse scandals emerging in the priesthood.

It therefore seems reasonable to extrapolate from the organisational or group level to the profession as a unit of study. There are many discussions of what determines a profession: I am here using a wide definition, which includes theoretical discussion of the field, and is best described as 'community of practice' (Brown and Duguid 2001, cited in Bartlett et al. 2007). I have also chosen to consider the internal working of the professional identity and ethics rather than corporate or organisational ethics because the former is a longer lasting aspect of a practitioner's career, which may involve several employers but one profession.

I am hypothesising that professional ethics have been founded on the ideal-typical model and that this acts as a 'persona' for the professional group. According to Jung's ideas of compensation, the more a group insists on its probity (and blames others for misrepresentation or, if pushed, 'bad apples' in its own ranks), the more obscure – and *potent* – its own shadow becomes. The emphasis on promotion rather than self-examination, common to most professions, illustrates this trait. As Larson (1977) and others claim that professional identity depends on the 'other' to determine its own boundaries, Jungian integration might challenge the notion of the profession. Jung suggests that ethical capacity is stimulated by the experience of struggling with the shadow elements of one's own personal or group identity; I suggest this offers a new direction for thinking in professional ethics. As Pieczka and L'Etang (2001) demonstrate, public relations faces all these challenges to its jurisdiction and identity, whether one considers it a profession or, as they do, an occupational group. So, can a Jungian approach address these issues?

CASE STUDY – PUBLIC RELATIONS

Jacquie L'Etang summarises the current debates in the field of public relations elsewhere in this volume; it does not need repeating. The key point I wish to emphasise is the tension between self-images of public relations as portrayed in core texts (Cutlip et al. 1985; Grunig et al. 1992) and those images held by critics like Stauber and Rampton (2004), Miller (2008) and others. The following section outlines some of the possibilities for applying Jungian ethics to public relations: a fuller exploration is contained in a recent paper (Fawkes 2009).

The Symmetric/Excellence Theory is accorded the status of a paradigm by Botan and Hazleton (2006) and while it has the laudable aim of improving public relations practice by quantifying and codifying best practice and demonstrating how others can improve, it has distanced itself from the darker aspects of public relations practice. In a kind of mirror image, the critics look only at the abuse, distortion and outright lying by PR people and organisations. They tend to take a very narrow view of the field, concentrating on corporate communications which involve corruption and distortion.

While many practitioners might like to see themselves as 'public relations professionals [who] promote mutual understanding and peaceful coexistence among individuals and institutions' (Seib and Fitzpatrick 1995 :1), they may suspect they are often engaged to 'spin the news, organise phoney "grassroots" front groups, spy on citizens, and conspire with lobbyists and politicians to thwart democracy' (Spinwatch.com).

The most powerful locus of contradiction and confusion is persuasion, about which the author has written elsewhere (Fawkes 2006a, 2006b and 2007), as have others, notably Moloney (2006), L'Etang (2006), Pfau and Wan (2006). The supporters of PR have tended to marginalise persuasion, despite Grunig's (2001) revision of the mixed-motives model, and – interestingly – seem to share the critics' conflation of persuasion and propaganda, with neither able to envisage persuasion as a legitimate communication tool.

It is also notable that many approaches to public relations ethics, apart from the rhetorical approach, lack real depth, often assuming either that market forces will iron out ethical problems or that the symmetry of the system and the distance from persuasion will act as ethical guarantors. Given that PR has been known to claim a role as 'ethical guardian' of the organisation (a claim that is fiercely disputed by L'Etang 2003), one might expect more rigorous analysis of ethical theory and practice. Public relations might even seek to become the natural promoter of the corporate conscience suggested by Goodpaster (2007), though it would need to engage more deeply with philosophical issues to qualify for this role. Bowen (2007) explores Excellent ethics from a Kantian perspective but current, post-Kantian, debates in professional ethics are not widely reflected in PR literature. One exception is Harrison and Galloway's (2005) application of virtue ethics to the various versions of the public relations practitioner, noted earlier.

DISCUSSION

If the above characterisation of public relations as a field is accurate then the notion of 'excellence' constellates as a *persona* archetype, emphasising the best in practice and theory and promoting public relations. Sample quotes include: 'Public relations has a moral purpose, which is social harmony' (Seib and Fitzpatrick 1995: 1); or more recently, 'Public relations is the champion of democracy and the guardian of common sense' (Vercic 2005). Core text books, the professional organisations and trade magazines are notably lacking in self-criticism (McKie 2001; Moloney 2006).

Jung is clear that a persona is necessary to conduct business in the world, to behave in ways acceptable to society and that elements of the individual (or group) are selected for presentation and others kept back as private. The danger is in over-identifying with this public face and forgetting it is not the whole story. That diagnosis would be supported by Pfau and Wan (2006:102), who argue that 'controversy over optimal approach has stunted public relations scholarship', a view shared by other authors (McKie 2001; Holtzhausen 2000, for example) who have commented on the normative, prescriptive weight of the excellence theory, and it may be that this paradigm for public relations research has become monolithic, stifling other ideas.

One might also read the insistence on propaganda as belonging to historical rather than contemporary public relations as rejection of 'unacceptable' personal characteristics or shadow material. It is also symptomatic in the individual of a weak ego (Stein 1998) which must deny and defend itself against what threatens its fragile identity. The enormous difficulties in defining the field may also be evidence of this immaturity.

The applicability of Jung's approach is further evidenced by the gusto with which the critics pick up the rejected, shadow material and fling it back at PR. The latest of these, Miller and Dinan's (2008) *A century of spin*, provides copious illustrations of PR deployment of deception and misrepresentation in government and corporate communications. It is also worth noting that they are unable to come up with any defence of PR – there is no discussion of the communication tactics used by voluntary organisations, trade unions or environmental campaigners, for example. This is also characteristic of shadow dynamics – the emphasis on the Otherness of the other precludes connection, shared ownership or recognition of the self in the other.

I suggest that the tension between the ideal-typical characterisation of PR's professional bodies and leading academics and the propagandist accusations of its critics outlined earlier is reflected in a more muted way between the same ideal-typical versions embodied in codes of conduct and the easy use of advocacy as an ethical 'get-out clause' by many practitioners. A Jungian approach would encourage engagement rather than rejection of these elements of the whole: what do they have to tell PR about itself? What do these voices illustrate? What if they are not all wrong? How can one have a professional internal dialogue if there is no capacity to listen? And how can one have professional ethics if they are based on the denial of large swathes of practice?

The move towards integration of the field would surely involve the painful but honest appraisals of PR's involvement with propaganda, past *and* present (a proposal for an Institute for Propaganda Analysis is made in Fawkes and Moloney 2008). It would involve the acceptance that on the one hand excellence is a laudable goal and genuinely reflects the experience and aspirations of many practitioners throughout the field; and on the other hand that their colleagues (or themselves in different circumstances) are often actively involved in using questionable methods to promote their employer's views. It might lead to discussion of what really is legitimate in current PR – the debate that many of the critics ignore. Jung would encourage us to look for the similarities, the points of connection within the field, rather than to label some good and others bad. Instead of drawing up codes to tell the difference, public relations might rediscover the fallible, approval-seeking, boastful and dishonest aspects of our collective personality. How would this be done and do all practitioners need to participate? My current conception of the role of a Jungian approach is one of starting a debate, opening a space for discussion which allows the light (or dark) in. I do not envisage mass therapy.

Public relations practitioners shape corporate, organisational and societal communications. There is a tendency to idealise the organisation, the profession and the practitioner, despite the hostility of critics. Guggenbuhl-Craig's (1972 [1968]) suggestion that the shadow of a doctor is a quack or charlatan, the shadow of a priest a false prophet seems to me to resonate with public relations' fear of the flack, the propagandist, about which I have written elsewhere (most recently Fawkes and Moloney 2008).

As I understand it, a Jungian approach to public relations ethics would start by acknowledging the propaganda role in public relations, past and present, without condemnation or judgement. In order to change direction, if that was collectively desired (a big 'if') these behaviours would need to be set in a wider context to provide an equivalent to the transcendent function suggested by Jung. I do not expect public relations to 'get God' but it does seem salient that professions in general and public relations in particular seek to locate their authority in the concept of society, as discussed earlier. The frequent claims that public relations works for the benefit of society need to be scrutinised and challenged but this may prove to be a common goal to which different viewpoints could agree to aspire. The sociology of professions, touched on earlier, offers some aids to this discussion.

If the field were prepared to have such a debate with itself, it might be surprised by its potential for transformation: in abandoning the safe but hollow idealism of the ideal-typical or the cynical and under-examined defence of advocacy, the profession might begin a search for deeper guidance about ethical conduct. It is worth repeating Samuels' (1985: 65) comment: 'There is a compelling moral aspect to integration of the shadow: to unblock personal and communal relationship and also to admit the inadmissible, yet human.'

CONCLUSION

This paper has sought to demonstrate that professional ethics is in a state of flux, reflecting changes in the status of the professions (and aspiring professions) and new ideas emerging from post-modernism. As the search for virtue or value highlights an inward journey, the work of Carl Jung is suggested as a possible guide to such adventures. Jung's conceptualisation of the self and the journey, through accepting the shadow, to integration were then explored as a moral basis for ethical behaviour and insight. These ideas were applied to the emerging profession of public relations, by visualising the core debates within public relations about its function and role in society in terms of archetypal struggles between Persona and Shadow.

The paper is exploratory rather than exhaustive but I hope it has demonstrated that Jung's writing on moral development is germane to current debates on ethics and that his concept of integration offers a way forward for the development of a more coherent professional ethics, not only in public relations but for others grappling with issues of ethics in rapidly changing times.

- The paper first appeared in *Ethical Space*, Vol 6, No. 2 pp 30-39, 2009.

  An earlier version was presented to the Third International Conference on Teaching Applied and Professional Ethics in Higher Education hosted by the Centre for Applied and Professional Ethics (CAPE) and the Professional Associations Research Network (PARN), Kingston University, July 2008

REFERENCES

Abbott, P. and Meerabeau, L. (1998) *The sociology of the caring professions*, London, UCL Press, second edition

Abramson, N. R. (2007) The leadership archetype: A Jungian analysis of similarities between modern leadership theory and the Abraham myth in the Judeo-Christian tradition, *Journal of Business Ethics*, Vol. 72 pp 115-129

Bauman, Z. (1993) *Postmodern ethics*, Oxford, Blackwell

Bartlett, J., Tywoniak, S. and Hatcher, C. (2007) Public relations professional practice and the institutionalisation of CSR, *Journal of Communication Management*, Vol. 11, No. 4 pp 281-299

Bishop, P. (1999) C. G. Jung and Nietzsche: Dionysos and analytical psychology, Bishop, P. E. (ed.) *Jung in contexts: A reader*, London, Routledge pp 205-241

Bishop, P. E. (ed.) (1999) *Jung in contexts: A reader*, London, Routledge

Botan, C. H. and Hazleton, V. (2006) (eds) *Public relations theory II*, Mahweh, NJ, Lawrence Erlbaum Associates

Broadbent, J., Dietrich, M. and Roberts, J. (1997) *The end of the professions? The restructuring of professional work*, London, Routledge

Brown, J. S. and Duguid, P. (2001) Knowledge and organization: A social-practice perspective, *Organization Science*, Vol. 12 pp 40-57

Christopher, E. and Solomon, H. M. (eds) (2000) *Jungian thought in the modern world*, London, Free Association

Cooper, D. E. (2004) *Ethics for professionals in a multicultural world*, Upper Saddle River, New Jersey, Prentice-Hall

Cutlip, S. M., Center, A. H. and Broom, G. M. (1985) *Effective public relations*, New Jersey, Prentice-Hall, sixth edition

de Vries, M. (1991) *Organisations on the couch: Clinical psychology in organisations, behaviour and change*, Josey Bass, SFCA

Dawson, T. and Young-Eisendrath, P. (1997) *The Cambridge companion to Jung*, Cambridge, Cambridge University Press

Dent M. and Whitehead, S. (2002) *Managing professional identities, knowledge, perfomativity and the 'new' professional*, London, Routledge

Fawkes, J. and Moloney, K. (2008) Does the European Union (EU) need a propaganda watchdog like the US Institute of Propaganda Analysis to strengthen its democratic civil society and free markets?, *Public Relations Review*, Vol. 34 pp 207-214

Fawkes, J. (2009a) Integrated ethics: a Jungian approach, conference paper to be presented to International Jungian Studies Conference, Cardiff, July

Fawkes, J. (2009b) The shadow of excellence: A Jungian approach to public relations, conference paper to be presented to International Communication Association conference, Chicago, May

Feldman, B. (2004) Towards a theory of organizational culture: Integrating the 'other' from a post-Jungian perspective, Singer, T. and Kimbles, S. L. (eds) *The cultural complex: Contemporary Jungian perspectives on psyche and society*, New York, Brunner-Routledge pp 251-261

Fitzpatrick, K. and Bronstein, C. (eds) (2006) *Ethical public relations: Responsible advocacy*, Thousand Oaks, CA, Sage

Fligstein, N. (2001) Social skill and the theory of fields, *Sociological Theory*, Vol. 19 pp 105-125

Goodpaster, K. E. (2007) *Conscience and corporate culture*. Malden, Mass, and Oxford, Blackwell

Grunig. J. (2001) Two-way symmetrical public relations: Past, present and future, Heath, R. L. (ed.) *The handbook of public relations*, Thousand Oaks, California, Sage pp 11-30

Grunig, J. E. and Hunt, T. (1984) *Managing public relations*, New York, Holt, Rinehart and Winston

Grunig, J. E., Dozier, D. M., Ehling, W. P. Grunig, L. A., Repper, F. C. and White, J. (eds) (1992) *Excellence in public relations and communication management*, Hillsdale, New Jersey, Lawrence Erlbaum

Guggenbuhl-Craig, A. (1972 [1968]) The psychotherapist's shadow: Contribution to international congress on the reality of the psyche, Wheelwright, J. B. (ed.) New York, New York, G. P. Putnam's Sons for C. J. Jung Foundation. https://ofj.org/library/the-reality-of-the-psyche-the-proceedings/

Harrison, K. and Galloway, C. (2005) Public relations ethics: A simpler (but not simplistic) approach to the complexities, *Prism* 3. Available online at http://praxis.massey.ac.nz, accessed on 14 October 2008

Haslam, S. A. (2004) *Psychology in organisations*, London, Sage

Heath, R. L. (ed.) (2001) *The handbook of public relations*, Thousand Oaks, California, Sage

Hede, A. (2007) The shadow group: Towards an explanation of interpersonal conflict in work groups, *Journal of Managerial Psychology*, Vol. 22, No. 1 pp 25-39

Henderson, J. L. (1990) *Shadow and self*, Wilmette, IL, Chiron

Holtzhausen, D. (2000) Postmodern values in public relations, *Journal of Public Relations Research*, Vol. 12, No. 1 pp 251-264

Jones, R. A. (2007) *Jung, psychology, postmodernity*. Hove, East Sussex, Routledge

Jung, C. G. (1984) *Modern man in search of a soul*. London, Routledge and Kegan Paul

Jung, C. G. and Hull, R. F. C. (1958) *The undiscovered self*, London, Routledge and Kegan Paul

Jung, C. G. and Storr, A. (1998) *The essential Jung*, London, Fontana, second edition

Jung, C. G. (1983 [1963]) *Memories, dreams, reflections*, London, Flamingo

Kultgen, J. (1988) *Ethics and professionalism*, Philadelphia, University of Philadelphia Press

L'Etang, J. (2003) The myth of the 'ethical guardian': An examination of its origins, potency and illusions, *Journal of Communication Management*, Vol. 8, No. 1 pp 53-67

L'Etang, J. and Pieczka, M. (eds) (2006) *Public relations, critical debates and contemporary practice*, Mahwah, NJ, Lawrence Erlbaum

Larson, M. S. (1977) *The rise of professionalism: A sociological analysis*, Berkeley, London, University of California Press

McKie, D. (2001) Updating public relations: 'New science' research paradigms and uneven developments, Heath, R. L. (ed.) *The handbook of public relations*, Thousand Oaks, California, Sage pp 75-91

MacIntyre, A. (1984) *After virtue: A study in moral theory*, Notre Dame, IN, University of Notre Dame Press, second edition

Matthews, R. (2002) Competition archetypes and creative imagination, *Journal of Organisational Change*, Vol. 15, No. 5 pp 461-476

Miller D. and Dinan, W. (2008) *A century of spin: How public relations became the cutting edge of corporate power*, Pluto Press, London

Moloney, K. (2006) *Rethinking public relations: Spin and substance*, London, Routledge

Mount, E. (1990) *Professional ethics in context: Institutions, images and empathy*, Louisville, KY, Westminster/John Knox Press

Oakley, J. and Cocking, D. (2001) *Virtue ethics and professional roles*, Cambridge, Cambridge University Press

Parkinson, M. (2001) The PRSA code of professional standards and member code of ethics: Why they are neither professional nor ethical, *Public Relations Quarterly*, Vol. 46, No. 3 pp 27-32

Pfau, M. and Wan, H. (2006) Persuasion: An intrinsic function in public relations, Botan, C. H. and Hazleton, V. (2006) (eds) *Public relations theory II*, Mahweh, New Jersey, Lawrence Erlbaum Associates pp 101-136

Pieczka, M. and L'Etang, J. (2001) Public relations and the question of professionalism, Heath, R. L. (ed.) *The handbook of public relations*, Thousand Oaks, California, Sage pp 223-235

Samuels, A. (1985) *Jung and the post-Jungians*. London, Routledge and Kegan Paul

Schweiker, W. (2004) *Theological ethics and global dynamics in the time of many worlds*, Malden, Oxford, Blackwell

Seib, P. and Fitzpatrick, K. (1995) *Public relations ethics*, Fort Worth, Harcourt Brace

Seidler, V. J. (1994) *Recovering the self: Morality and social theory*, London, Routledge

Singer, J. (1995) *Boundaries of the soul: The practice of Jung's psychology*, Sturminster Newton, Prism, second edition

Singer, T. and Kimbles, S. L. (eds) (2004) *The cultural complex: Contemporary Jungian perspectives on psyche and society*, New York, Brunner-Routledge

Smith, N. H. (1997) *Strong hermeneutics: Contingency and moral identity*, London, Routledge

Smith, P. C. (1991) *Hermeneutics and human finitude: Toward a theory of ethical understanding*, New York, Fordham University Press

Solomon, H. M. (2000) The ethical self, Christopher, E. and Solomon, H. M. (eds) *Jungian thought in the modern world*, London, Free Association pp 191-216

Sommerlad, H. (2007) Researching and theorizing the processes of professional identity formation, *Journal of Law and Society*, Vol. 34, No. 2 pp 190-217

Stauber, J. and Rampton, S. (2004) *Toxic sludge is good for you*, London, Robinson

Stein, M. (2004) On the politics of individuation in the Americas, Singer, T. and Kimbles, S. L. (eds) *The cultural complex: Contemporary Jungian perspectives on psyche and society*, New York, Brunner-Routledge pp 262-273

Stein, M. (1998) *Jung's map of the soul*, Chicago, IL, Open Court

Storr, A. (1999) Foreword, Bishop, P. E. (ed.) *Jung in contexts*, London, Routledge pp xi-xviii

Suddaby, R. and Greenwood, R. (2005) Rhetorical strategies of legitimacy, *Administrative Science Quarterly*, Vol. 50 pp 35-67

Watson, T. (2002) Speaking professionally: Occupational anxiety and discursive ingenuity in human resourcing specialists, Dent, M. and Whitehead, S. (eds) *Managing professional identities, knowledge, perfomativity and the 'new' professional*, London, Routledge pp 99-115

Weber, M. (1964) *The theory of social and economic organization*, New York, Free Press

Vercic, D. (2005) Public relations is the champion of democracy and guardian of common sense, *Behind the spin*. Available online at http://publicsphere.typepad.com/behindthespin/current_affairs/index.html, accessed on 12 October 2005

Wernick, A. (1991) *Promotional culture*, London, Sage

NOTE ON THE CONTRIBUTOR

Johanna Fawkes, PhD, is currently Visiting Fellow at Leeds Beckett University, UK. She was Principal Research Fellow at the University of Huddersfield (2016-2018), leading an international research team to produce the Global Capability Framework for Public Relations and Communications Management. Since 1990, Johanna has developed public relations degrees at all levels at universities in the UK and Australia, following a career in local government and trade union communication. She has delivered international keynote speeches and published widely on public relations' identity, performance and ethics. Her first book, *Public relations ethics and professionalism: The shadow of excellence*, introducing a Jungian approach to ethics, was published by Routledge in 2015. Her second, *Depth public relations: After the masquerade* (Routledge, 2023) explores connections between public relations, a global culture of performativity and climate collapse. She now lives in Andalucia, Spain.

Chapter 19

'Radical PR' – catalyst for change or an aporia?

Jacquie L'Etang

Jacquie L'Etang traces the history of the 'Radical PR' group, assesses its achievements to date – and looks to the future.

INTRODUCTION

This is a story about a group of scholars trying to change the direction of a discipline. There are many alternative endings to the story.

'Radical PR' was the name given to an international gathering of like-minded academics at the Stirling Media Research Institute (SMRI) in July 2008. It was a plunge into the unknown for scholars who travelled to Stirling from Australia, New Zealand, USA, South America, Scandinavia and Europe. What was it all about?

'Radical PR' evolved as a loose concept through a series of overlapping personal relationships among those who had articulated dissatisfaction and frustration with the dominant research agenda in the field of PR over a number of years. The characteristics of this group could be summarised as being among those PR scholars who approached the subject of public relations from multi- and inter-disciplinary contexts, going beyond functional applied work to consider wider issues of the occupation and its social impacts. I shall start by recounting briefly something of the overall nature and preoccupations of the public relations discipline.

THE PUBLIC RELATIONS DISCIPLINE

Public relations is the occupation responsible for the management of organisational relationships and reputation. It encompasses issues management, public affairs, corporate communications, stakeholder relations, risk communication and corporate social responsibility. Public relations operates on behalf of many different types of organisation both at the governmental and corporate level, to small business and voluntary sectors. Public relations arises at points of societal change and resistance.

Although in the UK work has been published on public relations since the 1920s, it was not until the late 1980s that degrees were established. Until that date, publications were largely restricted to practitioner texts. In the US, however, academics had been working consistently since the 1950s, largely from a business perspective, publishing student texts. Scholarly research in Germany was on-going from the early 1960s, and often engaged with societal contexts, but on the whole these ideas did not reach or impact Anglophone audiences. US academic research, which integrated organisational sociology and communications, tended to advance the discipline along functional lines, and, in the 1980s a large-scale international project (US, UK, Canada) led to the formulation of a theoretical base focused on effectiveness and excellence. Research that has subsequently emanated from this normative theory has been largely instrumental, applied and quantitative.

INTER-DISCIPLINARITY

The public relations discipline has struggled with its identity since it has been located in many different academic 'homes', including marketing, management, communications, media, journalism. Academic public relations writing reflects that '57 varieties' interdisciplinary context. Those in media studies and marketing tend to see PR as publicity or low-level technical publicity work, rather than a strategic and complex operation with diverse facets in promotional culture. Others in media and cultural studies have seen PR as spin and propaganda, the handmaiden of capitalism and corporate and political paymasters. Some conspiracy theorists have elevated public relations to a hidden, mysterious, dark and powerful force that manipulates the media. Such critiques are instructive, but have a tendency to focus on the media relations side of the work, often in a political context; to assume powerful media effects; and to elevate their authors to morality playwrights. It is not that these views may not be justified to some degree, but they do appear to be built on an unreflexive ideological partisanship that is intrinsically hostile and self-righteous. Irritatingly, some authors have scarcely a nodding acquaintance with either functional or critical work within public relations – as though such a subject and its academics are not worthy of close attention.

The complexity of public relations as a concept and practice really demands multi- and inter-disciplinary research that is longitudinal, mixed method, ethnographic and case study-based research in a variety of different sectors of the economy and micro-cultural contexts. Only such collaborative efforts can begin to capture a better understanding of this intriguing practice. At present, there really is a lack of empirical data. My personal view is that activities akin to public relations are intrinsic to organised human society and individual impression management, and that such work takes place 'between the hyphens' in multiple communications. The different academic homes provide part of the story, but like the Indian fable about the six blind men and the elephant, all of them have a valid, but incomplete, perspective.

PARADIGMS IN THE FIELD

In 1994, Magda Pieczka labelled the US approach to public relations as 'the dominant paradigm'. The dominant paradigm is functional, yet idealistic, largely drawing on literature from organisational sociology, psychology and management to elicit variables relevant to public relations practice. It comprises a not entirely comfortable marriage between the priorities of organisational effectiveness and idealistic ethical communication practice in which public relations practitioners 'balance' organisational and societal needs utilising 'two-way symmetrical communication' – a form of discourse ethics. One of the major difficulties of the dominant paradigm is its failure to account adequately for the role of power, and the significance of social dominance as the basis for much human interaction within and between organisations, but there are other weaknesses too, including the existence of a limited and somewhat prescriptive research agenda. Within the dominant paradigm there are several sub-themes: relationship management, which focuses on organisations and stakeholder/publics; communitarian, which argues that the appropriate role for public relations is community-building; rhetorical, which argues that the role of public relations as organisational rhetoric is beneficial to societies as it facilitates public debate and helps respective groups to arrive at consensus. Occupational roles and gender have also been a major focus of research, although this has also tended to be quantitative work exploring the role of US middle-class women.

Public relations as a practice and as a field struggles with issues of social legitimacy, and connections to propaganda, so ethical issues, especially corporate social responsibility (CSR) are also foregrounded in much literature. The predominant assumption within public relations scholarship appears to have been that new research will continue to add to that which is already there, rather than strike out on new tracks of discovery. US theory has aimed to build a universal scientific explanation and framework. This ambition has had some stifling effects, particularly on publication. Not only has it been hard for some scholars to get their work published, but also it is noticeable that US scholars do not always acknowledge the existence of work that was emerging in Europe from at least the late 1980s and that articulated alternative ideas to the US paradigm or even critiqued it e.g. Botan and Hazleton 2006; Bowen 2008. Historically, it has been difficult to articulate critical perspectives from within the field, and, speaking personally, I was very lucky that *Journal of Business Ethics* took some of my early work. It was difficult presenting work at conferences that was different and sometimes negative, both about public relations, and also about existing theory. Perhaps because there was relatively little theoretical work, the impact of a single framework had much greater impact. The dominant paradigm became a taken-for-granted consensus about the research agenda.

A small amount of critical research highlighting the role of power was developed largely in Scotland and New Zealand in the mid-1990s (L'Etang and Pieczka 1996; Motion and Leitch 1996). Contributions included post-colonial (Munshi 1998) and subaltern approaches (Dutta-Bergman 2005) and rhetorical work, which explored public relations practitioners as 'discourse workers'. Post-modernism has become a focus for some conceptualisation (Holtzhausen 2000), and there are promising signs of the emergence of ethnographic work in the field (Hodges 2006). There have been several histories from various cultures and it is fair to say that a sociology of public relations is now an emergent force (Pieczka 2006; Edwards 2006). There have also been some isolated Special Issues. The earliest appeared in the *Australian Journal of Communication* in 1997 'Public relations on the edge' edited by Leitch and Walker (Vol. 24, No. 2, 1997) which constitutes 'what is still the most influential collection from this part of the world' (Petelin 2005).

It was nearly a decade later before any such work appeared in the mainstream public relations journals notably two in *Public Relations Review*: one on 'Global public relations: A different perspective ' edited by McKie and Munshi from Waikato, New Zealand (Vol. 31, No. 4, 2005), 'Public relations and social theory' (Vol. 33, No. 3, 2007); and two in the *Journal of Public Relations Research*, one on 'Public relations from the margins' edited by the US scholar Moffitt (Vol. 17, No. 1, 2005) and one on 'Identity, difference and power' (Vol. 17, No. 2, 2005). Nevertheless, scholars operating outside the main frameworks are rather scattered, something that 'Radical PR' hoped to begin to address.

RESEARCH POTENTIAL

Public relations is present at all political, economic, socio-cultural and technological change in contemporary, post-modern promotional cultures. It engages with cultural beliefs and practices, communicative action, discourse ethics, organisational cultures and climates, formation of public agendas and debates, interest-group activism. Public relations is a diverse affair, present, for example, in music and the arts, technology, sport, tourism, religion, as well as corporate and political worlds. Within cultural studies, public relations has been seen as one of the 'cultural intermediary' occupations. In my view, public relations research should be a priority for scholars of many types and a multi-paradigmatic meeting place for enlightening our understanding of promotional culture.

DRAMATIS PERSONAE AND CRITICAL MOMENTS

Speaking personally, I had been very fortunate to work with Magda Pieczka for 16 years at SMRI. We collaborated on two books of critical essays (1996, 2006), the first of which caused a strong reaction, but may have played a role in beginning to open up debate about the politics of the PR field. Pieczka, (now at Queen Margaret University, Edinburgh) edits the *Journal of Communication Management*. She organised an SMRI seminar in 2000, which was attended by a number of critical scholars, especially from New Zealand. Professor McKie, from the University of Waikato, who has published on PR, chaos, post-modernity and environmentalism, became a regular visitor, and during his stay in 2007, we started to develop ideas that led to Radical PR. I set up a small group or Steering Committee adding to the names already mentioned: Jesper Falkheimer, from Lund, and Professor Jordi Xifra, from Girona.

Falkheimer had stayed at Stirling for several months during his sabbatical in 2006 and collaborated with me and my colleague Jairo Lugo on an article on public relations and tourism; Xifra had published several books on PR in Catalan and Spanish as well as articles in English. I knew from a week's visit to Girona, that Jordi and I shared much in common and we collaborated on a project for the *American Behavioral Science* Special Issue on Public Diplomacy (forthcoming, 2009). The collaborating institutions were University of Stirling, University of Waikato, University of Girona, Queen Margaret University and the University of Lund.

In liaison with the Steering Group I put together an (unsuccessful) application for network funding from the British Academy. This process, and other similar experiences, emphasise the fact that there are no public relations scholars who sit on national peer review grant-awarding bodies. Neither, to my knowledge, do any public relations specialists sit on any of the national Research Assessment panels. These absences highlight the political economy of public relations academia in the UK. The subject tends to be valued by institutions for its ability to recruit students to applied vocational courses; the discipline's research potential has not been recognised. In a very small way 'Radical PR' was a first step to forming an interest group that could diversify the subject, and subsequently help change perceptions of the public relations field.

WHAT DID 'RADICAL PR' AIM TO DO?

Our project aimed to set in motion a movement to reform the field of public relations. The practice of public relations is increasingly recognised as central to political and public life and has a massive, sometimes co-ordinated, global impact. However, the discipline of public relations lacks intellectual credibility with other fields. While islands of research and theory exist, there is no formal linkage and no established network to drive radical reformatting, let alone institutionalise it in sustainable form.

We sought to liberate the public relations field from its normative, functional, conformist agendas and realise the potential of public relations research to shed new light on contemporary life and inform cultural practice. Our purpose was to establish a network to redress the problems of isolation and generate new bodies of work to replace the current insular body of knowledge centred on narrow positivism that fails to acknowledge the field's power dynamics. In particular we hoped to leapfrog some of the middle generation and excite and interest those at the beginning of their academic careers. Consequently we were delighted to attract some highly original doctoral students.

Our starting point was to draw together people from a growing international cohort of scholars beginning to explore cultural, sociological, and theoretical aspects of public relations from interdisciplinary perspectives. This was not to be a conference as such, but the beginning of a process that would facilitate networking and engender confidence among those who had often worked alone for years in 'host' departments (such as media or cultural studies or marketing or business). Together we drew up a wish-list of invitees and were overwhelmed when virtually everyone accepted and committed to the project. When we failed to get funding, many dipped into their own pockets to make the (often extensive and expensive) trip to Stirling.

Our initial aim was to create an identity and platform for collaboration to instigate these radical changes. The project was built on the platform of informal contacts, and work in progress in different parts of the world. We aimed to: provide space for the articulation of alternative research agendas; engage a range of multi-cultural scholars from the margins of public relations, and cognate disciplines; and to provide a forum for new academics, and students at the doctoral and post-doctoral level. The initial list of project collaborators was drawn from a cross section of academic generations but aspired to excite and interest those at the beginning of their academic careers and considering a shift into the public relations field.

RUMOURS OF 'RADICAL PR'

Our initial idea had been for a small planning seminar, but several months into the initial planning process, something strange started happening. Scholars not on our initial list from institutions in Australia, the USA and elsewhere started contacting us for further information of 'the conference'. It was fantastic to realise that there were many more people than we had envisaged interested in pursuing alternative agendas. We re-worked our concept to allow people to give papers on some specified key themes. These were global in scope, had currency and were designed to catalyse the PR field and its connections with contemporary debates. Our focus on societal impacts rather than organisational need was intended as a powerful corrective to the dominant paradigm in the field. They were:

- PR and nationalism: stateless nations, nation-building, national identity;
- activism and campaigning: activism, anti-racism, corporate social responsibility;
- international relations, diplomacy, inter-cultural communication;

- public relations as a cultural practice: tourism, sport, religion;
- technology and discourse communities;
- theory developments: 'sociology of public relations'; cultural theory and PR.

'RADICAL PR' – THE EVENT

Within the time constraints available we endeavoured as a group to spend enough time discussing the nature of alternative research agendas. This was scary because it meant leaving apparent blanks in the programme to allow group discussion. However, I knew from running an SMRI event the previous year (on intersections between PR, religion, tourism and sport) that one can trust good academics to make such a format work, and even though many people had never actually met previously, there was a sense of camaraderie and shared enterprise. We spent time discussing: What is *not* radical enough in current PR? And went on to debate whether 'Radical PR' was the right label. There was considerable, and ultimately unresolved discussion about the appropriate title. A number were uncomfortable with the term 'radical' and while many other terms were put forward, there was no unanimous agreement. In fact, my original concept (before my strategic self wrote the first draft of the research grant application) had been for 'Wild PR'.

There were also a number of papers, too extensive to review here (abstracts are available on the website http://radicalpr.wordpress.com) but which included:

- Nilam Ashra: Inside stories: Understanding the daily lives of communication practitioners through discourse
- Rob Brown: Symmetry's consequences
- Timothy Coombs and Sherry Holladay: Cooperation, co-optation, or capitulation: Factors shaping activist-corporate partnerships
- Pat Curtin: Negotiating the meaning of Corporate Social Responsibility in a globalised context: A textual analysis of Mattel's CSR policies and its response to the 2007 recall crisis
- Christine Daymon: Humanising public relations research
- Kristin Demetrious: Adverse reactions: The negative effects of public relations in the public sphere
- Paul Elmer: Beyond Bourdieu: Body work in the cultural industries, or Bananarama rebuffed: it ain't only what you do, it's the way you do it, too

- Kate Fitch: Shifting sands: The slippage between publics and communities in public relations

- Caroline Hodges and Christine Daymon: An 'insider' in Mexico: Researching the occupational culture of public relations practitioners

- Øyvind Ihlen: Rhetoric to the rescue: Serving the public interest with rhetorical and critical approaches to public relations

- Julia JahFansoozi and Eric Koper: Exploring public private relations in cocoa research for development

- Ryszard Lawniczak: Transitional PR

- Gustavo A Yepes López: Perception about corporate social responsibility: Colombian case

- David McKie: National projection: Theorising competitive advantages, countries, and strategic leadership

- Margalit Toledano: PR and nationalism: How nation-building challenges shaped strategic communication in Israel

- Jordi Xifra: A public relations approach to stateless nation-building and public para-diplomacy: From 'real public relations' to 'noo public relations'

EVALUATION – A PERSONAL VIEW

There is much still to be done in public relations, both empirically and conceptually. Global issues of poverty, war, financial collapse, avian flu, human rights and the environment all have a public relations dimension in terms of networks of influence, policy and persuasion. Better connections need to be made to historical antecedents, philosophy and public communication. The role of public relations in society, its connections to class, elite organisations such as think tanks, and celebrity could also be better understood. Within organisations, it is hard to understand how public relations practitioners can act as other than propagandists, and it is harder still to understand how best such practitioners can engage with the organisational psyche in order to formulate and project organisational identity externally. Public relations scholarship needs to find time and space to engage in conversations with those from other disciplines, as well as those from practice.

Personally, I really hoped that others would be interested in taking the discipline along new and different paths and to be creative, as an antidote to the predictable organisation-management focus of most of the literature.

The 'Radical PR' event suggested that the discipline may be close to a 'tipping point'. It is apparent that various members of the meeting are continuing with informal exchanges, research and writing projects. However, the organisational side has not fared so well, for example the website slid into disuse, although recently efforts have been made to revive this with some cross-blog postings in which members of the dominant paradigm and others have debated the value of Radical PR and critical theorists (http://www.prconversations.com/?p=471). Perhaps the best way of seeing 'Radical PR' is as a critical incident or moment that generated potential. Only time will tell whether it signalled a major junction or a *cul de sac*.

ACKNOWLEDGEMENT

I should like to acknowledge the contributions of David McKie, Jordi Xifra, Magda Pieczka and Jesper Falkhiemer who contributed to the formulation of the British Academy grant application on which some sections of this article are based. However, the views expressed in this article are personal.

- This paper was first published in *Ethical Space*, Vol 6, No. 2 pp13-18, 2009

REFERENCES

Botan, C. and Hazleton, V. (2006) *Public relations theory II*, Mahwah, New Jersey, Lawrence Erlbaum Associates

Bowen, S. (2008) A state of neglect: Public relations as 'corporate conscience' or ethics counsel, *Journal of Public Relations Research*, Vol. 20, No. 3 pp 271-296

Dutta-Bergman, M. (2005) Civil society and public relations: Not so civil after all, *Journal of Public Relations Research*, Vol. 17, No. 3 pp 267-289

Edwards, L. (2006) Rethinking power in public relations, *Public Relations Review*, Vol. 32, No. 3 pp 229-231

Hodges, C. (2006) 'PRP culture': A framework for exploring public relations practitioners as cultural intermediaries, *Journal of Communication Management*, Vol. 10, No.1 pp 80-93

Holtzhausen, D. (2000) Postmodern values in PR, *Journal of Public Relations Research*, Vol. 12, No. 1 pp 93-114

L'Etang, J. and Pieczka, M. (eds) (1996) *Critical perspectives in public relations*, London, ITBP

Motion, J. and Leitch, J. (1996) A discursive perspective from New Zealand: another world view, *Public Relations Review*, Vol. 22 pp 297-309

Munshi, D. (1998) Media politics and the Asianization of a polarised immigration debate in New Zealand, *Australian Journal of Communication* Vol. 25, No. 1 pp 97-110

Petelin, R. (2005) Editing from the edge: De-territorializing public relations scholarship, *Public Relations Review*, Vol. 31, No. 4 pp 458-462

Pieczka, M. (2006) Editorial, *Journal of Communication Management*, Vol. 10, No. 4 pp 328-329

WEBSITES

http://radicalpr.wordpress.com

http://www.prconversations.com/?p=471

NOTE ON THE CONTRIBUTOR

Jacquie L'Etang is Honorary Professor at the University of Stirling working in collaboration with Alenka Jelen. She taught PR at Stirling from 1990 and was Director of the MSc. in Public Relations at the University of Stirling 1993-2012. She was Research Chair at Queen Margaret University, Edinburgh 2012-2015. During the 1970s and 1980s she worked in public relations at the British Council and at the London School of Economics. She is author of *Public relations: Concepts, practice and critique* (Sage, 2008), *Public relations in Britain: A history of professional practice in the 20th century* (LEA, 2004) and *Sports public relations* (Sage, 2008); co-editor of *The Routledge handbook of critical public relations* (with McKie, Snow and Xifra, 2016), co-editor and co-author of *Public relations: Critical debates and contemporary practice* (LEA, 2006) and *Critical perspectives in public relations* (ITBP, 1996). She has written book chapters and articles on topics such as public diplomacy, anthropology, rhetoric, ethics, corporate social responsibility, professionalism, sport, tourism, health and propaganda. In the final years of her full-time academic career she focused almost exclusively on historical and historiographical analysis of public relations exploring relationships between historicity and knowledge with societal change.

Chapter 20

Taking the BS out of PR: Creating genuine messages by emphasising character and authenticity

Kevin Stoker and Brad Rawlins

The realms of advertising and public relations, and the nowadays closely related realm of politics, are replete with instances of bullshit so unmitigated that they can serve among the most indisputable and classic paradigms of the concept.

Harry G. Frankfurt, 2005

Spin is not advocacy. Spin does not take a point of view. Spin is distortion that deliberately misleads the audience.

Robert Dilenschneider, 1998

We often hear about 'spin' and 'spin control'. There is nothing wrong with the concept so long as spinning does not turn into lying.

James Patterson, 1999

Keywords: bullshit, public relations, authenticity, professionalism

'One of the most salient features of our culture is that there is so much bullshit.' So begins Harry G. Frankfurt's (2005: 1) best-selling book, *On bullshit*, based on a lecture he gave 20 years ago. If Frankfurt thought BS was plentiful in the late 1960s, it has flourished a great deal since then. Why? Some have attributed its growth to the refinement of spin in the political sector, the proliferation of media and sources of information, the cutbacks in newsrooms which create a greater dependency on publicity agents, postmodern attitudes towards subjective truth, and a certain apathy toward elected officials and media by the public. Whatever the reason, Frankfurt's mix of philosophy, personal insight and subtle sarcasm helps explain the contemporary crisis of trust.

According to the 2009 Edelman Trust Barometer, a survey of 1,500 global opinion leaders in North and South America, Europe and Asia, the credibility of business, government and the news media was at the lowest point since the survey began. The trust deficit has also been measured by the Golin/Harris trust index, Gallup and Roper ASW polls, and studies done by Randstad North America. According to the Edelman study conducted over the last three years, the person most likely to be trusted fit in the category of 'a person like yourself', such as colleagues, friends and family. Official spokespersons, in both business and government, have seen steady declines in credibility. Only non-government organisations (NGOs) and other independent experts such as academics have maintained or increased trust (Edelman 2009).

A series of high profile acts of deception by journalists at prominent US news organisations, such as *The New York Times*'s Jayson Blair, the *New Republic*'s Stephen Glass, and *USA Today*'s Jack Kelley, damaged media credibility worldwide (Medsger 2004). Public relations also suffers from a trust deficit. A PRSA/Harris poll conducted in November 2006 on media and public relations revealed that 41 per cent of the general public, 29 per cent of business executives and 43 per cent of congressional members disagreed that public relations practitioners 'help their clients provide fair and balanced information to the public and other groups'. According to philosopher Sissela Bok (1999), all kinds of lying – lies to protect others, white lies, lies to liars and noble lies for the public good – harm not only the liar and the objects of the lie, but undermine the very fabric of society. High-trust societies are built on shared ethical values and preconceived notions of ethics and morality (Fukuyama 1995). But unlike the news media, public relations practitioners have not been dogged by allegations of lying as much as they have been criticised for spinning and manipulating the truth (Medsger 2004). That may be because the public values authentic communication and knows when communication is insincere and misleading. In other words, most rational people have a bullshit detector. For that reason, Frankfurt's theory of BS resonated with the public because it described a phenomenon with which people could identify but not necessarily define. Once defined, however, it exposed moral flaws in professional communication and more especially in public relations practice. We will explore Frankfurt's theory and provide suggestions on how to cut the bull out of PR.

ON BS

Frankfurt wrote his lecture on BS because of the lack of concern for the truth that he saw in society. Trained as an analytic philosopher, Frankfurt defined the nature of a thing recognised by all but understood by none. As one reviewer put it (Noah 2005): 'Frankfurt's definition is one of those not-at-all-obvious insights that become blindingly obvious the moment they are expressed.'

He lamented that in a society where BS was so pervasive, 'we have no clear understanding of what bullshit is, why there is so much of it, or what functions it serves. ... In other words, we have no theory' (Frankfurt op cit: 1).

Although Frankfurt does not provide a direct definition of the subject, a summary of his book would define BS as communication that misleads people, short of lying, about the sincerity of the communicator, who is unconcerned and careless about the truthfulness of the message. BS is not false; it is fake. Let's explore this definition in each of its parts.

First, BS is misleading communication, but its intent is not to mislead persons about facts or ideas, but, rather, about impressions. In particular, BS is used to create favourable impressions of the speaker. Frankfurt uses the example of a Fourth of July orator who 'goes on bombastically about "our great and blessed country, whose Founding Fathers under divine guidance created a new beginning for mankind"' (ibid: 18). He calls this humbug (a concept closely related to, and used to establish the premises of BS), not because the speaker regards his statements as false, but because he is trying to convey a certain impression of himself. As Frankfurt explains:

> He is not trying to deceive anyone concerning American history. What he cares about is what people think of *him*. He wants them to think of him as a patriot, as someone who has deep thoughts and feelings about the origins and the mission of our country, who appreciates the importance of religion (ibid).

BS falls short of lying. Liars communicate with the intent to deceive. They wilfully communicate information that they know is false with the intent to mislead others about that information. In the account given above, the orator is not lying. As Frankfurt explains: 'He would be lying only if it were his intention to bring about in his audience beliefs that he himself regards as false, concerning such matters as whether our country is blessed, whether the Founders had divine guidance, and whether what they did was in fact to create a new beginning for mankind' (ibid). So BS isn't lying, but it is used to misrepresent us, or to mislead others about what we really care about.

Frankfurt asserts that BS may be worse than lying because lying acknowledges truth but BS does not. As Frankfurt explains: 'The liar is inescapably concerned with truth-values. In order to invent a lie at all, he must think he knows what is true' (ibid: 51).

> It is impossible for someone to lie unless he thinks he knows the truth. Producing bullshit requires no such conviction. A person who lies is thereby responding to the truth, and he is to that extent respectful of it. When an honest man speaks, he says only what he believes to be true; and for the liar, it is correspondingly indispensable that he considers his

statements to be false. For the bullshitter, however, all these bets are off: he is neither on the side of the true or the side of the false (ibid: 56).

It is the lack of connection to a concern with truth that Frankfurt considers the essence of BS. The BS artist does not care whether what he says is true or not, he just picks out, or makes up, what best fits his purpose. For this reason, Frankfurt considers the bullshitter as a greater enemy to truth than the liar. Both liars and BS artists conceal part of themselves in order to mislead us: the liar hides that he is attempting to lead us away from what he considers to be true; the BS artist hides that he's not really interested in the truth. One feigns truth, the other feigns sincerity.

There is a carelessness, or lack of exactness, in BS that is also troubling. To illustrate this point, Frankfurt uses an account of the philosopher Ludwig Wittgenstein (1889-1951) reprimanding a sick colleague for saying she felt like a dog that had been run over. Wittgenstein reportedly replied: 'You don't know what a dog that has been run over feels like.'

Why was Wittgenstein upset at such an innocuous statement? Because, as Frankfurt surmises: 'Her description of her own feeling is, accordingly, something that she is merely making up. She concocts it out of whole cloth; or, if she got it from someone else, she is repeating it quite mindlessly and without any regard for how things really are' (ibid: 30). Therefore, Wittgenstein perceives her as speaking thoughtlessly about the way she felt. 'Her fault is not that she fails to get it right, but that she is not even trying' (ibid: 31) Why doesn't the BS artist try to get it right, or exact? It's not from a lack of effort or resources. As Frankfurt notes:

> The realms of advertising and of public relations, and the nowadays closely related realm of politics, are replete with instances of bullshit so unmitigated that they can serve among the most indisputable and classic paradigms of the concept. And in these realms there are exquisitely sophisticated craftsmen who – with the help of advanced and demanding techniques of market research, of public opinion polling, of psychological testing, and so forth – dedicate themselves tirelessly to getting every word and image they produce exactly right (ibid: 22-23).

What contributes to BS? 'Bullshit is unavoidable whenever circumstances require someone to talk without knowing what he is talking about' (ibid: 42). When this happens, what comes out amounts to hot air. Hot air is empty, without substance. It doesn't contribute anything useful. For Frankfurt, there are similarities between hot air and BS. 'Just as hot air is speech that has been emptied of all informative content, so excrement is matter from which everything nutritive has been removed. Excrement may be regarded as the corpse of nourishment, what remains when the vital elements have been exhausted' (ibid: 42-43).

WHERE'S THE BS IN PR?

Too often you hear people dismiss information as 'just PR', a bunch of PR, or simply PR, meaning that it already has the connotation of BS. There are several tactics and strategies that contribute to this perception. We would argue that two practices, that of spin and of being a hired gun, are especially harmful.

Spin and hype

Public relations, when it is reduced to spin and hype, is BS. There are many different definitions of spin. For some, spin 'is a lie, plain and simple' (Paul 2005). For others, it is an acceptable technique in a toolbox of powerful tactics 'for the aggressive engineering of perceptions' (Patterson 1999). According to the Merriam-Webster dictionary, spin means: to evolve, express or fabricate by processes of mind or imagination. One journalist from a national newspaper echoes that sentiment: 'Spin doctors work with myth, not with facts' (cited in Dilenschneider 1998).

Sometimes spin is pure falsehood. The famous case involving Hill and Knowlton's front organisation, Citizens for a Free Kuwait, engaged in clear-cut lying about Iraqi atrocities in Kuwait in the lead-up to the 1991 Gulf conflict. When spin is used this way, it might win some battles, but it loses the war over trust and credibility (Hargreaves 2003: 38-39).

Most spin is not concerned with truth, but with results. As one editor of a major magazine said: 'Spin doctors take shortcuts with the truth. To them, the end justifies the means' (cited in Dilenschneider 1998). Therefore, the spinmeister isn't concerned with the truthfulness or accuracy of the message, rather the results. This lack of sincerity for the truth defines spin as BS according to Frankfurt's theory.

Journalist Bryan Appleyard (1999, cited in McNair 2004) discerned this insincerity when writing about the explosion of spin in British politics. He said: 'At a quite refined intellectual level the PRs [sic] and the spinners do not believe in truth and are pretty confident that they will not be found out because nobody else believes it either.' Dilenschneider (op cit) also said: 'Spin doctoring is to public relations what pornography is to art.' This is an apt simile, because pornography has no real value to society, yet poses as art to keep its first amendment protection. Spin does the same thing. It purports to assist our democratic process, but lacks sincere and useful information and, therefore ,'subverts the free flow of information in the public sphere, thwarting the citizen's exercise of rational choice' (McNair op cit: 325). Spin is justified as part of our modern political process when, in fact, it only serves to benefit the self-interests of certain parties, while ignoring the interests of society as a whole.

When PR is reduced to spin, it's bad for you, it's bad for your company, and it's bad for your clients. More importantly, it's bad for the profession. Most importantly, it's bad for society, our collective community where we all reside as citizens. In George Orwell's *Nineteen eighty-four* (1949), he envisioned a society repressed by a dictator who used deception and misdirection. In Aldous Huxley's

Brave new world (1932), society is flooded with so much trivia it can no longer distinguish fact from factoid. As Patterson described the difference: 'Orwell feared truth would be denied us. Huxley feared truth would be drowned in a sea of irrelevance' (Patterson op cit: 733). Again, one tactic is to lie, the other is to use BS. Both harm society.

Hired gun techniques
Many practitioners defend acting on behalf of an organisation's self-interests using what Fitzpatrick and Gauthier (2001) called the attorney-adversary theory of public relations. This approach takes its lead from the judicial system, where the accused has a legal right to an advocate in the adversarial environment of the courts. In the 'court of public opinion', public relations practitioners act as hired advocates. Patterson and Wilkins (2002) explain adversary theory as promoting one-sided or highly selective messages in a marketplace of opinion where multiple opinions are offered. The primary duty of such advocates is to 'vigorously defend the client in public arenas' (Barney and Black 1994: 240). Such advocates need not be concerned with balanced messages nor the effect of their message beyond the immediate interest of their client (ibid). Such a lack of concern can lead to information that is misleading and incomplete, and thereby falls under the definition of BS.

The advocacy theory has been criticised on many levels. Some question the appropriateness of the attorney metaphor. While the judicial process relies on two parties presenting both sides of an argument before an impartial judge or jury, public relations presents information in an environment that is sometimes void of diverse arguments and that can have direct consequences to the audiences receiving the information. As Fitzpatrick and Gauthier noted (op cit: 197): 'With access to only one version of truth, how can the public take responsible action?' Baker (1999: 73) claimed that professional persuasive communicators have an additional responsibility to their publics that is absent from the legal persuasion metaphor. She also argued that it could not meet such moral norms as beneficence, nonmaleficence, reversibility, universalisability and respect for human dignity. Martinson (1998) has criticised the singular duty to plead the cause of a client or organisation in the 'marketplace of ideas' by examining its lack of attention to distributive and social justice.

Additionally, the advocacy model has been compared to a hired gun, where the PR professional has no vested interest in the organisation, its behaviours or its values, but uses its expertise to get messages placed through connections with certain media outlets. The advocate, or hired gun, model for public relations allows the PR practitioner a certain distance from the organisation and products being represented. The practitioner then can use 'plausible deniability' if the messages he or she creates are not entirely factual. However, from a BS perspective, more important is the lack of sincerity, concern or commitment on the part of the advocate. He or she may not be lying *per se*, but the lack of concern for the truthfulness of the message would be something that could transpire more easily because of the roles being played.

TAKING THE BS OUT OF PR

In a speech given in November 2005, Bill Nielsen, former vice-president of communications for Johnson and Johnson, said if public relations practitioners expected to 'stand for the truth and be believed', they had to tell the truth. Good character includes such simple ideas as a sense of civic duty, an innate sense of fairness, the ability to always care, pervasive honesty, respect – for organisations, institutions and for people who may hold different points of view – and personal integrity that is beyond reproach (Nielsen 2005: 5).

Character
To find an ethical solution to the problem of BS in public relations, the industry might create a new code of ethics or place greater emphasis on the public interest. But these solutions are just as susceptible to the insincerity of BS as other extrinsic motivations and influences. The first step to taking the BS out of public relations is taking the BS out of the practitioner and the organisation. A more authentic approach to public relations places responsibility for moral action on practitioners as individuals and organisations as a collective community of individuals. The ethics of virtue addresses issues of character and integrity and focuses more on individual moral substance than on codes of ethics and mission statements. Nielsen contended that character would play a critical 'role in recasting our work together going forward not only at the professional and organisational level but at the societal level as well'. Character, he continued, 'will determine our collective future including the new talent we must continue to attract to build on today's momentum' (ibid: 1).

Nielsen chaffed at the idea of reputation management despite its popularity among today's management. He called the label a 'misnomer' because 'reputation is earned through good character and behaviours that are observed and judged by others who accord reputation value' (ibid: 4). Reputation results from good management, Nielsen continued. He quoted Abraham Lincoln, who said: 'Character is like a tree and reputation like its shadow. The shadow is what we think of it, the tree is the real thing.' The irony is that management has put more focus on what external publics think than on cultivating organisational virtue, the source of good reputation. Nielsen urged fertilising the tree, not the shadow.

The theory that best expresses Nielsen's philosophy is virtue ethics which is concerned with character traits and habits that lead to right action. For example, an honest person has cultivated the virtue of honesty and chooses honesty, not because it is the best policy, but because of a desire for honesty and an aversion to dishonesty. Since the motive for honesty is a character trait of the person, the attributes of the individual and the act are in harmony. For the virtuous practitioner, honesty is a habit, a trait of character and conscience commitment, not a duty or reasoned calculation of good versus bad outcomes. The virtuous organisation may consist of a collection of individuals with character but more likely its character traits are embedded in constitutional elements, such as its operations, practices, rituals and culture. It is the values that old members look for in new recruits or expect to inculcate through training, cultural rituals and expectations, and rewards and discipline.

Persons or organisations with character cultivate virtues as part of their character development. Right action is the product of good character. Duties, rules and the greater good play secondary roles to being virtuous and having moral goodness. Moral action is learned from doing what the virtuous person would do. Aristotle, the founding philosopher in virtue ethics, 'recognized that one acquired virtuous character by acting like the person who had such character' (see Alderman 1982). Virtuous models, such as Jesus and Socrates, serve as exemplars of character. They stayed true to their beliefs even though their commitment to character resulted in their deaths. They eschewed fakery and condemned those who used communication to draw attention to themselves rather than to their message. They also used narratives to explain the way virtuous people should act. More important, their personal narratives reinforced what they taught or communicated. This congruity between private beliefs and public expression represents the first step toward achieving authentic communication – sincerity.

Sincerity

> If sincerity is the avoidance of being false to any man through being true to one's own self, we can see that this state of personal existence is not to be attained without the most arduous effort.
>
> Lionel Trilling, 1971

For the last 400 years, sincerity has helped define Western culture. The BS artist, on the other hand, values expediency and invokes sincerity or insincerity depending upon the desired public impression. Trilling defined sincerity as 'congruence between the avowal and actual feeling' (1971: 2). Simply using one's expertise becomes problematic if the public relations practitioner creates a message inconsistent with his or her true feelings. Sincere communication should accurately reflect the beliefs and values of the communicator. If the values communicated differ from the personal values espoused by the communicator, it represents a moral disconnect that deceives the audience as to the communicator's true beliefs. A common example of this kind of communication is when a public relations spokesperson claims an executive has resigned to spend more time with his or her family. The truth or falsity of the message is not as important as deflecting criticism and scrutiny from outside interests. The public relations practitioner knows the information is insincere, but communicates the information as if the executive sincerely wants a family-friendly position.

Another potential disconnect emerges from differences between individual character traits and organisational character. Virtue scholars disagree as to whether organisational character is a product of collective action or the goals, principles and procedures that shepherd right action (Wilbur 1984). For public relations, the latter definition is most likely true. Again, the question is whether one's personal values mesh with the organisation's character. The incongruity between the two is illustrated in the experience of a consultant for a multinational corporation who asked the company's top management to spend the morning reflecting on their top five to seven personal values (Pruzan 2001). He then had the managers merge into groups of seven and determine what values were most important to the group. In the afternoon session, the consultant went through the same procedure, only this time he asked the executives to identify what the five to seven most important values of the organisation were. The results surprised the consultant as well as the managers; their personal values failed to match up with their perception of the organisation's values.

This disconnection between personal and organisational values poses a problem for public relations practitioners who communicate organisational values to the public. Their role in an organisation as communicators of an organisation's values, vision, identity and intentions often means they disseminate messages contrary to their personal beliefs. As individuals representing the organisation, they must somehow identify, articulate and sometimes defend actions that they themselves did not directly plan or execute. History is replete with examples of public mouthpieces relaying information they assumed to be true but later learned was incomplete or inaccurate. No matter what the personal integrity of practitioners, their sincerity is irrevocably tied to their confidence in the character of top management and management's commitment to the organisation's values. The practitioner's loyalty is only morally defensible if he or she, first, believes in the morality of the organisation and its leaders, and second, believes that he or she can influence the decisions of those leaders (Stoker 2005). In an age of economic downturns and intense media and new media scrutiny, organisations are relying more and more on individual practitioners to apply a BS test to company communication.

Another potential disconnect arises from the agency-client relationship. In the most ideal situation, the character traits of the person would match those of the organisation. The practitioner could act as a conscience for the organisation because personal aversions to unethical behaviour would be consistent to collective or institutional aversions to unethical behaviour. For example, if the organisation refuses to disclose bad news, the practitioner could identify the action as deceptive and thus inconsistent with the organisation's aversion to deceptive behaviour. In other words, the practitioner identifies the virtue trait associated with the action and urges the client to be sincere in its communication.

Just having the expertise to represent a company does not fulfil the practitioner's moral responsibility. To use one's expertise to communicate an inauthentic message would be insincere, not only for the practitioner but for the organisation. To overcome this problem, the practitioner would have the moral obligation to help an organisation abandon actions that the practitioner and publics consider damaging, correct the damage that has occurred and change so that the damaging behaviour does not re-occur. These changes should bring the organisation's values more closely in line with the personal and professional values of the practitioner. Then the practitioner could authentically use non-moral virtues, such as advocacy, expertise and independence to assist in rebuilding the moral character of the company. As the organisation communicated values consisted with its character, it would become more sincere and more authentic.

Authenticity
Striving for more authenticity in communications is the final step to reducing BS in public relations. Nielsen's concept of PR people with character will go far to advance the integrity of the field. But good character alone may not fully reduce or eliminate BS from public relations. To reduce disconnects between character and public action, practitioners will need to have moral autonomy. To make authentic moral decisions, they must be able to act independently of all influences that might nullify their humanity and their commitment to character, truth and genuine communication. Even people of good character can succumb to extrinsic aesthetic pressures. Aesthetic pressures are often associated with beauty, but philosophers might also define aesthetics as physical, emotional or psychological needs. It might be hard to do the right thing when it could cost one his or her livelihood. It is difficult to avoid faking or softening the message if it harms the reputation of friends and colleagues. It also is tempting to use colourful, clever language, even humour, to draw attention away from the message. Thus, in addition to sincerity and character, BS-free public relations demands authenticity.

The definitions of authenticity vary from the dictionary's emphasis on being original, real and genuine to the philosophers' elusive concept of becoming an individual, an actor who achieves selfhood. Most philosophers focused on the negative aspects of inauthenticity, worrying more about the individual who surrenders self to social norms and values than about the positive implications of an individual who becomes truly authentic (see Golomb 1995). Part of the reason for this rejection of societal structures and institutions stems from a fear that outside forces would rob individuals of their freedom and thus their responsibility for their own lives. The existentialist philosophers distrusted religion, government, culture, tradition, or anything that might inhibit individuals from becoming distinctive and independent.

The last century has witnessed an evolution of society in which the oppressive structures of the past have given way to greater pluralism and freedom. The internet has increased access to new ideas, created virtual communities and expanded commerce. Though inequities still abound, there is more opportunity for individual choice, even in countries once dominated by totalitarian regimes. It would seem that the existentialists' fear of becoming part of the crowd, losing the chance to make choices and being enslaved by tradition and culture have abated. The truth is, however, that the corporate world, with its infatuation with buying, selling and the bottom line, has marginalised the individual in ways the existential philosophers could not have foretold. Position, power and authority bestowed by society or by the corporate world endanger our very nature, our very selfhood. The opinion of others, the label placed upon us by society, becomes more important than our 'sentiment of being', one's regard for who he or she is as a human being, a knowledge of one's own existence (Trilling op cit: 92-93).

Being authentic requires a strong sense of self. Citing philosophers concerned with a sense of self, Trilling provided the following explanation of how strength and authenticity are related:

> The sentiment of being is the sentiment of being strong. Which is not to say powerful: Rousseau, Schiller, and Wordsworth are not concerned with energy directed outward upon the world in aggression and dominance, but, rather, with such energy as contrives that the centre shall hold, that the circumference of the self keep unbroken, that the person be an integer, impenetrable, perdurable, and autonomous in being if not in action (ibid: 99).

In the same way that Nielsen has stood up against the tide moving the industry toward reputation management, authentic public relations practitioners think for themselves and help organisations and professions see the world a way that is at once individual and collective. The individual must stand tall for his or her beliefs and interpretation of the events in order for others to identify with him or her. Nielsen was expressing his view of the future of PR, but it resonated with many in the audience who shared similar experiences, values and beliefs. At the same time, it may have been mocked or ridiculed by others who saw it as praiseworthy rhetoric, but not rooted in the reality of the practice. An authentic person is not as concerned with how well the message is received as much as how well it represents his or her true thoughts. This is the opposite of BS as Frankfurt defined it. Some might question whether the lone practitioner can even have enough influence in a rule-governed organisation, but as Utilitarian John Stuart Mill argued, it is not incumbent that people transform an entire company or society, but that they seek to serve the private utility of those around them (Mill 2002 [1859]). We have to trust that sincere, authentic communication has universal appeal and will resonate with like-minded people everywhere.

Public relations achieves authenticity when it gains the strength to eliminate or reduce the disconnections between the personal and the professional and achieve moral congruity among internal beliefs, conscious commitments and external actions. To accomplish this task, practitioners must be able to separate themselves from external forces that demand conformity and develop courage of character. The authentic public relations person would be a work in progress, strong in character but open to further development and refinement. This requires confidence and humility, commitment and tolerance. Indeed, the authentic public relations practitioner heeds Nielsen's challenge of becoming a person of character, to becoming a truly BS-free communicator.

CONCLUSION

If the profession of public relations hopes to reverse the negative perception that it is replete with hacks and flaks, then it must embrace sincere and authentic practices that develop the character of honesty and integrity. Such efforts can't be 'purely strategic' in an effort to manage perceptions and images, thereby becoming inauthentic themselves. The first step has to be for each practitioner to look inward and evaluate his or her practice for occasions of insincerity and inauthenticity. If these practices have had temporary success in advancing organisational goals and objectives, they have also had lasting detrimental effects on the overall credibility of professional communicators. Like stalagmites on the floor of caves, which are formed from the dripping of mineralised solutions, the cumulative effect of these practices leaves deposits of cynicism and mistrust that build up resistance to truthful and genuine messages.

According to an Arthur W. Page Society (2007) white paper on *The authentic enterprise*, 'authenticity would be the coin of the realm for successful corporations and for those who lead them' (p. 6). This can only hold true if corporate communicators are steadfast in their commitment to these principles. There is no question that this can be a very difficult task for the practice of public relations, because words and messages deal as much with perceptions as they do with reality. But as long as the messages hold true to the genuine actions and character of an organisation, the efforts can remain authentic. Where the fabric of authenticity begins to unravel is when organisations attempt to please all parties and be liked by all.

If you are authentic, you can't be everything to everyone, which is certainly a temptation within the public relations practice. But that doesn't mean that an organisation can't be something different to each of its publics, depending on their connection to the organisation. In the parable of the blind men and the elephant, each of the blind men perceived the elephant as something different – a fan, a rope, a tree trunk – depending on what they touched. The elephant wasn't trying to be these things; it was just being an elephant (being authentic). Often stakeholders are blind to the other operations of an organisation. Consumers may not be aware of how employees view the company, etc. But if an organisation tries to be one thing to employees and something else to consumers, then, in today's more transparent communication environment, the incongruities will be exposed. Authentic organisations try to stay consistent with their values, even if different publics interpret them differently.

The challenge for the authentic communicator is reconciliation. First, to be sincere, as Trilling defined it, communicators must reconcile themselves and their values with those of the organisation they represent. Second, communicators must reconcile misperceptions of publics with the genuine actions and values of an organisation. If the organisation is being misunderstood, the authentic communicator must use accurate, sincere and genuine messages to correct those misunderstandings. Third, the authentic communicator must use two-way communication to determine whether the organisation is acting in ways that are inconsistent with its espoused values and practices. In this case, the communicator needs to help the organisation listen to its stakeholders to reconcile its own behaviour.

- This paper was first published in *Ethical Space*, Vol. 7, Nos 2 and 3 pp 61-69, 2010

REFERENCES

Alderman, Harold (1982) By virtue of a virtue, *Review of Metaphysics*, Vol. 36 pp 127-153

Appleyard, Bryan (1999) We are all liars now, *Sunday Times*, 30 May

Arthur W. Page Society (2007) *The authentic enterprise*. Available online at http://www.awpagesociety.com/site/resources/white_papers/, accessed on 23 April, 2008

Baker, Sherry (1999) Five baselines for justification in persuasion, *Journal of Mass Media Ethics*, Vol. 14, No. 2 pp 69-81

Barney, Ralph and Black, Jay (1994) Ethics and professional persuasive communications, *Public Relations Review*, Vol. 20, No. 3 pp 233-248

Bok, Sissela (1999) *Lying: Moral choice in public and private life*, New York, Vintage

Dilenschneider, Robert L. (1998) Spin: A high risk strategy: Bulldog reporter and PR newswire media relations conference, New York, 28 April

Edelman (2009) *2009 Edelman trust barometer*. Available online at http://www.edelman.com/trust/2009/, accessed on 1 May 2009

Fitzpatrick, Kathy and Gauthier, Candace (2001) Toward a professional responsibility theory of public relations ethics, *Journal of Mass Media Ethics*, Vol. 16, Nos 2 and 3 pp 193-212

Frankfurt, H. G. (2005) *On bullshit*, Princeton, NJ, Princeton University Press

Fukuyama, Francis (1995) *Trust: The social virtues and the creation of prosperity*, New York, The Free Press

Golomb, Jacob (1995) *In search of authenticity: From Kierkegaard to Camus*, London, Routledge

Hargreaves, Ian (2003) Spinning out of control, *History Today*, March pp 38-39

Martinson, David L. (1998) A question of distributive and social justice: Public relations practitioners and the marketplace of ideas, *Journal of Mass Media Ethics*, Vol. 13 pp 141-151

McNair, Brian (2004) PR must die: Spin, anti-spin and political public relations in the UK, 1997-2004, *Journalism Studies*, Vol. 5, No. 3 pp 325-338

Medsger, Betty (2004). Journalists who lie, journalists who die. Available online from http://www.poynter.org, accessed on 3 February

Mill, John Stuart (2002 [1859]) *The basic writings of John Stuart Mill: On liberty, The subjection of women, and Utilitarianism*, New York, Modern Library

Nielsen, Bill (2005) The character of public relations at 2005, 44th Annual Distinguished Lecture and Awards Dinner, Institute for Public Relations, 10 November. Available online at http://www.instituteforpr.com/lecture.phtml?article_id=44th_lecture, accessed on 1 May 2009

Noah, Timothy (2005) Defining bullshit: A philosophy professor says it's a process, not a product, *Slate*. March. Available online at http://www.slate.com/id/2114268/, accessed on 1 May 2009

Paul, Mike (2005) The PR industry's Pinocchio reputation needs a nose job, *PR News*, Vol. 39, No. 61 p. 1

Patterson, James (1999) Ethics still count, *Vital Speeches of the Day*, Vol. 65 pp 731-734

Patterson, Philip and Wilkins, Lee (2002) *Media ethics: Issues and cases*, New York, McGraw Hill Companies Inc., fourth edition

Pruzan, Peter (2001) The question of organizational consciousness: Can organizations have values, virtues and visions?, *Journal of Business Ethics*, Vol. 29 pp 271-284

Stoker, Kevin (2005) Loyalty in public relations: When does it cross the line between virtue and vice?, *Journal of Mass Media Ethics*, Vol. 20, No. 4 pp 269-287

Trilling, Lionel (1997) *Sincerity and authenticity*, Cambridge, MA, Harvard University Press

Wilbur, James B. (1984) Corporate character: Corporate governance and institutionalizing ethics. Proceedings of the Fifth National Conference on Business Ethics. Lexington, MA, Lexington Books

NOTE ON THE CONTRIBUTORS

Brad Rawlins is the interim Dean of the College of Liberal Arts and Communication at Arkansas State University. He has served in various administrative positions at Arkansas State, including as the senior academic officer of a campus he helped open in Querétaro, México. He is involved in the accreditation of journalism and mass communications programmes and his research interests continue to include elements of ethics, trust and transparency.

Kevin L. Stoker, PhD, is Professor and Director of the Hank Greenspun School of Journalism and Media Studies at the University of Nevada, Las Vegas. He researches in media ethics, history and philosophy. In 2020, he published the book, *Paradox in public relations: A contrarian critique of theory and practice*, with Routledge. He's also an avid cyclist and bogey golfer.

Chapter 14

Communicating mental illness and suicide: Public relations students' perceptions of ethical practice

Kate Fitch

Mental illness and suicide are complex issues which have significant social and economic implications. This study investigates the perceptions of public relations students in Australia towards ethics, following exposure to resources developed to educate students about the ethical challenges in communicating mental health issues. The findings suggest students recognise ambiguity around 'professional' ethics in relation to these issues; the need for personal responsibility in ethical public relations practice; that ethical development is incremental and that they learn most effectively through major assignments. The study includes recommendations for the teaching of ethics in relation to complex issues such as mental health.

Keywords: public relations, ethics, education, mental illness, suicide

INTRODUCTION
Mental illness and suicide are significant social issues. For example, in Australia mental illness is estimated to cost the economy A$20 billion each year (Council of Australian Governments 2006). More people die from suicide than from the combined total of motor vehicle accidents and homicide in Australia, where it is the leading cause of death for men aged under 44 and women aged under 34, and suicides cost the economy an estimated A$17.5 billion annually (ConNetica Consulting 2009, 2010). These figures do not address the social and emotional impact on family, friends and work colleagues. Challenges in addressing mental health issues include considerable stigma and misconceptions about these issues in the community (Herrman, Saxena and Moodie 2004; ConNetica Consulting 2010).

The Response Ability Project for Public Relations Education is managed by the Hunter Institute for Mental Health, a not-for-profit organisation funded by the

Australian government as part of the Mindframe National Media Initiative. The project develops teaching resources for higher education so that public relations graduates, as future communication practitioners, will be more aware of, and able to respond sensitively and appropriately to, issues relating to mental illness and suicide in professional contexts. A pilot study was run in several universities in 2009 (Mason and Skehan 2009), and the resources made widely available to Australian public relations educators in 2010.

This study investigates the recognition by final-year public relations students of professional ethics, and of the communication challenges around mental illness and suicide, following the use of Response Ability resources. The aim of this research is to investigate how public relations students respond to the introduction of complex social issues such as suicide and mental illness in their curricula in order to understand the pedagogical and curricular implications. The broader issue is the need to understand how students recognise professional responsibility and, indeed, the ethical challenges which they may need to engage with in their future careers.

The study makes specific recommendations regarding the teaching of ethics and ethical practice, particularly in relation to social issues around mental health, to public relations students. The research design uses surveys and a focus group to investigate students' knowledge after exposure to Response Ability resources in at least two units (i.e. the discrete subjects which make up the public relations major). The findings allow the development of recommendations for teaching public relations ethics in higher education, particularly in relation to complex and sensitive social issues such as mental illness and suicide.

BACKGROUND

Public relations and ethics

Public relations educators and professional associations differ in their perceptions of public relations ethics (Breit and Demetrious 2010). For example, ethical practice in the industry is orientated towards the client, profit and competitive advantage; however, in public relations education, where public relations is perceived as a communication (rather than a management) discipline, there is more focus on the broader social role of public relations (Breit and Demetrious 2010). One issue is that public relations is potentially very powerful in terms of shaping public opinion, and can have a significant impact on community attitudes and behaviour (Bowen 2005), meaning 'practitioners have the obligation to act … in a socially responsible way' (Starck and Kruckeberg 2003: 37). Fitzpatrick and Gauthier argue ethical standards should include 'considerations such as the welfare of others, the avoidance of injustice, respect for self and others, and the common good' (2001: 198). Public relations education must, therefore, consider the practitioner's ethical responsibilities 'to yourself as a person, your profession and the wider community' (Breit 2007: 308).

Public relations, education and mental health

Mental illness and suicide are complex issues which have significant economic and social implications. In 2007 in Australia, one in five people suffered a mental disorder, where a mental disorder refers to an anxiety, mood or substance abuse disorder (Australian Bureau of Statistics [ABS] 2009). Suicide is the leading cause of death in men aged under 44 and women aged under 34 in Australia (ConNetica Consulting 2010). Challenges in addressing mental health issues include the considerable stigma associated with mental illness and suicide and a lack of accurate information about mental health in the community.

Public relations practitioners may play a role, by recognising the need to develop socially responsible and ethical communication practices to reduce stigma and discrimination around mental health issues in the community; to be mindful of the link between communicating specific information around suicide and the potential for copycat behaviour; and to recognise that public relations practitioners may have to make choices regarding 'the use of appropriate language, branding and promotions, communication materials, managing media relations and managing your clients, colleagues and partners', where a knowledge of these complex social issues can influence socially responsible practice (Hunter Institute of Mental Health 2010a: 1).

Mental health issues, therefore, raise ethical challenges for public relations practitioners who must consider the social impact of their communication activity. These issues also challenge public relations educators as research suggests many students fail to make the connection between practical tasks and academic learning, or to demonstrate reflexivity around their role and responsibilities as future professionals (Fitch 2011). In addition, 'students learn when they build on their previous experiences, have authentic learning tasks and engage in meaningful activity, and have social interaction and critical dialogue around social issues' (Cooper, Orrell and Bowden 2010: 49). The challenge for educators is to design a curriculum which encourages a 'critical dialogue around social issues' such as mental illness and suicide.

THE RESPONSE ABILITY FOR PUBLIC RELATIONS EDUCATION PROJECT

The Mindframe National Media Initiative was developed in response to a growing body of research, which demonstrated certain representations of suicide in the media could influence the risk of copycat behaviour in vulnerable people (Pirkis and Blood 2001, 2010) and that media representations tended to portray mental illness in negative and stereotypical ways (Pirkis et al. 2001, 2008), which can influence community attitudes and lead to stigma and discrimination. The Response Ability project began in 1998 and aimed to influence journalism education to promote the responsible and accurate representation of suicide and mental illness in the media; it developed a range of multimedia resources for use in teaching (Sheridan

Burns and Hazell 1998; Greenhalgh and Hazell 2005; Skehan, Sheridan Burns and Hazell 2009).

In 2009, six Australian universities participated in a pilot project, Response Ability for Public Relations Education, and the resources were made more widely available in 2010 (see www.responseability.org). The website provides curriculum resources, including case studies, fact sheets and discussion questions for both lecturers and students, and is designed to introduce students to the ethical issues involved in communicating about mental illness and suicide. According to the Hunter Institute of Mental Health, 'the aim of the resources is to enhance the knowledge and skills of students so they are prepared to respond appropriately to communication issues surrounding suicide and mental illness' (2010b).

Public relations educators found the Response Ability resources 'useful, easy to use, of high quality and well presented' (Mason and Skehan 2009: 19). Students found the resources interesting and relevant, but few accessed the website or demonstrated improved knowledge of communication issues concerning mental illness and suicide (ibid). In addition, students often failed to recognise the issues in terms of their relevance for communication ethics and professional practice; rather they continued to offer responses to survey questions which suggested interpersonal communication with individuals who were either experiencing a mental illness or considering suicide (ibid).

METHODOLOGY

This study investigates how students perceive ethics in public relations in relation to mental illness and suicide. The investigation provides useful insights for incorporating ethics into public relations curricula, particularly in relation to communicating complex social issues such as mental health. The research design employs a survey and a small focus group, which allows a complex and potentially controversial topic to be managed with sensitivity (Daymon and Holloway 2011). The researcher's university granted ethics approval (ethics permit 2011/009). In order to maintain a distinction between students' unit assessment and their participation in this research, students were recruited from a final-year unit where the researcher had no teaching role.

Participation in the research was voluntary. Forty-five students completed a survey regarding their attitudes towards, and their awareness of, mental health issues in relation to public relations practice. Students responded to open-ended questions designed to assess knowledge of the Response Ability principles, understanding of ethics and how their studies contributed to that understanding. A thematic analysis was conducted to identify dominant and sub-dominant themes. In addition, units identified by students as useful in developing their understanding of ethical practice in relation to mental illness and suicide were ranked in terms of frequency. Students also rated their level of agreement with a number of statements about public relations practice. The researcher recoded responses into a nominal scale of disagree/agree and used chi-square to investigate demographic differences.

Following initial coding of the surveys, eight undergraduate students were invited to participate in a focus group; four students (two female, two male) accepted. A focus group offers 'rich data that is cumulative and elaborative' (Fontana and Frey 2000: 652) to emerge from the interaction between participants (Krueger and Casey 2000), allowing the researcher to investigate in more depth the themes which emerged from the surveys. An independent facilitator led the focus group discussion regarding professional and personal understandings of ethics in relation to communication and mental health, using stimulus material (a hypothetical scenario involving the suicide of a colleague and the Public Relations Institute of Australia's [PRIA] Individual Code of Ethics) to encourage students to discuss the ethical issues and responsibilities from a public relations perspective. The discussion was recorded using a digital voice recorder and transcribed. The transcription was analysed in terms of the dominant and sub-dominant themes. As a form of member-checking, a two-page summary of the analysis was offered to focus group participants (Lincoln and Guba 1985). Participants agreed that the summary accurately represented the focus group discussion.

SCOPE AND LIMITATIONS OF THE STUDY

This study reports public relations student perceptions of ethical challenges in relation to mental illness and suicide. Participants are enrolled in a public relations degree located in a communication school at an Australian university; their responses may not be generalisable.

The research project investigated more broadly student understandings of professional ethics. However, the focus of this paper is the student response to the introduction of mental health topics and their perceptions of the ethical implications for public relations practice. Although focus groups are not usually considered appropriate for sensitive topics (Fontana and Frey 2000), a small focus group is suitable for complex, potentially contentious topics (Daymon and Holloway 2011) and may be more comfortable for the participants (Krueger and Casey 2000). Focus groups 'take various forms depending on their purposes' (Fontana and Frey 2000: 651) and can be as small as two or three people (Wilkinson 2004; Daymon and Holloway 2011).

KNOWLEDGE OF MENTAL HEALTH ISSUES IN RELATION TO PROFESSIONAL COMMUNICATION

Knowledge of Response Ability principles
Following exposure to Response Ability resources, many students articulated the need to be 'sensitive' when communicating about mental illness and suicide. However, the survey results suggested they could not demonstrate knowledge of the

specific guidelines in the resources. For example, participants were asked to 'name three things that are important to consider when communicating about suicide'. Despite exposure to the resources in at least two units, 89 per cent of participants could not give three answers consistent with Response Ability principles. Eleven per cent of students could give three answers, and a further 53 per cent could give some (i.e. one or two) responses consistent with the principles. Similarly, participants were asked to 'name three things that are important to consider when communicating about mental illness'. Ninety-three per cent gave answers not consistent with Response Ability principles. Seven per cent of students could give three answers consistent with Response Ability principles and a further 56 per cent could give some (i.e. one or two) responses consistent with Response Ability principles.

As in the evaluation of the pilot study, a significant number of students understood the question in terms of interpersonal communication rather than the professional implications for public relations, suggesting the need for educators to emphasise professional obligations. The problem may relate to the way the question was worded as 'the answers provided seemed to reflect that students believed the question was about talking directly to a person who is thinking about ending their life/has a mental illness, rather than about communicating about these issues from a public relations perspective' (Mason and Skehan 2009: 19).

Communicating mental health issues
Focus group participants demonstrated familiarity with the Response Ability principles, in that they recognised the ethical implications for the practitioners and knew how to avoid conveying specific information regarding the location and method of suicides and to encourage help-seeking behaviour: 'You're not allowed to put any details of how they did it, and you have to provide contact numbers … for Lifeline and things like that.' The students were asked if they found discussing complex scenarios such as this useful in terms of their own learning and responded positively: 'Suicide, I think, is one of the hardest issues to communicate about because it's so sensitive' and 'Because these are things that you may have to deal with when you get out into the world.'

Students also stated that they thought working through such scenarios reinforced 'really how important it is to have certain ethical guidelines'. Ultimately, students recognised the responsibility for making socially responsible decisions rests with the individual practitioner: 'The responsibility I think still stays with you – you have a responsibility to the [organisation] and that person, especially in this situation to that person. And then there's the responsibility to yourself to act ethically too.'

Professional ethics and mental health issues
The students were critical of the Code of Ethics produced by the PRIA, primarily because it emphasised reputational issues for the industry rather than considered the social impact of public relations activity: 'It is mostly financial ethics rather than …

I don't even know what the word would be … but I guess emotional ethics.' Focus group participants did not find the code useful as an articulation of professional ethics, particularly following the discussion of suicide in the stimulus scenario: 'I don't find any of this relevant at all.' At the same time, students acknowledged the difficulty in developing a code which would address the diversity of public relations practice. However, the need to consider the impact of public relations activity on others i.e. the social dimension of public relations was a strong topic of discussion. Students perceived an over-emphasis in the Code of Ethics on risk and reputation management at the expense of social responsibility.

STUDENTS' PERCEPTIONS OF ETHICS AND EDUCATION

Developing understandings of ethical practice

Both survey and focus group participants perceived they learnt most about the communication issues around mental illness and suicide by completing a major assignment on the topic: 'You actually have to make a decision when you are making the campaign, instead of just talking about it.' This finding echoes the results of a study which interviewed journalism students who had entered an award designed to encourage responsible reporting of mental health: 'The majority of students indicated that they had learnt more about suicide and mental illness through their personal research in preparing a health or suicide piece,' despite exposure to Response Ability resources in their studies (Romeo et al. 2008: 127). Assessment tasks define learning objectives for students (Biggs 2003); exposure at university to such tasks was considered important by focus group participants: 'Because you don't really learn that much until you actually put it into practice.'

Eighty-nine per cent of students surveyed reported at least one unit from the public relations programme as useful in developing their understanding of ethical practice in relation to mental health issues. The most frequently cited unit was one which included a major assignment on mental health the previous semester. The next most cited units were: one which participated in the Response Ability pilot study in 2009 and continued to use the resources; a real-client unit, where students developed campaigns for not-for-profit organisations, and a research unit, which introduced research ethics and methodology. Neither of these units employed Response Ability resources, although both units encouraged students to consider the social impact and ethical implications of public relations activity.

Focus group participants perceived the emphasis on ethics in their public relations studies, in contrast to other disciplines, as important and valuable. However, units from courses (such as sociology and commerce); journalism (which has used Response Ability journalism resources extensively) and public relations units which had not used Response Ability resources (such as the real-client and research units) were identified by some students as contributing to their understanding of ethics and ethical behaviour in public relations practice in relation to mental health issues. This result is surprising, but confirms that students perceive their development of professional responsibility and understanding of ethical practice builds on their prior learning.

ETHICS OF USING MENTAL HEALTH ISSUES IN TEACHING

It is important to acknowledge one survey response, where a student wrote of their experience of completing a major assignment relating to mental health:

> I think I had a distasteful assignment lacking ethical consideration based purely and only on choosing an assignment topic of mental health – I learnt PR isn't about ethics and teachers 'teaching' me about considering people – an aim to offend NO-ONE is rubbish. I was disgusted with this assignment.

Although this response was the only negative comment received in the surveys (N = 45), it illustrates that some students find material related to mental health issues confronting, posing a challenge for educators who may consider scaffolding the ethical communication of mental health issues in a degree. The Response Ability project offers advice on teaching sensitive material and recognises that some people find the topics challenging.

Although this issue may be resolved by offering students a choice of assignments, such an approach means not all graduates will develop knowledge of mental health issues in relation to public relations practice. In the semester prior to this study, one lecturer responded to a similar concern about the use of mental health as an assignment topic, justifying its inclusion because of its significance to, and insufficient awareness in, the community. These student concerns suggest careful planning across a curriculum needs to occur to ensure that potentially challenging content, such as the Response Ability resources, are incorporated appropriately into the structure of a degree, and are not over-used, i.e. a programme-wide approach to the introduction of the resources should be adopted.

Cultural diversity and mental health issues

Survey participants viewed ethics as sensitivity to, or empathy with, others: 'Ethics, to me, is consideration of other genders, religious beliefs, politics, etcetera and the ability to maintain a compassionate view of the world.' Other students extrapolated the idea of sensitivity to others, by defining ethics as an awareness of the social impact of one's actions or behaviour: 'the consideration of how our actions will affect others.' Most participants recognised that ethics involved a determination of what was socially acceptable, with a significant cohort recognising that ethics would vary due to culture and context.

Therefore, students perceived ethics as a dynamic process, where ethics varies depending on the particular social context. This finding suggests that educators should be aware of the different cultural experiences students bring to the classroom

(Billett 2004) and should highlight the impact of culture and context on ethics in their teaching. However, this paper does not advocate that a cultural relativist approach should be adopted; rather, an understanding of socio-cultural contexts must be considered in relation to ethics and public relations.

Students have diverse experiences, which influence their learning and their understanding of ethics. Although chi-square tests revealed little statistical significance in responses by demographics for most questions, in relation to the statement: 'public relations practitioners cannot be responsible for the impact that their campaigns may have on members of the community, such as those people living with mental illness', a higher proportion of Australian students were more likely to disagree with this statement than international students. Such differences need to be addressed in the classroom, particularly given the diversity of students in, and the increasing internationalisation of, public relations education. Teaching resources should be multicultural and introduce cultural difference. In particular, understandings of mental health and attitudes towards mental illness and suicide vary across cultural, socio-economic and political contexts (Herrman, Saxena and Moodie 2004: 20-23).

Students in Malaysia, for example, are accustomed to graphic and detailed reporting of suicide in newspapers and may not recognise the impact of such reporting on suicide rates. The culturally diverse understandings of mental illness and suicide need to be taken into account when developing a public relations campaign. Embracing cultural diversity develops in students not only an awareness of difference but also explicitly the ways in which public relations practice can be socially responsible and culturally relevant (Chia 2009).

IMPLICATIONS FOR PUBLIC RELATIONS EDUCATION

This study is concerned with the ethical challenges in relation to mental illness and suicide for public relations, and makes some initial recommendations for educators to consider how they teach ethics in relation to these issues.

- Public relations activity needs to be considered in terms of its social impact (Starck and Kruckeberg 2003; Bowen 2005; Breit and Demetrious 2010), both on a community and – in the case of mental health issues – on vulnerable members of society (Fitzpatrick and Gauthier 2001). Some students and, indeed, practitioners, assume that professional responsibility relates to effective business practice, neglecting the social elements implicit in both 'social responsibility' and 'public relations'.

- Practical and contextualised learning tasks allow students to apply their understanding of ethics. If they are encouraged to reflect on and share their responses to the task, students have the opportunity to develop their knowledge of ethical communication.

- Public relations educators should set a major assessment item on mental illness and suicide. In this way, students will research the field and integrate theory with their understanding of professional practice. However, care should be taken in curriculum planning not to introduce multiple major assignments on mental health.

- Public relations educators could develop a real-client project or service learning activity involving mental health. Students may share their experiences and responses to the ethical issues they identify in a structured discussion (Fitch 2011), an approach supported by work-integrated learning scholarship, which advocates students reflect on practical experiences in order to better integrate theory and practice (Billett 2009).

- Public relations classes are diverse; at some Australian universities approximately half are international students (Fitch and Surma 2006). In addition, Australia is considered a multicultural country with one in four Australians born overseas (ABS 2006: 6). Introducing different cultural perspectives of complex social issues offers students an excellent learning opportunity.

CONCLUSIONS

One challenge in this study is the difficulty in isolating Response Ability resources as a single variable in terms of the impact on student learning in relation to ethics. Students, through both the survey responses and the focus group discussion, acknowledged the positive impact of a range of units, the diversity of the student body, and other activities such as paid work on their understanding of ethics in relation to public relations practice. This finding confirms that many factors contribute to students' professional development. From the student perspective, professional and ethical development is incremental and ethics demands a consideration of others, i.e. a recognition of the social impact of public relations, reinforcing other research findings (Bowen 2005; Breit and Demetrious 2010).

Specific knowledge and professional expertise in relation to communicating mental health issues should be scaffolded in a degree. Complex tasks, possibly for assessment, will improve students' understanding and knowledge of communication management in relation to mental illness and suicide. However, such tasks need to be carefully integrated into the curriculum to ensure that students develop appropriate conceptual knowledge to apply to different scenarios. In addition, educators should develop a context- and culturally-sensitive approach, which addresses the reality of both multiculturalism and internationalisation in contemporary public relations.

ACKNOWLEDGEMENTS

This study was funded by the Response Ability Academic Research Scheme, 2010.

- This paper was first published in *Ethical Space*, Vol. 9, No. 1 pp 14-21, 2012

REFERENCES

Australian Bureau of Statistics (2006) Migration, Australia 2004-05 (cat. no. 3412.0). Available online at http://www.ausstats.abs.gov.au/Ausstats/subscriber.nsf/0/9D6824AFE7734DA8CA25713F0016F8C4/$File/34120_2004-05.pdf, accessed on 12 May 2011

Australian Bureau of Statistics (2009) Mental Health, Australian Social Trends 4102.0. Available online at http://www.abs.gov.au/AUSSTATS/abs@.nsf/Lookup/4102.0Main+Features30March%202009, accessed on 12 May 2011

Biggs, John (2003) *Teaching for quality learning at university*, Buckingham, Open University Press/Society for Research into Higher Education, second edition

Billett, Stephen (2004) Workplace participatory practices: Conceptualising workplaces as learning environments, *Journal of Workplace Learning*, Vol. 16, Nos 5 and 6 pp 312-324

Billett, Stephen (2009) Realising the educational worth of integrating work experiences in higher education, *Studies in Higher Education*, Vol. 34, No. 7 pp 827-843

Bowen, Shannon (2005) Ethics of public relations, Heath, Robert L. (ed.) *Encyclopedia of public relations*, Thousand Oaks, CA, Sage Reference pp 294-297

Breit, Rhonda (2007) *Law and ethics for professional communicators*, Chatswood, NSW, LexisNexis Butterworth

Breit, Rhonda and Kristin Demetrious (2010) Professionalisation and public relations: An ethical mismatch, *Ethical Space*, Vol, 7, No. 4 pp 20-29

Chia, Joy (2009) Intercultural interpretations: Making public relations education culturally relevant, *Journal of University Teaching and Learning Practice*, Vol. 6, No. 1. Available online at http://ro.uow.edu.au/jutlp/vol6/iss1/5/, accessed on 12 May 2011

ConNetica Consulting (2009) The estimation of the economic cost of suicide to Australia. Available online at http://www.aph.gov.au/Senate/committee/clac_ctte/suicide/submissions/Add_info05.pdf, accessed on 14 July 2011

ConNetica Consulting (2010) Suicide and suicide prevention in Australia – breaking the silence. Available online at http://suicidepreventionaust.org.tmp.anchor.net.au/wp-content/uploads/2011/07/Breaking-the-Silence.pdf, accessed on 14 July 2011

Cooper, Lesley, Orrell, Janice and Bowden, Margaret (2010) *Work integrated learning: A guide to effective practice*, London and New York, Routledge

Council of Australian Governments (2006) National Action Plan on Mental Health 2006-2011. Available online at http://www.coag.gov.au/coag_meeting_outcomes/2006-07-14/docs/nap_mental_health.pdf, accessed on 14 July 2011

Daymon, Christine and Holloway, Immy (2011) *Qualitative research methods in public relations and marketing communications*, Abingdon and New York, Routledge, second edition

Fitch, Kate (2011) Developing professionals: Student experiences of a real-client project, *Higher Education Research & Development*, Vol. 30, No. 4 pp 1-13

Fitch, Kate and Surma, Anne (2006) The challenges of international education: Developing a public relations unit for the Asian region, *Journal of University Learning and Teaching Practice*, Vol. 3, No. 2 pp 104-113

Fitzpatrick, Kathy and Gauthier, Candace (2001) Toward a professional responsibility theory of public relations ethics, *Journal of Mass Media Ethics*, Vol. 16, Nos 2-3 pp 193-212

Fontana, Andrew and Frey, James (2000) The interview: From structured questions to negotiated text, Denzin, Norman and Lincoln, Yvonna (eds) *Handbook of qualitative research design*, Thousand Oaks, CA, Sage pp 645-672, second edition

Greenhalgh, S and Hazell, Trevor (2005) Student evaluation of the Response Ability Project, *Australian Journalism Review*, Vol. 27, No. 1 pp 43-51

Herrman, Helen, Saxena, Shekhar and Moodie, Rob (eds) (2004) *Promoting mental health: Concepts, emerging evidence, practice*. Summary report from the World Health Organisation, Geneva, Switzerland. Available online at http://www.who.int/mental_health/evidence/en/promoting_mhh.pdf, accessed on 14 July 2011

Hunter Institute of Mental Health (2010a) Issues and impact: Communicating mental illness and suicide (booklet). Available online at http://www.responseability.org/client_images/820717.pdf, accessed on 7 May 2011

Hunter Institute of Mental Health (2010b) Response Ability for public relations. Available online at http://www.himh.org.au/site/index.cfm?display=153913, accessed on 7 May 2011

Krueger, Richard and Casey, Mary Anne (2000) *Focus groups: A practical guide for applied research*, Thousand Oaks, CA, Sage, third edition

Lincoln, Yvonna and Guba, Egon (1985) *Naturalistic inquiry*, Newbury Park, CA, Sage

Mason, Nerida and Skehan, Jaelea (2009) Evaluation report: Response Ability for Public Relations pilot study, Newcastle, Hunter Institute of Mental Health. Available online at http://www.responseability.org/client_images/872504.pdf, accessed on 14 October 2010

Pirkis, Jane and Blood, R. Warwick (2001) Suicide and the media: A critical review, Canberra, Commonwealth Department of Health and Aged Care. Available online at http://www.mindframe-media.info/client_images/372860.pdf, accessed on 21 January 2011

Pirkis, Jane and Blood, R. Warwick (2010) Suicide and the news and information media: A critical review, Canberra, Commonwealth Department of Health and Aged Care. Available online at http://www.mindframe-media.info/client_images/900016.pdf, accessed on 21 January 2011

Pirkis, Jane, Blood, R. Warwick, Francis, Catherine, Putnis, Peter, Burgess, Philip, Morley, Belinda, Stewart, Andrew and Payne, Trish (2001) The media monitoring project: A baseline description of how the Australian media report and portray suicide and mental health and illness, Commonwealth Department of Health and Aged Care, Canberra. Available online at http://www.mindframe-media.info/client_images/372858.pdf, accessed on 21 January 2011

Pirkis, Jane, Blood, R. Warwick, Dare, Andrew, Holland, Kate et al. (2008) The Media Monitoring Project: Changes in media reporting of suicide and mental health and illness in Australia: 2000/01-2006/07, Commonwealth Department of Health an Aged Care, Canberra. Available online at http://www.mindframe-media.info/client_images/900018.pdf, accessed on 10 May 2011

Romeo, Michael, Green, Kerry, Skehan, Jaelea, Visser, Amy, Coan, Lyndall and Hazell, Trevor (2008) Researching and reporting on suicide or mental illness: A student perspective, *Australian Journalism Review*, October, Vol. 30, No. 1 pp 123-130

Sheridan Burns, Lynette and Hazell, Trevor (1998) Response … Ability: Youth suicide and the National University Curriculum Project, *Australian Journalism Review*, Vol. 20, No. 2 pp 111-128

Skehan, Jaelea, Sheridan Burns, Lynette and Hazell, Trevor (2009) The Response Ability project: Integrating the reporting of suicide and mental illness into journalism curricula, *Journalism and Mass Communication Educator*, Vol. 64, No. 2 pp 192-204

Starck, Kenneth and Kruckeberg, Dean (2003) Ethical obligations of public relations in an era of globalisation, *Journal of Communication Management*, Vol. 8, No. 1 pp 29-40

Wilkinson, Sue (2004) Focus group research, Silverman, David (ed.) *Qualitative research: Theory, method and practice*, London, Sage pp 177-199

NOTE ON THE CONTRIBUTOR

Dr Kate Fitch is a Senior Lecturer in the School of Media, Film and Journalism at Monash University in Melbourne, Australia. Her research foregrounds critical and sociocultural understandings of public relations, drawing on historical, feminist and social justice perspectives. Her first monograph, *Professionalizing public relations: History, gender and education* (2016) remains the only book-length, historical investigation of the industry in Australia. Her second book, *Popular culture and social change: The hidden work of public relations* (2021), offers a critical account of the broader societal impact of public relations. Dr Fitch is the co-editor of *Public Relations Inquiry*.

Chapter 22

The object of public relations and its ethical implications for late modern society – a Foucauldian analysis

Kristin Demetrious

This paper draws on a Foucauldian framework to show two distinct ways in which forms of public relations work in the public sphere to suppress the emergence of other coherences and discursive formations, particularly in relation to social movements. It argues that, not only are these practices socially divisive, antagonistic and politically offensive, but they are counter-productive within the conditions of late modernity and must change. Identifying and understanding the causes and effects of unethical public relations will open up new research agendas that help to explore alternative approaches to communication in the public sphere which avoid these consequences.

Keywords: object of public relations, ethics, Foucauld, social movements

INTRODUCTION

For citizens going about daily life – working, shopping, playing sport – the apparatus of unethical public relations and its effects are often hidden and unseen. This is not surprising because public relations' core characteristics of invisibility and persuasion are considered the means to its effectiveness. However, over the last three decades critics of public relations have been vocal about the social effects. A concern is the concealed presence of self-interested 'PR' and its influence in areas such as news media where citizens are likely to engage in interpretative discussion around contested public issues. Another is that some public relations practitioners act in highly unethical ways in relation to activist groups that challenge their activities (Nelson 1989: 131). Critics argue that this is because practitioners bow routinely to the self-interest of their employers, leading to unscrupulous behaviour and deliberate harm to the reputation of the opposition. These factors have highlighted the need to examine the profession's ethical foundations and to acknowledge that public relations as a communicative activity has a fragile relationship to economy, civil and state sectors and democracy that needs to be monitored (Nelson 1989; Stauber and Rampton 1995; Beder 1997; Hager and Burton 1999).

According to media ethicist Breit (2007: xvii), the contemporary public relations industry is a powerful element in a rapidly transforming media environment where technological, social economic and cultural change is 'valorising information' and turning media and communication into 'international commodities'. However, she argues that it is also a problematic profession from a social point of view. This is because it is highly influential and has the potential to exploit news and media outlets 'to the point of setting agendas and becoming primary definers themselves' (ibid: 10). She argues that public relations – which in Australia is largely self-regulatory – must therefore be practised in a reflective way. But this paper asks how do public relations practitioners 'reflect' when often they do not understand what it is precisely that they 'do'? New technologies, such as the internet and 'social media' developments such as Second Life have increased the realm of activity for 'PR' but in tandem with these techno-economic-communicative developments, new critical tools are needed to explicate these social-linguistic processes in order to analyse their broader sometimes negative effects. Knowledge in this area will help to inform decision making in public relations and conduct of individual practitioners by defining stronger and clearer ethical positions, responsibilities and accountabilities (ibid: 308-309).

In tackling these questions, this paper seeks to address a gap in the current discussions and to investigate how public relations practitioners act especially in relation to social groups such as activists and what it is they produce. It will firstly canvass a range of differing professional and academic worldviews within public relations that are relevant to the discussion of activism and communication; secondly it will overview two important communicative theories (Habermas 1995; Foucault 1972) that can be applied to explain some of the unethical activities associated with public relations. Next, the paper will detail a case study of unethical public relations in New Zealand and then apply the Foucauldian and Habermasian theories to several of the campaign texts – discussing the different ways these theories help to understand them. Lastly, the paper will discuss new strategies in teaching and practice of media and communication that point to fairer and more collaborative forms of social and professional relations taking into account the multi-dimensional concepts of ethics, responsibility and accountability in decision making.

THE OBJECT OF 'PR'

An important question in unpacking ethical issues around the practice of public relations is to establish how, as a profession, it relates to others in society and treats its stakeholders. According to Nelson (op cit), Stauber and Rampton (op cit) and Beder (op cit) public relations has a deep and historic animosity to activism. Indeed, much mainstream USA public relations literature lacks reference to and/or frames activists adversarially as undermining their legitimate activities. For example, the work of public relations analyst Larissa Grunig (1992) contains a specific reference to activism but only as something to be 'managed'. She says studying activism helps 'practitioners deal in more than an ad hoc way with the opposition their organizations face from activist groups' (ibid: 503). Deegan reflects a similar defensive view in *Managing activism* (2001), a book endorsed by the Institute of Public Relations, when he discusses that few business organisations are prepared for 'the growing threat' of an 'activist attack', and advises a proactive, rather than reactive, approach in learning how to 'manage' them. In particular, he argues that 'risk communications' (ibid: 94) is a specialist area in the management of public backlash or outrage, if for example 'there is a temptation to gloss over' an 'accidental toxic spillage' ... 'when communicating with key audiences' (ibid: 93).

This explanation of 'risk' is quite unlike sociologist Ulrich Beck's holistic definition of 'risk' as 'hazardous side effects' of the modernisation process. Beck (1992) says that risk in this sense presents global dangers for humanity but importantly signals a break in the logic driving political, social and economic development. As a result of this sub-political movements or activists will occupy a more central social space as the locus of politics (ibid: 20-21). Deegan's ideas about risk are localised and concerned with the micro-management of organisations in trouble with communities over some breach.

He argues, in this case, that 'risk communications' is largely a matter of managing perceptions, because, 'activists often exaggerate the risks associated with an organization' (op cit: 94). Echoing this theme, in 2005, the Victorian branch of the Public Relations Institute of Australia (PRIA Victoria) advertised a workshop conducted by public relations consultant Ross Irvine designed for practitioners to 'beat' activists 'at their own game'. It defined activists as 'special interest groups, lobby groups or NGOs (non-government organizations)' and argued that activists 'believe they know what is best for us – they have assumed moral leadership on many issues globally and they pressure businesses, governments and society to embrace their ideology' (PRIA Victoria 2005). Overall, these sentiments demonstrate that some views about legitimate forms of public relations include a complex and continuing antagonism with civil sector groups such as activists.

However, Larissa Grunig (op cit), Deegan (op cit) and the PRIA Victoria (op cit) are not representative of all the voices within the field of public relations. There are a range of other critical, differing and reflective views about activists. Smith and Ferguson, for example, approach the subject of activism from a more theoretically diverse and socially unifying perspective arguing: '[W]e treat activists, not only as challenges for public relations practitioners but also as practitioners themselves. In developing our views, we draw from political science, sociology, communication and public relations' (Smith and Ferguson 2001: 291). Cheney and Christensen accept criticisms of the professional area by acknowledging that 'public relations can perhaps be accused of trying to maintain discussions within relatively limited Western corporate arenas' (2001: 182). This marked divergence in views about the treatment of activist stakeholders within the field of public relations reflects a level of unresolved tension which this paper argues has significant implications for the future practice and theory of public relations.

THEORISING MEDIA, SOCIETY AND MEANING MAKING

One of the principal theories used by academics and ethicists to understand what it is that public relations practitioners 'do' and the relationship of this to modern society is the work of Habermas (1995). First published in 1962, Jurgen Habermas's *The structural transformation of the public sphere: An inquiry into a category of bourgeois society* is a socio-historic discussion of the public sphere; which can be defined as a conceptual space, separate from the state, where citizens, in a free and open way, engage in dialogue and debate focused around issues for the common good. Habermas examines its evolution, the transformation of its functions and, last, its possible reorganisation and renewal. In theorising media relationships through his communicative concept, Habermas brings into relief a grey, shifting and indistinct area of commercial, state and civic activity focused on the development of representation, authority and legitimacy. In particular, his analysis of public relations is useful to understand the media apparatus that maintains and reproduces power structures in activist debates. It is through this analysis that Habermas sheds light on ideals and the role of public opinion and rationality in shaping the social directions taken by society, government and business in late modern society.

According to Habermas, the genesis of the public sphere can be traced to early Greek and Roman democracies within the social patterns of the polis or city and the idea of lexis or discussion. He explains how the process of citizen discussion clarified issues of social importance: 'only in the light of the public sphere did that which existed become revealed, did everything become visible to all. In the discussion among citizens, issues were made topical and took on shape' (ibid: 4). For Habermas (ibid: 3-5), the idea of the public sphere, as a centre of self-interpretation that promotes the good of its members, gained acceptance in succeeding societies and periods, including modernity. Habermas argues that the changed social and economic conditions associated with the rise of European trade and capitalism created a new middle class with substantial power. These conditions empowered citizens who developed a distinct communicative activity that compelled authorities to justify themselves and their activities to the collective opinion of the people. The public sphere was the realm of communicative activity 'now casting itself loose as a forum in which the private people, come together to form a public, readied themselves to compel public authority to legitimate itself before public opinion' (ibid: 25). By the eighteenth century, Habermas claims, people were using communication 'without historical precedent' as the organising point and the process by which to critique their lives using reason (ibid: 27).

For Habermas, the practices of public relations – unlike advertising which is overt and recognisable as such – are deeply embroiled in the political realm of the public sphere. He claims that the addressee of public relations is the private citizen, not the consumer as such (ibid: 193). For Habermas, this is because public relations is the instrument of specialised commercial interests and its goal is the creation of self-serving public consent in which acceptance takes place. Therefore, for public relations to be successful consumers must be given a false consciousness and believe that they are actually making a decision based on their own judgement about what is good for society. As a result of the proliferation of this activity, Habermas concludes that rational agreement arising from exchanges of different opinion has disappeared from the public sphere because it is ousted by public relations (ibid: 195).

Indeed, he argues (ibid: 193) that invisible public relations which conceals commercial interests and masquerades as discussion for the common good exploits the 'classic idea' of a group of private people using reason to come together as a public for its own self-interested ends. For Habermas, moreover, this form of publicity in modernity is dangerous for democracy because it strengthens prestige and position, without drawing attention to unwanted discussion. Organisations and functionaries become interested in representation, not just from the outside, but through the public sphere as a form of legitimisation (ibid: 201). Public relations is, therefore, more subversive, politically oriented and powerful than advertising because it exploits and invades the process of the formation of public opinion. Hence the work of Habermas provides a useful theoretical framework in which the 'invisible' relationship between public relations and society can be explained and understood.

However, the theories of Habermas have limitations and can be described as approaching analysis from the discipline of the 'history of ideas'. According to Foucault, the history of ideas is a conventional research analysis style that 'sets out to cross the boundaries of existing disciplines, to deal with them from the outside, and to re-interpret them' (1972: 137). He says it takes account of the history of the literature, of science and of philosophy in trying to make connections and sense of themes and relationships, in hoping to 'rediscover the immediate experience that the discourse transcribes' (ibid: 137). As a result, the approach preoccupies itself with its own theme, with establishing continuities 'beginnings and ends' – and hence overlooks knowledge (ibid). In applying this, Habermas can be interpreted as concentrating on understanding *effects* of power within the particular conditions of modernity. Indeed, his (1995: 162) primary concern is the effects of a culture of consumption on the development and maintenance of rational critical debate, particularly in relation to the public sphere.

McHoul and Grace (1993) argue that Foucault approaches analysis from a different point of view. He ontologically detaches himself from the present and seeks to look at the rules that run through discourses but not 'in terms of the defining characteristics of modernity' (McHoul and Grace 1993: 60-61). However, according to Foucault, analysis from the history of ideas should not be abandoned altogether; rather an archaeological approach will yield deeper and more rigorous knowledge. For example, an archaeological approach to the study of communication identifies discourses and the rules by which their practices operate, not the 'thoughts, representations, images, themes, preoccupations that are concealed or revealed in discourses' (Foucault 1972: 138-139). It is also interested more in the object at the core rather than the things that the discourse is saying: 'It is not a return to the innermost secret of the origin; it is the systematic description of a discourse-object' (ibid: 139-140). Considering procedural questions, however, Foucault (ibid: 199) anticipates his work's methodological weaknesses. For example, he concedes that by looking for general rules of discourse he could overlook the significance of temporal phenomena or specific conditions and that he also fails to investigate the role of the speaking subject.

To investigate unethical public relations and its effects, this paper will draw on these two different analyses of power, that is, as a structural discursive investigation (Foucault 1972) and in terms of the significance of temporal phenomena and specific conditions of modernity (Habermas 1995). Therefore, this two-fold analysis provides a rich, complex understanding of power in late modern risk society and addresses the limitations Foucault identified firstly, with an archaeological approach (op cit: 135-140) and secondly with an approach which investigates solely modern society (McHoul and Grace op cit: 60-61). This conceptualisation positions the research not just as an examination of a particular case study of unethical public relations and activism, but more broadly as a study of communicative change and transformation of social structures First published in 1969, *The archaeology of knowledge* (Foucault 1972) proposes a conceptual re-evaluation of methodological approaches to historical analysis and epistemological assumptions such as 'unities' and 'tradition', in an attempt to find what governs their rules of formation. In this work, Foucault explores discourse as central to power and knowledge and historical development. However, as discussed, for Foucault, an investigation of an individual discourse only reveals a narrow and specific understanding. Rather, he is interested in how specific formations such as medicine and law – and public relations – come to exist in the first place.

Foucault's notion of discursive formation is a foundation concept of discourse. 'Discursive formation' refers to the creation of the discourse and the method by which statements disperse and appear through regularity, order and strategic choices (ibid: 38). Discourses are languages with history belonging to a particular formation. Foucault argues that unities or groupings and their discourses, such as medicine or political economy, should only be accepted if they are subject to 'interrogation; to break them up and then to see whether they can be legitimately reformed; or whether other groupings should be made' (ibid: 26). Once ideas about unities are questioned, 'an entire field is set free' (ibid: 26). Therefore, discourses do not remain static, they move, bend and eventually transform – but how does this take place? Foucault argues that 'contradictions' have an important role in understanding how the process of change occurs and how new strategies and concepts come about. He argues that there are two distinct forms of contradiction. On the one hand, some contradictions operate at an intrinsic and surface level from the same discursive formation, under the same conditions of operation of the enunciative function 'without in any way affecting the body of enunciative rules that makes them possible' (ibid: 153). On the other hand some 'are *extrinsic* contradictions that reflect the opposition between distinct formations' (ibid: 153; italics in original).

Foucault's notion of objects in discursive formations is also one of the central research concepts that I use in understanding unethical public relations. He argues that objects do not exist somewhere waiting to be found. Instead, they have a 'normative' relationship with a society or one which can be defined as conforming to social expectations that 'imply legitimacy consent and prescription' (Abercrombie, Hill and Turner 1994: 288). Foucault cites the normative example of 'motor disturbances, hallucinations and speech disorders' that were once understood to be manifestations of madness, but were subsequently redefined through psychopathology (op cit: 40). Foucault's analysis of these socially constructed 'objects' is to find out 'the first *surfaces* of their *emergence*' (italics in original) in order to understand what they do (ibid: 41). He argues that to understand the object and its definition other social phenomena of the day, such as the authority that limits their use, must be investigated. In the case of madness, Foucault names medicine as the authority that established, named and set limits around the object (ibid: 42). Foucault says that a particular mix of social conditions is necessary for the appearance of an object, and that an underlying system of rules enables its transformation. He argues: '[T]hese rules define not the dumb existence of a reality, nor the canonical use of a vocabulary, but the ordering of objects' (ibid: 49).

In summary, Foucault's ideas about objects and contradictions in transformation and change underpin my questions about public relations as a legitimate 'unity' and my search for a stronger and more inclusive one that includes stronger ethical foundations and tolerance for civil as well as state and business sectors. Drawing on the ideas of Foucault it also questions the fundamental basis of public relations as a unity and explores its potential for reformation and regrouping.

PUTTING A NAME TO IT – THE OBJECT OF UNETHICAL PR

The next section sets out an interesting case study of unethical public relations which occurred in New Zealand and includes forms such as 'astroturfing' and 'greenwashing' amongst others (Nelson 1989; Stauber and Rampton 1995; Beder 1997). Astroturfing refers to a 'fee for service' artificial grass roots public support offered by public relations companies. For example, a talkback radio segment might be bombarded with calls from 'genuine' concerned citizens claiming to support a contested fast food development; in reality, these people are 'stooges' working for the organisation. Greenwashing is the use of public relations to manipulate public views that corporations are acting in environmentally responsible ways. According to Australian consumer watchdog organisation Choice, at the moment 'consumers are getting bombarded by greenwash' and that 'sorting the dodgy green claims from the genuine ones can be a minefield' (Choice 2008). The case study was chosen because it provides a comprehensive description of a campaign and textual evidence, and also because of the ensuing bitterness between members of the public relations profession in the wake of an investigation.

CASE STUDY: TIMBERLANDS

In late 1999, New Zealander Nicky Hager and Australian Bob Burton made a formal complaint about unethical public relations to the Public Relations Institute of New Zealand (PRINZ), concerning the conduct of two of its members. They claimed that elaborate and highly unethical forms of public relations had occurred designed to undermine public debate about the future of West Coast New Zealand's temperate rainforest. Following this PRINZ instigated an internal investigation to establish the validity of the claims, but this was abandoned after a dispute between the institute and the members under investigation (Harrison 2004). Instead, PRINZ asked independent lawyer, Hugh Rennie, QC, to report back to the national executive with findings and a recommendation on the allegations of breach of ethics. The key players in this case study are: the state-owned enterprise Timberlands West Coast Ltd, a logging company owned by the New Zealand government; PR company Shandwick New Zealand employed by Timberlands to 'neutralise' disagreement about its activities; community action groups: the Royal Forest and Bird Protection Society, ECO, Greenpeace, Buller Conservation Group, Native Forest Action (NFA) and Victoria University Environment Group (VEG); and lastly, the New Zealand public relations professional association, PRINZ (Harrison 2004; Hager and Burton 1999; PRINZ 2001).

Hager and Burton's subsequent book, *Secrets and lies: The anatomy of an anti-environmental PR campaign*, claims Timberlands hired Shandwick New Zealand to mount a $1 million PR campaign to win government support for continued rainforest logging and to discourage their opponents. They claim the PR campaign began with activists receiving aggressive counter tactics for their involvement. Other claims include: buying local support through sponsorship; cultivating political allies to act as spokespeople and lobbyists; persuading newspapers to run favourable stories; infiltrating environmental group NFA to access information, monitor communication, tape-record their activities and then approach newspapers accusing them of being a front group for the Labour and Green parties; paying a bogus member $50 per hour to report back on VEG activities photographing or videotaping protestors and noting their clothing and brand names on file; using extremist discourse to describe and attack the activists and 'create the impression that they were insignificant, irrational outsiders' (Hager and Burton 1999: 38); creating front group Coast Action Network which claimed to represent the 'majority of West Coaster[s] who have had a gutful of propaganda aired by extreme conservation groups' (ibid: 39); and using scare tactics, for example legal letters to protestors threatening to sue for up to $100,000 (known as 'strategic lawsuits against public participation' or SLAPPs) (ibid: 41).

The evidence for the claims made in *Secrets and lies* was provided when one of the authors sought to confirm his growing suspicion that the Timberlands activists were the subject of an unjust but carefully planned and sustained communication campaign. Drawing on New Zealand's small group networks he looked for PR practitioners or insiders who were willing to divulge information about the covert campaign. In 1999 evidence of the campaign, which became known as the 'Timberland Papers', was passed over, with hundreds of pages of photocopies that included PR strategies, minutes, legal advice, correspondence etc.

The papers showed that the environmentalists' suspicions, far from being unfounded, underestimated the scale of the PR campaign against them. Here was detailed planning of how to cause trouble for the environmental groups and anyone who helped them: researching their vulnerabilities and deciding on the best tactics for countering them. Here were matter-of-fact discussions about infiltrating environmental groups to acquire information that could assist the campaign (ibid: 14).

In *PRINZ allegations of breach of ethics final report* (the Rennie Report), QC Rennie investigated five of Hager and Burton's 18 claims. Two of the five claims investigated were upheld: first that Shandwick New Zealand paid a student to spy on the activists and second that Shandwick New Zealand had a responsibility to caution clients in the adoption of the 'mindset of conflict', which in this case resulted in the promotion of terms like 'extremists' to describe Timberlands' opponents. Indeed, Rennie said: 'Such denigration of citizens with strongly held opinions about the use of a public asset is in danger of Goebbels-type misuse' (Rennie in PRINZ 2001: 32).

However, three of the five claims investigated were dismissed. They were: Shandwick's media campaign was judged to be comprehensive and extensive but not unethical; the tactic of drafting letters for use by Timberlands community supporters was dismissed because it was deemed that individuals had free choice to sign, and the creation of front groups like Coast Action Network could not be proved in this case, but if true this was deemed to be unethical.

THE AFTERMATH

Following this PRINZ undertook a review of its Constitution and its Code of Professional Practice to address the inadequacies Rennie identified. However, the two Shandwick New Zealand executives, Sorensen and McGregor, publicly resigned from PRINZ, furious about the scrutiny of their activities, saying:

> For the Institute to treat two individuals with a total of 32 years public relations experience in this way is appalling. They bent over backwards to entertain complaints from those who simply sought to promote themselves and in the process ignored the rights of their members and the Institute's obligations to them (cited in Harrison 2004: 6).

While *Secrets and lies* co-author Hager issued the following statement:

> I think that the case shows that some people in the PRINZ national executive were keen to take a stand on unethical behaviour. The Institute's declaration that it is unethical to attack citizens who are exercising their democratic rights is a very important decision … Since public relations campaigns have a strong potential to undermine democratic processes, there is an urgent need to find a more effective way of ensuring ethical PR behaviour (Hager, 11 May 2001).

ANALYSIS

This paper seeks to understand the different ways in which public relations practice demonstrated in the Timberlands case study is unethical in relation to activist groups and how this affects the public sphere and the profession as a whole. This section investigates in detail two examples of the public relations used by Shandwick. The ideas of Habermas (1995) will be used to analyse public relations is a particular form of social relations within the period of modernity, a Foucauldian analysis (1972) will be used to show the two distinct ways in which this occurred.

According to Hager and Burton (1999: 176), this Timberlands advertisement (below) was 'played at saturation levels during the period when Timberlands was attempting to ensure a flood of local submissions in favour of its beech logging plans' and featured children's voices (excerpt below):

> *Presenter: What did you like about Timberlands?*
>
> *Child: The thing that I like about Timberlands is because they take care of our forest and show what they can do.*
>
> *Child: The thing I like about Timberlands is you learn quite a lot.*
>
> *Child: The best thing I liked about Timberlands was pruning the trees.*
>
> *Child: The thing I like about Timberlands was going to the skid.*

> *Presenter: What a great impression Timberlands have left in these kids' minds. Next time you're out about in the forest, have a think about what Timberlands are doing for the West Coast* (ibid: 176).

Applying the ideas of Habermas (1995: 194) reveals that Shandwick PR used this tactic as a form of greenwashing to engineer consent in the public sphere by creating a climate of consensus that would enable the commercial activities of Timberlands to continue, at the same time neutralising unwanted discussion. The use of symbols and images such as children was deliberate to make it difficult for target publics to understand the advertisement as the promotion of system rationality, because it seems to contradict ideas about what and how it should look and behave. Drawing on the symbolism of the child, which connotes integrity, innocence and truth, the advertisement implied overall harmony between business, state and community groups. However, a Foucaldian analysis shows that in this case Shandwick also sought to address *intrinsic* contradictions within a discursive formation and developed statements that were intended in genial ways to lead the subject, through a series of symbols imbued with meanings, into a coherence that supported and naturalised the logic of simple modernity.

In doing this, Shandwick responded to what it believed were surface or intrinsic contradictions, that is, ones occurring *inside* a discursive formation, by seeking to adjust these for audiences within the public sphere through promotion also known as 'spin' and 'fluff', but in ways intended not 'in any way affecting the body of enunciative rules that makes them possible' (Foucault op cit: 153). In late modern society it is reasonable to suggest that the effect of harmonising intrinsic contradictions through public relations on a local level is likely to be tolerated by publics. However, depending on the extent to which it takes place, the engineered harmonising of intrinsic contradictions by public relations is no less socially damaging than the aggressive asphyxiation of extrinsic contradictions. Indeed, Habermas (1995: 195) has shown how the invisible seepage of commercial and political discourses into the public sphere causes its slow, subtle junking that puts at risk critical public opinion shaped by 'rational agreement between publicly competing opinions' in a society.

However, a different form of unethical public relations is evident in this excerpt below. According to Hager and Burton (op cit: 165) this poster was distributed that asked West Coast residents:

> Do you realise the extreme environmentalists are having an 'Adventurous' weekend in Reefton, Queens Birthday weekend, at West Coast peoples expense? ... WHAT MORE DO THEY WANT!!! DON'T LET THEM DESTROY OUR LIVES – If you believe in the survival of the West Coast Future, and would like to join us, please contact Coast Action Network (ibid).

In this example, the use of discourse such as 'extreme', 'destroy', and 'survival' points to the management of *extrinsic* contradictions. Drawing on Foucault (1972) this shows that public relations responds differently if it believes that statements issued by counter-sources will lead audiences *outside* the boundaries of the particular discursive formation (ibid: 153). In this case it acts aggressively to suppress and/or discredit the source so that their statements are not distributed or provide alternative statements that lead the subject back into the dominant discourse. QC Rennie referred to this as the PR consultancy's 'mindset of conflict'. For example, Shandwick, in a calculated way, intended the statements to be antagonistic and as a result would construct dichotomies such as 'us and them' and 'good and bad' etc. to stop alternative statements from emerging, so that thought would be funnelled back into the bureaucratic and instrumental systems dominant to this point. In relation to extrinsic contradictions, public relations acts like a fence around the dominant discourse promoted by industry and the state, both to keep in the speaking subject and to keep out new statements that might lead them to an alternative discursive formation (ibid). Furthermore, this case study shows public relations attempts to asphyxiate extrinsic contradictions set in motion by activists in order to maintain the dominant discourse (ibid: 149).

In summary, the Timberlands case study shows two highly unethical forms of public relations at work which can undermine the public sphere and the agency of individuals to participate fully as active citizens within a democratic society. The proponents used public relations both to suppress and neutralise the contradictions the grassroots activists raised. However overall, this paper argues that it is the extreme ways in which it was used to extinguish the extrinsic contradictions 'that reflect opposition between distinct discursive formations' as opposed to the ways it was used to deal with the intrinsic contradictions or 'those that are deployed in the discursive formation itself' (Foucault 1972: 153) which makes it highly socially and politically offensive and which raises serious questions for the profession and society.

IMPLICATIONS

Primarily my analysis about the response of public relations to contradictions in these activist debates show the different ways business and state organisations use public relations to suppress the emergence of other coherences and discursive formations. Two styles have been identified: the harmonising of intrinsic contradictions through spin and the aggressive asphyxiation of extrinsic contradictions.

Significantly, the tensions within the field of public relations, such as those demonstrated in the literature review and in the Timberlands case study between PRINZ and the two members under investigation, can also be explained by Foucault's ideas around contradictions. He says that intrinsic contradictions such as these point to 'inadequacy of the objects; divergence of enunciative modalities;

incompatibility of concepts and an exclusion of theoretical options' (Foucault 2005: 171-172). This paper examines public relations' relationship to activism and the extreme actions such as astroturfing and greenwashing which reveal, clearly, the object of public relations at its core. It argues this schism points to the inadequacies of 'PR' as an object and suggests the divisions within the field cannot be reconciled theoretically within current frameworks. However, irregularities such as this also reveal a new discursive formation is present because they are evidence of a new way of thinking that has found different coherences. The challenge is, therefore, not to try to reconcile these views but to set in motion a new ethically-driven approach which affects the ordering of objects.

Politically offensive communication practices such as those demonstrated in the Timberlands case study have raised an urgency to examine the role of ethics and public relations in relation to democracy. If we are involved with public relations we cannot help but be tainted by the poor practices of others. Indeed these acts are a source of confusion and of ambiguity that needs to be clarified. The Foucauldian framework adds to the work of Habermas (1995) and provides new analytical tools to identify sub-categories of unethical public relations practice that enable an evaluation of its effects within wider social contexts. In turn this establishes new categorical relations within the field that assist with research and in developing new approaches for practice. For example, Foucault's ideas show that organisations, to avoid the negative effects of unethical public relations organisations in the public sphere, need to accept a permeation of ideas which open up the possibilities to prevent, minimise and solve problems or socially controversial issues that are by-products of the social production of wealth (Beck 1992). Therefore, in practice, a defining characteristic of ethical communication is that it does not attempt to asphyxiate *extrinsic* statements outside its discursive formation in order to restore a hidden unity that serves its own organisational self-interest (Foucault 1972: 149-153). Nor does it attempt to harmonise surface or *intrinsic* contradictions within its discursive formation to create cohesion through symbolism and discourse resulting in the spin and fluff of public relations.

For some people, the relationship between business, politics and the media is formless and its effects on society are difficult to understand and see. Breit (2007: 347) discusses the difficult role that individual journalists and public relations practitioners have within a sometimes inadequate regulatory environment and recommends adopting a 'broader view of the media's social responsibility' because of the wider collective effects this will pass on. Media Social Responsibility (MSR) is defined as the adoption of an ethic in which individuals and groups individuals practise and interact with stakeholder in ways that reflect on 'honesty, fairness, and respect for the rights of others' (ibid).

This paper proposes to build on the notion of MSR in order to develop greater theoretical choices within the field of public relations which will assist the creation of the object of unethical public relations. Drawing on the discussion so far (Breit op cit, Habermas 1995, Foucault op cit, Hager and Burton op cit), MSR could be an approach to professional communication characterised by:

- Permeation of ideas which open up the possibility of alternative strategies that are capable of leading to a new discursive formation (Foucault op cit).

- A systematic attempt to integrate notions of managing contradictions to address conceptual weaknesses within the current codes of ethics (Breit op cit: 308).

- Interaction with intra-organisational public sphere, goal-oriented within the prevailing social governance systems to develop meaningful exchanges between social and state organisations and institutions and the pursuit of the ideal that it is possible to dilute the antagonism between social groups and promote mutual satisfaction and critical public opinion (Habermas op cit: 248)

CONCLUSION

Foucault's theories of the unities of discourse and the formation of objects, enunciative modalities, concepts and strategies and the function of statements shed light on how individual subjects are constrained in their agency to effect change. His work shows a new level on which language interacts to form relationships that, in turn, affects social action. The notion of the 'individual' who determines history through sheer Herculean self-will is upturned by Foucault's analysis. In its place, the subject, mostly unaware of a great repository of discourse from which they can draw, hybridise and construct – objects, unities and concepts – to form and disperse statements, transferring them into new modalities and other codes, invisibly shaping them as seemingly natural speaking positions.

Foucault gives the critical tools to see how the public relations industry creates discourse to control and manipulate the process of discursive formation. Public relations, using tools such as greenwashing and astroturfing within the public sphere, artificially creates and disperses objects, statements and concepts in concentrations that inflate their particular discourses to the extent that others are overwhelmed. The result is a discursive monoculture for society. Clearly, unscrupulous communication practices such as those demonstrated in the Timberlands case study have entrenched tensions between activists and the public relations industry but, moreover, they are also counter-productive for the organisations involved. If businesses continue to apply simple approaches in their public relations when dealing with resistance from activist groups, they will not only contribute to significant social havoc through conflict and antagonism but they will waste the collective resources of the state and risk their long-term business viability.

In this paper, I have discussed socially and politically offensive forms of public relations and the tensions within the field itself which need urgent attention. I believe that reconciling these issues requires innovation and a synthetic approach, drawing on a range of interdisciplinary social, political, communicative and discourse theories, to identify coherences in order to develop a conceptual analysis that leads to new understandings of these relationships. This critical view of public relations also reflects Foucault's ideas that unities should only be accepted if they are subject to interrogation and found to be sound. He argues once ideas about unities are questioned 'an entire field is set free' (Foucault op cit: 26). It is beyond the scope of this paper to do much more than map out some of this territory for renewal in the field. However, I speculate that if such a more rigorous communicative approach moved from the margins to the mainstream, then regulatory frameworks in the profession could be strengthened, taxonomies and sub-categories in the analysis of unethical public relations could be developed, greater sanctions for wrong doing in public relations by individuals and the organisations they represent and their effects on citizens in the public sphere could be described and understood to produce knowledge, counter ignorance and provide the tools for change.

REFERENCES

Abercrombie, N., Hill, S. and Turner, B. S. (2000) *Dictionary of sociology*, London, Penguin Books, third edition

Beck, U. (1992) *Risk society: Towards a new modernity*, London, Sage

Beder, S. (1997) *Global spin: The corporate assault on environmentalism*, Melbourne, Scribe Publications

Breit, R. (2007) *Law and ethics for professional communicators*, LexisNexis Butterworths Australia. Available online at http://www.choice.com.au/viewArticle.aspx?id=106128&catId=100570&tid=100011

Cheney, G. and Christensen, L. T. (2001) Public relations as contested terrain: A critical response, R. L. Heath and G. Vazquez (eds) *Handbook of public relations*, Thousand Oaks, CA, Sage pp 167-182

Choice (2007) ACCC and green electricity claims, www.Choice.com.au, December. Available online at http://www.choice.com.au/viewArticle.aspx?id=106128&catId=100570&tid=100011, accessed on 7 May 2008

Deegan, D. (2001) *Managing activism: A guide to dealing with activists and pressure groups*, The Institute of Public Relations, London, Kogan Page

Foucault, M. (1972) *The archaeology of knowledge*, London, Tavistock

Foucault, M. (2005) *The archaeology of knowledge*, London, New York, Routledge

Grunig, J. E. (ed.) (1992) *Excellence in public relations and communication management*, New Jersey and London, Lawrence Erlbaum Associates Publishers

Habermas, J. (1995) *The structural transformation of the public sphere: An inquiry into the category of bourgeois society*, Cambridge, Massachusetts, the MIT Press

Hager, N. and Burton, B. (1999) *Secrets and lies: The anatomy of an anti-environmental PR campaign*, Munroe, ME, Common Courage Press

Hager, N. (2001) Reaction to the Public Relations Institute decision on the professional conduct of Klaus Sorensen and Rob McGregor of Shandwick New Zealand Ltd in the Timberlands PR Campaign (statement) 11 May

Harrison, J. (2004) Conflicts of duty and the virtues of Aristotle in public relations ethics: Continuing the conversation commenced by Monica Walle, *PRism*, Vol. 2, No. 1. Available online at http://praxis.massey.ac.nz/fileadmin/Praxis/Files/Journal_Files/Issue2/Harrison.pdf, accessed on 21 November 2005

McHoul, A. and Grace, W. (1993) *A Foucault primer: Discourse, power and the subject*, Melbourne University Press, Carlton Victoria

Nelson, J. (1989) *Power in societies*, Toronto, Ontario, Macmillan Company

PRIA Victoria (2005) *Activists: How to beat them at their own game*. Available online at https://www.tai.org.au/file.php?file=NL44.pdf, accessed 24 October 2008

PRINZ (2005) The Timberland case. Available online at http://www.prinz.org.nz/site/news.nsf/0/098b1d3c62a16607cc256f0a007cdd92?OpenDocument, accessed 21 November 2005. PRINZ News, 15 May

Rennie, H. (2001) *PRINZ allegations of breach of ethics final report: Findings and recommendations of Hugh Rennie QC to the national executive*. Available online at http://www.prinz.org.nz/site/news.nsf/0/1ab21abce2368268cc256f0a007cdd90/$FILE/Mr%20Rennie's%20Report.pdf, accessed ON 21 November 2005

Smith, M. F. and Ferguson D. P. (2001) Activism, Heath, R. (ed.) *Handbook of public relations*, Thousand Oaks, London, New Delhi, Sage Publications

Stauber, J. and Rampton, S. (1995) *Toxic sludge is good for you! Lies, damn lies and the public relations industry*, Monroe, Maine, Common Courage Press

NOTE ON THE CONTRIBUTOR

Dr Kristin Demetrious is an Associate Professor of Communication at Deakin University, Australia. She is the author of *Public relations and neoliberalism: The language practices of knowledge formation* (OUP, 2022) and *Public relations, activism and social change* (Routledge, 2013). Currently a joint editor for *Public Relations Inquiry* (Sage), she has researched the relations of power in public relations for over twenty years, with particular interest in post-war US public relations, Australian political communication, risk producing industries' use of PR, PR workplaces and gender, ethics and ethical theory, activism, civil society and social change, as well as social media.

SECTION 4

And finally:
Speaking out on ethics

Chapter 23

Christchurch mosques shooting: Reflections and confessions

Rukhsana Aslam

Many essays have been written about the Christchurch mosques shooting in New Zealand on 15 March 2019. Academics, journalists, activists and strategists have analysed the event from all angles. They have talked about the gun laws, Islam, its representation in the Western media, white nationalism, the social media, internet regulation and the lessons learnt from it. This paper is more personal. It talks about the perspectives of the people who lived through that day. It includes their reflections and confessions on what happened and why it happened. It is also about the mistakes made and the lessons learnt by the NZ media and what, in turn, it taught the world – particularly about the importance of the principles of peace journalism.

Keywords: terrorism, Christchurch mosques shooting, Islamophobia, media and conflict, peace journalism

INTRODUCTION

15 March 2019 was a shocking day. Both for those who live in New Zealand and for the world.

It was the day when 51 Muslims were killed in the city of Christchurch, New Zealand. The Muslim men, women and children were killed and dozens injured in broad daylight between 1 and 1.30pm while they were saying their Friday prayers in the city's two main mosques – the Al-Noor mosque and the Linwood mosque. Some 49 of them were killed on the spot and two lost their lives a few days later in hospital. About as many were injured, some critically. Among them were toddlers, school children, teenagers, professional men and women, housewives and grandparents. The shooter, a 28-year-old Australian citizen and self-proclaimed white nationalist, was indiscriminate in his killing.

As the live streaming of the shooting showed, he walked towards the Al-Noor mosque killing whomever he found and was on his way from the Linwood mosque to further targets when he was arrested by the police.

To put the event in perspective, terrorism is rare in New Zealand's recent history. Tucked away deep in the southern hemisphere of the world, New Zealand is nearer the Antarctic than the United States of America. It has more sheep than the approximately 4.8 million people who live there; with 200 ethnicities, 160 languages – and some 57,000-plus Muslims. It is a nation that takes pride in its openness, diversity and heritage. The Kiwis love everything outdoors: sports, nature, fireworks, BBQs and drinks. For the shooter to choose Muslims in New Zealand as targets because he wanted to show the world that 'no place was safe' was a shock – not only for the New Zealanders but for the world.

The previous act of terrorism that New Zealand academics and journalists remember and still write about occurred in July 1985, when French secret service agents bombed and sank the Greenpeace protest vessel, the *Rainbow Warrior*. They killed one person.

According to researchers at Victoria University: 'In terms of per capita deaths, the Christchurch event, when 1.07 people died per 100,000 of population, was of a similar order of magnitude to the 11 September 2001 World Trade Center terrorism event when 2,996 people or 1.05 people per 100,000 died' (Chapple and Prickett 2019).

GOING BACK TO THE DAY

As a Pakistani-born Muslim woman, a journalist-turned-academic in media and conflict, I have lived through the 'war on terror' in Pakistan and witnessed on television the wars fought in Kuwait, Iraq, Afghanistan and Syria, along with countless acts of terrorism in the past few decades. Such events no longer surprise me: they just sadden me.

I first heard about the shooting in Christchurch through a text on my phone just as I was starting my Friday prayers. My first fear was that it was an act of terrorism by an Islamic extremist. So, I continued doing what I was doing. By the time I finished, it became clear that the Muslims were the victims and the shooter was a white nationalist. My fear turned to grief – but also relief. That was when I switched on the television, hoping there might be a clip in the afternoon news.

The news was broadcast all across the world media. The NZ media were also present at the scene. Reporters and crew from television channels, newspapers and radio gathered to give live accounts of the terrible events. Grabbing a corner around the area where the mosques were located and cordoned off by the police, they first interviewed members of families of those who had gone for their Friday prayers to the mosques but who never came out.

As a former journalist, I knew that the NZ journalists would do what they are trained to do: report professionally and objectively. As is the long-practised norm of journalism: to be neutral and dispassionate while doing a story is the principle that we journalists live by. We are trained to put aside our emotions, block our feelings and not get involved in situations when we write our reports or say our words before the camera, especially in conflict situations.

Hence, I expected the NZ journalists to link the Christchurch shooting with the anti-Islamic sentiments expressed by many in the Western world since the 9/11 attack on the World Trade Center in New York. I expected them to talk about Islamic extremism and the jihadists and to call the episode a 'sad event', blaming it on the religion of Islam and its followers.

To my utter disbelief, I saw John Campbell's voice break down when he talked about the 'staggering' number of deaths and his head drop in speechlessness in front of the hospital in Christchurch as he learnt about the scale of the tragedy. I watched Lisa Davies's eyes glisten with tears before the camera as she continued her reporting late into the night. I found Patrick Gower's face going white with grief when he met the families desperately searching for their loved ones. Inside the studio, anchorperson Hilary Barry kept shaking her head, saying it was a massacre and that the Muslim worshippers who were killed that day were 'like lambs in the slaughter house'.

Then, just hours after the attack, I saw New Zealand's young Prime Minister Jacinda Ardern call the day 'our darkest of days'. Those who had died were not only the Muslim worshippers, she told parliament. 'They were New Zealanders. They are us. And because they are us, we, as a nation, we mourn them' (Ardern 2019). As she condemned the 'terrorist attack' against New Zealand, she vowed not to name the shooter: 'He is a terrorist. He is a criminal. He is an extremist. But he will, when I speak, be nameless.' To the people, she implored: 'Speak the names of those who were lost rather than the name of the man who took them. He may have sought notoriety, but we in New Zealand will give him nothing. Not even his name.' It was the first time I witnessed a political leader and head of the state say such strong words.

In the days that followed, my surprise continued. Ardern's words 'they are us' became the slogan to unite people of all ethnicities. Countless stories of acts of kindness, compassion and generosity came to the fore. Donations in the millions of dollars; free halal food provision; voluntary services and counselling; mountains of flowers and toys against city railings; police patrols and community vigilance outside the mosques all across the country; images of white women wearing head scarves to show solidarity with Muslim women. It amounted to a breath-taking show of solidarity and compassion from a nation towards one of its communities. A most unusual phenomenon in the Western world was taking place in Aotearoa, the land of the long white cloud.

Amidst all these reports, the NZ media sprang another surprise by upholding what Ardern had said in her speech. After the initial reports on the shooter's identity, his manifesto, his arrest and appearance in the courtroom, his name and face were dropped. The media talked about the victims, the survivors, the first responders, the initial reactions, the individual and collective acts of kindness, the gatherings and the rallies. It debated the gun laws, the worldwide spread of Islamophobia, the simmering current of white supremacist nationalism in New Zealand and even the failure of the security agencies in detecting such elements in the country. But naming of the shooter in media reports, comments or analysis was minimal. That was unprecedented.

Exactly one week later, on 22 March 2019, when the burials were to take place after the Friday prayers, the *New Zealand Herald,* the *Dominion Post* and the *Press* dedicated their front pages to the victims and their faith. The *New Zealand Herald* showed fifty hearts enshrined in the arch of a green mosque with the title: 'A call to prayer' and accompanying slogan: 'In unity, there is strength.' The *Press* simply left its entire front page blank except for the one big word 'Salam' in Arabic with its translation in English 'Peace' underneath. At the bottom of the page were printed the names of the fifty victims. The *Dominion Post* published the exact time of the call to prayer, 1.32pm and the message: 'Today we remember' on the front page. The remaining half page carried the names of the victims. (The 51st victim lost his life six weeks later in hospital.)

At exactly 1.32pm, New Zealand came to a stand-still for a minute's silence in remembrance of the victims. The Imam of the Christchurch mosque, who survived the attack, gave his message of thanks, unity and love in Christchurch's Hagley Park and, as he led the prayers in the open grounds of the park, hundreds of New Zealanders stood guard behind the worshippers. According to Waqar Rana, 48, an IT professional, who had flown from Auckland with many other Muslims to attend the funeral: 'It was a sight unseen and the experience unforgettable!'

REFLECTIONS AND CONFESSIONS

By this time, I had to step back and take stock of what was happening. I was not the only Muslim in New Zealand to feel like this. There are hundreds of us who carry the emotional baggage and sense of unknown fear for being a Muslim, especially after the 9/11 attacks in the US; such is the spread of Islamophobia in the Western media.

Jamila Khatoon, 55, who manages the till at her family store, told me about her sense of 'great fear' for her large joint family from Jordan after the shootings. Especially as all the men in her family had left for Christchurch the next day as volunteers to help the government prepare the victims' bodies for burial. But she also said the immense support of the people and the government she was seeing on television was a great help in allaying her fears.

Farzana Noorzai, an Afghani Muslim primary school teacher, experienced first-hand the huge impact of the Christchurch tragedy on the Muslim community. She described her initial response and later:

> As a mother, I questioned the safety of my children. I questioned the safety of myself as a Muslim woman with a head scarf. I feared for our mothers and sisters. I felt empty. I felt emotional. I wanted to scream, the pain was unbearable. Nothing seemed to ease the pain. … [But] as I kept changing

TV channels, my attention was soon focused on the messages of unity, sympathy and kindness from our Prime Minister right through to our TV1 and TV3 news reporters. We cried and mourned together. I didn't feel like an outsider any more. I started believing again that there is still hope and kindness in the world (Bruce and Noorzai 2019).

Sana Kidwai, 39, an Auckland-based Indian Muslim, said it was not the first time that the Muslim community had been attacked and killed in a country for their faith, but it was the first time that a country and its media had acted to support them. His wife Subia, 37, a teacher in Auckland's Ormiston Primary School, said she kept waiting for the NZ media to lay the blame on the Muslim immigrants in New Zealand to bring violence to the country, but the Kiwi journalists 'took me by surprise'. Ali Tajik, 45, from Pakistan, had a Palestinian friend among the victims. He said the biggest issues for small immigrant families in such cases were the burial costs, the care of the families and the future income. He welcomed the fact that the government took that burden from the victims' families. Although he was still coming to terms with the loss, his friend's family was being 'looked after' by the government and the community.

As a former journalist and now an academic, I was wondering more about how to understand the empathy and the compassion that the NZ media had shown during the week. The journalists who reported on the attacks were as seasoned, experienced and professional as a journalist can hope to be. Campbell, a journalist since 1989, is the winner of a Qantas Media Award and the Best Presenter category for the New Zealand Film and Television Awards twice. Gower, the national correspondent of TV3, has twenty years' experience behind him and Barry has been among the country's most well-known faces on television for many years.

Why had they reacted so? Campbell told Barry in the studios that nothing had prepared him for the experience. 'A community within Christchurch was singled out for a reason, and that reason was hatred,' he said. 'This ultimately is an act that has no place anywhere, it's shattering to be here actually.' His voice shook and he quietly hung his head in despair. Campbell had covered the Christchurch earthquakes in 2011. But this was different. 'The city has been through so much but this is so very pointed, and very personal, Hilary, and hateful,' he said. 'It's terror, pure and simple ... a grotesque act of villainy' (*Stuff* 2019a).

For Gower, it was the first time in his career that he had seen something 'truly evil'. Standing near the Al-Noor mosque, he interviewed a young man named Abdi who had lost his three-year-old brother Mucad Ibrahim and was recounting what had happened. 'Everything was just going too fast. I just thought it was fireworks. Everyone was running, and I just started to run and just lost the boy,' Abdi said. 'And that broke me,' Gower said later. 'It wasn't because it was really sad, it was because for the first time in my life I really comprehended something that was truly evil' (*Stuff* 2019b).

Mahvash Ali, a Pakistani-born-New Zealander and a journalist, says she broke down crying on the pavement when she saw blood on the windows of the mosque. She can still remember the feeling of 'hate, fear and grief that permeated the city that day'. The sympathy, the support and the flowers starting coming the next day.

Megan Jones, documentary producer, thinks the reason it so affected Kiwi journalists and people alike was 'because it happened in our own backyard'. We are talking over a cup of tea as we work on our proposal for a documentary on the Christchurch shooting in the light of peace journalism. 'The principles of Whanau (family) and Aroha (love) are deeply embedded in the Kiwi way of life. And this act is the extreme and ultimate violation of both,' she says.

She also tells me how she wore a head scarf and stood outside Auckland's Ponsonby mosque with hundreds of other Kiwi men and women to show solidarity with the Muslim sisters. And *no*, the experience did not make her feel any less of a woman or different. Contrary to her earlier perception of the hijab as a 'symbol of oppression of women', it now means 'more like a symbol of choice and unity'.

I also asked her to reflect on the NZ media's restraint over naming the shooter. 'It was about not becoming a tool to promote one man's hatred and violence against a community that was our own.

'Jacinda was right when she said in her speech that we as New Zealanders pride ourselves on being open, peaceful and diverse and that the shooter sought notoriety through his act and manifesto,' she reflects. 'There's no question in our mind as journalists that the man should remain forgotten whereas the victims be remembered. It will probably be the same when he is tried in the court.'

Indeed, the question on how to cover the trial of the gunman in the coming months has become a major concern for the NZ media companies as they work together to agree on the protocol. A statement from the NZ Media Freedom Committee, comprising the senior editors of TVNZ, *Stuff*, New Zealand Media and Entertainment (NZME), Mediaworks and Radio New Zealand (RNZ), on 1 May 2019, said: 'We are aware that the accused may attempt to use the trial as a platform to amplify white supremacist and/or terrorist views ideology' (*Stuff* 2019c).

The signed protocol of the committee to cover the trial fairly but ethically agrees on limiting the coverage of any statement, symbol or image that in any way champions the white supremacist or terrorist ideology, especially the accused's 'manifesto' document; using pixelated images if unavoidable and selecting experienced journalists to cover the trial. They also stress the need to be mindful of the language, the tone and the words used to cover the trial.

The fact the industry is putting so much thought into the trial coverage impresses many and media commentators such as Tim Murphy (2019) have lauded the NZ media for delivering 'first-class public interest journalism' in covering 'one of the biggest, saddest and most shocking news stories in the country's history'.

But some, such as Ali, associate producer of the current affairs programme, the *Project*, are also critical of the shortcomings of the NZ media. While she does not deny 'the incredibly sympathetic reporting' in the New Zealand media after the mosque attacks, she argues there was 'a big failing on their part not to have detected the existence of the white supremacist elements and highlight the threat that had been lurking in the city for months, even years'. She continues:

> The Muslim community had been pointing out it to the police but these stories didn't come out until now. … It's not that discrimination or violence against the Muslims, especially the hijab-wearing women, didn't exist in the country. They've been here for years but the NZ media has ignored them like an ostrich burying its head in the sand.

Ali is not too far off the mark in her criticism here. Gower admitted it too. In his opinion piece (*Newshub*, 13 May), he wrote that people often thank journalists for doing a story. But when the Muslims thanked him after the Christchurch mosque attack, it affected him differently. 'I was ashamed and embarrassed.' He had failed them. 'Over the years, I've reported on threats to New Zealanders, like Islamic State, earthquakes and climate change. … But in 20 years, I've not done one story on white supremacy.' The reason was not that it didn't exist but that he, along with the other Kiwi journalists, thought it harmless.

> Honestly, I and many other Kiwi journos didn't see it as a real threat. This was an American problem, or European problem. … To many of us, white supremacists were a punchline. Like some racist uncle you saw at family reunions. But we should have known there are heaps of uncles, and nephews, and aunts, and sons and while we laughed, they just got stronger. And armed. … But I didn't know. Because we didn't look into it (Gower 2019a).

Paula Simpson had her own confessions to make. 'It's hard to know you're racist when you're surrounded by people like yourself,' she wrote in a personal essay 'Confessions of a former racist' in the *Spinoff*. Living a 'standard Kiwi kid life', eating her vegetables and going to church on Sundays, she didn't think she was a racist:

> I didn't notice other people's skin colour but, by heck, I knew that reverse racism was a thing and the Māori were fleecing us Pākehā. I didn't know much for sure, but I knew Asians were good at maths and Maoris were good at singing, but not school (Simpson 2019a).

She resented the fact that the Māori lived on state benefit and in state houses 'while I pay tax' but never saw her 'white privilege'. 'I had never even thought about a job interviewer judging me on the colour of my skin. Because I had never had to.'

When the 9/11 attacks happened, she found that Islam was 'scary' as she saw their stereotyped images in the media. 'Nope, I'm not racist but I wish those Islam people would go back to where they came from [with some foggy idea of Saudi Arabia as being home to all these Muslims].'

It was years later when she moved to India that her interactions with Muslims left her 'embarrassed and horrified at my judgements and Islamophobia'. She met a Muslim man, Mohammad Reza, and his family and developed a relationship with him, and she realised: 'Doesn't seem like rocket science, but I had to learn that Islam is just a religion. You get nutters in every religion. And that there's about 1.5 billion Muslims in the world, and that they are just people like me.'

As she became aware of her own prejudices, she recognised them in others: in the provocative comments of some NZ media personalities, in articles online, on Facebook. But there was acceptance too. When she brought Reza to New Zealand to meet her family, 'they loved him' and 'we had a great trip'. Reza even went to the Invercargill mosque to say prayers one Friday afternoon while she waited in the car and watched Muslims and Kiwis 'living happily side by side':

> When the news of the shooting broke on Friday, my heart shattered. I read the manifesto and I saw the same fear, the same lies, the same words that I knew other Kiwis had written on Facebook and *Stuff*. This is not my New Zealand, you say. I'm sorry. This is your New Zealand. Maybe you just couldn't see it.

While the article was appreciated by many for being so candid, it also attracted comments from 'incredibly angry people'. '[T]he vast majority of abuse I faced was from white men,' she noted. So much so that she wrote another article, 'Why are white men so angry?', and asked the question: 'Why is this OK?' (Simpson 2019b).

There is also much evidence to back up what individuals like Ali, Gower and Simpson are saying. Paul Spoonley, pro vice-chancellor of Massey University, conducted research on hate speech in New Zealand a few years back. There was 'plenty of evidence of local Islamophobic views, especially online', he said, but there was also 'a naivety among the New Zealanders, including the media, about the need to be tolerant towards the intolerant':

> We tend not to think too much about the presence of racist and white supremacist groups, until there is some public incident like the desecration of Jewish graves or a march of black-shirted men (they are mostly men) asserting their right to be white (Spoonley 2019).

LESSONS LEARNT

Simpson learnt through love: personal interaction and communication broke down her barriers. For Gower, the lesson was painful and hard: the 'real threat' has not gone. And as he promised to do better, he warned others not to ignore the threat:

It's time to get this right. It won't make up for the past but might stop future threats coming at us like a freight train. I get it now, and I promise to do better. And to all the young journos: these guys are a real threat to New Zealand. Dig in, investigate and don't make the same mistakes I did (Gower 2019a).

His story 'Christchurch attack: The dark truth about New Zealand's white supremacists' was the first in the series of stories that *Newshub* announced it was beginning 'on a subject important to Kiwis right now' (Gower 2019b). Colin Peacock (2019), editor of Radio New Zealand's *Mediawatch* show, talked about how the attack in Christchurch had made a mark on the NZ media. The attack 'has forced New Zealand news media to re-think the way they work, whose voices they amplify – and why', he commented.

Some journalists apologised for their earlier comments that were racist or disrespectful towards the other communities. The *Herald* now has a pool of staff working on investigating stories on extremism in communities and cultures in NZ which encouraged or hid it. According to the *Herald*'s senior investigative reporter, Matt Nippert, the journalistic project could run for years.

On the social media front, internet regulation had become the primary task, Peacock said. The internet providers had joined hands to block access to the website circulating the shooter's video and manifesto; the advertisers had pulled back from social media including those run by the government and private businesses. Moreover, the online news media, including *Stuff* and the *Spinoff*, turned off their comment sections after the attack for a few days to avoid them going 'toxic'; and country's largest blog, Kiwiblog, changed its policy from accepting anonymous comments to publishing only comments by 'people using their real names'.

There are broader lessons for New Zealand to learn as a society. These include the 'radicalisation' of alienated communities; the use of global communications technology as a 'breeding ground for extremism and hatred'; the existence of 'the dark web, where hate group websites "go dark" behind encrypted platforms and go out of reach of tech companies and security services' (Burton 2019). More importantly, it is time for New Zealand to come out of its 'tendency to assume we are living in a largely benign international environment', according to Burton, a senior lecturer at the NZ Institute for Security and Crime Science, at the University of Waikato. 'This is part of a troubling isolationist tendency in New Zealand politics that contributes to us not taking security seriously and investing in it accordingly. The Christchurch attacks have shattered these illusions,' he wrote in *The Conversation* on the four lessons learnt after the attack. But the biggest lesson is that 'Muslims are the biggest victims of terror across the globe' in a post-9/11 era. A 2011 report from the US government's National Counter-Terrorism Center (NCTC) states: 'In cases where the religious affiliation of terrorism casualties could be determined, Muslims suffered between 82 per cent and 97 per cent of terrorism-related fatalities over the past five years.' The fact that New Zealand has not yet 'adequately recognised the threat from neo-fascist ideology puts its communities at risk', Burton writes. For while 'the extremist who committed this attack acted alone, the ideology that motivated him has spread around the globe and is infecting our politics and discourse'.

Scott Atron (2017) says that violent extremism is 'the dark side of globalisation' that reflects the 'collapse of communities' and broken communication. It can only be mended with engagement not denunciations. He writes:

> Individuals radicalize while seeking identity in an increasingly flattened world. We have replaced vertical lines of communication between generations with horizontal peer-to-peer attachments that can span the globe, but paradoxically within ever-narrower channels for information. Without broad awareness and serious effort at guidance, we risk fanning violent passions to our likely detriment and that of others across the world (Atron 2017).

… AND THE LESSONS TAUGHT

Indeed, there is a lot of truth in what the people said above. The NZ media has a lot to learn – and as a society too – but let's also acknowledge what they have taught the world. 'For me, this is another sign that the way New Zealand dealt with the horrific attacks on Christchurch mosques might become a model for handling these sorts of incidents in better ways than common in the past,' Brigitte Nacos, an expert on terrorism and mass media at Columbia University in New York City, told Kiwi journalist David Williams, of *Newsroom*. She is the author of *Mass-mediated terrorism* (2002) that explores how terrorists 'exploit global media networks and information highways to carry news of their violence along with "propaganda of the deed"'.

Moreover, by focusing on the victims, survivors and their families, the NZ media helped the country to concentrate on the positive messages of community support and compassion rather than the message of hate and violence. It showed that kindness and tolerance for others has a place in the world, according to Bruce and Noorzai (2019). They hope New Zealand media outlets and journalists 'will continue to show the rest of the world that this is possible, through continuing to produce inclusive, balanced and nuanced perspectives of all communities in Aotearoa'.

Khairiah Rehman, an academic at Auckland University of Technology, said in a panel discussion on *Mediawatch* (Rose 2019) that the NZ media were 'leading the way' in the world in their 'representation of diversity and the different voices in societies'. On the same panel, Mohammad Hassan, former RNZ journalist, who now works for TRT World, said the week had been 'a great case study of how to deal with issues that involved the Muslim community'. He thought it had taken the NZ media 'a very long time to figure out' how to talk about terrorism against Muslims. But by 'opening up those spaces and giving those spaces to Muslim voices', they were changing the media landscape. Now, it was important that 'these voices are not forgotten' (ibid).

As a scholar on peace journalism, I would point out two important things that NZ journalists achieved: they tried to lower, if not break down, the barriers that exist between the people of different faiths; and they helped people to connect. TV presenter Jeremy Corbett brought the scholars of three religions – Islam, Christianity and Judaism – together on the *Project* (15 March) to talk about the issues of faith. He also went to Auckland city's mosque, met the young Imam and said prayers along with other men. On the women's side, Mahvash Ali, the associate producer of the segment, did the same. She later told me it was a day to remember: 'As I stood praying, on my one side was a white woman in a skirt wearing a head scarf and on the other side a Māori woman with her tattoo. Together, we prayed.' They both learnt something that day.

The call by New Zealand women to wear the head scarf on the day of the memorial helped connect the women of all faiths in the country on social media. 'Almost without exception, Kiwis were supportive of #headscarfforharmony' (Davies, 4 April). The members of online Facebook group 'Muslim ladies in Auckland' urged each other to bring as many scarves with them to the mosque as a 'gift for our guests'. A Fiji Muslim woman, who sold Islamic clothing and accessories, brought her entire stock of three hundred head scarves. A Chinese cloth merchant took out all the spare loose cloth he had and cut them into headscarves. The *Project* presenters Jesse Mulligan and Kanoa Lloyd talked about the 'best way' to console the families or 'reach out' to the Muslim men and women – even if it was permissible to hug. The *Spinoff* ran an article on the hijab: *why* and *how* it was donned (Ali, 22 March). Of course, there were voices who did not agree – and they were challenged. Such as, by Davies who wrote in *Stuff*:

> We did it as a visible sign of support, recognising the veil can be used as a tool of oppression and of liberation. ... And more than this, we did it to become enmeshed with our Muslim friends; you target them, you target us (Davies 2019).

There were several other media stories on TV1 and TV3 of people trying to find ways to reach out to the Muslim community. People preparing halal food for the injured and affected families; some flying it over on airplanes; taxis not charging those who visited the injured in the Christchurch hospital; florists working round the clock to make bouquets for the graves and students doing the fund-raising.

Some stories were shared personally. Rana told me that when he and his friends had to fly to Christchurch for the funeral, the company that operated the car park near the Auckland airport did not charge them, saying: 'It's on us.' On the way back, Air New Zealand upgraded their tickets to Business Class as they had bought the tickets earlier at full price before the fares had been reduced for the occasion.

A freelance photographer, and a friend (she didn't want to be named in the article), said that she felt morally obligated to apologise to many Muslim women during a rally in Aotea Square in Auckland city centre. 'As I apologised to them for the mosque attack, they apologised back to me for the acts that had been committed in the name of Islamic extremism in the past. What can you do after that? We hugged.'

Perhaps after all the scrutiny and analysis of the Christchurch shooting, the media images that will stay with the world will be that of people connecting: PM Jacinda Ardern hugging a Muslim woman with her head covered; the female Kiwi constable wearing a hijab as she stood guard at the Memorial Park Cemetery in Christchurch; and a nation coming together with the signs of 'They are us'.

And who can forget the words of faith and forgiveness from Ambreen, the Pakistani woman who lost her heroic husband and son in the attack (*Project*, 21 March). Or the inspiring words of Al-Noor mosque's Imam Gamal Fouda, also a survivor, who said at the funeral that the Muslims of New Zealand were 'heartbroken; but not broken' (*Stuff* 2019d).

LOOKING THROUGH THE PRISM OF PEACE JOURNALISM

What is truly remarkable for me as a media scholar is that at the time when the NZ media faced the biggest story of extremism and terrorism in the history of the country, the stories on the mainstream media were about people; the talk was about support and compassion; the focus was on peace and diversity and the debate was on how to address the issues. The principles of peace journalism were shining bright as they so rarely do.

Too often the regime of objectivity dominates newsrooms. Showing human compassion and emotion on screen, in fact, makes for even better journalists. Mistakes are made – and there is no shame in acknowledging them publicly. Indeed, opening up spaces for those who are normally misrepresented or underrepresented helps people to connect. Talking about the issues publicly helps society heal wounds that are inflicted through terror and violence. If conflict sells, there is also an audience for stories on peace and tolerance. While governments may make decisions, the media can play a role in pointing towards the right solution. And finally, when the people, media and leaders join hands, things can change.

Of course, a lot remains to be done: journalists in New Zealand still need to bring together people of different faiths, race and colour to start dialogues; they need to search for common ground between communities so that similarities are found and differences mitigated; they need to report in ways so that barriers are broken and bridges built. This means more meaningful and courageous debates:

about gun control, internet regulation, free speech, freedom and religion. But journalists have been 'inspired to investigate' (Peacock 2019) and that bodes well for the Kiwi media.

Until then, I reckon they do what a boy in a story did. He told the people of his village, who had gathered to praise the proud bear-hunter for his bravery: 'He can fell bears but I can eat a whole bear.' The villagers were stunned since the feat appeared next to impossible. They asked him how could he do that. He replied: 'One bite at a time.' For Kiwi journalists, the same goes: one story at a time!

- The paper first appeared in *Ethical Space*, Vol. 16, No. 4 pp 48-56, 2019

REFERENCES

Ali, Mahvash (2019) Phone interview, 25 September 2019

Ali, Mahvash (2019) Wear a headscarf today if you respect what it means, *Spin*off, 22 March. Available online at https://thespinoff.co.nz/society/22-03-2019/wear-a-headscarf-today-if-you-respect-what-it-means/, accessed on 14 October 2019

Ardern, Jacinda (2019) 'He is a terrorist – and nameless', PM Jacinda Ardern declares to nation, *Asia Pacific Report*, 19 March. Available online at https://asiapacificreport.nz/2019/03/19/he-is-a-terrorist-and-nameless-pm-jacinda-ardern-declares-to-nation/, accessed on 1 October 2019

Atron, Scott (2017) Don't just denounce radicalized youth, engage with them, *Washington Post*, 15 August. Available online at https://www.washingtonpost.com/opinions/dont-denounce-radicalized-youth-engage-with-them/2017/08/15/2e514cfa-81d8-11e7-902a-2a9f2d808496_story.html, accessed on 12 October 2019

Bruce, Toni and Noorzai, Farzana (2019) NZ media shows world high-quality coverage of Islam, *Newsroom*, 1 April. Available online at https://www.newsroom.co.nz/@ideasroom/2019/03/28/508794/nz-media-shows-world-high-quality-coverage-of-islam, accessed on 30 September 2019

Burton, Joe (2019) Four lessons we must take away from the Christchurch terror attack, *Conversation*, 18 March. Available online at https://theconversation.com/four-lessons-we-must-take-away-from-the-christchurch-terror-attack-113716, accessed on 25 September 2019

Chapple, Simon and Rickett, Kate (2019) Christchurch terrorist failed to sow distrust, *Newsroom*, 8 August. Available online at https://www.newsroom.co.nz/@ideasroom/2019/08/08/745202/did-the-christchurch-shooting-change-our-trust, accessed on 12 October 2019

Davies, Sharyn Graham (2019) I chose freely to wear a veil, just as many Muslim women do, *Stuff*, 4 April. Available online at https://www.stuff.co.nz/national/christchurch-shooting/111757204/i-chose-freely-to-wear-a-veil-just-as-many-muslim-women-do, accessed on 14 October 2019

Gower, Patrick (2019a) I was ashamed and embarrassed ... I've not done one story on white supremacy, *Newshub*, 13 May. Available online at https://www.newshub.co.nz/home/new-zealand/2019/05/patrick-gower-i-was-ashamed-and-embarrassed-i-ve-not-done-one-story-on-white-supremacy.html, accessed on 30 September 2019

Gower, Patrick (2019b) Christchurch attack: The dark truth about New Zealand's white supremacists, 12 May. Available online at https://www.newshub.co.nz/home/new-zealand/2019/05/christchurch-attack-the-dark-truth-about-new-zealand-s-white-supremacists.html, accessed on 30 September 2019

Jones, Megan (2019) Personal communication, May

Khatoon, Jamila (2019) Personal communication, 18 March

Kidwai, Sana and Subia (2019) Interview, 29 September

Murphy, Tim (2019) Media Room: Our media did us proud, *Newsroom*, 22 March. Available online at https://www.newsroom.co.nz/2019/03/22/500861/mediaroom-our-media-did-us-proud, accessed on 1 October 2019

Newsroom (2019) Collage of the front pages of NZ newspapers published on 22 March. Available online at https://www.newsroom.co.nz/2019/03/22/500861/mediaroom-our-media-did-us-proud#, accessed on 30 September 2019

Newshub (2019) Because it matters, 12 May. Available online at https://www.instagram.com/p/BxRiHkLB46W/?utm_source=ig_embed&utm_campaign=dlfix, accessed on 30 September 2019

Peacock, Colin (2019) How Christchurch mosque assault has made a mark on NZ media, *Asia Pacific Report*, 25 March. Available online at https://asiapacificreport.nz/2019/03/25/how-christchurch-mosque-assault-has-made-a-mark-on-nz-media/, accessed on 30 September 2019

The *Project* (2019) The heroism of Mian Naeem Rashid and the strength of his widow, Ambreen, TV3, 21 March. Available online at https://www.threenow.co.nz/tv/the-project/home/vids/20181/ambreen-naeem.html

Rose, Jeremy (2019) *Mediawatch* NZ: Reporting Islam before and after 15/3, *Pacific Media Report*, 31 March. Available online at https://asiapacificreport.nz/2019/03/31/mediawatch-reporting-islam-before-and-after-15-3/, accessed on 30 September 2019

Simpson, Paula (2019a) Confessions of a former racist, *Spinoff*, 16 March. Available online at https://thespinoff.co.nz/society/26-03-2019/confessions-of-a-former-racist/, accessed on 14 October 2019

Simpson, Paula (2019b) Why are white men so angry? *Spinoff*, 28 April. Available online at https://thespinoff.co.nz/society/28-04-2019/why-are-white-men-so-angry/, accessed on 14 October 2019

Spoonley, Paul (2019) Christchurch mosque shootings must end New Zealand's innocence about right-wing terrorism, *Conversation*, 15 March. Available online at https://theconversation.com/christchurch-mosque-shootings-must-end-new-zealands-innocence-about-right-wing-terrorism-113655, accessed on 30 September 2019

Stuff (2019a) John Campbell calls terror attacks a 'terrible insult' to Christchurch, 15 March. Available online at https://www.stuff.co.nz/national/111327227/john-campbell-calls-terror-attacks-a-terrible-insult-to-christchurch, accessed on 25 September 2019

Stuff (2019b) The Christchurch attack interview that 'broke' TV reporter Patrick Gower, 19 March. Available online at https://www.stuff.co.nz/national/christchurch-shooting/111383948/the-christchurch-attack-interview-that-broke-tv-reporter-patrick-gower, accessed on 30 September 2019

Stuff (2019c) Christchurch terror attack: How New Zealand media will report the trial, 1 May. Available online at https://www.stuff. co.nz/national/christchurch-shooting/112352367/christchurch-terror-attack-how-new-zealand-media-will-report-the-trial, accessed on 14 September 2019

Stuff (2019d) Christchurch mosque shooting: Al Noor mosque Imam Gamal Fouda's speech, 22 March. Available online at https://www.stuff.co.nz/national/christchurch-shooting/111496112/christchurch-mosque-shooting-al-noor-mosque-imam-gamal-foudas-speech?rm=m, accessed on 30 September 2019

Williams, David (2019) Avoiding click-hate: Lessons for the terror trial, *Newsroom*, 19 June. Available online at https://www.newsroom.co.nz/2019/06/18/640954/avoiding-click-hate-lessons-for-the-terror-trial, accessed on 14 October 2019

NOTE ON THE CONTRIBUTOR

Dr Rukhsana Aslam is a Pakistani-born-Kiwi-Muslim and journalist-turned-academic with a doctorate in Media and Conflict with focus on peace journalism. She has decades of experience as a working journalist and an academic in Pakistan. In New Zealand, she has been closely associated with the Auckland University of Technology (AUT) for many years. She takes on independent consultancy on peace journalism training projects in various countries and engages in dialogue with students, journalists and peace workers on various platforms. Her current research project is about the strong media voices in Pakistan that were rendered 'voiceless' in the ongoing political conflict between former Prime Minister Imran Khan and the retired military chief.

Chapter 24

Ethics and the poetics of editing

Susan L. Greenberg

Susan L. Greenberg highlights the thinking behind her latest book which, she says, offers a first ever attempt to define a poetics of editing and proposes a new field of 'editing studies' to support interdisciplinary work on this aspect of textual production.

My most recent book, *A poetics of editing* (Palgrave Macmillan, 2018), the result of long research and reflection, began as an attempt to make sense of my own experience as a media professional. Coming to scholarship later in life, I noticed that editing tended to be considered only as a secondary aspect of other concerns, and so its analysis was highly fragmented. At the same time, my experience in everyday life was that the *topos* of 'editing' was doing a lot of work as a way of understanding the world, if only by negation. An anti-editing rhetoric has evolved, expressed as a struggle between institutional control and the unedited and, therefore, authentic work of an individual.

The book, therefore, aims to bring this invisible form of 'making' into full view through a mix of description, definition and theory. It offers a first-ever attempt to define a poetics of editing and proposes a new field of 'editing studies' to support interdisciplinary work on this aspect of textual production; just as reception studies provides a frame for the understanding of reading and readers.

The book's descriptive work includes a comparison with other forms of textual mediation such as self-editing and translation, and a historical account that pinpoints the emergence of the modern editor. The definition talks of editing generically as a decision-making *process* which aims to select, shape and link the text, to deliver the meaning and significance of the work to its readers, involving, then, a triangulated relationship between author, editor and text. In brief, editing is the art of seeing a text *as if it is not yet finished.*

The ethics of editing is typically broached in terms of an analysis of power relations, using the interpretive frame of 'gatekeeping', or an analysis of standards and codes of practice; for example, concerning attribution of sources, or the history of textual edits. By taking a comparative, generic approach I raise a different range of ethical issues.

One line of argument concerns our understanding of gatekeeping. Professional mediation is open to critique because it has a familiar and explicit identity and set of practices; but many decisions about selecting, shaping and linking text have now moved to new and, therefore, relatively less transparent places in the 'circuit of communication'. I argue that these newer cultures of production should be made more explicit so that their own codes, identities and power relations can meet the same scrutiny.

The newer forms of mediation are competing with the old for power and influence by bidding for avant-garde status in a time-honoured way, defining themselves in terms of opposition to the dominant positions. The use of 'mainstream' as a derogatory trope for professional editing has its roots in the early weblog movement of the 1990s and the abbreviation MSM was first used by conservative bloggers opposed to the 'liberal' media after 9/11. Wherever it is found on the political spectrum, anti-MSM 'authenticity' demands the expression of strong, partisan, personal feelings, and opposition to 'experts' or other professional sources of constraint. But I make the case that constraints in a rule-based process can protect the weak and promote agreed public goods. The 'obstacle' of expert editing can help people think critically about what is being put into wider circulation, questioning what is otherwise taken as given.

The potential for editing to support debate and change is best supported, I argue, through a materialist poetics that draws on a mix of traditions and insights. A poetics of editing offers both a set of principles for a concrete form of making, and a broader contextual perspective about the production of texts, in which the 'objectivity' of editing – as defined in the book – allows us to take a step backwards from an acknowledged point of subjectivity

A key contradiction in digital culture, I contend, is that it struggles to reconcile the desire for authenticity – a form of idealist romanticism – with a lack of trust in the mediated world, arising from an idealist anti-humanism. Both impulses get in the way of efforts to communicate across individual subjectivities. Just as an 'alienated objectivity' can arise from a failure to engage with an objectified other, we need the new diagnosis of alienated subjectivity to describe circumstances in which the narrator fails to engage with an objectified self.

Moreover, I argue, the struggle to resolve such contradictions creates disappointment which, in turn, seeks a target. Editing serves in this role in the sense that it stands as a metonym for a set of related 'others', enemies whose existence is needed for the purposes of self-identification. If all the world is a fragmented text, an attack on the people who work to repair that condition can feel like a form of speaking truth-to-power.

In his landmark 1980 speech 'Modernity: An unfinished project', Jürgen Habermas describes this unfinished business as modernity's failure to stop rationality from splitting into branches that do not communicate with each other. For people to achieve emancipation in the everyday 'lifeworld' they need to reach an understanding of themselves and others. But for this to happen, the three different moments of reason – cognitive, moral and aesthetic – must 'interpenetrate one another'; a difficult task in the face of strong anti-modernist forces.

I propose that the practice of editing has the radical potential to help connect these forms of sense-making. It does so by being open to the multiple motives in a text, while also creating the capability to make decisions. The text is opened up and then closed down again, so that it can change status from private to public and continue movement around the circuit of communication, maximising the text's survival. Binary states – creative and critical, subjective and objective – cannot be ignored. But they can be acknowledged and navigated. It is the relationship between the two which fosters creativity.

- This paper was first published in *Ethical Space*, Vol. 16, Nos 2 and 3 pp 34-35, 2019

NOTE ON THE CONTRIBUTOR

Susan L. Greenberg is an Honorary Research Fellow in the School of Humanities and Social Sciences at the University of Roehampton, UK, where she led a postgraduate Publishing MA and the narrative nonfiction strand in the Creative Writing programme. Previously, she worked as a reporter and editor. Greenberg holds a PhD in Publishing from University College London and has supervised and examined doctoral work in publishing, journalism and creative writing. She is editor of the 'Editors and editing' list within the CUP series 'Publishing and book culture', and an advisory board member for the journal *Literary Journalism Studies*. Publications include *A poetics of editing* (2018), and 'The Polish school of reportage' in *Global Literary Journalism* (2012). Email: s.greenberg@roehampton.ac.uk

Chapter 25

Journalist or supporter? The ethical and professional challenges for freelance local sports reporters in France

Matthieu Lardeau

A local freelance journalist, covering the news of a sports club every week, balances on a knife-edge between journalistic distance and proximity to their subjects. At what point are they more supporter than journalist? Matthieu Lardeau, an academic and sports journalist, reflects on his own experience in the field.

Keywords: Complicity, friendship and journalistic rigour

'Well, we don't really talk about it, eh? You saw nothing, heard nothing...' How often does a journalist hear this said by one of their interviewees? A journalist should be in direct contact with their sources and their field to bring together both professional and ethical obligations: to impartially witness the event they are covering in order to be able to observe and collect its constituent elements without recourse to secondary sources, and to be the first interviewer of the protagonists and witnesses of this same event to collect their testimony as soon as possible. But to what extent do sports journalists' relationships with their informants compromise this obligation?

This question, which brings together the ethical, professional and epistemological issues of the journalistic profession, has been considered in both academic and professional literature (Bradshaw and Minogue 2020; Ruellan 1993, 1997) for journalists working for national news media or even established regional media. However, some groups of journalistic content producers have arguably been overlooked: freelances and especially the local press correspondents. An auxiliary labour force for the team of staff journalists, freelances mainly cover sports news in the French local press. A relationship of complicity, even friendship, is naturally woven with the personalities of these clubs or teams, a relationship which often calls into question certain rules or ethical standards: accuracy of information, respect for people, independence (Agnès 2015; Kovach and Rosenstiel 2014), affective non-involvement/involvement of the journalist with their field and more generally the management of the distance/proximity relationship with their sources.

I propose to analyse this problem by comparing it to my long experience as a local sports press correspondent in the local or regional French press. Cumulatively, I have fulfilled this role for 14 years, either side of being a full-time professional journalist for a total of six years. I will first discuss the role of a local press correspondent in France, particularly in regard to the ethical and professional standards and rules of journalism. Then, I will discuss in more detail the difficulty in managing the proximity/distance relationship with the subject.

THE LOCAL FREELANCE REPORTER: AN AMBIGUOUS STATUS

When considering the role of local press correspondent (LPC) we must consider the legal position of the incumbent and the frontiers of professional journalism – are they actually freelances or *de facto* employees? (Ruellan 1993, 1997; Thiery 2020). Are they subject, like journalists holding press cards, to the same professional and ethical obligations?

The status of the LPC in France is defined by article 16 of the French law of 27 January 1993 in the following terms: 'The local correspondent of the regional or unit press contributes, depending on how events unfold, to the collection of any local information relating to a specific area or to a particular social activity on behalf of a publishing company. This contribution consists of providing information submitted prior to verification or editing by a professional journalist before potential publication.'

A LPC covers news in a geographical and/or sectoral domain (sports, local life etc.) which has been entrusted to them by the departmental management of a local daily or weekly: they cover events, suggest articles to their management or sometimes submit ready-written articles. If accepted for publication, these articles may be partially or fully edited and/or rewritten by a professional journalist who, therefore, assumes the responsibility of producing content that meets professional requirements.

Unlike a professional journalist whose journalistic endeavours are their main remunerative activity (supported by the holding of the press card), the LPC cannot be legally recognised as a professional journalist and must therefore have another main source of income. However, depending on the circumstances, a situation can arise for experienced LPCs to produce articles which do not require the intervention of so-called professional journalists because their length of experience allows them to deliver articles which are acknowledged as respecting the ethical and professional rules of journalism. This can be seen when the professional journalists who oversee LPCs quickly read over the articles sent by them, giving great confidence *a priori* to the submissions and making few if any corrections to the document.

The lack of distinction between journalists holding a press card and LPCs is also observed in certain newspapers of the regional daily press (RDP), the departmental daily press (DDP) and the regional weekly press (RWP) that authorise their LPCs to sign – or byline – their articles, just like professional journalists. In the various newspapers for which I worked as a LPC, I have had periods during which I bylined my articles just like my superiors (with first name and last name, or initial of the first name and last name, or double initials) and other periods during which the LPC was still allowed a byline., However, a note was placed in front of the byline ('corr.' or 'cor.', abbreviation of 'correspondent') allowing for the LPC to be distinguished from a professional journalist.

Nonetheless, these distinctions between LPCs and professional journalists are, in my experience, of limited significance to readers and interviewees: the latter equate LPCs with professional journalists. Indeed, often the LPCs' interviewees consider them to be 'more journalist' than the professional journalists because they are their regular interviewers in the field, whereas they rarely meet the journalists who run the service.

Finally, the LPCs can find themselves in a very unusual situation when they have worked for the same editorial office for several years, such as every weekend in the case of sports news. In such circumstances, their journalistic experience allows them to master the professional expectations of their writing and, therefore, they end up integrating, often unconsciously, the ethical and professional rules and standards even though their LPC status does not require it. As a result, professional journalists tend to view some LPCs as journalists in their own right. Thus, the legal dimension on which the status of LPC is based – that of the LPC not being an employee and in that sense not having a subordinate relationship – is blurred and the editorial staff which employ a lot of LPCs end up considering them as full members of the team of journalists.

This situation can cause team issues for the managers of the LPC teams in the sense that, if a LPC does not wish to work on certain weekends or even sometimes during the week, or does not accept the request to cover an event or demonstration – because they do not like it, it does not interest them or they do not consider the request sufficiently profitable financially or professionally – their superiors may claim that they are not making an effort to ensure sufficient regular monitoring of their sector or their sports teams. For example, in order for regional dailies to fill their sporting timetable every Monday (and sometimes Friday or Saturday), the LPCs' writings are essential; without them, most of the pages could not be produced by the few professional journalists (Cuny and Elobo 2018).

Thus, regular and experienced LPCs are *de facto* considered to be professional quasi-journalists by their bosses, which creates a paradoxical situation: the law requires that the LPC is not in a subordinate or dependent relationship with their sponsors, but the practice makes them very regular contributors, to the point that some have been LPCs for several decades. As a consequence, these LPCs actually act like professional journalists with their bosses controlling the work of 'their' LPCs, while also considering them to be professionally equipped or qualified to work with large autonomy.

SHOULD THE LOCAL FREELANCE REPORTER COMPLY STRICTLY WITH JOURNALISM ETHICS?

In this arrangement, should LPCs be expected – when they do not have a legal obligation to do so – to be subject to the professional and ethical standards and rules of professional journalists? To begin answering this, we will take the example of sports journalism. Sports journalism can be considered as one of the rare specialist areas of the profession to be able to claim the practice, sometimes and at least theoretically, of so-called 'objective' journalism, that is to say a practice of writing reports of sports competitions which are characterised by changes in numerical scores and/or objective actions. Specifically, these facts can be observed by any spectator, without the journalist's approach interfering in the evolution of a match's score, the emergence of a dominant team or individual at a given time, and the timing of player changes. Likewise, post-match interviews aimed at collecting statements from trainers, coaches, captains, etc., cannot, in principle, be dependent on the particular point of view of the journalist since it is a highly codified exercise which consists of repeating word for word, as a quotation, the comments made by the people interviewed.

In this aspect of 'objective' sports journalism, the ethical dimension of journalism arguably remains peripheral, due to the highly codified exercise of reporting a sports competition. In just a few dozen lines or seconds, the aim is to bring to the attention of the public the objective outcome of a sporting event and the comments made by the people interviewed. In some senses this is a highly theorised account of straight, fact-based reporting. Complications to this model arise when those covering contests aim to provide 'colour' pieces which are inherently more subjective, or ask post-match questions which are intended to elicit answers to a particular agenda of the reporter's choosing (Bradshaw and Minogue 2020).

HOW CLOSE IS TOO CLOSE?

The professional and ethical questions that arise for the LPC relate to the management of their relationship with their informants in the field, particularly in the case of local sports journalism. The sports LPC is first and foremost a liaison and communication agent between sports clubs and the newspaper editorial staff, but they may also be a strong supporter of the sportspeople and sports clubs on their beat for which they provide regular coverage.

The main pitfall that awaits a sports LPC – like a professional journalist operating at the national level – lies in being both an observer and a committed participant in their area (Gimbert 2012), in this case being a supporter of the team or athlete they cover every weekend or very regularly. By necessity, the LPC, like any journalist, must establish close links with their informants to create the most favourable conditions for collecting information, in particular information that the interviewee does not wish to disclose or does so according to their own agenda. This proximity very often results in the creation of friendly relationships that invite closeness or even familiarity. Week after week, when the LPC follows the same teams or clubs and creates connections which may lead to a positive or favourable treatment for the club or team, sometimes the need for honesty or balanced information may be compromised. The possible 'supporterism' or boosterism of the LPC following 'their' team or 'their' club can be expressed on several levels: by supporting their club against that of a neighbouring town, or against a club from another department or region.

However, this risk of 'supporterism' is mitigated by the duty of fair journalistic treatment by the professional editorial staff who proofread the articles. But, in my experience, LPCs generally remain ethical in their presentation of a balanced treatment of the facts from the different protagonists. For example, before the start of a sporting event, I always introduce myself, greet and speak to the managers (president, coach, players) or even the supporters of opposing or visiting teams, giving them even more time than the host team that I already know; likewise, I try to give a fair, if not equal, treatment to the two teams in the article.

THE LOCAL FREELANCE AS A LIAISON AND COMMUNICATION OFFICER TO SPORTS ASSOCIATIONS

Some of the LPCs activities do not pose an ethical problem when it comes, for example, to being an agent of information transmission between a club and the newspaper and vice versa. In the vast majority of real-life situations, this exchange of information is part of my conception of the local journalist, namely an actor mediating between the news protagonists and the public. However, arguably like many journalists or LPCs, I have frequently stepped outside of my role as an outside observer and journalist to behave like a member of the management of the club or sports association whose news I was covering.

By way of illustration, as a sports LPC for a weekly in the large city of Seine-Saint-Denis, I covered the matches of the local basketball team which played at the national level and hosted teams from provinces and small rural towns. Often, their players, staff and supporters came to Seine-Saint-Denis for the first time and upon their arrival at the sports centre, expressed their fear of visiting this area of the Parisian suburbs, of being attacked, of their coach being targeted etc. I then see myself as having stepped out of my role as an external observer to take on that of a member of the club management – which I was not – or of a 'mediator' to welcome them, talk to them as soon as they arrived at the sports centre, accompany the staff and the players to the locker rooms and then sit in the stands next to their supporters throughout the match to reassure them. It required, leaving the role of external observer, to act as a resident of this city of Seine-Saint-Denis and a friendly face at the local basketball club with the purpose of improving the negative image these people had of the city. However, there is an unwritten rule in sport: that athletes or sports teams who play away may be made to feel apprehensive about moving to an unfamiliar, even hostile environment. That is part of the challenge of a sporting event and it is not expected that the host will make visitors particularly comfortable, psychologically.

Actually, these ethical questions emerge when it comes to responding to extra-journalistic requests from clubs. Frequently, I have been asked to advise them on their communication strategy with the various media – including potentially those for which I was working – to ensure better media coverage and for their marketing strategy. Occasionally, I received requests, which I refused, from large sports organisations to write editorial content and communication, while, at the same time, I was required to cover the sports news as a LPC.

A LOCAL JOURNALISM OF 'COMMITTED OBSERVATION'

My long experience as a sports LPC has led me to be, like I think any LPC, a committed observer of the life and news of sportspeople and sports clubs that I have covered for many years. However, I feel that the commitment was demonstrated in a contained manner in the sense that it never exceeded the professional codes of local sports journalism, which require the expression of a minimum engagement on the part of the journalist in the covered event, or ethical and professional standards and rules. The pyramidal organisation of a newspaper's editorial staff allows a second reading of a document sent by an LPC to a journalist who did not attend the event and, therefore, maintains the distance and the necessary perspective. In so doing, the second journalist fulfils the role of 'guardian' of the ethical and professional requirements by proofreading and correcting, amending, or even rewriting the LPC's article.

- This paper was first published in *Ethical Space*, Vol. 18, Nos 3 and 4 pp 100-106, 2021

REFERENCES

Agnès, Yves (2015) *Manuel de journalisme* [*Journalism: A manual*], Paris, La découverte

Bradshaw, Tom and Minogue, Daragh (2020) *Sports journalism: The state of play*, Abingdon, Oxon, Routledge

Cuny, Thomas and Elobo, Taliane (2018) Correspondants locaux: Les soldats de l'ombre [Local correspondents: Soldiers in the shadows]. Available online at https://assises-journalisme.epjt.fr/correspondants-locaux-les-soldats-de-lombre, accessed on 29 October 2021

Gimbert, Christophe (2012) Le correspondant, un amateur de local engagé par son territoire [The correspondent : A true local committed to his area], *Sciences de la société*, No. 84-85 pp 51-65

Kovach, Bill and Rosenstiel, Tom (2014) *The elements of journalism, What newspeople should know and the public should expect*, New York, Three Rivers Press, third edition

Ruellan, Denis (1993) *Le professionnalisme du flou. Identités et savoir-faire des journalistes français* [*The professional blur: Identity and know-how of French journalists*], Grenoble, Presses universitaires de Grenoble

Ruellan, Denis (1997) *Les 'pro' du journalisme: De l'état au statut, la construction d'un espace professionnel*, [*The journalism 'pro': Building a professional space from state to status*] Rennes, Presses universitaires de Rennes

Ruellan, Denis (2005) Expansion ou dilution du journalisme? [Journalism: Expansion or dilution?], *Les Enjeux de l'information et de la communication*, Vol. 1 pp 77-86

Thiery, Daniel (2010) Le correspondant de presse local: Un professionnel du photojournalisme amateur [The local press correspondent: An amateur professional photojournalist], *Communication & Langages*, No. 165 pp 31-46

NOTE ON THE CONTRIBUTOR

Matthieu Lardeau is Associate Professor in Organisation Studies and researcher at CleRMa, University of Clermont Auvergne, France. His research focuses on the sociology and management of journalism and the media industry. He spent about 20 years in the media industry as journalist, chief editor and head of business/communication as well as a freelance reporter for metropolitan newspapers.

Chapter 26

Brian Winston:
The 'transformative academic'

Richard Lance Keeble

Richard Lance Keeble pays tribute to Professor Winston, a leading world authority on television news, documentaries, freedom of expression and media ethics.

The special issue of *Ethical Space* Vol. 19, No. 2, of 2022, was dedicated to the memory of Brian Winston, the first chair of the Institute of Communication Ethics, the original publishers of *ES*, who had recently died aged 80 following a fall.

For half a century Brian wrote on television news, documentaries, freedom of expression and journalism ethics. He presented his ideas with great energy and often provocatively, moving on from work in TV to a number of prominent university posts in the US and UK. An inspirational and extraordinarily committed teacher, just months before he died he presented a talk to a conference of the Association for Journalism Education via Zoom from his hospital bed.

Professor David Chiddick, former Vice-Chancellor of the University of Lincoln, said: 'Brian helped turn shibboleths of traditional universities on their head' and described him as 'a generous, inclusive, empowering and transformative' academic.

THE MANY SIDES OF BRIAN

In one of his many profiles of Orson Welles, the great theatre critic Kenneth Tynan tells this story: Welles is invited to give a lecture in a small, mid-Western town but very few people turn up and there is no-one to introduce him. So Welles decides to introduce himself. 'Ladies and gentlemen,' he begins, 'I will tell you the highlights of my life. I am a director of plays. I am a producer of plays. I am an actor on the legitimate stage. I am a writer of motion pictures. I write, direct and act on the radio. I am a magician. I also paint and sketch. I am a book publisher. I am a violinist and a pianist.' 'Isn't it strange,' he ends, 'that there are so many of me – and so few of you!'

Like Orson Welles, there were so many Brian Winstons. There was Brian the polymath; the conversationalist and story-teller; the expert on media theory, documentaries, journalism ethics, freedom of expression, media technologies and their histories; the distinguished winner of the US Emmy in 1985; the enormously energetic and often provocative speaker at conferences around the world; author, editor and co-author of 20 major books, the last one, on fake news, written with his son, Matthew; the author of more than 50 book chapters and almost as many journal articles; the winner of a range of prestigious awards for his writings on media technologies, freedom of expression and for increasing the understanding of human rights. And there was Brian the *bon viveur*; the journalist; the controversialist regularly writing to newspapers with his views; the loyal friend to many; the dedicated father and grandfather.

Brian was very fond of telling a particular joke. Every morning during his trans-Atlantic voyage, an eastern European Jewish immigrant arrives at his breakfast table to be greeted by his companion, a Frenchman, with the phrase 'Bon appetit.' On the first morning, somewhat surprised, the immigrant replies courteously: 'Goldberg,' shakes the hand of his companion and sits down. On the third day of the voyage the mistake is pointed out to him. So on the fourth day he arrives primed. Before the Frenchman can speak, Goldberg utters a loud and cordial: 'Bon appetit,' to which the Frenchman replies urbanely: 'Goldberg.'

THE SEARCH FOR UNDERSTANDING

Brian told me that most Jewish jokes are based on such misunderstandings. And in a way, Brian's career as an academic and teacher sought – at root – to replace misunderstanding with understanding. Significantly, the joke appears on the very first page of his first published text, *The image of the media* (1973) following a quote from a Joni Mitchell song: 'They've paved Paradise and put up a parking lot' – his writings bursting with eclectic cultural references like this.

After studying law at Merton College, Oxford (and remaining a devoted and active alumnus ever since), Brian began a two-year stint as a researcher for Granada TV's World in Action in 1963. Then, from 1965 to 1971, he worked as a producer/director for a range of programmes on the BBC and Granada.

As an academic, his career started in 1971 as media course director at Alvescot College, Oxfordshire or as the blurb for *The image of the media* put it: 'Too old at thirty for the hectic and glamorous life of a TV producer, he retired to darkest Oxfordshire to put nearly a decade of practical experience and thought into print.'

Since then his posts included research director in the Sociology Department, University of Glasgow. From this came the seminal texts, *Bad news* (1976) and *More bad news* (1980), which challenged head-on the commonly held view that television news in Britain, on whatever channel, is more neutral, objective and trust-worthy than press coverage. Not surprisingly, the BBC, its halo punctured, was hostile even before publication, threatening the group with the possibility of copyright action, protesting to the university's Principal and putting pressure on the Social Science Research Council to limit the freedom of the researchers.

In 1976, Brian moved to America to be Visiting Adjunct Professor at New York University. Prominent positions followed – at Pennsylvania State University, Cardiff University and the University of Westminster.

In *Misunderstanding media* (1986), Brian takes the maverick role in which he so often delighted, challenging the widely-trumpeted notions around the 'information revolution'. To support his argument, he formulates a 'law' of the suppression of radical potential suggesting that new telecommunication technologies are introduced only insofar as their disruptive potential is contained.

He develops his ideas relating to the 'invention' of the cinema in *Technologies of seeing: Photography, cinematography and television* (1996) where he highlights the need for 'thick' rather than monocausal explanations – with the primacy of society as the main agent in setting technology's agenda.

In *Media, technology and society* (1998), he returns to his notions challenging the concept of the 'information revolution' taking in the complex histories of the telegraph, the telephone, television, calculators, computers, microcomputers, broadcasting networks, communications satellites, cable television and the internet.

In *Messages: Free expression, media and the West from Gutenberg to Google* (2005), he stresses the media's importance as an essential driver of free expression which underpins all human rights.

Two of his books, *A right to offend* (2012) and *The Rushdie* Fatwa *and after: A lesson to the circumspect* (2014), tackle the issues surrounding the *Satanic verses* controversy. He concludes: 'The right to free speech and the right within it to offend, because without it we have no free speech, must be maintained. At whatever cost.'

The Act of documenting: Documentary film in the 21st century (2017), written in collaboration with Gail Vanstone and Wang Chi, considers the complex issues relating to audience reception and challenges the essential Eurocentrism of the dominant debate. While his last book, *The roots of fake news: Objecting to objectivity* (2021), written with his son, Matthew, a teacher in the School of Media, Communication and Sociology at the University of Leicester, elevates the fake news debate to a completely new, high level, taking in its historical, philosophical, legalistic, scientific and ethical dimensions.

Retiring only very recently, he was one of the longest-serving academic staff members at the University of Lincoln, joining in 2002 and serving for periods as Dean of the Faculty of Media and Humanities and Pro-Vice Chancellor. In 2007, he was awarded the university's highest academic post being named The Lincoln Professor.

I first met Brian (who had a fiery temperament) in the 1990s at meetings on the continent of the European Journalism Training Association where he was a charismatic leading voice. Since then I worked with him on a wide range of educational and publishing projects – and it was he who appointed me professor at the University of Lincoln in 2003. I owe him such a lot.

Just before Brian died, *It's the media, stupid!*, a collection of essays I edited in his honour, was published by Abramis. Luckily, he was able to read through the final PDF. Three chapters from that *festschrift* are carried in this special *ES* issue. The first, 'Humans as cultural beings in theory and practice', is by Clifford Christians, one of the world leaders in communication ethics who has long been closely associated with *Ethical Space*.

Christians bases his essay on the notion that humans, as the one living species constituted by language, are therefore fundamentally cultural. According to Christians's philosophy-of-the-human, humans know themselves through their symbolic expressions. 'Communication is the creative process of building and affirming the human order though symbols, with cultures the human habitat that results. ... When humans are defined as cultural beings, human affairs are fundamentally interpretive, rather than a matter of scientific explanation presuming neutrality. Since humanity is embedded in an existing cultural world, its sense of being is necessarily historical.'

In this philosophical context, theories are not to be seen as scholastic paradigms of mathematical precision; rather, they tap into the imaginative power that gives an inside perspective on reality. From here, the essay moves on to consider Habermas and critical inquiry, the ideology of instrumentalism, Harold Innis's notion of the 'monopoly of knowledge', perspectivism, Clifford Geertz's stress on 'thick description' (replacing the thinness of statistically precise objectivism) – and much more.

Christians ends with a wonderful celebration of Brian Winston who 'exemplifies the humanities perspective of this essay. As a world class critical theorist, his hermeneutical depth on mediated symbolic systems demonstrates how interpretive scholarship ought to be done in a global era of cross-cultural complexity'.

Questions relating to harm, offence, insult, free expression, censorship, broadcasting regulation and journalistic codes of conduct were at the heart of many of Brian Winston's writings. Julian Petley, in a paper titled, 'Doing harm: How the UK government threatens to impose online censorship', focuses on the notion of harm, deriving from John Stuart Mill, that Brian Winston employs to indicate where the limits of freedom of expression should lie. According to Winston, claims relating to offence and insult have increasingly expanded definitions of harm and, in the process, narrowed the bounds of freedom of expression. Building on these ideas, Petley examines the regime of online regulation currently proposed by the UK government in the form of the Online Safety Bill. This 'threatens to create an unwieldy, unaccountable and unnecessary state apparatus of online censorship, operates with far too broad and vague a notion of harm, and will see material expelled from the online world which is entirely legal in the offline world'.

Across thirty years as a broadcast journalist, Pratāp Rughani has reported on people facing conflict, atrocity or their aftermaths. In South Africa, Rwanda, Aboriginal Australia, the UK and elsewhere he has conceived his documentary filmmaking 'as a kind of arena in which many experiences can unfold, with enough open space for an audience to make sense of competing perceptions and experiences and settle on their own view'. In the final paper drawn from the *festschrift*, 'Towards restorative narrative', Rughani calls for the creation of 'a more relational media – socially designed and biased enough to nurture the connective tissue between communities, drawing on practices from restorative justice including deep listening and searching for shades of grey'. Rughani tells of his experience shooting the documentary *Justine* (2013), about a young woman who rarely speaks and reports enthusiastically on the techniques of the pioneering Vietnamese video artist, Trinh T. Minh-ha, who describes her aspiration in moving image practice as 'restoring proximity of the subject and recognising the place of subjectivity'.

Rughani closes his essay on an important questioning note: 'Can a story production process now emerge that re-conceives media as ethically responsible "connective tissue" to configure a public space to enable storytellers, subjects and audiences to understand and relate to their diverging perspectives?'

Other chapters in *It's the media, stupid!* include Tom Waugh on 'The documentaries of Magnus Isacsson (1948-2012)', Deane Williams on 'Naïve realism: Repositioning Kracauer's theory', Kate Nash on 'Covid-19 conspiracy documentary: Claiming the real in a context of uncertainty', Annette Hill on 'The act of watching documentary', Raphael Cohen-Almagor on 'The price of ridiculing the prophet: The *Charlie Hebdo* affair', Ivor Gaber on 'Fake news, double spin and strategic lying in the post-truth era' and Martin Conboy on 'The media of the past determining the politics of the future?'

Brian always wanted to write an autobiography. He recorded loads of interviews with friends and colleagues – but never got round to it. As *It's the media, stupid!* was being completed we hit on a marvellous idea: I would interview him on Zoom about his life and ideas – and we would carry the transcript at the end of the book. I have friend and *ES* joint editor Donald Matheson to thank for alerting me to Zoom's ability to transcribe all video: so following six interviews I had enough material for a kind of 7,000-word substitute 'biography'. Brian was, above all, a conversationalist: for him, the acquisition of knowledge was a dialogic process. In a way, then, the interview at the back of the book perhaps best captures the Brian we knew and so admired.

BRIAN'S 'REFUSAL TO BE PIGEON-HOLED'

Next in this *Ethical Space* issue, two colleagues and friends pay tribute. After Brian stepped down as chair of the Institute of Communication Ethics in 2007, he was followed by Fiona Thompson for two years – and then by John Mair in 2009. Mair, editor of more than fifty texts, writes: 'Brian wrote for several of my curated book collections – on the BBC, on the pandemic and others. Always original. You gave him an idea – though usually it was the other way round – and he would run with it, put it through his institutional memory and wide reading and deliver before the deadline.' While Ivor Gaber, Brian's colleague on the editorial board of the *British Journalism Review,* highlights his 'refusal to be pigeon-holed, and his absolute commitment to factuality and the historical method'.

Florian Zollmann, a PhD student and then teacher colleague of Brian at the University of Lincoln for a number of years, reviews his last book, *The roots of fake news: Objecting to objective journalism* (Routledge, 2021) which he wrote with his son, Matthew. Zollmann concludes: 'Winston and Winston have produced a formidable study on the roots of the "fake news" crisis and how it could be mitigated. The book is a must read for scholars, students and journalists interested in understanding how the intricate relationship between journalism, truth and "fake news" has built up over centuries.'

Finally, in the tribute section, Stephen J. A Ward, in reviewing *It's the media, stupid!*, describes the essays as 'intelligent and stimulating' and adds: 'There is historical continuity amid the ten chapters: some of the main issues have been around for a long time: freedom of expression, media harm and the perennial debate on objectivity. There is also novelty: the social and media contexts in which the issues occur have changed, and the chapters reflect this evolution.' Ward also takes the opportunity to question the approaches to objectivity of a number of contributors – a challenge very much in the Winstonian tradition.

- This tribute first appeared in *Ethical Space*, Vol. 19, No. 2 pp 2-3, 2022
- **Richard Lance Keeble** is editor of *It's the media, stupid! Essays in honour of Brian Winston,* published by Abramis, of Bury St Edmunds, ISBN: 9781845497866, £14.95

Chapter 27

Why ethics matter

Tony Harcup

Tony Harcup argues that most of ethics can be boiled down to a few simple things such as listening, caring, being respectful, approaching people with a little empathy and humility – and generally trying to put oneself in others' shoes.

As we grow older, not only are there more funerals to attend but there are also more anniversaries to mark. Rather like funerals, anniversaries can be prompts for reflection as well as reminiscence. They might even be occasions to think about the future as well as the past. Such is the case with the realisation that *Ethical Space* is now entering its third decade. It was also in the air at two recent anniversaries with even more personal resonance for me, dating back to a time when 'ethics' would almost certainly not have been in my vocabulary.

Not that I was a particularly unethical youth. Although ethics may not have been articulated in so many words, a concern for what I would now recognise as ethical practice was most definitely a thing. Such thoughts were swirling at a gathering to remember a working-class writers' group that I had been part of as a teenager in the East End of London. I was asked what our ethos had been. It was an interesting question. When we formed 50 years earlier, we had set out no formal objectives and would never have heard of anything as grand-sounding as a mission statement. What we did have, I suppose, was a sense of *caring*. Caring not just about our own writing as individuals but also about the people and places around us.

Between us, our inclusive and supportive little writing group known as the Basement Writers produced poetry and prose that we published in print and sometimes performed in person at public readings. It may not have been journalism, yet it undoubtedly involved the telling of stories that were rooted in reality. *Our* reality, and the reality of the local community of which we were a part. Telling our stories was, I see now, a form of self-representation. Ethics were at the heart of it even if we didn't necessarily realise it. In case that makes it all sound very po-faced, I should point out that we had a right good laugh too.

Around the same time, in the autumn of 1973, a different group of people in another part of the UK were planning to launch a local alternative newspaper. Called *Leeds Other Paper*, the first issue was published in January 1974, in the midst of a cost-of-living crisis, and featured the tabloid-style front page headline: 'DON'T LET THE BASTARDS CARVE US UP'. This scruffy new paper was not big on impartiality, as the collective producing it made transparent in that debut edition:

> *Leeds Other Paper* exists to provide an alternative newspaper in Leeds; i.e. a newspaper not controlled by big business and other vested interests. It is our intention to support all groups active in struggle in industry and elsewhere for greater control of their own lives. The production will be intermittent at first – we are not professionals and we are few in number. We hope to grow, however, into a regular newspaper. If you wish to help in any way – articles, contacts, distribution etc – your assistance will be greatly appreciated (*LOP* No. 1, January 1974).

By the time I discovered the paper upon moving to the city the following year, *LOP* (as it was known to its friends) had become considerably more journalistic in tone. It retained its commitment to covering local people's struggles, though, as well as its welcoming attitude to newcomers. The first issue I saw defined its ethos in the following words:

> We publish *Leeds Other Paper* because we hope people will find it useful and interesting and because we enjoy doing it. We are not aligned to any particular political party but try to support groups and individuals struggling to take control over their own lives – whether it's in the factory, the housing estate, or the home. We can't however explain all our aims and ideas in a few sentences: the paper itself should give you a better idea of what we're trying to do. If you like the paper and want to make it better or help us get it out to more people, we'd be pleased to hear from you. Much of our material comes from sympathisers and groups working in various parts of Leeds and we'd like to get more news that way. We have weekly meetings every Monday evening, and new people are always welcome (*LOP* No. 20, September 1975).

Still a teenager, I accepted that invitation, went along and got stuck in. I have been a journalist and/or journalism educator of sorts ever since, and I like to think that all my work has retained at least some of the spirit of *LOP*, and of the Basement Writers for that matter. That spirit being an informal set of ethics, starting with listening to people at the bottom of the pile and proceeding to help amplify such voices.

I joined the National Union of Journalists as soon as I began to get paid for doing journalism, and it was through the union rather than any training course that I was formally introduced to the concept of ethics in the shape of the NUJ Code of Conduct. Dating from 1936 but updated several times since, this succinct code lays down some key principles on ethical issues such as accuracy, privacy, harassment, intrusion and the public interest. More detailed codes are available, as are more extensive editorial guidelines, reporting guides and style guides, but I think there's a lot to be said for something short and sharp that sets you thinking without trying to cover the minutiae of every eventuality.

If you look, you can find hundreds of codes of ethical conduct around the world, literally from A (Albania) to Z (Zimbabwe), produced variously by unions, employers, charities, professional societies, press councils and regulatory bodies (Mediawise n.d.). Ethics may now be more widely codified than ever but, as Barbie Zelizer (2017: 93) observes, 'codes of ethics in journalism have not done much to eradicate unethical behaviour'. Harsh, but true. A code on its own will not prevent all egregious behaviour any more than a criminal law can eliminate crime. But it might help us to identify such behaviour, to think about it, and – in an unknowable number of instances – to avoid it. It is a continuous and iterative process, or at least it ought to be. Codes are frequently updated, briefings issued and fresh guidelines drafted when new issues arise, as with recent efforts by news organisations and unions alike to get to grips with the ethical – and other – implications of artificial intelligence (Cools and Diakopoulos 2023; NUJ 2023).

As well as codes and guidelines, you can now find shelves and shelves of academic books on media ethics in general, and journalistic ethics in particular, which is a far cry from the days in which ethics would be knocked off in 'a two-hour session on a wet weekday afternoon halfway through a one-year course [that] was very much the standard teaching for would-be journalists until towards the end of the 1980s and early 1990s', as Chris Frost (2016: 3) recalls. Wilful ignorance is no excuse, and reading even a smidgen of the growing library of media ethics books and journal articles can better equip us to navigate 'real ethical dilemmas [that] have no straightforward answers, and ... engage in a better-informed conversation about ethics and its vital place in journalism culture and practice', as Price et al. (2022: 2-3) put it.

Ethical issues and dilemmas are many and varied, extending far beyond the most obvious areas of angst such as in what circumstances it might be justified to invade somebody's privacy, whether or not to run a story that relies on a confidential source and how to avoid intruding unnecessarily into someone's grief. Among the wider ethical issues worthy of serious consideration is representation – of women, for example – yet the topic has tended to be either absent or treated as marginalia in too many tomes on journalistic ethics, as Franks and Toms (2022: 227) note. This is odd because questions around how people are represented, to and by whom, are surely central to a cultural practice such as journalism. At least, they should be, shouldn't they?

Inspired by the work of scholars such as Meenakshi Gigi Durham (1998), Nancy Fraser (1986) and Linda Steiner (2018), I have found that one useful way of thinking about such issues is by attempting to apply a theory that emerged from feminist critiques of the relationship between knowledge and power and has come to be known as feminist standpoint epistemology (Harcup 2020). This essentially means trying to view events from the standpoint of those in any situation who are the least powerful and foregrounding such perspectives rather than uncritically reproducing dominant discourse. This theoretical approach recognises the epistemological gap between an 'understanding of the world available if one starts from the lives of people in the exploited, oppressed, and dominated groups and the understanding provided by the dominant conceptual schemes' (Harding 1991: 276). That seems to me to be a profoundly ethical project. It is also, more or less, what we were trying to put into practice on *LOP* back in the 1970s.

Of course, it is not always a simple matter to identify who are the most subjugated group in any given situation – discord over trans rights springs immediately to mind – and it must be recognised that oppressed people do not have a monopoly on insight, wisdom or kindness. But feminist standpoint epistemology may at least give us a starting point, and maybe even equip us with a map and compass, to help explore whatever terrain lies ahead of us.

Other ways of viewing wider ethical considerations beyond the series of discrete issues typically found in codes of conduct include the ethics of caring (Harcup 2020; Mathewson 2022; Robinson2011; Steiner and Okrusch 2006) and the ethics of listening (Dreher 2010; Gilligan 1993; Harcup 2020; Robinson 2011; Wasserman 2013). In this context, caring has more to do with justice than charity, and for media workers it can entail privileging the 'counter-stories of marginalised or subordinated people', as Steiner and Okrusch (2006: 115) put it. Journalists have 'an ethics or a responsibility to listen' to such stories, argues Tanja Dreher (2010: 99). This ethical approach to listening has been described as 'not just hearing the words that are spoken, but being attentive to and understanding the concerns, needs and aims of others in the dialogue' (Robinson 2011: 847).

However, by putting such an emphasis on listening to and caring for those who may have the quietest voices, and by reporting on society from the bottom up rather than the top down, I most emphatically do *not* mean that we should abandon other ethical norms such as a concern for accuracy, verification and fairness. While I do not wish to suggest that *LOP* always got everything right, journalistic due diligence certainly saved us from running some hairbrained stuff on occasions. Journalists ought not to be in the business of simply amplifying howls of rage; rather, we ought to apply our reporting skills within the context of a commitment to ethical ideas such as listening and caring. That's because ethics *matter*.

Ethics matter because, if we never think about what might be right, wrong, positive or harmful about our work, then we might as well be replaced by AI bots with no social conscience churning out commercialised 'content'. Without some sense of ethics, we are likely not just to be lousy journalists but lousy human beings too. That does not require everyone to read all the ethics literature available, nor to be able to recite relevant codes of content in their entirety, but it does need those of us producing journalism or other forms of media output to retain some commitment to the good of humanity. From time to time, it may also require a struggle to create sufficient time and space for ethical journalism – and for human journalists – to survive in what remains of the news industry (Harcup 2023).

Ethical journalism does not have to be complicated. As journalist Barnie Choudhury put it, when talking to Sallyanne Duncan (2023: 188) for her book, *Ethics for journalists*:

> The most important things for me are my ethical and moral values which lead to my conscience. Trust is at the heart of my ethical values. My primary concern is how can I win the trust of those about whom I am reporting and giving a voice. Of course, I want the story, but not at any cost. … I want to be able to go back to that source, that interviewee, that leader and know I wrote or edited a piece which was honest and authentic. … So, my starting point with any story I cover is to try to walk in their shoes.

That is simply put and none the worse for it. Indeed, with all due respect to the contributors to this journal over the past two decades, me included, perhaps we are sometimes in danger of over-complicating and over-theorising things. Most of ethics can be boiled down to a few simple things such as listening, caring, being respectful, approaching people with a little empathy and humility – and generally trying to put oneself in others' shoes. In essence, if we treat people how we would like to be treated ourselves, we will not go too far wrong.

REFERENCES

Cools, Hannes and Diakopoulos, Nicholas (2023) Writing guidelines for the role of AI in your newsroom? Here are some, er, guidelines for that, *Nieman Lab*, 11 July. Available online at https://www.niemanlab.org/2023/07/writing-guidelines-for-the-role-of-ai-in-your-newsroom-here-are-some-er-guidelines-for-that/

Dreher, Tanja (2010) Speaking up or being heard? Community media interventions and the politics of listening, *Media, Culture & Society*, Vol. 32, No. 1 pp 85-103

Duncan, Sallyanne (2023) *Ethics for journalists*, Abingdon, Routledge, third edition

Durham, Meenakshi Gigi (1998) On the relevance of standpoint epistemology to the practice of journalism: The case for 'strong objectivity', *Communication Theory*, Vol. 8, No. 2 pp 117-140

Franks, Suzanne and Toms, Katie (2022) Representing women: Challenges for the UK media and beyond, Price, Lada, Sanders, Karen and Wyatt, Wendy (eds) *Routledge companion to journalism ethics*, Abingdon, Routledge pp 227-234

Fraser, Nancy (1986) Toward a discourse ethic of solidarity, *Praxis International*, Vol. 5, No. 4 pp 425-429

Frost, Chris (2016) *Journalism ethics and regulation*, Abingdon, Routledge, fourth edition

Gilligan, Carol (1993) *In a different voice*, Cambridge and London, Harvard University Press

Harcup, Tony (2020) *What's the point of news? A study in ethical journalism*, Switzerland, Palgrave Macmillan

Harcup, Tony (2023) The struggle for news v*alue* in the digital era, *Journalism and Media*, Vol 4, No. 3 pp 902-917. Available online at https://doi.org/10.3390/journalmedia4030058

Harding, Sandra (1991) *Whose science? Whose knowledge? Thinking From women's lives*, New York, Cornell University Press

Mathewson, Joe (2022) *Ethical journalism: Adopting the ethics of care*, Abingdon, Routledge

Mediawise (n.d.) *Codes of conduct archive*, Mediawise. Available online at http://www.mediawise.org.uk/codes-of-conduct/codes/

NUJ (2023) *NUJ briefing on artificial intelligence*, National Union of Journalists, October. Available online at https://www.nuj.org.uk/resource/nuj-briefing-on-artificial-intelligence-october-2023-.html

Price, Lada, Sanders, Karen and Wyatt, Wendy (eds) (2022) *Routledge companion to journalism ethics*, Abingdon, Routledge

Robinson, Fiona (2011) Stop talking and listen: Discourse ethics and feminist care ethics in international political theory, *Millennium*, Vol. 39, No. 3 pp 845-860

Steiner, Linda (2018) Solving journalism's post-truth crisis with feminist standpoint epistemology, *Journalism Studies*, Vol 19, No. 13 pp 1854-1865

Steiner, Linda and Okrusch, Chad (2006) Care as a virtue for journalists, *Journal of Mass Media Ethics*, Vol. 21, Nos 2 and 3 pp 102-122

Wasserman, Herman (2013) Journalism in a new democracy: The ethics of listening, *Communicatio: South African Journal for Communication Theory and Research*, Vol. 39, No. 1 pp 67-84

Zelizer, Barbie (2017) *What journalism could be*, Cambridge, Polity

NOTE ON THE CONTRIBUTOR

Tony Harcup is an Emeritus Fellow in Journalism Studies at the University of Sheffield in the UK. His books include *Journalism: Principles and practice* (Sage), now in its fourth edition, which has been used on journalism courses around the world since it first appeared in 2004.

Chapter 28

The long, slow tasks of decolonising communication ethics

Donald Matheson

UNRAVELLING OF ASSUMPTIONS

The end of a book that has gathered together 20 years of communication ethics is a good place to think about what the next book might look like. For me, if that next volume is to have ambition and to do justice to the critical heritage of *Ethical Space*, it must tackle the major issue of the long legacy of colonialism in ethical thinking. In particular, if ethical theory and analysis are to be fit for a decolonising world – one in which European and North American frameworks are not the only bases to work from and one in which ethics achieves material and cultural benefits for those in the global South as well as the North – there needs to be a long and slow unravelling of assumptions and at the same time a re-ravelling of ethical thinking in different places. It requires more than an embrace of diversity and more than symbolic actions, such as taking down statues of colonisers like Cecil Rhodes at universities, useful as those moves are.

But how do we rethink the grounds for thinking about ethics? One approach, appropriate to a country founded on a bicultural relationship between indigenous and settler cultures such as Aotearoa New Zealand is to give status and authority to the disempowered indigenous frameworks so as to begin to rework relationships between people. This chapter works through some of that thinking. In doing so, it does not make recommendations for other places, as situations differ, but, in Appiah's (2023: 264) words, aims to send the 'flow of insight' against the usual flows.

A useful starting point for this is to note that colonialism is foremost a colonising of the mind, in which people in all global contexts are caught up. The consequences for those in the global North and those in the South are different, but the patterns of thinking that privilege the few affect everyone. That is unlikely to change much so long as societies are grounded in the languages, calendars, institutions, religions, ways of living, forms of art, economic structures and political practices of former colonial powers. This is also true of ethical norms, from ideas of good or bad to the tools through which we work through ethical tensions, to the theories of living well together underpinning them. We can propose proto-norms, such as truth, dignity and non-violence (e.g. Christians 2019), but as soon as we move towards applying or understanding these, a few ways of thinking immediately take precedence, even claiming universal status. Dignity, for example, quickly becomes a matter of respect for individuals, with all the baggage of the Cartesian separation of self and other and European traditions of the sovereignty of the individual. This is true also of unethical practice. As Jamaica Kincaid (1988) said of Antigua in *A small place*, the ethical shortcuts and accommodations and the turn towards authoritarianism and oppression of others among formerly-colonised peoples are learned behaviours, rooted in centuries of colonial government. Unravelling these kinds of structures is a task for us all. And, of course, the more distant colonial thinking may seem – the more it feels like a problem of the global South and the more likely it is to be invisible within structures of privilege that those in the North benefit from.

That means unravelling colonialism within ethics is a task particularly pressing for those who work within privileged university or media institutions. Museums in the rich world are a useful parallel case, as their displays and storerooms are physical manifestations of assumptions that the North collects global culture and memory, orders it, explains it to others and benefits from it – in ways that would be near-impossible to imagine if reversed. This epistemology of injustice, in which enlightenment and progress have been built on and legitimated conquest, stealing, enslaving and killing, leads directly to a task of 'dismantling the Master's house', in Giblin et al.'s (2019) phrase. Vawda (2019: 79) writes:

> A key aspect of museums' current and future role is to deploy their resources in epistemic ways that confront firstly, the variously acquired objects from the former colonies in the museums, and misrepresentations and omissions of colonialism in the exhibitions, but secondly, to confront the epistemic injustice of coloniality in and of the museums themselves.

We need to do something similar in the field of communication ethics. The arguments for a global media ethics are still, for example, voiced largely by English-speaking scholars, writing in English for scholarly presses or journals based in New York or London. Our debates are structured by terms and orders of knowledge and academic conventions whose universality has been assumed. Likewise, the goals of ethics remain embedded in projects initiated by the likes of Aristotle, Marx or Ellul.

So how to unravel some of this? This article is not a call to throw existing debate away, such as that represented by the 20 years of *Ethical Space* gathered in this book. Instead, it explores different ways of thinking about and doing ethics as a starting point for future steps. This makes particular sense from where I write, Aotearoa New Zealand. I live in a nation that, sporadically and unevenly, engages in a conscious process of decolonising. Its founding document is a treaty between indigenous Māori and the British Crown in 1840, Te Tiriti,[1] that was, for most of its history, misinterpreted, knowingly breached or ignored but, since the 1970s, has been returned to in national public debate. Aotearoa (as many are now calling the country) is, therefore, one place from which to think about what decolonising communication ethics can and could look like.

Our largest media organisation, *Stuff*, four years ago researched its own misrepresentations of Māori and other non-European groups and apologised for what it found on its front pages. Its staff believe it is one of only two media organisations globally to have acknowledged past wrongs in this way. My employer, the University of Canterbury, declared itself in 2021 to be in partnership with the local tribe, Ngāi Tūāhuriri. The 2017-2023 New Zealand government set up co-governance arrangements between the state and Māori in health, water resources and local government and bilingual naming in the public service and on road signs (although the newly-elected conservative government has reacted against those initiatives and may reverse some of them). Debates about decolonising this place may provide some resources to think about how to evaluate public communication and set out to build better forms of it. In particular, it provides some resources to think about how indigenous and European ways of working through what is right (tika, in Māori) can usefully interact, without the indigenous immediately being made into an 'other' – an interesting but lesser object. Māori ways of thinking are particularly useful here, as they are, in the words of Anne Salmond, one of our leading anthropologists, fundamentally relational. She draws on Māori tōhunga (priestly experts) and scholars to argue that, in te ao Māori (the Māori world), reality is not:

> … conceived of as a singular entity, composed of arrays of bounded entities in different realms and on different scales… [but] as arrays of open-ended, continuously reproducing networks of relations (Salmond 2012: 124).

That relational focus makes talking across difference a basic part of Māori ritual, identity-formation and ethics. That in turn redefines ethics as concerned with the relationships themselves, rather than the intentions and values of the parties to them.

THE INADEQUACY OF CULTURAL SENSITIVITY

Ethics as a matter of good relationships is therefore very different from accommodating diversity or showing cultural sensitivity. Diversity thinking does not in itself take us very far from one culture's norms. For example, in the Australian context it is common for media reporting on First Nations Australians to warn that reference will be made to the dead. The SBS's internal guidelines explain that protocols for mourning the dead among some clan groups require that naming the dead be restricted:

> [I]t's common practice that when there is a member of the community that has deceased, the person's name is changed due to cultural beliefs and the images of that person are suppressed. This maybe just for a period of time, some cases could vary between six-to-12 months, but liaising with the community is paramount (SBS 2017).

The guidelines, written by a staff member at NITV, Australia's indigenous broadcaster, advise media makers to follow the guidance from community leaders on whether to use the individual's name or a circumlocutory phrase and whether images of the person can be used. The ABC's editorial policy on respecting indigenous people and culture (ABC 2021) similarly requires journalists to warn viewers and listeners when a broadcast contains images and voices of First Nations people who may no longer be alive, so they can choose to avoid it.

In themselves, these guidelines and resulting practices should be celebrated, because they show respect for other people's cultures. They have also evolved in recent years to become more accommodating of First Nations perspectives. But they leave power firmly in the hands of one culture in representing others. The ABC guidelines, for example, emphasise warnings and spend less time on the question of whether or not distressing use of images or voices should be used at all. In the context of the cultural violence done against Australian First Nations since first contact, the colonial relationship remains undisturbed here. That is, the ethics here remains a white Australian ethics of respect for cultural diversity.

A further step is to add to communicators' ethical toolkit by drawing in and interpreting ethical frameworks from non-European cultures. Perhaps most widely discussed in the ethics literature is ubuntu, the African concept that 'I am me through others' or 'human interdependence' (Gade 2012). In the South African context, the idea has become an influential part of the ethical toolkit. However, as Rao and Wasserman (2007: 46) noted already 15 years ago, the term cannot simply be added into a global media ethics, because 'the overarching framework into which these concepts have been imported remains Western'. Indeed, it is hard to imagine what a global media ethics would look like, because ethics must always, as Rao and Wasserman go on to note, be reflexive and situational. That is, ethical ideas make sense in terms of the context and culture in which they are used, in terms of who uses them and in terms of wider power relations that they challenge or justify. That does not mean that other places cannot learn from ubuntu; the point is that the same reworking needs to happen everywhere.

FROM POSTCOLONIAL TO DECOLONISING

It is not credible to try to step outside the colonial context into a post-colonial future while little else changes. As Stuart Hall (1995) wrote already in the 1990s, the quotation marks 'cluster thick and fast around the question of the "post-colonial" and the notion of post-colonial times'. Colonialism is not over; there is little to celebrate; academia is only partly disengaged from colonising processes. As Hall also noted, at the heart of the problem with the notion of the post-colonial is that it tends to be disconnected from analysis of the distribution of power. The use of the term 'decolonising' is more useful because it emphasises the action of people to do that. Mignolo (2012) frames the task as specifically one of building decolonial futures through changing the 'rules of the game'. He writes: 'Without decolonizing knowledge and changing the terms of the conversation, the rules of the game would be maintained and only the content, not the terms of the conversation, would be disputed' (ibid: 23).

In Aotearoa, we have become used to the rules of the game being contested and alternative ways of thinking about good communication and social life being proposed. Those proposals are themselves contested, as noted above, because they disrupt the normal ways of doing public communication. 'It's going to be confusing if you add more words,' complained a conservative politician, Simeon Brown, who became Transport Minister in November 2023, about bilingual road signs (Quill 2023). But the to and fro of challenge opens up a space of in-between that itself has ethical potential.

That, however, has to begin with genuine engagement with te ao Māori rather than Simeon Brown's desire to make things easy. Formal public Māori communication practices in particular act out ontologies that are quite different to those in other parts of Aotearoa society, producing a very different ground for publicness. A central concept is that of whakapapa. Translated often as family history or lineage, Māori scholars note that it literally describes 'the process of layering one thing upon another' and so is always a figurative term that imagines personhood and family as a layered, collective self (Ngata 2011 [1944]: 6, cited in Mahuika 2019). The term refers also to physically embodied connection (O'Regan 1987), as it extends to relationships with place, with aspects of the natural world and with social order. According to Mead (2016), whakapapa underpins a person's claim to belong to a tribal group, to come from somewhere and to the responsibilities and rights that come with that. The importance of whakapapa means that formal public talk in Māori contexts, which takes place archetypally on the marae (home ground), is governed by a ceremonial process of finding connection between manawhenua (people of the marae) and manuhiri (visitors) that is acted out in the space before the meeting house. Discussion begins with a process of mihimihi (greeting) where manuhiri and manawhenua set out their whakapapa while standing on the marae atea (the forecourt). When welcomed next into the whare tīpuna (the house of the ancestors) talk shifts to finding shared whakapapa and building connections with the host. Public talk, then, begins with these ontological moves of placing oneself in connection in different ways at different moments of discussion. If there is to be argument, for example, it happens outside on the atea.

This is not just empty convention or protocol. In this layering of relationships, Māori publicness gives importance to the 'more-than-human', for example, both in the sense that personal identity is strongly connected to the place that someone's family is from but also in the sense that people have responsibility to those places. Parsons et al. (2021: 238) write that relationships through whakapapa to land, mountains, rivers and the sea 'inextricably bind' people as kin to their environment. This has significant consequences for public action. Wairewa Rūnanga, the tribal organisation in my home town, to take a very local example, has produced a multi-generational plan to repair a severely eutrophied lake and restore traditional food sources in it – a timeframe and ambition well beyond discussion and decision-making frameworks elsewhere in the community and directly linked to their whakapapa (Mahaanui 2013). The long-term task of cleaning the lake was largely outside the scope of other forms of public debate. Another consequence has been the state's recognition of people's relationship with ancestral rivers, forests and mountains by recognising the legal personhood of what European thinking would see as parts of nature (including in Acts of Parliament relating to the forests of Te Urewera and the Whanganui River). Similarly, Ngāti Rangi, a tribe who live on the flanks of the volcano, Mt Ruapehu, have argued successfully that people should adjust their buildings and roads to accommodate possible lahars (volcanic mud flows) rather than bulldoze or dynamite the crater lake, because of their kinship relationship with the mountain (Gabrielsen et al. 2017).

Salmond, cited above on Māori ontology, uses that frame to describe how the rangatira (chiefs) who signed the treaty with the British Crown in 1840 would not have been thinking in terms of bounded nation states, inhabited by citizens who were either of one nation or another, and who had property and voting rights that could be gained and lost by treaty. Rather than signing a treaty to gain rights as British in return for ceding sovereignty, they were forging a relationship with Queen Victoria and her kin:

> Kin networks are open-ended and flexible, with people activating different links in different circumstances (so that Maori kin groups are more contextual than corporate; and *ahau*, the self, is at once constituted by and inclusive of its networks of relations). They are also constantly changing, with some relationships being forged by insult and fighting, others by adoption, friendship and marriage, accompanied by gift exchange, while others, of limited value, are forgotten (Salmond 2012: 123).

This is not mere history, but explains the expectations and engagement of Māori political heritage and tensions in the relations of Māori political entities with the state today.

One concrete instance of changing the rules of publicness can be found, again, in museums. Te Papa Tongarewa The Museum of New Zealand, operates in relation to Māori culture, artefacts and people – and increasingly others – according to the principles of what it calls mana taonga. The processes of managing and exhibiting objects that the museum has acquired over time are connected back to the people whose treasures they are, in 'living relationships' that take for granted the legitimacy of those relationships and the validity of those people's perspectives. In doing so, it puts them back in control of curation. In practical terms, the museum's staff travel the country to liaise with tribes. The use and storage of objects is subject to consultation and the owners' stories about those objects are incorporated into curation. In addition, the museum contains a marae, allowing Māori publicness to be practised as part of opening exhibitions and educational activities. Anthropologist Philipp Schorch and curator Arapata Hakiwai (Schorch and Hakiwai 2014) argue that it is the fostering of these whakapapa links that gives the public actions of the museum legitimacy and thereby 'interpretive authority'. In contrast to state action that gains a measure of legitimacy through being debated by all, here a particular decolonising, bicultural legitimacy is gained through building public connections between past and present, treasures and the people and the places where their meaning arises. Others are then invited to take part in those connections. It is significant that the focus is much more on the relationship-building than on science or other forms of rationality in managing the collections, thereby changing the way the museum connects with its society.

CONCLUSION

Other places will have other structures for doing good communication. The point of introducing tikanga, or ways of working out what is right, in Māori communication is not to place it on a pedestal (there are things that are often criticised, within and outside Māoridom, such as the gendering on most marae of who speaks when). I hope it has achieved two things. The first is to describe how public communication in the country is being changed as Māori perspectives are given centrality in some parts of public life. From the national museum to understanding of the country's founding document to the inclusion of the 'more-than-human' in legal definitions of the public, the rules of the game are changing so much that it is no longer possible to think of communication ethics in this place as belonging to Anglo-American traditions. The second is to offer up an example of where decolonising thinking can lead.

The relational ontology at the heart of Māori communication practices has parallels with thinking in journalism studies (and many other parts of communication studies) but should not be enveloped by that thinking or reduced to an example. Beckett (2011) among others calls for greater focus on the relationships that media organisations set up with their audiences and the way they claim a space in public debate. Using an economic analogy, he argues that relational qualities such as trust, authenticity, transparency and collaboration are becoming ever more highly valued in the contemporary 'moral market'. The ethics of care, some versions of virtue ethics and cosmopolitan ethics are used similarly to focus on relationships and to think beyond liberal traditions. In Aotearoa, however, the debate begins elsewhere and the parallels are of limited use. A decolonising frame asks us to think about who has the power to shape the terms of discussion. It is only by accepting the fundamental status of thinking such as Māori tikanga for the people who draw on it that we can develop ethical frameworks that step outside the colonial heritage.

NOTE

[1] The Māori name, Te Tiriti, is used as it describes the Māori-language version of the document, which was signed by rangatira (chiefs), rather than the quite distinct English-language version. The representative of the British signed both versions (Waitangi Tribunal 2016)

REFERENCES

ABC (2021) Respecting Indigenous people and culture in ABC content, *Editorial policies*, Australian Broadcasting Corporation, November. Available online at https://www.abc.net.au/edpols/respecting-indigenous-people-and-culture-in-abc-content/13633944, accessed on 6 December 2023

Appiah, Kwame Anthony (2023) *The ethics of identity*, New Jersey, Princeton

Beckett, Charlie (2011) *Supermedia: Saving journalism so it can save the world*, London, Blackwell

Christians, Clifford G. (2019) *Media ethics and global justice in the digital age,* Cambridge, Cambridge University Press

Giblin, John, Ramos, Imma and Grout, Nikki (2019) Dismantling the master's house, *Third Text*, Vol. 33, Nos 4 and 5 pp 471-486. DOI: 10.1080/09528822.2019.1653065

Gabrielsen, Hollie, Procter, Jonathan, Rainforth, H., Black, T., Harmsworth, Garth and Pardo, Natalia (2017) Reflections from an indigenous community on volcanic event management, communications and resilience, Fearnley, Carina J., Bird, Deanne K., Haynes, Katharine, McGuire, William J. and Jolly, Gill (eds) *Observing the volcano world*, Cham, Springer pp 463-479. Available online at https://doi.org/10.1007/11157_2016_44

Gade, Christian B.N. (2012) What is ubuntu? Different interpretations among South Africans of African descent, *South African Journal of Philosophy, Suid-Afrikaanse Tydskrif vir Wysbegeerte*, Vol. 31, No. 3 pp 484-503. DOI/abs/10.1080/02580136.2016.1222807

Hall, Stuart (1995) When was the 'post-colonial'? Chambers, Iain and Curti, Lidia (eds) *The postcolonial question: Common skies, divided horizons*, London, Routledge pp 242-260

Kincaid, Jamaica (1988) *A small place*, New York, Farrar, Strauss and Giroux

Mahaanui (2013) *Mahaanui iwi management plan*, Christchurch, Mahaanui Kurataiao

Mead, Hirini (2016) *Tikanga Māori: Living by Māori values*, Auckland, Huia Publishers, revised edition

Mahuika, Nēpia (2019) A brief history of whakapapa: Māori approaches to genealogy, *Genealogy*, Vol. 3, No.2 pp 32. Available online at https://doi.org/10.3390/genealogy3020032

Mignolo, Walter (2012) Decolonizing Western epistemology/Building decolonize epistemologies, Isasi-Daz, Ada Mara and Mendieta, Eduardo (eds) *Decolonizing epistemologies: Latina/o theology and philosophy*, New York, Fordham University Press pp 19-43

Ngata, Apirana T. (2011 [1944]) The Porourangi Māori Cultural School, Rauru-nui-a-Toi Course, lectures 1-7, Gisborne, Māori Purposes Fund Board/Te Rūnanga o Ngāti Porou

O'Regan, Tipene (1987) Who owns the past? Change in Māori perceptions of the past, Wilson, John (ed.) *From the beginning: The archaeology of the Māori*, Auckland, Penguin pp 141-145

Parsons, Meg, Fisher, Karen T. and Crease, Roa (2021) *Decolonising blue spaces in the anthropocene: Freshwater management in Aotearoa New Zealand*, London, Palgrave

Rao, Shakuntala and Wasserman, Hermann (2007) Global media ethics revisited: A postcolonial critique, *Global Media and Communication*, Vol. 3, No.1 pp 29-50

Quill, Annemarie (2023) 'They should be in English': National to ditch te reo Māori traffic signs, *Stuff*, 26 May. Available online at https://www.stuff.co.nz/bay-of-plenty/300890230/they-should-be-in-english-national-to-ditch-te-reo-traffic-signs, accessed on 7 December 2023

Salmond, Anne (2012) Ontological quarrels: Indigeneity, exclusion and citizenship in a relational world, *Anthropological Theory*, Vol. 12, No. 2 pp 115-141. Available online at https://doi.org/10.1177/1463499612454119

SBS (2017) Indigenous cultural protocols: What the media needs to do when depicting deceased persons. NITV, 27 July. Available online at https://www.sbs.com.au/nitv/article/indigenous-cultural-protocols-what-the-media-needs-to-do-when-depicting-deceased-persons/97xq2otnt, accessed on 6 December 2023

Schorch, Philipp and Hakiwai, Arapata (2014) Mana taonga and the public sphere: A dialogue between Indigenous practice and Western theory, *International Journal of Cultural Studies*, Vol. 17, No. 2 pp 191-205. Available online at https://doi.org/10.1177/1367877913482785

Vawda, Shahid (2019) Museums and the epistemology of injustice: From colonialism to decoloniality, *Museum International*, Vol. 71, Nos 1 and 2 pp 72-79. Available online at https://doi.org/10.1080/13500775.2019.1638031

Waitangi Tribunal (2016) Section 3: The signing of the Treaty of Waitangi, *Treaty of Waitangi past and present: Aotearoa the way it was*. Available online at https://www.waitangitribunal.govt.nz/publications-and-resources/school-resources/treaty-past-and-present/section-3/, accessed on 6 December 2023

NOTE ON THE CONTRIBUTOR

Donald Matheson is co-editor of *Ethical Space: The International Journal of Communication Ethics* and Professor of Media and Communication at the University of Canterbury, Aotearoa New Zealand. He writes on communication ethics, journalism, public communication in social media and discourse analysis.

Index

The Age 10, 147-165

Annan Committee 42

Arendt, Hannah 3

Artificial Intelligence (AI) 1, 19, 396

Aslam, Rukhsana 3, 17, 363-377

Assange, Julian 13, 63, 223-238

Authenticity 16, 18, 318, 327-329, 379, 406

BBC 6, 8, 41, 42, 43, 44, 49, 50, 51, 52, 53, 54, 56, 57, 60, 64, 81, 91, 97, 98, 101, 102, 104, 106, 108, 109, 120, 121, 130, 152, 218, 282, 285, 389, 392

Blog/blogging 11, 15, 106, 120, 172, 174, 225, 227, 228, 235, 278, 279, 316, 371, 379

Boochani, Behrouz 11, 183-196

Bourdieu, Pierre 8, 91, 92, 93, 94, 99, 100, 137, 314

Bradshaw, Tom 5, 18, 20, 381, 384

Brazilian News Atlas 11, 166-180

Brexit 112, 124

Brooks, Rebekah 9, 105-111

Bullshit 3, 9, 16, 318-331

Castillo, Antonio 3, 10, 131-146

ChapGBT 1, 19

Character 16-17, 35, 191, 292, 294, 318, 324-325, 326, 327, 329

Charitable journalism 3, 12-13, 216-222

Chilevisión 136, 138, 139

Chomsky, Noam 8, 80, 87, 135, 264

Christians, C. 1, 2, 5, 18, 255, 391, 401

Churchill, Winston 24, 27, 34, 114

Climate change 12, 14, 254, 255, 257, 258, 259, 260-261, 262, 263, 264, 265, 266, 267, 268, 269, 270, 369

CNN 96, 97, 98, 99, 102

CNN Chile 138

Code of ethics 293, 294, 298, 302, 324, 336, 337, 338, 354, 358, 378, 379, 386, 391, 395-396, 397

Colonialism 3, 11, 19, 186, 190, 400, 401, 403, 404, 407

The Conversation 12, 156, 217, 218

Corporate social responsibility (CSR) 308, 310, 313, 315, 317

Daily Express 25, 29, 36, 56

Daily Mail 9, 36, 52, 63, 107, 109, 110, 112, 113, 118, 119, 121, 123, 124, 127n

Daily Mirror 9, 54, 112, 113, 118, 119, 122, 123, 124, 125, 127n

Daily Telegraph 29, 50, 51, 63, 67

Demetrious, Kristin 17, 314, 333, 340, 341, 345-360

Democracy 6, 15, 29, 32, 38, 45, 48-49, 56, 62, 65, 71, 82, 133, 168, 223, 224, 225, 226, 227, 230, 233, 234, 235, 243, 244, 255, 256, 257, 263, 283, 300, 301, 346, 349, 357

Domeneghetti, Roger 3, 9, 112-130

Drudge Report 227

Editing, ethics of 378-380

Facebook 91, 148, 159, 170, 224, 225, 235, 370, 373

Fake news 18, 141, 389, 390, 392, 393

Fataluku Research Project 12, 197-215

Fawkes, Johanna 3, 15, 291-307

Fitch, Kate 3, 17, 315, 332-344

Fontoura, Marcelo 2, 11, 166-180

Foucauld, Michel 17, 345, 346, 354, 357

Frankfurt, Harry G. 16, 318, 319, 320, 321, 322, 328

Geneva Conventions 7, 81, 82-83, 84, 87
Glasgow University Media Group 133, 135
Globalisation 8, 91, 92, 93, 101, 200, 276, 372
Goggin, Gerard 3, 13, 223-238
Greenberg, Susan 3, 18, 378-380
Guardian 7, 23, 60, 61, 62, 63, 65, 66, 67, 70, 71, 72, 81, 83, 84, 85, 86, 110, 113, 185, 229, 234, 279, 281
Gurleyen, Pinar 3, 14, 254-275

Habermas, Jürgen 256, 346, 348-349, 350, 354, 355, 357, 358, 379, 391
Hackett, Robert A. 3, 14, 224, 235, 254-275
Harcup, Tony 2, 14, 19, 36, 242, 394-399
Herman, Edward S. 8, 80, 87, 135, 264
Hoggart, Richard 6, 41, 42, 45, 46, 47, 48, 49, 51, 55, 57
Hoggart, Simon 110
Huffington Post 185, 225, 232
Human rights 3, 7, 10, 14, 63, 65, 69, 78-90, 133, 135, 141, 185, 187, 188, 193, 218, 235, 240, 246, 247, 250, 279, 284, 315, 389, 390

Independent 81, 83, 84, 85, 86
Institute of Communication Ethics 6, 18, 388, 392
Interviews 14, 15, 25, 91, 94, 101-102, 151, 152, 155, 160, 203, 206, 210, 239, 240, 247, 278, 280, 283, 284, 285, 287, 338, 364, 367, 369, 381, 383, 384, 385, 392, 398
ITN 96, 98, 101, 102, 109
ITV 41-58

al-Jazeera 279, 285
Jung, Carl 15, 291-307

Keeble, Richard Lance 3, 5, 8, 14, 18, 239, 241, 242, 243, 267, 388-393

Lardeau, Matthew 18, 381-387
Leeds Mercury 6, 23, 37
Leeds Other Paper (*LOP*) 19, 394, 395
L'Etang, Jacquie 3, 16, 300, 308-317
Luckhurst, Tim 3, 5, 6, 23-40
Lüdtke, Sérgio 2, 11, 166-180
Lynch, Jake 235, 240, 241, 242, 266, 267, 270

MacIntyre, Alasdair 2, 292, 294
Mail on Sunday 107
Manchester Guardian 23, 28, 37
Mann, Arthur 5-6, 23-40
Matheson, Donald 2, 5, 19, 392, 400-408
McDonald, Willa 3, 11, 183-196
Media studies 46, 309, 331
Mental illness 3, 17, 332-344
El Mercurio 134, 135, 137
Moral relativism 1, 298
Multicultural 112, 313, 340, 341
Murdoch, Rupert 6, 9, 15, 53, 56, 107, 109, 230, 280, 281-285, 286, 287
Murrell, Colleen 3, 8, 91-104
Muslim media 14-15, 276, 278

News of the World 53, 54, 69, 70, 105, 108, 110
New Yorker 3
New York Times 66, 81, 139, 229, 319

Objectivity 98, 258, 259, 265, 266, 268, 284, 285, 374, 379, 390, 393
Observer 35, 36, 55, 71, 81, 86

'Parachute journalism' 91, 92

Peace journalism (PJ) 3, 8, 13-14, 17-18, 239-253, 254, 266-267, 268, 270, 363, 368, 373, 374-375

Petley, Julian 3, 6, 18, 41-58, 62, 66, 72, 391

Pilkington Report 6, 41-58

Podcast 10, 140, 141, 172

Poetics of editing 18, 378-380

Poole, Elizabeth 3, 14-15, 276-288

Professional ethics 15-16, 17, 291-307, 332, 333, 336, 337-338

Propaganda 7, 14, 15, 32, 78, 80, 87, 135, 245, 263, 264, 265, 266, 267, 300, 302, 309, 310, 353, 372

Public relations (PR) 5, 15-17, 291-360

Q News 14, 279

Rationality 1, 292, 348, 355, 379, 406

Rawlins, Brad 16, 318-331

Reid, Marian 3, 12, 197-215

Ricketson, Matthew 3, 10, 147-165

Rughani, Pratāp 18, 391-392

Sanders, Karen 1-4, 19

Sincerity 16, 320, 321, 322, 323, 324, 325-327

Snowden, Edward 7, 59-77

Spin 16, 107, 134, 300, 301, 309, 318, 319, 322, 355, 356, 357, 392

Stoker, Kevin 16, 318-331

Stourton, Edward 108-109

Stuff 367, 368, 370, 371, 373, 374, 402

Suchenwirth, Lioba 3, 13-14, 239-253, 267

Suicide 3, 17, 98, 152, 332-344

Sun 9, 63, 69, 70. 105, 112, 113, 118, 119, 121, 122, 123, 124, 127n

Sunday Age 152

Sunday Pictorial 54

Sunday Times 6, 51, 56, 69, 81

Sun on Sunday 125

Sydney Morning Herald 185, 226

The Times 24, 25, 29, 31, 35, 36, 37, 48, 81, 83, 84, 85, 86

La Tercera 134, 137, 138, 139

Townend, Judith 3, 12-13, 216-222

Truth/truthfulness/truth-telling 3, 16, 17, 35, 72, 96, 223, 224, 225, 226, 229, 230, 231, 244, 260, 267, 268, 292, 318, 319, 320, 321, 322, 323, 324, 325, 327, 328, 329, 355, 371, 372, 379, 392, 393, 401

Tulloch, John 3, 6, 8-9, 105-111

Vancouver Sun 265

Vanity Fair 107, 108

Wake, Alexandra 3, 10, 147-165

WhatsApp 11, 183, 192

WikiLeaks see Assange, Julian

Winston, Brian 18, 388-393

Witnessing 19, 136, 148, 149, 150, 151, 153, 160, 161, 162, 183, 185, 233, 327, 364, 365, 381

Yorkshire Post 5, 6, 23-40

Zollmann, Florian 3, 7, 8, 78-90, 393

www.ingramcontent.com/pod-product-compliance
Lightning Source LLC
Chambersburg PA
CBHW071944220426
43662CB00009B/981